KNIGHTS OF THE QUILL

KNIGHTS OF THE QUILL

CONFEDERATE CORRESPONDENTS
AND THEIR CIVIL WAR REPORTING

Patricia G. McNeely

Debra Reddin van Tuyll

Henry H. Schulte

Purdue University Press
West Lafayette, Indiana

Printed in the United States of America.

Library of Congress Cataloging-in-Publication Data

McNeely, Patricia G., 1939–
    Knights of the quill : confederate correspondents and their Civil War
reporting / Patricia G. McNeely, Debra Reddin van Tuyll, Henry H. Schulte.
        p. cm.
    Includes bibliographical references and index.
    ISBN 978-1-55753-566-5
    1. United States—History—Civil War, 1861–1865—Press coverage. 2. United
States—History—Civil War, 1861–1865—Journalists. 3. War correspondents—
United States—Biography. I. Van Tuyll, Debra Reddin. II. Schulte, Henry H.
III. Title.
    E609.M375 2010
    973.7'8—dc22

                                                                    2010006209

Cover art: The Newspaper Correspondent. Drawing by Edwin Forbes. Courtesy

*This book is dedicated to the men and women
who reported the Civil War for Southern newspapers,
especially those whose names remain unknown.*

Contents

Preface: Why We Wrote This Book   ix

1   Knights of the Quill: The Press in the Crucible of War   1

SOUTH CAROLINA

2   William Ashmead Courtenay: A Knight on the Field of Honor   27

3   Felix Gregory de Fontaine: Chronicling the Horrors of War   45

4   Robert W. Gibbes: The 'Mind' of the Confederacy   95

5   Joan: A Citizen Journalist of the Confederacy   104

6   Bartholomew Riordan: Spying on Washington, D.C.   127

7   Leonidas W. Spratt: Preserving the Legend of "Stonewall" Jackson   140

8   Henry Timrod: Reluctant Correspondent who became Poet Laureate   160

FLORIDA

9   L.H. Mathews: General Bragg's Nemesis   181

ALABAMA

10   John Forsyth: Love and Hate in the Strife-Torn South   203

11   Henry Hotze: Propaganda Voice of the Confederacy   216

12   John H. Linebaugh: On the Move for the *Memphis Daily Appeal*   238

13   Samuel Chester Reid, Jr.: Renaissance Adventurer   247

14   William Wallace Screws: "Most Useful Citizen of His Day"   265

15   William G. Shepardson: Swashbuckling Newshawk on the Chesapeake   276

GEORGIA

16 Peter W. Alexander: Friend of the Foot Soldier 311

17 James Roddy Sneed: "No Greater Tyranny
than a Muzzled Press" 341

18 John S. Thrasher: Revolutionary and Reformer 362

LOUISIANA

19 Durant da Ponte: Through a Young Diarist's Eyes 379

20 Henry H. Perry: Confederate Apologist and Reporter 395

TEXAS

21 Charles DeMorse: Reporting From the Indian Territories 409

22 William Doran: A Texas Hero Takes Up His Pen 436

23 James P. Douglas: Fighting for the South with Pen and Sword 453

24 R. R. Gilbert: A Texas Humorist Goes to War 465

VIRGINIA

25 George William Bagby, Jr.: Confederate "Croaker" 483

26 James B. Sener: Covering the War from His Hometown 513

27 John R. Thompson: A Poet Makes an Impact as "Dixie" 543

28 Virginia: "From a Lady Correspondent" 556

TENNESSEE

29 Henry Watterson: Rebel with Many Causes 571

Epilogue 597

Appendix 601

Source Notes 607

Index 699

About the Authors 727

Preface

Why We Wrote This Book

AFTER LISTENING ALL DAY TO PRESENTATIONS OF CIVIL WAR RESEARCH papers at a 2005 conference in Chattanooga, Tennessee, three journalists-turned-college-professors began talking into the night about the men and women who risked their lives to report the war for the South.

They wondered about the nameless correspondents who wrote under pen names to keep from being imprisoned by the enemy or shot as spies. Why would "Sparta," "Dixie," "Grapeshot," and "Personne" go into battle armed only with scraps of paper, dull pencils, and quills and ink to scribble stories for newspapers hundreds of miles away? Why would they sleep on beds of mud or snow for days on end? Why would they drink polluted water and eat raw corn or burned bread and fat cooked over an open fire?

The professors pondered the passions that drove the correspondents into the heat of battle for the sake of a story. They wondered about who influenced what they wrote and why Southern newspapers faced less censorship than Northern newspapers. Why did the Confederate correspondents get by with vicious criticism of civilian and military leaders that would have gotten the typical Northern newspaperman arrested or the newspaper closed down "instanter" as they would have said back in the 1860s? Mostly, though, they wondered what those reporters were really like as human beings.

That turned the conversation to what historians already knew about the South's war correspondents. The quick answer was, "Not a lot." One of the trio recalled that a Confederate newsman once described members of the Southern editorial brotherhood as "knights of the quill,"[1] a moniker very much at odds with the more common depiction of Civil War correspondents as "bohemians." James B. Sener, one of the first Southern reporters to use the phrase, certainly was more knight than bohemian. He was an attorney with an undergraduate degree from the University of Virginia and a law degree from Washington College, and after the war, he would become chief justice of the Wyoming Supreme Court. Many of the other Southern correspondents who came to mind that night seemed to fall more into the knight category, too. The three professors ticked off a list that included the son of a French nobleman, a dozen or more lawyers, a former U.S. diplomat, several physicians, a priest, and at least two well-educated women, one of whom followed her son into war.

If all, or even most, Confederate correspondents came from such elite backgrounds, would their war correspondence be any different from that of the Northern "bohemians" who appeared to have come from a wider variety of social backgrounds? Could that account for the changes in Southern journalism during the Civil War? News did move to the front page, as it already had in the newspapers of the urban North. The emphasis of Southern journalism shifted from commentary to information, factual information presented in a non-partisan manner. The new standard for quality journalism required that writers sift truth from rumor, or at least tell readers when they were reporting rumors.[2]

In essence, practices adopted to cover America's bloodiest war pushed Southern journalists toward what are considered to be more professional practices, and intriguingly, this seems to have happened, not because of some industry-wide push or reform movement. Instead, it appears to have been a natural response to circumstances and readers' needs.

Was this because true hard news demands to be told in a different way than political coverage, which had dominated much of journalism throughout the country and throughout most of the 19th century? Or could it have been that the South's journalism was suddenly pushed toward new standards because of an influx of a new type of journalist—men who were from the upper reaches of society, who brought the outlook of professionals, albeit from other fields, to their newspaper work?

At least during the war period, the distinctions between the actual journalism of the North and South were not profound.[3] The news industries had different experiences—Southern newspapers had far fewer people and less available labor, far fewer available resources, and an outlook that defined news, at least in the beginning of the war, as something quite different from facts presented in a straightforward manner. Only in the 1850s had many Southern newspapers added reporters to their staffs.

It would stand to reason that there should be some distinctions between Southern and Northern journalism of the time; the professors agreed. Southern journalists were, for the most part, products of a slave society. Their daily association with slavery would have given them a different worldview that would have influenced the way they constructed their journalism. Scholars established long ago that journalists' personal characteristics and perspectives influence how they decide what constitutes news, as well as how they structure and package it. Modern theorists refer to journalists as gatekeepers—those who decide what information will reach an audience. The process of making those decisions is called framing.[4]

The three professors were intrigued by these questions, and it was disquieting that there were so few places to go for answers. The lack of knowledge about

Southern correspondents, they agreed, was due to the disparity in scholarly attention to the Confederate press. The Southern press has typically received short shrift in most survey treatments of Civil War journalism, and there are few book-length studies of the Confederate press. Much more has been written about the Northern press and its correspondents. Without much effort, the trio quickly came up with a list of eight books about the Northern Civil War press.[5] The three could name only one book that dealt specifically with the Southern press in the Civil War. They reeled off the names of several other books that dealt with the Southern press in advance of the Civil War, but those works focused on the content produced by journalists, not the journalists themselves.

Those earlier books examined how the press, North and South, fomented the Civil War. Both the editorializing of the antebellum Southern press and its partisan, political nature were singled out as contributors to the sectional polarization that erupted into civil war. Historians used terms such as "archaic" and "benighted" in some of those works to convey the idea that the antebellum Southern press was worthless for two reasons: the more rural Southern press had not adopted the practices of urban journalism, and Southern journalists never questioned the region's slave labor system.

These sour-grape comments may have resulted from claims in an 1857 screed, *The Impending Crisis* by Hinton Helper, that indicted nearly every Southern institution for unquestioned acceptance of slavery—including journalism. He argued that slavery and sectional politics had stifled independent thought in antebellum Southern journalism.[6] However, Helper's seemingly principled stance on slavery is suspect. Prior to 1857, he had advocated the expansion of slavery and complained about the meddling of abolitionists in issues that were none of their concern. Helper had similarly indicted the California Gold Rush when he failed to strike it rich. In all, he was a bitter man and something of an opportunist.[7]

Helper's indictment of the Southern press was almost as complete as his indictment of slavery. Southern newspapers, he wrote, had made no improvements and were tainted by "the imbecility and inertia which attaches to everything which slavery touches."[8] Even the South's rural papers fell far shy of the rural papers in the North, Helper contended. "What that country-press was twenty years ago, the country-press of the South is now."[9]

Helper's criticism extended beyond press quality. He charged that Southern editors were whipped by the planter elite. He wrote that "no Southern editor dared appeal to a mass of readers by assuming the stance of the common man, in serious opposition to the propertied and powerful elite."[10]

For students of 19th century Southern culture, this statement seems odd. Contemporary scholarship about the exact nature of the relationship between upper- and lower-class whites has softened the notion that planter hegemony was wielded like an iron fist. As the sectional debates of the 19th century grew more heated, the interests of all Southerners aligned, regardless of class.[11] There was also evidence to indicate that the South's journalists were not likely to be intimidated by the planter elite that historians are so fond of writing about; they were the elite.[12]

Although Helper was the first to indict Southern journalism, other writers pushed ideas that seemed to support his position. For example, Frederick Hudson, James Gordon Bennett's managing editor at the *New York Herald*, maintained that journalism history should only embrace those people and practices that led to the development of the metropolitan brand of daily journalism.[13] Hudson's 1873 history of American journalism contains few mentions of the press outside the Northeast. He divided his book into six periods and mentioned the Southern press in only two of those periods. Critics at the time were skeptical of Hudson's blatant bias in favor of the big-city style of journalism, but it was an ideology that has had broad appeal and influence.[14]

Historian George Henry Payne was among those who were influenced by the ideas Hudson and Helper put into circulation.[15] Instead of relying on primary sources, Payne adopted Helper's conclusions and wrote that the influence of slavery held back Southern journalism by causing a "lack of enterprise and lack of freedom which made them seem inferior to their brethren at the North."[16] He argued that this was because, "There can be no great editors or journals, where brute force and material wealth so completely control, and the result was that the Southern men of idealism were ignored in their own communities, or they went north."[17]

If that were true, then a great deal of early American journalism would have to be classified as unworthy, including that of the colonial period, which has been praised for fomenting the Revolutionary War, because slavery existed throughout the colonies and early nation. Payne obviously believed that a man "of idealism," his criterion for a good editor, could be neither a supporter of slavery nor a slave owner. Other historians have also made this argument, but it is an unsupportable contention.[18] While neither was a journalist, one has only to hold up George Washington or Thomas Jefferson to counter that being a man of idealism and being a slaveholder are not mutually exclusive categories.

As products of a slave society, Southern journalists were infused with values peculiar to that society. Historians who expect Southern newsmen to reject the established social norms of their time in order to be considered worthy of the journalistic calling are imposing ideas and ideologies of a later period. In the 21st century, all agree that slavery was wicked and that its abuses have created social, political, and economic troubles that still plague the country. That was not the understanding of most antebellum Southerners as the nation debated the issue in a series of divisive sectional conflicts that culminated in a bloody civil war. It is an idea the country has had to grow into.

Noted journalism scholar James W. Carey strongly believed that if one is to understand a phenomenon, he or she must understand both the facts and "the structure of imagination that gives them their significance."[19] He meant that historians must try to understand what led their subjects to be the way they were. People become who they are not only because of innate personality traits and biology alone but also because of their culture. The ideas, beliefs, and attitudes of Southern journalists would have been shaped in part by societal ideas, beliefs, and attitudes, one of which was that slavery was the proper station for blacks. Most Americans in the 20th and 21st centuries are uncomfortable with the blatant racism of antebellum attitudes about slavery. This discomfort, however, does not change the fact that the men and women discussed in this book lived in a different time and held different ideas.

As that Chattanooga evening wore on, the three professors agreed that they should produce a book that would tell the stories of the men and women who covered the Civil War for Southern newspapers. They would examine their stories, study their personal lives and professional experiences, and delve into their backgrounds to see how those factors affected their work as war correspondents. Before the evening was over, the seeds had been planted for a project that would become *Knights of the Quill,* a book that would add facts to the inadequate record about Southern journalism in the Civil War period and perhaps add more chips to the argument that 19th century Southern journalism was quite relevant to journalism history.

Knights of the Quill consists of heavily researched biographies that cover a wide range of Southern correspondents. Many of the best-known Southern correspondents are included—those few whose names were inscribed on the Civil War correspondents' memorial arch at Gathland State Park, Maryland, but also included are some little-noticed journalists, including several from the trans-Mississippi region and two women who have been nearly overlooked by historians.

A few unlikely candidates are included as well. Henry Hotze, the Confederacy's chief propaganda agent in Europe, is included because he created and published London's Confederate newspaper, the *Index,* as is at least one journalist who never set foot in the field: Robert W. Gibbes, Jr. Gibbes was not a correspondent but he headed a groundbreaking Southern press service. Ultimately, these correspondents represent the many different kinds of people who covered the war. *Knights* also offers a chapter laying out the environment in which the reporters worked and discusses many of the structural problems they faced in getting their stories and transmitting them back to their newspapers.

The ultimate purpose of this book is to reassess Confederate journalism within a thoughtful framework and to draw some conclusions about this understudied area of journalism history. The authors hope to replace the claims of "dullness and triviality" that have been attributed to the Confederate press with a clearer view of its vibrancy, endurance, and vitality. Equally important, the authors hope to save the fast-disappearing memories of these courageous men and women who frequently risked their lives to write prolifically and passionately about the skirmishes and battles of the Civil War.

Heartfelt thanks are due to the 14 dedicated authors who helped put *Knights of the Quill* together and for laboriously tracking down details of many correspondents' lives. It has made the effort worthwhile. Thanks go to David Sachsman and Kittrell Rushing, hosts of the Symposium on the Nineteenth Century Press, Civil War, and Free Expression, held each year at the University of Tennessee at Chattanooga. They encouraged the project, allowed recruitment of authors from the conference attendees, and included panels on the correspondents in their program. And finally, thanks to family members for undertaking a host of necessary but inconvenient tasks in order to give the authors time to research, compose, and edit these chapters.

Patricia G. McNeely
Debra Reddin van Tuyll
Henry H. Schulte

1

The Confederate Press in the Crucible of War

Debra Reddin van Tuyll

WAR CORRESPONDENTS ARE MEN AND WOMEN OUT OF LEGEND. THEIR reputations portray them as gritty, glamorous, fearless journalists who will go anywhere and to any lengths to get the story from the battlefield. The term "war correspondent" conjures up images of Peter Arnett, Bernard Shaw, and John Holliman reporting from the balcony of their Baghdad hotel during the opening bombardment of the Persian Gulf War in January 1991. While fire from bombs, missiles, and antiaircraft guns rained down like an illuminated gully-washer that night, the three journalists alternately hid under their beds to avoid capture and crawled out on the balcony to report what was happening around them.[1]

Because of their daring deeds, and the impact of their work, war correspondents have been called many things. Hero. Myth Maker. Propagandist. The first professional war correspondent, the *London Times*'s William Howard Russell, gave himself a slightly longer title: "miserable parent of a luckless tribe." Russell's experiences covering Great Britain's Crimean War and America's Civil War clearly left him on the cynical side.[2] Russell was one of those "mostly rough, sometimes ready" war correspondents who came to exemplify the nickname: "Bohemian." That name fit the correspondents who followed armies and tramped around the battlefields, many of whom easily fit the image of the 19th century reporter: "poorly dressed and poorly mannered . . . insensitive, rude, and dishonest" men who drank heavily and pried into other peoples' business.[3] The terms "journalist" and "gentleman" were considered to be mutually exclusive in those days, especially when applied to the war correspondent.

This image of the Civil War correspondent as "bohemian" has been enhanced by memoirs of the correspondents themselves and by later histories.[4] Few of these works present the experiences of former Confederate newspapermen who chose to put the war behind them or else were too busy trying to eke out a living in the postwar South to produce memoirs. Attempts to discern the story of Confederate war correspondents is further complicated by the fact that the identities of only a handful are even known.

The situation was different in the North. Union General Joseph Hooker did historians, and Northern journalists, an enormous favor when he insisted, and General Ulysses S. Grant agreed, that all reporters who covered Union armies sign their dispatches with their initials. That has made it easier for historians to determine the identities of Northern reporters and to track down their stories. Further easing the work of historians, many Union reporters left memoirs and other personal papers. With identifiable subjects and available primary sources, Civil War historians have had the raw materials necessary for studies of Northern correspondents, which is perhaps the likeliest explanation for the greater number of works about their experiences.

The result is that far more is known about those Northern bohemians, the group that has come to define the Civil War correspondent in both the scholarly and the popular mind. Correspondents who were hired by Southern newspapers to cover the war came from a different mold. For the most part, they approached their newspaper work from the vantage of other careers and with greater training and education. As a rule, they also came from the middle and upper classes. These were not working-class artisans whose talent as wordsmiths had advanced them from the composing room where they got their start as apprentices and printers' devils. The Southerners had college or professional educations, and their families had means enough to own slaves in greater proportions than the general population. Their perspectives and outlook on the war they were covering had been shaped in more rarified air.

Demographic data on the South's war correspondents and editors, collected from the 1860 census, show that as a group, journalists were better educated and owned more slaves than the general population of the region. Only about 25 percent of Southern families owned slaves by 1860. About 40 percent of editors and about 51 percent of correspondents owned at least one slave.[5] Almost 70 percent of Southern journalists were college educated or professionally trained (see Appendix 1 for details).[6] Clearly, the South's war correspondents provide an exception to the "reporter-as-bohemian" model. In fact, it can be argued that the South's correspondents had backgrounds and social positions more like those of contemporary news gatherers. These journalists did not necessarily possess personal social and political power, but they were often related to or associated with people who did.

A good example would be Theodoric Carter, a correspondent for the *Chattanooga Rebel*. Carter himself had no wealth listed in the 1860 census, nor was he listed as owning any slaves. However, the 21-year-old lived at home with his parents, and his father was listed as having $67,000 in net wealth (combined real and personal property) and owning 29 slaves. Clearly, this level of wealth and slave-owning put the Carter family in the upper reaches of Southern society.

This is not to argue that all Confederate journalists were from wealthy slave-owning families. There are many instances in which the young men who became war correspondents had little or no wealth listed in the census and owned no slaves. In some instances, this could be explained by age, as it was in Carter's case—he had not yet inherited or earned independent wealth. War correspondence was a young man's work then as it is now. While a handful of the correspondents were on the downward slope toward age 50, the majority were still in their 20s and 30s. They were in the early stages of their careers and had not yet had the opportunity to amass wealth. Most would rise to positions of prominence with the passage of time. Some, like Henry Watterson, would go on to become important editors who would use the power of the press to help rebuild the South. Others would become a secretary of state, a chief justice of a state Supreme Court, and a personal secretary to a governor. At the time of the Civil War, they were at the dawn of their careers.

There were well-educated, wealthy men from prominent families who served as Civil War correspondents for Northern newspapers, men like Charles Graham Halpine, Adams Sherman Hill, and Henry J. Raymond. However, their numbers were diluted by the sheer volume of correspondents for Northern newspapers who came from more diverse backgrounds.

One historian has speculated that the South's professional men disproportionately sought careers in journalism because there was little else for them to do. Agriculture, which was the dominant industry in the South, did not offer the same kind of opportunities as the commerce-centered industries in Northern cities. Further, most Southern newspapers had not succumbed to the newfangled model of journalism that was sweeping Northern cities: the crime-and-scandal-ridden penny press. Southern newspapers retained their political character, a topic of prime interest to readers who had weathered the political storms resulting from the slavery debate and particularly of interest to the social elites who were more likely to be slave owners. Simply put, politics paid, particularly as the debates over slavery grew more fractious and Southern political opinion became more unified and radicalized. Who better to take charge of framing the rhetoric than an upper-class gentleman who might otherwise face underemployment?[7]

The typical Southern newsman on the eve of the Civil War was a well-educated man of prominent social standing, the perfect person to lead public opinion. He was sufficiently educated to gain respect, or at least of a social position elevated enough to have connections on the inside track of events and issues. When it came time to send reporters into the field, some of the editors volunteered, but others hired correspondents to follow the drums of war. As editors looked around for reporters to send off to Virginia or Tennessee or Arkansas, they chose men with whom they were connected in some way—often the connection was by political party or some sort of previous journalistic tie. As a result, these paid correspondents came from backgrounds very similar to those of their editors.

The *Charleston Mercury*'s staff offers examples of the educational pedigrees that were common among Southern newspaper staffs during the Civil War period. *Mercury* Editor Robert Barnwell Rhett, Jr., was a Phi Beta Kappa graduate of Harvard University. Of Rhett's four wartime correspondents, three had attended college and one had an additional professional degree. His Richmond correspondent, George W. Bagby, Jr., attended Delaware College and graduated with a medical degree from the University of Pennsylvania. Rhett's short-term correspondent in the western theater, Henry Timrod, attended the University of Georgia, and Leonidas W. Spratt, the *Mercury*'s first Virginia correspondent, had a degree from South Carolina College (now the University of South Carolina) and had also read the law. Bagby was the son of a Lynchburg, Virginia, merchant. Timrod had been born into a life of privilege in a moneyed family with its own plantation. Even though the family lost everything after Timrod's father died an early death and their plantation burned, his mother managed to send him to the best schools in Charleston when he was an adolescent. As an adult, Timrod was poverty stricken, but it was genteel poverty. He suffered, but he had numerous social connections who helped him through his bleakest moments. Spratt sprang from a political family. He was a first cousin of President James K. Polk, and his relations have continued to serve in the high reaches of American government. His great-great nephew, Congressman John Spratt of South Carolina, has been a member of the U.S. House of Representatives since 1982.

The same type of stories can be told for many of the South's other war correspondents. Felix Gregory de Fontaine, the *Charleston Courier*'s premier correspondent, apparently did not have a college degree, but he was the son of a French nobleman and had been educated by private tutors. The *Savannah Republican*'s Peter W. Alexander was a lawyer and a graduate of the University of Georgia.[8] John Linebaugh of the *Memphis Daily Appeal* was an Episcopalian priest and an attorney. Charles DeMorse of the *Clarksville* (Texas) *Standard* and James Beverley Sener of the *Richmond Enquirer* and the *Richmond Dispatch* were attorneys. Sener was a graduate of the University of Virginia with a law degree from Washington College (today, Washington and Lee University). These men were patricians. They were knights of the quill.

The term "knights of the quill" was used during the war to refer to journalists from both the North and South. On at least one occasion, the term "birds of passage" was used for journalists who made brief appearances on the battlefield but then scurried homeward soon afterward, the sort of reporter to whom today's epithet "drive-by media" might be applied.[9]

Sener, a correspondent for the *Richmond Enquirer*, referred to himself and other war correspondents with Lee's army as knights of the quill when reporting on the difficulties they were having in obtaining Northern newspapers. A Northern correspondent had used the same term a year or so previously in a story about reporters who were covering a visit by President Lincoln to West

Point. However, given other characterizations of Northern correspondents in the literature, use of this term seems out of place when applied to them.[10] The term seems more appropriate as a descriptor of the Southern editors and correspondents who tended to come from the upper echelons of society.

Confederate correspondents have been criticized for their enthusiastic and patriotic support of the Southern cause, what some historians have seen as propaganda.[11] This critique fails to consider that journalists, for the most part, were social and political insiders who had a personal stake in the outcome of the Confederate revolution. This was an ideological revolution, as well as an actual revolution. Press culture in the antebellum and Civil War South was far more complex and far less monolithic than some have portrayed it.

By the same token, most aspects of press culture were quite similar across the regions. Regardless of whether a newspaper was published in Augusta, Maine, or Augusta, Georgia, typography, printing technologies, advertising sales, postal regulations, and miserly subscribers who did not pay their bills were daily concerns of every owner and editor. In that way, newspaper production conformed to scholar James W. Carey's description of journalism as an "industrial act," a product whose conventions are "as much a product of industrialization as tin cans."[12] Although journalism in both regions shared much in common, the regions differed in their understanding of the nature and purpose of news. Journalism in the Civil War South took on a different form and had a fairly distinct purpose.

Oriented toward agriculture, Southerners lived apart from one another, yet were intimately connected through church, community, and family. Joan, one of the South's women correspondents, alluded to this when she wrote how Southern yeomen might work at manual labor all day and then walk miles to care for someone who was ill. Those connections meant Southerners had less need for newspapers to keep them up-to-date on neighborhood gossip than their kin in Northern cities who lived more closely but more anonymously.

Although Southerners did need to be connected to the larger world, that world loomed as a threat to their system of slave labor. As a result, the majority of Southern newspapers were political organs published for elite readers who had a keen interest in protecting the region's peculiar labor system. Politics and commerce dominated their pages, not the "crime and crisis" news that marked the front pages of the North's metropolitan dailies.[13] This kind of journalism succeeded because Southern readers wanted newspapers to be vigilant witnesses to the vicissitudes of Washington politics and to function as an early warning system when threats appeared on the horizon.

American newspaper readers in the early- to mid-19th century, those in the North as well as in the South, were not looking for the kind of journalism that would be dominant in the 20th century: dispassionate, detached, and authoritative.[14] They could not, for it did not yet exist. However, the Civil War would advance the movement in that direction, as public demand for information outran the desire for political commentary in both the North and the South. Southern journalists had some help moving in this direction in 1863 with the creation of a new press association and a superintendent who required journalists to adopt practices and standards that were the vanguard of modern professional practices.

John S. Thrasher, superintendent of the Confederacy's most successful news service, the Press Association of the Confederate States of America, was a leader in reforming Southern journalistic practices. He imposed new rules on his staff and on subscribing newspapers by requiring dispatches to be short, accurate, and devoid of any opinion or commentary.[15] Thrasher's rules were intended to make his correspondents more efficient and the news they produced more acceptable to all newspapers, regardless of their political interests. However, the impact was enhanced by changes that were taking place in the way some Southern journalists were thinking about their work. Even editors who were not ready to give up on personal, opinion-based journalism were recognizing that their patriotic sentiments should be balanced with enough independence that they should be willing to point out errors by the government and demand "with dignified impartiality and firmness" changes to address those errors.

The *Memphis Appeal*'s editors, for example, believed that newspapers had a responsibility to point out errors and incompetency in the conduct of the country's political and military business. That was "the mission which has been confided to it [the press] by the Government and country, and the great cause which absorbs all hearts," the paper argued.[16] Such attitudes were common in antebellum newspapers, although the "duties of patriotism" then would have been construed to be pointing out the errors of the opposition party while arguing that the paper's affiliated party had discerned the right and proper path forward. Confederate editors were beginning to understand their obligations to hold political leaders accountable, showing evidence that they were not immune to the movements toward professional standards and values that were occurring elsewhere.

For all of Thrasher's reforms, Southern newspapers did not have an easy time getting the war covered. Newspapers with very large subscription lists were unknown in the South. Southern newspapers were more likely to have only a few thousand subscribers and their available resources were meager. Rather than place paid correspondents in the field, many editors relied on dispatches from volunteer correspondents, usually soldiers serving in the units they wrote about.

Editors tried several times throughout the war to create wire services to solve some of their news-gathering problems. From 1861 to 1863, at least three services were established, but none was successful. Finally, newspaper editors from the Confederate heartland met in Atlanta in March 1862 to begin discussing the problem of getting battlefield news for their newspapers.[17]

They met again in Augusta in January 1863, and at that meeting, editors from Georgia, Alabama, Mississippi, and Tennessee established a combined professional organization and cooperative news agency, with Thrasher as superintendent.[18] The new service, headquartered in Atlanta, also worked to address problems Southern newspapers were having, such as access to military information, conscription of newspaper employees, and provisions for food and forage for field reporters.[19]

Despite its commitment to high-quality journalism, the Press Association was not always any more popular with the newspapers it served than earlier services. There was much grumbling, for example, when newspapers had to pay for long articles about the Confederate Congress that contained little usable news. Nevertheless, the association was the most successful of the Southern press associations. By January 1864, less than a year after its establishment, the association was functioning at full speed. Virtually every Confederate newspaper published from late 1863 until the end of the war carried the press association's copyrighted "Telegraphic News," another of the association's innovations. For the first time in American history, news stories were copyrighted. For Thrasher, the step was a matter of self-defense. An unscrupulous telegraph agent in Mobile, Alabama, had been diverting dispatches to individuals who wanted the news sooner than it would appear in newspapers, and Thrasher copyrighted the dispatches to protect the agency's property.[20]

Confederate war correspondents who worked for newspapers rather than wire services were sometimes professional and sometimes amateur. The amateurs were most often soldiers, but a few were women or civilian men. At least one historian has dismissed this amateur category as not qualifying as "genuine correspondents," but he was wrong to do so.[21] These amateurs should be thought of as the first generation of what today are "citizen journalists." In many cases, they were far more than mere commentators. Joan, one of the Confederacy's three women correspondents, wrote from Virginia for the *Charleston Courier*, gathering information from the War Department, the hospitals where she did nursing work, soldiers who had come to the city from the front, and travelers passing through.

Although she only wrote for a few months, Joan's correspondence was valuable because she excelled at getting news from another prized source of information: Northern newspapers, or, as they were sometimes called, "foreign journals."[22] Later in the war, these would become so scarce outside Richmond that the press association in 1864 hired a correspondent whose sole job was to get information from Northern newspapers. Joan's letters almost always included news summaries from Northern journals, a common practice at the time.

At least two other women wrote for Southern newspapers, a woman known only by her pseudonym, "Virginia," who wrote about Alabama troops stationed in Norfolk, Virginia, for the *Mobile Advertiser and Register*, and "E.L. McE.," who reported on General Joseph E. Johnston's army at Fairfax Station for the *Knoxville Register.*[23] E.L. McE. has proven elusive, for it has been impossible to locate copies of the editions of the *Register* for which she wrote.

Many of the Confederacy's correspondents were soldiers, a good number of whom had been editors or printers before the war. The list includes W.P. Price and C.M. McJunkin, editor and assistant editor of the *Greenville* (South Carolina) *Southern Enterprise,* and Hugh Wilson, an editor at the *Abbeville* (South Carolina) *Press.*[24] Melvin Dwinell, editor of the *Rome* (Georgia) *Courier,* wrote more than 200 letters while serving as an officer in the 8th Georgia Regiment. He was one of the more prolific correspondents, despite being wounded at Gettysburg and seeing action in 23 battles or skirmishes.[25] Major W.W. Humphreys of the Army of Northern Virginia became the war correspondent for the *Anderson* (South Carolina) *Intelligencer* when the paper resumed publication in February 1865. It had shut down in 1861 when Humphreys and the rest of its staff had formed a rifle company and mustered into the Confederate army. One of the editors, who had been wounded and sent home, restarted the paper and made arrangements for Humphreys to provide correspondence from Virginia.[26]

Historians have paid scant attention to the soldier correspondents from either North or South, but they were an important link between local units at war and their loved ones at home. Usually, these correspondents wrote for hometown newspapers, and their letters detailed their experiences.[27] The best soldier correspondents told the truth, whether flattering or not to Confederate troops. A correspondent for the *Savannah Republican,* for example, reported that soldiers in his unit would amuse themselves by rifling through the pockets of dead Federal soldiers, making lewd comments when they found love letters or a picture of a woman.[28] The worst were exaggerated puff pieces intended to flatter their officers.

Editors sometimes solicited battle reports from soldiers who were in town following an action. One of the *Memphis Appeal*'s stories about the Battle of Shiloh was obtained in this way. The *Appeal* editor had encountered a soldier in town the day after the battle and asked him to write an account. The soldier, who signed his letter J.W.R., complied but said his letter would be brief because the fighting had worn him out "in body and mind." The report was littered with romanticized references but it also described the action he observed.

> Stephens' and Douglas' regiments are on the left, obeying the order of our gallant, great, but unpretending "Frank"—"Drive them into hell." In this charge Capt. Rogers fell wounded—and poor John of the gallant 5th, paid the price of liberty. Alas! Alas! for these regiments. Like Bates' and Smith's, they're completely riddled; and though they have forced the enemy from his position, they cannot long stand against overwhelming numbers.

Hark! What shout is that in our rear? Whence these martial orders, re-echoed from officer to officer? Halt! Halt! Dress! Forward, march! Breckinridge, far as the eye can reach along the hills, leads his martial host. Already the enemy's left are [unreadable word] on his gunboats—has given way—his center shaking, and shouts of victory pierce the air.

Suffice to say our gallant leaders, Beauregard, Bragg, Johnston, Gladden, Polk, Ruggles, Hindman, Cheatham, Bowen, Clark, Breckinridge, Loring, Wood, Slaughter, and Hardee, were charging a line three miles in length of a desperate and determined foe. That they whipped them at every point, and at night fall, are masters of the field.[29]

Editors also published private letters from soldiers at the front brought in by the recipients. In January 1863, the *Macon Telegraph* published a description of how Confederates prepared for fighting near Fredericksburg, Virginia. Sergeant Herbert Varner of the Macon Light Artillery wrote to T.A. Harris of Macon that he and the other soldiers in camp were awakened at 4:30 in the morning with shouts of "Get up, Boys! Prepare to march! The signal gun has fired." The soldiers scurried to their duties.

Suffice it to say that a few moments labor in the snow with the frozen wheels of our guns and ammunition wagons, and the quite unhandy task of arranging frozen harnesses to our horses, found us ready for the struggle—drawn up in front of our encampment, waiting orders, which were speedily transmitted to us. It would have done your heart good to have seen with what a cheerful spirit our army marched to the battlefield that cold, misty morning. As our heavy Parrot guns passed them, they gave expression to the satisfaction they experienced in seeing these huge "dogs of terror," by frequent cheers for "Lung Tour," &c. So blockaded was the highway with troops that it was nine o'clock before we were thrown into position . . . On arriving at our position, so dense was the mist, that nothing was discernable immediately to the front except the dim outlines of towering steeples to the churches in the city below. The roar of battle was incessant; but not a soldier engaging in the fight could be seen. Gradually, the mist cleared away—there lay the city deserted and in gloom, a tempting prey to Yankee artillery, which now raked its streets with shot, shell and canister, battering down its walls, and setting fire to its finest dwellings . . .[30]

Varner warned that the next morning would bring with it "a terrible battle, but so misty was it that there was little firing before the forenoon." By that time the fog had lifted its veil and the battle resumed, Varner wrote that the enemy's bayonets "glistened with dazzling light and their huge line of troops stood defiantly firm." The jockeying continued.

The long line of infantry, with cavalry to their left, is put in motion; they advance directly against our position. They are numerous—say fifteen thousand—and we all look to our commanding General, anxiously waiting to hear the command, "Commence firing!" He surveys them complacently with his glass, removes it slowly, and turning round, says calmly: "Open on them—slowly and with precision." No sooner had we fired our first guns than the entire crest of hills bordering the valley was alive with flames of fire, belching forth from our cannon, and hurling missiles of destruction into the compact ranks of the enemy . . . Our artillery drove the advancing column of infantry behind the banks of the river, which protected them from our fire. . . They remained under cover of the hills near the river bank till darkness set in, and so ended the first day's operations . . .[31]

Rumors flew through the Confederate lines on the morning after the second day of fighting, according to Varner. The artillerymen were hearing that Burnside wanted to renew the attack, but his officers were refusing to go back into battle. "I heard many prisoners say that Burnside had ruined himself and the cause of the North by fighting Lee at Fredericksburg—by the unwise policy of exposing his men to no advantage on that battle ground, where they said, Lee's army could whip the entire Northern army."[32] Varner added that the Union divisions "fought more bravely than Yankees were ever known to fight. But that is readily explained: they drank all the liquors in the city and were truly drunk— some of them so much as to stagger wildly over the field and many too drunk to carry their guns." By Tuesday morning, however, the fighting was over. "Not a Yankee was to be seen on this side of the Rappahannock. Their retreating columns were seen marching down the river," and for good measure, the Confederate artillery fired two parting shots at the Yankee rear, Varner reported.

Stories by soldier-correspondents varied in quality, but the best, like Varner's, had a "you-were-there" immediacy that is the mark of excellent reporting. Soldier-correspondents often wrote with great optimism and enthusiasm about their exploits, as did Varner, and some have interpreted their zealous patriotism as propaganda.[33] An equally valid argument can be made that such stories were examples in print of the *esprit d'corps* of soldiers. Throughout the war, soldier morale tended to be higher than that of civilians, and it was not uncommon for soldiers to encourage the folks back home about the progress of the war. Stories with the immediacy and vibrancy of Varner's letter allowed readers to experience the action. One cannot read Varner's letter without feeling the bite of frost on his cheeks and the impatience of the horses to get moving.

Covering the Civil War as a field reporter was arduous work for miserable pay. Correspondents traipsed after armies, often on foot and in bad weather. Those working for individual newspapers fared a little better with regard to salaries. Henry Timrod, a well-known literary figure, was one of the better paid correspondents. He received $6 a day plus traveling expenses when he covered the Corinth campaign for the *Charleston Mercury*. George W. Bagby, Jr., who also wrote for the *Mercury*, never received more than $3 a story.[34] While that may not sound like a lot, Bagby was prolific. Most days, he wrote at least one, and often two, letters, and he wrote for more than one newspaper, some with more generous pay scales than the *Mercury*. The *Nashville* (Tennessee) *Union and American*, for example, paid Bagby $5 a story.[35]

Wire service salaries in 1863 ranged from $10 to $100 a month, depending on the amount of time assignments required. Reporters working closer to the action were better paid; however, they had greater expenses. The Southern Associated Press, a short-lived Confederate wire service, was paying its Fredericksburg correspondent $100 a month in 1863. A year later, the Richmond newspapers matched that salary for their Fredericksburg correspondents. Because of the spiraling cost of living in urban areas, some correspondents, such as those stationed in Richmond, received supplemental pay. Richmond wire service reporter J. Henly Smith was receiving an additional $4 a day subsistence allowance in the spring of 1864.[36]

Translating these figures into meaningful numbers is difficult because of the problems with Confederate currency and inflation and the difficulty in accurately translating dollars across nearly 150 years. However, based on calculations using an online inflation calculation in conjunction with calculations of the value of Confederate dollars in gold, that $100 salary in 1863 Confederate dollars would translate to about $570 in 2008 dollars.[37]

In addition to salaries, mounted reporters received an allowance to cover the cost of maintaining a horse. It was with some trepidation that the press association board of directors agreed in early 1864 to provide horses for their field correspondents—provided the reporter paid a security deposit on the horse to ensure its "return in the same good order" that he received it. Providing horses for correspondents was an expensive prospect, but the expense was worthwhile. According to Superintendent Thrasher, in the year the wire service's reporters had been without horses, their dispatches had been slow and desultory.[38]

Unlike Northern correspondents who could purchase food from the Union army, Confederate correspondents had to supply their own rations. So if they had no opportunity to get to town to resupply, they would often go hungry or have to forage for food on their own. The situation became so critical that Thrasher sought legislation that would require the army to sell food and forage to correspondents. Senator Louis Wigfall of Texas introduced the measure in Congress on May 18, 1864, but it failed because of obstruction by Senator Benjamin Hill of Georgia. Thrasher then asked the secretary of war to recommend that generals allow press association correspondents to purchase supplies from military stores. The secretary declined, arguing that the generals could issue such an order if they wished. Correspondents were left on their own to find provisions.[39]

A common image of the war correspondent is the stalwart, solitary journalist braving the guns of war on his own, but Confederate correspondents sometimes banded together in their travels. The editors of Savannah's two dailies, William

Tappan Thompson of the *Morning News* and James R. Sneed of the *Republican*, traveled together to Charleston to cover the bombardment of Fort Sumter.

Only a few months later, as Union and Confederate troops met outside a Virginia village called Manassas, correspondents made their way *en masse* to what would soon become the site of the Confederacy's first victory. The party included Leonidas W. Spratt of the *Charleston Mercury*, Felix Gregory de Fontaine of the *Charleston Courier* and the *Richmond Enquirer*, Peter W. Alexander of the *Savannah Republican*, and William Shepardson of the *Columbus* (Georgia) *Times* and the *Montgomery* (Alabama) *Advertiser*. Alexander and de Fontaine were still traveling together the following spring, accompanied by New Orleans correspondent H.H. Perry, although it was not clear whether they were fleeing the approaching Union armies or going to cover the pending fight at Corinth, Mississippi.[40]

After following the army all day, correspondents prepared their dispatches at night. Alexander of the *Republican* followed a standard practice, first drafting a short dispatch to be sent by telegraph. The next day, he would follow that with a lengthy letter that he often worked on all night. At dawn, he would gallop off to get the dispatch in the mail.[41]

Military censorship or unavailability of a courier often delayed correspondents' reports. Press restrictions in the Confederacy consisted primarily of limitations on access to the armies and to the telegraphic wires. Telegraphic restrictions were among the first imposed.[42] They were considered necessary because news could move faster than armies for the first time.[43] However, such restrictions merely slowed the transmission of information, since correspondents could still send their dispatches by mail or courier. Access was a bigger issue. Without direct access to the armies, correspondents had to wait for publication of official dispatches, which could take months. Soldiers who had fought in a battle made their way to a town where they might be interviewed, as press association Superintendent Thrasher did in Atlanta after the Battle of Chickamauga, when General Braxton Bragg prohibited correspondents from joining the army.[44]

Despite access problems, Confederate newspapers never faced the level of censorship their Northern counterparts endured. One of President Jefferson Davis' proudest boasts was that the Confederate government had been able, for the most part, to protect press freedom throughout its short existence. The Confederate Constitution was proof, Davis asserted, of the new nation's intent to maintain fidelity to long-held American principles. The president maintained that the Confederate struggle was one for constitutional liberties and, although he might deplore partisan and mean-spirited attacks from newspapers, he accepted them as part of a free society.[45]

Davis maintained that the Confederacy, through its "unequal struggle," had never acted "to impair personal liberty or the freedom of speech, of thought, or of the press."[46] As late as the fall of 1864, he was publicly claiming freedom of expression as one of his prime values. In an interview with Mrs. Rose Green-how, a famous Confederate spy and author, Davis said his commitment to free speech was what kept him from suppressing the *Richmond Examiner*. She quoted him as saying, "Better suffer from that evil which is temporary, than to arrest it by a still greater one. It is a dangerous thing to interfere with the liberty of the press; for what would it avail us if we gain our independence and lose our liberty?"[47] Historians point out that the press fared better in the Confederacy than political dissidents.[48]

This apparent paradox in Southern attitudes—ambivalence regarding freedom for slaves coupled with unshakable commitment to individual liberties—may strike modern readers as bizarre. To understand this thinking, one must remember that the South's "peculiar institution" offered daily lessons on what it meant to lose one's freedom. Those lessons, coupled with their privileged position, taught white Southerners to guard their freedoms jealously—even fanatically.

Civilians matched the Davis government in their tolerance for dissent. Only twice did Confederate mobs attack newspapers, and the attacks were in the same town over the same issue. In the summer of 1863, a mob of Georgia soldiers wrecked the *Raleigh* (North Carolina) *Standard* office because of the editor's pro-peace stance, and the next day a mob of *Standard* supporters sacked the opposition newspaper's office in retaliation. The Confederate Congress preferred to let the military negotiate access and content issues with journalists. This was a solution that the U.S. Supreme Court would settle on in the 20th century with regard to controlling reporter access to courts. In a 1976 decision, the Court admonished judges to control the parties over whom they have authority, such as lawyers, bailiffs, and witnesses, and to avoid placing restrictions on reporters.[49] Nevertheless, military commanders were often constrained by the Davis administration's insistence that the Confederacy follow a strict constructionist approach to constitutional issues. It was a stance that would prove inconvenient in the latter days of the war when some Davis men, and perhaps the president himself, found that a degree of ruthlessness, not constitutional idealism, was necessary to win wars.[50]

Despite their demands for freedom, Southern journalists also believed they had the responsibility to support the public good, and that meant being careful with information that would reveal military secrets. When General Pierre G.T. Beauregard expelled all reporters from his army because of what he considered an indiscreet dispatch published in the *Memphis Appeal*, the *Savannah Republican*'s Alexander responded that he agreed the offending journalist should be punished. However, he argued that punishment should not be extended to those journalists who had not published the information. He wrote, "There is no reason why the innocent should be made to suffer, and especially the people who have been lavish of their means and their blood in support of our cause."

Alexander mounted another, even more persuasive argument, at least to modern ears. He wrote:

> This war is the people's war. Their sons and brothers make up the army, and their means, and theirs alone, support and maintain it. And shall they not be allowed to know anything that is transpiring within that army? When their sons are maimed or slain in battle, shall they be denied the poor privilege of seeing a list of the killed or wounded? Is the army to be a sealed book to the country? Even in the despotic France and monarchial England, literary men have been encouraged to accompany their armies, and to write freely of their movements; but it has been reserved for a free (?) America alone to place a muzzle upon the Press . . .[51]

Alexander argued that the offending telegraphed report could not have given away any sensitive information because it did not arrive until after the enemy already knew the Confederate army's location. Further, Alexander doubted Federal commanders needed to examine Southern newspapers for information about troop movement. He pointed out that Confederate lines were porous and that "spies, dressed in the garb of citizens, enter and leave our lines without much difficulty." Deserters and disaffected citizens were also known to carry information to the enemy, he added. Alexander concluded, "An attempt, therefore, to saddle any part of the blame upon the correspondent in question is unjust and disingenuous. A scapegoat is wanted, however, and this writer has answered the occasion." Alexander's objective in writing his letter was "vindication of the freedom of the Press, and of the rights and respectability of literary men everywhere."[52]

Reporters sometimes provided sensitive military information through ignorance. Most of the reporters in the field, even many who were also soldiers, had scant military experiences to draw on in evaluating what information could safely be published. Many Southern correspondents were too young to have served in the Mexican war, the only major American war that would likely have occurred in their lifetimes.[53]

Official cautions about what correspondents should and should not report began at the outset of the war. As soon as the fighting started, Secretary of War Leroy Walker warned correspondents not to give away military secrets. He specifically told them to publish nothing about force size, number of weapons, condition of the troops, or possible military movements.[54] Similar cautions were repeated by people serving in the army. Albert Rhett, a captain in the Brooks Guard and brother of *Charleston Mercury* Editor Robert Barnwell Rhett, Jr., wrote another brother who was working at the paper, urging what has been virtually universal practice by the American press through all the country's wars: "Be exceedingly careful how you write in the Mercury, or publish anything to give the enemy a knowledge of our numbers or equipment."[55]

The Confederate government itself never adopted a censorship law, even when military authorities asked the War Department to intervene.[56] The response generally was that no laws were available to prohibit publication of military information, and the government was not particularly interested in adopting any. Rules of military conduct did give officers a few options for dealing with correspondents. They could expel individual correspondents, as General Joseph E. Johnston did in December 1861. Johnston banned reporters from his army and reminded soldiers and officers that conveying information to the enemy, even when done unwittingly, would aid the enemy, and was punishable by death.[57] Braxton Bragg also banished reporters from his headquarters in 1862.[58]

Beyond this sort of military control, Confederate civilian authorities believed that it should be left to journalists to do the right thing, to readers to be satisfied with information that could be published without harm to the army, and to commanding officers to enforce existing military regulations regarding reporters who overstepped their bounds. President Davis summarized Confederate attitudes in a letter to General Bragg: "To preserve the liberty of press, yet restrain its license, is possible only where it is controlled by a sound taste and sentiment in its patrons."[59]

Even General Robert E. Lee could not budge the Confederate government's reticence. In July 1862, Lee wrote to the new Confederate secretary of war, George W. Randolph, to complain about an article in the *Richmond Daily Dispatch* that disclosed troop locations. He demanded that Randolph stop that sort of publication.[60] Randolph sent copies of the letter to the newspapers in Richmond, and he added a note saying he hoped it would not become necessary for his department to intervene. Despite his subtle threat, Randolph never sought censorship legislation, nor did the Confederate Congress take up the matter on its own.[61]

Three days before Lee wrote his letter, General Earl Van Dorn, commander of the southern Mississippi and eastern Louisiana military district, declared martial law in that area and ordered the arrest of any journalist who published information about troop movements or anything that would impair public confidence in the military or the government. The order also made it a death penalty offense to communicate with the enemy.[62]

Van Dorn's order provoked a lively debate in the Confederate Congress, more because the general imposed martial law and suspended the writ of habeas corpus than because of his threat to journalists. Van Dorn was denounced as a threat to the pillars of freedom, and later that summer, Senator T.J. Semmes of Louisiana introduced legislation to restrain military commanders from unconstitutionally exercising civilian powers. Van Dorn bowed to public pressure and revoked his order.[63]

Military censorship reached its peak in 1862. By early 1863, press association Superintendent Thrasher was making efforts to improve press access. One of his first steps was to travel through the Confederacy, meeting with generals to work out those issues. When General Beauregard began delaying dispatches, Thrasher called on him personally and explained the need for access and timely transmission. He also agreed that his reporters would share what they learned about the enemy with Confederate military authorities. Beauregard was impressed with Thrasher and urged other Confederate generals to cooperate with him.[64]

Although some newspapers had their own rules for news dispatches, the rules were generally similar to those of Thrasher. The *Charleston Courier*, for example, refused to publish stories about the number or position of forces, points likely to be occupied by the enemy or doubts about their strength, the arrival or departure of troops, events of the future, or hints at actions to be taken. The *Courier* also declined to list strength estimates for Confederate forces and only reported on what was believed to have actually happened during battles or what was available from official military reports.[65] The *Courier*'s position amounted to what some might consider self-censorship, although others might call it responsible publishing.

Whether it was responsibility or self-censorship, some Southern editors may have been more cautious because of the region's greater unanimity of purpose.[66] Even hard-line libertarians like the editor of the *Augusta Chronicle and Sentinel* agreed that newspapers ought to keep military secrets. "A man who happens to own a printing press should not be allowed to print sentiments intended to aid the enemy . . . No paper should be allowed to print treasonable sentiments," Editor Nathan S. Morse wrote.[67] This is an ironic statement from an editor who later in the war would be accused of being a traitor himself for advocating for peace and criticizing Jefferson Davis. However, Morse would have been among the first to argue that critiquing the performance of public officials was one of the most important responsibilities of the press and ought to occur, even if it aided the enemy by undermining civilian morale. He would see a distinction between such criticisms and reporting on troop movements and military plans.

Not surprisingly, the *Charleston Mercury* was an exception to an otherwise fairly tractable press on the issue of protecting military secrets. Its editors believed the public had a right to know everything about the war since it was providing the men and the money for it,[68] although the newspaper also admitted, if somewhat reluctantly, that "no one favors indiscreet publications useful to the enemy."[69] The *Mercury* was an anomaly among 19th century newspapers. It was firmly committed to the notion that the public had a right to know not only about government operations but about those of the military as well. Throughout the Confederacy's brief existence, the paper crusaded for open meetings of Congress and battled any attempts to restrain the press. When General van Dorn issued his 1862 order making it a capital offense for any journalist to publish information about troop movements or any information that would erode public confidence in military or civilian authorities, the *Mercury* responded with an indignant editorial that reminded readers of the free speech clause in the Confederate Constitution.[70] That clause, the *Mercury* pointed out, was supposed to be a shield against press suppression. "The Constitution under which we live, expressly provides that—'Congress shall make no law abridging the freedom of speech or of the press,'" the editors wrote.[71]

Press restraints were only one reason that correspondents were not always Johnny-on-the-spot to report firsthand on military affairs. Illness and injury were other frequent impediments. The long days, often sleepless nights, constant exposure to the elements and camp illnesses, lack of food, and bad water were a constant threat to correspondents. "L," a correspondent for the *Carolina Spartan* of Spartanburg, South Carolina, missed nearly a month in the field when he came down with typhoid fever. Ivy W. Duggan, a popular soldier-correspondent for the Sandersville, Georgia, *Central Georgian,* was hospitalized three times in 1861 for various camp diseases. The *Central Georgian* editor commented, "Mr. Duggan's patriotism is greater than his strength."[72] Injuries were also common. De Fontaine, reporting for the *Charleston Courier,* was dragged nearly 70 yards by his frightened horse. Although he received no major injuries, he dealt with the painful aftereffects for several months.

Correspondents ran risks of even greater sacrifices: death, or capture—by the enemy and by friendly troops. The *Augusta Daily Chronicle and Sentinel*'s Milledgeville correspondent, "Rover," had a close call near Madison, Georgia, while covering Sherman's March to the Sea in late 1864. He was traveling from Eatonton to Madison, listening for Confederate pickets to call out alarms if Yankee soldiers were in the area. Suddenly, a Confederate scout "came dashing down the road crying, 'to the woods, to the woods,' and we wooded," Rover wrote. He waited several hours in the rain before returning to the road to see if he could move on. "We had not traveled more than a hundred yards, before a party of cerulean clad equestrians came dashing up, and in a very polite and insinuating manner briefly requested us to halt. The request was accompanied with most significant cocking of carbines and pistols, which, brought to a horizontal attitude in one's front are very persuasive, especially to an unarmed civilian and we halted." The Union soldiers questioned him intensively about the locations of Confederate troops in the area and then let him go.[73]

The work of the Confederacy's correspondents filled an important social need. Readers wanted to know about battles, especially when there was fighting nearby, and casualties. When fighting was distant, readers avidly consulted newspapers to find out how local boys and men fared in the battles.[74] Journalism historians have disagreed about how well Southern correspondents met readers' needs for war information. Phillip Knightley found Southern correspondence to be subpar, but it should be noted that he felt the same way about most early war correspondents.[75] Others, including J. Cutler Andrews and 20th century Mississippi reporter/editor Hodding Carter, II, believed that the Civil War produced good journalism and far more of it than has often been possible in other wars.[76]

Sherman's men destroying railroad tracks in Atlanta, Georgia. Photograph from the
Library of Congress

Andrews suggested that the quality of Southern journalism was not as poor as
some historians have portrayed it. He concluded that the best Confederate correspondence was easily as good as the best work of Union reporters.[77]

The best correspondence was outstanding in both quality and effectiveness.
Peter W. Alexander of the *Savannah Republican*, by most estimates, including
competitors, was one of the best correspondents in the South. The *Charleston Mercury* called Alexander "The War Correspondent . . . who has hitherto
earned the reputation of being one of the most discriminating and best informed of letter writers with the Army of the Potomac."[78] Alexander's prestige
was enhanced in late 1862, following the Battle of Sharpsburg, when he began a campaign to ensure that the South's ragged soldiers were adequately fed,
clothed, and housed in the coming winter.[79] Alexander's story created a sensation throughout the Confederacy. The *Savannah Republican* reported several
weeks later that every exchange newspaper it received had reprinted the story.[80]
Republican Editor James R. Sneed used Alexander's story and the response to
it to point out the value of a correspondent's work, especially with regard to

reporting on army corruption: "[H]e has shown a fearless courage in exposing official delinquencies and inefficiencies."[81]

Another of the South's most significant correspondents was the *Charleston Courier*'s de Fontaine, who was already roving through the South in 1860, writing about abolition for the *New York Herald*. His articles were so extensive that they were published in 1861 as a book, *History of Abolition; its Four Great Epochs,* which was reprinted in 2009. The stories that he wrote about the Montgomery convention and the founding of the Confederate government were reprinted in *Army Letters from Personne*, a magazine that de Fontaine published after the war.[82] He wrote the first story to be published in the North about the firing on Fort Sumter. He covered dozens of skirmishes and battles and wrote prolifically from the field through the entire war with the exception of four months in early 1864. During that time he produced columns and editorials for the *Daily South Carolinian*, a newspaper that he had bought in Columbia, while simultaneously writing a book of war anecdotes, *Marginalia, or Gleanings from an Army Note-book,* which was reprinted as recently as 2006.

Shortly after the war ended, the *New York Times* called de Fontaine the South's "ablest war correspondent."[83] De Fontaine was in the field for virtually the entire four years of war, and his stories bore witness to some of the most dramatic moments of the conflict. De Fontaine's story recounting his survey of the battlefield at Ball's Bluff in Virginia demonstrates his mastery at making war real for his readers. He watched the sickening sight of pigs running away from the battlefield, one with a human hand in its mouth, being chased by six others. Further along, he and his companions came upon a trench where the remains of Union soldiers had been hastily, and improperly, buried. One pig gnawed on "a piece of shoulder, another was gnawing at a leg, while a third was pulling out the bowels of a half decomposed corpse. Gathering a pile of stones, we did all in our power to prevent the awful desecration by covering the bodies for a time, and a file of men was promptly detached to complete the work which the Yankees had so cruelly left undone."[84]

De Fontaine's writing showed a keen awareness of the need to balance the gruesome, demoralizing stories like this one with something to uplift his readers' spirits. His stories often included comic sections told in a light-hearted, waggish style, sometimes with a sharp moral lesson. De Fontaine was keenly aware of the paradoxes of human nature and the absurd. He offered a good example in the fall of 1861in a feature about the artillery units of the Army of the Potomac.[85] His concluding paragraph was clearly intended to poke fun at the officers of those units. De Fontaine wrote that the five commanding officers were all "supreme, absolute and incorrigible bachelors in the loneliest sense of the term." They were as "full of unappropriated affection as a prism is of color, young, good-looking, chivalrous, domestic, overflowing with the milk of human kindness and admiration for the gentler sex, neither of them has the courage to pucker his lips . . ." De Fontaine continued with the "revelation" that the men were taking bids for ladies willing to take on a lifetime of darning socks and sewing buttons. His P.S. to the article clarified the officers' requirements: "Widows and maidens over forty or weighing more than two hundred and seventy-five pounds, avoirdupois, will receive no attention."[86]

Other reporters made significant contributions. Leonidas W. Spratt was the *Charleston Mercury's* earliest Virginia correspondent. An attorney by training, Spratt had worked in the 1850s as a crusading newspaper editor whose cause was reopening the slave trade. Spratt eventually sold his newspaper to the *Mercury* owners, but he continued to work for the Rhetts and took to the lecture trail to build support for his dream of renewing importation of slaves.

One of Spratt's most important contributions to Civil War history came from one of his final dispatches in the *Mercury*. Writing after the First Battle of Manassas, Spratt added an anecdote to a July 24, 1861, dispatch. His story focused on the news that the body of General Barnard Bee was being returned to South Carolina. However, Spratt, in describing Bee's death, included a description of events just prior to the general's death. Spratt wrote that Bee's men were being overwhelmed by enemy forces. As the general was desperately looking for a way to rally their spirits, he spied another Confederate general. Bee pointed to the general and shouted to his terrified troops, "There is Jackson, standing like a stone-wall."[87] Spratt's anecdote preserved for history the moment when General Thomas Jackson received his famous nickname.

Most scholarly attention given to Confederate correspondence has focused on men like Alexander, Spratt, and de Fontaine who reported on military affairs, but another group of correspondents covered the politics of the war. Political news coverage exploded as the Southern states debated secession after Lincoln's election. The *Atlanta Intelligencer* and the *Augusta Constitutionalist* sent reporters to Florida in January 1861 to cover that state's Secession Convention. The *Intelligencer* sent its associate editor, John W. Leonard, who reported that Floridians were "true as steel."[88] Many newspapers would send correspondents to Richmond to cover sessions of the Confederate Congress.[89] The *Mercury* hired Richmond native George W. Bagby, Jr., a physician who had turned to journalism in the 1850s. Bagby, who wrote under the pseudonym "Hermes," would become a fearless critic of Jefferson Davis and an important press dissenter.[90] Bagby's invective became so strident that *Mercury* Editor Robert B. Rhett, Jr., a man not known for his measured words nor conciliatory editorials, ordered Bagby to moderate his assessments of the president.

Much Civil War correspondence was little more than bombastic bravado, unrealistically optimistic and often downright wrong. However, those inaccurate reports were often based on what correspondents had learned from the officers in charge of the units in action who did not know or understand what happened during an engagement. It took days or weeks for more accurate

The Civil War correspondents' memorial arch was erected in 1896 in Gathland State Park, Maryland. Photograph by Debra Reddin van Tuyll

reports to become clear. To demand complete accuracy for battlefield reports in the immediate aftermath of a fight is to ask for the impossible from both generals and correspondents.

Given the circumstances, Confederate correspondents did as good a job as possible covering the war, and they excelled on other stories. The reporters were

Hermes, the Greek messenger god, on
the Civil War correspondents' memorial
arch, Gathland State Park, Maryland.
Photograph by Debra Reddin van Tuyll

especially adept at keeping the plight of the ragged, hungry soldier in front of
the public. They offered well-written descriptions of life in camps and on the
battlefield and provided real insight into how the war was going.[91] They were
not unlike the members of their "luckless tribe" across history. They reported
the battles and the politics and the effects of the war, sometimes secondhand
and often without a clue to the truth. Editors and audiences alike believed that
newspapers played a valuable role in the South's doomed struggle for freedom.

". . . fifty years or a century hence, no memorial of our epoch will be more
valuable than a file of newspapers published at the present time," wrote *Augusta
Chronicle and Sentinel* Editor William S. Jones in the winter of 1861.[92] W.J.
Yates, editor of the Charlotte, North Carolina, *Western Democrat,* made virtually the same claim four years later as the war neared its end. "The best history
of the present war that has been, or ever will be, written is already penned," he
wrote days before the fall of Richmond. "It will be found in the newspapers of

the Confederacy."[93] An important Georgia weekly, the *Athens Southern Watchman*, believed that "next to our organized armies, [newspapers] are the most powerful engines within our country for the attainment of its independence."[94]

Readers believed newspapers were important, too. Immediately after the fall of Fort Sumter, as far away as Montgomery, Alabama, the *Charleston Mercury* was in huge demand. The *Mercury*'s Montgomery correspondent wrote that "On Sunday, THE MERCURY was in great demand, and large sums were offered for a single copy containing the account of the battle."[95] Diarist Cornelia Phillips Spencer wrote that her fellow North Carolinians, many of whom had never subscribed to more than their county weekly, came to see dailies as an absolute necessity during the war. She wrote that there was considerable "general anxiety to have the latest news, and above all from the army."[96]

Journalists had the power to affect public opinion and morale even while moving away from the partisan model of earlier times and toward more detached, impartial reporting. Although newspapers were not the only source of information that might affect public opinion, they were an important one, according to social and political theorists such as Benedict Anderson and Talcott Williams. These scholars contend that newspapers function as "a common consciousness" that makes formation of public opinion possible, and they argue that without news media, it would be impossible for information to spread through society and become the foundation for concerted public action.[97] Those who wrote for Confederate newspapers would have agreed. "The power of the newspaper press," wrote Joan, a correspondent for the *Charleston Courier*, "is not half appreciated by us. It *makes* [emphasis hers] public opinion."[98]

South Carolina

Batteries of the Confederate states bombard Fort Sumter as the Civil War begins. *Harper's Weekly*, April 27, 1861. Courtesy of South Caroliniana Library, University of South Carolina, Columbia

Dozens of reporters poured into the South during the tense last months before the Civil War began, and as shots were fired at Fort Sumter on April 12, 1861, the demand for news became intense. South Carolina's two most influential newspapers, the *Charleston Courier* and the *Charleston Mercury*, fielded correspondents whose prolific and detailed articles were frequently reprinted by other newspapers and are still being quoted by historians today.

The *Courier*, a consistent opponent of disunion and nullification, hired at least two correspondents: Felix Gregory de Fontaine, who wrote as "Personne," and "Joan," who has never been identified. De Fontaine was a reporter for the *New York Herald* when he filed the first story to reach the North after the start of the Civil War. However, he joined the *Courier* and the Confederate army after the fall of Fort Sumter and became one of the most significant correspondents for the South. Joan, who was one of the Confederacy's three female correspondents in the war, accompanied her son to Virginia where she wrote for four months from the War Department, hospitals, and Richmond.

In addition, the strident *Mercury*, which had campaigned for secession and war, fielded a steady stream of correspondents, including Henry Timrod ("Kappa"), William Ashmead Courtenay ("Kiawah"), Leonidas William Spratt ("L.W.S."), and Bartholomew Riordan ("Adsum").

After joining his friend de Fontaine at the front, the sickly Timrod reported in a quinine-induced stupor for less than three months before returning to South Carolina. Timrod's mind was filled with the horrors and devastation that he had witnessed, and he wrote poetry from his heart that would make him the Poet Laureate of the Confederacy. His work, which is still included in most anthologies of American poetry, was resurrected in August 2006 when Bob Dylan borrowed from Timrod's poetry for the lyrics of his best-selling album *Modern Times*.

Timrod might have been forgotten had it not been for Courtenay, a friend and fellow correspondent from Charleston, who created a foundation to publish Timrod's poetry after the war. Courtenay's war correspondence forced him into a duel at the start of the war. He survived the duel and the war and afterward devoted much of his time and his great wealth to preserving history.

As Spratt was preparing to leave his job as a correspondent for the *Mercury*, he wrote a final article that created a Civil War legend. His news story about the return of the body of General Barnard Bee to South Carolina contained the anecdote that stamped General Thomas Jackson with his enduring nickname "Stonewall."

Riordan slipped into Washington, D.C., to spy on the Federals before returning to South Carolina to become managing editor of the *Mercury*. Later in the war, he also became the Charleston-based reporter for the Press Association of the Confederate States of America, which was organized by Southern newspaper editors looking for a reliable way to get battlefield news.

South Carolinian editor Robert W. Gibbes, Jr., became president of the combined wire service and professional association. Although Gibbes never reported in the field, he used his position and prestige to advocate for the correspondents and to battle army censorship and conscription of journalists.

2

William Ashmead Courtenay: A Knight on the "Field of Honor"

Patricia G. McNeely

Because of his criticism of military conditions in the Confederate army, correspondent William Ashmead Courtenay began and very nearly ended his service in the Civil War trying to defend his reputation on the field of honor. Soon after he arrived on the Virginia battlefield in October 1861, soldiers in the South Carolina Palmetto Guard accused Courtenay of writing a story in the *Charleston Mercury* that was "false and slanderous, and totally unworthy of a true Carolinian."[1]

Outraged, Courtenay considered their charges to be an attack on his character and challenged one of their officers to a duel. No one was injured in the confrontation, and Courtenay, who prided himself on his accuracy and honesty, continued his editorial crusade against the wretched army conditions that had led to the duel. As the war was drawing to a close, Courtenay accused another officer in Hardeeville, South Carolina, of mistreating military horses. When the officer tried to blame him for starving the animals, Courtenay demanded satisfaction. The duel was aborted after months of correspondence when it became obvious that the offending officer was never going to meet him on the field of honor.[2]

When the war ended, Courtenay turned his efforts to building businesses in transportation and manufacturing in a state writhing in the political and economic turmoil of Reconstruction. While his businesses were growing, he became an art patron and mayor of Charleston and was endorsed as a gubernatorial candidate by several newspapers.

Decades later, Courtenay was still writing about the war, and he played a pivotal role in creating Henry Timrod's legacy as poet laureate of the Confederacy. By the turn of the century, Courtenay was one of the wealthiest men in the South. His range of business, political, cultural, and literary activities was so extensive that the *Charleston News and Courier* summarized his life on June 11, 1909, by saying that he had been a "'Captain' on the tented field, 'Mayor' of

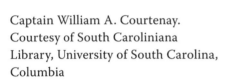

Captain William A. Courtenay.
Courtesy of South Caroliniana
Library, University of South Carolina,
Columbia

Carolina's metropolis, 'President' of a great manufacturing plant and crowning all was 'Doctor' in the world of letters."

Born in Charleston on February 4, 1831, Courtenay and his older brother, S. Gilman, were raised by their widowed mother Elizabeth and other female relatives.[3] When Courtenay was 12 years old, he attended Dr. John C. Faber's academy for three years before going to work in his brother's publishing and book-selling business.[4] He joined the Washington Light Infantry, a South Carolina militia unit, on April 29, 1851, but continued working for his brother's book company until October 1, 1860, when he became business manager of the *Mercury*, one of the most stridently secessionist newspapers in the South.[5]

Six days after Abraham Lincoln was elected president on November 6, 1860, South Carolina Governor Francis W. Pickens ordered Courtenay's infantry unit to guard the U.S. Arsenal in Charleston, where military supplies and 22,000 muskets were stored. South Carolina seceded from the union on December 20. After the first shots of the Civil War were fired at Fort Sumter on April 12, 1861, Courtenay was one of 180 infantrymen ordered to occupy Fort William Washington on the east end of Sullivan's Island.

Courtenay was separated from his infantry unit in Charleston in the fall of 1861 when he was transferred to Virginia as a quartermaster in General James Longstreet's corps.[6] He arrived in mid-October after rains had turned Manassas

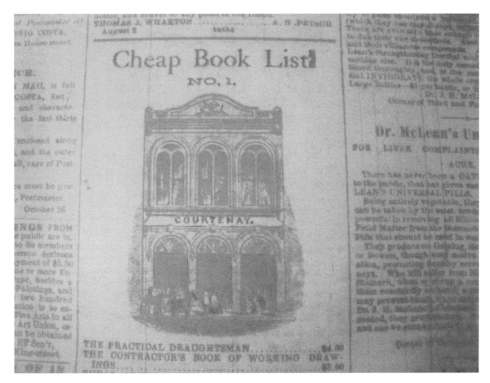

An advertisement for Courtenay's book shop, which was located at 9 Broad Street in Charleston. *Charleston Courier,* September 2, 1861. Courtesy of South Caroliniana Library, University of South Carolina, Columbia

Junction into a river of mud. "The rain was pouring down—a sort of second deluge," he wrote. "The red clay had been trodden by the thousands who traverse it, into a sort of tough paste, with a mean depth of about six inches."[7] Rain and mud were not his greatest problems, however. After waiting two hours to get an official permit, he could not find his suitcase. After searching desperately on the platform, he asked a man wrapped in an oilcloth if he knew where he could find his baggage.

> "Baggage!" the man replied. "Indeed, if you have not kept it under your seat all the way, it's gone sir—GONE; nobody ever recovers baggage HERE—it goes either one of two courses—STOLEN or LOST—most often larceny; but, sometimes, articles get mislaid and then they are discovered after some drenching rain has reduced everything to ruin; it's all d—n nonsense to look for baggage HERE."[8]

Courtenay searched the rest of the day until, cold, hungry, and wet, he warmed himself beside a campfire before crawling into the quartermaster's storehouse and sleeping on a pile of salt. At early dawn, an Alabama soldier gave Courtenay a cup of hot coffee before he went back to hunt for his valise, which

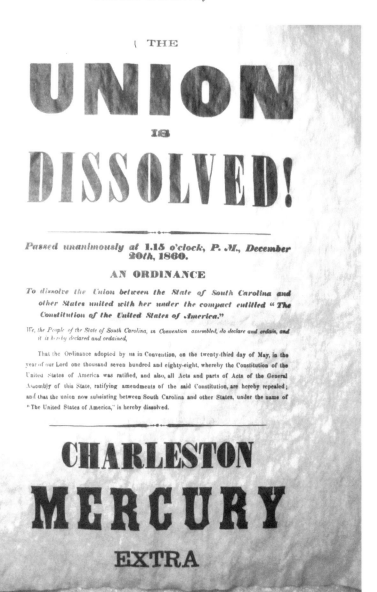

Charleston Mercury extra announcing secession. Courtesy of South Caroliniana Library, University of South Carolina, Columbia

he found, somewhat flattened, but in good shape. Courtenay had not been in his tent a day before he started writing under the pseudonym "Kiawah." Like most correspondents, he had chosen a pen name to protect himself and to facilitate his ability to gather information. Even though he had just arrived in Virginia, he was already critical of the direction of the war.

Seen as we all see it here, groping and foundering about from Munson's Hill to Fairfax Court House, apparently without meaning or object, sometimes advancing—again

Munson's Hill, the advance post of the Confederate army on the Potomac River. *Harper's Weekly,* October 5, 1861. Courtesy of Rare Books and Special Collections, University of South Carolina Libraries

retreating—our army is a huge machine dormant, with its extremities engaged in those delightful irregularities, known in a soldier's life as out-post duties. Sitting outside my tent, with my eye fixed on a mountain top in Maryland, due north, I wonder in the sleepy mood that I am in, if the "Army of the Potomac" will get there before December's blasts freeze up the camps, and winter quarters are voted, with grim unanimity, "a military necessity."[9]

At the end of his article, Kiawah appended a note that was intended only for his editor Robert Barnwell Rhett, Jr., but the postscript was published in the *Mercury* October 18, 1861.

P.S. . . . I have talked a great deal with the officers, and I find that our South Carolina troops are fast getting disgusted. I think it is reasonably certain, that nearly all the twelve months men will go home in the spring. They say they have been "sold" and would go home now if they could. The health of the camp is improving.[10]

By "sold," Courtenay meant that the army was "controlled and kept inactive to further a political policy—a policy not consistent with the views of Disunionist—the policy of Reconstruction, proclaimed at the stump by our Vice President."[11] Without realizing that a storm was brewing over his comments, Courtenay described the square mile of tents "spread out over hill and valley as far as the eye could see" and the bustle of activity in the nearby town that had been turned into a military outpost.[12]

Crowds gather in its streets—officers gallop to and fro—cavalry file in, and artillery trains rumble heavily along, on their way to their new quarters—sentinels stand on the turnpike and before headquarters, and you see on either side all the evidences of war. The hotel is closed—not, as is the case with many elsewhere, for want of travellers—but strange to say, for want of rations. Barns are turned into commissary storerooms, stables have been supplied with bellows and anvil, and horse-shoeing is going on incessantly.[13]

Not knowing then that he would later help save the legacy of Charleston poet Henry Timrod, Courtenay ended his first article longing for Timrod's pen "to do justice to the landscape."[14] Courtenay's idyllic descriptions of army life changed quickly to anger and disappointment as rain turned their camp into stagnant channels of mud with thick choking smoke clustered over campfires sputtering with green, wet wood. Putting on his oil cloth early one morning, Courtenay took a walk through the miserable camp and wrote angrily as the anonymous Kiawah.

It is quite early, and the boys are getting breakfast together. Intent upon the contents of a tin pan, I find one in his shirtsleeves. He has the rations of raw flour for his mess; near by is a bucket of water, and in a frying pan a piece of fat bacon, with which to grease the tough dough. After a rough kneading, it is put in the oven, spread out with the hand, and left to bake; and in due course of time, it is pronounced "done." Upon examination, you find it brown outside, raw inside, and only palatable on account of the grease—otherwise, it would choke you. [15]

Repulsed by the wretched bread and fat that the soldiers were cooking for breakfast, Courtenay continued through the camp where he was equally appalled by the pathetic process of making coffee in camp.

[H]e has the rations of coffee, which have just been burnt in the fire. These are put into a stocking and laid on an oak log with one hand—with the other, heavy blows are struck with a billet of wood or an ax; this process is in lieu of a coffee-mill, which is not to be had. There are several ways of "grinding" coffee; the most novel, however, is to get a smooth board and a glass bottle; the grains of coffee are deposited on the board, and the bottle is used as a roller. After great effort, the grains are broken, not into very small particles, but as well as is possible under the circumstances ... The French—but why mention them—even the detested Yankees, issue ground coffee in paper packages of one ration each, packed in boxes of one hundred or two hundred each. So with sugar, tobacco, salt, pepper, &c. But the rations of coffee are fast giving out; and whiskey, better known as "army lightning" is reported on the way to be issued in gills to the men.[16]

Aware of private boats running the Federal blockade of the eastern coast, Courtenay suggested in his article that the government should consider risking a cargo run to Rio de Janeiro to bring back coffee for the troops. Denying that he was just finding fault with everything in the army, he said his descriptions were a "plain picture of our camp life." As much as anything else, his letter was an effort to rouse the folks back home to send food, clothes, and blankets to their sons and husbands at the front who were suffering from eating raw and burned biscuits and rancid fat while sleeping in the cold, rainy weather with scarcely a blanket for each man. "[A]nd what will be the result in a week or two is easily foreseen," he wrote. "Either send clothing and blankets for our soldiers, or enlarge your hospital accommodations."[17]

Courtenay became so angry with wretched conditions in camp that he lashed out at Confederate leaders, who had already appointed a congressional committee to investigate troop living conditions. He was concerned that the committee would "white-wash" executive inefficiency, so he suggested that a month of strict camp discipline for the committee with a gill of brandy or "army lightning" every day would work a wondrous change in conditions in the camp.

> It is suggested that the Confederate Congress be supplied with leaky tents and army rations, and brought up to Bull Run in November, to transact the public business on the banks of this muddy stream; that the President and Secretary of War be bivouacked near by, to keep the Congress in countenance. [18]

At the outset of the war, most people in both the South and the North thought the conflict would be brief, probably less than six months. When Courtenay joined the South Carolina Palmetto Guard at Manassas, Virginia, he found evidence of this when he interviewed a Federal prisoner who told General Pierre G.T. Beauregard that the North was in earnest . . .

> . . . that the money could be raised, and that the South would be subjugated. He created the impression that (General George B.) McClellan would soon be in motion with an overpowering force and that the army of the Potomac would be *crushed.* As to all this, the gentleman may believe it, but General Beauregard and the army are dubious. Another prisoner thought that the war would be over in two or three months at farthest, and that we would make it all up somehow or other, *in time for the spring trade.*[19]

As Courtenay settled into camp life, he found himself eating so much raw, blackened dough and charred fat cooked over a smoking open fire that he almost lapsed into poetry when he saw the bakery at Manassas. His rapture turned almost as quickly into anger when he learned about the elaborate paperwork that hungry soldiers had to process to get one loaf of bread a day.

> We look in and see that there are several ovens and the pile of light loaves are tempting enough to a man who has eat raw dough for three weeks. Strange to say, the loaves had no prices—"not for sale." Even a soldier could only get one, by an order, signed and countersigned by high officials. Strange things happen in war, thought I. BREAD—well baked BREAD—only to be had as a special dispensation.

Think of it, ye city people! luxuriating daily in warm crisp loaves, from Claussen or Marshall—think of your brave volunteers craving for well baked bread.[20]

As a successful businessman with a keen eye for organization and efficiency that would bring him great wealth after the war, Courtenay immediately saw how the army could provide better bread in unending quantities. Although he may have been making recommendations through proper military channels, he apparently was getting no results, so he continued sending an avalanche of criticism and suggestions for improvement to the *Mercury* for publication. In addition to his advice to send blockade runners for coffee, Courtenay shared a fount of unending ideas with his readers.

Says an officer near by, to whom I expressed my surprise at there not being a supply for all the army: It's quite impossible to have ovens in the army: before they can be built, the army may be moved. Not at all, I replied. In the Crimea, the French Commissariat had portable sheet iron ovens, which served admirably. Ah! indeed! was his astonished reply. I thought of telling him that each French battalion had its oven of portable sheet iron—that raw flour was never issued in the French army, and need never be in ours: but I thought it was wasting breath; for aught I knew, he might have been a protégé of some great man, and was already sufficiently informed about all army matters; so I passed on, still thinking that each regiment of our army might very soon have a portable oven in camp if the authorities would only give an order.[21]

Hailing from an agrarian state that prided itself on rice, corn, and fresh vegetables, Courtenay called on the hometown folks to send some of that good food in the soldiers' direction along with candles so they wouldn't have to go to bed at 5 p.m. every night.

By the way, is there any RICE and GRIST in Charleston? If so, are the railroad charges the prohibition to its reaching the army? In the name of common sense, can't we get rice and hominy, instead of raw dodgers. And candles—it's dark at 5 o'clock p.m. We can't see to read or write—go to bed in despair, and wake up two or three hours before sunrise, wishing for daylight. The luxuries of Sugar and Coffee have disappeared altogether, and Sugar is 5 cts. a pound in New Orleans.[22]

Cold weather had arrived in Virginia along with Courtenay, and he went to bed early on October 27, 1861, because he had no candles or light wood. He woke at sunrise the next morning, shivering in 32-degree weather. "[E]xtremities cold as ice, with two heavy blankets for cover, and any number of bands playing 'Away down South in Dixie,' for reveille," he wrote, as he complained about "thirteen hours of darkness out of twenty-four, without the comfort of reading or writing. We spend about two hours of it squatting before the fire, with our chin on our knees, and talk over the incidents of the camp; but this is tiresome, and we lay ourselves out, in our blankets with ample time for meditation."

When Courtenay decided to gallop his horse around Fairfax County to take a look around, he wrote that he was appalled at the destruction he found everywhere.

Along the route of the contending army, every where was the aspect of desolation. Barns are empty, crops destroyed, cattle slaughtered, fences burnt, orchards stripped, and the farm houses are, in too many instances, shorn of their valuables. Better far, would it have been for Virginia, had her sons occupied, at any sacrifice, her Northern boundary along the south bank of the Potomac, rather than have incurred this disgrace and loss. It is no exaggeration to say that four-fifths of the fences in this section are destroyed. What an item! . . . It will be more honorable as well as less costly, both in life and treasure, to face the enemy as soon as they show themselves and give the bayonet. Welcome them with bloody hands to hospitable graves.[23]

Courtenay visited dozens of soldiers and officers in camp before settling in with the popular surgeon of the regiment who had visitors at all hours of the day and night.

About midnight we are startled with a cry of "Doctor! Oh, Doctor! _____ is dying and wants you to come and see him." Surgeon unrolled his woolens and begins a hasty toilet. While this is being conducted with every diligence, by the starlight, questions are propounded as to the case:
"What does he complain of?"
"He's very bad off, Doctor!"
"What has he been eating?"
"Don't know, Doctor."
"Went down to Manassas yesterday?"
"Yes, Sir."
"Eat raw corn on the way back?"
"Believe so, sir."
Doctor started out with a shawl around him and is away about twenty minutes . . . The doctor returns, his patient had been down to the Junction, eat and drank a variety of things, returned to camp and eat half a dozen dodgers, and as many ears of corn, half roasted; natural consequence is "about to die" in the night—don't die, however, and is very penitent next day.[24]

Several hours before dawn, Courtenay was awakened by men building campfires in the night to warm themselves. They were too cold to sleep. The troops were awaiting the arrival of anything that would lessen their misery.

[W]e find out that when it is too cold to sleep under a seven dollar cotton blanket, the boys sit around the camp fires to keep warm and sleep in the day time *in the sunshine*. This is a tolerably good idea. The only trouble is, the sun don't shine every day, and good warm blankets would be better to rely upon. I supposed

Governor Pickens bought 10,000 pair of the cargo of the last arrival, and that these will soon be on. Better hurry them up, they are wanted.[25]

Soon after Kiawah's postscript about the "sold" soldiers appeared in the *Mercury*, members of the South Carolina Palmetto Guard sent an angry letter to the editor of the *Mercury*. Courtenay's personal note had been intended for the editor of the *Mercury* and was not meant for publication. However, the note was the *Mercury*'s kind of news. Even if the editor had known that the postscript was for his eyes only, he probably would have published it anyway. His father had worked stridently for secession in the *Mercury* for more than a decade, and when Rhett, Sr., was overlooked for president of the secessionist republic or for any leading role in the new administration, the *Mercury*'s editorial position shifted to criticism of Jefferson Davis and the Confederate leadership.

Soldiers in the Palmetto Guard were furious about the article, calling it "false . . . slanderous and totally unworthy of a true Carolinian." Although Rhett, Jr., took responsibility for publishing Kiawah's off-the-record comments, he made it clear that he would do it again. "The responsibility of its publication is ours," he wrote. "We believed then—and we believe now—its purport to be true, and, therefore, we published it."[26] The editor wrote:

> The Palmetto Guard has thought proper to take exception to these statements and have adopted a certain preamble and resolutions, which our readers will find in our columns, although by no means bound to publish them, from a respect either to their tone or substance. In one of these resolutions, the statements of our correspondent are denounced as "false and slanderous and totally unworthy of a true Carolinian" . . . They also seem to suppose, that these statements were intended to reflect on our Generals on the Potomac. Neither of these inferences are correct.[27]

Rhett defended Kiawah's comments and said that he interpreted Kiawah's assertion that the officers "are fast getting disgusted" to mean that they were disgusted with sitting around doing nothing. "If they have any chivalry or zeal for the service, can they be anything else but 'getting disgusted?'" he asked.[28] As to Kiawah's comments about the 12-month volunteers going home in the spring, Rhett wrote:

> Can anyone doubt the reasonableness of this assertion? What did the troops go to Virginia for? To stay behind entrenchments, live in the mud, and to die of disease, from cold, and a wretched commissarist? We have supposed our troops went to fight, and to drive the Yankees out of the Frontier States. If they are not allowed to accomplish this object, after a year's disheartening and demoralizing inactivity, is any one so silly as to suppose that they will continue, after their term of service has expired, in such an inglorious employment?[29]

Ruins of Mrs. Judith Henry's house on the Bull Run battlefield near Manassas where Courtenay fought a duel with Captain G. B. Cuthbert on November 21, 1861. Photograph from the Library of Congress

Courtenay was astonished at the reaction of the Palmetto Guard and in-terpreted the published comments as a reflection on his honor. He challenged Captain G.B. Cuthbert to a duel, which was one of two duels that were sched-uled on the cold morning of November 21, 1861, near Manassas. The men and their seconds huddled with their weapons of choice on the slope below the Henry house where signs of the First Battle of Manassas were still clearly vis-ible. Adhering strictly to the Code of Honor, Courtenay and Cuthbert paced away from each other before exchanging shots that passed harmlessly through their clothes. Both men declared themselves satisfied before shaking hands and stepping aside for the second duel, which was being fought over a game of chess. Cuthbert took offense again in March 1862 at comments written about him in the *Mercury* by Courtenay's editor, but the second duel was averted, this one between Cuthbert and Rhett, Jr., after a flurry of letters between the two men.[30]

The dark days of winter arrived in camp on clouds that showered them with snow, sleet, and rain, and the wind moaned through homespun shelters as the Confederates settled into winter quarters for three months. "Huts are now in order, and already these rude shelters meet the eye in every camp," Courtenay wrote. "We creep snugly into them and are thankful that wood is plentiful."[31] The monotony was broken by a full dress army ceremony complete with a salute of 15 guns announcing the arrival of Generals Joseph E. Johnston, Pierre G.T. Beauregard, and Robert G. Van Dorn.[32] Although most war correspondents complained from time to time about the wretched food, clothes, and living conditions in the army, Courtenay criticized the system in almost every article he wrote. In addition to writing the usual pleas for help from the folks back home, he continued suggesting specific ways to improve the supply system and army life. He railed steadily about soldiers' conditions until May 15, 1862, when he was assigned to the general staff of the Third Military District.

Two weeks later, on June 3, 1862, he was reassigned as post quartermaster in Hardeeville in the Beaufort district of southeastern South Carolina. Since his cover as Kiawah had been blown by the duel, the decision to reassign him to a remote supply outpost was either an effort to silence him or an opportunity for him to put his ideas into motion as a supply officer. He arrived in late November 1862 at the isolated depot on the railroad line between Charleston and Savannah, Georgia. The remote outpost was to be his home until the end of the war.[33] Since Courtenay was in charge of supplies, his editorial complaints about camp conditions disappeared. Furthermore, his isolated post kept him so far away from skirmishes and battles that his correspondence for the *Mercury* was reduced to regimental news about deaths, injuries, and other random information that he picked up along the way.

Soon after he arrived in Hardeeville, Captain W.E. Earle rode to Courtenay's headquarters, seeking him out. The captain said his light battery had been ordered to the vicinity, and he wanted advice on a good locality for a company camp. While Courtenay was pointing out different suitable sites, Earle talked about his problems drilling and preparing the men in the light artillery service. He said he had been unable to find a handbook for the light artillery drill and had to depend on whatever verbal instructions he could get. Courtenay brushed up his bookstore skills and sent to Charleston for his personal copy of the latest edition of the U.S. Light Artillery Manual, which was illustrated with plates of every part of the gun, carriage, caisson, and projectiles along with every detail of the drill. Courtenay watched with pleasure as Earle followed directions in the manual to organize and drill his battery and wrote, "I record here that I never in the army, or out of it, witnessed more painstaking, constant work done than went on in 'Earle's Battery.' Hour after hour, day after day, for months the drills were kept up, and the result was very soon seen—one of the best disciplined and most efficient light batteries in the service."[34]

While Earle was organizing his soldiers, Courtenay began fighting another battle on paper. He initiated an investigation into mistreatment of army horses under the care of W.L. DePass in February 1864. When the Army board found

Courtenay was stationed for much of the war in Hardeeville, South Carolina, which was located near the Charleston and Savannah Railroad. *Harper's Weekly,* March 4, 1865. Courtesy of Rare Books and Special Collections, University of South Carolina Libraries

that the horses were in a "neglected condition," DePass claimed that his "horses had been without long forage for six weeks," which was a slap at Courtenay, who was in charge of supplies. Courtenay was outraged by what he called a "false claim" that impugned his integrity as an officer and was adamant in his demands for DePass to make a satisfactory statement to the board that would clear him of wrongdoing.

> Upon the receipt of this direct and unequivocal testimony, I wrote you under the date of July 26th, setting forth—first—the fact that you were the author of the language, which had done me injury as an officer, and secondly, I proved by my books that the statement made by you to the Board was false, you stating to them, that you had received a number of pounds of long forage, less than your requisitions, not that you had received most . . . for six years. I (am) proving by my books, that you had something less than half rations, upon which the cavalry horses subsisted during the same period, without the necessity of a Board of survey and without being in a "starving condition."[35]

Despite several efforts by Courtenay, DePass failed to make the necessary statement to the board by October 1. When it became obvious that DePass was not going to take responsibility for the neglected horses, Courtenay claimed that he had been insulted and demanded "satisfaction as usual under the circumstances."[36] While efforts to organize a duel were under way, General William T. Sherman's troops were preparing to march toward Savannah. In advance of his evacuation of Atlanta, Sherman telegraphed General Henry Wagner Halleck on November 11, 1864, ordering him to break the 103-mile railroad line that ran between Charleston and Savannah by December 1. Hidden by an early morning fog, 5,500 men, infantry, cavalry, and artillery began moving up the Broad River on November 29 from the Federally occupied base at Hilton Head. They were headed for the deep water at Boyd's Landing above Beaufort.[37] The Confederates were surprised by the Federal advance, but word of their movement spread quickly because of a series of outposts and picket stations where mounted sentinels stood watch over the railroad lines and bridges.[38] Without knowing where the Federals would attack, Colonel Charles J. Colcock ordered the Confederates to the entrenchments at Honey Hill near Grahamville.

> Not only was the handful of soldiers quietly preparing to face fearful odds, but the small community of Grahamville was stirred to resistance! As soon as the news of the presence of the enemy became known, Captain George P. Elliott, commissary of the post, appealed to the citizens, old and young, to organize a company and go to the breastworks; this was promptly responded to, and this small force was there during the day, mostly armed with double-barrel guns.[39]

By nightfall, the Federals were encamped within a few miles of the railroad, threatening Grahamville and Coosawatchie.[40] Confederate reinforcements were on the way from Charleston and Savannah, so the small band of artillery and cavalry prepared to stand its ground until help arrived.

> It was a night of watchfulness and anxiety—unless the expected infantry reinforcements arrived before daylight the fearful odds of more than twenty-five to one would be encountered in the morning. Every one of this small band of Confederate soldiers, in front of the enemy that night, deliberately made up his mind that the Federal army was to be held in check, whatever the odds, whatever the sacrifice.[41]

Early on the morning of November 30, the full force of 5,500 Federals attacked at Honey Hill, just a few miles from Courtenay's base in Hardeeville. The Confederate force waiting for them consisted of 120 dismounted cavalry and two guns.

> Sergeant Julias A. LePrince was at one of the guns; he was a sufferer from chills and fever, and that was the alternate day for his attack; sure enough, in the very midst of the fight, the gallant sergeant was shaking very perceptibly and burning up with fever, but by sending spare men off to the rear, to fill his canteen with

water which he was drinking in large quantities, he kept to his gun. An officer finally noticed him and promptly said:

"Sergeant, you ought not to be here; go (to) the rear!"

But the sergeant quietly remarked: "If I go to the rear, shaking as I am, people might think I am scared!"

He stayed by his gun until the action was over late in the evening.[42]

When reinforcements arrived at mid-day, the Confederates finally had a force of 1,500 soldiers fighting 5,500 Federals.[43] Armed volunteers were standing guard late that afternoon when General John H. Howard, who was 70 years old, grabbed his favorite double-barrel gun loaded with buckshot and rode toward the enemy.

> When within range, he opened fire with both barrels, and was in favor of charging down upon them, but the officer in command prudently withdrew his small force. I have heard the General express the regret that Broad River was between the enemy's camp and the mainland, and that we had no ships to go after them. I think his ambition was to sacrifice his life for the State and "the cause."[44]

By nightfall when the Union army retreated, 746 Federals had been killed, wounded, or captured, while the greatly outnumbered Confederates had lost only eight men. When Courtenay wrote a definitive description of the battle in later years, he said, "It was just wonderful what the boys did—Why, a rabbit could not have crossed the road."[45]

In later years, U.S. Army Captain C.C. Soule blamed the Federal loss on "very bad management" that allowed two pieces of artillery and one company of dismounted cavalry "to hold in check for three hours an entire brigade—these faults cannot be overlooked."[46] However, the crushing and humiliating defeat at Honey Hill was of little concern to Sherman, whose troops were so deep in Georgia by then that he was able to send a message on December 22, presenting the city of Savannah to President Lincoln as a Christmas present.[47] When Sherman began transferring part of General Oliver Otis Howard's Army of the Tennessee from Savannah to Beaufort in early January 1865, another skirmish broke out along the railroad near Hardeeville. Desperate attempts to recruit more Confederates failed, and the Federals began burning and pillaging their way through South Carolina in a two-pronged movement toward Goldsboro, North Carolina. Sherman's troops destroyed most of the railroads in South Carolina and left towns in their path in smoldering ruins, including Grahamville and Hardeeville, where Courtenay was stationed.

Courtenay probably fled to Charleston to defend his family, and sometime in the spring of 1865, he moved to the upper part of South Carolina where he started a transportation business carting cotton the 84 miles from Newberry to Orangeburg.[48] The possibility of a duel erupted again when DePass pretended to schedule times for the confrontation in Columbia. However, DePass's deliberately late letters and misleading information finally annoyed Courtenay so much that he wrote that he had concluded "some months ago, that I had been defeated in my effort to redress my wrongs and had determined not to renew the demand."[49]

> I would not be surprised at anything now-a-days, we seem to be in a transition state, everything coming out in reverse of the old condition, and it is just possible, that the generally recognized rule that it takes two to make a bargain, has been entirely abrogated and under the new dispensation, the party having the first say, carries the day.[50]

The attempted duel became an unhappy memory for Courtenay as he immersed himself in rebuilding his life after the war. After the railroads were repaired in the spring of 1866, he discontinued his transportation business and returned to Charleston with his wife, Julia Anna Francis, whom he had married on October 19, 1854. He established a shipping business and spent the next 22 years managing steamship lines to Baltimore, Philadelphia, New York, and abroad.[51] Edith, the first of their 10 children, was born in 1867 and was followed by Campbell, 1868; Carlisle, 1869; Ashmead, 1870; Julia, 1875; St. John, 1877; Arthur, 1879; Edward Courtenay, 1881; Elizabeth, 1883; and Edward C., 1885. Arthur, Edward Courtenay, Elizabeth, and Edward C. all died during the year they were born.[52]

While his family was growing, Courtenay served as mayor of Charleston from 1879 to 1887 and on the boards of visitors for the Naval Academy in 1882 and of West Point in 1887.[53] A hurricane destroyed most of Charleston's waterfront during his first administration, and the 1886 earthquake leveled much of the city during his second administration, but he is remembered for helping rebuild the city's infrastructure and government. Along with R.C. Winthrop of Massachusetts, Pierpoint Morgan of New York, and former President Rutherford B. Hayes of Ohio, Courtenay was elected to a seat in 1887 on the Peabody Educational Trust board, which was charged with administering more than $2 million in funds to improve education in the Southern states.[54]

When he left public office in 1887, a New York shipbuilder named a rescue vessel for him and, in spite of Courtenay's objections, a group of Charleston citizens commissioned a marble bust of him for the Council chamber. Sculpted by Edward Valentine and unveiled December 19, 1888, the inscription read:

WILLIAM ASHMEAD COURTENAY
Mayor of Charleston, 1879–1887
As Chief Magistrate
He administered the government with
firmness, impartiality and success.

> Even amid the disasters of cyclone[55] and earthquake,
> signally illustrating the safe maxim, that,
> "PUBLIC OFFICE IS A PUBLIC TRUST."[56]

Courtenay was elected president of the Bessemer Land and Improvement Company in Alabama in April 1889 but moved back to Charleston in 1890. He was being mentioned as a gubernatorial candidate and was endorsed by several newspapers[57] until the nomination of Benjamin R. Tillman of Edgefield ended the speculation.

In 1894, he founded the Courtenay Manufacturing Company, a cotton mill at Newry in Oconee County. Newry was named after the small town in northern Ireland where Courtenay's grandfather Edward was born before immigrating to Charleston in 1791.[58] Courtenay named his home Innisfallen, after an island in the Lakes of Killarney section of Ireland made famous by the poet Thomas Moore.[59]

Near the end of the century, Courtenay decided to keep a promise he had made to his former schoolmate and friend Henry Timrod during a chance meeting at a railroad station in January 1865.

> He was then in feeble health, depressed in spirits, and in the midst of that general desolation which only those knew of whom shared the calamities that overtook our dear southland at the close of the war. On that, to me, most sad and well re-membered occasion, and the last time I ever saw him, I recall his plaintive regrets at the then hopeless task of collecting and publishing his poems. He spoke of his repeated disappointments in life, but kept dwelling with deep feeling on the non-publication of his literary works. Finally I said to him: "Harry, we are all in a great deal of trouble. The future is very uncertain and promises may be difficult to fulfill, but if my life is spared, and I can accomplish your wish, I promise you I will do it." He instantly seized my hands and exclaimed eagerly: "Will you? Will you?" "Yes," I said. "I will certainly do it, if I can."[60]

Timrod died eighteen months later, on October 7, 1867. Nearly 30 years later, Courtenay made good on his promise to Timrod and began a one-man campaign in 1898 to revive the poet's fading reputation. He formed the Timrod Memorial Association and arranged for Houghton-Mifflin to publish in 1899 a complete edition of Timrod's poems with a memoir and a portrait of the author for $1.50 a copy.[61] Courtenay said the third volume of Timrod's poetry had not been published because the copyright had been entangled for the past 20 years in the bankruptcy of his publishers.[62] Courtenay recalled that Henry W. Longfellow, alluding to the city of Charleston, had said, "To have been the birthplace of Henry Timrod is a distinct honor; the day will surely come when his poems will have a place in every cultivated home in the United States."[63]

Courtenay acquired pledges from editors in Baltimore, Washington, Richmond, Nashville, Wilmington, Asheville, Charleston, Augusta, and other Southern cities agreeing to sell Timrod's poems. Editors in Atlanta also pledged support for the bronze monument that Courtenay erected in Washington Park in Charleston.[64] Courtenay presented a portrait of Timrod to the Timrod Library (now Richland County Library) in Columbia.

Courtenay's interest in preserving and honoring South Carolina's history became his passion during the last years of his life, and he donated thousands of dollars for statues, books, and artifacts. He helped raise money for a granite obelisk honoring the Civil War dead of the Washington Light Infantry in Charleston and became one of 35 founding members on the board of directors of the newly established South Carolina Audubon Society.[65] For his extensive efforts to establish memorials to Civil War heroes and history through gifts to libraries and historic organizations, Courtenay was awarded an honorary doctor of law degree by the University of Nashville in June 1900 for his service as "philanthropist, patriot and patron of letters."[66] He became one of the founding commissioners of a state Historic Commission to safeguard materials relating to South Carolina, an organization that was the forerunner of the South Carolina Department of Archives and History.

Courtenay moved in September 1906 to Columbia, probably to live near or with his daughter Julia, who was married to Louis Morgan Barnwell of Columbia.[67] Courtenay died March 17, 1908, in Columbia at age 77 and is buried in Magnolia Cemetery in Charleston.

3

Felix Gregory de Fontaine: Chronicling the Horrors of War

Patricia G. McNeely

THE "MAGNIFICENTLY TERRIBLE" THUNDER OF ARTILLERY RUMBLED through Charleston, South Carolina, as New York reporter Felix Gregory de Fontaine hurried through crowded streets gone wild with excitement. Residents had been startled out of their sleep on the morning of April 12, 1861, by the sound of "angry guns" being fired at Fort Sumter by Confederates. Lights flashed from every house, and "in the twinkling of an eye . . . an agitated throng are rushing towards the water front of the city to catch their first view of battle," he wrote.

> Grave citizens whose dignity under ordinary circumstances is unimpeachable, are at the top of their speed, dressing as they run and throwing out explosive "hoorays" as if they must have a safety valve for their enthusiasm or be suffocated. There are men *sans* coat and vest, women *sans* crinoline and children in their night gowns.[1]

De Fontaine watched the battle rage until the news embargo lifted around 3 o'clock that afternoon when he telegraphed the first news report to New York after the Civil War began.[2] It was published the next day under a 17-deck headline on the front page of the *New York Herald.*

> Civil War has at last begun. A terrible fight is at this moment going on between Fort Sumter and the fortifications by which it is surrounded . . . The excitement of the community is indescribable. With the very first boom of the gun thousands rushed from their beds to the harbor front, and all day every available place has been thronged by ladies and gentlemen, viewing the solemn spectacle through their glasses . . . Troops are pouring into the town by hundreds, but are held in reserve for the present, the force already on the island being ample. People are also arriving every moment on horseback, and by every other conveyance. Within an

Felix Gregory de Fontaine. Courtesy of Tony and Maryjane Islan

area of fifty miles, where the thunder of the artillery can be heard, the scene is magnificently terrible. [3]

Most reporters for Northern newspapers had been arrested or run out of town during the tense last days before the war began, but de Fontaine was able to move about freely because he was known as a Southern sympathizer. More importantly, he had developed a close and lasting relationship with General Pierre G.T. Beauregard, another gentleman of French descent who had taken command of the South Carolina troops as they were gathering in Charleston.[4]

De Fontaine's father, Chevalier Louis Antoine de Fontaine, was a wealthy French nobleman whose title was the equivalent of being a knight.[5] He had accompanied Charles X into exile in Edinburgh, Scotland, in 1830. After living a few months with the king at Holyrood Palace, the chevalier sailed for New York where he was married in 1833 to Laura S. Allen, an American who was related to the Revolutionary war hero Ethan Allen.[6] Their first child, Felix Gregory, was born in Connecticut on July 14, 1834.[7] The chevalier, who spoke several languages, traveled extensively in the United States and arranged for his son to be privately tutored.[8]

As a teenager, the younger de Fontaine became one of the early shorthand writers in America by learning phonography, a system of writing rapidly with abbreviated words. His "condensed long hand" was so proficient that he described the method and provided exercises in a book that was published in 1886.[9] He would be described in later years by novelist, poet, and newspaper partner William Gilmore Simms as a "smart, active, intelligent little fellow, amiable & genial, and sufficiently pushing to make his way in the world."[10]

The slender, dark-haired young man began his career at the *Boston Herald*, where he was known as "Little Felix."[11] A full-time reporter by age 16,[12] he wrote verbatim shorthand reports in 1850 of the notorious trial of Harvard chemistry

Charleston residents rushed to see the bombardment of Fort Sumter. *Harper's Weekly*, May 4, 1861. Courtesy of South Caroliniana Library, University of South Carolina, Columbia

Professor John H. Webster, who was found guilty of murder after the victim's false teeth were found in Webster's furnace.[13]

After his stint in Boston, de Fontaine moved to New York to join the staff of the *Herald,* where he became a close friend of the editor, James Gordon Bennett. Using his shorthand skills, he reported the trial of Congressman Daniel E.

Confederate General Pierre G. T. Beauregard.
Courtesy of South Caroliniana Library, University
of South Carolina, Columbia

Sickles, who was found guilty of killing Philip Barton Key on February 27, 1859, in Washington, D.C. De Fontaine's version of the trial was published as a book later that year in New York.[14] After the trial, de Fontaine, who was known for his "cheery, jovial disposition,"[15] traveled through the South writing articles about the history of abolitionism. De Fontaine blamed fanatic abolitionists for causing the Union to dissolve and for spoiling chances for gradual emancipation in the South. The articles were printed in the *Herald* on February 2,1861, and reprinted as a book later that year.[16]

His extensive reports from the South and the subsequent book made him one of the first correspondents already on assignment in the conflict that became the Civil War.[17] He continued to write prolifically through South Carolina's tumultuous secession in 1860 and during the creation of the Confederate government in Montgomery, Alabama, in 1861. When it became certain that war was inevitable, de Fontaine moved on to Charleston to report the first shots fired at Fort Sumter. He would be one of the few correspondents who wrote during the entire conflict and to continue after the war had ended. He is also one of the

A. S. Willington. Courtesy of the *Post and Courier*, Charleston, South Carolina

few who reported almost exclusively from the battlefields during the war, with the exception of four months in early 1864, when he wrote editorials about the war for a newspaper he bought in Columbia, South Carolina, while also writing a book, *Marginalia, or Gleanings from an Army Note-book*, that was still being reprinted in the 21st century.[18] De Fontaine is also the only correspondent known to have established a magazine devoted to memories of the Civil War after the conflict ended.

De Fontaine was 26 years old when Bennett sent him to South Carolina to cover the National Democratic Convention in April 1860.[19] Bennett had begun his own journalism career in Charleston in 1823 under the tutelage of A.S. Willington, who had been one of the founders of the *Charleston Courier* in 1803. He was still the editor when the Civil War began. The two editors had remained close personal and professional friends, and the *Herald* usually reflected Bennett's sympathy for the South.

De Fontaine was still in South Carolina when Governor William Henry Gist notified other Southern states on October 5, 1860, that South Carolina was considering seceding from the Union. After Abraham Lincoln was elected on November 6, de Fontaine reported the explosive events that led to South Carolina's secession on December 20, 1860.

After the stormy secession, de Fontaine rode the train to Montgomery, Alabama, to cover the creation of the new government of the fledgling Southern republic. He reported the adoption on February 8, 1861, of the provisional constitution, one of the documents that he would rescue at the end of the war, and the election of President Jefferson Davis of Mississippi and Vice President Alexander Stephens of Georgia. De Fontaine described crowds cheering as the Confederate flag was raised over the Alabama State House on March 5. He returned to New York at the end of March but barely had time to grab a change of clothes before boarding the *Columbia*, a steamer bound for Charleston, on March 31, 1861.[20]

De Fontaine was one of more than a dozen correspondents from Northern and Southern newspapers who reached Charleston in time to witness the first shots being fired at Federally occupied Fort Sumter on April 12. He telegraphed a steady stream of bulletins to the *Herald* until Major Robert Anderson accepted Beauregard's offer to evacuate the fort "on his own terms."[21] Anderson lowered the Federal flag over Fort Sumter on April 14.

The *New York Herald* condoned secession until the eve of Fort Sumter, but Bennett sent word on April 19 to President Lincoln that the newspaper was ready to throw its support to the administration.[22] Although de Fontaine had been born and raised in the North and was reporting for a New York newspaper, his loyalty was to the South, and when Bennett shifted his support to the Union, Willington hired de Fontaine as a correspondent for the *Courier*. Unlike the nearby *Charleston Mercury*, which campaigned for secession, the more moderate *Courier* opposed disunion and South Carolina secession. However, when the war began, the 79-year-old editor reluctantly added "Confederate States of America" to the *Courier*'s nameplate on February 23, 1861. His heart was never in the war, and he died of apoplexy the next year.[23]

The fall of Fort Sumter was greeted with enthusiastic demonstrations in the Confederacy, which would grow to nine states, including Virginia, by late May when Richmond became the newly designated Confederate capital. When the First South Carolina Regiment left for Virginia in May 1861, de Fontaine accompanied the men as a military correspondent with the rank of major.[24] He would become one of the highest paid correspondents in the war, drawing a salary from the *Courier* in the range of $6 a day plus traveling expenses, which was as much in one day as a private made in two weeks.[25] Before the war ended, he was writing for at least six other newspapers, and he also wrote for the Southern Associated Press and the Press Association of the Confederate States of America, which paid $25 to $30 a week, plus expenses. Most correspondents wrote under pen names to protect themselves from possibly being shot or hanged if captured. De Fontaine wrote most frequently under his favorite pen name "Personne" (person) for the *Courier*, the *Richmond Daily Enquirer*, the *Mobile Daily Advertiser and Register*, and the *Savannah Republican*. By 1864, he was writing for his own newspaper, the *South Carolinian*, which he bought that year. He was also known as "F.G. de F" for the *Richmond Whig* and occasionally for the *Savannah Republican* and as "Quel Qu'un" (someone) for the *Memphis Daily Appeal*.[26]

De Fontaine interviewed dozens of generals, soldiers, and Union prisoners on the battlefields, as well as top-ranking officials in the Confederate government, including President Davis. He covered dozens of skirmishes in South Carolina, North Carolina, Virginia, Maryland, Tennessee, and Georgia. He also covered most of the major battles, including the first and second battles of Manassas, the Battle of Shiloh, the Battle of Antietam, the Battle Above the Clouds in Chattanooga, Tennessee, and the fall of Atlanta, Georgia.

He was a prolific writer who made every effort to report news accurately. He occasionally corrected mistakes that he had reported, and he complained about the difficulties of sifting through rumors to find the facts. He frequently named his sources and occasionally used direct quotes. De Fontaine usually wrote three or four 1,200-word newspaper articles a week; occasionally some were as long as 8,000 or 9,000 words. Throughout the war, he wrote detailed and elaborate descriptions of the terrain where the soldiers were camping and fighting.

Dispatches to newspapers were sent either by couriers who rode back to the nearest telegraph office or post office or by military telegraph in the field. However, de Fontaine's articles usually took several days to reach the editors and another day to be published. At the end of the war, the *New York Times* called him the "ablest war correspondent in the South."[27]

De Fontaine saw his "first important engagement of the war" in early June in skirmishes at the mouth of the James River in Virginia when 3,500 Federals, marching from Newport News and Hampton, were defeated on June 10 by 1,200 Confederates at Little and Big Bethel. These skirmishes were not as large or bloody as subsequent battles; only 79 Federals and 8 Confederates died, but the correspondent was seeing the awful consequences of war for the first time.

The scene after the battle, to one unaccustomed to spectacles of this nature, was frightful. In the swamp through which the New York Zouaves advanced to assault our lines, there were bodies dotting the black morass from one end to the other, and the gay uniforms contrasted strangely with the pallid faces of their dead owners. One boyish, delicate looking fellow was lying in the swamp with a bullet hole through his breast. The left hand was pressed on the wound from which his life-blood poured; the other was convulsively clenched in the weeds that grew around him. Lying on the ground was a Testament, that had fallen from his pocket, dabbled with blood. Inside the cover was the printed inscription: "Presented to the defenders of their country by the New York Bible Society." A United States flag was also stamped on the title page.[28]

De Fontaine had been disappointed by what he considered blunders and bad decisions by Confederate military leaders during the first few months of the war, but the repulse of the Federals at Bethel Church gave him the opportunity to send home some "encouraging" news.

> Heretofore, we have been experiencing little else than a series of surprises. When Anderson walked from Fort Moultrie into Sumter, it was a "surprise." When troops reinforced Fort Pickens, it was a "surprise." When Fortress Monroe was reinforced, it was a "surprise." When Ellsworth and his Zouaves marched into Alexandria, it was a "surprise." The landing at Newport News was a "surprise." The occupation of Grafton was a "surprise": And, lastly, the attack at Phillippa was a "surprise" . . . But the victory at Bethel Church has turned the gloomy current into livelier channels.[29]

He was in Richmond when word came on June 18 that the Confederates had evacuated Harpers Ferry to avoid being cut off by Federal Generals Robert Patterson and George McClellan, who were advancing from the north and the west. De Fontaine, who by then was also writing for the *Enquirer,* left Richmond on July 20, 1861, arriving barely in time to cover the first battle at Bull Run the next day. Union General Irvin McDowell had led 35,000 troops from Washington, D.C., to Bull Run, a small creek 22 miles west of Washington that ran near Manassas, where Beauregard waited with 22,000 Confederates at the Stone Bridge over the creek. The roar of a 30-pounder shattered the early morning calm while de Fontaine was hitching a ride to the bridge on a passing ambulance. He was passed by a regiment of breathless but cheering Virginians running from the railroad station at Manassas Junction to join the battle.[30] He saw squads of men who had been in the battle and had come out exhausted.

"Wounded men with heads bloody, hands shot away, legs mangled and otherwise hurt, were slowly wending their way with their comrades towards the Junction," he wrote. "Near the scene, in a shaded hollow, on the banks of a narrow creek, large numbers of the wounded were gathered and undergoing various operations at the hands of the surgeons, who, covered with blood and dust, plied the knife, saw and needle."[31]

> The enemy were mowed down by hundreds . . . and (the bodies of) men lay in every field and patch of woods. The horses of the artillery were dead and dying in piles around their batteries and the Yankees were receiving a succession of shocks which it was not possible to long withstand. Still they fought obstinately and well,

General Beauregard's camp of Confederate troops at White Springs, Virginia, near the Manassas Gap Railroad. *Harper's Weekly,* July 13, 1861. Courtesy of Rare Books and Special Collections, University of South Carolina Libraries

yielding not so much to numbers as to the irresistible onsets which followed on infantry and artillery alike.[32]

As General Joseph Johnston's fresh Confederates swept in from the Shenandoah Valley in time to stop the Federal advance, President Davis arrived from Richmond by train in time to watch the Federal troops retreating back to Washington and to celebrate the unexpected Confederate victory. Davis urged the generals to pursue the retreating army and capture Washington, but the plan was scrapped when Beauregard and Johnston reported that the army didn't have enough food, equipment, or transportation for such a pursuit and warned of a possible counterattack by fresh Federal troops who had just arrived.[33]

In what would become a habit, de Fontaine rode over the field exploring the woods and thickets after the battle and describing the bloody, gruesome scene that he would find with increasing regularity in the coming months and years.

The spectacle is too horrible for description. Men and horses are scattered over the ground for several miles, lying in every possible attitude and mangled by every possible wound. Broken artillery wagons, earth torn up, corn and grain

The Fourth South Carolina regiment working in the trenches at night at Manassas Junction, Virginia in 1861. One of the soldiers is reading a newspaper by the light of the campfire. *Harper's Weekly*, August 10, 1861. Courtesy of Rare Books and Special Collections, University of South Carolina Libraries

trampled down, fences laid low, houses riddled, trees and bushes cut to pieces, all bespeak the terrible character of the opposing fires.[34]

In the space of about an acre, de Fontaine counted more than a hundred enemy soldiers lying in all directions. "It was a horrid sight to look upon for the first time," he wrote. "One little gully in which the enemy had made a stand was filled with dead bodies."[35]

The victory set off a rush of enthusiastic stories in Southern newspapers that added to the widespread belief that the war would soon be over. However, de Fontaine and the other leading Southern correspondent, Peter W. Alexander of the *Savannah Republican*, fell ill from fatigue and exposure for about two weeks after the battle. De Fontaine spent some time recovering and writing while in Culpeper, 60 miles southwest of Washington,[36] before returning to Richmond, where he was hired by W.H. Pritchard to write for the Southern Associated Press.[37] De Fontaine loved to tell anecdotes and always tried to add a little humor to his stories when he could. When de Fontaine rode the train out of Richmond on August 4 to visit General John B. Magruder's Army of the Peninsula, he described the crowded, dusty, hot trip, where he had to . . .

... occupy six inches of a metaphorical seat, the remainder of which is divided
between a very fat Irish woman and a very large basket. Old lady in a decided state
of distillation. At once discovered an odor of strong water as if she had freely indulged in burning fluid and sugar, seasoned with onions.—Her face is broad, red,
moist, and oleaginous, suggestive of a scarcity of soap and water, and is a sort of
base from which protrudes a gigantic twenty-four pounder of a nose—a patriarchal ornament on which a beard has grown ... For the last half hour ... the stout
dame has subjected me to an inquisitorial bombardment, compared with which
that of Sumter was mild and trivial. I let off my artillery in minute monosyllables.
She finally leaves at a way station.[38]

De Fontaine was finding it difficult to sift through rumors that were circulating with increasing regularity through camps and towns. He described the
problem to his readers to help them understand some of the difficulties he faced
reporting the news.

Rumor has been the ruling God and men have worshiped at the shrine of the
deity. . . . The slightest suspicious intent excites the acutest apprehensions. Are the
cars detained over one train—a battle is in progress. Are orders received from
BEAUREGARD about munitions . . . —instantly the whole town is in a furor.
"Hostilities are certainly about to commence"—Arlington is to be attacked and
Washington taken immediately; the Potomac has been crossed by Johnston and
he is in full march through Maryland; the street corners are therefore thronged,
the innocent bulletin boards are encompassed with a cloud of witnesses; the cor-
ridors of the hotels daily perspire with your loquacious contents, and the telegraph
is surrounded frequently until late at night by curious inquirers after the "latest
news from Manassas." There is always a moral certainty that a battle is going on.
Men seem to feel it in their bones, and you can no more reason them out of their
office to obstinacy than instill into a mule a knowledge of didactic poetry.[39]

In addition to rumors, official sources sometimes provided incomplete or inaccurate information, problems that de Fontaine tried to deal with by citing
sources by name or general description when he was not an eyewitness and by
correcting his mistakes and misinformation with subsequent stories. However,
army censorship, which started as soon as the war began, was more of a problem than rumors and misinformation. The army prohibited correspondents
from providing information that could be used by the enemy. Since most of
the stories from the front were not published for several days because of delays
in getting stories to newspapers, correspondents didn't believe what they were
writing would be useful to the enemy.

Army censors thought otherwise and prohibited the correspondents from
writing about specific locations, numbers, and troop movements. Tiptoe-
ing around the censors, de Fontaine tried to provide enough information and

Correspondents frequently wrote about the dozens of ways that soldiers found to amuse and entertain themselves in camp. Here Mississippians practice with the Bowie knife. *Harper's Weekly*, August 31, 1861. Courtesy of Rare Books and Special Collections, University of South Carolina Libraries

description for readers to get a general idea of where he was and to visualize conditions at the front, but the restrictions frequently tested his creative abilities.

> In writing from my present whereabouts, two reasons compel me, like the Flying Dutchman, to hail from the somewhat indefinite port of nowhere. First, it would not be prudent to name the spot, and second, it is a geographical impossibility. "It's not that far that my education extends." I simply know that I am in the woods. A stroll of half an hour has carried me from the canvas village of the Hampton Legion to the forest banks of the Potomac, and here, as Jonah rested under his guard, I have sat me down under the shade of a wild persimmon to indite another of my random sketches from the seat of war.[40]

In quiet moments, when the troops were waiting for battle, de Fontaine described the bravery of soldiers in combat and the courageous death of fallen comrades. However, just as often, he described ordinary living conditions in camp. Soldiers frequently organized greased-pig races, sack races, and blindfolded attempts "to stick a hot poker in a certain target with any quantity of immense practical jokes," but he considered racing the most enjoyable.[41] De

Fontaine also wrote personal stories about soldiers—their routine activities, their hobbies, their dreams, and their pets, like the pet chicken kept in the tent of Lieutenant Colonel J.B. Griffin, second in command in Wade Hampton's Legion from South Carolina. De Fontaine was amused by the "veritable Yankee chicken" that lived in the tent with the colonel.

> When the [chicken] is present, ten chances to one that she is either on his table or roosting on his shoulder. As the bantling neither lays nor crows, the height of Miss Chicken's ambition is to do her setting on the head board of the Lieutenant-Colonel's bed, whither she retires with as much regularity and punctuality as he does himself. The animal's bones are not to be picked this side of Washington city.[42]

Downtime at camp was sometimes broken by the appearance of President Davis. On September 28, he arrived unexpectedly at Fairfax Station to be escorted through the streets "to the cheering of the assembled crowds."[43] "His Excellency arrived—just as he does everything—unostentatiously," but "when it was announced that the President was approaching, the soldiers broke through all discipline, and rushing to the road, gave vent to their enthusiasm in prolonged hurrahs" before he was escorted to camp. De Fontaine suggested that the visit might be to escape the "turmoils of official duty" while consulting with the three commanding generals and inspecting the army. "Perhaps also to be present in case of a battle," he wrote.[44]

However, instead of the anticipated battle with the Federals advancing on Fairfax Courthouse, the Confederates began a hasty late-night retreat toward Centreville. De Fontaine rode up and down through the almost endless winding procession of "private carriages, transportation wagons, ambulances, noisy drivers, braying mules, stalled teams, ladies on horseback, droves of cattle, sheep and pigs, families on foot, children without shoes and stockings, and mothers with babes in their arms."[45] As he rode around the caravan surveying the refugees, he described one of the pitiful families trudging through the night.

> [R]iding up to the father who was bent nearly double under the weight of a sackful of cooking utensils, I said to him, "Where are you going?" "God only knows, sir, but anywhere rather than fall into the hands of the Yankees." "But where do you expect to stop tonight?" "In the woods, sir, unless we can reach Centreville, which is four or six miles away." "Why don't you wait until morning—the Yankees won't be here for three days to come?" "Well, sir, I'm afraid to trust them, and I would rather know that my family are safe, if we do have to travel on foot all night." I tried to induce the man to go home again, by giving him every assurance possible that he would not be molested, even if he remained—for he was too poor to steal from—but no consideration would induce him to retrace his steps, and I left him trudging on with a half dozen little ones and a feeble wife, realizing for the first time in this struggle, the terrible devastating effect of war.[46]

De Fontaine left Centreville four days later, headed for Manassas with Dr. William G. Shepardson, a correspondent for newspapers in Alabama, Georgia, and Virginia. They turned toward the Potomac when they heard heavy booming guns from the direction of the Confederate batteries on the lower river. Expecting to find a major battle under way, the two correspondents rode their horses at full speed toward Dumfries, 22 miles away.

> When almost half way there, . . . a man passed me on a sorry-looking mule—one of those quaint, ancient-like individuals, who seem to have been born late on Saturday night, are found nowhere but in Virginia and would be prizes in the British Museum as a cross between an American Scarecrow and Egyptian Mummy. Notwithstanding the blank stupidity written all over him, I thought I would venture the question—"What's the news, friend—what are they firing at below." "Well—I dunna," was the drawling response—"I—reckon—as—heow—we're a firin' inter the Yanks. I hearn say they was a tryin' ter land down to Occequois."[47]

Although the information was indefinite, it was the only shadow of intelligence that they had received since starting. Without stopping to rest their animals, they pushed on at full speed only to find when they arrived at Dumfries that the town was "as staid and quiet as a Sunday—not a ruffle on a human face, or anything else to indicate the occurrence of upheaval" on which they had risked so much speculation and horseflesh.

"What's all that firing about today, sir?" he asked a man in the street. "Oh, nothing—just a couple schooners." "Anybody hurt?" "Nary body, but they made a big fuss doing it—fired a heap o' guns."[48] The correspondents had missed the action of seeing Confederates capture several Federal schooners headed for Washington. Disappointed and exhausted, de Fontaine hunted up quarters for the night, which he found "in a fourth-rate farm house, where the dining room was a bed chamber, the uncovered door a bed and my knapsack a pillow."[49]

Still looking for a battle to report, de Fontaine headed toward an anticipated skirmish at Bacon Race, which caused him to miss the major Battle of Ball's Bluff near Leesburg, Virginia, where equal forces of about 1,700 men clashed on October 21. He did not witness General Nathan "Shanks" Evans' victory, which turned into another costly retreat for the Federals.[50] But when de Fontaine arrived to survey Ball's Bluff after the battle, he came upon a grisly scene: pigs were eating Yankee corpses that had been buried in shallow graves, and a party of men were rowing from body to body rifling through the pockets of dead Yankees floating by with their deathly white faces upturned for crows to pick on.[51]

> On our way hither, we passed across the battle field where I saw one of the most sickening sights, and an instance of human depravity of which I ever had conception. Riding towards the water's edge, we met a pig running at the top of his speed with a human hand in his mouth, half a dozen of his grunting companions in full

chase. Further along, we came to the trench where the Yankees had buried their dead, and here another drove were busily at work rooting up and eating the horrid remains. One had a piece of shoulder, another was gnawing at a leg, while a third was pulling out the bowels of a half decomposed corpse. Gathering a pile of stones, we did all in our power to prevent the awful desecration by covering the bodies for a time, and a file of men was promptly detached to complete the work which the Yankees had so cruelly left undone.[52]

Although Ball's Bluff was a victory for the Confederates, a reporter for the *New Orleans Crescent* accused General Evans of disobeying orders in fighting the battle in the first place and of making a mistake in the second place by not attacking the Federals on the opposite side of the river the next day. Like other correspondents who never hesitated to editorialize about the war, de Fontaine defended the actions of the South Carolina general at length in the article that he constructed from interviews with soldiers and officers who had fought in the battle. He wrote that instead of committing an error, "the course of the General was dictated by the soundest military sense, good judgment and regard for the lives of those under his command."[53]

De Fontaine carried his tools of the trade, pencils and paper, to write his always lengthy newspaper articles or "letters," sometimes in the comfort of a room or tent, but frequently on the ground leaning against a tree or under a wagon or wherever he happened to be.

> In fact, I am writing in the midst of a crowd of hungry fellows who are waiting for dinner, with a large board for my desk, a stone for a seat, and no end to temptation to anathematize internally every individual who comes within two feet of me, for he is sure to be looking over my shoulder.[54]

He was perturbed that his articles about Ball's Bluff were not published for a week, which was a greater lag than usual, because the telegraphers were delaying the transmission of his letters. General Order No. 78 had established limits on messages that related to the movement of troops, especially when it related to the position of particular corps, as well as the movements and strength of any portion,[55] and information could not be transmitted until it was approved by an officer. However, some of the operators overzealously appointed themselves as unofficial censors and delayed sending newspaper stories even when they had been approved.

> I take this occasion also to say, apologetically, that more than once the readers of the Courier have been deprived of telegraphic news which, duly endorsed by superior officers, unexceptionable, ought to have gone at once, but was detained after leaving Manassas, Fairfax and Dumfries solely by the stupid obstinacy of telegraphic martinets who supposed themselves to be subserving the public good. You will, therefore, be kind enough to bestow your anathema upon them and not me.[56]

The post office was not much better, and by the next month he was complaining to readers about its service. "Please ask Postmaster (John H.) Reagan, editorially, to put a little more gum on his postage stamps. Like bad children, they require a terrible licking to make them stick to their letters."[57]

While Beauregard and President Davis were disagreeing about the course of action at Manassas, the provisional president was elected to a six-year term on November 6. Two days later, Confederate commissioners James Mason and John Slidell were seized by the Federals aboard the *Trent*, a British packet en route to Europe from Havana, Cuba. Their capture gave the South hope that Britain would finally become an ally, a possibility that de Fontaine mentioned from time to time. While the Confederates were hoping for international support that never materialized, conditions were beginning to deteriorate in the South. He noted that the number of ill soldiers was increasing because of bad weather, damp ground, and exposure.

> The Destroyer has stalked so frequently into camps during the present campaign that his presence no longer creates commotion. Men suffer and die, while their calloused comrades in adjoining tents are playing cards, performing on musical instruments and indulging in song and jest. "Poor man, he was a good fellow," is their obituary notice. The remains are borne away in a rude casket, to be deposited in mother earth; no bell tolls the funeral march, no weeping mourner drops a tear, and a cross, a pile of stones, or a rough rail fence marks the last resting place of the dead soldier. The heart suffering that has followed the trail of the present war will be a part of its history never written.[58]

Confederates were also facing an even greater problem—soldiers whose one-year enlistment would end by the following April. De Fontaine wrote: "How many thousand of these there are, I will not undertake to say, but the number is so considerable that apprehension may be experienced as to their probable course of action on returning home."[59]

Although he traveled with the army, de Fontaine was responsible for his own transportation and lodging. He followed the troops by train, on borrowed horses, passing wagons or ambulances, and sometimes on foot. He stayed in hotels and houses when they were available, but most of the time camped in tents with the soldiers and slept on the ground in the open when necessary. While waiting for the second attack at Manassas, he was rooming in an "amended hen-roost, through whose thousand openings the wind makes the melody of an Eolian harp. There one is tied down to the circumscribed range of a tent."[60]

When the second attack at Manassas had not materialized by Christmas 1861, de Fontaine stayed in a hotel in Norfolk, Virginia, where he reported that the holiday was celebrated with the fervor of a national anniversary. "The streets were thronged from morning till night," he wrote. "Fire crackers spluttered and went off with impertinent bangs, the boys blew toot horns and paraded in masks, the girls went to the ivy decked churches and the old people gave dinner parties, where stewed oysters, calves foot jelly, ravenous appetites and fabulous numbers of pretty speeches blended in the most amicable confusion."[61] However, the frivolity and merriment did nothing to erase de Fontaine's memories of bloody fields where battles had raged and soldiers had been killed in the past year, and he wrote sadly the day after Christmas about home and friends lost in the war.

> There are vacant chairs at the table and fireside, and the sad faces and somber garbs of mothers, sisters, wives and little ones are eloquent with the story of sacrifice they have suffered for their country's good . . . The fathers, sons and brothers who made their "merry Christmas" a year ago, now sleep in the cold embrace of death, beneath the sod of a distant State, their silent homes marked only by a rude slab of wood, or a name notched in a tree, or a mound of turf— no flowers planted near by loving hands, no tokens about the grave to show that the footstep of friend has ever trod the hallowed spot.
>
> Fierce bullets and merciless diseases have done their work of destruction upon our noble men, and left behind a train of mournful memories that will make the war of the Southern Confederacy a stalking ghost at some Christmas tables for life henceforward.[62]

The holiday mood faded in Norfolk the day after Christmas when word spread that Federal officials had nullified the possibility of war with England by releasing Mason and Slidell and admitting that their arrest had been illegal.[63]

While de Fontaine was returning to Manassas at the end of the first year of war, Shepardson, who was de Fontaine's companion on the Dumfries trip, wrote an article under the pen name "Bohemian" that enraged General Joseph E. Johnston. The article gave the location of various Confederate brigades and described the location of their winter quarters in the December 30, 1861, issue of the *Dispatch*. When Secretary of War Judah P. Benjamin told the general that the law provided no punishment for the security breach, Johnston issued an order expelling all newspaper reporters and correspondents from his army. After de Fontaine heard the news, he was "living like a pig in the mud" in Manassas and fuming about the weather and Johnston's order.[64]

> The weather is even worse than our spirits. Snow, rain, drizzle, fog and slush have been our torments for the last three weeks. Nature has been hung in the blackest of mourning, while we poor fellows wander up and down in the sackcloth and ashes of discontent. Of news there is not an item worth the record. The army is as barren of the article as a sucked orange is of juice. Even were it to be had, the recent order of Gen. Johnston makes it a death penalty for a correspondent to say aught to the people at home that concerns the welfare of their sons and brothers who are here to fight the battles of the Confederacy.[65]

De Fontaine rode south toward Augusta, Georgia, in early February, while Union forces headed toward the Cumberland River to attack Fort Donelson, Tennessee. The battle resulted in a stinging defeat for the Confederates on February 16 when Generals John Floyd and Gideon Johnson Pillow retreated into Nashville. At the same time, General Ulysses S. Grant was promoted in Washington to major general of volunteers. The Federals celebrated their first major victory, which opened their path into the heart of the Confederacy.

For his stories about the Confederate loss, de Fontaine interviewed an officer who had been wounded at Fort Donelson and had been part of the exodus out of the Union-occupied area of Tennessee. "People rushed through the streets in every direction," de Fontaine wrote. "Wagons were collected; furniture and valuables packed up; the depots thronged with men, women and children anxious to escape on the various roads, and the one grand thought permeating the entire community was, 'how shall I save myself?'"[66]

After de Fontaine arrived in Augusta, he wrote about those last days in Tennessee, describing how Confederate military authorities were setting fire to the steamboats to keep them from falling into enemy hands.[67] Reporting second-hand news, de Fontaine wrote that the telegraph office in Nashville had burned up all dispatches "to save trouble to the senders when the Feds come."[68] They were right to be burning documents because a few days later, General Don Carlos Buell's Federal troops occupied Nashville on February 25, 1862, after forcing the Confederates under General Nathan Forrest to retreat. Nashville was an important base for the Federals, who held it for the remainder of the war.[69]

De Fontaine soon left for Atlanta where editors were organizing to fight Johnston's order to expel journalists from the army. Newspaper editors were convening in Atlanta on March 11 and March 12 to discuss problems with censorship and wartime reporting. Johnston's order to expel correspondents from his army was causing significant problems in gathering news from the battlefront. At the direction of the newspaper editors, de Fontaine and two other journalists, J.R. Sneed, editor of the *Savannah Republican*, and J. Henly Smith, editor of the Atlanta *Southern Confederacy*, met in Savannah to draft a series of resolutions criticizing Johnston's action and calling for the War Department to rescind the order.[70]

From that meeting, de Fontaine headed to Tennessee. En route, his borrowed portmanteau and everything he owned were taken for the third time in four months. "I begin to feel very much like Adam when he wore only one suit of clothes," he wrote. "If they have been taken by accident, won't somebody send them back. If designedly, will the thief allow his benevolence to stretch sufficiently far to communicate the terms on which he is willing to make an exchange?"[71] He followed Generals Albert Sidney Johnston and Beauregard into battle where just a week later, de Fontaine watched Johnston die on the field during the surprise attack on Grant's forces at Shiloh Church, Tennessee, April 6–7, 1862.

Gladden continued to rally his troops enthusiastically, after his arm was shot away. Breckinridge had four horses killed under him, the first being a six thousand dollar animal recently presented and his clothes were completely riddled with balls . . . Poor Sidney Johnston was struck . . . and bled to death in twenty minutes.[72]

After Johnston was killed in "the rain of death amidst which they rode," Beauregard replaced him as commander, "dashing into the thickest part of the battle, and inspiring the troops who won the day."[73] When the battle was over, de Fontaine trudged through mud and cold rain to inspect homes and hotels that had been converted into hospitals for wounded soldiers and were filling rapidly. "The wounded still continue to come in, and the houses in Corinth are rapidly filling up," he wrote. "The hotel has been turned into a hospital, and five hundred men are already here covering the floors."[74] De Fontaine reported that a fifth, if not a fourth, of the Confederates were out of combat and, according to a prisoner that he interviewed, nearly a third of the enemy. He settled in for the night like a sardine wedged in with more than 300 wounded soldiers on the floor of the only hotel in town and expecting to be sleeping outside in the mud by the next night.[75]

> While I write I am sitting on the floor of one of the corridors, with the bodies of the living and the dead ranged on either side and opposite as far as the eye can reach. Groans fill the air, surgeons are busy at work by candle light, a few women are ministering to the wants of the suffering, the atmosphere is fetid with the stench of wounds, and the rain is pouring down upon thousands who yet lie out upon the bloody ground at Shiloh.[76]

All of the railroad cars were being used to transport hundreds of sick and dying soldiers, he wrote, "but the cry is, 'Still they come.'"[77] The next day, de Fontaine rode over the fields, describing scenes of the dead and still dying and the lingering smells and sounds of the battle that he later called "one of the greatest and bloodiest fights in the record of modern history."[78]

> No reality in the entire range of human experience can be more grandly solemn than to stand on a battle field and gaze around upon the bloody picture of mangled, dying and dead humanity, which the red hand of carnage has left behind. The sounds of strife have been hushed; the ground no longer trembles under the tramp of legions, and the air has ceased to vibrate with the rolling of musketry, the thunder of artillery, and the wild shouts of men. Naught disturbs the silence of the spot save the whispering of the leaves, the caroling of the birds, and the subdued voices of friends searching for the dead, mingled with the moans of the wounded and their pleadings for relief.[79]

"Nine tenths of the wounds are in the extremities, and if proper care is taken will not result fatally. Unfortunately, however, the condition with the roads and the distance of the battlefield from Corinth, rendered it impossible to bring away all the wounded, and hundreds have laid for two days and nights through a pelting northeast storm, upon the cold ground without anything to eat or any kindly hand to render assistance," he wrote.[80] Such an experience could do nothing less than humble a man, de Fontaine believed. "After the excitement of the battle has passed away and before the bodies over which you may have carelessly trodden a few hours before, you now bend in reverence and read lessons whose imprint will never leave your memory," de Fontaine wrote. "Hearts buoyant with hope and fervor have been forever stilled; lips with which you have been wont to commune are parted in death; eyes that have looked familiarly into your own, now dim and glassy, are turned towards the cold sky, and faces are pallid with the ghastly marble of the grave upon them."[81]

> The blood still flows from the unstaunched wounds of the living, or has thickened and dried upon their persons, and passing by, pitiful glances follow you as if they silently implored the assistance which it is not in your power to render. The ground is cold and wet, yet there they lie, unable to move, waiting, while minutes seem to drag into hours, for the arrival of the comrades who are to remove them to the hospitals . . . And how these poor fellows shudder and groan with anguish at the rough manipulations of those who have come to their relief. How I have seen strong men weep under this burden of agony, and pray for death to relieve their sufferings.[82]

De Fontaine ended his vivid report with a plea: "Ah! If those who ruthlessly make war could stand upon the battle field and see its results, long would they hesitate before they placed human life in the balance to weigh against the accomplishment of their designs."[83]

By the next night, all space was filled with wounded soldiers. De Fontaine, who had been without rest or food for 20 hours, slept in the mud and ate only a little raw bacon before he settled in for the night. He was still in Corinth, living in the open and trying to find clean clothes and a toothbrush when his friend Henry Timrod, a journalist from South Carolina who became the poet laureate of the Confederacy, arrived on April 24, 1862. Timrod had signed on as a special correspondent for the *Mercury*, but his timing was terrible. In addition to the casualties from Shiloh, sick and wounded soldiers arriving from embattled New Orleans poured into the hotels and private homes in the area. By the time New Orleans surrendered a few days later, no space was left in Corinth.

The correspondents slept on the ground, under wagons or porches, leaning against trees or wherever they could find shelter, but they could find no place to hide from a 36-hour "plague of rain" and a "howling East wind" that finally ended on May 5. Meanwhile, General Buell was moving into the area with 17,000 fresh Federal troops. De Fontaine was roused from his bed in the mud on May 7.

A night alarm! . . . Suddenly—Whish-sh—sh-sh shoots up a long golden serpent, streaming the dark blue like a meteor, lingers for an instance in mid air, then breaks into fiery corruscations, and disappears. It is a signal from one of the headquarters . . . Like the touch upon the wonderful lamp of Aladin, it calls into life a thousand varied scenes. The "long roll" rings its warning far and wide. Quick sharp commands echo through the woods. The country is now alive with passing couriers. Infantry, artillery and cavalry that seem to have sprung from the earth, so quickly have they responded to the alarm, are moving in detachments to and fro, and the heavy tramps of men and beasts, the music of the regimental bands, the shrieks of fife and rattle of drum, all tell of the sleeping monster aroused from his lair.[84]

The Confederates drove back two Federal brigades amid intermittent skirmishing at Farmington, Mississippi, on May 10, but more Federal troops were moving toward Corinth, where the Confederates were stationed. De Fontaine was so ill for two weeks after the battle that he could not write.[85] Like the soldiers, de Fontaine and Timrod, whose pen name was "Kappa," were still sleeping on the ground by May 15, finding food wherever they could and suffering from bouts of chills and fever.

The weather is warm and enerating. Comforts of life are scarce. Hard bread, water, molasses and bacon, very tough and indigestible, constitute our fare; a very hard plank and a pair of blankets serve as a bed; you scrape the dust off your person with a shingle; and after washing in water brought from a mud puddle, dry your face on a pocket handkerchief, then dry it. We wash our own clothes, do our own cooking, and when rations give out, "beg, borrow and steal." About three times a week we have the chills, with which my friend "Kappa" and myself were wont to shake "like the dry bones in the valley of Jehosophat." Of late, however, we have grown too lazy to shake, and lie and look charitably on each other . . .[86]

The next day word came that the Federals had captured Norfolk, forcing the Confederates to blow up the *Merrimac* because there was no safe place to move the cumbersome ironside. Bad news of another kind spread rapidly through the ranks concerning an insulting order about the Confederate women of New Orleans that was issued on May 15 by Federal Major General Benjamin Butler.

. . . officers and soldiers of the United States have been subjected to repeated insults from the women (calling themselves ladies) of New Orleans, in return for the most scrupulous non-interference and courtesy on our part. It is ordered hereafter when any female shall, by word, gesture or movement, insult or show contempt for any officer or soldier of the United States, she shall be regarded and held liable to be treated as a woman of the town plying her avocation.[87]

De Fontaine wrote that the army was alive with indignation. "I have never seen men more aroused, and when the note of battle rings out, no sound will be more welcome and none will leap more gladly into the breach than those who have been inspired by the stirring appeal to their humanity in behalf of the now outraged name of 'Woman!'"[88]

He expected the enraged Beauregard to lead the Confederates into battle at any minute. Instead, the general expelled the correspondents from his army on May 27, 1862, including de Fontaine, Alexander, Timrod, and Henry Perry, who had been with the *Picayune* until the fall of New Orleans but was now writing for the *Memphis Appeal*.[89] After the general ordered the evacuation of Corinth, the troops retreated 50 miles to Tupelo, Mississippi, on May 29. However, the order did not come soon enough, and 2,000 Confederates were taken prisoner by Federals moving into the city.

De Fontaine and Timrod escaped by horseback toward Memphis, where the Federal fleet had passed Fort Randolph and Fort Wright without firing a shot and anchored within two miles of the city.[90] After almost a month of sleeping in the rain and mud and eating scraps of food, de Fontaine was so ill that he had to be carried on a sickbed to watch the two-hour naval battle for control of Memphis. From his vantage point, he could plainly see through his field glass the features of the officers and men on the decks and hear their voices, and he watched the Federal gunboats "vomiting fire, thunder and destruction" before the city fell to the Federals on June 6.[91]

> Never was a city more completely stripped of everything that could reward a Yankey's cupidity, or gratify his desire for destruction. Every dollars worth of public property has long since been removed. All Cotton for miles around has been burned; no man holds more than fifteen hogsheads of sugar; the bluffs are bare save where blackened heaps show the altars from which has ascended the incense of the peoples patriotism; the last train this morning removed the Postoffice and military officers, and the bridges have been burned. [92]

De Fontaine reported that Memphis was quiet but not under martial law, "though two regiments of Illinoisians and a Federal dictator gave it the semblance of military rule," he wrote. "The streets were guarded at night by Yankee troops in lieu of the ordinary city police, but no arrests were made, and no effort was made to interrupt the activities of the citizens." Stores were closed and no business was being transacted. "Contrary to expectation, not the slightest Union sentiment was observable and from many of the chamber windows of the fair daughters of the city Confederate flags continued to wave their dainty proportions, and bespeak the sturdy obstinacy of the inmates," he wrote.[93]

Northern newspapers were selling on the streets for "two bits" each, de Fontaine reported. The proprietors of the *Daily Appeal* published their newspaper in Memphis until two hours before the Federals arrived when they moved the office and its contents to Grenada, Mississippi, which was becoming a strong defensive position for the Confederates. De Fontaine had planned to stay in Memphis a day or two longer, but a friend sent him a note saying that the Federals knew he was in the city and "were making inquiries as to his whereabouts." He had been traveling the streets disguised as a "respectable farmer," but changed his look when some ladies gave him their brother's clothes. In his new disguise, he said he "couldn't recognize his own self" in the dark. His friend sent a buggy and servant to guide him through the country, and he left under cover of night for a four- or five-hour ride south to Hernando, Mississippi. Under the shadow of the depot, he wrote a letter on June 9 while waiting for the train to take him to Grenada.[94]

> Good-bye to Memphis, to Yankee rule, to Yankee gunboats, Yankee atmosphere and Yankee buntings. I breathe free and now that I am once more under the folds of the good old "stars and bars" can write of matters pertaining to the last two days in a manner which a few hours ago would have stamped treason on my valuable entity, and conjured up a nightmare of prison bars and dungeon walls.[95]

As he rode the train through Jackson, Mobile, Montgomery, and Atlanta on his way back to South Carolina on June 21 to recover his health, de Fontaine wrote about the disturbing apathy and sluggishness of people in the cities along the railroad.

> Nowhere along a route now of nearly a thousand miles have I observed any acres of Cotton except that which has been gathered in piles ready for the torch. But of corn there is no end . . . Of wheat, oats, and vegetables I saw less upon the rail road, but I learn that every farm and plantation in the Cotton states will yield more than its usual proportion of these articles.[96]

While he was thinking about wheat and vegetables, de Fontaine turned to criticizing the army's diet and health care. He said that nine tenths of the sicknesses at Corinth, notwithstanding the bad water and other deteriorating influences, could have been prevented if the troops had been given a chance three times a week to enjoy a change in their ordinary rough fare of hard bread and "spoilt" bacon. He proposed an Army Vegetable Society to carry out his suggestions.

> Thousands of soldiers have, within the last year, died of diarrhea, dysentery, bowel and other kindred complaint, which, in their early stages might have been made to yield to the simplest medicines. But medicines, especially upon the march or on picket, are not to be had; occasionally the camp chest itself does not afford them. The soldier, meanwhile, suffers his malady to grow upon him, until suddenly he finds himself beyond the reach of medical care, and becomes little better than potter's clay, or is sent home debilitated and broken down for life. Times

Federal General Fitz-John Porter's troops were attacked by an overwhelming force of Confederates on June 27, 1862 at the Battle of Chickahominy in Virginia. *Harper's Weekly,* July 26, 1862. Courtesy of Rare Books and Special Collections, University of South Carolina Libraries

almost without number I have heard men wish for some specific that would afford them relief, and seen them, as a dernier resort, go to the sutlers' tents and pay five prices for miserable stuff, one dose of which would make a hog squeal the chromatic scale for a week.[97]

De Fontaine proposed that soldiers be provided with vials of medicine for diarrhea and that the army carry patent medicine chests on a small scale for everything from toothache drops to "poor man's plaster: and mustang liniment." He said that he had been caught in painful predicaments so often that "hereafter no circumstance will tempt me to travel without them."[98] However, he had no medicine that would cure his friend Timrod, who was desperately ill with tuberculosis. The poet had also left Memphis in June for the Columbia home of his sister, but he never recovered or returned to the battlefront.[99]

Fully recovered, de Fontaine headed north to Richmond, too late to see the Battle of Seven Pines and the Seven Days Campaign, each of which turned the banks of the Chickahominy River into bloody cemeteries. As he rode toward the battlefields, he made a rare complaint about his chosen profession: "I should have chosen some other field of existence than that which involves ten hours of daily bobbing up and down on a hard trotting horse, under a sun whose shading recesses are warmed up to 98 degrees, and through a country now so desolated that when a man sits down to a meal, he must be satisfied if he gets enough to fill a hollow tooth."[100]

When he arrived, he interviewed dozens of hungry soldiers in the nearly 100 degree heat to reconstruct the battles for the *Charleston Daily Courier.*

> . . . the Battle of Seven Pines proved far more disastrous to the regiment than any other in which it has been engaged . . . Such was the intensity of the fire from both the arms of the service, however, that for a long time it was not possible to advance a foot. Volley after volley was poured with unerring precision into our midst. Every shot apparently had its mark, and our men fell rapidly. The Federal bullets barely skimmed the ground, and in many instances the balls which struck our recumbent soldiers would pass through both arms and legs. Still, the position was held until after dark when the order was given to 'up and charge 'em.' The boys rallied with a will, and went to their bloody work as if they were something more than mortal, but human nature could not withstand the thunderbolts that flashed from the Federal artillery at the onset, and they were obliged, after a determined but ineffectual attempt, to obey the order to retire.[101]

Before the battle ended, 7,997 Confederates and 5,739 Federals were dead. Seven Pines was a prelude to General Robert E. Lee's peninsular campaign, which began on the north side of the James River near Richmond. Seven Pines was followed by a series of battles called the Seven Days Campaign, which included battles at Oak Grove, Beaver Dam Creek, Gaines Mill, and Savage's Station. Writing from Gaines Mill after the battle, de Fontaine described the devastation.

> Turning to the right and plunging into the woods, every step is marked with the evidence of a terrible contest. Probably no part of the field speaks more plainly to the imagination than this, where the bullet-scarred trees, the shattered limbs lying upon the ground, the severed saplings, the splinters made by passing cannon balls, the earth strewn with Yankee caps, canteens, bullets, fragments of shells, portions of clothing, knapsacks, straps, etc., etc., all indicate that a whirlwind of destruction had swept over the spot and left its blight behind. Here is . . . where every State in the Confederacy sealed with the life current of its soldiers its devotion to the cause.[102]

De Fontaine joined South Carolina's Palmetto Sharpshooters who had converged on the retreating Federals for the fifth skirmish on June 30 at Frayser's Farm, later called the Battle of Glendale, while Jackson's divisions were stopped at White Oak Bridge two miles down the road. De Fontaine described the condition of the men who survived the bloody battle and tornado of fire through which they had passed.

Out of Company H, in Giles' regiment, numbering about fifty men, there are but four whose persons or clothing did not bear the marks of a bullet. The flag was struck thirty times, and the colors of the Palmetto Sharp-shooters were struck twenty two times. The company of Captain Kilpatrick, in Jenkins' regiment, had but one man left untouched; two other companies brought out but three un-scathed. Colonel Jenkins is himself a curiosity as an illustration of the doctrine of "special Providence." Strapped to the back of his saddle was an India rubber coat. This had fifteen bullet holes through it. His sword, resting against his side, was struck twice, once just under the guard, by a minie ball, and the second time by a grape-shot, which carried away about ten inches of the end. His sword knot was cut; bridle rein severed, so that he had to lean over to pick up the dangling portion; his horse shot twice, and himself struck by glancing shots three times, all of which have left their mark on arm, body and knee. There has probably not been a more miraculous escape from death or injury during the entire series of battles.[103]

Counterattacks by fresh Federals, led by Generals Joseph Hooker and Philip Kearny, saved the line of retreat and established a strong position at Malvern Hill, where the sixth and last of the Seven Days Campaign ended. Lee's 80,000 Confederates assaulted 80,000 Federals under the command of Generals George B. McClellan and Fitz John Porter on July 1, 1862.

Balls strike the left flank and crash on through the double files, maiming twenty and thirty at a time. The sullen "thug" of the grape shot as they bury themselves in the bodies of the men is an appalling sound—one that can never be forgot-ten— but all sensibility has now disappeared, and the one thought is victory or death. The Federals, from their entrenchments in front, at short range, are like-wise pouring in a terribly destructive fusillade; but it is nothing compared with the awful showers of iron that plow so mercilessly through our ranks from the batteries on the left. Whole Companies are decimated. In some not more than a half a dozen men remain untouched.

The ground is covered with our dead and wounded, and they are falling every second. Is there no help for this carnage? None. Other troops are not at hand to engage the attention of the batteries and withdraw their fire . . . The stern, pale faces of the few survivors are turned towards the Colonel in command to read if possible their fate, but no voice can be heard in such a storm, and a single wave of his sword points out the path of duty.[104]

De Fontaine was deeply moved by the bloody fighting that left 16,000 Feder-als and 20,000 Confederates dead and dying on the fields. "Tread lightly, for you are in the midst of a mighty cemetery," he wrote. "The earth has drunk the blood alike of friend and foe, and both lie together where they fell."[105] De-spite their victory, the Federals withdrew to the James River, where they were protected by patrolling gunboats. While their wounded soldiers were being transported back behind Federal lines, de Fontaine visited their field hospitals where they were being treated.

And here I beheld another sight, which few men, thank God, have ever witnessed. In the middle of the yard something was lying upon the ground. At the first glance I supposed it to be a roll of dirty blankets, but observing that it had motion, I walked up to it. "Don't look there," said one of the Yankee nurses, "or you will see what will follow you to your dying day." Just at that moment the blanket was turned down by the object beneath—you could hardly call it a human being—and a faint voice ejaculated, "Water!" I could hardly believe my senses. There lay a man with the right side of his face, including the eye, nose, right ear, and the entire right lobe of the brain shot away, and a deep cavity in their place, in which might have been inserted two large fists. Maggots, mosquitoes, ticks, flies and vermin of every description filled the gaping hole by millions. They were crawling through his hair, in his mouth, over his face, and some had entered and were eating out the half closed eye on the opposite side. The man had been wounded in this terrible manner in the battle of Friday, and since that time, for nearly three weeks, had lingered in the condition I have described—a mass of corruption, suffering the torments of the damned, and yet unable to die. It was a spectacle which made one shudder and reel with heart sickness.[106]

When he arrived in Richmond, de Fontaine wrote several lengthy and comprehensive articles to help his readers picture the gruesome sights of the battles that had raged for the past few weeks. He recalled the horrendous sights and sounds that he had seen as he walked around the battleground. He remembered eyes glaring at him from the bushes and men imploring him for water with their "mutilated limbs, some with an angry scowl upon their faces, as if their hate could never be quenched; some groaning with agony, or in the pangs of dissolution; some smiling, some tearful with the thoughts of home, mothers, wives and sisters, some in pain and some at peace forever."[107] De Fontaine had watched the never-ending spectacle of horribly wounded men being loaded into ambulances and wagons that lurched back and forth from the battlefield to neighboring houses or temporary shelters under the trees.

Surgeons (stripped to their bloody work) are busy with knife and saw lopping off limbs, extracting balls, and dressing wounds. Hospitals here and there in the sheds, out-houses and shady pieces, are surrounded with litters and their sad looking contents, while amputated legs and arms lie about in ghastly profusion. Blood flows so freely that you can smell it in the atmosphere. The dead are on every side, and such looking dead as can be seen no where except upon a battle field. Some are pale and placid, with no mark upon them save the little round hole in the breast from which oozed their life's current. Some have been shot in the face, eye or forehead, and some terribly mangled by round shot or shell, which has torn away great fragments of their bodies.[108]

Soldiers with deep religious convictions and men who had never before prayed fell to their knees after the bloody battles finally ended. De Fontaine, who frequently attended religious services in camp or his own private "church" under the leafy trees in camp, reported that "the recent battles had done more to make religious converts than all the homilies and exhortations ever uttered upon the pulpit . . . Attendance at various religious services in camp has never been higher and the religious element never more predominant."

> There is something irresistible in the appeal which the Almighty makes when he strikes from your side, in the twinkling of an eye, your friend and comrade, and few natures are so utterly depraved as to entirely disregard the whisperings of the "still small voice" which makes themselves so vividly heard at such a moment. A man who has stood upon the threshold of eternity while in the din and carnage of a fight, has listened to eloquence more fiery and impressive than ever came from mortal lips.[109]

While de Fontaine settled into a hotel in Richmond, writing steadily about the horrors of the past few weeks, he could hear the booming noise of Federal gunboats steaming up and down the James River shelling both sides "almost daily and nightly."[110] Officers in colorful uniforms arrested anyone who couldn't show a "pass," gamblers "picked their teeth on the doorsteps of their establishments and ogled the women on the street corners, while speculators, Congressmen, planters, business men and beautiful ladies hurried through the streets."[111]

Rested and reinvigorated, de Fontaine arrived at Orange Court House, Virginia, on August 18 in time to see the Confederates begin a great advance. On August 20, General James Longstreet was at the head of the column that crossed the thigh-high Rapidan, a tributary of the Rappahannock River running near Fredericksburg. Because the army was marching 15 miles a day, de Fontaine wrote his articles as a diary. "Scene exciting and amusing," he wrote. "Nearly whole day thus occupied." He reported that the army was moving cautiously on August 21 because the enemy was nearby. "From a hill on the other side of the Rapidan we have a magnificent view for miles. Three columns—long, black winding lines of men, their muskets gleaming in the sunshine like silver spears, are in sight, moving in the direction of Fredericksburg, or down the opposite bank of the river."[112]

The Confederates made camp on August 21 in the woods where thousands of troops lined both sides of the road for miles. Campfires glimmered in the trees, muskets were stacked along the edge of the forest, and the soldiers were busy rolling up their blankets and sitting around the fires watching the roasting ears of corn and discussing the "coming events which cast their shadows before. . . ."[113] Like the soldiers, de Fontaine wrote, "we live on what we can get—now and then an ear of corn, fried green apples, or a bit of ham fried on a stick, but quite as frequently do without either from morning until night."[114]

Deserting Confederates and Yankee spies were treated the same way; after a trial, they were sentenced to death and executed, either by hanging or a firing squad. Although numerous soldiers from both sides had been hanged or shot in the field, de Fontaine did not describe an execution until August 22, 1862, when Charles Mason from Perrysville, Pennsylvania, was sentenced to die. He was accused of killing a Confederate courier and wearing his uniform to the front to report that General "Stonewall" Jackson had sent a message to reverse the order of the column. When the spy couldn't provide enough information about the Hampton Legion, he confessed that he was a Yankee who belonged to the Union army. He was tried in the field and sentenced to hang.

> The execution took place this afternoon under the direction of Gen. Evans in the presence of his brigade and a large number of soldiers. The prisoner was mounted on a horse, his hands tied behind him, and he was driven beneath a tree. The rope, which was little larger than an ordinary bed cord, then being adjusted, he was ordered to stand upon the saddle. As he did so, a soldier gave a sharp cut to the animal, and in a second more the spy was jerking convulsively from the limb above him. He met his fate with great stoicism, and appeared perfectly satisfied with what he had accomplished, but to the last denied all participation in the act of shooting Longstreet's courier. He said that he had an uncle and aunt who lived in Clark County, Virginia, and that the latter had made him the Confederate uniform which he wore.[115]

Covering the war was becoming increasingly difficult for de Fontaine. Armed with a pistol and rifle, he was not expected to fight, but he faced the same problems of survival as the soldiers. More importantly for him, he had to keep pencils and enough paper to write about the battles and find a way to mail or telegraph his stories to several newspapers. As he marched with Longstreet's men up the south side of the Rappahannock, de Fontaine described the difficulties of writing on the move.

> Writing on a march is not the most convenient or agreeable task in the world, however tantalizing may be the cacaothes scribendi of the scribbler. Though he may have any amount of mental pabulum on hand ready to be moulded into shape, there are few times or places when he can set himself consistently down to the work and do full justice to his material. The shelter of a house is not to be thought of; a tent is a palace; pen and ink are tabooed, and a man is forced to seek his epistolary comfort either at the crumbling end of a lead pencil, with a shady tree or its equivalent for a sanctum, and fence rail for his writing desk, or dispense with the same altogether. He must labor spasmodically in sunshine and storm, jerking out his thoughts whenever he can get a chance, and though he may have to lay himself out at full length beneath a baggage wagon, as I am at this moment doing, be content with accommodations which, if not princely, he must

teach himself to believe are at least ample and independent. It is an ignominious rostrum from which to talk to twenty thousand people, but it is nevertheless a fitting illustration of the straits to which all connected with the army are more or less reduced.[116]

His descriptions of the hardships and horrors of army life and death are detailed and vivid, and he frequently described the wretched food or sometimes scarcity of food, as well as the unsanitary conditions, shabby clothes, the frequently bare feet of soldiers in the field, and the increasingly desperate attempts of the soldiers to find food and shoes.

> I look around me and see barefooted and ragged, bearing only their muskets and a single blanket each, yet all inspired by the hope of another battle. I have seen some, too, who were hungry—stragglers who would come up to the camp fire, tell a pitiful story of sickness or fatigue, and then ask for a bit of bread and meat . . . Speaking of bare feet, I suppose that at least forty thousand pairs of shoes are required today to supply the wants of the army. Every battle contributes to human comfort in this respect, but it is not every man who is fortunate enough to "foot" himself upon the field. It has become a trite remark among the troops, that "all a Yankee is now worth is his shoes," and it is said, but I do not know how truly, that some of our regiments have become so expert in securing these coveted articles, that they can make a charge and strip every dead Yankee's feet they pass without coming to a halt.[117]

De Fontaine wrote his articles like letters to the folks back home. He frequently wrote in the first person and, like other correspondents, became an advocate for the soldiers, sometimes making personal pleas for help from his family of readers.

> There has been a criminal neglect somewhere in not supplying the army with shoes and clothing. At least a fourth of the troops are destitute of shoes, and common sense tells us that the best soldiers in the world, this condition, cannot and will not march or fight. If the General Government fails to take this matter in hand, let the noble women of the land do so, and promptly . . . Winter is approaching rapidly and a movement of this kind cannot take place too soon.[118]

While trying to stay close enough to the fighting to report the battles without being killed, de Fontaine was forced to scavenge for food like the soldiers. He reported that farmers throughout the region were complaining that the Confederates were as bad as the Federals about stripping the country of everything that could be eaten. "Now and then there may be one who, if he takes a dozen ears of corn, will pin a two bit bill to a fence post as a token of his honesty; but as a general thing ducks, chickens, pigs, and meat are remorselessly 'gobbled up' without the remotest conception of right or wrong," he wrote.[119]

Some generals tried to restrain the looting, but de Fontaine said only one or two partially succeeded, including Generals John B. Hood and Roger A. Pryor. "I have seen their brigades on a march of fifty miles, and where others were followed by stragglers who might be counted in the hundreds, I suppose that twenty-five would fully cover all who lagged behind the 'old Texan' Brigade and the Floridians."[120]

Worries about food disappeared quickly as de Fontaine followed the Confederates into the narrow Thoroughfare Gap that ran through the Bull Run Mountains, where ". . . the sharp echoes of the muskets and rifles bounded from rock to rock until lost in space." Wounded and dead soldiers had fallen along the way, and at one point, he saw nearly 40 bodies lying within a few feet of each other. He found a spot on a nearby hill to watch through a field glass the Second Battle of Manassas on August 29–30, 1862. The Confederates crushed most of General John Pope's army, which fled over the Bull Run but continued fighting near Centreville and Weldon, Virginia, before retreating toward Washington. The Confederates won the last Battle of Bull Run at Chantilly, Virginia, on September 1 before Lee's troops crossed the Potomac into Maryland. De Fontaine stayed within sight of the raging battles and worked so constantly and quickly that he was able to dispatch more than 7,000 words to the *Courier* on September 2 on the Second Battle of Manassas.[121]

> This is a portion of the history of the day which pen cannot full describe. But if the reader can imagine himself standing on the heights around the old Henry House and looking across the country in the direction from which we advanced, over the gullies, ravines and vallies which divide the opposite hills, he will see dead and wounded lying by thousands as far as the eye can reach. The woods are likewise full of them. It has been remarked by every one that the enemy on this vast hetacomb outnumber us five or six to one. They lie thickest upon the slopes and summits where their batteries were planted, and the infantry were drawn up as supporters, in many instances as many as eighty or ninety dead, marking the place where fought a single regiment. It is one of the singular coincidences of this strange battle that Hood's brigade encountered on Saturday precisely the same troops whom they met at Gaines' Mill in the battle before Richmond—the Duryea Zouaves, fierce fellows in red baggy breeches, red skull caps and blue embroidered jackets— and as on that occasion, literally mowed them down. In front of the Hampton Legion and Eighteen Georgia, I counted ninety-six of the dead, to say nothing of two or three hundred wounded, who were laying in every attitude, and groaning in every imaginable key.
>
> In front of the position occupied by Jackson's men the killed are even more plentiful. In many places you cannot walk three feet without being compelled to step over or around a corpse. Sometimes they are piled together, and very rarely you can see a Confederate soldier lying in the midst of a putrifying mass. Today

I found a wounded Federal, who has lain for the last two days and nights, where, by extending his hand on either side, he could touch the dead bodies of five of his companions. One of these he was coolly using for a pillow. How callous men become by familiarity with the scenes of war.[122]

De Fontaine camped with the troops on September 7 at Buckeystown, 10 miles into Maryland's interior, where the troops were allowed to go into town after making camp. He reported that Confederate money was taken without a murmur at all the stores and, for the first time during the campaign, Confederates could buy the articles they most needed at peace prices. Coffee was 25 cents a pound, sugar was 11 cents or 12 cents a pound, salt 50 cents a sack, boots $5 and $7 a pair, shoes $3, flannel 40 cents a yard, and everything else in proportion, including lager beer, ice cream, dates, confections, and preserves.[123] After the much needed respite, Confederate troops headed for Boonsboro in mid-September to fight the first battle in Maryland. When Federal General McClellan arrived in Frederick, he found a copy of General Lee's orders.[124] The mishap allowed McClellan to move rapidly and accurately to the Confederate positions near Harpers Ferry, Hagerstown, and South Mountain, where Jackson, Longstreet, and Jeb Stuart were posted.

De Fontaine watched the Battle of South Mountain begin soon after daylight on September 14 with

a vigorous cannonade, under cover of which two or three hours later, first the skirmishers and then the main bodies became engaged . . . To sum up the days work in a single sentence—we barely held our own. Advance we could not. The enemy in numbers were like a solid wall. Their bayonets gleamed from behind every rock and bush. Retreat, we would not, and thus we fought, doggedly, giving and taking the fearful flows of battle until long after nightfall. If we drove the Federals a few hundred yards, they in turn drove us. If we gained here, we lost there. Our very attitude, in simply holding our position with making the gallant charges which we have taught them to expect, encouraged them, and every hour their efforts appeared to grow in magnitude and strength . . .All this time the lion-hearted Longstreet was riding amid a shower of bullets, in the thickest of the fight. Twice did the shells strike the ground at his feet and cover him with dirt, while the musket balls that found in him a ready target buried themselves in the trees and branches on every side. Refusing his aides the privilege of sharing his danger, he stood alone at his post of honor, watching with a fearless yet hopeful heart the issues of the hour.[125]

General Lee was a short distance in the rear, de Fontaine wrote. "He too was calmly awaiting the fulfillment of the plans, and the expression on his face told how confidently he relied upon his brave boys for their accomplishment." The wounded, returning by the hundreds and borne on litters or limping along

Confederates crossing the Potomac before the Battle of Sharpsburg (also known as the Battle of Antietam). Illustration by Alfred Waud. September 1862. Courtesy of the Library of Congress

tortured by pain, were simple details to the general, noted de Fontaine. "A move was in progress upon the chess board that was to secure a great object, and every courier who came and went, every aide who mounted his horse and galloped hastily to the front bearing his orders, was only the minor agent in the operation of the scheme, that was spread as a map before his mental eye."[126]

The fight continued into the night, with neither side seeming to gain or lose, but the Confederates fell back early the next day to a position near Union-occupied Harpers Ferry, which fell to the Confederates in heavy skirmishing on September 15. The army moved so rapidly that the most severely wounded soldiers were left at Boonsboro, which was occupied by the Federals. By September 18, the Confederate and Federal armies had converged in the valley of the Antietam in Sharpsburg, Maryland, for the single bloodiest day of fighting of the Civil War. The Antietam Creek, which was not wider than 40 feet at any point, was fordable by infantry but impassible by artillery, except on the bridges.

If the battles of Shiloh, Donelson, Richmond and Manassas are considered among the greatest in modern warfare, that of Sharpsburg, whether in length, obstinacy

Confederates lie dead after the bloody Battle of Sharpsburg in Maryland. Photograph by Alexander Gardner. September 1862. Courtesy of the Library of Congress

or numbers, outranks them all. Few records of battles show more troops concentrated on a single field than were gathered here. If we look on the Federal side, we may enumerate the forces of McClellan, Burnside, Sigel, Sumner, Banks and Reno, all commanders of corps d'armee. One hundred thousand of their troops were trained soldiers, nurtured and disciplined in camp and field since the beginning of the war. Add to these the forces from Western Virginia, under Gen. Cox, likewise veterans, and the ninety thousand fresh levies, who, according to Northern accounts, joined the Yankee army after the late battle of Manassas, and we have an approximate estimate of nearly two hundred thousand men. It was a force gathered for but one purpose—to crush out before we left the soil of Maryland, and, as fast as steam could carry them, they flocked to the standards of their Generals from every camp and city in the North.[127]

The divisions, commanded by generals Longstreet, Jackson, D.H. Hill, R.H. Anderson, and Lafayette McLaws, were remnants of their former strength, he reported. "Whatever may have been the force with which we entered Maryland . . . has dwindled down more than a third," he wrote.[128] By mid-afternoon, Lee ordered General McLaws' division, which had been held in reserve, to move to Jackson's support. "And blessing never came more opportunely," he wrote. "Our men had fought until not only they, but their ammunition were well nigh exhausted, and discomfiture stared them in the face. But thus encouraged, every man rallied, and the fight was redoubled in its intensity."[129]

During an interval in the fighting, de Fontaine rode to the rear through the shattered town of Sharpsburg, where many houses had been struck by shells and one or two set on fire and destroyed. He wrote briefly and in haste from Shepherdstown, Virginia, on September 19, saying that the army had fallen back from its position for some unexplained reason and re-crossed the Potomac, leaving between 200 and 300 of their most severely wounded soldiers. Federals crossing the Potomac continued skirmishing with the Confederates on their way to Shepherdstown, Virginia, but the Federals retreated after losing 150 men and the Confederates made camp. De Fontaine said the army could not long remain camped in Shepherdstown.

We must either go forward or back. The country around us has been stripped of everything that can supply man or beast, and our provisions have to be drawn on wagon wheels for many miles. In less than a month, the roads will probably be impassible from mud, and the operations of the army be accordingly blocked.[130]

De Fontaine usually found a safe vantage point from which to watch the battles through a field glass and was never hit by enemy fire. However, he was ill twice during the war from fatigue and eating poorly, and he was injured once, when he caught his spur in his horse's bridle and was dragged 50 to 75 yards when his horse was frightened in late October. Even though no bones were broken, de Fontaine was severely cut and bruised. His injuries were complicated by internal inflammation that forced him to return to South Carolina during the third week of October.[131]

After recuperating in South Carolina until early December, he headed north to rejoin the Confederates at Fredericksburg, Virginia. On the way, he joined the front in southeast North Carolina before Christmas to report a series of rapidly moving skirmishes. As de Fontaine approached Kinston, North Carolina, fighting resumed early on December 14, near an old church where blood-stained floors showed that it had been used as a Union hospital. Federals had buried the dead from both sides in the adjacent cemetery before the Confederates regained Kinston and settled in for the Christmas holidays.

De Fontaine described Kinston as a "shanty town" where "the women all chew yellow snuff, and the men sit on the door steps and gape."[132] The editor of the Raleigh (N.C.) *Progress* was offended by de Fontaine's description of Kinston, saying that Personne, that "duck of a little fellow," was sent into North Carolina to ridicule and libel the people by the *Charleston Courier.* The editor accused Personne of being "a foreign hireling, who receives twelve or fifteen dollars a week and expenses," an accusation de Fontaine did not deny while claiming to be "as ragged as a pauper Falstaffion."[133] The editor said, "The chap, we learn, however, is quite young, and we may forgive something on the score

of his years, and hope that as he grows older he will grow wiser, and that time
will improve his manners and elevate his respect for our women."[134] De Fontaine apologized for his comments about the ladies but stood by his description of the Kinston area.

He stopped in Richmond on his way to Fredericksburg on January 23, 1863,
where he found that Richmond had changed so remarkably in the past six
months that "one has to indulge his fancy but little to imagine himself among
the throngs of Broadway."

> The city is overflowing with people of all castes, complexions, purposes and pro-
> fessions. Refugees are here in swarms, and, thanks to the noble, warm-hearted
> citizens, have found new homes, that replace for a time their own spoliated pos-
> sessions. Speculators are thick as locusts—the outpouring of every city and town
> in the Confederacy, while gamblers, courtesans, transient visitors, blushing
> brides, ecstatic bridge rooms, members of Congress, representatives in the State
> Legislature, Department clerks, officers of no account, officers . . . and citizens
> generally, have swollen the motley procession of humanity, until the city limits
> are scarcely capacious enough for its accommodation.[135]

A provost's guard stood on every corner, and everyone on the streets had to
show a pass, de Fontaine wrote. "Gentlemen or beggar, neat or nasty, high and
low, all have to stop before these inexorable sentinels, and 'show cause' why they
are there."[136]

While the Confederates were fighting in North Carolina, Lee had easily won
the Battle of Fredericksburg on December 13, when the Federal army attacked
the entrenched Confederates on the hills near the city. Almost 13,000 Federals
were killed, wounded, or captured, compared with fewer than 6,000 Confederates. The battle had been over for almost three weeks when de Fontaine arrived
in Fredericksburg on January 25, but he could still see evidence of the battle.

> The ground is rutted with the tracks of artillery, indented with the hurried prints
> of feet, and gashed by shells and round shot. Grass and corn have been trodden
> into the earth, fences are leveled, and stains of blood yet mark the spots where life
> has paid the remorseless forfeit of war. Dead horses load the air with putrifying
> odors and lie around in scores, while at frequent intervals the eye is arrested by
> the long fresh trenches in which the enemy have hastily thrown and buried their
> dead. Here and there may be seen a solitary mound with its rude wooden head
> board, and ruder hieroglyphics, marking the resting place of one more chosen
> than the others—but generally, the corpses were huddled together and thrown
> into the pits in every shape, without regard to order, decency, or respect. In one
> instance that came under my observation, the arm, shoulder and ghastly head
> of a Yankee soldier was protruding from the earth. Such is the spectacle that is
> repeated nearly every hundred yards until you reach the river bank.[137]

Federal and Confederate pickets exchange newspapers in the Rappahannock.
Harper's Weekly, February 7, 1863. Courtesy of Rare Books and Special Collections,
University of South Carolina Libraries

After surveying the battlefields, de Fontaine joined the Confederates on the
Rubicon River, within sight of the Federals on the opposite side. The arrival of
newspapers in camp would trigger a brief truce as a few Yankees from across
the river and Confederates rushed to pick up the latest news. "A paper held up
at any time," de Fontaine wrote, "will bring a dozen men flying down to the river
bank, each with a *Harper's Weekly, Leslie's Illustrated*, or some lesser light of the
newspaper firmament, each anxious for a barter."[138]

De Fontaine was writing for the Southern division of the New York Associated Press, which had been relocated from Louisville, Kentucky, to Augusta,
Georgia, after Federal troops occupied Louisville in June 1861.[139] Dissatisfaction with AP and continuing problems that correspondents and editors were
having reporting the news led de Fontaine and other representatives of the
Southern press to convene in Augusta, Georgia, on March 1, 1863, to organize the Press Association of the Confederate States of America, consisting of
43 daily newspapers in the Confederacy.[140] Newly appointed Superintendent
John S. Thrasher and President Dr. Robert W. Gibbes, Jr., immediately tackled
the increasing problem of military censorship of news.[141] Thrasher complained
that numerous officials, including the secretary of war, military commanders,

and the postmaster general, had given orders to "exercise a censorship over the Press reports and to dictate what shall and what shall not be transmitted by telegraph."[142]

The directors supported Thrasher in his opposition to extreme military censorship and told him to "use all means in his power to remove unnecessary restrictions." Because the directors also wanted more control over the news telegraphed from their correspondents, Thrasher was authorized to develop a list of General Rules for Telegraphic Reports, which included instructions to write simply and clearly while avoiding unusual and ambiguous words and abbreviations as well as unsubstantiated rumors. He asked correspondents not to repeat news and to keep their opinions and comments to themselves.[143]

On March 3 after the meetings, de Fontaine took the train from Augusta to Savannah in time to see four Federal ironclads in their third day of shelling Fort McAllister at Genesis Point, Georgia, about 25 miles south of Savannah. The ironclads headed out before dark, leaving only three casualties—a rabbit, a cat, and an old hen.

> The narrow escapes from mutilation or death were miraculous. On several occasions these heavy shells would burst in the very area in which the men were standing, and yet simply knock them down by the concussion or cover them with sand. The story of the cannonier who suddenly disappeared in the earth, leaving nothing but one ragged elbow protruding, and as soon as he got his head free sputtered the sand out of his mouth, and lustily roared, "All quiet on the Ogeechee," is said to be literally true.[144]

One of the most miraculous escapes was that of a barrel of whisky that was standing in the quarters of one of the officers. De Fontaine reported that a shell entered the side of the house, "passed directly under the whisky without disturbing it, knocked a wash basin into a shape worse than a cocked hat, upset an oil can, demoralized several pieces of crockery, spoiled the 'linked sweetness long drawn out' of a string of sausages, and passed out at the other end of the premises. This shows at least what 'good spirits' will do in a fight."[145]

Heading north to Charleston, de Fontaine arrived in time to write extensively about the attack on April 7, 1863, by a Union fleet of ironclads.[146] Still heading north, de Fontaine reported skirmishes along the way for almost three weeks before he reached Chancellorsville, Virginia, where he watched Lee win his greatest victory between April 30 and May 2. When Jackson was wounded by friendly fire, he was moved to a plantation office in Guinea Station where he died on May 10. After reporting the sad news, de Fontaine headed south before the Confederates won the Second Battle of Winchester, which cleared the way for the invasion of Pennsylvania.

De Fontaine had been happy as a bachelor and from time to time had signed his articles, "Yours in single blessedness."[147] However, he did not accompany

Lee to the Battle of Gettysburg because he returned to South Carolina to marry 20-year-old Georgia Vigneron Moore on June 10, 1863, in Spartanburg.[148] She was described in later years as "a bundle of nerves tied together with energy." Born in Abbeville in 1843,[149] she was the daughter of the Reverend George W. Moore, a Methodist clergyman,[150] and the sister of Colonel John V. Moore of Orr's Rifles. Moore died from wounds on September 1, 1862, after leading his regiment at the Second Battle of Manassas.[151]

De Fontaine and his bride moved to Charleston, where she had attended Miss Bates' Seminary on Church Street before the war.[152] He arrived in time to report the second Federal bombardment of Battery Wagner on Morris Island on July 18, 1863. At the head of the attack was the 54th Massachusetts Colored Infantry, whose story was told in the 1989 movie *Glory*. When de Fontaine visited the scene after firing had ceased, he wrote extensively in the July 20 and July 21 *Courier* about the devastating attack, saying that no battlefield in the country had ever contained so many mangled bodies in such a small space. The Federal bombardment of Battery Wagner, Morris Island, and Fort Sumter continued until September 6 when Confederates abandoned Wagner and Morris. Fort Sumter, which had been reduced to a pile of rubble, and Charleston held out, but the Federals continued to bombard the city from time to time.[153]

De Fontaine took the train to Atlanta in early October, where he stopped long enough to visit Thrasher at the Press Association and to "read fresh from every morning's press, the *Appeal* and *Register*—both industrious refugees—and the *Confederacy* and *Intelligencer*."[154] Heading north, De Fontaine was at the Chickamauga Station in Georgia when General Bragg received President Davis for an informal review of the troops on October 10. The President rode down the line, and the various brigades presented arms as bands played and flags drooped "in the official presence."[155] The troops were recovering from their costly victory on September 20 at the Battle of Chickamauga, where 18,454 Confederates were killed, wounded, or missing and 16,170 Federals were killed, wounded, or missing in two days of heavy fighting.[156]

De Fontaine joined General Bragg's troops in their camps in front of Chattanooga on the Tennessee-Georgia border. The opposing troops were camped without tents in full view of each other a mile and a half apart in woods and fields. Through his field glass, de Fontaine could see a large number of tents on the opposite side of the Tennessee, sufficient, he said, to indicate a strong reserve.

> The note of battle is once more sounding in the ear of the army. Our artillery, posted around the base of Missionary Ridge, at various points in front, and in the Lookout Mountain, opened this morning at 10 o'clock, and have continued a steady fire up to the present moment—five o'clock P.M. The enemy are replying from a large battery on the centre of their line, from another on the right and others situated in the Raccoon Mountain across the river . . .

Although Confederates occupied Fort Sumter on April 14, 1861, Union forces would try for nearly four years to take it back. In this illustration in 1863, the fort was almost reduced to rubble, but the Confederate flag was still flying over the fort. Courtesy of Library of Congress

While I write the enemy have begun to shell vigorously and missiles are flying in every directions towards the left. Lookout Mountain is alive with the echoes of detonating guns and bursting projectiles, and the greyish white puffs of smoke spiraling out from the umbrageous sides of the grand old pile . . . The crest of Missionary Ridge, as far as the eye can reach along the army line, is dotted with groups of men watching the progress of the fight and marking the aim of the antagonistic fires. You have only to imagine yourself on the edge of a huge basin broken . . . with mountains all around you catching the shadows of the clouds, with two great armies in hostile array ready at any moment to be precipitated into a deadly conflict, with the air filled with thunders of artillery rolling and bounding from every cranny, and on across the country, two hundred thousand spectators eager from curiosity while groups of the enemy lying in the fields out of range, pickets firing at each other, shells whistling by, sunshine glistening on the accoutrements of the Yankees behind their batteries and along their lines, the river looking like a mirror, the mountains throwing their broad arc, flecked shapes upon the valley below and the clouds thick with the sulphurous vapors of the guns.[157]

As he watched while Bragg's army reached the heights of Lookout Mountain, de Fontaine was bitterly critical of the army's progress because he believed, accurately, that the golden opportunity had slipped from their hands. "The enemy has been permitted to occupy a strong hold, from which direct attack cannot dislodge him, and within ten miles of a battle field, on which he was disastrously defeated with a loss of more than half of his artillery, and one quarter of his army, allowed to reorganize, reinforce, and prepare to resume the offence," he wrote.[158]

De Fontaine joined the troops in their camps before the bloody battles to control Tennessee. Even though a battle was imminent and supplies were short, the soldiers were willing to share what little they had.

"Was invited to supper," de Fontaine wrote. ". . . directly . . . produced from a bag that had gone the rounds of a Western campaign, a bone, five biscuits and a pinch of salt. Five minutes more and a tin cup, that served at once for fire and table—was set before us, oderiferous (sic) with the fumes of smoking hot coffee. Our table was a rock, our spread a blanket and an appreciative appetite compensated for every other want."[159]

He spent the night on Lookout Mountain with the soldiers on an India rubber blanket spread on a bed of leaves. He had to sleep with two other men who told him to "take the middle. With a tolerably stout officer on either side, all three occupying no more than four feet breadth wise, packed like sardines and straight as liberty poles, my friends on the uphill side constantly rolling against me, and I, in turn, pressed against my down hill neighbour, you can imagine the situation, and why it was that before morning the latter unfortunate was obliged to prop himself up with rocks to keep from rolling to the bottom of the hill."[160]

De Fontaine sent a list of killed and wounded to the *Courier* on October 29, along with the chilling news that many of their wounded and dead sons and fathers had been abandoned on the field when the troops fell back to defend the crossing at Lookout Creek. Without comment, he reported that Grant had arrived in Chattanooga.[161]

As another Northeastern storm began, he reported with growing dismay that the Federals controlled the valley below, which set the scene for the battles to follow on Lookout Mountain and Missionary Ridge: "The enemy now occupy Lookout Valley, west of Lookout Creek—possess the railroad up to a point three or four miles distant, and are entrenching at various positions. Chattanooga is, therefore, virtually a permanent base for Federal operations."[162] De Fontaine watched as 1,200 Confederates withdrew after fighting the hopeless Battle Above the Clouds on Lookout Mountain before he too was forced to escape with the retreating Confederates after the Battle on Missionary Ridge, which was lost in desperate fighting on November 25.

"Those who could escape from the ditch, did so, and made their way down the hill, the remainder of the command taking the same course," he wrote. "Those who gained the interior of the fort, with few exceptions, and others who could not escape from the ditch, were captured . . . A large number were killed in the ditch; others while retreating down the hill, when the Federals re-opened fire."[163] De Fontaine estimated that 50 Confederates were killed or wounded and 200 Confederates were captured, but he put the total Confederate loss in the three brigades at 650 killed and wounded.

Under a flag of truce, General Ambrose Burnside offered General James Longstreet the privilege of removing the wounded and burying the dead. During the day-long truce, Confederates and Federals were allowed to visit. "Many of the refugees from Knoxville had an opportunity of communicating with their families in the city," de Fontaine wrote. "Scores of these gentlemen joined the army hoping to reach home and be restored once more to their wives and children, but they have again been doomed to disappointment and exile."[164]

The Federal victory eliminated the last Confederate control of Tennessee, and de Fontaine joined Longstreet's miserable soldiers as they settled in for the winter in the rugged mountains of east Tennessee. He wrote his last report of the year on December 11 from near Rogersville before returning to Columbia, where he joined efforts of the Press Association of the Confederate States of America to keep Congress from conscripting journalists. Association President Gibbes successfully argued in a letter to Congress that the power of the press lies partially in the fact that it is not "dependent upon the individual will of Government officials."[165] A medical doctor by training, Gibbes was Confederate surgeon general of South Carolina. However, he had also been engaged in journalism since 1853 when he began publishing the *South Carolinian* in Columbia. By 1864, he was ready to retire from the newspaper business. With backing from two Charleston friends, de Fontaine bought the newspaper on January 13, 1864. As part of the deal, the partners wanted him to hire his sick and penniless battlefield colleague Henry Timrod. De Fontaine wrote dozens of unsigned articles for the *Carolinian* while writing a book of anecdotes and interviews about the war. He finished writing *Marginalia* in May 1864 and, leaving Timrod in charge, returned to the field to cover Grant's Wilderness Campaign. Confederates and Federals fought the three-day battle on May 5-7 in Spottsylvania and Orange counties, Virginia, where Lee inflicted more casualties on the Federals than his own army suffered. Unlike Grant, Lee had no replacements.

De Fontaine returned to Columbia in early July to find his newspaper thriving in spite of problems with devaluation of the currency and shortages of ink and newsprint. His partners were publishing a daily four-page tabloid that was almost half full of advertisements.[166] Satisfied with the condition of the newspaper, de Fontaine rode the train to Atlanta where he wrote a sad letter on July 8, 1864: "One gloomy fact is patent above all others, namely, that the citizens of Atlanta are deeply, darkly, desperately blue," he wrote. "I have yet to hear a cheerful word, or yet to see the expression of any other than the most sanguine hopes."[167] Even though he knew General William Tecumseh Sherman's troops were camped outside the city, he tried to write encouragingly.

They read impending events in the most portentous signs. Our army has been still further withdrawn to the banks of the Chattahoochee. The enemy are within twelve miles of the city, and the population is agog with excitement. Affrighted ones are removing their goods, chattels and personal corporosities with all possible speed; the curbstone philosophers are in a quandary, puzzled as they speculate, and wild in their indulgence of the most extravagant theories . . . In reality, there is yet little cause for alarm. From the beginning Gen. Johnston is said to have regarded the Chattahoochee as his choicest position, and to have expressed every confidence in his ability to hold that point. Hence his present step is one wholly consistent with his entire plan of campaign, and promises that success which, could not penetrate the mind of that great chieftain, might perhaps be seen looming up in the magnificent preparations of a complete and decisive victory.[168]

De Fontaine's tone did not reflect the reality of the growing danger in Atlanta as Sherman ordered his troops in a semi-circle around the city to destroy supply lines.

The great struggle for Atlanta commenced today, immediately surrounding the city on the North side, in the form of a semi-circle, and opened with artillery, which continued until about two o'clock. [General William J.] Hardee and [General Joseph] Wheeler were detached the night before by Gen. [John B.] Hood, and by this time struck the enemy's left, making a flank movement, when Hood's old corps, under Cheatham, advanced from breastworks more than a mile, capturing a large number of guns, dogs and prisoners. The battle is not yet concluded—Hardee still pressing on the Federal flank, having captured sixteen guns and about two thousand five hundred prisoners. The total number of guns on hand from twenty-two to twenty-four prisoners, nearly four thousand.[169]

After several days of heavy skirmishing, both sides rested until mid-August when Sherman resumed his efforts to destroy Confederate supply lines and Hood was finally forced to evacuate Atlanta.

By July 20, no newspapers were left to publish in Atlanta and de Fontaine was the only correspondent of any note who was still reporting from Hood's army.[170] Vandalism was increasing, and de Fontaine lost everything he owned for the fifth time when his possessions were pillaged. "I dwell on the subject with peculiar dissatisfaction because of my own losses, which leave me minus of everything, from tooth brush to blanket, except the clothes in which I stand," he wrote.[171] As the indiscriminate plundering raged, he left Atlanta at the end of July on one of the last trains still operating before Sherman's troops destroyed the last supply lines around the city. About 60 percent of Atlanta lay smoldering and in ruins when Sherman's troops occupied the city on September 2.

De Fontaine was back in South Carolina in time for the birth of his and his wife's first child, Georgia A., on September 23, 1864, and to pick up copies of his new book, *Marginalia, or Gleanings from an Army Note-book,* a collection of war anecdotes that has been reprinted as recently as 2006.[172] After spending some time with his family and writing a few more articles about Atlanta, he headed for Richmond in November 1864. Passing through the Petersburg area where Lee's troops were under siege, de Fontaine wrote from a hut partitioned with canvas strips that served as the headquarters for one of the generals.

He wrote that desertion was increasing in the Confederate army and that more than 60,000 soldiers were absent without leave. He lamented the lack of good officers and did not approve of the system of soldiers electing their own officers. He said popularity rather than competence had become the criterion for selection,[173] and he speculated about another major problem threatening the Confederacy: the declining value of money. De Fontaine's financial partner, George A. Trenholm, had succeeded fellow Charlestonian Christopher G. Memminger as secretary of the treasury in June 1864 and had developed a plan to bolster the almost worthless currency, which had been collapsing since early 1863.[174] De Fontaine called on Congress to adopt the plan proposed by the new secretary of the treasury to strengthen the value of Confederate money.

> War cannot be long and successfully maintained without strong sinews in the shape of money. Congress has tried to make them, but failed, and notwithstanding the abundance of Confederate notes in circulation, the soldier has at last come to think of them as little better than waste paper. A dollar will buy him an apple; two, an onion; ten, a melon. One night's lodging away from camp eats up the month's pay of a private, and twelve plates of oysters absorbs that of a Brigadier-General. The consequence is, that, for himself, the soldier cares nothing. For clothes and subsistence, he depends on the Government; for his luxuries he will sell the shoes from his feet or the shirt from his back. But he has a wife and children, and it is not unnatural that he should measure their necessities by his own. If money is worthless to him, how much more so must it be to those at home who supply their wants from a monthly purse![175]

Skirmishing continued in the Petersburg area until Sherman was marching toward Savannah, which fell to the Federals on December 21 and presented as a Christmas present to President Lincoln the next day. No longer optimistic, de Fontaine headed to South Carolina where he arrived in early 1865 to warn Columbians of Sherman's inevitable approach. He hurriedly shipped all his newspaper material and equipment that could be moved to Chester, South Carolina.[176] De Fontaine's partner Julian Selby wrote:

> After frequent reports that were received as to the intentions of "Tecump" (Sherman), and the promises made to the soldiers as to the license that would be allowed them when they captured the capital of South Carolina, it was decided

to remove the printing material to the upper part of the State. Mr. De Fontaine undertook to manage the job and to look after it when it reached its destination.[177]

De Fontaine left Columbia on the last train to Charlotte on February 14 before Sherman's troops advanced on the city. His partners Selby and Timrod kept enough printing material to issue a "thumb sheet" two or three times a day—"not a pleasant occupation, with shells dropping in the neighborhood of the building," Selby wrote.[178]

After reaching Charlotte, de Fontaine described the evacuation of Columbia as Sherman's troops began shelling the city on February 15; his partners Simms and Selby wrote detailed descriptions of the destruction. The march of Sherman's army "was a continual flame—the tread of his horse was devastation," Selby wrote after their newspaper office was consumed in the fire that destroyed Columbia on February 17.[179]

De Fontaine began publishing the *Carolinian* in Charlotte on March 14 and resumed publication in Chester, South Carolina, on April 2, 1865,[180] the same day that Richmond was evacuated by the Confederate government. As the Confederate government began to disintegrate, most of the archives were destroyed or shipped on wagons and trains to Greensboro and Charlotte, North Carolina, and Chester and Abbeville, South Carolina, where the Confederate government dissolved on May 2, 1865. Some papers, however, were left behind in Richmond, and those were either burned or scavenged by souvenir hunters when Federal forces occupied the city.

Enormous quantities of Confederate archives piled up in Charlotte and Fort Mill, South Carolina, where much of it was burned because the railroad bridge over the Catawba River into South Carolina had been destroyed.[181] When nearby Salisbury was captured, some records were moved to Chester and turned over to the postmaster.[182] De Fontaine drove a cotton wagon to the railroad station where he rescued a load of abandoned Confederate papers, which included copies of the provisional and permanent constitutions, copies of opinions of the attorney general, and hundreds of other government documents.[183] Although he used some of the papers to publish his newspaper, many of the papers became part of the War Department collection of Confederate archives, the Stanton Papers in the Library of Congress, and the New York Library.[184] The provisional constitution that he rescued is in the Museum of the Confederacy in Richmond, and the permanent constitution that he saved is housed at the University of Georgia.

In the waning days of the war, the de Fontaines moved to Charleston. De Fontaine tried to get a pardon in Washington, D.C., on August 20, 1865.[185] He resumed publishing the *Daily Carolinian*, with Simms and Timrod as associate editors,[186] but they were facing heavy competition. The *Charleston Daily News* began publication on August 14, and the *Courier* was returned to the Confederate owners on November 16, after being published by Federal editors since

Felix Gregory de Fontaine and his wife, Georgia Vigneron Moore, with their three children, Georgia A. (right), Wade Hampton (center), and their youngest, Edith Vigneron. This picture was taken circa 1878. Courtesy of Tony and Maryjane Islan

February. On March 29, 1866, de Fontaine visited New York[187] shortly before the birth of their second child, Wade Hampton, in Charleston.[188] De Fontaine was experimenting with morning and evening editions of the *South Carolinian* and was planning to start a morning newspaper in Columbia called the *Columbia Carolinian*. However, de Fontaine was facing financial problems and could no longer afford to pay his associate editors. The newspaper was discontinued "for want of support" in May 1866.[189]

In an article headlined "An Encouraging Symptom," the *New York Times* chortled over the failure of de Fontaine's newspaper. "We heartily rejoice that these journals have been discontinued for 'want of support.' We wish the whole brood of Southern newspapers, of which they are samples, could share the same fate. They are doing more to damage the South in every way, and to keep the whole country embroiled in hot and angry sectional controversy, than scores of loyal journals can cure or counteract. They represent the class of insolent braggarts who did so much to betray the South into rebellion, and so little to help her out."[190] Simms started writing for the *Courier* while Timrod tried unsuccessfully to open a girl's school with his sister in their home in Columbia in

September 1866.[191] Timrod died October 7, 1867, hemorrhaging from his lungs in the last stages of tuberculosis.

De Fontaine began publishing a German-language weekly newspaper in Charleston, *Die Charlestoner Zeitung*, with John A. Wagener[192] as editor and C.G. Erckmann as publisher. However, toward the end of the year, de Fontaine left *Die Zeitung* in their hands and moved his family to Bergen Point, New Jersey. He became managing editor of the *New York Evening Telegram*. "We left our hearts in the South, but took our heads to the North," his wife wrote.[193] In 1870, de Fontaine became financial editor of the *New York Herald* and later drama and music editor.[194] Their third child, Edith (sometimes spelled Edythe), was born in July 1876.[195]

By the time de Fontaine moved to New York, he had written hundreds of newspaper articles for at least six newspapers and the Press Association, as well as three books. While he was working for the *Telegram* and the *Herald*, he wrote lengthy articles about the Civil War for magazines and other periodicals and he wrote or edited nine more books. [196] Four of his books are still in print. *Marginalia, or Gleanings from an Army Note-book*, which he wrote in 1864, was reprinted in 2006. *The Fireside Dickens: A Cyclopaedia of the Best Thoughts of Charles Dickens*, which he wrote in 1883, was reprinted in hardcover in 2007, and *Birds of a Feather Flock Together: Or Talks with Sothern*, which was originally published in 1878, was reissued in hardcover in 2008.

De Fontaine returned to Columbia, South Carolina, in 1895 to establish the War Record Publishing Company. He compiled the articles that he had written during the war into a scrapbook by pasting his newspaper articles on official papers of the Confederate Department of Justice that he had rescued at the end of the war. Using the articles as references to jog his memory, he began publishing *Army Letters of Personne*, a monthly magazine of war letters and memories of the Civil War. In the first edition of his magazine, he urged soldiers to write their memories and their stories before death overtook them.

The story of the war will never be fully told until we get the details from the lips and pens of the private soldiers. Volume after volume written by the general officers on both sides have made us fairly familiar with the strategy and tactics of the struggle: with the movements of divisions, the gallantry of brigades and brave dash of regiments and battalions, but of the individual heroism of the men in the ranks, the adventures of the scout, the encounters on the skirmish line, the life on picket and the thousand and one incidents that the boys like to talk about around the campfire, the simple narratives are too few. The private soldier replies, "I've got it all in my head, and when I have time, I mean to write it out." That's what's the matter, old soldiers; you have had these grand reminiscences in your heads for 30 years, and with careless indifference to the future that is almost criminal, you are permitting them to remain there untouched and unrecorded. You are getting

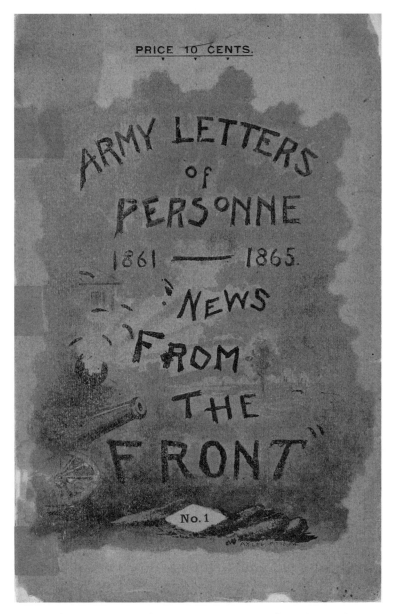

Cover of Army Letters of Personne. Courtesy of South Caroliniana Library, University of South Carolina, Columbia

old, tremulous and forgetful. One of these days may not come to you until, with
failing voice and shaking limbs, you realize it has come too late. [197]

Two issues of the magazine had been published by the first week of December 1896, when de Fontaine went hunting with friends in Hopkins, a small
town near Columbia. He caught pleuropneumonia. As he was dying, he said,

Second page of de Fontaine's magazine, Army Letters. Courtesy of South Caroliniana Library, University of South Carolina, Columbia

"The silver cord was already loosened and the golden bowl was broken." His wife Georgia and his youngest daughter, Edythe, were with him when he died on December 11, 1896. He was 62. His casket was accompanied from Trinity Church (now Cathedral) by an entourage of the Governor's guards in full-dress gray uniforms and members of Camp Hampton United Confederate Veterans.

He was buried in Elmwood Cemetery[198] in Columbia with full military honors, including the customary volleys fired over his grave in the presence of veterans of the Confederacy "now realizing that one by one they are fast being gathered home."[199]

At the time of his death, their son, Wade Hampton, was living in New York serving as the head of the Lettuce Cream Manufacturing Company, a cosmetic company on Fifth Avenue. Their oldest daughter, Georgia, was married to E. Ogden Schuyler[200] and lived in Bergen Point, New Jersey.[201] After de Fontaine died, his widow's health began to fail. She died of heart failure less than a year later, on October 16, 1897, in Englewood, New Jersey, at age 54.[202] She was buried in Elmwood Cemetery, beside her husband. She had written three plays, an operetta, a novel, a children's history, and enough poems to fill a volume. She was a member of the Daughters of the Confederacy and the Daughters of the American Revolution.[203]

Felix Gregory de Fontaine and his wife, Georgia Vigneron Moore de Fontaine, lie today in unlocated graves in Elmwood Cemetery in Columbia.

4

Robert W. Gibbes: The "Mind" of the Confederacy

Debra Reddin van Tuyll and Patricia G. McNeely

Aₗₜₕₒᵤ𝒈ₕ Rₒбₑᵣₜ W. Gₗббₑₛ, Jᵣ., ₙₑᵥₑᵣ ₛₑᵣᵥₑ𝒹 ₐₛ ₐ 𝒻ᵢₑₗ𝒹 ᵣₑₚₒᵣₜₑᵣ, he was an influential advocate for the war correspondents and president of the Press Association of the Confederate States of America, founded by the South's daily newspaper editors in Augusta, Georgia, in 1863. Without his efforts, the correspondents would have been far more frustrated and less successful in covering the war, and editors would have had to settle for second-rate and irregular stories.

As the first president of the Press Association, Gibbes helped organize the wire service and worked alongside Superintendent John S. Thrasher to battle the Confederate government for copyright protection of wire dispatches, exemption of journalists from the draft, and greater access to the military and its actions. Always ready for a new challenge, Gibbes moved seamlessly into his role with the Press Association, having already worked in almost a dozen different professions and avocations by the time the Civil War began. Although he started his career as a chemistry professor without a college degree, he became a surgeon, writer, editor, publisher, meteorologist, historian, art collector, and two-term mayor of Columbia, South Carolina.

He added "journalist" to that list in 1840 when he took his first newspaper job, a position that would place him on a trajectory to file what was probably the first open meetings lawsuit in South Carolina, and perhaps in the United States.[1] Newspapers from around the country rallied around Gibbes and praised his decision to stand up to the Columbia mayor who threw him out of a city council meeting. In the aftermath of the case, *Frank Leslie's Illustrated Newspaper* praised Gibbes as "essentially American . . . a physician by choice . . . an editor by ability, and a politician of leading influence."[2]

Gibbes learned early the value of cooperative professional efforts, and that experience motivated him to organize and become president of the South Carolina Press Association, one of the first state press associations in the country.

Dr. Robert W. Gibbes, Jr., was president of the Press Association of the Confederate States of America and Surgeon General of South Carolina during the Civil War. Courtesy of South Caroliniana Library, University of South Carolina, Columbia

The organization was discontinued during the turmoil before the war and not resurrected until 1875.

When the war began, Gibbes enlisted in the Confederate Army and became surgeon general of South Carolina. Five of his sons also enlisted; four became officers and one represented the Confederacy in England. Gibbes became widely known for his passionate defense of worthy principles, most notably, freedom of the press.[3]

He was born in Charleston, South Carolina, on July 8, 1809, to a Revolutionary War hero, William Hasell Gibbes and his wife, Mary Philip Wilson Gibbes.[4] Young Gibbes attended South Carolina College (later renamed the University of South Carolina), but he was not allowed to graduate because he was part of a student rebellion aimed at gaining permission for students to live off campus. Students eventually acquired the privilege they sought, and although the college never awarded him a degree, Gibbes was hired as President Thomas Cooper's assistant in the Department of Chemistry, Geology, and Mineralogy.[5] While teaching at the college, Gibbes continued his education at the Medical College of South Carolina and graduated with a medical degree in 1834.

He began practicing medicine in Columbia, but his interest in agriculture also led him to begin writing for the weekly *Carolina Planter* in 1840. He resigned from the newspaper after a year but continued to write prolifically about science and medicine for state, national, and international magazines and newspapers for the next 12 years. Novelist and fellow journalist William Gilmore Simms was initially unimpressed with Gibbes' articles. In a letter to a friend in 1849, Simms said, "Poverty is the word for Gibbes. He is a poor devil and a devilish poor writer."[6] Simms had changed his mind, at least to a degree, about Gibbes by the end of the Civil War when he said that "perhaps no other person in South Carolina has more distinguished himself by his scientific writings, and by his indefatigable research which illustrates them."[7] However, Simms made no comment about Gibbes' journalistic efforts.

In 1852, Gibbes gained control of another Columbia newspaper, the *Palmetto-State Banner*, which he renamed the *Columbia Banner*. The owner had moved to California in the middle of "a scandal that rocked the town," although it was not clear what the scandal was.[8] A year after buying the *Banner*, he purchased the paper's primary competitor, the *South Carolinian*, for $10,000. The *South Carolinian* was a Democratic newspaper with a circulation of about 3,000 that included subscribers in North Carolina, Georgia, Tennessee, Mississippi, Alabama, Arkansas, Missouri, and Texas.

After Gibbes bought the *Banner*, he urged the state's newspapers to establish a state press association, and on December 1, 1852, 23 editors and publishers from 20 newspapers met in Columbia at the Fireman's Hall to organize the South Carolina Press Association. Gibbes was elected president of the organization, which continued to hold annual conventions until 1857, when it became inactive; it was reorganized in 1875.

Gibbes earned a national reputation as a journalist after he was barred from reporting an open meeting of the Columbia City Council in September 1855. Mayor E. J. Arthur, a member of the Know-Nothing (American) party, had awarded the city printing contract to Columbia's Know-Nothing newspaper, and he apparently believed that contract also conferred on the newspaper the exclusive right to report on city council meetings, a position he had communicated to Gibbes. The feisty editor showed up to cover the meeting, despite the mayor's warning, and when Gibbes refused to leave the chamber, Arthur instructed Columbia Police Chief John Burdell to eject Gibbes. After the case was heard in March 1857 by the Richland District Court of Common Pleas, the jury found in Gibbes' favor.[9]

In his instructions to the jury, the presiding judge spoke eloquently of the right of reporters, and citizens, to attend meetings of their elected representatives and to discuss, critique, write about, and publish the proceedings of those meetings. In his comments to the jury, the judge made the following points, according to a report of the proceedings.

> Town Hall . . . is not private property . . . [E]very citizen has the right to enter if he does not interfere with the decorum of the proceedings. This is a matter of common right; that he shall know what his representative does and says . . . [I]t follows, that if a corporator and voter has the right to attend a public meeting, there is no power on the part of that body to say to him, you shall be expelled unless you will pledge yourself not to report its proceedings. Every man who is there, exercises the right to hear. How would it operate if it were otherwise? And what is reporting the proceedings? It does not necessarily follow that they must be published in a newspaper. Then any body may be expelled who will not promise not to say any thing to his neighbor. When he puts it in the paper, he only gives it a wider scope.[10]

According to the report of the proceedings, the judge turned to the issue of what exactly constituted press freedom and concluded that it was a "mixed bag," so to speak. The judge said that he had not found a definition of press freedom in his career, but he knew that Alexander Hamilton had believed that truth published for justifiable ends ought not be punished. He thought this was the definition the jury ought to use in its deliberations.

> What is the difference between liberty of speech and the liberty of the press? What is that which is printed but speech in another form? It is but speaking to a greater number than can hear the common voice, by means of signs—as the painter speaks from the canvas and the sculptor from the marble, the impressions of his own brain. The liberty of the press and the liberty of speech have the same protection in the Constitution of the United States. And the liberty of the press is not confined to the newspaper press by any means.[11]

The judge considered it his duty to say that as a matter of law, the freedom of the press is guaranteed by the Constitution to every citizen of South Carolina. However, as he told the jury, it was not easy to determine what that meant. "But while the freedom of the press is and must be protected, it has, of late years in this country, attained a very different character from what it was when these words were used. It is a matter of great question whether, upon a broad scale, it does not do more harm than good in these United States," he wrote.

> Why, the "apostle of liberty," Jefferson, was the man who said that if all the lies of a newspaper were strung together it would be difficult to find anything left. Well, this might not be true, but in New York the press has done infinitely more harm than good for years past. But be that as it may, the freedom of the Press is guaranteed in the Constitution of the United States, and if this Council were led to commit an assault and battery from an intention to invade the liberty of the Press it is an aggravation of their offense . . . [T]he freedom of the press is guaranteed in the constitution and, with all its mischiefs, we must take it.[12]

Gibbes had sought $10,000 in damages from the mayor and police chief, and although the jury sided with him with regard to the verdict, they and the judge disagreed as to the value of the harm done. They awarded the editor $25 from the mayor and six-and-a-quarter cents from the police chief. With that money, Gibbes commissioned a silver goblet lined with gold. He had it engraved to read:

> The Freedom of the Press is guaranteed by the Constitution of the United States. To eject a corporator from a public meeting because it is suspected or avowed by him that he means to publish a report of the proceedings is not Lawful.[13]

Frank Leslie's Illustrated Newspaper published a profile of Gibbes a few months after the trial, and its editors commended Gibbes for his defense of press freedom: "For his noble defense of the liberty of the press, he deserves, and receives everywhere, the thanks of his fellow-citizens."[14]

Gibbes was a staunch supporter not only of press freedom but also of secession and Southern independence, and he believed the press had a role to play in achieving that independence. He was among the representatives of 43 newspapers who gathered in Augusta, Georgia, in February 1863, to organize the Press Association of the Confederate States of America. On the second day of the gathering, Gibbes was unanimously elected president.[15] He would spend the next year helping to organize the wire service and addressing problems with news-gathering common to all Confederate newspapers.

In his role as president, Gibbes dealt with the practical side of operating a wire service and led the association's efforts to resolve problems that plagued Southern reporters and newspapers. He clearly understood the role of the press and was devoted to helping journalists fulfill that role. Gibbes wrote eloquently about the importance of journalism to the South's war for independence when he delivered his first and last presidential address to the Press Association members in April 1864.

> Your presence here to-day is auspicious of good to our beloved Confederacy and our noble people. While our sons and brothers are on our borders, asserting

and defending the heritage of independence, won by the swords of our fathers, and, until recently, acknowledged by our Northern co-States and the nations of the earth, while war rages, unjust, unprincipled, ruthless, perfidious and dia- bolical war, waged by the fiendish malignity of treacherous Federal associates, conducted with disregard to every characteristic of humanity, and urged with cruelty, pillage, arson, rapine and murder, seeking to destroy and subjugate a pa- triotic people entitled to freedom, you are here peacefully representing the mind of the Confederacy met together in general council to consult for the best means to give the people knowledge, to keep them constantly advised of the progress of their cause, and to promote their intellectual requirements. [16]

Gibbes called the spectacle "a striking one," saying that "amid the excitement of revolution—the grand uprising of a whole people imbued with the principles of inherent sovereignty and conscious power—you meet quietly and calmly to give the world assurance of the fact, that, intending to continue free, our people are even now thus early claiming to cultivate the blessing of peace, their intel- lectual interests. Gentlemen, as the exponents of the mind and will of the Con- federate people, you have with one accord already shown that they are worthy of their revolutionary parentage."[17]

Gibbes was not simply trying to influence his audience. There can be little doubt that he believed what he was saying—both about the South's bid for in- dependence and, most importantly, about the importance of journalism and journalists to their communities. He proved this not only with that 1857 lawsuit but also in the way that he conducted his own newspapers.[18]

He believed that newspapers should be dignified, patriotic, and conservative. They should be above name-calling, although he rarely ignored any editorial insult hurled in his direction. He also advocated journalistic independence; political principles espoused by newspapers ought to be those of the editor, not some political party, and he pledged that his editorial opinions would always be based on his own convictions "in accordance with what I conceived South- ern policy."[19]

As president of the Press Association, Gibbes did more than theorize about the role of the press. He helped solve practical problems, such as unauthorized sales of news dispatches. The Press Association sought copyright protection to keep its dispatches from being stolen and sold to individuals who were bribing unscrupulous telegraph operators of the Southwestern Telegraph Company in Mobile, Alabama, to divulge dispatch content before it could appear in news- papers. Mobile was a hub for the association's transmissions. Individual corre- spondents would telegraph their stories and a company agent would then collect and amass them into a single transmission.[20] Gibbes announced the decision to copyright dispatches, and the rationale for it, in his presidential address at the first annual meeting of the association's board of directors.

The daily concentration at numerous points for publication of reports from scenes which attract public attention, holds out to other parties than those having the labor and expenditures of the Press Association the temptation also to become publishers. I regret to say that in some sections of our country the managers of the telegraph have sought and found their profit to the injury of the Press by availing themselves of the fruit of our labors . . . Through these means the very labors of the Press Association to serve the public and give increased interest to their journals, are made to become instruments for the injury of its members and actually destructive of journals important to the welfare, spirit and economy of the people.[21]

Copyrighting of dispatches, which had already begun, was only partially successful in stopping the thefts, Gibbes reported. The Southern Express Companies, an important Southern freight and parcel hauler, had complied with the law, but the Southwestern Telegraph Company decided to fight back. It had sought the aid of an Alabama congressman to oppose the copyrighting of news dispatches. Press Association Superintendent John S. Thrasher, the man charged with day-to-day management of the wire service, had been lobbying the Judiciary Committee of the Confederate House of Representatives to keep the copyrights in force, but it appeared now, Gibbes told the directors, that it might be necessary to take the matter to court. He sought the directors' advice on how to proceed: "The copyright of the news reports has another important bearing upon the interests of the Association," he wrote. "If your labors are protected by the shield of the law, and their benefits cannot be attained except through the legitimate channel of adhesion to the Association, and equal participation in its burthens, the inducements to cooperate with it will be increased, and of separate action will be diminished in equal degree."[22] This achievement of copyright for news appears to have been the first time a legislative body had deemed news worthy of legal protection.

Gibbes was an enormously effective representative for the Press Association, but his association with the wire service ended when he sold his Columbia newspaper. Gibbes resigned as president of the association when he sold the *South Carolinian* in 1864 to Felix G. de Fontaine, a noted Southern war correspondent who was chiefly associated with the *Charleston Courier.* At the time of its sale, the *South Carolinian* was widely recognized as the most outstanding daily in that area.[23] When Gibbes decided to sell the paper to de Fontaine, he ensured that the *South Carolinian* would be in skilled enough hands to continue its legacy of high-quality journalism.[24]

Gibbes' wife, Carolina Elizabeth Guignard Gibbes, died in early 1865, just weeks before Union General William T. Sherman's troops destroyed Columbia. Federal soldiers ransacked and burned Gibbes' house, which contained collections of some of the finest art and artifacts in the state. One of the few items that he was able to save was the silver and gold goblet that he had commissioned

Most of Columbia, South Carolina was destroyed in Sherman's raid on February 17, 1865. *Harper's Weekly,* April 8, 1865. Courtesy of Rare Books and Special Collections, University of South Carolina Libraries

View of Columbia's Main Street from the State House after Sherman's raid on February 17, 1865. Photograph by Richard Wearn. Courtesy of South Caroliniana Library, University of South Carolina, Columbia

Residence of Dr. Robert W. Gibbes, Jr., after the devastation of Sherman's raid on the city. Close examination of this photograph reveals a balding man standing on the front steps. Although the photo was taken from too far away to permit positive identification, the man may have been Gibbes. Photo by Richard Wearn, Columbia. Courtesy of South Caroliniana Library, University of South Carolina, Columbia

with the $25 and six-and-a-quarter cents he won in settlement of his open meetings lawsuit. The goblet is still owned by direct descendents living in Columbia.

Only days after the city was sacked, Gibbes wrote a letter to "your Excellency" (possibly the governor), dated "Ruins of Columbia, February 28, 1865." Gibbes painted a vivid picture of a devastated city. "Rations are nearly out—a pint of corn apiece is all they get now," Gibbes wrote. "The river is very high and there is no crossing . . . The pillage was terrible—the Yanks say Columbia was the richest place in plunder they visited . . . I saved nothing but the suit of Clothes I had on. My daughter and her six children lost everything. My house & Robert's were destroyed—James' house escaped miraculously after he had distributed his clothes and abandoned it."[25]

Gibbes died October 15, 1866, at age 57.[26] He is buried beside his wife at Trinity Cathedral in Columbia.

5

Joan: Citizen-Journalist of the Confederacy

Debra Reddin van Tuyll

JOAN WAS AN UNLIKELY ANTEBELLUM SOUTHERN WOMAN. SHE WAS A mother with a martial spirit. She traveled from South Carolina to the Virginia war zone on her own to ensure that she would be near if her son were wounded doing his duty as a Confederate soldier.

To support herself, she did not work as a domestic, a laundress, a nurse, or a governess, the more likely employment options for a 19th century woman forced by circumstances to work outside her own household.[1] Instead, Joan turned to an occupation not generally open to women, especially those of the upper classes: journalism. It was in this work that Joan made her one bow to convention. She used a pseudonym to cloak her identity, a choice that has served Joan well for nearly 150 years, for despite extensive and diligent efforts, her actual name remains a mystery.

Women like Joan—white, educated to some degree, and at least moderately well off—typically lived sheltered lives in the 19th century. When they wrote, they primarily did so for only two audiences: themselves and their families. As historian Elizabeth Fox-Genovese explained, "It was one thing to write; quite another to claim the public and unfeminine mantle of authorship."[2] The situation was a bit different in the North, where even well-to-do women were less set apart from the public sphere. That is not to say that it was common for Northern women to work in journalism, but it was not entirely unheard of, either. As early as 1847, Jane Swisshelm Grey became editor of the *Pittsburgh Saturday Visitor*, and she would work in the field as an editor, and even Civil War correspondent, for many more years.[3] Southerners were more conservative, however, and while an occasional woman might surface as a magazine contributor or "editoress" of a country weekly or a temperance journal, like Mrs. A.M. Gorman of the Raleigh, North Carolina, *Spirit of the Age*, rarely did they appear in any major news-editorial role for a mainstream daily. When a Southern woman did write for publication, she would almost always do so anonymously.[4] A good example would be Louisa S. McCord, one of the South's ablest antebellum apologists.

McCord wrote widely in all the leading publications, such as *DeBow's Review* and the *Southern Quarterly Review*, and she always signed her articles with her initials or a pen name.[5] McCord was of impeccable social standing. Both her husband and her father were leading men in South Carolina. No one would dare snub her had she chosen to write under her own name, yet even she conformed to the social conventions of the day.

The bounds of proper feminine behavior loosened during the war, however. As more Southern men volunteered for and were drafted into the Confederate military, gender roles and relations were "ripped apart." This was probably truer in industries other than journalism, but even among newspapers, female labor became acceptable, as the presence of several women among the ranks of Southern war correspondents indicates.[6] Many women took on jobs and roles they never would have considered before the war. One of those women was Joan, who spent four months in the summer and fall of 1861 as a Virginia correspondent for the *Charleston Courier*. Joan's decision to go to Virginia and take up "scribbling" for a newspaper would have given society's matrons a strong case of the vapors in an earlier time, but it gained a degree of approval when the war started. The public's growing desire for news was only partially the reason. Women everywhere were volunteering their labor for a variety of previously male-dominated tasks. They did so to aid the cause, and their volunteering was taken for what it was: a patriotic commitment to the cause of Southern independence.[7]

Joan's experiences can be read not only as a typical tale of how the Civil War affected women but also as an antecedent of a 21st century reportorial practice: citizen journalism. In modern America, citizen journalists are amateurs who report on local affairs. Joan went a bit farther afield in her reporting. She willingly walked into a distant war zone and wrote about what she found there, but she was reporting on South Carolina troops for South Carolina readers. Those troops and readers just happened to be caught up in a bigger story of national importance. One difference between Joan and most contemporary citizen-journalists, who work for free, was that Joan was compensated for her work for the *Charleston Courier*, even though her stories were neither polished nor particularly sophisticated. However, her writing was profoundly passionate, a factor that must have weighed heavily in the decision to run her stories on the *Courier*'s front page, often right next to the work of the paper's other correspondent in Virginia, the thoroughly skilled Felix G. de Fontaine, or Personne, as *Courier* readers knew him.[8]

Although far fewer in number, Joan's homely letters would have been no less valuable than Personne's polished dispatches to readers whose sons and husbands were among the troops about whom both correspondents reported. In fact, Joan's impassioned denunciations of "fiendish" Yankees, her allusions to Mother Goose tales, and her constant—and sometimes tedious—religious and patriotic diatribes would have resonated with readers.[9] Joan's letters convey a

Army hospital near Richmond. Photograph from the Library of Congress

feeling of authentic experience by one to whom the outcome of the war mat-
tered profoundly.

For several reasons, including her anonymity and the newspaper for which
she wrote, Joan's correspondence has been largely ignored. The fire-eating
Charleston Mercury has captured far more of historians' attention than Joan's
more mainstream employer, the *Charleston Courier*. Further, so little journalism was produced by Civil War-era Southern women that classifying and analyzing it was difficult for historians, for there are so few starting places.[10] In
Joan's case, the only materials available for study are her few months of writing
for the *Courier*.

That writing is significant not only because it is of a genre not often associated with Southern women of Joan's time. It is significant, too, because Joan's
experience was different. Joan not only wrote letters for a newspaper, she also
followed her son to Virginia. She did not simply languish in Richmond, however.
She worked in the hospitals and she wrote letters for the *Courier* that covered
topics ranging from hospital policy to troop welfare to battles to Confederate
politics. Like most Southern women, Joan was motivated to do her part to help
win the war. Opportunity placed her in the Confederate capital, and inclination
led her to pick up a pen to aid the cause.

The *Courier*'s editors were fully aware of the sacrifices Southern women
were making to support the war, and that was one reason why they hired Joan
as a correspondent. When she decided to head for Virginia, Joan wrote to the

editors, seeking employment as a correspondent. She told them she wanted to go to Virginia to be near her son so that she "may help to nerve him for the bitter scenes before him and minister to his wants if the conflict leaves him living and a sufferer." However, she apparently needed the additional income that she hoped to acquire by writing for the *Courier*. The editors were delighted to help so devoted a woman whom they dubbed "A Spartan Mother."[11]

In the years after the war, the *Courier*, by then the *News and Courier*, ran a regular column, "Our Women in the War," consisting of articles written by women throughout the South about their experiences. In 1885, the newspaper published a collection of 79 columns.[12] Concluding that the stories of women were largely untold, the editors acknowledged the following in the book's introduction:

> It seemed to us that no Confederates were more worthy of our loving remembrance than those who bound their warrior's sash when he went forth to fight; who suffered worse than death a thousand times, when battle raged loud and long; who were stung and wounded by privations that the hardy soldier never knew, and who, besides, were exposed to the injuries and taunts of the infamous raiders who, during and after the war, visited Southern homes and stripped them of what was holiest and dearest, because it was dear and holy.[13]

While Joan revealed little demographic or identifying information in her writing, her character, attitudes, beliefs, and nature were on full display. Her writing revealed her to be a bright, curious, educated, well-traveled woman who was at least old enough to have a 20-year-old son in the army. Another story hints at the presence of a husband in the same unit as her son, but the statement is not made clearly enough to determine whether Joan was actually a wife or a widow.[14] She must have been moderately well off financially, but probably not wealthy, for she did write to the *Courier* in hopes of being hired as a paid correspondent.

Joan admitted that her interest in working for the *Courier* was selfish—she wanted to be near her son. She disavowed any public service motive: "But do not understand me to profess that I [unreadable word] to write in order to add to the interest of your paper, or relieve the anxiety of throbbing hearts."[15]

Despite her protestations, Joan's desire to write for the *Courier* was also a way to serve the Confederacy, similar in motive to a man volunteering for Confederate service. Writing for the newspaper gave Joan a means of supporting a cause in which she believed passionately: Southern independence. Passion alone, however, did not get the bills paid, and Joan had to meet the calls on her purse for bed, board, travel, and even postage. She was going to Virginia whether the *Courier* hired her or not. A salary would be a welcome addition to her pocketbook, but clearly it was not essential.

Joan revealed enough about where she grew up to indicate her home was in the country rather than the city. She had alluded to this in a letter describing the appearance of Richmond. She commented that the houses in Richmond were of different architectural styles and that the first time she had ever seen anything similar was a visit to Charleston for the first time. On that trip, she wrote, she saw for the first time houses constructed to suit the individual styles of their masters.[16]

This comment offered another clue as to Joan's place of residence. In many 19th century communities, there would have been a degree of variety in residential architecture. However, that would not have been the case in many, if not most, textile mill towns such as those that dotted upcountry South Carolina. The houses in mill towns were generally exactly alike. There might have been some variations between the houses for workers, foremen, and managers, but within a job classification, all the houses were the same.

Other evidence points to Joan's residence being in the hinterlands of South Carolina. In one letter, she described the many different kinds of people who were coming into Richmond regularly. In her writings about whether Richmond was a Southern city, she referred to the presence of the ubiquitous "market cart" pulled by a weary horse. The cart would be occupied by a ". . . scantily clad woman in the saddle with her longbonnet and longer pipe smoking as she goes, the man plodding along by the side of the cart on foot; and perhaps a child or two inside of it, too young to be left at home." This scene, Joan wrote, is played out in every town from Virginia to Texas. "When you have seen one, you have seen a thousand of them—so common in the South that they do not attract the slightest attention."[17]

The people she described were from a class known as "yeoman farmers," a group referred to by one historian as "self-working farmers." They owned enough land to sustain their families but not enough to be large-scale cotton producers.[18] Yeoman farmers typically owned 200 or fewer acres and five or fewer slaves, if any. They might have grown a bit of cotton each year in order to have a cash crop, but most of their land would have been dedicated to agricultural production for the benefit of their families.[19] Joan wrote nostalgically about growing up among people just like these—not as one of them, but as a daughter of the privileged class. She showed a depth of understanding in her comments, and her privileged status had wisely not led her to dismiss these people as "no account." They were "oftentimes as noble in heart as they are coarse in exterior," she wrote. After working all day, they would walk miles to look after someone who was ill. They might be illiterate and unaccustomed to luxuries, "but the nobler, finer feelings of the soul are not unfrequently in active play."[20] They were people who would give what they had to help a stranger, and Joan's years living among these people had given her a strong respect and admiration for them.

Although Joan may have spent most of her life in upcountry South Carolina, she had done some traveling—to Charleston, which would be expected, but also to New York City. When she traveled there in the winter of 1859-1860, she expected one of her primary entertainments to be attending lectures. She was disappointed, however, because the lecturers were most frequently abolitionists who did nothing but abuse slaveholders. The lectures, she said, made her blood boil.[21]

Joan was well aware of the issues of the day and had strong—even fanatical—opinions about them, especially about the nobility of Confederate leaders and the righteousness of the Southern cause. She was convinced that God was on the side of the South. That being the case, she believed there could be no doubt about who would win the war. In her opinions, Joan showed herself to be anything but a meek, compliant, and dependent woman. She may have lived in a world where land ownership conveyed masterhood on men and dependence on women, children, and slaves, but that notion did not produce subservience, a gentle tongue, or any sort of reticence in the *Charleston Courier*'s correspondent.[22]

In character, Joan was more harridan than belle. She was a patriot of the truest stripe, a faithful Christian who devoutly believed in—and preached at length about—the sovereignty of God and His will for Southern victory. She was also a tender mother and, perhaps, a wife. But she could also be a sharp-tongued, shrewish fishwife, although she would probably be shocked at that characterization. She was thoroughly versed in the antebellum social conventions and rules of propriety for Southern women and diligent in enforcing their observation, at least where others were concerned.

One of Joan's concerns was the sobriety of Confederate troops, a topic to which she could turn with pencil flying. "The sobriety of our army constitutes its strength and efficiency," she declared. "When this element in it is violated it will be shorn of its glory. Neighborhoods will dread the presence of encampments in their vicinity, acts of pillaging and plunder will be of daily occurrence, and outrages against property frequent; such is the case always where liquor rules." Joan argued that even just a few drinks could turn a gentleman into a brute and deprive him of reason. She also believed that serving in the army made the temptation to drink even greater because soldiers "would naturally seize upon anything calculated to drown in forgetfulness many sorrows." She believed the Confederate government ought to step in and stop drinking by soldiers. "It is enough for them to give their youth, and the strength of their manhood to their country," she argued, "let her not, while they are saving her, present to them the fascinations of a cup which when drained to the dregs, inebriates, debases and ruins them body and soul.[23]

The fact that Joan corresponded for the *Courier* was evidence that she no longer felt entirely bound by contemporary conventions, although she did not acknowledge in her letters that the rules for female behavior were loosening. In fact, she wrote just the opposite. Her correspondence demonstrated that she still expected other women to be decorative, decorous, demure, even prim, and she was quick to criticize any woman whose behavior fell short of those standards, although she would sometimes add a compliment to absorb some of the sting of her cutting remarks. She observed at her catty best, "Ladies have another custom which is never seen with us—passing about in the streets with uncovered heads, often going some distance from home without bonnets, not, of course, in the heat of the day, but when the sun is declining and at night." She found Richmond women to be lacking in the discerning tastes possessed by women from other parts of the Confederacy. "Richmond ladies have but little taste in dress as far as my observation goes, and less extravagance," she wrote. "This may be because of the deep and absorbing patriotism which permeates every rank and station, and leads all to forget themselves in their country's welfare and her defenders."[24]

The only exception to Joan's rigid social standards was herself, although she probably would have argued she was acting out of devotion to family and country and ought not be held accountable for overstepping her bounds as a woman. Nevertheless, as both Joan and the mavens of South Carolina society knew by second nature, true ladies did not go off to a war zone to live in a boarding house and write for public consumption, nor did they take up residence in an army camp.

But war's necessities changed things, and chief among them were the duties and responsibilities of women, which, along with privilege, were the defining components of an elite, white Southern woman's identity in the antebellum period.[25] The war extended a woman's duties beyond the norm of the individual household by adding a societal level. No longer was a woman responsible only for and to those within her own household—husband, children, slaves. She also had a duty to aid in her country's bid for independence. Her role as "republican mother" in the new Southern republic led her to peek out, and then step through, her household gate into the larger world.

Southern society rationalized this expansion of a woman's duties by likening her new work as simply another form of mothering. By going to Virginia as a citizen correspondent for the *Courier,* Joan contributed to this expansion on ideas about a woman's proper role in war. In Joan's writing, the *Courier* found an additional way to connect to its readers hungry for war news.[26]

Having a woman writer also gave the *Courier* the opportunity to connect with readers whose interests might have been overlooked: women. Joan's stories offered a different vantage point for observing, analyzing, and commenting upon the military and political aspects of the war.[27] She did not self-consciously tell woman-to-woman stories, nor did she write only about women's interests, although those often crept into her stories. Her stories zeroed in on topics that would matter to women in ways that might be overlooked by a male reporter.

That did not, however, keep Joan from sending in articles that would interest both sexes.[28] She kept people back home informed about what was happening at the seat of war, the quality of hospitals, the health of troops, and national politics, a topic on which Joan turned in her first letter from Richmond.

In that first letter, Joan reported that Confederate Vice President Alexander Stephens had been on the train she took to Richmond. "In his quiet, unobtrusive way he took his seat in a car where he would be most likely to escape observation," she wrote. "When he was drawn out by parties into conversation, as he was occasionally, we all listened spell-bound to his matchless eloquence."[29] A few days later, in an analysis of what Congress was doing with regard to financial matters, Joan wrote that she had complete confidence in all the Confederate leaders: "But whatever plans may be adopted by our Congress for raising the means necessary to carry on the war, they will no doubt be the very best that could be devised," she wrote. Joan believed Confederate statesmen were the best who had ever served any country and that they were diligent in conducting the fledgling nation's business. She was particularly pleased that citizens seemed to realize how strong their leaders were. "It is so pleasant to see such confidence in our rulers as is everywhere exhibited; and as to the means necessary to support our political fabric, (we say it in no spirit of pride or vain boasting), these Confederate States hold as a subject that which reigns as king over the commerce of the world." Joan had no doubt that the Confederacy would win its independence and that it would emerge as one of the leading nations of the world. "Until 'seed time and harvest fail,' we are obligated to stand pre-eminent above and before all other lands," she argued. "If we only make ourselves as good as the Lord has made us great, we shall become the glory and praise of the whole earth."[30]

She also had great confidence in the South's generals and civilian leaders. Speeches by Generals Pierre G.T. Beauregard and Joseph E. Johnston could stir "every drop of blood" in Joan's veins. She wrote poetically that all patriots and Christians should be proud and thankful that God had protected their homes and freedoms and had given them "such Generals" to conduct the war.[31]

In Joan's opinion, however, no public figure exceeded Jefferson Davis in nobility or devotion to the cause. To Joan, Davis was "the brilliant scholar, the accomplished orator, the gifted statesman, the clear-sighted financier, the able diplomat, the heroic warrior, the lofty patriot, the finished gentleman." No man could compare to "our peerless President. One age and country does not produce two such men."[32]

She illustrated this with a description of a visit the president made to a nearby camp to review units on parade. Davis arrived, mounted on "his splendid iron grey—almost white—horse." Those present crowded near the president, and Joan heard him ask the commanding officer about how the troops were faring. The president wanted to know about their health, lodgings, and food and instructed the colonel to apply to the Confederate commissary for anything necessary for his men.

Joan reported the president as saying, "I hope you will not leave Richmond until the comfort of your men is secured as far as it can be." She was moved by his concern. "There was among that listening crowd one heart which daily, hourly, throbs with anxious interest for the soldier's comfort, upon which those benevolent words of this peerless man were engraven, to be obliterated never, until death shall blur them," she wrote. Davis' apparent concern for Confederate troops had truly won her loyalty that day. "There is nothing too trivial for his attention," she wrote, "and nothing escapes his notice that can promote another's comfort. He seems to regard the people as his family, himself the patriarchal head."[33]

Joan was intensely patriotic—an ardent Southern nationalist. The *Courier*'s choice of a name for her—"Spartan Mother"—was also a good description of her attitude toward the war: winning Southern independence was paramount. In Joan's mind, the South was pure and blameless. It had endured grievous wrongs far too long; she believed that it was time to end the abuse. The North was the unreasonable aggressor whose objective was to subjugate the South, to turn free white men into slaves—and she cited scripture to prove it. "The hatred of our enemies is as uncompromising as it is incomprehensible," Joan claimed. "It seems astonishing that they should pursue us with such malignity. We have never wronged them; we are but seeking to defend our own homes and establish our own liberties, and for this they lay waste to our fair land, and threaten to hold us in manacles." She continued:

> Do they wish us to contribute of our substance of old to their support? We were willing even to have done this. We gave them all our products to ship, thus casting into their treasury a large percentage of our crops. We allowed them to import all our goods, and received them from them after they had passed through many hands each making his own share of profit out of them and all coming from our pockets. Still we complained not; indeed, we preferred that they should manage this exporting and importing business for us and were willing to pay them for it so we were spared the trouble attendant upon it. We suffered them to impose heavy duties on manufactured goods to our great detriment, in order to build up their own interests, and one way and another, we contributed seventy percent towards maintaining the expenses of the United States Government, and only asked in return that our property might have the protection which we had a right to demand from the Government; a protection granted to other citizens of the Republic, whose share of the public burdens was much less than our own. The almost literal reply of the party now in the ascendant was, 'My father made your yoke heavy but I will add thereto; my father chastized you with whips but I will chastize you with scorpions.'[34]

The scripture Joan quoted was taken from the story told in Chapter 12 of 1 Kings about King Solomon's son Rehoboam who ascended to the throne of Israel upon his father's death. When Rehoboam's people asked for relief from heavy obligations to the government, he refused, even though his advisers assured him that if he lightened those obligations, the people would be loyal to him forever. Joan obviously saw a parallel between King Rehoboam's decision and the Union's, between an abused Israel and an abused South.

Joan was so convinced of the rightness of the Southern cause that she was willing to accept, even encourage, extreme measures for dealing with traitors and Yankees. For example, she heartily approved of General Beauregard's summary execution of a railroad conductor who had accepted an $800 bribe to delay a train full of reinforcements headed for the front.[35] Her hatred of Yankees was so white-hot that she refused to believe the organization of peace meetings in the United States signified a sincere desire on the part of at least some Northerners to find a way to end the conflict.

"Yet these peace meetings are only isolated; the northern mind is by no means permeated with the desire for peace," she wrote. In the same article, Joan observed that the Northern peace supporters "had better look out for how they promulgate such opinions or they may wake up some night with five hundred Federal soldiers around them . . . And be cut off from the privilege of habeas corpus."[36] She was correct; the Lincoln government—particularly the military— did much to suppress Copperhead sentiment throughout the Northern states, and Lincoln did make use of his power to suspend the writ of habeas corpus (as did Jefferson Davis at times).[37]

Nor was Joan above complaining when Northern prisoners were treated leniently or when accusing Federal troops of the worst sort of atrocities, including firing on Confederate field hospitals. But she became indignant when Northern papers accused the Confederate army of doing the same thing—and worse.

> The New York papers now charge this [firing on hospitals] upon the Confederate Army; and on the principle that it is best to tell a big one while they are about it, they have added that we set fire to their hospital, burning up the surgeons and all the wounded and fired into their ambulances and killed the wounded prisoners, pinning them to trees with bayonets and then cutting them to pieces. That ought to do in the way of lying for one day's issue of a paper.[38]

The *Courier*'s correspondent could not understand why Southern and Northern troops would meet under truce flags to chat, trade knives and newspapers, and sometimes even send gifts to one another after these encounters. "This all seems like very queer proceedings to me," Joan commented, clearly perplexed by the seeming perfidiousness of the meetings. Her preference, she wrote, would be to shoot one of the Northern "hirelings."[39]

On at least one occasion, however, Joan did admit that not all Yankee soldiers were brutes. She included in one of her letters a report from a wounded Confederate soldier who was stopped by a Yankee and given water while fleeing from the battlefield at First Manassas.[40]

Joan was willing to make any personal sacrifice to secure the South's independence, and she believed other Southerners ought to feel that way, too. She offered her highest praise to those who put the torch to their own homes and crops rather than allow them to fall into the hands of the enemy. After describing the Union assault on Hampton, Virginia, Joan added, "I do not wonder the citizens were willing to burn up their homes. No spot polluted by such barbarians could ever be home to me again."[41]

Her anti-Union invective extended to the inclusion of atrocity stories in her letters—sometimes, only what she imagined those atrocities might have been like had they occurred. In the aftermath of First Manassas, she wrote: "There are few of us here but what are continually drawing comparisons of what might have been our lot if the Lincoln mercenaries had succeeded in entering the city. With their thirty-thousand pairs of handcuffs, they would soon have placed the men in a helpless condition and pillaged, burned and destroyed at their pleasure."[42]

Although the war and the troops were two of Joan's most important topics, much of what she wrote dealt with general military affairs and troop welfare. The reasons for Joan's limited battle coverage were twofold. First, she spent much of her time in Richmond where she could only get information from interviews with soldiers, private letters from soldiers, Northern newspapers, and official reports from the government. Second, little important military action occurred in the late summer and fall of 1861, the period during which Joan corresponded for the *Courier*.

Only two skirmishes occurred while Joan was working for the *Courier* that warranted mention in the *Encyclopedia of Military History*'s summary of Civil War battles: the Battle of Cheat Mountain in western Virginia (September 12–15, 1861) and the Battle of Ball's Bluff, near Leesburg (October 21).[43] Consequently, Joan's military reporting dealt less with the glory of the battlefield and more with the tedium of soldiers sitting in camp and waiting for the next engagement. Her letters assured readers, most of them chaffing for a forward movement since First Manassas, that soldiers and generals were ready to fight—that the South's military leaders were just waiting for the proper moment. "One can only appreciate the enthusiasm which pervades the camps and which makes them seem as if they were in the midst of the festivities of some gala day," Joan wrote. In the same article, she continued, "Yet no one complains [about hazardous duty]; all are eager for their time to come."[44]

The lack of significant military action did not stop Joan from addressing martial topics, especially those related to the First Battle of Manassas, the first major battle of the war, and the first Confederate victory. Joan arrived in Virginia just days after that encounter, and First Manassas was a frequent topic in her letters. One of her earliest stories reported (inaccurately) casualty numbers. She reported that Confederate losses included fewer than 40 killed, wounded, and taken as prisoners. She also mentioned Union losses. The first Union casualty estimates to arrive in Richmond reported 40 Union officers and 3,000 troops taken as prisoners. Her source was both vague ("our first news from the battle") and, of course, inaccurate.[45] Confederate losses for the battle totaled 1,981 to the Union's 2,706.[46] Northern newspapers were no more accurate in their casualty reports. Joan triumphantly contradicted the *New York Herald*'s figures of Union losses: "The *Herald* of last Friday says their official returns show 386 killed, 25 wagons lost (we took 150 richly laden,) 17 cannon *spiked* [emphasis hers] and lost, (we have 67, none of them spited, they were in too great haste), &c., ad infinitum."[47]

Because there was little actual news to report, Joan often fell back on that staple of 19th century personal journalism: personal opinion. In Joan's case, that opinion often took the form of scripture-based mini-sermons. In one dispatch, she reported having heard that the Confederate army had moved out from Manassas, which resulted in considerable anxiety as people wondered if the next grand battle was about to happen. Whatever did occur, Joan reminded her readers that . . .

> . . . "God is our refuge and strength, a very present help in time of trouble" and at His feet we bow and crave His blessing on our arms, His mercy on our homes. As He led and guided His children of old, He has signally shown His mercy unto us in a thousand ways, since first we sought to establish our independence; that He will aid us to the end and enable us ultimately to secure the desired objects, we do not for a moment doubt. Meantime, we may meet with reverses; we must be prepared to receive them and submit to them as part of His discipline.[48]

According to Joan's martial gospel, Confederate victories had not been produced by Southern arms or armies but by God's will. She reminded her readers, "The battle is the Lord's alone."[49] Joan also wrote her share of color stories, little sketches of camp or civilian life or battlefield anecdotes that sometimes were true but also embodied an old tale intended to reinforce a belief or attitude. One of the most common was about the faithful slave who followed his master onto the battlefield and was one in spirit with the Southern cause. While some of the stories were undoubtedly true, most probably had the same genesis as the tales slaveholders had told for years about contented bondsmen singing gospel hymns in the field who knew their place and were content to stay in it. These were "pre-urban" legends passed on to assuage widespread white fear of slave insurrection, a fear that deepened during the war.[50]

The most vivid of these kinds of stories from Joan cited "an old negro" who claimed to have fought in the recent battle at Manassas. The man claimed to have participated in the battle of Manassas and that "he went there as a drummer but when the fight became general, he threw down his drum and picked up a musket, and did some terrible execution if we believe his own tales." According to Joan's story, enough people were anxious to hear those tales, whether they believed them or not, that "he has a crowd after him at the street corners all the time, white as well as black, anxious to hear incidents of the battle field and is quite a hero among them."[51] Joan observed this incident herself, so it would be doubtful that she was using it as an "I-don't-know-whether-this-actually-happened-but-I-know-it's-true" tale to reinforce Confederate confidence in the loyalty of their bondsmen. Whether the drummer-turned-soldier's tale would meet the truth test is less certain.

In another letter, Joan included a sketch, taken from a private letter she had received from a soldier, about amenities and meal preparation at a camp near Manassas. The writer had taken over cooking duties for his group, and the men had concocted a table from an old door for which they had even found a table-cloth. The letter reported that the table worked just as well as if it had been made of mahogany. The writer confided that his current main staple for cooking was green corn and that if he could find some milk, he was ready to experiment making a corn pudding. He had just that day bought a duck and some duck eggs that would be added to his larder.[52]

In another article, written after Joan joined her son's unit in the field, she recounted her first-hand observation of meal preparations in camp. That story dealt with how cooking duties were parceled out. The men were "constantly making new arrangements about the division of labor," Joan reported. Often, they would rotate duties or, if that did not work, they would try to find a servant to do the cooking for them. The cooks usually were unskilled, most having been trained to be body servants, according to the soldier's letter, so the next resort would be to get the servant who cooked for the commanding officer to cook for soldiers, too. That arrangement generally failed because the slave forgot to do something for his officer, putting an end to the cook's moonlighting.[53]

Joan spent nearly a month making arrangements to join her son's unit at the front, and much of that time was spent waiting for a passport that would allow her to travel from Richmond to Fairfax. The trip itself was fraught with adventures. Joan set off for the front lines on Saturday, September 14, a trip of just under 100 miles from Richmond. Joan wrote that she was going to the front to reunite with "the hearts I so earnestly longed to hold communion with once more."[54] By 3 p.m., she had made it as far as Bristoe and stopped for the night at a house filled with troops, including one who was still recovering from wounds received at Manassas.

She mentioned the soldier because his story allowed her to paint the enemy as a diabolical, craven mob of hoodlums, one of her favorite themes. According to Joan's letter, on the day before the battle at Manassas, drunken Union soldiers had run the soldier and his family away from their home near Fairfax. The Yankees absconded with "everything that could be carried away, and what could not be transported was destroyed—invaluable family portraits slitted up in their frames, and some pictures torn out and thrown on the floor, and the frames carried away, bullets put through looking glasses, &c."[55]

Joan returned to that theme in a later letter in which she reported a conversation with an old man from the same area. It gave her an opportunity to again portray Yankees as scoundrels and cowards. The old man, she wrote, said the Yankees unsuccessfully tried to ransack his house and catch his horse on the way to Manassas. After the battle, two of those soldiers slouched back into the old man's yard, "crouching like dogs before him, begging him in humble tones for something to eat." The old man told Joan he had needed no one to tell him the Yankees had been defeated.[56]

The next day, Joan completed her journey. She managed to arrange a ride with another Fairfax refugee, a woman who hoped to return to her home. They started toward Fairfax in the woman's carriage but were able to get only as far as Manassas, three miles from Bristoe (now known as Bristow). At Manassas, guards insisted that the two women have passports from an officer before being allowed through the checkpoint.

"It seemed so strange that in our own land and country a man with a loaded gun should deliberately walk out before the horses heads and order us to halt until he could find out whether it was proper for two harmless, inoffensive women to pass up the road," Joan mused in her letter. To find the officer meant a walk of about a quarter mile "through countless groups of soldiers looking with curious eyes at the unusual sight of a woman in their camps." Joan finally made it to the officer's station and was thoroughly interrogated before receiving the passport.

The encounter with the guard thrust Joan into one of the most profound consequences of the war for women of the upper classes. Their men were away fighting, and elite women were on their own. If they left the protection of their homes and the private sphere, they had to deal directly with the consequences of stepping outside the bounds of societal proscriptions. Their privileged status, which had previously offered protection from such encounters, was already beginning to crumble. Although the war had not entirely changed the nature of gender relations in the South, Joan observed, "We were, though, everywhere treated with the utmost courtesy and kindness, and had some pleasant wayside chats with gentlemen at different stations."[57]

That evening, Joan reached the camp she sought, where she was a surprise visitor who received "an honored mother's welcome" from the boys she knew back home. Her son was doing picket duty near Washington and would not return until the end of September.[58] "All seemed glad to greet a visitor from the outside world," she wrote.[59] Joan ate her evening meal from a tin plate, seated at a rude table made by "nailing barrel staves to two long hickory poles and placing the leaf thus formed on camp stools."[60] She noted other camp innovations, including cots manufactured from forked tree branches and the addition of shelves and bunk beds to tents.[61] That night, she bedded down in her son's tent.

A cryptic comment in her September 24, 1861, letter to the *Courier* hints at the presence of her husband serving in the same unit. She described the evening spent in the company of soldiers from her son's unit, but added that she slept in her son's tent that night, "in the kind companionship of him whose love has been the sunlight of my life since girlhood's opening dawn."[62] She could have been merely making reference to being surrounded by her son's things, but the reference sounds more like something that would be said about a husband or a lover than a child, particularly since she claimed to have known this person since her girlhood.

At the front, Joan continued to convey news to the *Courier*'s readers, although the frequency of her correspondence declined precipitously. In the letter describing her trip to the front, Joan warned her editors not to expect much from her in the way of correspondence. "It will be hard," she wrote, "to gather news here except in our own immediate surroundings, for by the time a rumor has traveled ten miles, even if it were fact when it started, it is so distorted that it is idle to believe a word of it."[63] Joan's report was prophetic, for she would write fewer than ten letters in the next two months.

A good example of Joan's news reporting during her stay at the front appeared in the letter she wrote after her son returned from reconnaissance duty near Mason's Hill, a plantation that overlooked Washington, D.C., Fort Ellsworth, the Potomac, and Alexandria, Virginia. His unit returned to the main army with a number of tales about their assignment literally at the front lines.

One of those stories, from the Mason plantation, once again held up the specter of the faithful, Yankee-hating slave. When Union troops swept through the plantation property, they took all the Mason slaves with them, according to Joan. One of the slaves escaped from his Union captors, and since his return home, he had taken to shooting Yankees whenever he saw one, she reported. The Confederate soldiers were doing their best to stop him and "other independent scouts, who are in the habit of shooting at the enemy's pickets" because they were giving the Southern soldiers a bad reputation. "The Yankees say they would not mind so much being shot at by white men, but that these South Carolinians who are, in their eyes, the embodiment of evil, have brought their negroes there to fire at them and it is too much for them to bear."[64]

Whether she was writing from Richmond or the front, Joan focused regularly on health in the camps and hospital care for wounded and ill soldiers. She believed hospitals were an important component of the war effort because they helped conserve the army's most important resource: soldiers.[65] She used her letters to advocate several hospital reforms, including removal of ill soldiers from camps so that others would not be infected,[66] a measure that was eventually adopted, although Joan did not know why the change in policy had occurred.[67] "It has been the policy of late to have none in the sick tents of the regiment, but send them immediately to the rear as soon as they are attacked, whether because the season is becoming so inclement, or because a conflict is considered so imminent, I cannot say," Joan wrote.[68]

She also believed that each state should establish its own hospitals for its soldiers. "I understand that Mississippians and Louisianans are talking of opening hospitals for the sick of their own State," Joan wrote. "This ought to be done. Every State represented ought to have a hospital here."[69] She would later report that Mississippi, Louisiana, and Georgia had followed Alabama's example and established hospitals in Richmond.[70]

Joan was especially anxious that the solders be provided for in the coming winter. The fall's heavy rains and cooler weather prompted her to call for "diligent preparations" to ensure the comfort of the troops during the cold weather season. Those preparations, according to Joan, ought to include production of large quantities of flannel shirts, drawers, socks, and mittens. However, the greatest need was blankets since the supply available for purchase in the Confederacy had been exhausted. Joan suggested that each family in the South donate at least one blanket to the troops.[71]

She was more specific about plans to house soldiers on the outskirts of Richmond during the winter. Barracks were being erected, and more were planned. Joan regretted that the buildings would not be as picturesque as the tents, but agreed that they would provide better winter accommodations.

> Extensive preparations are being made for the comfortable accommodation of the soldiers in Richmond during the winter months. Buildings are to be erected and are in progress of erection sufficiently capacious to accommodate thirty thousand troops. They are long wooden buildings, to be arranged with a hall through the center, and berths on each side. They are being built in the outskirts of the city, and will, when completed, entirely supersede the picturesque tent encampments which now dot every hill side in every direction wherever an eligible spot can be found. If the rough structures are less pleasing to the eye than the white winged tenements in which our brave soldiers now find shelter, the sense of the superior comfort, and security from inclement weather which they afford, abundantly compensates for the want of grace and beauty.[72]

The new construction would not be extensive enough to house all the troops around Richmond, and Joan reported on innovations some soldiers were making to ready their tents for winter: a means of equipping their tents with fireplaces. The soldiers dug holes in the dirt floors of their tents and lined them with stones. They also created a flue to carry the smoke out. The fireplaces were small but effective at keeping tents warm and dry.[73]

Joan's interest in soldiers' health was reflected in many of her letters. In her first letter from the front, Joan reported that the present location of the unit she was visiting was healthier than that of the camp near Manassas. Still, typhoid plagued the troops—one doctor reporting as many as 50 cases under his care.[74] Joan believed some of the illness was caused by poor water near some of the camps, but she reported that the water quality at the new location near Fairfax was much better than it had been at Manassas and that food was abundant, especially beef and flour. In fact, the soldiers she accompanied had more of some foods than they could use. Other supplies were scarce, including candles, soap, sugar, and coffee. She attributed the shortages and other problems to inefficiency or incompetence among those in the Commissary and Quartermaster's services, a constant problem for the Confederate army throughout the war, and to selfish and inattentive officers.[75]

Joan also reported on topics such as politics, women, censorship, and press operations. She included an occasional hard news story, such as a bridge collapse that resulted in derailment of eight train cars. The severest injuries had been among a group of soldiers from Kentucky on their way to the front. The soldiers had been singing "My Old Kentucky Home" when the train plunged down an embankment outside Richmond. Joan's informant was a gentleman who was on the train but escaped unharmed. "Poor fellows," Joan wrote as the men returned to Richmond. "They left us so joyous and exultant a few brief hours before the sad accident, which sent some of them into eternity and left others maimed for life." According to her story, eight cars fell down an embankment and splintered into pieces. Injuries were made worse because many of the passengers were gored by the bayonets affixed to their rifles. Joan interviewed a survivor who believed that "nothing but the mercy of God spared any of their lives."[76]

These Kentucky soldiers were particularly worthy of praise and admiration, Joan told her readers. They had left their homes "to aid us in our hour of peril." She continued:

> Their brave hearts revolt at the tyranny to which their fathers bow so meekly, and every pulse of their noble natures responds with sympathetic interest to our great struggle for constitutional liberty. They pledge us the aid of their strong arms; the benefit of their powers of endurance which have been nurtured by their mountain training; the use of their [unreadable word] rifles, for which they have a world-wide reputation. They number within a fraction of a thousand and are all gentlemen. They have come here armed and equipped at their own expense. We give them a brother's welcome. If their patriot blood stains our soil, we charge it upon our sons who are native and to the "manner born" to avenge them five to one. If their mother state repudiates them we will claim them for our own.[77]

Another of her news stories told of 11 Union prisoners of war who escaped from a Richmond prison. Joan wrote of one prisoner who had the audacity to write his wife that he would be home in a week or two. Three were quickly recaptured, but the others remained at large.[78]

Joan occasionally included political news in her letters, including a comment on the Trent affair, the diplomatic incident that occurred when officers of the USS *San Jacinto* detained two Confederate envoys who were traveling to London on a British ship to seek recognition of Southern independence. Joan wrote there was much dismay that James Mason and John Slidell would be subjected to such "ruthless and unscrupulous" tyranny. She hoped, as many others did, that the arrests might turn Great Britain against the United States since the commissioners had been forcibly removed from a British ship.[79] She wrote that "the universal feeling is that the Government which has committed this outrage upon the high seas has injured itself far more than the transaction can, by any possibility, injure us."[80] Slidell and Mason were eventually released, but Confederate hopes for a rift in the relationship between the United States and Great Britain were not realized.

Joan also wrote about women, especially those who fulfilled their duties as women through nursing, feeding, and clothing Confederate soldiers. However, she had nothing but contempt for women who stepped out of that role and engaged in what she considered contemptible behavior, such as aiding Federal soldiers imprisoned in Richmond.

> One lady here is making herself very conspicuous by loading up her carriage with delicacies every morning, and visiting them [Union prisoners], and distributing them around. She takes a grown daughter with her, and they say she furnishes them with means to write, and sends their letters. No man in Richmond would dare to do this, and when a woman takes shelter behind her sex to perform a dastardly act, she ought to be measured by the standard of a man and brought to an account.[81]

She was equally incensed when she learned that several Northern women had come to see the battle at Manassas, including two daughters of a Massachusetts senator and the daughter of newspaper Editor Thurlow Weed. Joan wrote that, according to a rumor, Miss Weed had come from New York specifically to be accorded the honor of hoisting the Federal flag over the capital building in Richmond. Joan commented that if women were to be tolerated on the battlefield, the taking of women as prisoners of war ought to be tolerated, too.[82] Joan returned to that incident in a second letter when she mused about what military thinkers would make of senators' daughters who go to battlefields "to witness the carnage or, to use their own words, the fun?" Joan believed that the nature of women made them unfit to witness events on a battlefield. "Oh, who can believe that any could be thus depraved, that she could so far forget her sex, herself, her woman's heart, as to seek pleasure there," Joan demanded.[83]

The *Courier*'s correspondent could also mete out praise to other women when she thought it was warranted. She noted the industry of Richmond's church women in one letter, writing: "In almost every Church edifice in the city, some lecture room or vestry room has been appropriated to the use of seamstresses, and you see them day after day at their post at work for the soldiers." The facilities, she wrote, were often equipped with as many as six sewing machines and women who were clearly committed to their work. Joan noted that "some of the ladies who work here have been at it for months, but still keep on with unabated diligence; to the post day after day, as if every interest of life were swallowed up in the all-absorbing one of making our soldiers comfortable."[84] In fact, some women worked so diligently at their sewing that their meals had to be brought in to them.[85]

In another letter, Joan wrote of a conversation with a woman from Weldon, North Carolina. The women of that town filled a train car as often as once a week with food for their menfolk serving in Virginia. These women set aside one day each week for cooking for the soldiers. This was apparently a ritual repeated throughout the Confederacy, for Joan noted that an astounding number of private boxes were being sent to soldiers, adding to the scores of bags, weapons, munitions, and other equipment already being carted around Richmond by a huge number of wagons and horses. Many of those private boxes were never delivered, Joan wrote, because they were misaddressed or not labeled at all.[86] Later, in order to resolve the congestion, she would call for a new depot in Richmond to deal only with items sent to soldiers and to cut down on waste that resulted from disorganization.[87]

Another womanly activity that often provided letter material for Joan was the work of caring for wounded and ill soldiers, and Joan frequently turned to this topic. In one letter, she illustrated the tender care soldiers were receiving in Richmond homes by telling the story of how a Mrs. B. and her daughters nursed a young soldier from Texas. The soldier ultimately died, after playing out a melodramatic scene that Joan related to her readers. The soldier awoke in the middle of the night, according to Joan's story, and announced that he was about to die. Mrs. B. was summoned to his bedside, and he told her that he knew he was not far from death. He assured her, however, that he was not afraid to die because Jesus was with him. The young soldier asked Mrs. B., whom he had come to call "Mother," to comb his hair, just before he died. Joan's praise was fulsome for this woman and the others in Richmond who looked after soldiers. However, Joan had nothing but disdain for a woman who had applied to look after only convalescing soldiers because she did not have the nerve to dress a wound or to look after an ill soldier. Joan was impressed with the number of homes that had quickly been opened to soldiers. "It is an honor to humanity that the instances have been so numerous," she reported.[88]

Women had another pastime that attracted Joan's attention—one more frivolous than cooking and sewing for soldiers, but one that gained the correspondent's approval: admiring men in uniform. The admiration, Joan argued, was justified.

Ladies have always been accused of admiring soldiers because of their brilliant uniforms, but I think they have fairly earned the right to have this charge withdrawn. The courtesy which they receive now, always and everywhere, cannot be attributed to this cause. We daily see men whose carriage and demeanor exhibit the marks of the thoroughbred and polished gentleman, clad in cloth coarser than they have been wont to give their negroes, and made with almost as much simplicity as servants clothing; grave colors, unrelieved, perhaps, by a single braid, and nothing to denote the military except the closely fitting body and the little upright collar . . . Notwithstanding their plain, sometimes disfiguring dress, they are as great favorites with the ladies as ever, and not only those of gentle birth and breeding, who can always recommend themselves, but those of ruder tastes and more primitive habits. Ladies look up to them as almost more than human, standing as they do with sword in hand to defend their rights and protect their homes. Aside from this, they are bound together by a common tie, for who has not a son or brother, friend or father, in the camp.[89]

Joan's observation spoke to an important aspect of the Civil War, one that has drawn attention from women's historians. In the antebellum period, there was a gender-based "quid pro quo" between white men and women in the South. Men would protect and provide if women agreed to obey. The war upset that balance; Southern men learned that they could not protect without the help of women to take over management of farms and plantations and especially slaves or to take manufacturing jobs to keep the materiel of war in production. Southern women learned that they did not need a man to protect or provide for them; they could—and did—fend for themselves, just as Joan was doing in Richmond.[90]

Joan's journalistic interests extended beyond those of soldiers and the women who admired them. She also took up topics that traditionally would have been within the purview of men. One of those issues was censorship, although Confederate censorship did not concern her. She did her best to comply with injunctions from the Confederate War Department, and like most Confederate correspondents, Joan willingly obeyed orders to withhold information that would aid the enemy. She believed that, although "the public mind is thirsting for news," and many developments were taking place, she could not in good conscience reveal what those developments were because of her obligations to keep troop movements secret.[91]

However, Joan occasionally found some justification for disobeying War Department injunctions against transmitting certain information. One of her common excuses was the telegraph. She believed that since she was passing along information by letter rather than telegraph, her revelations were moving slowly enough to do no harm and ought to be allowed. "Army movements are not allowed to be promulgated through the telegraph," she wrote, "consequently we cannot expect such news through our own channels, but I suppose letter writers may be allowed to discuss what is in everybody's mouth" or what had already been published in Northern newspapers.[92]

Joan doted on reporting instances of newspaper censorship and closure in the North. She reveled in reporting that mobs had attacked the offices of three New York newspapers in late August 1861 to silence their calls for peace.[93] One of Joan's most vitriolic diatribes against Lincoln and his government was set off by the censure of the *New York News*, the *New York Day Book*, the *Journal of Commerce,* and several Baltimore newspapers, each of them continually in trouble with the Lincoln government.[94] She was livid because the papers had been shut down, even though they had only reported the truth about the strengths of the Southern army and the weaknesses of the Northern army. She cited "the magnitude of our resources, the ability of our Government, the devotion of the people to it and to their rulers, the perfect unanimity existing among us, and the enthusiasm of our citizens upon the subject of their independence."[95]

This was Joan at her passionate—but uninformed—best. Before long, the reality of the South's lack of resources would become apparent and so would the region's factionalism and lack of devotion to the cause, factors that would play havoc with civilian morale.[96] For the moment, though, Joan could wax eloquent in her denunciations of Lincoln as a tyrannical censor. "Have a care, proud despot," she warned the Union president. "The men you deal with have been [emphasis hers] *freemen*." She continued:

> Though your heel be on them now, there is a might and power in the spirit of freedom implanted in the human heart which, when it is in full play, can burst any shackle earth can bind. It lies dormant now, but you have no guarantee that it can long continue thus; and when it rises, as rise it surely will with giant strength (for there are noble spirits among you who will not always bear this thralldom) it will hurl you not alone from the position you now occupy,—a position once so honored, now so desecrated,—but from the face of the earth which your foul presence pollutes.[97]

Individual citizens were being deprived of their civil rights, Joan reported. On a daily basis Southern citizens and sympathizers were being detained and jailed in Northern cities without being charged, she told her readers. "The main objective seems to get their money away from them, and shut them up out of spite," Joan wrote. She also reported that Northern officials were opening the letters these prisoners received and publishing their contents. "Could men sink lower than this?" she asked.[98] Apparently they could, for a few weeks later, Joan accused Union military authorities in Baltimore of waging war on "gentlemen's cravats and children's stockings." Any red and white tie or any stocking made of red and white yarn had been banned because those were the colors used to signify secessionist sentiments.[99]

Like other Richmond correspondents, Joan used newspapers as one of her primary information sources. Her letters nearly always summarized the latest reports from one or several of the Northern newspapers that circulated freely in Richmond.[100] She also indulged in occasional critiques of press performance and, like most media critics, usually found journalists wanting. Joan accused the Northern papers of showing the "worst possible taste" when they analyzed and commented upon the performance of government or the military. She was particularly annoyed by press admonitions to the government. "This spirit of dictation by the press to the powers that be has become in Northern journalism a crying evil. It is no light thing to cast reproach upon those who are high in positions of trust and power."[101]

Despite the problems with newspapers, Joan believed they had value. "People abuse the newspapers very much," she wrote, "but after all they are so much more reliable than any other source of information that we ought not to find fault with them."[102] She believed that most editors tried to tell the truth but sometimes were fooled by an overwhelming number of reports into letting error creep in. "If editors gave credence to what proves false, they should not be censured," Joan wrote.[103]

Newspaper content concerned Joan because she believed the press had a powerful effect. "The power of the newspaper press is not half appreciated by us. It *makes* [emphasis hers] public opinion," she wrote.[104] She also believed that those who run newspapers have obligations to their readers. She believed that newspaper coverage could warp a public man's better impulses and cause him to "stoop to baseness, of which very probably they would not otherwise have been guilty."[105]

Joan lived up to many of the same tenants of journalistic practice in place today. She tried to base her reports on personal observations or what she learned in interviews. When Joan did resort to reporting rumor, she reminded her readers that she could not vouch for the veracity of the information. In one letter, she reported hearing that there had been "hard fighting going on at Newport News" but added that she had not been able to confirm this claim with "any reliable sources."[106]

Joan understood that it was never acceptable to make up news.[107] In reporting that Fort Pulaski, which guards the sea entrance to Savannah, fell after being bombarded for six hours by four ships, Joan wrote that her source was a Savannah resident, but "one to whom I traced a sensation report once before." She wrote that she had no confidence in the story, although in this case it turned out to be almost true; Pulaski had fallen, but it had withstood bombardment for 30 hours.[108]

Joan's story chronicles cultural changes that allowed Southern women to take their first steps into the world of war reporting, of Southern journalism's acceptance of women among the news-editorial ranks as something other than a poet or "editoress" of temperance or other special interest publications. It is also a story that bolsters arguments that the Civil War profoundly changed the place of elite white Southern women within their society by creating a "striking fluidity of female gender roles." Southern men returned from war as the defeated, their claims to be "protector" in shambles. Southern women had learned during the war to assume roles previously closed to them, including that of journalist. The household gate had been opened. It would never again close completely.[109]

6

Bartholomew Riordan:
Spying on Washington, D.C.

Patricia G. McNeely

AFTER CONCLUDING THAT CORRESPONDENTS WERE GETTING INCONSIS-
tent and contradictory information, Bartholomew Rochefort Riordan decided
to risk being seized as a traitor and made a hasty visit to Washington, D.C., soon
after the war began. The South Carolina reporter wanted "to see for myself what
was transpiring there under the LINCOLN dynasty" and what was happening
in the Federal capital.[1] He managed to escape unharmed back across the enemy
lines to the Confederate camps in Virginia where he wrote prolifically about his
adventures for his South Carolina newspaper, the *Charleston Mercury*.

Riordan soon returned to South Carolina where he spent most of the rest
of the war editing and reporting as managing editor of the *Mercury*. However,
he continued reporting regularly for other Confederate newspapers when he
became one of 20 correspondents in 1863 who covered the war for the newly
formed Press Association of the Confederate States of America. He had only to
step outside his office near the waterfront to gather news about the assaults on
Charleston that continued until February 1865, when the city was evacuated.

Although Riordan wrote daily reports for the Press Association, his widely
published briefs and stories were published without a byline, so most of his war
writing is anonymous. His greatest contribution to American journalism would
come after the war when he joined forces with Confederate Captain Francis
Warrington Dawson to create the *Charleston News*. The editors soon merged
their fledgling newspaper with the dying *Courier* to create one of South Carolina's most powerful and influential 19th century newspapers, the *News and
Courier*, which continues to publish today as the *Post and Courier*.

Riordan was born in Virginia in 1839.[2] A devout Catholic, he was educated
at Mount St. Mary's College before starting his journalism career at the *Washington Union* in Washington, D.C.[3] Riordan quickly decided journalism was not
his calling and moved to New Orleans to be a cotton factor's clerk.[4] Before long,

Bartholomew Riordan. Photograph
courtesy of the *Post and Courier,*
Charleston, South Carolina

he once again "drifted to journalism" at the *New Orleans Picayune* and the *New Orleans Delta*.[5] An old college friend, whose first name is not known but whose last name was Randall, had also turned to newspaper correspondence, as well as poetry. He described their life in New Orleans.[6]

> We were both more or less Bohemians and had slender purses, but we were young and full of life, taking trouble romantically. Both of us had friends of wealth and position, so that our social existence was very charming. If I had the talent of a novel writer, I could weave an interesting romance of our career in Louisiana, but it is just as well to let the dead part bury its dead in silence.[7]

When Riordan was sent to South Carolina to cover the Democratic convention for the *Daily Delta* in 1860, he liked Charleston so much and made such a flattering impression on the editor of the *Charleston Mercury* that he remained in South Carolina.[8] By the fall of 1860, Riordan was managing editor of the *Mercury*.[9] He was described in one of the New York newspapers as the factotum on the *Mercury* staff . . .

> . . . who is obliged to read so many exchanges that it is a wonder he is not made an idiot in the flower of his youth; that being who clips, who wagers, who writes out the "markets," who deciphers raving and incomprehensive telegrams, who looks after the editorials, and has an eye on the local column, who reads miles of proofs, who must know who dies and who gets married, who attends to that mysterious and awful duty the "making up" of the paper, who "sees the paper to

press," who, finally, works like a galley slave from 12 o'clock in the day to 3 o'clock in the morning of the next day, day in and day out, year in and year out, until the hot, unwholesome atmosphere of the editorial "den," drafts, a continual cramped position, want of physical exercise, and a perpetual mental strain, cause the scissors to drop from his stiffened fingers, and necessitate the writing, by a brother quill, of a dead head obituary.[10]

A few days after the Civil War began, Riordan headed north as a correspondent, writing under the pen name Adsum.[11] He arrived in Richmond, Virginia, on April 26, in time to report the movements of the South Carolina volunteers who camped for the night in an unfinished almshouse before moving to the old state fairgrounds to pitch their tents. "The worn and dingy uniforms of our men contrast a little strangely with the bright new trappings of the Virginians," he wrote, "but the ladies have not been slow to assign the difference to its true cause—long and faithful service upon the cheerless sand hills of Morris Island."[12]

> I have heard more than one enthusiastic Virginian, glancing wistfully at the torn and grimy clothes of those whom our State has sent, declare that they envied their brethren of South Carolina the possession of those tattered and smoke stained garments, which afforded so striking a testimony to the sacrifices and privations through which Fort Sumter has been wrested from the Northern Government.[13]

He described the camp fires blazing cheerfully, and wrote that he was glad to see large amounts of fresh beef and other accompaniments before hopping the train to Alexandria, Virginia, just across the river from Washington, D.C. "The sights I saw along the line of the Virginia Central and Orange and Alexandria Railroads convinced me that a great revolution in opinion had taken place, and prepared me to find Unionism less rampant than formerly in this vicinity," he wrote.[14]

> As the train flew by on its way, in many a fallow field I beheld heavy bodies of the sturdy, hard-fisted yeomanry diligently drilling without uniforms or arms, and evidently moving with the single purpose to fight to the death for their homes and firesides. In this region the farmers are generally poor, and can ill afford to spare time from the plough for needless military duty. But they are now aroused in earnest. Most of them, having turned over the cultivation of their crops to negros, under the superintendence of those too old for active service, are marching out by thousands, determined never to return until the independence of the South has been acknowledged. [15]

Riordan saw companies drilling along the railroad with every variety of weapon—ancient flintlock muskets and rifles, shotguns, old-fashioned horse pistols, dilapidated sabers, and, in some cases, hickory pikes or cornstalks. "I am glad to say, however, that this state of things is being changed with wonderful

Riordan made his way from Alexandria to Washington, D.C., over this long bridge, which was guarded by the U.S. artillery. *Harper's Weekly,* May 18, 1861. Courtesy of Rare Books and Special Collections, University of South Carolina Libraries

energy," he wrote. "Not a train comes up from Richmond that does not bring its load of field pieces, columbiads, mortars, and small arms. Ten days more will suffice to place in the field at least 50,000 Virginians, well armed, tolerably drilled, and, above all, determined to conquer or die."[16]

Arriving in Alexandria, Riordan reported Southern flags flying everywhere, from public buildings, hotels, stores, and residences. "Half the male population of the town is under arms," he wrote. "New military companies are forming, and the old ones are filling up their ranks. The mothers and the maidens have caught up the Southern feeling, and are urging fathers, sons, brothers and lovers to muster in the good cause."[17]

> The outskirts of the town are closely guarded by pickets, and the wharves are paced day and night by sentinels, who note and report every movement of the Federal steamers, whose possession of the river is, as yet, undisturbed. In a word, the "against Yankee rule and plundering," so gloriously begun in Charleston on the twentieth of December last, now stretches, in all the might of popular endorsement, from the Rio Grande to the Potomac.[18]

He said the Long Bridge, an ancient and dilapidated structure, was the only remaining link of communication in the region between the United and the

Union troops attacking Confederate prisoners in the streets of Washington, D.C., soon after the war began. *London Illustrated News,* September 14, 1861. Illustration from the Library of Congress

Confederate States. All means of conveyance that crossed to the Washington side of the river had been seized by the Federals, so Riordan found it difficult to persuade any Alexandria drivers to risk their teams on the other side.[19]

"Finally, by paying double what had formerly been the fare between the two cities, I obtained the privilege of a seat in a shaky and venerable omnibus, drawn by four consumptive looking beasts, whose slow movements and well defined ribs afforded a sufficient guaranty against their being either seized or coveted by anybody," Riordan wrote.[20]

He described people "hastily packing up the more valuable of their effects, and in great numbers . . . quitting their homes. It was a mournful sight to see every avenue leading from the city blackened with the dense procession of carriages and vehicles laden with furniture sadly and slowly pursuing their way towards the towns and villages of Maryland." The correspondent described the "terrible plight" of the "poor people of the city who have not yet left."[21]

It is a second Reign of Terror. Each man fears that his neighbor is a spy, for it is known that the Administration is freely using the government funds to maintain numerous and organized bodies of spies and secret informers. This corps is composed partially of the secret police of the city, and partially of wretches drawn from the lowest purliens of Northern cities. Such is the crew at whose mercy the people of Washington have been placed by ABRAHAM LINCOLN. I know that the citizens are ready to rise up the moment they (can) do so with a chance of success. The army and navy, shorn of its brightest ornaments, is demoralized and disaffected. The volunteers from the North are already repenting their sudden enthusiasm for a broken Union and a flag disgraced. The Seventh Regiment has declared that it will never cross the Potomac. Those whom nothing else could move are shocked and scandalized at the atrocious cowardice and barbarism of the Western Vandal, who, it is known, has mined with gunpowder and means to blow to atoms the most magnificent structures ever reared upon the American Continent.[22]

Riordan warned anyone heading north to the battlefields to bring spare arms because buying any kind of firearms was impossible. He wrote that he saw a man leaving for the South who sold his revolver for $100, and the purchaser thought he was lucky to get one even at that price.

The people of this town, who, two weeks ago, never thought of danger, are now sharpening rusty old swords of Revolutionary memory, and diligently cleansing up their flintlock blunderbusses. It is too bad that with such weapons our brave Virginians should have to face the cut-throats and invaders from the North, who are armed cap a pie with the latest inventions of Yankee ingenuity.[23]

Although Riordan wrote profusely, only a few of his letters made it to the *Mercury* because of delays at the post office, and he soon returned to Charleston to work as an editor at the newspaper for the rest of the war. One of his main jobs was supervising correspondents in the field, including Richmond correspondent George W. Bagby, Jr. In that role, Riordan maintained an extensive correspondence with the reporter, even helping Bagby buy clothes and plot a never-undertaken escape to Europe.[24]

In addition to his editorial duties, Riordan began writing for the Press Association of the Confederate States of America after it was created in February 1863. When the siege of Charleston began in April 1863, Riordan sent 50-word bulletins twice a day.[25] The armada that assembled outside Charleston was one of the largest and heaviest afloat.[26] Federals began an incessant bombardment of Batteries Wagner and Gregg on Morris Island from July through September 6, when General P.G.T. Beauregard ordered the evacuation of the garrisons. Riordan reported heavy assaults in late October 1863 when the thundering guns of the Federals were hitting Fort Sumter with the heaviest bombardment to that time.[27]

Riordan reported on the Federals firing constantly and rapidly on October 28 at the sea face of Fort Sumter with 300-pound Parrott guns. "No damage of consequence to the fort, but the sea wall is pretty well battered," he wrote. The fort was bombarded even more severely on October 29, and a man was killed at

Shells burst in the streets of Charleston, South Carolina. Sketched by an English Artist. *Harper's Weekly,* January 9, 1864. Courtesy of Rare Books and Special Collections, University of South Carolina Libraries

Interior of Fort Sumter after bombardment from Morris Island. *Harper's Weekly,* January 9, 1864. Courtesy of Rare Books and Special Collections, University of South Carolina Libraries

The war left Charleston in ruins. Photograph from the Library of Congress

the fort, Riordan wrote.[28] The attacks, which continued until the end of the war, brought both Harriet Tubman, a runaway slave and a leader of the Underground Railroad, and Clara Barton, founder of the Red Cross, to South Carolina with the Union troops.

Charleston was not strategic from a military viewpoint but it was of great symbolic value to the Federals. Fort Sumter had been reduced to rubble with only one remaining gun—a 32-pounder, and as the bombardment continued, Riordan began to intersperse complete articles with his bulletins for the Press Association at a fixed salary of $100 a month.[29]

He reported heavy and continuous bombardment of Fort Sumter all night on October 30 from nearby batteries Gregg and Wagner and the Centre Battery. "The fire on Sumter from Gregg, Wagner, and three monitors, has been incessant since 10 o'clock this morning," he wrote. "The monitors drew off at seven this evening, but Gregg and Wagner are still firing rapidly from 300 pound Parrott guns.—Six hundred and seventy-nine shots have been fired at Sumter, eighty-eight of which have missed. They were nearly all directed at the sea face." He reported that one of the monitors burst a gun and retired, with her turret disabled. "No further casualties reported this morning. Heavy firing from 200 and 300 pound Parrott's still progressing, but the heaviest bombardment of Fort Sumter to date was on October 30."[30]

> From sundown on Wednesday to sundown on Thursday 1,215 shots of all calibre, from 15-inch mortars to 300-pounder Parrotts and downwards, have been thrown into and against the fort. The only casualties have been the slight wounding of seven privates of the 12th Georgia regiment. This evening the enemy opened fire from a mortar battery at Cummings's Point upon the northeast angle of the fort, which seemed to be the special object of attention, and sustains the brunt of the firing to-day. They appear to avoid firing on the city side of the fort. The enemy's batteries engaged were those at Gregg, Wagner, and Cummings's Point, in addition to three monitors. The bombardment of Sumter still goes on, but the fire is a good deal slackened. Our batteries continue to fire slowly and deliberately, the enemy at present paying no attention to them.[31]

President Davis visited South Carolina in November 1863, noting that Charleston had been singled out as a particular point of hatred to the Yankees. He said he did not believe the city would ever be taken, but if it should, Charleston should "be left one mass of rubbish."[32] His orders would be obeyed; by the time the attacks ended on February 17, 1865, most of Charleston was in ruins and Fort Sumter had been reduced to rubble.

Riordan kept up a steady flow of bulletins and stories for the Press Association. Although his articles appeared without a byline, his briefs and bulletins appeared in many member newspapers throughout the Confederacy. Near the end of the year, Atlanta fell in heavy fighting, and Federal troops began their march through Georgia. Sherman's troops took Savannah in December 1864 before marching into South Carolina, and Riordan left when Charleston was evacuated in February 1865.

As Federals were assaulting and burning Columbia on February 17, 1865, Riordan was on his way to Virginia to join the staff of the *Richmond Examiner*. While he was there, he met Francis Warrington Dawson, a Confederate captain from England who had joined the staff as the war was ending.[33] Riordan and Dawson became close friends. When Riordan returned to South Carolina to become assistant editor of the *Charleston Courier*, he persuaded his old boss at the *Mercury* to hire Dawson in late November 1866.[34]

Riordan had been thinking about owning his own newspaper, and in 1867, Riordan, Dawson, and Benjamin Wood of New York purchased the *Charleston News*.[35] Riordan and Dawson took over operation of the newspaper, while

The interior of Fort Sumter after the evacuation by the Confederates on
February 18, 1865. *Harper's Weekly*, July 2, 1865. Courtesy of Rare Books and
Special Collections, University of South Carolina Libraries

Wood maintained a financial interest. Riordan thought he would have to hire
an editor until Dawson could get enough experience to take over, but Dawson
performed so well that he quickly became the most powerful and influential
editor in South Carolina. An exact opposite of the flamboyant Dawson, Riordan
was quiet and studious. His friends said, "He shrank from the public gaze and
he had no political ambitions. His judgment in matters of business was excep-
tionally correct. He wrote with great clearness and force. His methods were
scholarly, his taste artistic."[36]

Riordan and Dawson published the *Charleston News* until April 1873, when
they purchased the *Courier* and merged the newspapers into the *News and
Courier*.[37] Riordan was editor of the *News and Courier* in 1874 and 1875 and
living at 56 Tradd Street in Charleston with a relative named John B. Riordan.
Although Riordan had married sometime before the war and had children, little
is known about his family.

When Riordan was living in Charleston, he was described by a friend as a
"first-class newspaper man and in alliance with the brilliant Captain Dawson,
made the *News and Courier* a power in the land."[38] Riordan handled the business affairs of the newspaper, including the advertising, and in 1877, Riordan
and Dawson bought Wood's interest.

Cannons in front of the Mills House Hotel in 1865. Photos by E. and H. T. Anthony, New York. Courtesy of South Caroliniana Library, University of South Carolina, Columbia

Even though the newspaper was growing and expanding, Riordan decided to start another business in New York. A friend who saw Riordan in 1882 after he returned to New York, said "curiously enough, he had gone back to the cotton business, which had no attraction for him in youth."[39]

While establishing the New York business, Riordan continued his work at the newspaper, which was incorporated as the News and Courier Company in 1884. The newspaper doubled in size from four to eight pages and began statewide delivery by rail as it became the dominant newspaper in South Carolina. However, the next year, Riordan inexplicably sold his interest in the newspaper and permanently left Charleston.[40] His decision may have been caused by a stroke

The Press Corps of the *Charleston News*, started by Riordan and F. W. Dawson after the war. Riordan is the seventh from the left with his left hand in his pocket and his right hand near the center post on the porch railing. Dawson is standing in front in the center of the stairs. Courtesy of the *Post and Courier,* Charleston, South Carolina

that happened about that time. Years later in 1897, a friend who had known him from childhood, wrote that Riordan had suffered a stroke earlier in his life. He wrote, "Many years ago, he was partially paralyzed, and never wholly recovered from the stroke. There was a marked slowness of mental action and a slight limp in one leg, but his intellect was otherwise unimpaired and his bodily vigor unabated up to a recent period."[41]

Although Riordan's sudden departure from South Carolina and the newspaper business was puzzling to his friends, he was also known to be moody and melancholy from time to time.

> He was, in many respects, a remarkable man, and though of a dominantly practical turn, there were elements of fine sentimentality in his nature that no battle with the world could subdue. I think, however, that he had a tendency to serious and even melancholy moods, and there were events in his pilgrimage on earth that deepened these emotions. Life as we both planned it in our boyhood together

was very differently ordered, and I look back with pathos to the various happenings that frustrated all of our sensational devisings. This, however, is a common experience and all men recognize how human proposing is not the disposing of Providence.[42]

Although he was president of the Mason Cotton Gin Cylinder Company by 1886, Riordan soon left that business to join the New York Cotton Exchange and become a cotton broker.[43] With his son, James Riordan, and other financial backers, he established Riordan & Co., Cotton Commission Merchants. After Riordan's death, his childhood friend wrote that Riordan "had devoted his best effort to the establishment of this business and placed it upon so sure a foundation that the firm will go on as usual though the founder has passed away."[44]

Riordan's partner, Dawson, the unarmed champion of law and order who had managed to avoid many duels, was murdered March 12, 1889, when he accused his married neighbor, Dr. Thomas Ballard McDow, of paying inappropriate attention to Dawson's French governess.[45]

Riordan died March 21, 1897, in New York. Mourning his death, his friend wrote, "I have heard that my old friend found such happiness as the world can give to his devoted children, and I have reason to believe that he died a holy death."[46]

7

Leonidas W. Spratt:
Preserving the Legend of "Stonewall" Jackson

Patricia G. McNeely

As he was preparing to leave his job as a correspondent for South Carolina's *Charleston Mercury*, Leonidas William Spratt wrote a final article that created a Civil War legend. His news story about the return of the body of General Barnard Bee to South Carolina contained the anecdote that stamped General Thomas Jackson with his enduring nickname "Stonewall" and created an unforgettable image of a man who would become one of the South's most beloved generals.

A few days after writing the story, Spratt abruptly announced that he was ending his work as a battlefield correspondent and began a series of public lectures in Virginia to raise money for wounded soldiers. While he was on the lecture tour, he was accused of being a spy and arrested by the Confederate army. Spratt barely escaped imprisonment by documenting his extensive secession speeches and his record as "one of the most uncompromising of all of the advocates of Southern rights, having been battling for the cause for over a quarter of a century."[1]

Still fiercely loyal despite his arrest, Spratt resumed his eyewitness accounts of the war in public lectures in Charleston before joining the Confederate army as a private in April 1862. He was quickly promoted to major and became general counsel for General Maxcy Gregg before being promoted to colonel and becoming judge advocate for General James Longstreet for the duration of the war.[2]

A first cousin of President James K. Polk, Spratt was born near Fort Mill, South Carolina, on August 3, 1818, the youngest of eight children of James S. and Margaret McRee Spratt.[3] Unlike most of the Spratt men who were "tall and spare with angular faces,"[4] he was "small, very erect and slender with brilliant beautiful eyes."[5] After graduating in 1840 from South Carolina College (now the University of South Carolina), Spratt moved to Quincy in the panhandle area of

General Barnard Bee. Courtesy of South Caroliniana Library,
University of South Carolina, Columbia

Florida to practice law. A decade later, he returned to South Carolina, where he
was admitted to the state bar in 1850 and began practicing law in Charleston.[6]

Soon after he moved to Charleston, Spratt married Caroline Cooper on October 28, 1850.[7] Their first child, also named Leonidas William Spratt, was born
March 9, 1853, the same year that Spratt became co-editor and co-publisher of
the *Charleston Southern Standard*, a newspaper he used to launch a massive
campaign to reopen the slave trade.[8]

Although the importation of slaves into the United States had been outlawed
since 1808, the campaign was so widely disseminated that *New York Tribune*

General Stonewall Jackson *Harper's Weekly,* March 14, 1863.
Courtesy of Rare Books and Special Collections, University
of South Carolina Libraries

Editor Horace Greeley called him "the philosopher of the new African slave
trade."[9]

Spratt's main argument was that the North would capitulate to efforts to
reopen the slave trade if the South threatened to secede.[10] In addition to his
newspaper articles, he published articles in *De Bow's Review* and a book, *The
Foreign Slave Trade: the Source of Political Power and of Material Progress, of
Social Integrity, and Social Emancipation to the South.*[11] An accomplished and
electrifying orator, Spratt made frequent speeches. In one of his appearances
before the South Carolina legislature,[12] Spratt argued that the North would not

dare resist reopening the slave trade if it were presented as the only alternative to secession and, if he were mistaken and secession ensued, there would be no cause for regret.[13]

This was a bittersweet period for Spratt. His family and newspaper were expanding, but tragically, his second child, Mary, who was born in 1854, died the next year. While his family was expanding, his newspaper had grown in four years to 1,200 subscribers with $17,000 in annual revenue.[14] He sold it in 1857 for $800 to Robert Barnwell Rhett, Sr., who owned the *Mercury*, the only other newspaper that came close to matching Spratt's secessionist fervor. The purchase, in effect, tripled the *Mercury*'s circulation.[15] Although Spratt continued writing and editing for the Rhetts, he was never the editor of the *Mercury*.[16]

The next year, in what would become his best-known legal battle, Spratt successfully defended the crew of the brig *Echo*, an American slave ship that had been captured off the coast of Cuba by a U.S. Navy vessel and brought into Charleston harbor in 1858.[17] The slave ship operators were charged with piracy and violation of the U.S. Act of 1820, which prohibited transporting humans for slavery. President James Buchanan ordered the slaves returned to Africa. Although the judge warned the jury that South Carolina was subject to the laws of the United States, the jury acquitted the slave traders, a decision that gave notice that no slave trader would be convicted in a South Carolina court.[18] Later in 1858, Spratt was elected to a two-year term in the South Carolina House of Representatives; and in 1859, the "fire eater that nobody knows" helped convert the Southern Commercial Convention into a vehicle for secession and made a passionate prosecession/proslavery speech at the Vicksburg Convention.[19]

Spratt's wife died on July 21, 1860, leaving him with his seven-year-old son who most likely spent time with relatives in Charleston and Fort Mill as Spratt pursued his political agenda. After he signed the Ordinance of Secession,[20] Spratt began pushing for a constitutional convention and the organization of a provisional government for the seceding states.[21] He was sent as a commissioner to Florida in early January 1861 to persuade that state to secede. [22] When Spratt finished his speech at the secession convention, 15-year-old Susan Bradford wrote in her diary, "You never heard such cheers and shouts as rent the air, and it lasted so long."[23]

After Florida seceded on January 10, 1861, elated South Carolina Governor F.W. Pickens wrote a note to Spratt saying, "Give our cordial congratulations to the Convention and say we will stand by Florida as we intend to stand by our own guns. We are now prepared and hope to do our duty."[24]

Wherever he could find an audience, Spratt was writing letters and articles and delivering speeches. When the Confederate Congress adopted a provisional constitution modeled after the U.S. constitution in February 1861 in Montgomery, Alabama, he exploded with criticism.

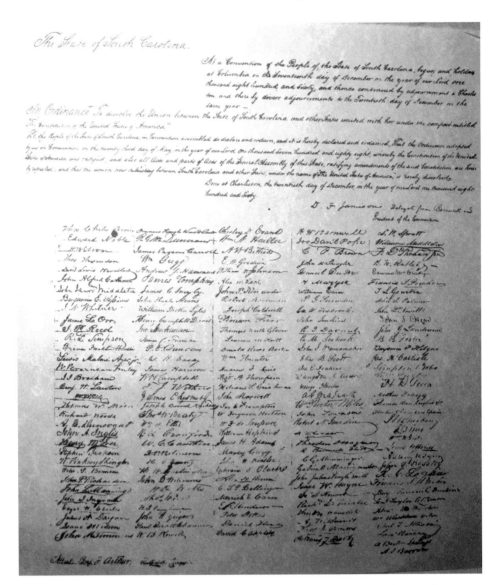

L.W. Spratt was the only correspondent who signed the South Carolina Ordinance of Secession. His signature is at the top of the far right column. Courtesy of South Carolina Department of Archives and History

The South is now in the formation of a Slave Republic. This, perhaps, is not admitted generally . . . The contest is not between the North and South as geographical sections, for between such sections merely there can be no contest; nor between the people of the North and the people of the South, for our relations have been pleasant, and on neutral grounds there is still nothing to estrange us. We eat together, trade together, and practice, yet, in intercourse, with great respect, the courtesies of common life. But the real contest is between the

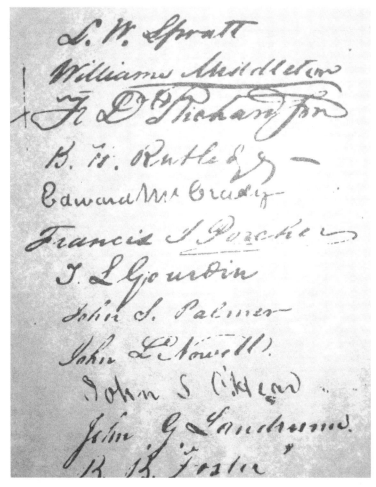

Spratt's signature, at the top, is shown as it appeared on the
Ordinance of Secession. Courtesy of South Carolina Department
of Archives and History

two forms of society which have become established, the one at the North and
the other at the South. [25]

By leading the procession of Southern states out of the Union, Spratt wrote,
South Carolina had "erected at least one nationality under the authority of which
the powers of slavery may stand in that fearful contest for existence which at
some time or other is bound to come."[26]

We are erecting a nationality upon a union of races, where other nations have but
one. We cannot dodge the issue; we cannot disguise the issue; we cannot safely
change our front in the face of a vigilant adversary . . . We may postpone the crisis by disguises, but the slave republic must forego its nature and its destiny, or

The Palmetto State Song is a secession song that was created in Charleston, South Carolina by Henry Siegling in 1861. The illustrated cover for sheet music is a celebration of the South Carolina state convention on December 20, 1860, where the ordinance of secession was passed unanimously, thereby severing the state's ties with the Union. The song was "respectfully dedicated to the signers of the Ordinance of Secession." The cover illustration shows the interior of the crowded hall, where on a stage several of the 169 delegates are gathered around the secession document. Above them hangs the flag of South Carolina, with a palmetto appearing under an arch. Above the arch is an allegorical mural with a palmetto tree in the center, under which Music (or Poetry, holding a lyre), Liberty, and a third female figure repose. The central vignette is flanked by a farmer (left) and sailor with an anchor. Two additional allegorical figures appear in niches on either side of the stage. Courtesy of Library of Congress it must meet the issue, and our assertion of ourselves will not be easier for admissions made against us. Such are the two forms of society which had come to contest within the structure of the recent Union. And the contest for existence was inevitable.[27]

Spratt's strident demands for recognition of the Confederacy as a slave republic and his belief that war was looming were rejected by more moderate Confederates, who saw state rights as the primary reason for secession and who did not believe that war was inevitable. The *Mercury*'s Washington correspondent reported February 16, 1861, that "the Peace Congress had reached a 'most lame and important conclusion,'" but praised Spratt for his actions at the conference.[28]

> Mr. SPRATT'S masterly letter cannot fail to excite attention wherever it is read. You may look for severe comments on it from the reconstructionists generally. But it will be of great service in opening the eyes of halfway Southern men to the true philosophic basis of the present movement, and to the majesty of the future that awaits us, if we hold unflinchingly to a pure and simple slave Republic.[29]

When the war began two months later, Spratt headed for the battlegrounds as a correspondent for the *Mercury*. Signing his articles L.W.S., he was in the field by early May 1861, reporting from Charlottesville, Virginia, where he was impressed by the widespread support of the war from people in Virginia. "There is, perhaps, no single gentleman in the whole section who has not contributed his $5 or $10 to a fund, for every company, and one gentleman has offered to stand drafts upon him to the amount of $50,000."[30]

Before moving on to Richmond, Spratt visited Harpers Ferry on May 14, 1861, where he wrote about the strategic value of the town to the Confederate army and the poor condition of the soldiers.

> Many of them, delicately raised, and nurtured, had eaten nothing from the day before. Their supplies were on ahead at Strasburg, some sixty miles away; there were no cars to take them on, and for hours they stood without breaking ranks, and with only water for a refreshment. To one lad, with a frank and open face, I gave the little provision which we had made for our own journey, and I can scarce remember ever to have seen a lad so grateful. He made a show of defending it with his bayonet, when a half a dozen charged upon him for a share, but soon gave in, and seemed all the happier in making the others as contented as himself.[31]

Spratt returned to Camp Davis near Richmond on May 20, where he described the difficulties of creating an army for the new republic. The army, he said, takes on energies and motives of its own "and stands and starts on its career as a potent and perilous creation."[32]

> Of the pains and labor—of the strain upon the social nature of a State in giving birth to an army—few, I fancy, have an adequate conception. We know of armies

as existing facts, but have never seen the labors necessary to produce them, and perhaps no State has ever presented a fairer exhibition of the painful process than Virginia does at present. Her social system is rocked with the unnatural effort. All her energies are turned to war. The currents of her peaceful life are all tapped by the requisitions of an army. It makes a drain upon her dairies, her meat houses, her stables, her granaries, her mills, her barn yards, her stock farms, her stores, her shops, her armories, her railroads, her liberality, her patriotism, her sympathies, and her society. The army becomes an omnivorous animal. Its capacious maw is clamorous for every thing.[33]

A few cases of measles had broken out in Camp Davis, Spratt reported. "They have been carefully cared for in a hospital to themselves, and it is not apprehended that the disease will spread to any extent. They will be moved to another hospital today to be cared for by the Sisters of Charity, who have volunteered to take charge of them."[34] During their down time, soldiers were finding ways to occupy their time by playing games, singing, and writing letters to the folks back home. He was surprised to find that . . .

> . . . two fine puppies have been adopted into the first regiment, which are already the darlings of the men, who seem never to tire of being worried by them, while a frisky little white kitten has found its way even into headquarters, and clambers over the shoulders of all the officers, even up to the General himself, without the slightest sense of embarrassment.[35]

Spratt's descriptions of ordinary camp life and soldiers' diversions soon turned to complaints about the rain and "shockingly cold" weather that made life in the camp dreary and uncomfortable even before he had seen his first battle. "The weather has changed, and I have had my first experience of camp life in the rain," he wrote. "A northeast wind has been blowing for two days; cloaks and oil cloths are in requisition, men hurry to and from their meats; there is no unnecessary lounging out of tents, except to hug the camp fires."[36] Before moving on to Manassas Junction, Spratt reported that the seat of the Confederate government had been moved to Richmond and that the Federals had invaded Virginia.

> At 8 o'clock the train arrived, bringing the intelligence that Alexandria had been taken and ever since men, women and children, in all sorts of conveyances, and in all degrees of destitution, have been arriving . . . The bridges were torn up as the trains passed, and those so unlucky as to have been left, have had to make their way round as best they could. Some have come in carriages, some in hacks, some in carts, and some on foot. . . . There seemed to be no disposition to do gratuitous injury; but a few arrests of citizens were made, and no opposition was offered to the escape of those who left the city; but the town was occupied, the railroad depot was taken possession of, and everything was in the hands of a military and a hostile power.[37]

The "enemy has finally and emphatically departed from his defensive policy and . . . a war of subjugation has been inaugurated," Spratt wrote, as he described the Federal advance on May 27 toward nearby Fairfax, between Alexandria and Manassas Junction.[38] He planned to follow the army in a buggy, which was to take part of his baggage, but the buggy never appeared and Spratt was forced to abandon almost everything he owned before heading for Centreville.

"I left the balance by the roadside to which it had been carried, with still more; and with a gun, pistol, overcoat and demijohn of brandy, which last, as I never drink myself, would have seemed as unnecessary as anything I could have elected," he wrote.[39] When he arrived, Spratt learned that a train loaded with Confederate soldiers had crashed full-speed into a stationary train also packed with soldiers. Several were killed or injured, and in the resulting chaos, the soldiers could not separate their bags, pitch tents, or prepare supper.[40]

The Federals took Morgantown in late May before attacking Fairfax Court House. After a brief skirmish on June 1, the Union army retreated to a fortified position at Arlington Heights. While waiting for another attack at Fairfax, Spratt was surprised at the lack of concern of people in the area.

> It is strange how soon a people become indifferent to danger. The tract of country between this position and the enemy must soon become a battleground, but few have left it—few have put their things in readiness to leave. All are engaged about their customary avocations. Women, as well as men, await the issue.[41]

Without waiting any longer for a battle, Spratt headed for Richmond on June 4. When he returned to Fairfax, he was distressed to report that the little white "headquarters kitten" had disappeared. He reported that the kitten had last been seen on the top of a baggage wagon on the arm of a man named Ormsby, nibbling at his fingers and clambering over his head and shoulders, to the great satisfaction of both of them.

> But Homer sometimes slept, and so also slept Ormsby through the weary hours of the long night from Richmond to Manassas, and the kitten has not since been seen or heard of.
>
> Not so the puppies, which I also mentioned as attached to the First Regiment. The men in charge of them may have slept, but, also, doubtless, slept the puppies, and, reappearing after their ride, they have since been as thriving and mischievous as ever. One has been named Bonham and the other Beauregard, and there is quite a diversity of opinion which can whip—and which, in fact, is the most competent to any other of the responsibilities and powers of doghood.[42]

As the two opposing armies gathered for battle, Spratt reported that one of the officers was dashing around trying to get someone to hold a bag containing $27,000 in cash that belonged to the regiment. Not wanting to take the bag into battle, he turned the money over to a Colonel Boylston "and went dashing on to battle with more pleasure in getting rid of $27,000 than many more would have had in earning it."[43] Spratt wrote that Confederate soldiers led by Colonel Maxcy Gregg ambushed and captured a train at Vienna on June 17.[44] En route to Manassas, Spratt reported a skirmish at New Creek,[45] followed by reports of the movements of the troops as they gathered for another battle.[46]

About 5,000 Federals were moving to reopen the Loudoun and Hampshire Railroad, an effort that Spratt said would be blocked, if possible, by the Confederates.[47] Most correspondents editorialized to some degree, including Spratt, who wasted no time in surveying the situation, deciding what needed to be done, and providing his assessment of what the Confederate army should do:

> But if it were not gratuitous—if the enemy were even more formidable than he is—there are reasons why that position should be held. It commands the road to Staunton and down through the whole valley of Virginia; it commands the road through Manassas Gap to the rear of this position, and on to Richmond; and if, therefore, the disproportion or danger were greater, he should hold it. He could stand until reinforcements could be sent, or, if need be, he could fight.[48]

Spratt also described problems the army was having acquiring enough wagons for transportation. At one point, officials discussed suspending operations until the army could manufacture enough wagons. "Pertinacity prevailed, however," he wrote. "The authorities consented at least to try the old Virginia wagons, and it has been found that they do transport a bed or bacon as well as the best regulation wagon could do."[49]

Firearms were also a problem. Spratt reported that more than 40,000 men had not been mustered into the field because the privately owned, double-barreled guns and rifles in the state were not regarded as an "available arm."[50]

By June 26, 1861, Spratt had moved on to Manassas Junction, where he wrote:

> The feeling is that there may be fighting elsewhere, but that there must be fighting here, and the place, therefore, for meeting people is not unlike New York used to be in September. But, unlike the visitors of New York, they are singularly indifferent to accommodations. Tent room and a blanket is all they stipulate for. With a competent servant, they can forage for their own food; and among the same class of men, I can safely say, I never have heard less complaint upon the score of entertainment . . . There are as yet no ladies, and there will not be; I suppose. They cannot pack as close as men; and would, of course, be miserable with the single carpet bag, which is all the conditions of this life allows.[51]

However, Spratt had misjudged Southern women and soon reported that relatives who were following their husbands, sons, and fathers into battle were beginning to move into nearby lodgings. "The ladies, however, cannot be kept entirely away," he wrote. "The wives and mothers and daughters of men and officers are already coming into the farmhouses around. Still others will come on as the season wears or the contest closes, and Culpeper Court House and a Sulphur Spring, some 40 miles away upon the Manassas Gap Road, secure among the mountains, may yet become, for this season at least, the most fashionable places at the South."[52]

When Generals Joseph Johnston and Thomas Jackson, who had not yet earned his legendary "Stonewall" nickname, arrived at Martinsburg in preparation for a battle, they found that Federal General Robert Patterson had not received the flag of truce that would have enabled him to release the women and children from the battle area. After the flag was delivered, Spratt reported, Patterson was then unwilling to lose the protection of the women and children, whose presence would prevent an attack. "It is hard that a ruthless and insolent invader should be at liberty to skulk behind the cribs and petticoats of women and children and find protection," Spratt wrote.[53]

Instead of waiting for an attack, a Federal force that Spratt estimated at 18,000 men soon marched 10 miles from Martinsburg toward General Johnston's forces at Bunker Hill, but Johnston fell back to Winchester.[54] The weather turned hot, and the Confederates erected arbors of brushwood running between the tents. "The long shady lines were the most comfortable things I had seen for a long time," he wrote. And it was in the shady arbors that the men assembled on Sundays for church.[55]

Spratt reported the defeat at Laurel Hill of General Robert S. Garnett, who retreated with his troops to Corrick's Ford near Parsons where he became the first general officer to be killed in the war. Spratt wrote that Garnett's defeat was not surprising, "especially in view of the fact that the Federalists had more than 15,000 men, while our force was less than six thousand . . ."[56]

> . . . it appears that Gen. GARNETT's force had become divided upon the Tygart Valley river, and that the enemy, concentrating his entire force on the one section, consisting of some three thousand men, cut it off . . . It is particularly to be regretted that the first engagement, the first contest for the attack to empire, should have occurred at this point. The enemy were there in the best condition to advance, and we in the worst condition to resist them, and for a time it may induce the feeling that they are, in fact, able to clear the track as they have said they are.[57]

Spratt reported on July 10 that the Federals had advanced on Fairfax, but General Milledge L. Bonham's troops fell back to Centreville before marching to Bull Run, about four miles from Manassas, to take up their positions for the battle. Before leaving Fairfax, the Federals burned the courthouse, jail, two hotels, and the female academy, which had been General Bonham's headquarters, according to Spratt. They also burned the Harrison House at Germantown and several private houses at Centreville. "They are in a bad humor, and we have tried our best to give them a reason for it," Spratt wrote.[58] He reported an attack at Blackburn's Ford on July 18 that was repulsed by Longstreet's men.

The enemy from the higher ground, on the other side of the creek, had, apparently, the advantage of our infantry on this; but almost at our first fire, they recoiled. They came again to the charge, and were again repulsed; again they returned, and again they were driven back. Several companies of riflemen were ordered to pursue them across the creek, which they did with the utmost gallantry, and from this repulse, they did not again return, but continued on to Centreville, where they took up their position.[59]

During this time, the Washington Artillery, with only four field pieces, poured shot into the enemy with murderous effect, Spratt reported. "Sherman's Battery contained eight field pieces, but it was fairly whipped," he wrote. "Several times the Federals were forced to change position, and at last were driven from the field." The Confederates were fighting an enemy variously estimated from 6,000 to 15,000, Spratt wrote. "Our troops had no advantages of any kind. The whole force at this point was less than 2,500; they were on lower ground. They had no breastworks, no masked batteries, no rifled cannon, and the enemy must confess that he has been whipped on a fair and open field, by less than half his force."[60]

As forces headed for Bull Run, Spratt wrote that all the people around for more than four miles had been ordered to leave their homes and move to safety at the rear of the Confederate troops. En route, he reported shots being fired.

The two batteries of artillery stationed on the rising ground on either side of the creek, more than a mile apart, had a regular duel. They had the field to themselves . . . The scene of conflict is painful. I mentioned yesterday that, under a flag of truce, the enemy undertook to bury their dead, but did not bury all. I now learn that they did not even ask to bury their dead, or make any effort to do so, and a gentleman on the ground, and at pains to count them, states that more than sixty men were found rotting in the field. Some were doubtless, carried off, but it argues a singular wont of humanity that they should permit those to be unburied. Many of them were buried by our men, but the task was so offensive that the party was forced to desist.[61]

Spratt and other correspondents, including Felix Gregory de Fontaine of the *Charleston Courier* and *Richmond Enquirer*, Peter W. Alexander of the *Savannah Republican*, William G. Shepardson of the *Columbus* (Ga.) *Times* and *Montgomery* (Ala.) *Advertiser*, and David G. Duncan of the *Richmond Dispatch* started from Manassas Junction at 7 a.m. on Sunday, July 21, 1861.[62] More than 35,000 Federals were gathering from several directions to attack 32,500 Confederates in the general area around Bull Run, a lazy creek meandering near Manassas. The correspondents had left in such a hurry that they had no field glasses with which to watch the distant battle, but they were able to borrow a powerful opera glass from Colonel William G. Bonner.[63] While they were

First battle of Manassas. Photograph from the Library of Congress

waiting, they were joined by Edmund Ruffin, the fire-eating Virginia farmer who advocated state rights and secession and had fired the first shot at Fort Sumter. "He had come to the conflict with his eighty odd years weighing upon him, and his flowing locks, to take part in this fight, encouraging our young men by his presence and example," Spratt wrote. "Agile as a youth of sixteen, with rifle on his shoulder, his eyes glistened with excitement as he burned to engage the Yankee invader."[64] Watching from his vantage point above Bull Run, Spratt wrote his reports in bulletins.[65]

HALF PAST TEN O'CLOCK A.M.—There is firing on our flanking column. The enemy has opened their battery upon it half way. The column responds. The firing becomes rapid musketry! Generals BEAUREGARD, JOHNSTON and BONHAM, have just come to the hill where I have been standing. The whole scene is before us—a grand moving diorama. The enemy have sent a ball from their rifled cannon at us. Another. They pass over us with a sound that makes our flesh crawl. All have left the spot but Generals BEAUREGARD, BONHAM and JOHNSTON, and their aides. The firing has ceased at the head of our flanking column. It is renewed again, nearer, I think, to the enemy. Another ball exactly over our heads. A very sustaining force follows our flanking column. The enemy, firing at our Generals, has dropped a shot among the wagons in the edge of the woods below, and they dash off. Another shot follows them as they fly, and plunges in the ground but a few feet behind one of them.

ELEVEN O'CLOCK—The firing has been awful. The heads of the flanking and resisting columns are distinctly visible from the smoke that rises above them; and they stand stationary for a long time, but at last the enemy column goes back—a column of dust rises in their rear—a shout rises that roars loud as the artillery from our men—the enemy fire slackens our reserves advance—the dust rises on to the position lately occupied by the enemy—we triumph, we triumph, thank God!

QUARTER BEFORE TWELVE O'CLOCK—The enemy make another stand. Again, there is the roar of musketry, long like the roar of distant and protracted thunder. Again, the roar, but always at the head of the enemy column. A column of dust rises to the left of our forces and passes to the enemy right. It must be intended to flank them. It is fearful to think how many heart strings are wrung by the work that now goes on—how many brave men must be mangled and in anguish.

TWELVE O'CLOCK, NOON—The batteries first opening have been silent for half an hour, and the whole extended valley is now the thick of the fight. Where the enemy last took his stand retreating, the fight is fearful—the dust is denser than the smoke. It is awful. They have been repulsed three times—so it is reported by a courier—and now they have taken their bloodiest and final stand.

HALF PAST TWELVE O'CLOCK—The firing now is at its height. Never until now have I dreamed of such a spectacle; for one long mile the whole valley is a boiling crater of dust and smoke.

QUARTER BEFORE ONE O'CLOCK—The fray ceases; Gens. (P.G.T.) BEAURE-GARD AND JOHNSTON dash on to the scene of action, and as we cannot doubt that the enemy has again fallen back, it looks as though they were on their way to Washington.[66]

As the Federals began their retreat back to Washington, Confederate President Jefferson Davis reached the battleground. After arriving on the train that brought him to Manassas, the president mounted his horse and, accompanied by Colonel Joseph R. Davis and numerous attendants, galloped to the battlefield where wounded soldiers on the roadsides and in the fields raised their hands and gave "shout upon shout and cheer upon cheer."[67]

> . . . the honored Chief Magistrate of the Confederacy arrived upon the ground almost as the shouts of victory died upon the distance. They rose again for him, and again and again for the gallant military chieftains under whose able leadership the action had been won. And there was not one who looked upon that field, strewn with the fragments of war, and glittering in the beams of sunset, and upon those long lines of begrimed and bloody men, and upon the dark columns of the insolent invader, as crushed and cowed, he crawled from the field, who did not feel that he stood upon another historic point in human history.[68]

Davis conferred with his generals about whether the Confederates should pursue the Federals. While the generals were persuading Davis to end the battle and let the enemy return to Washington because the Confederates were too tired and their supplies too low, Spratt sat down with his pencil to describe the devastating scenes that he had just witnessed.

> The dead and dying lay about. The masses of horse lay under cover of the hills for the occasion that should invoke their action. Men stood to their arms along that bloody line, and looked a strange interest on the enemy. Was he to return and continue a fight of eight hours duration? Was he to change the point of his attack and force them, wearied and broken as they were, to another field, or, were they, broken and outdone, about to retire from a field to which they had become assured by experiences there was no harvest of power or glory to be won, but where they were, indeed, welcomed with bloody hands to hospitable graves. That this was their purpose, at length appeared. A shout arose upon the conviction, from 10,000 throbbing and exultant hearts.[69]

After the battle ended, Spratt wrote lengthy articles on July 20, July 22, and July 24 that he apparently mailed from Camp Pickens near Manassas.[70] Returning to Richmond, Spratt learned that General Barnard Bee's body was being returned to South Carolina the next day. The article that he wrote described Bee's courageous last stand at Bull Run, and it also contained the anecdote that gave Stonewall Jackson his famous nickname. The article was unsigned, but the *Mercury*'s only other Richmond correspondent, Dr. George W. Bagby, Jr., whose pen name was Hermes, was serving with the troops at Bull Run at the time and would not write his first story for the *Mercury* until that fall.[71] A descendant, U.S. Congressman John Spratt (D-S.C.), remembers relatives saying that his great-great uncle Leonidas claimed to have written the "Stonewall" article.

The article was telegraphed from Richmond on July 24 and published July 25 under a headline that read, "OUR SPECIAL ACCOUNTS FROM RICHMOND FROM OUR OWN CORRESPONDENT." The information had been obtained from a member of General Bonham's staff.

> The remains of Gen. BARNARD E. BEE leave (Richmond) to-morrow for Charleston. The name of this officer deserves a place in the highest niche of fame. He displayed a gallantry that scarcely has a parallel in history. The brunt of the morning's battle was sustained by his command until past two o'clock. Overwhelmed by superior numbers, and compelled to yield before a fire that swept everything before it, Gen. BEE rode up and down his lines, encouraging his troops, by everything that was dear to them, to stand up and repel the tide which threatened them with destruction. At last his own brigade dwindled to a mere handful with every field officer killed or disabled. He rode up to Gen. JACKSON and said, "General, they are beating us back."

General Stonewall Jackson in camp from a drawing by English artist Frank Vizetelly, who was working for the *Illustrated London News. Harper's Weekly*, February 14, 1863. Courtesy of Rare Books and Special Collections, University of South Carolina Libraries

The reply was: "Sir, we'll give them the bayonet."

Gen. BEE immediately rallied the remnant of his brigades, and his last words to them were: "There is JACKSON standing like a stone-wall. Let us determine to die here, and we will conquer. Follow me!"

His men obeyed the call; and, at the head of his column, the very moment when the battle was turning in our favor, he fell, mortally wounded. Gen. BEAUREGARD was heard to say that he had never seen such gallantry. He never murmured at his suffering, but seemed to be consoled by the reflection that he was doing his duty.[72]

The legend of "Stonewall" grew rapidly as the story was told and retold around campfires and reprinted in other newspapers, including the *Richmond Dispatch*. Preserving this story was Spratt's major contribution to Civil War journalism. Certainly, it was his last. Within a few days, Spratt abruptly announced in the *Mercury* that he was quitting as a war correspondent. He did not clearly explain his reason for leaving, although he alluded to difficulties he was having getting information.

Facts as to the operation of their Governments and their military or other agents, are, in a government like ours, due to the people. And I have thought it might be agreeable to their many friends at home to hear even the little I have felt at liberty to tell about them, and so have continued to write when there have been many reasons of private feeling which I should not. But the position of an outsider in a military camp is not pleasant, and I see no present reason why I should continue in it longer. If anything special occurs, I will still communicate it.[73]

Instead of writing for newspapers, Spratt decided to deliver public lectures about the war. He began a speaking tour that included Lynchburg and Richmond to raise money for wounded and sick soldiers.[74] Soon after he gave one of his speeches, Spratt was accused by a woman in Richmond of being a spy and was arrested by the Confederate army. He didn't write about his problems, but his arrest and subsequent release were reported in the September 23, 1861, *Richmond Dispatch*, probably by Shepardson, along with a chatty description of the problems correspondents were having as suspected spies.

It is a singular fact in the war that the ladies are foremost in everything, and that their patriotism and vigilance in guarding the interests of the Government is unceasing. A short time ago a well-known newspaper man, who has been for years a severe fire-eater and strongly in favor of opening the slave trade, was arrested at the instigation of a female custodian of the public welfare as a suspicious character. It was with difficulty he escaped imprisonment, although he showed a clear record, and proved that he had made Secession speeches ever since he was first elected to the Legislature of his native State, many years ago. With this circumstance in mind, I was much amused at an old lady a few miles below this place, who evidently kept a sharp look-out on all strangers who might prove emissaries of the Round heads.

The locality, for convenience sake, may be called Bristow.

Scene—the parlor of a hotel.

Dramatis persona—party of gentlemen conversing in one corner; ladies in the other, who continually cast side glances at a newspaper reporter who is writing out his notes at the centre-table.

Act 1st.—Reporter oblivious to all about him. Old lady walks back and forward, casting sundry glances on the strange hieroglyphics. Gents still conversing. Old lady whispers significantly to her companions, when the party put their heads together and converse in an under-tone. Reporter still oblivious. Finally, the work is completed, the notes go into a side pocket, the book is folded, pen wiped, and inkstand put away. Reporter prepares to leave the room by side entrance, but is intercepted by old lady, in behalf of community.

Old lady—"Have you been taking down what we've been saying?"

Reporter—"Certainly not, madam." (Aside: "what an old—")

Old Lady, (interrupting)—"Well, then, mister, be you a spy or anything?"

Reporter very suddenly subsides, but immediately draws sundry papers containing his record, which he spreads upon the table. To make matters still stronger, he claims relationship with Jeff. Davis, has known Aleck Stephens from his boyhood, went to school with Beauregard, was by Johnston's side at the taking of Chepultepec, and fought in the battle of Bull Run. Smiles of satisfaction gradually creep over all faces. Play concludes by finding all parties satisfied, old lady having introduced pretty black-eyed daughter to the roving Bohemian and suspected spy.[75]

After his arrest and release, Spratt returned to Charleston to conduct another public lecture on September 28, 1861. The *Mercury* promoted his Lecture on the Battle of Manassas Plains as a "correct idea of the first great battle of the war." Spratt "presents, upon a diagram, the movements of each division of the armies, indicates the points where the several battles were joined—for it was a day of battles—shows the spots where fell the lamented dead—exhibits the scenes presented by the different actions of the day, and gives, in fact, a picture of the battle, which only can be had from oral illustration."[76]

After being introduced by Governor Pickens, Spratt also apparently discussed problems on the battlefield—"the reasons why the right wing was not engaged—why there was no pursuit of the enemy . . . the relative merits of our troops in the way of fighting, and generally of the incidents that illustrate the course of that engagement."[77]

After his lecture engagements dwindled, Spratt decided to join the army on December 2, 1861, and was assigned to Captain G.C. Heyward's Company, Martin's Regiment, in the South Carolina Militia. Since he had his own horse, he was paid $12 a month for its use.[78] Although Spratt had joined the army as a private, he rose rapidly through the ranks, was promoted to major, and appointed general counsel for General Maxcy Gregg on April 16, 1862.[79]

Spratt had never been injured in battle, but while he was traveling on the train through South Carolina, he was bruised but not seriously hurt when two cars were thrown off the track and one turned over.[80] After recovering, he returned to Richmond to marry Mary A. Wadsworth on June 19, 1862, in the home of her father, John E. Wadsworth.[81] He soon returned to the battlefield where he was appointed on December 16, 1862, as a judge in General Longstreet's military court, a position he most likely held until the end of the war.[82]

On April 7, 1865, in the waning days of the war, Spratt, who had been promoted to colonel,[83] was admitted to the general hospital in Danville, Virginia, with "debilitas."[84] He returned to his hometown of Fort Mill, South Carolina, soon after the April 9 surrender at Appomattox Court House.[85] As the Confederate government began disintegrating in Richmond, President Davis coincidentally also fled south to Fort Mill. He presided over a Confederate cabinet meeting on May 4 on the lawn of the William Elliott White house, a short distance from where Spratt was hiding out in the old family home where he was born.[86] When the meeting was over, Davis spent the night in the neighboring

Confederate General James Longstreet, *Harper's Weekly*, July 9, 1864.
Courtesy of Rare Books and Special Collections, University of South
Carolina Libraries

Springfield House near Spratt's home before continuing to Abbeville, South
Carolina, and Washington, Georgia, where the government dissolved.

Spratt returned to Charleston to practice law. He and his second wife, Mary,
had two sons, James Wadsworth,[87] born on October 28, 1867, and Charles B.,
born in 1870.[88] The family moved to Richmond in 1872 before moving to Florida
in 1876,[89] where he became a judge in Jacksonville. He wrote three books, one
each in 1894,[90] 1896, [91] and 1902,[92] before he died on October 4, 1903, at age 85.[93]
Spratt and his wife are buried in Evergreen Cemetery in Jacksonville.

8

Henry Timrod: Reluctant Correspondent Who Became Poet Laureate

Patricia G. McNeely

HENRY TIMROD'S STINT AS A WAR CORRESPONDENT FOR SOUTH CAROlina's *Charleston Mercury* was brief, but the Civil War and his experiences at the battlefront were the inspiration for poems that created his legacy as the Poet Laureate of the Confederacy. He was a reluctant soldier when he left for the Western front, and the sights and sounds of the sick, wounded, and dying Confederates sickened him almost as much as sleeping on a plank on the ground and drinking polluted water.

After writing unremarkable articles for the *Mercury* for less than three months, the destitute, tubercular poet staggered back to South Carolina to spend the last years of the war yearning for peace and writing editorials interspersed with poetry about suffering and tragedy. The horror of the war and memories from the front haunted Timrod until, overwhelmed by tuberculosis and unrelenting poverty, he died in 1867.

Timrod became an important 19th century Southern poet who has been compared to better known writers such as Henry Wadsworth Longfellow and John Greenleaf Whittier. His poetry, which is usually included in Southern studies and most anthologies of American poetry, was resurrected in August 2006 when Bob Dylan borrowed extensively from Timrod's poetry for the lyrics of the best-selling album "Modern Times."[1]

Born in Charleston, South Carolina, on December 8, 1829, the poet was named for his grandfather, Heinrich Dimroth, who Anglicized his name to Henry Timrod when he immigrated to America from Germany in 1765.[2] Timrod's father, William Henry Timrod, was a self-educated bookbinder and poet whose shop became the gathering place for the literary and intellectual men in Charleston.[3] He and his second wife, Thyrza E. Prince, had four children. Henry, their third child, was known to his friends as Harry or Hal. His two older sisters were Adeline Rebecca, born in 1823, and Emily, his favorite, born

This portrait of Henry Timrod was painted
from a photograph circa 1897 and presented to
the Timrod Library (now the Richland County
Public Library) in Columbia, South Carolina by
W.A. Courtenay, also a *Mercury* correspondent.
Photograph by Patricia G. McNeely

in 1827, and his younger sister Edyth (sometimes spelled Edith) Carolina, born
in 1835.[4]

Timrod's father died in either 1837 or 1838,[5] leaving the family with money
and their own plantation, but the house burned when Timrod was 13 years old,
and his family lost everything.[6] Nevertheless, his poverty-stricken mother managed to send him to one of the best private schools in Charleston, where he met
Paul H. Hayne, a fellow poet, editor, and adviser, who became Timrod's life-long
friend.[7] Timrod began writing poetry when he was 15 years old. On the occasion of the death of one of his tutors, he wrote:

> *Not a grin was seen, not a giggle heard*
> *As the tutor breath'd his last*
> *Not a Freshman uttered a jesting word*
> *At the thought of labours past.*[8]

With funds provided by a Charleston donor, Timrod entered the University of Georgia in 1847 where he studied English literature and the classics and became a devoted student of the "masters of English song—Shakespeare, Spenser, Milton, Burns, and Tennyson," and his best-loved poet, William Wordsworth.[9] He quickly became "sentimental—very," sighing over the nameless woman whose "eyes had wov'n about my heart and brain,"[10] as well as Marie, Cousin Lou, Isabel, Arabella, Mary, Anne Waddel, Chloe, Rachel, and others.[11] Timrod began sending poetry under the *nom de plume* of Aglaus, a minor Greek poet, to the *Southern Literary Messenger* in Richmond where the best of his poetry continued to appear until 1853.[12]

With his heart more or less intact but suffering from health and financial problems, Timrod left the university after two years to study law in Charleston. He resumed his friendship with William Gilmore Simms, a leading Southern novelist who had known Timrod's father and recognized Timrod's genius at an early age. Timrod became part of an informal club established by Simms that also included Timrod's friend Hayne,[13] who became editor in 1857 of *Russell's Magazine*. The magazine, founded by popular Charleston bookseller John Russell and described by Simms as "eleemosynary literature," included Timrod's poetry and prose, but failed after the fourth issue.[14]

The study of law did not suit Timrod who soon left to resume his classical studies in the doomed hope of becoming a college professor. He wrote poetry while teaching and tutoring on plantations and in small schools in North Carolina and South Carolina. While he was teaching in Florence County, South Carolina, he lived with his sister, Emily Goodwin, in "Forest Cottage" where he met Emily's sister-in-law Katie Goodwin.[15] Although Timrod barely noticed her at the time, she would become the "Katie" of his poetry and his wife after the Civil War began.[16]

A volume of poetry called *Poems*, which contained a collection of Timrod's best verses from the previous eight or nine years, was published in 1860 in Boston, but the book "fell on the great world of letters, generally speaking, almost unheeded, shut out by the war cloud that soon broke upon the land, enveloping all in darkness."[17] The book probably would have been unheeded under any circumstance because most scholars considered his early poetry to be frail and immature. However, everything—his life and his poetry—changed when the Civil War began.[18] Timrod's former teacher and professor William J. Rivers wrote: "The terrible realization of our late history roused him as nothing else on earth could have roused him; and in the excitement of his soul he strung his lyre to more exalted themes, and poured forth in quick succession many spirited odes, which gave him rank among the foremost lyric poets of America."[19]

One of his first great poems, "The Cotton Boll," was published in the *Mercury* on September 3, 1861, while he was courting Katie. They were engaged by January 4, 1862, but Timrod was too poor to marry. In an effort to make some money, he enlisted March 1, 1862, in the 30th South Carolina Regiment, which was commanded by his friend, Colonel Lawrence M. Keitt. The colonel offered him the chance to enlist as a gentleman volunteer, which would have provided him a horse and the dignity but not the rank or pay of an officer. Timrod was too poor to accept, so he enlisted as a private to receive a salary.[20]

While he was preparing to leave for the battlefield, he wrote letters to his sister, in which he speculated that England would join the war on the side of the Confederates. However, a week later, he told her he had given up hope: "In spite of the prediction I sent you last week, I begin to despair of European intervention. We have over bid the power of King Cotton. When King Wheat gets upon his throne, he is just as strong."[21]

Before leaving for the front, Timrod signed on as a war correspondent for the *Mercury.* When he left South Carolina on his way to Corinth, Mississippi, on April 11, 1862, he was proud that he was making $6 a day and traveling expenses—"higher even than Personne's with the *Courier.*" Personne was the pseudonym of Felix Gregory de Fontaine, who had been writing for the *Charleston Daily Courier* since the war began. Timrod's salary was as much in one day as an army private made in two weeks. However, the depressed and frightened poet had grave misgivings about how he would fare in the war.[22]

> I am afraid to dwell upon the feelings with which I start upon my adventure. The letters from Personne and [Peter]Alexander[23] show that I will have to encounter great hardships and many . . . shocking sights. However . . . the hope of an early union with Katie will give me strength. But with my usual proneness to despondency, I cannot help some dismal forebodings.[24] General (Pierre G.T.) Beauregard's position on the Western front is a very difficult one. Rumors say he has been outflanked and surrounded, and if he should be defeated, I can look forward to nothing but death or capture. Either fate would be very bitter to me now. With the cup of happiness at last so near my lips, it would be agony unspeakable to see it dashed to the ground.[25]

Timrod's friend Keitt had arranged for the terrified poet to go at once to the quarters of Colonel John H. Savage of the 16th Tennessee Regiment in Atlanta "and he will take care of me," Timrod wrote. "This will smooth many a difficulty in my way . . . In what quarter of these Confederate states will I be when I next write to you. Perhaps I may never write to you again. It is horrible."[26]

After reaching Atlanta, Timrod boarded the train for Corinth, Mississippi, about 20 miles southwest of the battlefield at Shiloh, Tennessee. "Worn out with fatigue, dazed by the bustle of the camp and the novelty of his position,"[27] he finally arrived in Corinth on April 24, 1862, on a train especially appropriated for the Tenth Regiment of South Carolina Volunteers.

Timrod had chosen the worst possible time to join the army. More than 20,000 Confederates and Federals had been killed or wounded on April 6 and April 7 in

Worn out with fatigue, dazed by the bustle of the camp, and the novelty of his position, Henry Timrod finally arrived at the railroad junction in Corinth in April 1862. Illustration from *Harper's Weekly,* June 21, 1862. Courtesy of Rare Books and Special Collections, University of South Carolina Libraries

the bloody battle at Shiloh. The toll was nearly twice as many as the battle casualties at Manassas, Wilson's Creek, Fort Donelson, and Pea Ridge combined and was the first battle on a scale that became common during the next three years.[28] When the battle ended, General Beauregard ordered his troops to Corinth, which was considered a crucial strategic point by both armies.

"If defeated here, we lose the whole Mississippi Valley and probably our cause," Beauregard wrote.[29] However, Corinth proved to be a terrible location for the encampment because of the foul water that was causing thousands to fall ill from typhoid or dysentery.[30] The beleaguered Beauregard did not share any information with the correspondents, and Timrod, who was writing under the pseudonym of "Kappa," had nothing to report in his first article except "rumors, hopes, fears, doubts, arguments and speculations."[31] He was also competing with de Fontaine, who had been in the field from the beginning.[32] Although the two men had become good friends and would later be business associates, they were writing for rival newspapers in the same city.

The Confederates, who abandoned New Orleans on April 24 to avoid its destruction by Federal bombardment, also headed for Corinth where hotels and private homes were already packed with sick and injured soldiers from Shiloh.[33] Timrod reported that the enemy, very strongly reinforced, was at Hamburg, on the west side of the Tennessee River, but he said he had heard too many conflicting opinions to be able to report Beauregard's intentions.

While Kappa was hunting for something to report, he interviewed enough soldiers to conclude that the Confederate victory at Shiloh had been "needlessly lost."

At sunset on Sunday, the enemy, driven from every position, was crowded confusedly together within a space of about a quarter of a mile around the landing;

The town of Corinth, Mississippi, as seen from Beauregard's Headquarters. Illustration from *Harper's Weekly,* June 21, 1862. Courtesy of Rare Books and Special Collections, University of South Carolina Libraries

many of them had stacked or thrown away their arms; the road to the landing was gorged with wagons, cannon and carriages of every description; the transports were upon the other side of the river whither they had gone with what commissary stores could be hastily collected from the general wreck; and the gunboats composed the only force which still retained any power to do harm. Even this power they possessed rather in semblance than in reality.[34]

From the height of the bluffs that lined the banks of the Tennessee, the mortars had to be elevated to throw their shells to a distance of at least two miles. "Within the curve of projection," he wrote, "it was possible to walk with as much safety as in the celebrated passage beneath the Falls of Niagara." Timrod had interviewed Confederates and prisoners who agreed that a single charge was all that was needed at that juncture, and Grant's army would have laid down its arms.[35] He wrote:

The Yankees, like a flock of frightened pigeons, cowering beneath the expected swoop of the hawk, awaited this charge, with an alarm only equaled by their wonder at its delay. It was on the point of being made, when an order from headquarters to recall the pursuit arrested our victorious soldiers, and lost us a triumph which might have been complete.[36]

Timrod speculated that just some small additional effort at Shiloh could have resulted in a triumphant end to the Western campaign. After his lengthy description of mistakes made during the battle, he took the other side of the argument and explained the probable reasons for the decisions that could have led to the order and justified them from a military point of view.

"Many of the Confederate regiments had become scattered beyond all chance of collection; the soldiers were engaged in pillaging the captured camp of the enemy, or were leaving the field in great numbers, laden with booty, and the army was rapidly getting demoralized by its own successes," he wrote. "There was every ground, too, to suppose that [General Don Carlos] Buell was at hand with fresh and superior forces; nor could it be known at headquarters, which were at some distance from the last scene of battle, how small was the additional effort to put a triumphant end to the Western campaign."[37]

At the same time, Timrod was critical of the decision to fight the second day of the battle at Shiloh, saying that the soldiers were exhausted by 12 hours of fighting: "An officer was observed endeavoring to recall a wearied straggler from the field. 'It's no use, Captain,' was the reply. 'I'm just perfectly worn out, and I ain't gwine back.' And go back he did not."[38]

While waiting for the battle at nearby Farmington, Timrod described ominous warnings from a book titled *Armageddon,* published in the 1850s, that claimed the Bible predicted the Civil War.

> The author professes . . . to have discovered a true key for unlocking the mystery of Scripture; and in the application of this key to prophecies already fulfilled he displayed great ingenuity. But what is most extraordinary in the book is a prediction which it contains, and which is affirmed to have been derived from the Bible, to the effect that between the years 1862 and 1865, a great battle is to take place in the Valley of the Mississippi. The parties engaged in this battle are to be "thirteen free States of the South, and some despotic powers of the North": never dreaming at the time when this prediction was arrived at, that the term "despotic power" could by any possibility be applied to the Yankee portion of the United States . . . For the comfort of the superstitious, I must not omit to add that the victory, after three days of terrible fighting, is to be complete on the side of the thirteen states.[39]

Early on the morning of May 3, Timrod and two friends were riding on horses borrowed from General Leonidas Polk's staff along the lines of the entrenchments when they heard spirited gunfire. They rode four miles back to Corinth to exchange their borrowed horses for some inferior horses that would not be needed in the battle. They returned to the battlefield in time to watch the Federals drive the Confederates out of Farmington in what may have been the only battle that Timrod actually witnessed.

> The brigade of General [Henry] Marmaduke, posted on picket duty in front of Farmington, a little place situated some four and a half miles from Corinth, on the road to Eastport, was attacked by a heavy body of Federals, consisting

of infantry, cavalry and two batteries, or twelve pieces of artillery. The advance guard of the enemy was driven back with considerable loss, and our troops held the ground. Later in the afternoon the Federals threw forward their whole force, variously estimated at from four to ten thousand, attacked our brigade in front and on the flanks, and then a comparatively heavy fight ensued.[40]

Timrod reported enemy artillery fire that started late in the afternoon and played incessantly for nearly an hour upon the Confederate lines with shot and shell. "Our own guns were but four in number—known as the Swett Battery, from Vicksburg, Mississippi—and these responded handsomely from the front, and, protected the retreat, which, in view of the immense odds against us, was soon after ordered," he reported. "As we fell back, the enemy advanced, and are now in possession of Farmington."[41]

The firing ceased about six o'clock, with a loss to our men of about twenty killed and one hundred wounded. In two of the regiments, I learn, there was somewhat of a stampede, and my own eyes looked upon the shameful spectacle of men dribbling by two's and three's back to their encampments in the vicinity of Corinth. The force engaged on our side was not above twenty-five hundred; and while there may be an excuse for retreating before superior numbers, there was none in the world for the disgraceful dispersion of eight or nine hundred men by a few round of shot and shell.[42]

While Timrod lambasted the Confederates for falling back, he admitted that "the firing of the enemy is represented to have been excellent" as he anticipated more fighting. "To-morrow may bring with it the dreadful conflict. At farthest, we confidently expect it within three days," he wrote. Meanwhile, "our shields are bright, our lances set, and our breasts are to the foe."[43]

Competent officers generally agree that the battle will be fought chiefly with artillery, the nature of the ground, and the undergrowth preventing an infantry attack in the usual way. In some respects it will be a sort of Fort Donelson affair, without its disastrous finale. There will be fine opportunities for sharp shooters behind trees, and desperate charges at short ranges, but no one on our side fears the result. With Beauregard, Bragg, Price, Breckinridge, Hardee, Polk and Van Dorn, and the brave men awaiting their orders, we believe in our invincibility.[44]

By Sunday, May 4, Timrod reported that the Federals were within a mile and a half of the Confederate entrenchments and that both parties were undoubtedly ready for the final struggle. "But the weather has again become bad, and further operations will probably be suspended until the first clear day," he wrote. "Shakespeare's strange refrain, 'O the rain, it raineth every day,' is quite intelligible in this country."[45] He reported that the town and the surrounding woods were swarming with soldiers. "Large bodies of them are moving to and fro, cannons, wagons and ambulances are encountered in every direction, and of all the materials of war, there seems to be no end."[46]

On May 5, Timrod began worrying about the possibility that instead of fighting, the Yankees would simply attempt to cut off supplies and communications by destroying the rail lines. "They might thus enclose in a circle through which it would be difficult to break. Could they starve us out? Our supplies are large but they are not inexhaustible."[47] An hour later, he was reporting that the Federals had reached the Memphis and Charleston Railway and had burned two bridges on that road, about eight miles east, which cut them off from sawmills that the army had been using and interrupted their connection with Memphis. Like thousands of others in Corinth, Timrod fell ill with fever May 7, but he tried to continue writing as he lay stretched on a pallet . . .

> . . . from which I look up to a roof of naked rafters, tapestried with cobwebs, or down upon a floor, whereon the dust lies to the depth of an eighth of an inch in thickness, and every crevice of which is peopled with whole families of cockroaches, that, on the approach of night, sally forth and promenade my chamber in all directions; with nerves unstrung and quinine humming like a swarm of wasps in my ears; with the vivid recollection of yesterday's chill upon me, and the prospect of another ere I shall be twelve hours older; turning and twisting myself in every way in order that I may write with as little discomfort as possible."[48]

Kappa roused from his quinine-induced confusion to the sound of heavy firing on May 9. A cavalry man stopped outside his window to tell him that the Federals were advancing in line by every road along the entire front and skirmishing was taking place near Confederate entrenchments. He said a Confederate soldier was killed 200 yards away.

> Soon I saw some of the results of the skirmish, in the passage of ambulances containing the wounded, the groans of one or two of whom made the heart sick. Then came the news that our whole army had deployed a mile beyond our fortifications, and were to lay upon their arms all night. About nine o'clock, the deep boom of three of our own heavy 24-pounders—signals doubtless understood by our Generals, but unintelligible to us—seemed to give notice that the opening of the solemn tragedy could not be far off. We all retired to rest under the impression that battle would be joined today.[49]

Still reporting from his bedroom window the next morning, Timrod remained convinced that a Confederate victory was imminent. He reported that a stampede of Yankees had been caused when the Confederate cavalry under General Stonewall Jackson . . .

> . . . got behind the invading army, crossed the Tennessee River, captured two hundred of their troopers and destroyed Paducah, together with stores to the value of

six millions of dollars. It was the silence before the storm. The enemy are retreating towards the river, and the Confederates are in full pursuit. I hear the roll of the musketry and the thunder of the cannon, with an angry impatience at my necessitated inactivity. But I can procure no horse, and must await here the developments of the day . . . To-morrow I hope to announce you a splendid victory.[50]

Although the skirmishing was too far away for Timrod to see, he could hear the echoing artillery and he could see the awful consequences as wounded and dying soldiers were brought back into Corinth. The blood and gore were beginning to weigh heavily on his poet's soul.

> With every engagement that I hear of, there rises before me the vision of some tearful mother or sister; and I see, with the distinctness that rivals the hallucination of the opium-eater, the blanched lips of maidens and wives, over whose future shall henceforth rest—in some cases never to pass away except with life—the somber shadow of death! These are thoughts, however, which tend rather to nerve than to weaken the arm of a lover of one's country. He who most vividly realizes the woes of his land will strike the hardest to end, or at least to avenge them.[51]

Timrod reported that on May 10 a division of 15,000 to 20,000 Federals under General John Pope had occupied the village of Farmington. Confederates fleeing the area overheard Yankee officers say they had achieved their goal of breaking up the Confederates' connections in every quarter except in the direction of Memphis. "Beauregard is even now on the point of retreating, and thither, of all places, it was the wish of the Yankees that Beauregard should go," Timrod wrote.[52]

Timrod wakened to silence on Saturday morning, May 10. "The report is that the Yankees have retired—an officer tells me, though I can scarcely believe it—leaving their tents behind them," he wrote. "Looking through the one window of my domicile, which, partially shaded by a locust tree, gives upon a small yard enclosed by a dilapidated fence, I see nothing more warlike than a half-starved horse grazing upon the scanty grass of the enclosure."[53]

As the wounded and feverish soldiers poured into Corinth, taking all available space, Timrod was forced to give up his room. His friend de Fontaine was also ill, and the two correspondents were sleeping on the ground outside Corinth, finding food wherever they could and coping with chills and fever. Suffering with him, de Fontaine wrote:

> The weather is warm and enervating. Comforts of life are scarce. Hard bread, water, molasses and bacon, very tough and indigestible, constitute our fare; a very hard plank and a pair of blankets serve as a bed; you scrape the dust off your person with a shingle; and after washing in water brought from a mud puddle, dry your face on a pocket handkerchief, then dry it. We wash our own clothes, do our own cooking, and when rations give out, "beg, borrow and steal." About three

times a week we have the chills, with which my friend "Kappa" and myself were wont to shake "like the dry bones in the valley of Jehosophat."[54]

Timrod returned to the encampment on May 23 to find the army in a state of great excitement and expecting its fate to be decided within the next 48 hours, but heavy rains suspended all operations. He told *Mercury* readers that Federal General Henry Wager Halleck was fortifying his troops near the Confederate lines. "It is my opinion that he will not, if he can avoid it, be forced to fight until he feels himself perfectly prepared," Timrod reported. "He is mounting siege guns upon the neighboring hills, and when he is ready, he will probably proceed to batter this position with shell and ball for eight or ten days, killing very few, perhaps, and doing no great harm, but exhausting our men by the ceaseless watchfulness which they will be compelled to assume. That object attained, he will then, I suppose, advance to the general assault."[55]

Timrod interviewed a prisoner who said that the "enemy have lain for the last two nights on their arms, looking for an attack from us" and that large Federal reinforcements were on the way. "I regret to say that desertions from our army are very frequent. Fifty-eight men left a Tennessee regiment in one day," he wrote. "One wretch of this description—a deserter . . . —was captured and shot yesterday morning."[56]

Faced with increasing health problems caused by bad water in Corinth, as well as the prospect of being surrounded by a siege, Beauregard ordered his army to begin the 50-mile trek south on May 29, toward the safety of Tupelo, Mississippi. After calling the evacuation of Corinth the "equivalent to a great victory," Beauregard, who was also in poor health, took an unauthorized leave of absence to recuperate. President Jefferson Davis was so shocked and outraged at the retreat that he replaced Beauregard with General Braxton Bragg.[57]

Timrod was still shaking with chills and fever and no longer able to endure the hardships of camp life, so in June he headed toward the Columbia, South Carolina, home of his sister, Emily.[58] He rode the train south to Mobile, Alabama, where he met James Ryder Randall, author of "Maryland, My Maryland," who wrote later that Timrod's mind was unfit for such rude employment as war correspondent and "dwelt among the stars." [59]

He could hardly travel any distance without losing his valise; and he had that singular disease which makes one blind or nearly so at night. I had to carry him around, at dusk, as if he were sightless. Even in those days he was extremely fragile and a manifest victim of consumption. Yet he strove vigorously to combat with a world for which he was not robustly fitted and whose sordid objects were somewhat contemptible and unworthy."[60]

When Timrod arrived in Columbia, he was in the early stages of tuberculosis, the disease that would take his life soon after the war ended. His friend and

The evacuation of Corinth, Mississippi. Illustration from *Frank Leslie's Illustrated Newspaper*, June 21, 1862

teacher Dr. J. Dickson Bruns wrote: "The story of his camp life would furnish a theme for mirth, if our laughter were not choked by tears. One can scarcely conceive a situation more hopelessly wretched than that of this child, as it were, suddenly flung down into the heart of that stormy retreat, and tossed like straw on the crest of those crimson waves, from which he escaped as by a miracle."[61]

Timrod's old friend Paul Hayne was equally appalled: "Out of the refluent tides of blood, from under the smoke of conflict, and the sickening fumes of slaughter, [Timrod] staggered homeward, half blinded, bewildered, with a dull red mist before his eyes, and a shuddering horror at heart."[62]

By July 1862, Timrod returned to Charleston, saying that he was "advised by my physician not to return to camp, but in the absence of all employment, what else can I do? My mind and body are both in too sickly a state for study, and I cannot consent, while so many better men than myself are enduring the hardships of a campaign, to 'lay on the roses, and feed on the lilies of life.' On the other hand, I cannot help knowing that I could do but little service in the field."[63]

Returning to his military clerkship, but admitting that he was unfit for camp, Timrod applied for a discharge based on ill health.[64] He appeared before the medical examiner on December 3, 1862, and was found to be "incapable of performing the duties of a soldier" because of "Tubercular Phthisis." He was discharged on his birthday, December 8, 1862. The year that he spent on the roll of

Company B of the 20th South Carolina Volunteer Infantry Regiment had been spent "on detached service," for which he received no army pay.[65]

Although his time at the front had been brief and he had witnessed only one skirmish, the stark and mournful memories prompted Timrod to begin writing poetry again. "Charleston" was published in the *Mercury* on December 13, 1862. "The Unknown Dead," which was published in the *Southern Illustrated News* July 4, 1863, began:

> *The rain is plashing on my sill,*
> *But all the winds of Heaven are still;*
> *And so it falls with that dull sound*
> *Which thrills us in the church-yard ground,*
> *When the first spadeful drops like lead*
> *Upon the coffin of the dead . . .*[66]

Timrod enlisted again in July 1863, immediately after the Federal attack on Fort Morris, South Carolina, but a lung hemorrhage on that same day, which was caused by his tuberculosis, ended his military career. He became an assistant editor on the *Mercury* in August 1863, although the pay was still not enough for him to marry Katie, and he did not consider the work suited to his "tastes and habits."[67] His job was to collect facts and reduce them to publishable form, but he said the job was not conducive to writing. "The nervous state in which I am kept by the necessity of being always on the *qui vive* for the last items is utterly incompatible with poetical achievement."[68]

Timrod's battlefront friend, de Fontaine, returned to Columbia, South Carolina, in January 1864 to buy the *Daily South Carolinian* through a partnership with Theodore Wagner and his brother-in-law, George W. Trenholm, who were cotton exporters and shippers in Charleston. Trenholm was believed to be the wealthiest man in the South on the eve of the Civil War and had accumulated even more wealth during the war running the Union blockade. At one time during the war, he owned as many as 50 ships.[69]

Since Timrod had no money to invest in the newspaper, "it is presumed that his 'partnership' meant only that he should receive a portion of the profits in lieu of a regular stipend."[70] In spite of Wagner's generosity, Timrod complained. "Wagner, in making conditions in my behalf, rated me at the usual rate which poets go for," Timrod wrote, "and I was subordinate in pecuniary interest and therefore in practical authority not only to the senior editor (de Fontaine), but to the head printer of the journal (Julian A. Selby, an experienced printer and businessman)."[71]

Timrod's first editorial appeared on January 13, 1864. He preferred writing editorials to reporting, and his position with the *Daily Carolinian* finally provided him with enough money to marry Katie, who was living in Columbia with her brother George and his wife, Emily, who was Timrod's sister.[72] De Fontaine, writing on the occasion of Timrod's marriage on February 16, 1864, described Timrod in the time leading up to his wedding as a "nervous, restless, jerky, abstracted individual who was wont to upset our exchanges, read papers for hours upside down, write editorials and tear them up."[73]

Simms visited Timrod in May and wrote to Hayne: "I saw Timrod and was glad to find him in better health and spirits than he has had for years before." Simms credited this to temperance and employment and to the influence of Timrod's new wife.[74] Simms said he was becoming a fine prose writer and work on a daily newspaper would modify his tendency toward "the essayical." Timrod wrote dozens of editorials for the *South Carolinian*, but three are considered to be his "editorial best":[75] his romantic tribute to the Confederate raider "Alabama," which sank in the English Channel after "circumnavigating the globe" and destroying numerous Northern ships; "Spring's Lessons," written after Appomattox; and "Names of the Months Phonetically Expressive," his effort to find characteristics of each month in the sound of the month's name.[76]

Of more importance to Timrod, his benefactors Wagner and Trenholm offered to publish an illustrated collection of his poetry in England.[77] However, the project was abandoned because of difficulties getting the copy to England and because Trenholm left to become the second Confederate secretary of the treasury.[78] Wagner, who was known as a generous man "who wore his purse on his sleeve," gave the poet $1,000,"[79] which Timrod deposited in a bank until it gradually became worthless.[80]

Although he was deeply disappointed that the book was not published, Timrod wrote two more poems by September 1864 and dozens of editorials for the *Carolinian*.[81] He was highly offended when a friend asked if he occupied the editorial chair when de Fontaine was at the battlefront.

> I have occupied that chair since it passed into the hands of Messrs. de Fontaine and Co. With the exception of about a dozen furnished by Mr. de Fontaine during my absence or temporary illness, I have written every leader and leading editorial that has appeared in the paper since January of this year (1864). . . . I mention this not from any vanity—you will acquit me of that—but because it is of some pecuniary importance to me that the amount of labor which I have given to the Carolinian should be generally known.[82]

The energetic and hardworking Simms said Timrod's "labour is not exhaustive, nor very serious. He has only to prepare a couple of dwarf essays, making a single column, and the pleasant public is satisfied. These he does so well, that they have reason to be so. Briefly, our friend is in a fair way to fatten, and be happy, though his muse becomes costive and complains of his *mesalliances*."[83]

Timrod's wife, Katie, gave birth to a son, Willie, on Christmas Eve 1864. It was one of the happiest moments of his life, but Timrod continued to dream of publishing his book of poetry. While waiting for a train in January 1865, he spoke with an old friend, Captain William Courtenay, who had also been a correspondent for the *Mercury*. Courtenay promised to publish Timrod's poetry someday, if he could.[84]

Timrod's feeble but enthusiastic joy was short-lived. De Fontaine returned to South Carolina in January to warn Columbians of General William T. Sherman's inevitable approach and to hurriedly ship most of the newspaper material and equipment to Chester, South Carolina. De Fontaine left on February 14 on the last train out of Columbia to Charlotte, North Carolina, probably with his wife and newborn daughter, as Sherman's troops advanced on the city.

Timrod and Selby kept enough printing material to issue a "thumb sheet" two or three times a day for three days—"not a pleasant occupation, with shells dropping in the neighborhood of the building," Selby said. The *South Carolinian* newspaper office was destroyed with the rest of Columbia on February 17, 1865.[85]

When the Federal army took over in Columbia, Timrod's job disappeared and, in addition, as "one whose vigorous, patriotic editorials had made him obnoxious to Federal vengeance," he was forced to hide, probably in Forest Cottage near Florence.[86] When the Federal troops left, he "rejoined his anxious womankind, to behold, in common with thousands of others, such a scene of desolation as mortal eyes have seldom dwelt upon."[87]

While Selby was struggling to start a new newspaper, the *Phoenix*, de Fontaine published several issues of the *Daily Carolinian* in Charlotte, before moving to Chester, where he resumed publication on April 2, 1865,[88] the same day that Richmond was evacuated by the Confederate government.[89] The U.S. flag was raised at Fort Sumter on Friday, April 14, 1865, four years to the day after it was lowered by Major Robert Anderson. The next day, the flag was lowered to half mast when President Lincoln was assassinated.[90]

Timrod hoped to become one of the editors when de Fontaine re-established the *Carolinian*,[91] but while he was waiting, he wrote a letter in July 1865 to Northern poet Richard Henry Stoddard in an effort to find a job in New York.

> . . . I have been reduced by the destruction of this town to the most abject poverty. Literature is an unattainable and undesired luxury. I have tried to open a school, but can get no pupils, as nobody is rich enough to pay the tuition fees. All are alike ruined . . . I have a family to support, and they must starve. With what reception would a Southerner meet in New York? Could I hope to get employment there in any capacity whatever? Hack writer of a newspaper, editor of the poet's corner of some third rate journal, grocer's clerk—nothing would come amiss to me that would put bread into the mouths and a roof over the heads of those whom I love best in the world.[92]

Nothing was available in New York. Still without a job and living in poverty in South Carolina, Timrod wrote to his friend Hayne about his miserable condition.

You ask me to tell you my story for the last year. I can embody it all in a few words—beggary, starvation, death, bitter grief, utter want of hope. But I'll be a little more particular that you may know where I stand. You know, I suppose, that the Sherman raid destroyed my business. Since that time I have been residing with my sister Mrs. Goodwin. Both my sister and myself are completely impoverished. We have lived for a long time and are still living on the gradual sale of furniture and plate. We have eaten two silver pitchers, one or two dozen forks, several sofas, innumerable chairs and a bedstead.[93]

Timrod's anguish peaked on October 23, 1865, when his son, Willie, died, prompting an outpouring of mournful poetry, including "Our Willie" and "A Mother's Wail."[94] De Fontaine had started publishing the *Daily Carolinian* in Charleston by July 1865. The masthead on November 17, 1865, listed de Fontaine as editor and publisher, with William Gilmore Simms and Henry Timrod as associate editors. Timrod said de Fontaine had made "a grave mistake in carrying his paper to Charleston" because it "was languishing and will die" under the competition from that city's long-established newspaper.[95]

Timrod's job with the *Carolinian* didn't require him to move to Charleston; he was to write his editorials in Columbia and forward them by mail. Since he would have less supervision of the paper, he was to receive only ten dollars a week.[96] "I am to write them in Columbia and forward them by mail," he wrote. "Necessity compelled me to accept the offer—I have hacked for him for four months, and have not yet received one month's pay. The truth is, Fontaine *can't* pay."[97]

De Fontaine left in March for a trip to New York to visit friends at the *New York Herald* where he had worked before the war. Simms complained that Timrod did nothing to help him during the five weeks that de Fontaine was in the North.[98] Even though Simms was complaining about Timrod's laziness, he located the remaining 20 copies of Timrod's book and sold them at high prices to friends in Charleston who still had money. He gave Timrod a little money at a time because, as he said later, Timrod "suffers from the sin of impecuniosity."[99] The money did nothing to lift Timrod's spirits. Still in despair, he said, "I not only don't write verse now, but I feel perfectly indifferent to the fate of what I have written. I would consign ever(y) line I ever wrote to oblivion for one hundred dollars in hand. Simms had to urge me several times before I would take the trouble to send him my war lyrics."[100]

When de Fontaine returned from New York, he was planning to convert the *South Carolinian* from a morning newspaper to an afternoon newspaper in Charleston and also to re-establish it in Columbia as the *Columbia Carolinian*.[101] While waiting for de Fontaine, Timrod told Hayne he wasn't writing any poetry; however, he wrote "Ode," which is considered to be one of his best poems and was sung at the Confederate Memorial exercises in Magnolia Cemetery in Charleston June 16, 1866.

Sleep sweetly in your humble graves,
Sleep, martyrs of a fallen cause;
Though yet no marble column craves
The pilgrim here to pause.

In seeds of laurel in the earth,
The garlands of your fame are sown;
And, somewhere, waiting for its birth,
The shaft is in the stone!

Meanwhile, your sisters for the years
Which hold in trust your storied tombs
Bring all they now can give you—tears,
And these memorial blooms.

Small tributes! But your shades will smile
As proudly on those wreaths today,
As when some cannon-moulded pile
Shall overlook this Bay.

Stoop, angels, hither from the skies!
There is no holier spot of ground
Than where defeated valor lies,
By mourning beauty crowned.[102]

Timrod's financial connection with the *South Carolinian* ended that year. He submitted poems to Northern magazines and made an unsuccessful attempt to open a girls' school in the fall.[103] He found a little temporary work in November 1866 as a clerk in the office of Governor James L. Orr,[104] but he was unemployed again by April 1867 and hoping and waiting for de Fontaine to re-establish his newspaper in Columbia.[105] "Fontaine is about to establish a paper in Columbia, and that I am to be one of its editors, with a prospect of rather better pay and more work than I have hither to get," he wrote. "We hope to issue the first number next Monday. The paper is to be called the 'Columbia Carolinian.' The 'South Carolinian' will be continued in Charleston as an evening paper."[106]

He was still waiting when he had a severe hemorrhage of the lungs on September 13, 1867, apparently while he was reading proof sheets of his 1862 poems.[107] In a letter to Hayne on September 16, Timrod wrote, "Yesterday, I had another and still more copious hemorrhage. It occurred in the street—the blood came in jets from my mouth—you might have tracked me home in crimson."[108] The bloodstained proofsheets are preserved by the Charleston Library Society.

Emily was called to her brother's room September 20, 1867, where she found that Timrod had had "a much more violent hemorrhage than any of the preceding ones. The blood was pouring from his mouth with such violence as to

The house in Columbia, South Carolina, where Timrod died in 1867. Courtesy of South Caroliniana Library, University of South Carolina, Columbia

threaten strangulation."[109] Timrod lingered for two weeks before dying on October 7, 1867. He was not quite 38 years old. His sister Emily said he "died at the hour he years ago predicted. The whisper: 'He is gone' went forth as day 'purpled in the zenith.'"[110]

He was buried beside his son in the cemetery of Trinity Church (now Trinity Cathedral) in Columbia. Timrod's pallbearers were men who had helped him in various ways, including de Fontaine and General Wade Hampton.[111]

De Fontaine closed the *Daily Carolinian* and returned to New York in November 1867 to become a financial editor for the *New York Herald*, but he returned to Columbia in 1895 to establish the War Record Publishing Company and to start a magazine devoted to the Civil War. He wrote an article for the *Charleston Sunday News* on June 28, 1896, in which he quoted Courtenay as saying that Longfellow, after reading aloud "the beautiful Invocation to Peace," closed the book of Timrod's poems with the remark, "I do not wonder . . . that Tennyson exclaimed, 'The man who wrote those lines deserves to be called the poet laureate of the south!'"

De Fontaine resumed the effort to publish a volume of Timrod's poems, but died in December 1896, before it was published. After de Fontaine's death, Courtenay began a crusade to publish Timrod's poetry and honor his memory. He established a Timrod Memorial Association in Newry in Oconee County, South Carolina, and persuaded Houghton Mifflin to publish 4,000 copies of Timrod's poetry in late 1899.[112] He spent the profits on a bronze bust of Timrod that was erected in Washington Square in Charleston on May 1, 1901, and on a monument at his gravesite at Trinity Church.[113] Courtenay also presented a portrait of Timrod to the City of Columbia for the Timrod (now Richland County) Library in a ceremony on May 24, 1905. At the ceremony, Colonel Henry T. Thompson said that "Henry W. Longfellow, the poet laureate of America, said, 'The day will come when Timrod's poems will have a place in every cultivated home in the United States . . .'"[114] The South Carolina General Assembly passed a resolution in 1911 making the verses of his poem, "Carolina," the lyrics of the official state anthem.

Timrod's widow, Catherine Lloyd, who had remarried after his death and moved to the north, died on February 20, 1913, at Ridgefield Park, New Jersey, as the widow of Alfred Lloyd of England. She was the "Katie" of his poems, the subject of "A Year's Courtship," and the mother of Willie, their only child. It was the anguish of a mother's heart upon the death of her child that inspired Timrod to write "Our Willie" and "A Mother's Wail."

Timrod's poetry is included in most historical anthologies of American poetry, and he is regarded as a significant—although secondary figure—in 19th century American literature. In an ironic twist, Bob Dylan borrowed extensively from Timrod's poetry for the lyrics in his 2006 best selling album *Modern Times* without giving the poet any credit for the words that had literally been covered with his life's blood nearly a century and a half ago.

Florida

Union-occupied Fort Pickens, which is shown as it guarded the entrance to Pensacola (Florida) Bay in early 1861, was key to the use of the sprawling Pensacola Navy Yard. Confederate forces failed to capture the fort, and it remained in Federal hands throughout the Civil War. This picture first appeared in *Harper's Weekly* February 23, 1861 before appearing in the *New Orleans Daily Delta* April 10, 1861. Courtesy of Rare Books and Special Collections, University of South Carolina Libraries

FRONTIER FLORIDA HAD BEEN ADMITTED TO THE UNION ONLY 16 YEARS earlier, but enthusiastically seceded and went on a war footing. When lawmakers met in Tallahassee to endorse secession on January 10, 1861, the booming cannonading of Fort Sumter was but three months distant, and the tiny population of Florida seethed with secession fervor.

Nearly all the population of 140,000 residents—the smallest of any state—was concentrated in the northern third of Florida. More than 60,000 were African-Americans, most of them slaves working in an agriculture-based economy. Pockets of Union sympathizers existed, but Governor Madison Stark and Governor-elect John Milton were staunch supporters of secession. The delegates' vote to secede was an overwhelming 62 to 7, and Florida joined South

Carolina and Mississippi in the new Confederacy. Mississippi, Florida, and Alabama seceded within two days of one another.

As war approached, the focus of North and South was on coastal forts, including Pensacola, a deepwater port in far west Florida that contained major Federal installations, the Pensacola Navy Yard, and giant Fort Pickens guarding the entrance to Pensacola Bay. As Confederates began a major military buildup in Pensacola in early 1861, Fort Pickens was held by a few Federal soldiers. Both sides agreed to a truce: Federal authorities agreed not to reinforce the fort from the sea if Confederates would not attack the fort. Confederate General Braxton Bragg was assigned to the area of Pensacola and Mobile to bolster the Confederates, as a large press contingent from outside the state gathered in Pensacola, anticipating the war would begin there.

However, the April 12 attack on Fort Sumter by Confederate cannon ended speculation about where war would begin. As Bragg plotted the capture of Fort Pickens, *Pensacola Observer* reporter Lawrence H. Mathews disrupted his plans by publishing a story on that fateful day, April 12, that detailed Bragg's intentions. Federal forces reinforced the huge fort the same night, and thwarted the general's plans.

An angry Bragg ordered Mathews sent to Montgomery, Alabama, for trial, but Mathews was released soon after and continued writing for his newspaper. His was the first military arrest of a civilian in the war, and there would be thousands of others.

More than 25 weekly newspapers were publishing in Pensacola and other communities in north and central Florida as the war began. Editors busied themselves with news of their areas, leaving the collection of information from the war zones to outside reporters or newspaper exchanges.

Early in the war, the Federal navy bottled up the ports operating in Florida and gradually took possession of the coastline, leaving the interior to refugees from the coast. Florida became a breadbasket for the Confederacy, shipping corn, beef, and lumber north to the Confederate states under siege. In 1862, the *Savannah Republican* predicted that Florida and Georgia would harvest "a superabundant crop of corn" and suggested that it be fed to hogs, cattle, and sheep to help the war effort. By war's end, the Union controlled nearly all of the state and the press was in the hands of outsiders.

9

L.H. Mathews: General Bragg's Nemesis

Henry H. Schulte

As the North and South lurched toward war in early 1861, Pensacola, Florida, was in turmoil. Correspondents for Southern newspapers had gathered in anticipation of the first shots of the Civil War being fired on Union-held Fort Pickens, which guarded the entrance to Pensacola Bay. As Confederate General Braxton Bragg plotted the capture of the lightly defended fort on April 12, a mild-mannered correspondent for the *Pensacola Observer* disrupted his plans.

That day the *Observer* published a story detailing the "rumor" that sand batteries were being erected on Santa Rosa Island, the site of Fort Pickens, in preparation for a Confederate attack on the fort. The reporter was Lawrence H. Mathews, who wrote under the pen name "Nemo." He would be arrested by Bragg, sent to the Confederate capital in Montgomery for trial, and become the first of thousands of Confederate civilian political prisoners arrested by Southern military authorities.[1]

Born in Ireland on September 26, 1830, Mathews had worked for the *Observer* for five years. He had come to the United States in 1848[2] and moved south to Pensacola before the war.[3] For the *Observer* and as a correspondent for other Southern newspapers, Mathews had been reporting the events surrounding the stalemate in Pensacola between a small contingent of Union troops occupying Fort Pickens and hundreds of Confederate volunteers arriving daily to bolster Bragg's forces.

A fragile truce existed between the opposing groups. In late 1860, Fort Pickens was occupied only by a caretaker and his family. But on January 10, 1861, Union Lieutenant Adam Slemmer, occupying the barracks at nearby Fort Barrancas, decided to move his small contingent of men to the fort on the island, believing that he could better defend Union property there.[4]

With war threatening, Fort Pickens and the nearby navy yard facing Pensacola Bay were key pieces on the chessboard as the government in Washington and the Confederate government in Montgomery sought to secure port facilities

General Braxton Bragg. Courtesy South Caroliniana
Library, University of South Carolina

in Pensacola and elsewhere. Both sides realized the importance of the fort and
the navy yard to their plans. However, Confederate authorities faced a dilemma:
if they attempted to capture the fort, it would precipitate war. But if they waited
and Union warships reinforced the fort, it would remain under Union control
and use of Pensacola Bay and the navy yard would be lost.[5]

Political discussions designed to resolve the ongoing stalemates at both
Charleston and Pensacola resulted in the Fort Pickens Truce. Union officials
agreed not to expand defenses at the massive fort with troops offshore in Union
vessels, and the Confederates agreed they would not attack Fort Pickens. The
Confederates already occupied the navy yard and two other small forts fronting
the bay—Barrancas and McRee.[6]

After Abraham Lincoln was inaugurated on March 4, 1861, affairs at Forts
Sumter and Pickens assumed a more critical status. Confederate President Jefferson Davis assigned General Bragg to command all troops in and around Pensacola, and Bragg took over on March 11. His orders were to assess the situation
in Pensacola and relay his findings to the Confederate War Department. Bragg

Fort Pickens as seen across Pensacola Bay, Florida. *Harpers Weekly,* March 9, 1861. Courtesy of Rare Books and Special Collections, University of South Carolina Libraries

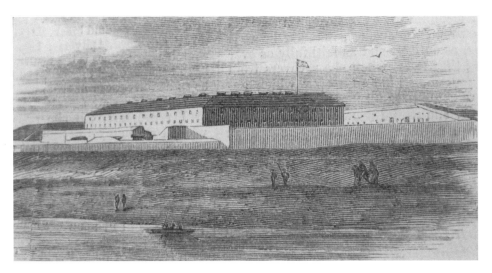

Fort Barrancas, which was across the narrow entrance to Pensacola Bay, supported massive Fort Pickens. *Harper's Weekly,* December 14, 1861. Courtesy of Rare Books and Special Collections, University of South Carolina Libraries

was uncertain that his troops could capture Fort Pickens without substantial cost to his forces.

"Fort Pickens cannot be taken without a regular siege, and (we) have no means to carry it on," Bragg wrote his wife. "Unless attacked, no fighting could take place for a long time, as we are totally unprepared for anything of the sort. Things are in a most deplorable condition." He described his troops as "raw volunteers . . . without discipline."[7]

The Confederate batteries opposite Fort Pickens. *Harper's Weekly,* April 20, 1861.
Courtesy of Rare Books and Special Collections, University of South Carolina
Libraries

Almost no copies of the articles that Mathews wrote for the *Observer* have
survived, but he was also writing letters to the *New Orleans Daily Delta* that
were published several days later under the initial "M." He reported on March
28 that Bragg's troops continued to construct sand batteries on the beachfront
on Santa Rosa Island adjacent to Fort Pickens. "General Bragg and his officers
under his command are untiring in their efforts to place every thing in good
order," Mathews wrote in the *Daily Delta* March 28.

> Here we are with the guns of Fort Pickens bristling to our view on the opposite
> side of the bay, and the "stars and stripes" floating to the breeze from the new flag-
> staff erected on the south-west corner of the building . . . War is in everybody's
> mouth, and people begin to look on it quite philosophically. Many who left here
> weeks ago have returned and resumed business. The number of troops at present
> here is nearly two thousand (later to rise to more than 6,000), the finest body of
> men that could be assembled anywhere in the world.[8]

Mathews was accurate about Fort Pickens' guns "bristling." At that time
the fort contained 250 big guns, although only a few were ever fired. He reported that "nothing is talked of from morning until night save the taking of
Fort Pickens." Readers of the *Observer* and the *Daily Delta* were being told by
Mathews that all the appearances of activity around Pensacola denoted war,
and soon "if the Northern Confederacy does not give up the forts in the states
which have seceded."[9]

Meanwhile, Federal officials were busy making plans. A dispatch in the *Daily
Delta* from Washington on April 4 reported major activity in the army and navy

General Bragg's camp as seen from Fort Pickens. *Harper's Weekly,* June 15, 1861. Courtesy of Rare Books and Special Collections, University of South Carolina Libraries

departments. "All the available vessels now in port are ordered to prepare immediately for sea," the *Daily Delta* correspondent reported. "The government is evidently preparing for war." He also told readers that the Federal government "is resolved on sending reinforcements to Fort Pickens."[10]

But while Washington was moving toward resolution of the Fort Pickens stalemate in its favor, reports from the Confederate capital at Montgomery noted "assurance that Fort Pickens can easily be conquered." Nemo/Mathews also assured his readers on April 5, "The news yesterday that Fort Pickens being about to be reinforced alarmed no one in this neighborhood."[11]

While Bragg hesitated, Mathews published in his April 12 report in the *Observer* that the general was about to take action. While Bragg stewed over Mathew's story that tipped off his plans, the reporter, not realizing that he was about to be arrested, reported on April 13 that the fort had been reinforced during the night from Union ships lying offshore.

> Last night, about 8 o'clock, seven guns were fired from the ships outside, and immediately afterwards lights were displayed around Fort Pickens, and the supposition is they are sending reinforcements from the fleet to the fort. The lights were kept burning all night. About fifteen hundred (Confederate) men were under arms in the Navy Yard all night, for what object is a mystery to us who are in the neighborhood.[12]

Mathews reported on April 13 "definite intelligence of the reinforcement of Fort Pickens." One of Bragg's spies reported that a company of troops "supposed to be artillerists, eighty in number, and a quantity of provisions and munitions were landed." Fort Pickens now had men to man the big guns. Actually,

50 artillerists and 30 sailors comprised the Federal force that moved into the fort.[13] Mathews also wrote in an April 13 report to the *Daily Delta* that the Confederate solution would be to take the fort by force, anticipating an oncoming struggle for the fort.

> The people here anticipate fighting in three or four days. Everything now indicates the solution to our difficulties by a resort to arms. Women and children are getting out of the way. Even our lady friends from Alabama have left until the affray is over.[14]

New York Tribune correspondent Albert Richardson, traveling incognito in the South, reported that "an officer in Bragg's camp told him that all preparations for capturing Fort Pickens were made, that the United States sentinels on duty on a certain night had been bribed, but that Nemo's intimation of the intended attack frustrated it, a copy of his letter having found its way into the (Union) post and forewarned and forearmed the commander."[15]

By April 14, Bragg had decided to arrest Mathews and bring him to his command post. The stalemate was being resolved, with heavily armed Union troops guarding the fort, up to 2,000, according to some accounts. The *Charleston Mercury*, whose correspondent "Troup" was writing from Montgomery, also recorded Mathews' arrest.

"A man by the name of Mathews, the correspondent of the *Pensacola Observer*, under the signature of 'Nemo,' was arrested yesterday, and sent under guard to this city. The charge against him is furnishing information to the enemy," Troup reported. "It was the intention of General Bragg to make an attack on Fort Pickens on Friday night, according to this correspondent, and the information, after being published, was sent to the fort. Lieut. Slemmer at once signaled the fleet and during the day one hundred men were landed on Santa Rosa Island, together with a large quantity of shot. The plans of General Bragg were frustrated."[16]

Another *Mercury* correspondent, "La Palma," writing from Pensacola, also detailed the Union's reinforcement of Fort Pickens and Mathews' detainment. "This correspondent, whose nom de plume was Nemo, was yesterday arrested and sent away by order of Gen. Bragg. His name is Mathews, and he is a schoolmaster of this place. He is a trifling fellow, and is suspected of being a spy for the enemy."[17] Mathews described his arrest in a letter of complaint he wrote to Confederate Secretary of War Leroy Pope Walker.

> Not one of my friends were allowed to speak to me there. I was not allowed to go to my house to get clothes, or money. I was ruthlessly torn from my motherless boy, five years old, carried to this city (Montgomery) a distance two hundred miles from my home and business. I arrived here on Monday afternoon, unconscious of any criminal act on my part.[18]

Federal ships reinforced Fort Pickens on April 16, 1861. *Harper's Weekly,* May 25, 1861. Courtesy of Rare Books and Special Collections, University of South Carolina Libraries

Mathews wrote Walker that he had been taken to Bragg on April 14, the same day that Fort Sumter surrendered to Confederate forces in Charleston. The *Observer* correspondent detailed his exchange with the general.

"Mr. Mathews, are you the correspondent of the Pensacola Observer?"

I truthfully replied that I was the correspondent of the Pensacola Observer, under the signature of Nemo, and of the New Orleans Delta, under the signature of M.

"Have you written the correspondence for the inside of the Observer of Friday the 12th last?"

I answered that I did.

"By what authority did you assert that the Confederate States were to raise sand batteries on the island of Santa Rosa?"

I replied that such was the general rumor for two days on the streets.

"You do not say it was a rumor, but the inference can be drawn therefrom is that I had confided the same to you."

I said, General Bragg, I think no such inference can be drawn as I never claimed any such prerogative, nor have I sought to find out your plans.

"You are a traitor, Sir," was his assertion.

This was too much and I earnestly expounded. General Bragg, whoever calls me traitor speaks falsely of me. I would shed my last drop of blood for the South.

"I place you under arrest, Sir."[19]

Bragg told Mathews' captors, "Allow him no communications whatsoever." In his letter to Walker, Mathews wrote that he was transferred to Montgomery for trial under sealed orders from Bragg. The correspondent was put up at the Exchange Hotel where he wrote his letter of complaint. Mathews asked Walker to inform him of the charges against him and to identify his accusers.

I am prepared for trial, be my fate what it may. I fear nothing but the terrible suspense that racks me, from my not knowing what I am impeached with. I have been a secessionist when there was no honor attached to that name. I am no less than one now that an attempt has been made to dishonor me. It is my political faith. I have lived by it and I am prepared to die by it.[20]

Meanwhile, press reports of Mathews' arrest were disrupting other journalists' plans. *New York Tribune* correspondent Richardson became increasingly concerned for his safety while visiting Mobile, Alabama. Northern reporters were no longer welcome in the South, especially those who represented the *Tribune,* and Richardson posed as a well-to-do merchant from New Mexico. He had planned to visit Pensacola, believing that war might erupt there over the Fort Pickens controversy.[21]

"In Mobile, the leading hotel was crowded with guests, including army soldiers en route for Bragg's army," Richardson wrote. "It was my own design to leave for Pensacola that evening, and look at the possible scene of early hostilities." However, Richardson decided to bypass Pensacola, and when he arrived in Montgomery, there were more stories of spy arrests, including detainment of Mathews. As Richardson noted in his autobiography published at war's end in 1865:

The morning newspapers, at our breakfast table, detailed two interesting facts. First, that "Jasper," the Charleston correspondent of the New York Times, had been seized and imprisoned in the Palmetto City. Second, that Gen. Bragg had arrested and sent under guard to Montgomery, "as a prisoner of war" the correspondent of the Pensacola Observer. This journalist was an enthusiastic Secessionist, but had been guilty of some indiscretion in publishing facts touching the strengths and designs of the Rebel army. His signature was "Nemo," and he now bade fair to be No One, indeed, for some time to come.[22]

Unknown to Richardson, Mathews was being held under guard somewhere on the floors above him in the Montgomery hotel. The *Tribune* correspondent was grateful for his decision to reject the visit to Pensacola and head north to safety. He wrote: "I now began to entertain sentiments of profound gratitude toward the young officer at Mobile who kept me from going to Fort Pickens. I continued my journey due North."[23]

One of the Confederate camps at Warrington, near Pensacola. *Harper's Weekly,* December 14, 1861. Courtesy of Rare Books and Special Collections, University of South Carolina Libraries

Richardson, who himself would be captured as a spy in the siege of Vicksburg and spend months in Confederate prisons, continued to hear tales of spy arrests as he continued his journey to Charleston. He hoped to remain for several days, but "the public frenzy had grown so uncontrollable that every stranger was subjected to espionage. One could hardly pick up a newspaper without seeing, or stand for ten minutes in a public place without hearing of the arrest of some northerner charged with being a spy."[24]

Correspondent Troup told his *Charleston Mercury* readers that he was uncertain of Mathews' future.

> What will be done with this prisoner I am unable to say, but it does seem as if such important information ought to have been known only to the commander himself, until time to commence the attack. Mathews is now under examination at the War Department.[25]

However, Mathews' case was heard quickly in Montgomery, with the Cabinet deciding that he did not commit treason, merely an indiscretion in reporting Bragg's plans. His arrest, quick trial, and subsequent release were widely reported by most of the South's newspapers. Considering the speed with which the issue was resolved, most of the South's press, including one of the papers he wrote for, the *Montgomery Advertiser,* reported both arrest and release in one story.

RELEASE OF "NEMO" of the Pensacola Observer. "Nemo" alias Mathews, the enterprising Warrington correspondent of the Pensacola Observer, was arrested by order of Gen. Bragg and brought to this city Monday on the charge of having communicated intelligence through one of his letters which gave the enemy notice of preparation for an attack on Fort Pickens. Mr. Mathews was released from custody, the Cabinet doubtless regarding his act as one of indiscretion. Mr. M is considered, by most who know him best, as an enthusiastic Southerner, and in his haste to furnish agreeable news for a local newspaper perhaps never thought of its injurious effect. Those who have read "Nemo's" letters extensively republished by the press, will certainly be slow to suspect him of any hostile intent to the Confederate States.[26]

While Mathews was universally portrayed as a reporter caught up in a sensitive censorship issue, historian Mark E. Neely, Jr., paints him in a different light—as a civilian political prisoner held by military authority. Neely cited Mathews' arrest as the first of thousands that ensnared many innocent civilians.

Thus, the Confederate army's first arrest of a citizen occurred on 14 April 1861, even before President Abraham Lincoln called out troops to suppress the rebellion. There would never be a day during the Civil War when Confederate military prisons did not contain political prisoners.[27]

Neely studied the prisoners and the system that created them through the records of 4,108 civilian prisoners held by military authority in the Confederacy. Although there were many more civilians held in prison, only those who could be identified by name through five years of research were included. Neely's conclusion:

Knowledge of the existence of thousands of political prisoners now reverses our basic understanding of the Confederate cause. Instead of protecting the southern rights and liberty to which politicians had extravagantly pledged their society before the war, the Confederate government curtailed many civil liberties and imprisoned troublesome citizens. Moreover, many white Confederate citizens submitted docilely to being treated as only slaves could have been treated in the antebellum South. Some here and there protested the system, but it operated throughout the existence of the Confederacy.[28]

Mathews was one of the fortunate civilians who managed to extricate himself from military custody and resume his career as a reporter and editor. His arrest and acquittal as a spy continued to occupy correspondents' reports as they pursued the story. More than a month later, *Memphis Appeal* correspondent "Nagle" interviewed Mathews and assured readers that Mathews was a strong partisan for the South.

I had the pleasure of making the acquaintance of Mr. L.H. Mathews whom you will remember was the correspondent "Nemo" of the Pensacola Observer, whose arrest, acquittal and so forth, was the subject of much comment over the land. I found him a quiet, gentlemanly man, whose whole heart is interested in the success of the Southern cause. In 1848, he was one of the friends and companions of John Mitchel, and exiled with the rest of the Irish patriots. Like most of intelligent Irishmen, he is of stout built and of medium height with heavy whiskers, a frank open countenance and mild blueish-grey eyes. Like every true Irishman, too, he is a strong partisan for the land of his adoption, the birthplace of his Louisiana wife, and the dear home of his children.[29]

Nagle told his readers that Mathews was the active editor of the *Observer* and "as careful of the rights and interests of our beloved South as you or I can be." Mathews never otherwise mentioned a Louisiana wife or family, and the Federal Census of 1860 lists only Mathews and a five-year-old boy living in his Warrington house near Pensacola. Mathews mentioned a "motherless boy" only in his letter to Secretary of War Walker.[30]

By the time Mathews was released and returned to Pensacola, Bragg's opportunity to capture Fort Pickens without major troops and arms had slipped away, and Union apprehension about the fate of the fort was alleviated. Despite a year of occasional clashes between Union and Confederate forces, the North held Fort Pickens throughout the war, frustrating Confederate efforts to make use of the sprawling Pensacola navy yard.

Mathews resumed his work for the *Observer*, covering the telegraphic news from the war zones and writing about local events and troop movements in and out of the area. Union vessels continued to patrol offshore, ensuring that Confederate forces would have no lack of problems if they attacked the fort. The *Observer* editor was effective in coming up with patriotic themes, taking material from the exchanges that showed how much Southerners were contributing to the war effort. In one story, Mathews reported that four widows living in the South had sent 19 sons to fight for their country. He wrote about a widow in Virginia who was doing even better than that: she sent seven sons into the service.[31]

There were signs that the owner of the *Observer* was struggling financially, as Mathews pleaded with subscribers to pay their 5 cents a copy for the newspaper. In a note at the top of a page, he wrote: "We would say to our friends, in a spirit of kindness, that it takes money to get up a daily newspaper—more than many of them are aware. It is therefore impossible for us to give copies of our paper gratuitously to any one."[32] Mathews was probably under some financial pressure himself, for he announced in the *Observer* on June 9 that he had reopened a school on the north side of town "prepared to admit a limited number of pupils. He will be well pleased to see his pupils again." The Federal census of 1860 had listed Mathews as a teacher.

Writing about the Pensacola Guards, the Confederate army unit Mathews would join in early 1862, he was effusive in his praise. He lauded their bravery and the affection that Pensacola citizens had for the soldiers. "Capt. (Alexander H.) Knight is a gentleman in every sense of the word," he wrote, "a kind commander who will attend to their wants with the kindness of a parent. He is well versed in military tactics." With this kind of praise, Mathews would have been well positioned to earn the confidence of Knight and his men when he enlisted the following year. Mathews listed 12 of the unit's officers and their rank and concluded his story with this message: "May they be as much the terror of our countries enemies as they are beloved by their acquaintances, is our most sincere prayer."[33]

Chatty goings-on in Pensacola aside, Mathews never lost sight of what he considered the need to bolster the Confederate side with rhetoric against President Lincoln and the North. While reporting the Confederate victory at Fairfax Courthouse, he wrote: "This is glorious news. It gladdens our heart to hear such brilliant achievements." Most of Mathews' reports included diatribes against the Union invaders of Virginia. Under a headline, "Invaders Routed With Loss of Life," he concluded the story:

> But we digress, our purpose is to announce the glad tidings to our readers that the miserable hirelings, who, Hessian-like, hire themselves out to slaughter their fellow-men in the South, have been again routed by our own brave sons, whose chivalry has become a house-hold word. And thus it must be the end of the chapter. The God of battles blesses our patriotic efforts, and victory must ever perch on our victorious banners.[34]

Although Bragg remained in Pensacola through the rest of 1861, there was little military activity, other than both sides shoring up their defenses. There was a flurry of interest on May 14 when President Jefferson Davis, accompanied by his wife, Varina Howell Davis, and Confederate Secretary of the Navy Stephen R. Mallory, arrived by train from Montgomery to inspect the troops and harbor defenses. Historian George Pearce suggests that during Davis' visit to Pensacola, he decided the cost of attacking Fort Pickens was too high and he concluded that Bragg's troops could be used to better advantage elsewhere. After Davis departed, Secretary of War Walker wrote to inquire whether Bragg was willing to give up some troops to the Virginia theater of war. After a series of exchanges, Bragg dispatched 2,500 troops.

The long quiet exploded the night of September 2, 1861, when Federal troops from Fort Pickens set out in small boats and set afire the massive Confederate navy dry dock that had been grounded in Pensacola Bay. The dry dock burned to the waterline. [35]

The Federals followed up by sending 100 men in small boats out into the bay the night of September 13 to disable the *Judah*, a ship being outfitted as a

Federals burn the giant Pensacola dry dock off Fort Pickens late in 1861. *Harper's Weekly*, October 12, 1861. Courtesy of Rare Books and Special Collections, University of South Carolina Libraries

Confederate privateer at the navy yard dock. The ship was set afire, and three men were lost on each side in the ensuing struggle, which represented the first lives lost in Florida in the Civil War.[35]

In retaliation, Bragg planned an intricate assault on Santa Rosa Island in the early hours of October 9, sending 1,000 volunteers to the island and burning a Federal camp. Federal troops from Fort Pickens responded, and Bragg's volunteers lost 18 men. Following the attack, Federal forces planned another retaliation on November 22, a bombardment that lasted two days. Neither side was able to deliver a decisive blow, continuing the yearlong stalemate.[36]

Confederate authorities in Richmond were impressed with Bragg's handling of military affairs in the Mobile and Pensacola areas and offered him command of the Trans-Mississippi Department on December 27, 1861.[37] Bragg begged off, protesting that Mobile's security was at risk. However, after Confederate defeats along the Tennessee–Kentucky line, Secretary of War Judah P. Benjamin ordered Bragg to that area on February 18, 1862: "The decision has been made, and the president desires that you proceed as promptly as possible to withdraw your forces from Pensacola and Mobile, and hasten to the defense of the Tennessee line." No troops were to remain in Pensacola, but continuing defense would be provided to Mobile.[38]

By February 27, Bragg had his staff "working day and night" to abandon Pensacola. Confederate troops were ordered to leave nothing the enemy could use, "to burn all from Fort McRee to the Mobile road." Bragg departed for Corinth, Mississippi, on February 28 with 10,000 troops.[39]

The day after Bragg left, Mathews enlisted in the army for three years and was assigned to Company K, 1st Regiment, Florida Infantry, as a private on March 1, 1862. Mathews' war records show he was paid a bounty for enlisting.[40] Transportation foul-ups caused lengthy delays in Confederate evacuation plans through March and April, but sawmills, wharves, lumber, cotton, and other items useful to the Yankees were destroyed. Conditions in the Pensacola area deteriorated rapidly as the Confederates moved toward their final days, counting down to May 9.[41]

On that day, the last troops began to evacuate and by midnight "every combustible thing from Fort McRee to the navy yard was enveloped in a sheet of flames." Pensacola dwellings were spared, and the Union took command on May 12. As it became obvious that Confederate forces were abandoning Pensacola, her citizens had gradually dispersed into Alabama. Pensacola's Board of Aldermen set up a government-in-exile in Greenville, Alabama, and the region steeled itself to Federal occupation.[42] For the remainder of the war, Fort Pickens served as a prison for political prisoners—captured Confederates and Federal troops requiring disciplinary confinement.[43]

By July 16, Mathews' army status had changed and he was assigned as a hospital steward. The surgeon in Pensacola at the time was Dr. John Scott, an Englishman who was commissioned surgeon in 1861 and remained in Pensacola until its evacuation in 1862, when he was sent to Montgomery. Since Mathews quickly found his niche as a steward, it is possible that Scott had a hand in it.[44]

The steward's job apparently agreed with Mathews, because he spent the rest of the war in that role. In both the Union and Confederate armies, hospital stewards were important figures. They ranked above the first sergeant in a company and, while members of the medical corps, were on the regimental commander's staff. The steward of a hospital, wrote Confederate nurse Phoebe Pember, "cannot exactly define what his duties are, the difficulty being to find out what they are not."[45] As a steward, Mathews was expected to oversee the administration of the field hospital for a regiment (only one steward to a regiment), supervision of other hospital attendants, purchasing and caring for hospital supplies, keeping hospital records, and supervising food services. Mathews was also authorized to apply dressings and bandages, extract teeth, apply cups and leeches, and administer injections. Hospital stewards were not issued firearms, although some carried their own for protection of patients in the field and the hospital drug chest.

Payroll records show Mathews earned $66 for three months. By November 1862, he was working as a steward in the area of Shelbyville, attached to Bragg's

Army of Tennessee. Bragg, who was Mathews' old nemesis in Pensacola, wrote an order on July 9, 1863, in Chattanooga relieving him of duty and ordering him to rejoin his regiment in DeSoto, Mississippi. Mathews' payroll records indicate he was attached to Walker's Hospital there until October 31, 1863.[46] At that time, the secretary of war appointed Mathews to serve at the R&D Hospital in Montgomery. By order of the secretary, however, he was reassigned in October 1864 as steward at the W&D Hospital in Montgomery. Mathews was listed in the Return of Stewards in Montgomery on December 1, 1864, by C.J. Clark, surgeon in charge at the hospital.[47]

After the war, the entrepreneurial Mathews probably could have succeeded as a teacher, in medicine, or in newspaper work. He chose journalism to the delight—and occasional consternation—of thousands of Alabama newspaper readers over a period of 25 years.

By 1870, Mathews was in Birmingham, Alabama, then only a village that was incorporated in 1871. He purchased the only ongoing newspaper, the *Birmingham Sun*, from the first owner/editor, Robert H. Henley, who was also the first mayor of Birmingham. With a wealthy co-owner, Thomas A. McLaughlin, Mathews changed the name of the paper to the *Independent* and published it for several years.[48] Blount County neighbor James W. Palmer later put the initial date of publication at 1871.

> Dear Brother Mathews—Will you allow me space in your newspaper for a reminiscence that might be of interest to some of your readers? I say brother because I have been a close reader of your paper since you started the Jefferson Independent in Birmingham in 1871, and I consider we have been co-workers in the line of reform.[49]

In purchasing the *Sun* from Mayor Henley, Mathews inherited the original Washington hand press that powered the *Jones Valley Times*, the first newspaper in the region in 1845. That paper had lived only two years, and a series of publications followed it, each inheriting the original Washington hand press. By the time Henley sold the *Sun* to Mathews, the press had changed hands six times. Historian George Cruikshank called the old press "the mother of the later publications."[50] By 1874, Mathews was listed as editor of the *Independent*, along with co-editor McLaughlin. Mathews was also listed as editor of the *Tri-Weekly Independent* on May 19, 1874.[51]

Mathews had a capacity for stirring up controversy, and other newspapers recorded his activities, including the *Gadsden Times*: "Col. James R. Powell assaulted the editor of the *Birmingham Independent* with a bludgeon the other day." The reason for the assault was not disclosed, but it would not be the last time that Mathews was involved in a physical altercation.[52]

Not long afterward, Mathews decided that Blount County was a more promising newspaper venue than Birmingham and moved to Blount Springs where he established the *Blount Springs News*. In August 1877, he was elected justice of the peace.

Mathews' first years in Blount County were involved in discussions and votes about changing the county seat. In 1877, an effort to move the county seat from Blountsville to Blount Springs failed, and Mathews moved his operations to Blountsville, renaming the newspaper the *Blount County News*. Another unsuccessful effort to move the county seat in 1883 led to prolonged editorial haggling among editors in the competing towns.[53]

On one occasion, Mathews' editorials so infuriated a rival Blount Springs editor that the man, John R. Perkins, editor of the *Blount Springs Advance*, resorted to physical violence early in 1883. The *Guntersville Democrat* reported the incident.

> Assault Upon the Press. Blount County holds an election next Monday to decide whether or not the county site shall be removed from Blountsville. The question of removal is exciting a good deal of interest, and several caustic articles have appeared in the News, which opposes removal, and in the Advance, favoring removal. John R. Perkins, one of the commissioners, not content with hurling defiance and abuse upon the News, and all others who oppose removal, through the columns of the Advance, a few days ago actually assaulted and beat the editor of the News. In the last issue of the News, its editor denounces this conduct of Perkins in not very complimentary language, and claims that it is nothing less than an assault upon the freedom of the press.[54]

The editor of the *Democrat* wrote that Mathews was a man "well advanced in years," while Perkins was a young man. "We hope that Mr. Perkins will be bound over to keep the peace towards all editors, and especially the editor of the *News*." The pertinent issues of Mathews' newspaper have not survived, but he is recorded as arming himself against future attacks. The *Democrat* reported:

> We visited the office of the Blount County News and found both Editors in, as we expected, and hard at work. The senior, who styles himself as "The Wild Irishman," gave us as is his custom a warm reception and formally extended us the "liberty of his office" and the use of his exchanges.[55]

The *Democrat* editor was escorted through Mathews' art gallery, "even extending the courtesy so far as to give us a peep into his arsenal, where we found an armory for defense against a second assault on the press."

By 1889, Blount County voters had successfully moved the county seat from Blountsville to the new town of Oneonta, and Mathews moved his newspaper once again, keeping up with the location of the county seat. His final change: he merged the *News* with the *Dispatch* to become the *Blount County News and Dispatch*. Under a headline, "Consolidated," in the new publication on August 11, 1887, the new owners, Mathews, John H. Ketchum, and A.D. Howell, wrote that the politics and principles "are unchanged and unchangeable. It shall be the sincere desire of the *News* and *Dispatch* to advance the cause of truth, virtue and justice; to promote the interest of Blount and its people, and to endeavor to make this great Country what God created it to be, the garden spot of Alabama."[56]

Mathews used every opportunity to promote the interests and growth of Oneonta, seeing the town as one that might develop into another Birmingham. But Blount County resources were simply shipped south to Birmingham, fueling that city's growth.[57]

Alabama readers and editors knew Mathews as the Wild Irishman of Blount County, a role he relished and nurtured. He was forever a staunch Democrat, and the columns of the *News-Dispatch* were filled with his partisan viewpoints, often racist. The editor usually chose sides on politically sensitive issues of the time, which angered citizens of Blount County as well as fellow editors in towns around the state. It was common for country editors to snipe at one another, but Mathews did so with such wit and humor that he earned the respect of fellow editors. Said the *Southern Aegis* in 1889:

> Long May Bro. Mathews Live. It is interesting to observe how Brother Mathews gives some editors a black eye for calling him old, and sticks to his youth, like a flea in the oleaginous oozings of a skinned pine pole. There is a tubful of encouragement in Brother Mathews' assertion that he is just in the prime of his manhood, as he leads some of us up the hill of time ten years or more. Long may our brother of the quill live to be a conspicuous lighthouse to those juveniles who think they are so much wiser than their daddies.[58]

Mathews' writing prowess grew with the years, and he never countenanced upstart newspapers in his territory. He did what he could to hasten their demise, and when they folded, he gleefully and sarcastically chronicled their death, as he did on the passing of an upstart, the *Mineral Age.*

> In Memoriam. Died at Blountsville, Ala. On Oct. 2, 1885, in the hope of a glorious resurrection at Warrior, Ala., Miss Minner Alage, the adopted daughter of L.R. Hanna, Esq., a pretended philanthropist of this county. It never had any legitimate parentage, and was begotten in iniquity, and died of slow starvation, a dose that had been prepared for its neighbor, the Blount County News. The ways of God are inscrutable, and hypocrisy today meets its true desserts as it did in the days of the Savior. The puny bantling was born at Chepultepec, Blount County, and was of very doubtful parentage, yet it was a sensitive thing, and told its adopted parent three weeks before its death that it didn't want to live, for the following reasons, to wit: The County officers paid no attention to it! The Probate Judge snubbed it; The Sheriff only noticed it three or four times; The Circuit Clerk never tipped his hat to it; and the Register in Chancery totally ignored it. Peace to its ashes![59]

While most of his years in the newspaper business were spent in Blount County, Mathews often returned to Birmingham to visit friends. He celebrated his birthday there in 1892. One of the attendees, the editor of the *Birmingham Age-Herald*, extolled his old friend in print on October 2, 1892.

> Father Mathews—Editor L.H. Mathews of the Oneonta News-Dispatch was in Birmingham the other day. He came down to celebrate his 63d birthday, the dear old man, and there wasn't one of us who wasn't heartily glad to see him. His head is white, but his soul is young, and all the men who toil upon the press of Alabama love him. He laughs, and is jolly; he tells the truth and is honest, and there is not a man in all the world who loves him not. He is probably the best loved of all the men who make the newspapers of Alabama, this noble old Father Mathews. May his shadow never grow less![60]

Ever the businessman, Mathews wrote a letter of gratitude during the 1895 holidays to all the readers who wished him well during a four-month illness. "To the many neighbors and friends who were so attentive and kind to us during our long illness, we return a thousand heartfelt thanks." But he couldn't resist adding a footnote: "Now a word to our delinquent subscribers, we need money, and respectfully ask you to pay up your indebtedness. Come up like good and true citizens and cancel these debts. We only ask what is ours by right. Wishing all a merry Christmas and happy New Year!"[61]

Mathews grew increasingly frail but continued publishing the *News-Dispatch*, as he searched for a buyer. He died on December 12, 1896, but the newspaper continued publishing until its demise on February 4, 1904. Although a Louisiana wife, a family, and a five-year-old "motherless child" were mentioned during his early years in Pensacola, Mathews' obituary listed no survivors. The *Southern Democrat* noted that Mathews was buried in an unmarked grave in Oneonta's Old Liberty Cemetery. "The exact location of his rascally bones has now been lost to time."[62] Dozens of Alabama newspaper editors noted Mathews' death. The *Montgomery Journal* wrote on January 7, 1897: "He was a true man, firm in purpose, but gentle in nature, and was a true patriot who loved his adopted country, as only a true Irish man knows how to love the home of the brave and the land of the free." Four months after he died, the *Birmingham State Herald* labeled him in its April 10, 1897, edition as "one of the most versatile writers on the press, and a cleverer and more sociable gentleman never lived."

"He spurned deceit," Blockton, Alabama, reader J.L. Whitten wrote. "He was incapable of treachery. He scorned demagoguery and chicanery. He had opinions and convictions, and died not hesitating to give them. The town of Oneonta, the county of Blount and the State of Alabama are poorer because his voice and pen are silent, and his noble heart has ceased to beat."[63]

Only the nearby *Southern Democrat* damned him with faint praise. Its editor wrote in the *News-Dispatch* on January 7, 1897: "While Mr. Mathews had some faults as all of us do, he was a successful newspaper man. He will be greatly missed by the people of Blount and the state press."

Except for his Irish heritage, Mathews said little about his past. In an 1889 column, Mathews reminisced about his adopted land, his love for it, and his sadness at Ireland's plight of that time. It is interesting to note that this sentence contained 85 words.

> Our dear old grandmother, of blessed memory, lived to the ripe old age of 106 years, and that too in down trodden, rack-rented, persecuted Ireland; while we, for the past forty years have basked in the sunshine of freedom, and for the past thirteen years have inhaled the mountain air, imbibed the health restoring waters, and occasionally in accordance with the scriptural injunction of the Apostle Paul to Timothy, we have taken a little something else to be found only in these mountain fastnesses.[64]

There is no record that Mathews ever wrote about his prewar years as a Florida newspaperman or his service as a hospital steward in the Confederate army. His obituary in the *Birmingham Age-Herald* on December 13, 1896, bestowed on him the title of Colonel and reported he had been in the newspaper business in Alabama for half a century, "longer than anyone else." His editor friends were giving him the benefit of the doubt since Mathews/Nemo could actually claim no more than about 25 years as an Alabama editor, nor could he claim the title of colonel.

Alabama

The war in North Alabama—Union troops burn the bridge over the Tennessee River at Decatur. *Harper's Weekly,* August 16, 1862. Courtesy of Rare Books and Special Collections, University of South Carolina Libraries

Aɫᴀʙᴀᴍᴀ, ᴛʜᴇ ꜰᴏᴜʀᴛʜ ꜱᴛᴀᴛᴇ ᴛᴏ ꜱᴇᴄᴇᴅᴇ ꜰʀᴏᴍ ᴛʜᴇ Uɴɪᴏɴ, ᴡᴀꜱ ᴛʜᴇ birthplace of the Southern Confederacy. Delegates from the seven seceded states gathered in Montgomery in February 1861 to organize the Confederate States of America and to draft a new constitution. Even before hostilities erupted at Fort Sumter on April 12, 1861, Alabama was preparing for war.

The new Confederate government relocated within months to Richmond, Virginia, where it remained until war's end, but Alabama was diligent in its support of the Southern rebellion. More than 120,000 Alabamans served in the Confederate forces, constituting virtually all of the population capable of bearing arms.

Alabama contributed six important correspondents to Confederate journalism: two lawyers, two politicians, a priest, and a surgeon.

Lawyer Samuel C. Reid would appear near the top of any listing of the best Confederate reporters. He had written four books before joining the army at the start of the war. At 42, he was one of the oldest of the South's war correspondents. Reid began his newspaper career at the *New Orleans Picayune,* while practicing law. When Union forces captured New Orleans, Reid lost his home base but continued writing for six other newspapers.

John Forsyth, editor of the *Mobile Advertiser and Register,* was a correspondent for a brief time but was politically influential throughout his lifetime. Forsyth owned the *Columbus* (Georgia) *Times* before returning to Mobile to resume his career as a journalist.

John H. Linebaugh, a former priest, wrote under the pseudonym "Ashante" for the *Memphis Daily Appeal,* a newspaper that moved so often to escape Federal seizure that it became known as the *Moving Appeal.* While Linebaugh was writing for the *Appeal,* when he could locate it, he offended General Braxton Bragg, as did other Southern correspondents. The general jailed Linebaugh for writing about troop movements before the battle but also possibly for suggesting that Bragg was unwilling to engage Federal forces, an idea that fanned the general's easily fanned anger.

Lawyer William W. Screws enlisted in the Confederate army when war erupted and, with no journalistic training, began writing letters home to the *Montgomery Advertiser.* He quickly turned into a reporter. He was yet another journalist who was arrested by General Bragg. Released after 10 days, Screws was captured late in the war by Union troops near Petersburg, Virginia. After the war, Screws became editor of the *Advertiser.*

William G. Shepardson, a surgeon who also reported during the entire war, incurred the wrath of Generals Bragg and Joseph Johnston. After leaving Virginia to escape arrest, Shepardson was captured at the Battle of Roanoke in North Carolina. A prolific and adventurous reporter, he was transferred to the navy in 1863 to serve aboard the notorious cruiser *Tallahassee,* one of the most effective Confederate raiders. During an 11-day period in late 1864, the *Tallahassee* captured or sank 33 Union ships.

Henry Hotze learned the newspaper trade from *Mobile Advertiser and Register* editor Forsyth, but his greatest contributions to the Confederacy were his public relations skills. The Confederacy sent him to England to influence the British to join the war on the South's side, but the war ended with England still in a neutral role.

10

John Forsyth:
Love and Hate in the Strife-Torn South

Erika J. Pribanic-Smith

Romanticized stories of the Civil War depict genteel gentle-men riding off bravely to defend the Southern cause, their hearts full of love for their region and disdain for the Northern aggressors who would take away the cherished institution of slavery. In the case of Colonel John Forsyth, by all accounts, this quixotic picture is no myth. A close colleague called him "highly cultured," "the soul of honor," and a gentleman "of the fast vanishing old school."[1]

His own editorials for the *Mobile Advertiser and Register* portray a love of the South and belief in its ways of life as strong as his hatred of those who sought to destroy them. Based on these ideals, Forsyth did do battle, not with a musket but with words as his weapon.

Although Forsyth's tenure as a Civil War correspondent amounted to mere weeks, he enjoyed a long career as a newspaper editor and an even longer in-volvement in the South's political processes. In those capacities, he became a figurehead for Southern democracy and frequently found himself at the center of local and national controversy. A supporter of slavery and staunch partisan, Forsyth played a monumental role in shaping the ideology that created sec-tional strife and eventually led to the battles he covered.

At the time of Forsyth's birth on October 31, 1812, his family was well known. His grandfather Robert, a Scottish immigrant, served as a major in the Conti-nental army during the Revolutionary War and so impressed George Washing-ton that the general appointed him marshal of the District of Georgia after he became president. Robert Forsyth's untimely death at the hands of a Methodist minister prompted Congress to allocate funds for the care of his family.[2]

Robert's second son was Forsyth's father, John, who married Clara Meigs, daughter of the first president of what is now the University of Georgia. John, Jr., was their first son and the fourth of their eight children. Born in Augusta, Georgia, the year his father was elected to the U.S. House of Representatives,

John Forsyth. Photograph from the Library of
Congress

Forsyth spent much of his youth in the nation's capital, except for the two years
his father served as minister to Spain. The elder Forsyth served a term as governor of Georgia in the late 1820s, but spent most of his political career in Washington as a congressman and as secretary of state under Presidents Andrew
Jackson and Martin Van Buren.[3]

Boarding school took Forsyth from Washington City to Amherst, Massachusetts, in 1828. Four years later, he graduated from Princeton as valedictorian
and returned to his birthplace of Augusta, where he studied law with Colonel
Henry Cumming. He also became something of a social butterfly, popular with
both men and women in Augusta's prominent circles. A longtime friend proclaimed that "in a time when courtesy and polish were characteristics of Southern gentlemen, Forsyth's manner toward women had a deference and delicacy
that was peculiarly his own." A much sought-after bachelor, he chose as his wife
South Carolina native Margaret Hull. The couple had two children: Charles and
John III.[4]

Forsyth was admitted to the bar in 1834 in Columbus, Georgia, where he
remained for one year before moving to Mobile, Alabama. President Jackson
appointed him U.S. attorney for the Southern District of Alabama, presumably

in part out of the president's respect for Forsyth's father. He served in that position for two years.[5]

In 1837, Forsyth and partner Epapheas Kibby purchased the *Mobile Commercial Register and Patriot* from Thaddeus Sanford and Samuel F. Wilson. A partisan editor, Forsyth remained loyal to the Democrats to a fault, engaging in numerous political battles with Whig papers such as the *Mobile Advertiser and Chronicle*. When he first took the helm, the *Register* enjoyed the benefits of serving the dominant party, but economic panic galvanized the Whig Party, which blamed the nation's financial downturn on policies begun by President Andrew Jackson and continued by Van Buren. Democrats such as Forsyth blamed the banking system. As the Whig Party took political power, the *Register* became the opposition paper—a position that Forsyth relished.[6]

However, family problems forced him to relinquish the position quickly. After his father died in October 1841, Forsyth returned the paper to its former owners and moved back to Columbus, Georgia, to settle the family estate, a task that took several years. Meanwhile, Forsyth maintained his newspaper connections in Columbus. He purchased the *Columbus Times*, a Democratic weekly organ, and was appointed by President James Polk as the local postmaster. During his 12 years as a partisan editor in Georgia, he suffered the same sort of political and personal attacks from Columbus' Whig journals as he had from opposition newspapers in Mobile.

It was at the *Columbus Times* that Forsyth got his first taste of war correspondence. As first lieutenant and adjutant in the 1st Georgia Regiment for five months during the Mexican War, he sent numerous accounts of his life as a soldier to his hometown newspaper.[7]

Territory gained from the Mexican War caused political strife as proslavery and antislavery forces debated what to do with the land. One suggestion, called the Wilmot Proviso, undid the Jacksonian party structure. Forsyth and his *Times* at first remained faithful to the Democratic Party, but after the election of President Zachary Taylor, Forsyth took a stand for Southern rights, sought to organize a new party, and openly began to advocate secession.

The Compromise of 1850, a series of laws that attempted to resolve the territorial and slavery issues that arose from the war with Mexico, crystallized these sentiments, and Forsyth became an Ultraist in the Southern Rights Party. Although he took tremendous criticism for his stance, the staff at the *Register* later attributed the "series of brilliant and much-quoted articles" in which he took "strong grounds against the so called Clayton Compromise" for garnering Forsyth "wide and new repute as a writer on national politics." Nonetheless, after the Southern Rights Party rejoined the Unionist Democrats in 1852, Forsyth retired from the *Times* and returned to Mobile with plans to build a lumber mill.[8]

Disaster intervened in Forsyth's project, however, when fire destroyed the newly constructed mill just before it opened. Forsyth joined with John Y.

Thompson and Jacob Harris to purchase his old *Register* in September 1854. By June of 1859, he was sole owner and editor. He would remain at the helm, in title if not in person, until his death 18 years later.[9]

Forsyth's faith had been restored in the Democratic Party, and he remained a devoted supporter for the rest of his life, although events of the coming decades dealt the party several hard blows. The first of these was the 1854 Kansas-Nebraska Act, which forged an ideological bond between Forsyth and Stephen A. Douglas. Douglas designed the legislation that created two new territories and allowed settlers to decide whether to allow slavery within their borders. Opponents denounced the act as a concession to the slavery proponents in the South.

The debate that followed from 1854 to 1856 split the nation into four parties: the Democrats, Black Republicans, Free Soil Know-Nothings, and Southern Know-Nothings. The latter two parties, which arose because of a tremendous influx of immigrants, drew Forsyth's ire for dividing and weakening the South "in its vital struggle with the powers of Abolitionism." Immediately following Forsyth's death, the *New York Herald* credited the "Know-Nothing excitement" for making Forsyth's name familiar to the country as a leader of his Democratic cohorts.[10]

During the heated 1856 election, Forsyth pushed for a national Democratic ticket, both as editor of the *Register* and as a delegate to the national convention. He considered the "Democratic faith" to be "an ambrotype of the great charter of 1787" and professed a lifelong adherence to the party because of its "noble struggle . . .to maintain the great doctrines of State equality, equal rights and personal, religious and civil liberty." Forsyth considered that effort to be of utmost importance during the crisis that the nation then faced.

> Once more is this embodiment of the spirit of revolutionary courage, and of the wisdom of the Fathers of the Republic in 1787, to be appealed to, to save the legacy of constitutional freedom from the touch of sectional hatred and religious fanaticism. If the Democratic party does not stand firm in this crisis—if it does not bravely plant its flag on the impregnable ramparts of the constitution as a rallying point to all the lovers of Republican institutions, . . . there is no other ark of refuge and safety from the murderous elements of hostility and hatred railed against it.[11]

While extolling the virtues of his beloved Democrats, Forsyth's editorials during the campaign warned against the evils of the Black Republicans. He declared the clash between the two parties to be "no common war," because of the opponent's savage temper and mercilessness.

> It is not a mere Knightly tournament, which, though sometimes dangerous, is yet the manifestation of the chivalrous virtues of courage, generosity, and courtesy—it is not a duel between sections on a point of punctilious honor; but it is internecine war—war to the knife and to the hilt, which is breathed in this ukase of the Abolition Autocrat. The Roman battle cry has gone forth against us, and

we of the South are summoned to our defensive arms and walls with "*delenda est Carthago*" ringing in our ears.[12]

Forsyth's editorials reflected not only a political partisanship but a violently sectional one, deeply rooted in his support of slavery. His sectionalism became even more apparent following the national convention in June 1856, which he termed "the most important political assemblage in the annals of American History since the Convention that debated and framed the Constitution."

Forsyth rejoiced that the entire Democratic Party had sided with the South in adopting a platform based on the doctrine of state sovereignty, by extension protecting the "indisputable *State Right*" of domestic slavery. He encouraged all Southern men to return the favor, joining in support of the Democrats to ensure that the Constitution, "which guarantees Southern safety," would remain the law of the land. Otherwise, he feared "the powers of the Federal Government shall pass into the hands of the Abolitionists and be wielded for Southern destruction."[13]

Forsyth's fierce sectional diatribes proved eerily prophetic. He proclaimed that the certain Democratic victory in the Presidential contest would "speak to the deluded agitators of the North a language not to be mistaken."

> It will warn them of the danger they incur by trampling upon us as an adversary they now vainly imagine too weak to resist. It will admonish them that they have no hope of "conquering by dividing" us, and that nothing short of revolution, bloodshed and civil war can accomplish the wicked purpose they have in view.[14]

After James Buchanan's nomination, lame-duck President Franklin Pierce rewarded Forsyth's party support by appointing him minister to Mexico, and Forsyth departed for his new post in July 1856. Forsyth proved an ineffective diplomat during his two-year tenure, wrapping Pierce's directives into treaties that accomplished his own political scheme. Both Pierce and Buchanan rejected the treaties he negotiated, and Forsyth objected to the treaties Buchanan drafted instead, undermining the efforts of two Buchanan supporters who came to Mexico to negotiate transit rights on the president's behalf. A Mexican revolution complicated matters during the stalemate between Forsyth and his own government. His actions were widely criticized in newspapers, in Mexico and the United States, and he ultimately resigned.[15]

Despite his falling out with Buchanan, Forsyth remained loyal to the Democratic Party as the 1860 election approached. His support of Douglas separated Forsyth from his Southern brethren, who adopted a firm state rights stance, but Forsyth wished to keep the Democratic Party intact to avoid turning the nation over to the Black Republicans. After he failed to garner a seat at the Democratic Convention in Charleston, he worked behind the scenes in an effort to secure Douglas' nomination. The controversial walkout of the Alabama contingent, led by fire-eater William Lowndes Yancey, offered Forsyth an opportunity, as he led a new—and possibly illegal—state delegation at the Baltimore Convention. Although his subversive actions helped secure Douglas' nomination, they also resulted in abuses of Forsyth and the *Register*, particularly by the *Montgomery Advertiser*, Yancey's journal.[16]

Partly at Forsyth's urging, Douglas became the first presidential candidate to campaign actively on his own behalf. He made two tours of the South, the last of which landed him in Mobile on election day. Douglas awaited results in the *Register* office, with Forsyth at his side. Upon Lincoln's election, Forsyth joined the call for secession, which earned him the label of traitor by Northern Douglas men who recommended a moderate approach. But Forsyth believed that with Douglas' defeat "the cause of the Union was lost." Forsyth told Douglas that "a quiet submission to Lincoln's administration would be taken and treated by the North as an unconditional surrender for all times to come" and that it was better to fight a long and bloody war than remain in the Union and be stripped of slave property. He argued that submission would result in the unthinkable prospect of having millions of free blacks turned loose among them.[17]

Alabama became the fourth state to secede. The Confederate Congress soon authorized a peace commission composed of Forsyth, Martin Crawford of Georgia, and Alfred Roman of Louisiana to negotiate friendly relations with the United States. Although the men traveled to Washington, their attempts at negotiations occurred largely by letter with Secretary of State William Seward, who apparently duped them by strategically delaying his response to the group's demand for recognition and agreeing to evacuate Fort Sumter, only to renege later. Ultimately, the commission failed to obtain the government's recognition of the Confederacy and evacuation of Southern forts. Forsyth declared that war was "inevitable."[18]

Soon after the war began, Mobile's city aldermen appointed Forsyth mayor, a position he held for six months. He also helped organize a ceremonial militia unit in Mobile, which promoted him to colonel. Both of Forsyth's sons enlisted in the Confederate Army, but John III was discharged because of poor health. Charles fought in many of the most famous Civil War battles and eventually reached the rank of colonel, but his career ended in scandal after his regiment retreated in panic and confusion from a battle at Cedar Creek, Virginia, in October 1863.[19]

Forsyth's brief stint as a Civil War correspondent occurred during the last quarter of 1862, when he joined General Braxton Bragg on his Kentucky campaign. At best, Bragg's relationship with the press was strained. He became known as the "Sherman of the Confederacy," thanks to the number of correspondents arrested at his command. In fact, the Confederate army's first citizen arrest was Lawrence H. Mathews, a correspondent for the *Pensacola Observer*, whom Bragg arrested on April 14, 1861. Mathews was charged with treason for publishing information that may have tipped off the enemy to the general's

Forsyth arrived in Kentucky just before the Battle of Perryville. *Harper's Weekly,*
November 1, 1862. Courtesy of Rare Books and Special Collections, University of
South Carolina Libraries

plans to capture Fort Pickens. John Linebaugh of the *Memphis Appeal* and William Wallace Screws of the *Montgomery Advertiser* suffered similar fates later
in the war, and the *Mobile Advertiser and Register*'s correspondent Samuel C.
Reid fled Tullahoma, Tennessee, under advisement that Bragg planned to arrest
him. Generally, Bragg strictly forbade newspapermen from entering his ranks
and frequently withheld information from correspondents, leading to a great
deal of criticism of the general.[20]

Recognizing the need for positive coverage to improve his image, Bragg summoned Forsyth, a close friend, to join him in Kentucky shortly before the Battle
of Perryville. Forsyth began writing from the field for the *Register* on October 14, 1862. In a September 27, 1862, letter from Bragg's headquarters at Bardstown, Forsyth described in great detail his adventurous journey.

We set out with wagons, tents and provisions, to camp out on the way, and
should all have been (but some were not) armed to guard against Bushwhackers
in Tennessee and "State Guards" in Kentucky. We soon discovered that the
Bushwhackers (Unionists of East Tennessee) were not to be dreaded. They were
themselves hiding from the Confederates in the mountains, and at their homes

only women and children were to be found . . . My powers of endurance were put
to the test before we got through. We followed the track of the army over Wal-
dron's Ride, up to the Sequatchie Valley and across the Cumberland Mountains
to Pikesville, wondering how General Bragg ever got his 1,800 wagons and tired
troops over these rough declivities.[21]

Forsyth reported that "nothing of special interest occurred" until the group
neared Glasgow, around which they detoured after a courier informed them
that Federal cavalry had raided the town. Although his party "took every pre-
caution" on their march, a company of the 7th Regiment, Pennsylvania Cavalry,
"dashed upon [them] at full speed." Forsyth lamented that his "unwilling visit
to the Federal camp" cost him a servant, two horses, weapons, and clothing. He
listed his "companions in misfortune" as "Major W.J. Wickes of Memphis, of
Gen. William Joseph Hardee's staff; Captain Kennedy, of Alabama; Dr. Sanders,
formerly of our State and now of Memphis; Dr. Mix, of La.; and Mr. Sheppard,
of Memphis."[22]

Forsyth was quickly released on parole, but after his ordeal, the fiery *Register* editor proclaimed himself "quite ready and willing to get even with the
Yankees when the first opportunity arises." Apparently prejudiced against all
things Northern, he complained that although he'd been remounted on a horse
captured from Union troops, he feared he'd find no equal to the confiscated
black mare he bought in Atlanta.[23]

Forsyth also used this correspondence to describe his plans for establishing a
newspaper office to travel with the army through Kentucky and publish "Bragg's
Army Register."

> You know that a man once inoculated with types, never gets over the fever. I am
> a living example of the truth of that principle—I have been all my life trying to
> get away from types, and yet they pursue me like Banquo's ghost. I thought I had
> escaped them in the army. But alas for human plans and expectations; I have just
> organized a corps of printers out of the army and obtained the presses, types and
> transportation for a newspaper office to travel with the army to go to work wher-
> ever it pitches its tents. The soldiers want news and Kentucky, plunged in Yankee
> darkness, needs enlightenment.[24]

In a second letter in that same issue, dated September 28, Forsyth demonstrated his admiration for Bragg and faith in the Confederate army. He described
the positions of Confederate troops throughout Kentucky: those under Generals
Kirby Smith at Lexington, Humphrey Marshall at Paris, and Carter Stevenson
at Danville. He placed Bragg's troops 39 miles from Louisville, claiming that
a single division of Bragg's army could occupy the city whenever the general
pleased. Bragg's march to Bardstown, according to Forsyth, would be "recorded
as one of the most remarkable in history." With "a fortitude and cheerfulness

above all praise," the troops had covered 300 miles of rough terrain, driving Union General Don Carlos Buell out of Tennessee. Forsyth assumed that General Sterling Price had done his part to clear all of Tennessee of Union rule and predicted that Bragg was strong enough to maintain Kentucky.[25]

Forsyth identified two potential problems, both of which he claimed were outside the Confederate army's control but which the "resourceful generals" were working to rectify. The first was what Forsyth perceived to be a lack of support from local male Kentuckians, whom he declared to be "cowed by Federal military rule." However, he noted a glimmer of hope among the women.

> While the men are backward, the women are irrepressible secessionists. As our army moved their smiles and tears, their handkerchiefs and Confederate flags would remind you that you were way down in Dixie. With such a spirit in the women there is hope for the men of the land yet. [26]

General Smith had recruited a few hundred men, but Forsyth had larger numbers in mind. If 50,000 of the Kentuckians would volunteer to help the Confederate cause, he asserted, "their freedom would be secured." Forsyth saw no point in fighting for their liberty if they did not believe in the cause enough to "strike a blow themselves." The other problem was a need for clothing and blankets, some of which Smith had procured at Union expense. Forsyth wrote that Kentuckians also should contribute to the Confederate cause by providing such items to shield the army against the coming cold weather.[27]

A week later, the *Register* published a letter from Bardstown dated September 30, along with an apology for its tardiness. Forsyth reported that the army's possession of the Kentucky village had been quiet, the natives hospitable, and the troops undisturbed by enemy forces. He speculated on the success of other Confederate generals in the area but did not reveal Bragg's plans "lest my letters should fall into enemy hands." Forsyth expressed hope that the Confederates could hold Kentucky and Tennessee so their armies could benefit from the ample provisions there and possibly send food back home. He reiterated his concern that Kentuckians had not volunteered and reasoned that if the Confederate government sent a supporting army, the locals would be "encouraged to give us two or three recruits for every advancing Confederate soldier."[28]

That letter appeared after Forsyth's single battle report. On October 18, *Register* readers were treated to a letter from Harrodsburg in which Forsyth described battles of October 8. His esteem for the Confederate troops remained obvious.

> At 3 o'clock P.M. they advanced in splendid line, with Gen. Bragg's orders to push along the whole line to close quarters. For one hour and a half the enemy maintained his ground bravely in the face of a murderous fire of artillery and musketry. Our troops fought like heroes until the enemy began to falter, when with

a shout our boys moved forward and drove them three or four miles, entirely off
the field. Meantime an attempt on our left had been repulsed.[29]

Forsyth estimated the Union loss at double the Confederacy's, despite the fact
that the enemy forces far outnumbered Bragg's. Generals Smith and Withers
experienced even greater success at Frankfort. In Forsyth's opinion, the Southerners bested their foe even while taking care of their fallen soldiers. While
the injured Confederates were removed from the field, Union wounded all were
left in the absence of a Union surgeon. Following the battle, Forsyth reported
Bragg's troops to be "in the highest spirits," and Bragg proclaimed his army to
be the best in the world. The following day, the *Register* published a brief telegraphed report in which Forsyth squelched rumors that Brigadier General D.W.
Adams had been wounded in the battle. He assured readers that "our Mobile
friends generally" were safe.[30]

Although Forsyth had predicted in his report that another battle was at
hand, Bragg withdrew his forces from Kentucky. The *Register* reported on October 24 that the Confederate army was retreating and supported the action,
despite the fact that the results were "very different from what was anticipated
when that splendid army set out on its noble march for the deliverance of Kentucky." The *Register* speculated that Kentucky may have been unprepared for
the movement, having "no real desire to be freed from the Lincoln despotism,"
and optimistically stated that the provisions the army gained from its brief stay
in the state were worth more than the cost of the movement.

"In this view," it concluded, "the expedition was not by any means a failure."
It is unclear who wrote this unsigned piece. A brief item published on October
26 announced Forsyth's return to Mobile the previous day, providing evidence
that he did not write it. However, Forsyth's colleagues at the *Register* clearly
shared his admiration for Bragg and faith in the Confederacy as a whole.[31]

The editorial encouraged readers to wait until the history of the Kentucky
campaign had been written before they passed judgment on the general's actions. Forsyth aimed to offer such a history in the *Register* on November 9 and
16. The published material, however, was not so much a history as a defense of
Bragg's actions.

In the first piece, Forsyth declared his unwavering support for the general
and his duty to "the cause of justice and truth" to correct the numerous mis-
statements "which give vent to the disappointment of those who are in a rage
with a General because he did not realize their absurdly exaggerated expectations and perform impossibilities." Those expectations Forsyth himself had
expressed in his correspondence weeks earlier. He pointed out the marked difference between planning a war with pen and paper and physically fighting it in
the field. Going against his prior assessment of Bragg's strength and his army's
greatness, Forsyth asserted that if Bragg had stayed in Kentucky, he would have

lost his army "and with it, the Southern cause from Tennessee to the Gulf of Mexico."[32] Forsyth principally blamed the Kentuckians for Bragg's failure.

> Gen. Bragg marched to Kentucky upon a military programme which ought to have been fully comprehended at home, and which was clearly set forth in his first proclamation to the people of Kentucky. He went at the head of a liberating army, not by its own force to conquer Kentucky from the hands of the Federals, but to aid Kentuckians in their own efforts to throw off the Abolition yoke. He said to that people, distinctly, if you would be free, rise in arms, and I have the power with your assistance to redeem you. If you do not value your liberties sufficiently to risk life and property in their attainment, I shall retire from the State and leave you to your fate.[33]

As Forsyth noted throughout his stay in Kentucky, however, the men of that state were not eager to pick up arms. After Bragg found "scowling Unionists" rather than "delegations from towns and counties coming out to hail his arrival," he did everything he could to stimulate an uprising. "The 50,000 armed men did not come," Forsyth lamented, "and after a march of nearly 300 miles, Gen. Bragg found the keystone of his entire plan dropped out." Despite his disgust "with the failure of the Kentucky spirit," Forsyth explained that Bragg had no choice but to fight on Kentucky soil to protect his own men against the army of Union General Buell. Beyond that, there was no point in remaining in the state.[34]

Forsyth repudiated claims that Bragg's Kentucky invasion had accomplished nothing, outlining eight positive outcomes of the movement: (1) evacuation of Buell's army from Tennessee, (2) sparing north Alabama from Federal occupation, (3) possession of Cumberland Gap, (4) the capture of up to 20,000 prisoners, (5) vast gains in arms and ammunition, (6) enough jeans to clothe the army of the Mississippi, (7) defeats of the enemy in three major and 20 minor battles, and (8) offering Kentucky an army to help her liberation, whether she accepted being another matter.[35]

In the second sketch, Forsyth reiterated that the campaign "failed only to answer the lofty expectations of the country for reasons beyond the control of either the general or his heroic army." He offered a brief history of the army, painting a picture of a group "destitute of every requisite of a soldier save courage" and hastily whipped into shape under Bragg's masterful guidance. Forsyth regaled readers with the glorious tale of the troops' "memorable march" and of military movements "brilliantly executed," allowing the Confederate army to secure north Alabama, southern Tennessee, and a large portion of the Memphis and Charleston Railroad "without a blow."[36]

Forsyth also defended Bragg against criticisms that he should have fought Buell at Mumfordsville and that Buell beat him in a race to Louisville. In response to the first claim, Forsyth asserted that Bragg offered Buell a battle and he declined it. To answer the second censure, Forsyth vowed that Bragg could have reached Louisville days ahead of Buell if he wanted to, but that he headed for Bardstown instead because it was rich in provisions his army needed. Finally, Forsyth recounted the number of enemy troops Bragg expected to face after Buell was reinforced at Louisville and heralded Bragg's common sense and prudence "for the safety of the brave army under his command."[37]

Forsyth's conclusion afforded Bragg and his men a great deal of glory.

> Whatever judgment contemporaneous opinion, disappointed in its exaggerated expectations, may pass upon this expedition, the historian will record it as one of the most remarkable campaigns of this great war, whether viewed in reference to the grandeur of the plan, the heroic endurance of the men, or the masterly retreat of the army from the mighty dangers with which it was surrounded.[38]

Just as Forsyth's antebellum rhetoric and political scheming had drawn scorn from his contemporaries, so did his clearly biased history of Bragg's failed campaign. One of the most scathing critiques came from the pen of Kentucky Provisional Governor Richard Hawes, who fled the state with the retreating Confederate army. Hawes' letter, published first in the *Richmond Enquirer* and reprinted in the *Register*, called Forsyth's history "replete with erroneous statements," not the least that Kentuckians had refused to take up arms in their own defense. Hawes argued that efforts were under way to raise local troops for the Confederate cause, which would have come to Bragg's aid had he not retreated so swiftly. Hawes placed the blame for the campaign's failure squarely on Bragg, asserting that it would have been successful had he crushed Buell's army at Mumfordsville, before Union forces captured Louisville.[39]

Forsyth rebuked Hawes' claims primarily by restating facts he had given in his "history" and by arguing that anyone could create a perfect strategy in hindsight. Forsyth's main objectives appeared to be defending his own credibility as well as Bragg's honor.

> My interest in Gen. Bragg is limited by my desire to see justice done to a brave soldier who has not taken off his harness for an hour since the war began; and my interest in the Kentucky campaign is limited by my wish to vindicate the truth of history. I wrote at first as I write now, without any bias that I can conceive of, to my judgment, my feelings, or even my prejudices. I confess to a high admiration for some of the very extraordinary characteristics of Gen. Bragg, and I equally confess to the pleasure I always feel, and a *penchant* to which I am always given, of taking sides with any man who I believe is unjustly assailed by that most reckless of all persecutors—*fashionable clamor*. I claim then, to be an impartial witness of what I saw, and a competent one according to my ability.[40]

For the remainder of the conflict, Forsyth served the typical war editor role of lifting public morale. As the war drew to a close, he realized the hopelessness of the cause, fleeing Mobile in advance of Union troops in April 1865, toting along much of his printing equipment and staff with the aim of publishing be-hind Confederate lines. The Union army confiscated his office and installed a supporter there to publish a new paper named the *Mobile Daily News*, with "late *Advertiser and Register*" printed under the nameplate. By July 1865, Forsyth managed to retrieve his property, and the *Register* returned to its old office.[41]

After the war, Forsyth initially supported the Reconstruction movement, signed his loyalty oath, and worked to organize a new state government that would ensure a speedy return of white domination. After the Civil Rights Act, however, Forsyth changed his mind about Reconstruction and published ever more racist attacks on freedmen. Throughout those trying times, during which the state and national governments were predominantly Republican, Forsyth remained loyal to the Democratic Party and was appointed to its national ex-ecutive committee in 1868. His denunciations of the opposing "radical" party led to further criticism, but rather than instigating the revolution he threatened following Grant's election, he worked quietly toward restoring white rule to the South.[42]

Increasingly absent from the newspaper because of his declining health, For-syth experienced his last hurrah in 1874. To his great satisfaction, the Demo-crats regained control of Alabama and the U.S. Congress. Forsyth himself was elected to the state legislature and was offered the speaker position, but he de-clined because of his feeble state. He served in his legislative position only a few days, virtually disappearing from the public eye after that. Forsyth died at his home in Mobile on May 2, 1877.[43]

In a famous letter Forsyth penned during the early days of Reconstruction, he noted, "How times change, and men with them, in the world of transitory events and opinions. The zenith of today is the nadir of tomorrow."[44] He ex-perienced many such peaks and valleys in his career, but despite the changing times, Forsyth himself changed little. He maintained from his youth to his dy-ing day a love of politics, a belief in democracy, and a talent for using his pen to make people think, whether they agreed with him or not.

After Forsyth's death, Northern papers eulogized him as the leading Demo-cratic editor of the South. He had been regarded as a leader by a large portion of the Southern press and he often had exercised "a measure of control over popular opinion and in matters of policy that no other Southern editor has equaled."[45]

11

Henry Hotze:
Propaganda Voice of the Confederacy

Joseph V. Trahan III

THE YOUNG, STRUGGLING CONFEDERATE REPUBLIC WAS IN CRITICAL need of European acceptance and, more importantly, recognition in 1861. The skillful persuader chosen to accomplish the goal was Henry Hotze, a brash young newspaper editor from Mobile, Alabama, who had developed significant political and journalism connections and knew the importance of influencing public opinion. Using 21st century public relations techniques that he developed on the job, Hotze became the propaganda voice of the Confederacy.

Although the 27-year-old communicator failed in his efforts to persuade England to recognize the Confederate government or to declare war against the United States, he created dozens of public opinion and propaganda techniques still used today. He conducted research and public opinion polls, identified influential public opinion leaders and persuaded them to deliver messages that he wrote, made friends with high-ranking government officials for whom he wrote speeches, and gained editorial access to some of London's most important publications.

When he decided that a newspaper would best serve his propaganda purposes, Hotze hired credible English writers to deliver the Confederate message in *The Index*, a weekly newspaper that he created and published for three years in London to persuade and influence members of Parliament. Historians called Hotze "the most effective and well-known Confederate propagandist in Europe"[1] and *The Index* "one of the most effective of all organs of propaganda before the period of the World War."[2] Hobbled by lack of money, Hotze borrowed from friends to publish the newspaper, but he was unable to carry out many of his other ideas, including publishing an import/export list to show how much the Union blockade of the Confederate coast was costing English wholesalers.

Hotze believed fervently in the Confederate cause, and he did not want to admit failure. Haunted by the possibilities of what he could have accomplished

Henry Hotze. Courtesy of the Museum of Mobile

in England with more money and time, he continued publishing *The Index* for four months after General Robert E. Lee surrendered in April 1865 at Appomattox Court House, Virginia. Hotze finally accepted defeat, and on August 12, 1865, he published the last issue of the newspaper, but he never returned to his adopted home in America.

Born in Zurich, Switzerland, on September 2, 1833, he was the son of Rudolph Hotze, a captain in the French Royal Service, and his wife, Sophie Esslinger Hotze.[3] He was educated in a Jesuit college before immigrating to the United States, where he became a naturalized U.S. citizen in Alabama in June 1855.[4] With his natural charm and support for Southern culture, Hotze established enough important connections in Mobile's powerful social circles to be appointed to the Mobile delegation to the Southern Commercial Convention in Montgomery in 1858. The appointment gave him the opportunity to network with fervent Southern-cause spokesmen such as William L. Yancey, Roger A. Pryor, and Edmund Ruffin.[5] He soon earned a provisional appointment as secretary of the U.S. Legation at Brussels where he served both as secretary and

The Cabinet of the Confederate States at Montgomery. From left, Attorney General
(later Secretary of State), Judah P. Benjamin; Secretary of Navy Stephen Mallory,
Secretary of the Treasury Christopher Memminger (standing); Vice President
Alexander Stephens; Secretary of War Leroy P. Walker (standing); President
Jefferson Davis; Post Master John H. Reagan; and Secretary of State Robert
Toombs. Illustration from *Harper's Weekly*, June 1, 1861. Courtesy of Rare Books
and Special Collections, University of South Carolina Libraries

Charge d'Affaires. However, when Congress failed to appropriate money to
maintain the post, Hotze returned to Mobile on the eve of the Civil War.[6]

Hotze's political and propaganda career was uninterrupted by this setback,
and he became an associate editor for the *Mobile Advertiser and Register*. He
was guided by the distinguished editor and diplomat, John Forsyth, from whom
he received the critical journalistic training he needed to fine-tune his natural writing style. Hotze also was named secretary to the newly created Mobile
Board of Harbor Commissioners,[7] a maritime experience that would serve him
well during his upcoming Confederate governmental service. When the sim-
mering powder keg between Northern and Southern brothers finally erupted
on April 12 at Fort Sumter, Hotze was already working for the young Confederacy as the liaison for a group of Mobile leaders who wanted to seize the
transport *Illinois*. His dispatches to Leroy Pope Walker, the first Confederate
secretary of war, were already displaying the necessary public relations skills
needed to build consensus and credibility, and Walker's final telegram granted
Hotze's group the authority to act. Although no evidence of the expedition's
success has been found, one thing is clear: Hotze was already developing his

relationship-building and writing skills that would prove valuable in his future
Confederate government service endeavors.[8]

However, before Hotze would serve in the Confederacy's diplomatic corps,
he would shoulder a musket for his adopted country. Hotze's brief Confederate
military career was spent in the Mobile Cadets, a military unit composed of
young aristocratic men from Mobile who were "united for the purpose of military amusement." The Cadets decided to place themselves on a war footing in
the service of Alabama's governor.[9]

On April 23, 1861, the Mobile Cadets were ordered to Montgomery, Alabama, to begin their Confederate Army assimilation process. Hotze kept a journal as his unit sailed aboard the *St. Nicholas* on the Alabama River en route to
Virginia.[10]

> We drill six hours a day on the upper deck, and the sun is excruciating. Many of
> us are "green" in the manual, and each of the older members acts as instructor to
> an "awkward squad." One or two of the more awkward ones were discovered late
> last night, long after "taps," rehearsing, in solitary despair, the hard-learned les-
> sons of the day. The thing was too ludicrous and, besides, too well-intentioned to
> provoke more than a formal reprimand from the officer of the board.[11]

Hotze had been given a berth in the captain's stateroom along with a little
corner at the first clerk's desk for his writing.[12] Like most correspondents, he
chose a pseudonym and began writing for the *Mobile Advertiser and Register*
as "Cadet."

> One of the last exploits of the great gun was to fire at a party of ladies walking
> over the beach! Afterwards it was announced in the Northern papers, that a flag
> of truce had been hoisted near our batteries. Of course, nobody ever saw or heard
> of that flag, but it is known that one of the ladies (I believe Miss Augusta Evans,
> of our city, the gifted authoress of Beulah) immediately after the shot passed over
> the heads of the party, waved a white handkerchief in triumph and derision at the
> cowardly foe.[13]

Hotze's friend, Mobile Mayor Jones M. Withers, was elected the regiment's
colonel before the unit arrived at Montgomery on April 28. When the regiment
was sworn into service at Lynchburg, Virginia, the elite Mobile Cadets officially
became Company A, 3rd Alabama Volunteers. Describing the moving ceremony, Hotze wrote: "The ceremony was an imposing one, and there was not, I
truly believe, a man in all the ten companies that did not feel the solemnity of
the occasion, and of the obligations he was assuming."[14] His journal covering
the period from late April through July is filled with routine camp life recollections. His writings include guard duty, tent mate descriptions, dress parades,
and other garrison duty details, but soldiering was becoming a bore to Hotze
near the end of June when he wrote:

Despising the enemy, despairing of winning any glory in meeting him, or of having any serious work to do, disgusted with the dull routine of camp life, we were gradually losing that stern sense of responsibility, that pride in our position with which we entered the ranks. A sort of demoralization not in the worst meaning of the word, but still serious enough to be painfully felt was spreading through the regiment.[15]

Hotze had left field duty at the end of May to join the regimental staff headquarters group as a clerk,[16] but his clerking duties were short-lived because in July he returned to Mobile, apparently on leave status. Hotze wrote: "My military experiences did not end with the date of the Battle of Manassas (news had come to his unit of the battle on July 23rd), but from that date I ceased to shoulder the musket as a private in the ranks."[17] So ended Hotze's lackluster Confederate military career, but his usefulness to the Stars and Bars was about to begin.

Walker ordered Hotze on August 31, 1861 to travel to Europe to determine why purchases of arms and munitions were being delayed. Walker instructed Hotze "to waste no time in placing himself en route, selecting the line of passage his judgment most approved."[18] Hotze arrived in Richmond on September 6, 1861, to obtain additional War Department instructions and messages.[19] Leaving Richmond, Hotze was delayed by slow trains, long stopovers, and a train wreck as he made his way to Canada to sail for England.[20]

Ever the inquisitive, keen-thinking public opinion student, Hotze recorded his U.S. travel observations. He found the North abuzz with war fever, brimming with confidence in its military forces' superiority, ignorant of the extent of their current national danger and the fact that the Union army's soldiers were from the bottom of life's barrel, fearful of Confederate spies, and unaware of the fact that arrests were increasing daily. Hotze's northern trip reconfirmed his belief in the Confederate cause's ultimate success.

Hotze reached his final destination of London on October 5. The following day he delivered his dispatches to Confederate agents William L. Yancey, Pierre A. Rost, and A. Dudley Mann.[21] He remained in England for two weeks, conferring with the Confederate agents about public opinion both at home and in Europe and discussing how the struggling Confederacy could counter the North's monopoly of English press with a press agent of their own. He researched the situation and formulated a proactive propaganda and public relations plan that would tell the Confederacy's story to all of Europe. He recommended that the Confederacy send a public opinion agent to London immediately to attempt to stem the anti-Confederate sentiment and create an avalanche of pro-Southern support. Hotze nominated himself to be that agent.[22] In this position he believed he would be better able to serve his Confederacy with the power of his persuasive pen instead of a rifle. He was about to embark on his Confederate propagandist career.

Hotze returned to Richmond on November 6, 1861, where he was immediately discharged from the Confederate Army and reported to the new Confederate Secretary of War Judah P. Benjamin. He laid before Benjamin his propaganda plan for reversing the anti-Confederacy flood to a pro-Confederate flow. Benjamin eagerly endorsed his interesting proposal and recommended that he present it to Secretary of State R.M.T. Hunter.[23]

What Hotze articulated to Hunter was a propaganda/public relations plan to reverse negative English public opinion toward the Confederacy and hopefully ensure recognition for the South. Hotze's plan: First—research/analyze current English public opinion through the English press and discussions with movers and shakers; second—develop a plan of action that would ensure the telling of the Confederacy's story; third—communicate part of the plan through the utilization of propaganda/public relations "billiards" tactics in which third parties such as influential English editorial writers would insert Hotze-influenced editorials in London's leading newspapers. The editors would receive their usual 2 to 10 guineas fee for each editorial and the Confederacy's story would be told through the words of Englishmen. Hotze told Hunter that his plan had merit with the following goals: propagating the Confederacy's cause in the English press; educating English opinion leaders and editors about the South; and finally, once informed, editors writing supportive editorials themselves. In effect, Hotze would "multiply himself in exerting favorable influences in the press." Finally, he would evaluate his plan by analyzing English public opinion fluctuations through the press and hope for the Confederacy's recognition by the world of nations.[24]

Hunter was sold on Hotze's bold plan and appointed him a Confederate commercial agent on November 14, 1861. Although Hotze was appointed a commercial agent to England, Hunter's letter of instructions made it clear that commerce would not be his main endeavor. His main mission would be one of winning the English press' support through his revolutionary propaganda plan.[25]

In a letter, Hunter told Hotze that he was ". . . to zealously strive to dispel foreign fears as to the reconstruction of the Union and to emphasize the universal sentiment of the Southern people to prosecute the war until their independence shall no longer be assailed."[26] Hunter also charged the young Confederate propagandist to "keep constantly before the public . . . the tyranny of the Lincoln Government, its utter disregard of . . . personal rights . . . and its notorious violations of the law."[27] With this charge, Hotze was given the opportunity he had asked for, stemming the Union propaganda tidal wave that had already been launched against the young Confederacy in early 1861.

By nominating himself for Confederate propaganda agent abroad, Hotze would attempt to become the Confederacy's point man in its struggle for English recognition. At age 27, Hotze had the confidence of Secretary Hunter and some meager funds allotted him as resources to accomplish this enormous task. He was granted a salary of $1,500 a year and a $750 contingency fund, "a rather absurd price to pay for the good will of a whole continent!" wrote historian Frank L. Owsley.[28]After Hunter suggested ways to try to manipulate the press, he instructed Hotze to report to James M. Mason, Confederate commissioner to England, and exhibit his credentials.

> You will avail yourself of every opportunity to communicate with this department, and keep it advised of the tone of the English press and the current of public sentiment with regard to the struggle in which the Confederate States is now engaged, transmitting with appropriate comments such printed extracts from the printed journals as you may deem to have an important bearing upon the question. You will be diligent and earnest in your efforts to impress upon the public mind abroad the ability of the Confederate States to maintain their independence, and to this end you will publish whatever information you possess calculated to convey a just idea of their ample resources and vast military strength and to raise their character and government in general estimation. You will zealously strive to remove any fears that may be entertained abroad as to the re-construction of the Union, from which we have separated, and that it is the universal sentiment of the people of the Confederate States to prosecute the war until their independence shall no longer be assailed. You will keep constantly before the public view in Great Britain the tyranny of the Lincoln Government, its utter disregard of the personal rights of its citizens and its notorious violations of law. Contrasted with this you can justly and forcibly dwell upon the fact that peace and order have reigned everywhere in the Confederate States and that the laws have been instantly and impartially administered. You will also impress upon the people of Great Britain the trade which may be established between our respective countries, and assure them of the almost universal opinion in the Confederate States that as few restrictions as possible should be imposed upon that trade and those only for revenue purposes.[29]

Hunter concluded: "Much discretion, however, is left to you, and the Department relies for success upon your address and dispatch."[30] Hotze also had Hunter's permission to extend his operations to France (if he desired to do so). However, Hunter must have thought that Hotze's mission would be very limited in scope because the tiny contingency fund and annual salary was all the Confederacy provided him to accomplish his mission.[31] "In the light of Hotze's accomplishment, the stipend and expense money . . . seem like a jest," historian Owsley wrote.[32]

For the meager investment, the Confederacy's State Department was gaining the services of a young man who would exploit every opportunity he encountered or created. All of young Hotze's previous career opportunities: consular service—member, journalist, soldier, and maritime commercial agent—had prepared him to tackle his new appointment. More importantly, he had other valuable qualities: congeniality, strong writing skills, effective oral communication

Confederate Commissioner John Slidell was one of the two
Southern diplomats captured by the U.S. Navy in the Trent
Affair. Illustration from *Harper's Weekly*, November 30, 1861.
Courtesy of Rare Books and Special Collections, University of
South Carolina Libraries

skills, keen powers of observation, and an intuitive ability to correctly gauge
official and public opinion.

At the end of 1861, Confederates had a surge of hope that England might recognize the young republic and declare war on the United States after Confederate commissioners Mason and John Slidell were seized by the Federals aboard
the *Trent*, a British packet en route to Europe from Havana, Cuba. Their capture
gave the South hope that Britain would finally become an ally. However, Federal
officials quickly nullified the possibility of war with England by releasing Mason and Slidell and admitting that their arrest had been illegal.[33] Soon after the
diplomats were released, the newly minted propagandist arrived in London on
January 29, 1862, to begin changing English public opinion to a pro-Confederate
tint. He began researching current English public opinion sentiment in the

press and in the minds of England's opinion leaders. When Hotze had first visited England in October 1861, he was optimistic about changing public opinion. However, when he arrived the second time, his initial assessment in the wake of the Trent affair revealed an English ministry that had a renewed determination to pursue a neutrality policy and to avert war with the United States. Hotze wrote with toned-down optimism two days after his London arrival in January 1862: "It would be premature, after a sojourn of barely three days to venture upon an expression of opinion on the tone of public sentiment here. So far as I have met individuals, and so far as the information extends which I receive from others, the impression left on my mind is favorable without warranting very sanguine hope."[34]

Hotze's ever churning mind now revved into high gear with his English press and public opinion leaders' analysis. He was beginning the first step of the modern public relations' process—research/fact finding. "There seems to be a lull in political discussions through the press probably owing to the approaching meeting of Parliament which assembles on the 6th instant," he wrote. "The papers have said little or nothing, beyond the mere announcement of the fact, concerning the arrival of our commissioners."[35]

Hotze's study of English newspapers revealed that an indefatigable and unscrupulous agency was at work in the press, which was losing no opportunity to damage the South in public estimation. This "agency" he correctly identified as Thurlow Weed, a New York publisher and politician, who enjoyed a large secret service fund. Hotze thought the manner in which he went about his work was repulsive to English tastes, and he said that Weed's example warned him that he could not be too cautious and circumspect.[36] Hotze correctly surmised that before he attempted anything in the English persuasion arena, he must accurately gauge current English public opinion by measuring the beliefs of those who wield real power. Hotze was warned by what he saw as Weed's clumsy dealings with the English, and he wrote, "I shall not venture to write until I feel the ground firm under me."[37]

Hotze began implementing the tactical aspects of his persuasive plan by cultivating a close, friendly relationship with the London newspaper editors. He intended to move slowly and with conviction in order to avoid offending the English. He knew the importance of influencing the press' editorial views, and on February 23, 1862, he reported his initial success to Hunter. Hotze wrote an editorial that was published in the *Morning Post* by editor A. Bothwich and seized the opportunity to present to the English reading public the "evidence of the unanimity of (Southern) resistance, and especially to point out the novelty and injustice of the theory . . . that a nation must be able to defend itself against all odds before it has a right to call itself a nation."[38]

Hotze was especially excited about his accomplishment because he had succeeded in proactively telling the Confederacy's story to the English, pointing

Union propagandist Thurlow Weed was Hotze's Federal counterpart. Illustration from *Harper's Weekly*, November 23, 1861. Courtesy of Rare Books and Special Collections, University of South Carolina Libraries

out the Union's injustices, and being able to publish his editorial in the English Prime Minister Lord Palmerston's official organ. He believed that the English press' editorial pages would now fall open to him. He would, however, utilize "the privilege moderately, neglecting no opportunity nor seeking to create artificial ones."[39]

Hotze needed more money to entertain and persuade opinion leaders such as Lord Campbell, Lord Derby, Lord Palmerston, Earl Russell (whom Hotze referred to as the "U.S. Government's apologist"), and William Bright ("who leads or represents no political party but himself"), to name just a few of those he attempted to influence. He truly believed that Lord Campbell "is a useful acquaintance and one of our most zealous friends."[40] Hotze analyzed public opinion "as not hostile, but rather as cold and indifferent."[41]

His next tactic was to play a little billiards by getting the English opinion leaders to tell the Confederacy's story and eventually gain recognition for the young Confederacy. Hotze wrote to Hunter:

> I have been fortunate enough to gain almost immediate access to a higher social sphere giving me a wider range of influence and immeasurably greater facilities for usefulness other than I hope to attain in so short a period of time. I am daily applied to for facts and arguments to be used in our favor and you will readily perceive that I cannot hold conversations on confidential topics in the common drawing room of a boardinghouse & etc.[42]

In March 1862, Hotze's public relations activities dramatically increased.[43] With the skill of a modern Madison Avenue public relations professional, he used English opinion leaders and editors to tell the South's story by letting the experts/credible English sources express the Confederacy's side of the story themselves.

Hotze soon learned that two of the most zealous supporters of the Confederate cause were James Spence, author of the pro-Southern *American Union*, and Lord Campbell of the English House of Lords, both of whom soon became Hotze's good friends. He favorably compared the importance of Spence's book to that of political philosopher Alexis de Tocqueville's *Democracy in America*. Hotze wrote that Lord Campbell had decided "to make a speech in the House of Lords in favor of our (Confederacy) recognition (and) has engaged me to write for him the points of argument which I most desire to have urged in that body."[44] He eagerly provided the necessary persuasive arguments to Lord Campbell within 10 days of his request.

Taking advantage of his newly acquired credible position with the English press, Hotze was able to soften the negative publicity produced by the fall of Forts Henry and Donelson in early 1862. He hastened to underrate the importance of the border states in conversations with British writers.

> Our (Confederate) Constitution was framed and the government organized for the states in the cotton region proper. The border states joined the Confederacy only after the war started, and if the North expended "blood and treasures" and succeeded in gaining temporary possession of the outer ramparts, the great states of Virginia, North Carolina, Missouri, Kentucky and Tennessee, the Southern Confederacy Citadel would still remain untouched.[45]

Many of Hotze's British editor friends seemed to agree with his arguments because many of them took his ideas and published them in their publications. The *London Times* used his exact words.[46] At about the same time, Lord Campbell rose in the House of Lords to deliver his pro-Southern recognition speech in which he denounced the blockade. After Lord Campbell's speech, which was influenced by Hotze, Earl Russell reluctantly wrote that "a reconstruction of the American Union was not possible."[47]

Hotze had to surmount some difficult problems. One of those was his lack of Southern news. He begged Hunter to send him important Southern newspapers so he could clip and transmit them to the English press. Hotze told Hunter, "If I had Southern intelligence, though ever so sparingly or irregularly, I should wield a real power in journalism here, which even my unremitting labor and hitherto singularly good fortune will not give me."[48]

Hotze was also fighting a running battle to keep the Southern press' intemperate language extracts from being published in England. He was constantly persuading English editors that the Southern cause was doing better on the battlefields than the Southern press was reporting. He suggested to Hunter that the Southern press should be censored "to restrain such public expression of individual indiscretion if not disaffection . . . Where one vital interest is common to all and overshadows all minor interests, all that conflicts with it is treason."[49]

In the few months he had been in England, Hotze had accomplished a great deal with zeal and initiative. Considerable success had accompanied his devotion to his duties and already English public opinion had begun a slow, favorable pro-Confederate turn. "I am almost daily applied to for information and advice and my Coast survey charts are in constant demand," he wrote.[50]

Consequently, Hotze now believed more than ever that he must produce a public relations tool that would accurately and aggressively tell the South's story. Even though he had gained editorial access to some of London's most important publications, such as Lord Derby's *Morning Herald, London Times, Morning Post*, and the *Standard*, he concluded that a newspaper would best serve his persuasion purposes. Hotze's principal reason for founding *The Index* was to provide an agency that would collect and disseminate Southern news from all sources. The newspaper would also educate a new corps of editors, opinion leaders, and decision makers about what was really happening in the South. Hotze planned to pay the editors for their writing, thus becoming their employer as well as their educator. In his April 25 letter to Hunter, Hotze revealed his plan and purpose.

> I have now, after mature deliberation, concluded to establish a newspaper wholly devoted to our interest, and which will be exclusively under my control, though my connection with it is known only to a few initiated, and will not be suspected by the public at large . . . You will see from the prospectus which I enclose my

plan for making the paper a machine for collecting, comparing and bringing before the public with proper comments the vast amount of important information
which is received in Europe though private channels. This was most difficult to
accomplish, and I did not seriously contemplate the new publication until I had
assured success.[51]

With financial assistance from two of his friends, H.O. Brewer of Mobile and
A.P. Waters of Savannah, as well as his own funds, he ensured a publication "in
a manner worthy of the cause for a period of three months." I hope to cause
you an agreeable surprise with the first number of *The Index*," Hotze wrote to
Secretary of State Hunter.[52] Now the Confederate propagandist had his lethal
persuasive tool.

The first issue of *The Index* rolled off the press on May 1, 1862. It was sub-
titled "A Weekly Journal of Politics, Literature, and News," contained 16 pages,
and sold for 6 pence. It was published on Thursday afternoons, until its final issues, which came out on Saturdays. Hotze explained the significance of
the name *Index* in his first issue: "If The Index should be fortunate enough to
point the way to a more speedy settlement of the unfortunate American War,
or it should serve as a guide to a better understanding of the real character
of a greatly calumniated people, we might well congratulate ourselves on the
choice of our title."[53]

By publishing *The Index*, Hotze would ensure that the English opinion leaders would receive the accurate Civil War Southern news in a planned and comprehensive manner. This was very important since England did not officially
recognize the Confederacy. No communication existed between the two governments because no Confederate official had official status in England.

Although Hotze was aggressively seeking recognition, he realistically reported back to Benjamin on August 4, 1862, that at least five-sixths of the lower
house and all the peers, with only two or three exceptions, were friendly to the
Confederacy, "but there are very few indeed who carry that friendship so far as
to oppose the Government in power. Thus the cabinet is left supreme arbiter
in American affairs. What actuates it mainly is an exaggerated fear of war, and
especially of the safety of Canada. When our arms are successful they flatter
themselves with the hope that the ardently desired independence of the South is
about to be secured without danger to themselves; when reverses befall us, they
lack the decision, I might say the courage, to act."[54]

> There are those also, both in and out of cabinet, whose American policy is
> summed up in an expression ascribed to Carlyle, "that the war is like the burning
> out of a very dirty chimney, at which the neighbors may look on with compo-
> sure and self-congratulation." These desire the utter ruin of the North to render
> Canada safe, and the utter annihilation of the South to remove, as they think, the
> most formidable competitor of India.[55]

The Index was representative of English journalism in every aspect. It was neat and unpretentious, with a one-inch Gothic-style banner. Its subtitle, "A Weekly Journal of Politics, Literature, and News," appeared immediately below the banner in bold type. The paper contained 16 pages, each measuring approximately 10 by 13 inches and divided into columns. The articles appearing in the columns were printed in their entirety without interruption except for continuation to a following page. Hotze had done his homework and understood the English press and how to accurately communicate the Confederacy's messages in both style and substance. *The Index*'s format scarcely varied during its publication life. A typical edition's contents were:

CONTENTS

Notes of Events of the Week 241
Cotton and Dry Goods Market Liverpool Letter 243
Manchester Letter 243
Latest Direct Intelligence from the South Battle of Gaines Mills. 243
Mr. Seward and Earl Russell 245
Foreign Correspondence:
New York 244
Paris 244
The Latest Intelligence 248
Position of the Federal Armies 248
The Cotton Manufacture and the Cotton Famine 249
The Sheffield Manifesto 250
The Two Campaigns 251
Editorials 252
Reviews:
A Northern View of the American War 252
On the Recognition of the Southern Confederacy 253
Letters to the Editor 247
Lieutenant Maury and The American Struggle 254
The Confederate Cause in Europe 255
Advertisements .... 256[56]

Additionally, the influence of *The Index* was multiplied because the English writers submitted material to several publications. Hotze elaborated on this to Secretary Benjamin in September of 1862.

The establishment of The Index enabled me on occasion to assume the position of employer of the pens of some of these gentlemen. Thus, at least half the articles in The Index are written by Englishmen, who, only a few months ago, had but imperfect knowledge of and little active sympathy with the South. It is my object and hope, by this means, to have found a fight will, from their positions, and to be more valuable to those of the ablest pens of our own country.[57]

Hotze begged for more funds for *The Index* when Edwin DeLeon, an experienced journalist and personal friend of President Davis, arrived in Europe with $25,000 for Confederate propaganda efforts. DeLeon recognized Hotze's competency but took a critical view of *The Index*'s effectiveness. On October 1, 1862, in reply to Hotze's financial aid request, DeLeon wrote:

> With regard (to) The Index I will speak to you with (the) frankness of a friend. I do not think it can be sustained; the tax of 40 pounds per week being too heavy to be long continued and temporary aid doing no good ... Moreover in the Herald & Standard you have daily organs of wide circulation representing political English parties while the correspondence of the Times, Post, Telegraph, throw a flood on our affairs. With a weekly paper and the limited circulation you can get ... you cannot hope to rival your native competition.
>
> I therefore do not feel at liberty to divert the funds under my control for the direction as suggested in your letter ... Consider therefore whether you feel conscientiously bound to continue such a thankless and terrible labor, as the conduct of The Index involves, and whether now (whatever was the case when you established it) your time and talents and energy could not better be bestowed upon papers of wide circulation in England or in contributions to German journals or periodicals. My judgment may be erroneous, but I have given you my convictions, and you will bear me witness that I have not intruded unasked advice and that no one acknowledges your services to the cause more fully than myself. [58]

DeLeon did not understand that *The Index* was not written for the ordinary English public but instead was targeted to England's public opinion leaders—writers, editors, cabinet and government officials, diplomats, clergy, and anybody that Hotze considered an opinion leader. He clearly understood the tactics of targeting messages to specific publics, as well as using credible experts to tell the story. DeLeon was not the only one who criticized Hotze's publication. Slidell, early in the publication's life, criticized it for not editorially attacking the British Cabinet for its failure to recognize the Confederacy.

Hotze's stable of *Index* English writers originally included James Spence, whose book Hotze highly praised but who was a lead writer for only three issues. Hotze's deep commitment to slavery caused him to make mistakes, and he was instrumental in ending Spence's contributions. Hotze was frightened by Spence's ultimate slave emancipation ideas that rendered the publication "unduly conspicuous."[59] Hotze also hired Percy Greg, who was a regular contributor to the *Manchester Guardian*, the *Saturday Review*, and the *Standard*. Hotze characterized him as "one of the most talented leader writers in London, who, besides being a valuable contributor to *The Index*, is one of our most efficient

supporters in the columns of the *Saturday Review* and other literary and political journals of high standing."[60] Hotze also had *Index* writers in the United
States in New York, Brooklyn, Washington, and Philadelphia, as well as in Richmond and Norfolk, and even occupied New Orleans. He paid journalists from
France, Italy, and to a lesser extent Germany, who provided *Index* articles.

Although English recognition of the Southern Confederacy was Hotze's main
goal, his toughest battle was publishing the Confederacy's propaganda journal. *The Index*'s circulation never exceeded 2,500, its advertising revenue was
limited, and it never became a self-supporting publication. After Hotze's tiny
$750 contingency fund was exhausted, he turned again to his friends Brewer in
Mobile and Waters in Savannah and also begged the Confederate government
for more money. *The Index* cost about 40 pounds to produce weekly, and Hotze
made just 20 pounds a week from subscriptions and advertising. He told Benjamin in his November 7, 1862, dispatch: "The value of an organ is not merely as
a means of reaching public opinion, but as a channel through which arguments
and facts can be conveyed unofficially to the Government itself, an agency
through which connections can be established."[61]

After Hotze appealed to Mason in December of 1862, he finally received 250
pounds from a reluctant DeLeon to support *The Index*.[62] DeLeon did not understand Hotze's strategy, which was to increase his persuasive propagandist
influence on England and, indirectly, the rest of Europe. DeLeon continued
his resistance, even though Benjamin praised Hotze's work and *The Index*'s
editorial contents and persuasive influence. Hotze finally appealed directly to
Benjamin, telling him that the 250 pounds would "relieve me from immediate
embarrassment" but that he needed more. Hotze was rewarded with an increase in his contingency fund from the $750 American fund to 2,000 pounds a
year along with more high praise from Benjamin, who wrote, "Your dispatches
continue to afford interesting and gratifying proof of the intelligent zeal with
which you are performing your duties, and it is desired by the Department
that you continue. I have had occasion to examine The Index more particularly
since I last wrote, and observe a progressive and marked improvement in its
contents."[63]

Benjamin also liked Hotze's plan of employing and educating English writers
on Southern viewpoints on the war. He believed this concept was both intelligent and practical for the Southern cause. Benjamin wrote Hotze:

> Your plan of engaging the services of writers employed in the leading daily papers
> and thereby securing not only their cooperation but educating them into such a
> knowledge of our affairs as will enable them to counteract effectually the misrep-
> resentation of the Northern agents appears to be judicious and effective.[64]

Hotze responded by saying, "My plan has been to abstain from attempting
to do too much at once, but as soon as one position was secured to use it for

Confederate diplomat James M. Mason was captured along with Slidell
by the U.S. Navy in the Trent Affair. Illustration from *Harper's Weekly*,
November 30, 1861. Courtesy of Rare Books and Special Collections,
University of South Carolina Libraries

attaining another." Thus the establishment of an organ was at one time the great
end, but when established, it became the means to carry out other plans.[65]

Hotze's main propaganda objective with *The Index* was official recognition
of the Southern Confederacy by England, even though *The Index* discussed a
wide variety of important Southern Cause topics during its four years of publication. Everything else was secondary to Hotze's primary Confederate government service.

Some quotes from *The Index* from May 22, 1862, through January 26, 1865, clearly illustrate this mission. On May 22, 1862, *The Index* editorialized that recognition did not mean intervention. As the war progressed, Hotze never dropped the subject of recognition of the Confederate states as an independent nation. On March 19, 1863, *The Index* declared that the Confederacy was "recognized on the stock exchange, recognized by common parlance and by public opinion the world over . . . (and) is unknown and unrecognized only by the diplomatic ceremonial." On June 2, 1864, *The Index* declared: "While we refuse to recognize the existence of any government in that country (Confederacy) . . . everything wears the air of complete organization and accomplished national independence." As late as January 26, 1865, with the end of the Confederacy in sight, *The Index* gave another version of its well-utilized theme: "The true obstacle to recognition by England is not slavery (for in the height of the abolitionist agitation she readily recognized Texas), but the apathy, or rather lack of initial power by her present government."[66]

Hotze told Benjamin that he had designed *The Index* to be "in appearance and contents acceptable to English ideas and it was essential to avoid the great error of American journalism, that of mistaking forcible words for forcible ideas. It was necessary to draw a marked contrast between *The Index* and the popular idea of an American paper."[67] "Thus the establishment of an organ was at one time the great end, but when established, it became the means to carry out other plans," he wrote. By January 17, 1863, Hotze was spending so much time on *The Index* that he reported to Benjamin that his eyes were beginning to fail.

Another of Hotze's public relations tools that he proposed in May 1863 was the publication of a classified list of the English products consumed by the Confederacy and their cost. This list would show English wholesalers the cost of the Union blockade of the Confederate coast. Hotze wrote:

> I propose to issue a classified list, with the estimated value, of the chief articles of foreign production which the Confederate states in a normal condition consume and pay for annually. This I would address to some twenty-four thousand wholesale dealers in Great Britain in the form of a letter, with each one's specialty marked in ink, so as to make each one feel himself specially addressed.[68]

This publication, Hotze estimated, would cost approximately 100 pounds, but the list was never published because of a shortage of funds. His list would have struck a blow for Southern recognition by using the one instrument that could truly sway English public opinion: their pocketbooks. However, Hotze posted blockade statistics for the Atlantic Coast in *The Index*, partly to influence public opinion against the blockade but also to encourage blockade-running.[69]

Symbols were also powerful tools that Hotze attempted to employ in his fight for Southern recognition. In June of 1863, he proposed placing the new Confederate flag next to the British Union Jack in every available space in the London streets. He wrote, "This which I design simply as a demonstration to impress the masses with the vitality of our cause, I expect to accomplish in time to produce some effect before the motion comes on for discussion."[70] (The motion that Hotze was referring to was the motion for Confederate recognition by Parliament.) Hotze clearly understood that not only must an oral message be repeated at least six times to be understood; it must be supported with consistent nonverbal messages of symbols. Unfortunately, this proposal also failed because of a lack of funds.

Hotze organized a series of large pro-Confederate meetings in outlying towns to bolster the motion for recognition that was being introduced in the House of Commons on June 30 by J.A. Roebuck. When the motion was withdrawn on July 13, Hotze wrote that all parliamentary action is past. "Diplomatic means can no longer prevail, and everybody looks to Lee to conquer recognition."[71] He consistently attempted to stay productively ahead of the public opinion changes, always giving professional public relations advice that was honest and blunt. Even after the fall of Vicksburg and General Lee's crushing defeat at Gettysburg in July 1863, the English community and journals still believed that the Confederacy would succeed. Hotze wrote to Benjamin:

> ... at no time during this war has our cause received such valuable assistance from journalism. It is unfortunately too true that the English nation has taken in our struggle rather what may be called a sporting interest ... and has not yet fully waked up to the universal issues of moral right, national liberty, humanity and civilization, which are involved in the contest.[72]

He recommended continuing to influence England's opinion leaders because they, rather than the general public, form and crystallize public opinion. However, even though Hotze believed in the effectiveness of his propaganda work, he also realized that it would take someone more persuasive than himself to win over all of Europe. He wrote: "I could wish that some solemn voice, louder and more authoritative than that of the mere journalist, a voice which can command at once the attention of the whole civilized world, might speak to the conscience of this nation."[73]

Benjamin continued to support *The Index*, writing on September 19, 1863: "The paper being to a certain extent an English journal, although devoted to our defense, the moderate and temperate tone in which it is conducted is not only necessary but eminently judicious."[74]

Pamphleteering was one of Hotze's public relations tools employed early in his propaganda battles. Some of his pamphlets included Spence's *The American Union*, which was translated into French and German; Frank Key Howard's *Fourteen Months in American Bastilles*, which chronicled the Union's cruelty to Confederate prisoners of war; and *Address to Christians Throughout the World*, which supported slavery throughout the world. Hotze believed that frequent repetition of messages to targeted publics would produce more chances for a successful reception of messages. Hotze told Benjamin, "Again, it is not one newspaper article, nor a dozen, but hundreds that affect public opinion at large. Reiteration is the most powerful argument with the hundreds of thousands who take their opinions at second hand."[75] Hotze said the operator who directs those efforts should be "invisible."[76]

Hotze continued to have critics in the Confederacy whose objections were based on misunderstanding about what he was attempting to do with *The Index*. Former Confederate Senator Clement C. Clay of Alabama wrote in 1864:

> I apprehend The Index has but few readers besides its patrons and our open and active friends, does not reach the minds of the great body of the English public opinions. Moreover, it has not met the oft recurring questions of public law where our rights and interests have been disregarded with requisite promptness and force. I have in memory several instances . . . where the wrong done by the English Government was palpably and not strongly presented for us.[77]

Despite the criticism, Hotze had established effective propaganda operations in France, Italy, Germany, and England by the middle of 1864, and *The Index* was being published and distributed in China and Australia. However, during September 1864, more than 300,000 people signed peace petitions that were sent from the people of Britain to America. Hotze, a realist, realized that he had been unsuccessful in achieving the ultimate goal: English recognition of the Southern Confederacy and the possibility of England joining the war on the Confederate side. Hotze wrote an unusually long and pessimistic letter to Benjamin on July 29, 1864.

> For over two years we have had a clear majority of the English press in our favor. The geography of the war, its causes, its events, the resources of the combatants, were not better understood or more elaborately treated even in America, and yet this did not prevent Lord Palmerston at the end of the session insulting a deputation of English gentlemen of the highest respectability by telling them that "they who in quarrels interpose will often wipe a bloody nose." . . . I fear we are doomed to continued disappointment, and money and efforts are alike thrown away.[78]

The end was now clearly in sight for the Confederacy and *The Index*. On April 25, 1865, news arrived from the Confederacy that General Lee had surrendered the Army of Northern Virginia on April 9 at Appomattox Court House, Virginia. James D. Bulloch, Confederate naval agent abroad, wrote Hotze on April 25: "The Confederacy cannot recover from the shock of Lee's surrender . . . So long as the President holds out, I will, but fancy he will in time be forced to acknowledge the inevitable result. I hope you will be able to keep up *The Index*. . . ."[79] Hotze intended to keep publishing *The Index* for as long as possible. He wrote a correspondent on June 1, 1865: "The Index will, of course, continue to vindicate the true history of the struggle and the principles which though overcome by force still survive, but it will be less exclusively Southern than heretofore . . ."[80] From April until August 12, 1865, Hotze continued to publish *The Index*, but on August 12, 1865, the newspaper's final issue hit the European streets. The publisher of *The Index* said goodbye to his loyal readers.

> This is the last number of The Index . . . The blockade of the South rendered it necessary for the representative of the Confederate Government, to have some avowed channel of publication; and, naturally, this position developed upon this journal. Under such circumstances, though we regretted, we had no right to complain, that in Europe we were looked upon as the mere organ of the Confederate Government, and that we were described in the United States as "the rebel organ."
>
> We are strongly tempted to address a few last words to our Southern readers . . . The long agony of the South will not be without a reward. Though defeated, the South is not dishonored. The history of her independent existence does not exceed four years, but it is a complete and brilliant record that will endure so long as virtue and heroism are venerated . . . The Southern Confederacy has fallen, but her gallant sons have not died in vain. Whatever flag waves over her capitols the South will be free. Under whatever Government her people live, their influence will be felt . . . Time will obliterate the ravages of the fierce conflict, and the South, chastened by the will of God, and exalted by her chastening, will yet be happy and prosperous as in bygone days . . . It is with a good heart, though with personal pain, we bid our Southern friends farewell.[81]

The Index's 172nd issue was its final. It had been a remarkable persuasion experiment by a talented man. *The Index* was published from May 1, 1862, until August 12, 1865, with little funds, English writers, and a dream of Southern recognition. At the time of its death *The Index* was circulating in England, France, Germany, Australia, China, Italy, and, of course, America. It was the Confederacy's main propaganda tool abroad. Hotze wrote:

> . . . owing to their exiled condition, [it was] too poor, or else had too many other demands upon its purse, or is I regret to add, in some instances too lukewarm, and withal too numerically small, to afford that support with even an approach to adequacy. Much of this might have been avoided, had it been possible to manage the paper as a commercial speculation and less as a political engine, but this was and is out of the question. The Index, moreover, commits daily a sort of intellectual suicide. In educating English writers to plead our cause, often purposely with greater emphasis in the columns of other journals, it has raised rivals even in the affection of its own supporters, and few suspect, none know, the silent unobtrusive agency through which it has operated upon its contemporaries.[82]

Even though *The Index* had support from England's opinion leaders, it was never able to convince Parliament to vote for Southern recognition, and Hotze's other public relations tactics, such as symbols, speechwriting, issues management, and pamphleteering, had limited success. After the war ended, Hotze never returned to his adopted home in America and continued working as a journalist in Europe, mostly in Paris. There, in 1868, he married Ruby Senac, the daughter of a Confederate navy paymaster. They had no children.[83] Near the end of his life, he returned to Switzerland, where he died on April 19, 1887, in Zug, a small town 20 miles south of Zurich, the town where he was born on September 2, 1833.[84]

12

John H. Linebaugh: On the Move for the *Memphis Daily Appeal*

Matthew J. Bosisio

THE DROWNING DEATH OF JOHN H. LINEBAUGH SAID A LOT ABOUT THE kind of Civil War correspondent he was: aggressive, opinionated, somewhat rash and nervous, and prone to bolt when potential trouble threatened.

Such was the case on the night of October 26, 1864, when the steamboat on which he was a passenger suddenly ran aground in the Alabama River. Rather than wait for daybreak and certain rescue, Linebaugh and several other uneasy passengers slipped over the side and attempted to reach the shore. He was the only one who failed to make it in the swift-moving current.[1]

Linebaugh had left Richmond, Virginia, five days earlier en route to Alabama to the area in which General John Bell Hood's Army of the Tennessee was operating. He represented several different newspapers, including the four that had recently organized themselves into the Richmond Mutual Press Association. Linebaugh's assignment was to cover Hood's march from northern Alabama to Nashville.[2]

He was quite familiar with the regiment, having reported on the army for several months while it was under the command of General Braxton Bragg. Linebaugh was working for the *Memphis Daily Appeal* at the time, and the army's movements were of particular interest to the newspaper's editors, who had to keep moving the newspaper's offices to escape Federal seizure. Linebaugh joined the staff in Atlanta, where the newspaper had fled from Jackson, Mississippi, after Federal troops entered that city.[3]

Even though he was 51 years old, Linebaugh was a neophyte journalist, only joining the *Appeal* staff after several other careers. Editors John Reid McClanahan and Benjamin F. Dill had been desperately looking for a war correspondent when Linebaugh appeared in June 1863. His lack of training, experience, and, some would come to say, courage made him a poor fit. The result was that his tenure with the newspaper lasted but nine months and was occasionally marked by notable and combustible events.

Originally from Kentucky, Linebaugh first trained for the law, and in December 1840, he was practicing in Tuscaloosa, Alabama. The work may not have appealed to him, however, because he did not remain long in that field.[4]

After two years of legal work, Linebaugh shifted gears and entered the religious life. He was recommended for orders in October 1842 and was assigned his first post as a deacon at St. Stephen's Church in Eutaw, Alabama. He augmented his duties at St. Stephen's with preaching at parishes throughout Alabama whenever requested. Linebaugh was subsequently ordained an Episcopal priest at the age of 33.[5]

In April 1846, he was given two separate mission assignments: St. Paul's Church in Selma and, each first Sunday, St. Luke's in nearby Cahawba. He "entered upon his duties with the most flattering of prospects of being extensively useful."[6]

Linebaugh's usefulness was required immediately. What he found at St. Paul's was a church in serious decline. The parish was struggling and heavily in debt. As he described it, there was not "much in the present condition of the Parish to encourage."[7] The church was unfinished and $2,400 in the red.

The new minister turned to the church's creditors and managed to persuade most of them to forgive nearly 75 percent of the debt. He was left with $637 to dissolve by December 1847. That amount, as well as refurbishing the church, was eventually accomplished through a donation from Christ Church in Mobile, a gift from a parishioner from Christ Church in Tuscaloosa, and various church functions.

Linebaugh reportedly also built up the budget by other creative means, including renting the church basement "as a warehouse for the storing of liquors . . . and other articles."[8] Within 18 months, he was able to declare that the state of the church was debt-free and "in a healthy condition."

His personal finances were another matter. By now married and with four children, Linebaugh reported in May 1849 that the parish he had rescued had, nevertheless, produced insufficient funds to meet the needs of the minister.[9] By year's end, he had cut his ties with St. Paul's and the Diocese of Alabama and had taken up duties as rector of St. James Church in Baton Rouge, Louisiana.

There, he happily encountered a stronger congregation than at St. Paul's and an overall condition that encouraged him "that a brighter day is dawning upon the Church in this Parish."[10] Churchgoers found him to be a sociable minister, but they also concluded that he was rather "too fond of the inebriating cup for his own good . . ."[11] Linebaugh lasted at St. James until 1852, when he was suspended by Bishop Leonidas Polk on unspecified charges "derogatory to the character of the then incumbent."[12] A stint at Emmanuel Church in Athens followed, as did his inglorious defrocking by the bishop of Georgia in 1856 following his "renunciation of the Ministry of the Protestant Episcopal church, and his intention not to officiate in future in any of the Offices thereof . . ."[13]

Linebaugh retreated with his family to an Alabama farm for a number of years and occupied himself in "agricultural pursuits" before finally showing up in Atlanta at the newly established offices of the *Memphis Appeal* in June 1863.[14] It was his first newspaper job. The *Appeal* had recently fled Jackson as Federal troops took the city. It was the third move for the newspaper after leaving Memphis the night of June 5, 1862, destination Grenada, Mississippi. The editors were happy with their new location, but nearly six months later, on November 29, they were forced to flee again as Federal troops advanced into Mississippi. Operations were set up in Jackson. The following spring, the *Appeal* was on the move to the east. From Atlanta, the editors assured their readers that their escape from Jackson was timely and successful.

> Our regular issue was made, as usual, on the morning of the day the Federals entered the city, but through the energy of our attaches and the aid of a number of friends, everything essential to the publication of the paper was brought off. We flatter ourselves our "evacuation" was a masterly one—as it was accomplished without loss, notwithstanding a number of shots were fired across Pearl river at our rear guard by the disappointed Yankees.[15]

Assigned to the Army of Tennessee, Linebaugh, now a cub reporter, decided to station himself at Dalton, Georgia, about 25 miles south of where the army had set up camp. His decision was considered unusual by the standards of war coverage at the time, and it kept him isolated from other correspondents assigned to the same army. Linebaugh defended his apparent aversion to camping with the army by telling his editors repeatedly that nothing was happening that was worth reporting.[16] It was the first in a string of incidents that found Linebaugh absent or fleeing from the point of news, often to the consternation of his editors.

One such incident found him in the heart of the action. On August 21, 1863, Linebaugh was attending a service at the Presbyterian Church in Chattanooga. Midway through the service, a Yankee shell exploded near the church, killing one man and injuring another. It was the beginning of an attack on the city.[17] Instead of covering the story, Linebaugh caught the first train to Atlanta. He later explained that he had done so because he had "a lady under my protection."[18] The *Appeal* was scooped by the *Mobile Advertiser and Register* with a story written by Chattanooga *Rebel* Editor Henry Watterson, who had also attended the church service.

When Linebaugh reported the news or wrote a column, he often worked under the pen name of "Ashante." He owned up to that signature in a letter to Vice President Alexander Stephens.[19] (The letter was written in April 1864, two months after he had terminated his employment at the *Appeal*.)

Readers came to know the pen name as Linebaugh's, if only from his writing style, a style that might best be described as effusive. He had "a penchant for foreign expressions, historical allusions, complex vocabulary, and wordiness demonstrated in necklaces of prepositional phrases."[20] While one obituary generously declared him to have been "a graceful and polished writer, a profound thinker, and a scholar of rare attainments and extensive classical reading,"[21] his readers found him to be anything but. One sentence that appeared in a column consisted of 139 words.

> That this occultation was to be expected, as the necessary prelude, nay, presage of our independence was the prophesy of the thoughtful and it is only those who knew not what revolution meant, or supposed it was a transition from one dream of criminal or inglorious repose to another, those who knew nothing of freedom in its aspects of dignity, and were willing to take servitude, even the degraded servitude of superimposed Yankee domination if it were gilded with wealth, or attended by an emasculate or traitorous enjoyment of delegated prosperity, in preference to the noble enjoyment of mental, moral, and political independence, the independence of a free-born heart, mind and will, who are cast down; so much cast down as to be now willing to make terms of peace upon condition of preserving a mess of miserable potage.[22]

He fell to using such words as "didactic," "afflucium," and "abhosta doceri," not exactly in the mainstream vocabulary of the day.[23] Linebaugh's response to his agitated readers was consistent with his usual response to any criticism. He lashed out: "Our English seems to be 'Greek and Latin' to some of our city contemporaries. Well, we are not surprised at that, as pure English, as well as good sense, is 'all Dutch' to many people."[24]

In the field, his trials and inexperience led to hit-and-miss reporting and to dispatch topics that were not always on point. There was little consistency. At times, his subject matter, for example, was on "theoretical strategies, Greek mythology, Wellington minutia, or religious admonitions,"[25] instead of on information pertinent to his beat. Other times, his reporting and commentary were "detailed and informative,"[26] especially when pressured by his editors.

Once, when writing about the towns he watched being evacuated in anticipation of the arrival of Federal troops, Linebaugh focused his detailed descriptions on the human element of the war.

> Men, women, children, servants moving off with steps quickened by the excitement of danger, or fear of being left behind, indulging in no retrospective leave takings or lingering regrets, or casting backward a look of love or sadness at their separation from home with its long role of tender and endearing attachments and association, while wagons filled with household goods, horses, cows, sheep, and even dogs, are seen wending their way along, as if, influenced by some strange

Linebaugh was concerned about Charleston, South Carolina. Shown here are the
Ruins of the Round Church and Secession Hall. Photograph from the Library of
Congress

or mysterious destiny, they were lost in dreamy doubt as to the present, and in
unexplained confusion as to the future. This tearing up household memories and
attachments by the roots, abandoning the territory upon which one was born,
giving up everything dear to interest and memory alike, to become an exile and
wanderer, is a sad, sad spectacle, and sadder experience; but an evidence of patriotism, sublimely truthful, and which proves that the world has not lost all its
heroism, but possesses still a claim to virtue, not less undisputed, than that which
makes the pages of history luminous with its luster.[27]

Concerned in particular about Charleston, South Carolina, and the possibility that the city might fall to the enemy, Linebaugh turned to his knowledge of
the classics and his vision of the future.

If Charleston must yield, she will be a prouder monument of glory and love of
country than has been witnessed since Marathon, and, like that ancient scene
of conflict, will make the name of Carolina as illustrious in the future of the
world as that of holy and classic Greece itself. It will be enough for her sons, when

wandering in exile on some foreign shore, to procure the homage of devotion and enthusiastic admiration to say, "I am a Carolinian. I am one of that little commonwealth that did all, and dared all, and surrendered and sacrificed all for the sake of honor, liberty and love of country." And surely, in the coming times, it will be a sufficient eulogy and epitaph.[28]

Linebaugh was not well liked by the men in uniform and was particularly detested by General Braxton Bragg, who was often criticized by the reporter,[29] including once when Linebaugh confided to readers that "it may be as his friends would seem to contend, that the chief of the army is an apotheosis."[30] In one comment, Linebaugh delivered a broadside against the general that was somewhat veiled and couched in the notion of liberty.

> We may have our opinion of Gen. Bragg, but that opinion we have never obtruded upon the public, save when we thought the highest interests of the cause demanded its expression . . . We are anxious, above all things, to avert subjugation, and have given our whole influence, without stint and without reserve, from the beginning of this war, to this object, but we are equally anxious to come out of this revolution with our national robes of constitutional liberty unspotted by the terrible ordeal through which they have passed. Personal liberty, liberty of opinion and liberty of the press, we desire to see unimpaired, for without them our success over the foe on our borders, will be worse than a barren success.[31]

In another, the correspondent defended his criticisms of the general as being on the basis of liberty and not as attacks on Bragg's reputation.

> While, as a citizen, I have felt free to criticize many acts of administration—acts inseparable from the endless ramifications and responsibilities of his peculiar field of duty—yet we have never impeached the purity and integrity of his political character. This we believe to be as pure as the sun in the heaven, and that Washington himself was possessed of a no more sound love of human liberty, or more sacred desire to transmit it untarnished and unimpaired to future generations.[32]

Regardless of what Linebaugh wrote, Bragg considered him a correspondent who violated blackout orders and spread false information.

The *Appeal*, like most newspapers, struggled with these kinds of reporting issues, as well as with censorship and sometimes arbitrary restrictions. The editors understood the importance of keeping sensitive information out of the hands of the enemy, which was widely assumed to be reading the Confederate press. But the editors, "fearing that information was often withheld only to protect the reputation of a commander, preferred to determine for themselves what news might be published."[33]

In one editorial, they complained that correspondents had been frequently in Bragg's camp "until a general order was recently issued by that officer, declaring that no news reports should be sent by telegraph from his camp." Linebaugh commented, "Similar orders have no doubt been issued by other military commanders, and by the Secretary of war, which tend to deprive us of the news."[34]

When it seemed appropriate, the *Appeal*, considered a "rabidly rebellious newspaper,"[35] did not hesitate to defend reporters who were obstructed or harassed. Once, the editors took to task Major General Earl Van Dorn for fining and imprisoning reporters whose stories he perceived to be merely "calculated to impair confidence in any of the commanding officers."[36]

In spite of the criticism, the *Appeal* seldom ran afoul of commanders. However, the animosity between Bragg and Linebaugh became increasingly troublesome, even though Linebaugh had at one point been complimentary of the general.[37] Matters came to a head between the two men early on September 16, 1863, only days before the battle began at Chickamauga in extreme northwest Georgia. An unsigned arrest dispatch was sent to Colonel A.W. Caldwell, commandant of the post at Rome, Georgia, ordering that Linebaugh be taken into custody. The order was executed and Linebaugh was held until that evening, when a signed arrest and transmission order arrived from Bragg. The correspondent was taken under armed guard 12 miles west to Kingston, Georgia, and held overnight.[38] The following day, Linebaugh was sent by train to Atlanta and consigned to "the common barrack prison."[39] He was held without charges.

When word reached Dill, the *Appeal*'s co-editor, the newspaper hired an attorney to file a writ of habeas corpus, challenging Linebaugh's arrest without evidence. Before it could be served, and on word that the writ was coming, Linebaugh was sent by boxcar to Dalton, then secreted away to the stockade in Ringgold, Georgia. He was there for 10 days before Bragg suddenly released him on October 4.[40] During his confinement, Linebaugh was prevented from covering the Battle of Chickamauga, arguably one of the great Confederate victories.

No formal charges were filed, but allegations of treason were widely rumored, based on the fact that Linebaugh had been reportedly writing of troop movements ahead of the battle. Another popular theory for his arrest was that Linebaugh had suggested that the general was unwilling to engage Federal forces, fanning Bragg's rising fury with the reporter.[41]

In any event, the editors at the *Appeal* were incensed. They said so (or perhaps it was Linebaugh himself) in an editorial three days after his release.

> As the case at present stands, Gen. Bragg, or whoever else ordered the arrest, has been guilty of a high political and civil offense for violation of the Constitution and the persons who were engaged in abducting the prisoner, after service of the writ, are liable, according to the laws of Georgia, to the penalties of kidnapping.[42]

The editorial noted further that the reporter's arrest "was without authority, and the absurdity of the charge itself, as of the arrest, is proved by their refusal to yield obedience to a civil mandate, issued to have a civil accusation disposed of judicially, the only way in which it could be disposed of, in accordance with the assumption promoting the arrest."[43]

For his part, and under his own name, Linebaugh unleashed his indignation in a front-page story in the *Appeal.* In it, he insisted that he had done nothing differently than any other correspondent or newspaper, noting that if he were "guilty of indiscretion," which he conceded was possible, so, too, were many.[44]

His article suggested that the real blame for any breach lay, instead, at the feet of field officers with loose lips. Linebaugh denied ever violating official confidences, and argued that he was incapable of it.

> While within the lines of the army I applied to many general officers for news, but for only such news as was communicable by the laws of its service, stating that it was intended for publication, and in every instance having permission to use it, relying upon the integrity and intelligence, and, in all respects, superior knowledge of the duties in the premises of the officers themselves, rather than my own judgment. Officers, in this regard, should know their own military rules and obligations better than a civilian. I cannot remember a single instance in which I ever violated, in my letters, an official confidence, and if I know myself, I am incapable of it. If officers cannot keep their own official confidences, but insist upon ventilating them by free and easy communication to eager ears, they cannot expect else than that they will "take the wings of the morning and fly to the uttermost parts of the earth."[45]

Linebaugh pointed out that his particular imprisonment was hardly an isolated incident among the various Southern armies.

> The experience of my incarceration made me acquainted with many others who, without friends or acquaintances, or pecuniary ability to fee lawyers, were languishing in confinement, in ignorance of the charges upon which they had been arrested. The fear is that "military necessity" is to become the law of the land, and that the possession of military authority in the hands of ignorant, passionate or tyrannical men is to become the authority and warrant of its exercise.[46]

But Linebaugh was not finished. He had one additional point to drive home regarding his arrest.

> If treason consists in giving "aid and comfort" to the enemy, based upon the possibility of a newspaper containing army news reaching the enemy, General Bragg's pet journals are as much guilty of treason as others, for they contain just the same news, telegraphic and general, as do others, and I have heard of no measures or special police to keep them from the enemy more than applies to others. Mr. Provost Marshal McKinstry, with his rare legal acumen and detective vigilance, can inform the public perhaps.[47]

Standing with the *Appeal* on principle, the *Huntsville Confederate* also blasted those responsible for Linebaugh's arrest. "While sustaining Gen. Bragg and Colonel [Alexander] McKinstry, however, we do not approve of the conduct of their subordinates in disobeying the writ of habeas corpus. The military should be subordinate to the civil authority, and the writ should have been obeyed promptly."[48] In general, however, most reporters and editors—while harboring no love for Bragg and his methods of dealing with the press—did not sympathize with Linebaugh, seeing him as a bumbling upstart "who never should have been hired as a war correspondent in the first place."[49]

In the end, the *Appeal*'s McClanahan and Dill may have arrived at the same conclusion. Unable to tolerate Linebaugh's reporting deficiencies any longer, he was pulled from the field, a scant four months after he was hired. He was later rehired and assigned desk duty in the *Appeal* office in November 1863, and there he continued his usual writing style through editorial commentary until February of the following year.

Linebaugh quit the newspaper and returned to northern Alabama for several months before resurfacing as the reporter for the new press service that had been organized in Richmond, the Richmond Mutual Press Association. However, Linebaugh died before reaching the destination of his first assignment.

By normal standards, Linebaugh had a difficult go of it throughout much of his adult life. He lost a son to the war and another to illness, did battle with readers and military officers, was criticized for his reporting, and bounced around the South, unable to settle comfortably in any particular career. But he provided a service at or near the action when the *Appeal* most needed it. Eyes and ears were needed on the ground, and editors McClanahan and Dill were willing to take a chance on him. In the end, however, his usefulness was measured in months of service rather than years and in copy that often drifted into "a style of rhetoric and classical allusion that was being outmoded by the war."[50]

Notice of John Linebaugh's untimely death was carried in a number of Southern newspapers, including the *Richmond Whig* a month after the fact. The obituary noted that he left "a wife and interesting family of children, besides a large circle of warm and admiring friends to mourn his loss."[51]

13

Samuel Chester Reid, Jr.: A Professional Goes to War

Mark K. Dolan

AFTER SHIPPING OUT TO SEA AT AGE 16, SAMUEL CHESTER REID, JR., became a surveyor, lawyer, Texas Ranger, newspaper reporter, and the author of four books before joining the Confederate army. At age 42, he was one of the oldest war correspondents for the South.

Reid was born in New York on October 21, 1818,[1] the same year his father helped design a version of the American flag that kept 13 stripes and added a new star for each state. Reid tried to follow in the footsteps of his famous father, a sea captain who held high positions in the Navy and for whom the USS *Reid* was named.[2] However, the sea held little allure for young Reid, and he returned home in less than a year to try his hand at surveying.[3] As part of the first U.S. Geological Survey of the Ohio River, he helped determine where the South began and, in effect, helped draw the Mason-Dixon Line, that mythic crossing for runaway slaves seeking freedom in the North. Reid developed a lifelong interest in mapping, and many of his later newspaper reports included distances and directions. Other jobs that Reid held also suggest this interest. In 1851, he took a job with the National Railroad Convention in Memphis, helping to map a rail line to the Pacific Ocean.[4]

Within a few years, Reid followed the Mississippi River south to Natchez where he studied law and classical literature with General John A. Quitman, who owned Monmouth Plantation in Natchez. Quitman held various political posts in Mississippi, including the governorship from 1835 to 1836.[5] Reid would also serve in the war with Mexico under the brigade commanded by future president Zachary Taylor. Quitman and Taylor both influenced Reid's thinking on the military and helped shape his intellect.

After he completed his studies, Reid settled in New Orleans to practice law. The Texas Rangers enlisted him in 1846, primarily, he wrote later, because he owned a horse. In his preface to his account of the Mexican-American war, Reid wrote that

Samuel Chester Reid, Jr. Courtesy of
Princeton University Press

he joined the Texas Rangers primarily because the idea of enthusiastically assisting his country in a foreign land appealed to him.[6] He apparently joined a scouting
expedition when he was 34 years old, more for adventure than patriotism.

Reid's authorship of several books contributes to understanding his life as a
roving reporter, as he has been called. His first book, *The U.S. Bankruptcy Law of
1841, With a Synopsis and Notes* (Natchez, 1842), was an outgrowth of Reid's law
studies. Six years later, he wrote *The Scouting Expeditions of McCulloch's Texas
Rangers* (Philadelphia, 1848), which included several anecdotes of local color,
mostly quoted material. Reid's anecdotes appeared in his later reporting, like
those of Mark Twain and other American humorists. In one, an officer recounted
being given shelter by a wealthy local family on an earlier foray into Mexico. The
family requested that he join them in a formal dance before dinner, despite his
ragamuffin appearance.[7] Later, he was given a hot bath while the daughters in the
family combed the officer's hair back into place with their fingers.[8]

Similar to the way he would later write his Civil War reports, Reid expanded
on the journey itself: how he left New Orleans and sailed across brackish Gulf
waters where several of the crew succumbed to dysentery under a searing, wind-
less sky. He wrote about the wax statues of the Virgin Mary in the windows of
mud houses and described the wedding of an American soldier, his leg recently
amputated, to a Mexican girl who was "determined to have him."[9]

In Reid's preface of his Texas Rangers book, he wrote that he had been persuaded by acquaintances to publish his experiences as "a journal of an expedition

remarkable for many events worthy of being preserved for the future."[10] He dedicated the book to General Taylor, who became for Reid a military role model. On a prefatory page he wrote to Taylor:

> The tribute is offered, not only as a token of the high regard and esteem in which you were held by the men and officers under your command, whose friend and leader you were; and of the high sense universally entertained for your military talents, for which you are justly distinguished; but also for the kind courtesies received at your hands while in the service of our great country.[11]

Reid's model for effective military leadership seems to have derived from his association with Taylor, whom Reid described as affable and demonstrating "kind courtesies" for the other men.[12] The fastidious General Braxton Bragg, with whom Reid would later squabble during the Civil War, was also mentioned in Reid's scouting expedition narrative. Reid's later criticism of Confederate army performance most likely grew out of his own military experiences.

After writing the Texas Rangers book, Reid began writing another book titled *The Life and Times of Aaron Burr, a Vindication,* but his manuscript was destroyed by fire in 1850. Just before the Civil War began, he wrote about the court proceedings of his famous sea-captain father, who commanded one of the most daring battles in naval history. *The Case of the Private-Armed Brig-of-War General Armstrong* (1857) recounted how the elder Reid skirmished with British frigates off the Azores islands. The British ships were en route with supplies to Jamaica, but the encounter bought time for Andrew Jackson to fortify New Orleans during the War of 1812. A lengthy diplomatic correspondence involving several countries followed the sea battle, questioning the degree to which the battle had been fought in neutral waters. Reid's book covered the proceedings before the U.S. Court of Claims.

His early books gave depth to his newspaper career.[13] He had started working for the *New Orleans Picayune* before the war began, simultaneously practicing law and journalism in the city. However, when the war broke out in 1861, the *Picayune* hired Reid to become a "special correspondent," as full-time paid writers were known at the time.[14] The newspaper paid Reid about $25 a week for his work, the usual wage paid by most newspapers.[15]

It was common practice at the time for correspondents to use pen names for anonymity. Reid appeared in the *Picayune* as "Ora" and later as "Sparta." His dispatches to the *Montgomery Advertiser* were also signed "Ora," although he wrote for the *Atlanta Intelligencer* as "290." He initialed several of his reports with the letters "S.C.R." as well as with an "R" or an "S." Several of his reports were left unsigned, indicating perhaps the hasty conditions of war reporting.[16]

Following the armies as they traveled throughout the South, Reid was able to witness and record several of the battles as they happened, as well as to evaluate the general mood of the public in cities and towns across the region. He prized accuracy in his reporting but underplayed the setbacks suffered by the Southern armies, softening the bad news. Although some of his letters fanned the pro-slavery sentiments of Southerners, Reid's best journalism was devoid of opinion, consisting instead of descriptions of the land and terse battle dispatches. His travel anecdotes and slices of daily life read more like personal journal entries, because his colorful dispatches contained a combination of rich descriptions, lengthy anecdotes, and factual news.

Reid also used his reports to boost morale when possible and to unite citizens by keeping them informed. This entailed more than listing army positions and recording casualties. Reid told his readers what the war meant in relation to their way of life. "Our Government and people this year will be made to learn and understand the extent and character of this war, which they previously had so little conception of," he wrote.[17] Moving around the South as he did allowed Reid to explore the differences and similarities of public sentiment across the region and to quell rumors with fact.

During his time spent as a war reporter, Reid witnessed a number of important battles: the Battle of Perryville, the Battle of Stone's River, the Battle of Chicka-mauga, the Battle of Lookout Valley, the Battle of Chattanooga, and the Battle of Kennesaw Mountain—a significant contribution for a single correspondent. Yet his descriptions and travel combined to show his love for the region. He traveled to Kentucky in September 1861 to report on what he hoped would be its seces-sion from the union and described a people determined to control their land. "The true men of Kentucky are rising, and are determined to free themselves from the Lincoln oligarchy. A spirit of true patriotism and the widest enthusiasm is spreading itself all over the southern portion of the state," he wrote.[18]

Reid used humor to make his writing more readable by giving it a more con-versational tone. In a letter from the Cumberland Gap, Reid recalled his march from Knoxville with General John P. McCown and staff, describing scenery along the way. As he passed through the settlement of Gravestone, he mock-ingly noted that it "consists of a few houses, a store, and any quantity of red headed children."[19] Another example of Reid's humor was reflected in a story written on September 4, 1861, obtained from "a very high authority" about a man named Abe Enlow—thought to be Abraham Lincoln—who after stealing a saddle fled to Kentucky where he changed his name in order to escape punish-ment. It was one of many jabs Reid aimed at the U.S. president.

> There is no one who has become lower since Abe Enlow has become a traitor President, under the stolen name Abe Lincoln. But we all said at the time that the boy who stole Jim Craycroft's saddle would never come to any good end . . . There can be no doubt, after this authority, as to who Abe Lincoln is. I wish this to take its chance on reaching you, but if any of Old Abe's get hold of it, it will be sure to miscarry.[20]

In a letter from the Cumberland Gap, Tennessee, Reid recalled his march from Knoxville with General John P. McCown and staff and described scenery along the way. *Harper's Weekly,* July 5, 1862. Courtesy of Rare Books and Special Collections, University of South Carolina Libraries

Reid included himself as a member of this Southern society, bonding himself to kinsmen and creating fervor for the South's cause. While in Tennessee on February 16, 1862, Reid was forced to leave his post after a mail carrier failed to arrive that morning. Recounting his trip to headquarters to send a telegram, he wrote:

> I called at headquarters today—enjoying a delightful walk of a mile and a half, ankle deep mud—and saw Major Gen. Polk, who is looking remarkably well, notwithstanding his severe labors. While there I learned a telegram had been received from Tuscumbia, stating that the enemy had taken possession of the telegraph office in Florence, and had found out everything that had been passing over the wires at the time . . .[21]

Yet, his letters also explained the difficulties Reid faced obtaining accurate information and the patience he displayed to obtain it. Rumors were rampant and passed quickly through camps, leaving correspondents like Reid to separate fact from fiction.[22]

Since verification was difficult to accomplish in the midst of battle, information printed in newspapers often consisted of little more than unsubstantiated gossip. Although, according to Reid, some correspondents were content to publish anything they received, Reid felt uncomfortable relaying hearsay and worked actively to stop rumors. He refused to print details that seemed sketchy or thin; if he did feel the need to pass it on, he would accompany the report with a disclaimer that it might not be true. He wrote: "I could send you a thousand floating rumors, which come from tergiversating, fluctuating, reliable gentlemen, but it is not worthwhile"[23] In this way, Reid's lively and intrepid commentary made him a favorite among those who depended on newspapers for their information. "I start at dawn tomorrow for the front," he wrote. "I send this by courier to Corinth, and also a dispatch of the news, which I hope may reach you. There are no telegraph lines from here, and the news will have to be sent by couriers to Corinth."[24]

Reid had a commitment to a free and independent press, and several of his reports cite other newspapers and magazines from which Reid had gleaned additional information. He rebutted articles published in Northern newspapers as a way of arguing for the Confederate cause. He also reported information about watercraft and other weaponry published in magazines such at the *Atlantic Monthly*, indirectly assisting the Confederate army as a collector of information.[25]

Reid's devotion to truth telling helped explain why he detested spies. The fear of Northern spies was prevalent in the Southern states, and so great was this threat that a man caught out of uniform and unable to identify himself could be executed on the spot. This fear, while not unsubstantiated, was propagated—at least in part—by those working for the press. Reid apparently shared this fear, since his dispatches revealed his preoccupation with covert infiltration: "The enemy, no doubt, has many spies out, hovering around us and is well posted as to many of our movements. I fear that there has not been that strictness observed in this regard which should prevail."[26]

Many of his reports described the capture and execution of the intruders, while others simply presumed the guilt of drifters, as in this report.

A spy, supposed to be one of Lane's Kansas jayhawkers, who had made his way here from Missouri, boldly came into camp today and asked for an audience with Gen. Polk, saying that he had the most important news to communicate. He is a miserable, cadaverous looking creature, and the personification and embodiment of all that is mean and despicable in the Yankee. The burthen of his secret was that a large portion of the people on the border were ready to join the Southern States if they could only receive assurance from President Davis that they would be well received and protected. He modestly asked for transportation and money to pay his expenses to Richmond, that he might communicate this "highly important, if true," communication to the president. On being asked where he was from, he answered North Carolina, but admitted that he was born in Massachusetts. He was but a base imposter.[27]

Correspondents worried about being captured and imprisoned or executed. The penalty for spying was usually death as illustrated by two Confederate spies named Williams and Peters, who were hanged by the Army of the Cumberland on June 9, 1863. *Harper's Weekly*, July 4, 1863. Courtesy of Rare Books and Special Collections, University of South Carolina Libraries

Reid's emphasis on small detail and natural beauty set his stories apart from those of some correspondents and it also revealed the difficulties of life as a correspondent. Faced with inclement weather and transportation problems, he found it difficult and tiring to get out timely dispatches. Mail carriers were sparse and telegraph lines, if present, were not always functional.[28] While in Corinth, Mississippi, he wrote on March 30, 1862, "The telegraph was down today between this to Memphis, nearly all day, and such is the press of military business over the lines that it is with great difficulty that anything can be got through."[29]

Reid also complained that the post office at Chattanooga was the worst managed in the Confederacy. Underscoring the importance of dependable communication both to the military and to the Southern press, he wrote, "Hardly a week passes but that a new commander is appointed on account of some whim or (sic) of the authorities; the consequence is that it is impossible to conduct the affairs and duties of the Post with any degree of regularity . . . "[30] Reid cited unfair treatment by the Northern press, even of its own officers: "General (George) Beal has been lately vilified by the Yankee press, especially by those Abolition hounds . . . of the Nashville sheet," who faulted Beal for protecting the property and belongings of Southern citizens.[31]

However, Reid's criticisms were never so caustic as to risk alienating his readers, and he kept their interests and values at the core of his reporting. His letters overflowed with Confederate patriotism and the issues about which he felt most passionately. But for Reid, patriotism did not mean blindly praising the military and remaining positive despite setbacks and mistakes. It meant covering the war with a critical eye.

Cautious optimism pervaded many of his letters, despite incompetence he perceived in the military's upper ranks. He railed against generals whose lax discipline he felt would prevent the Confederacy from gaining victory. While Reid was not always positive in his assessments of the Confederate army, he used his critiques as motivation for its improvement. For example, upon visiting Colonel Sam Marks and his "Bloody 11th Louisiana" regiment on March 28, 1862, he reported that they were in "splendid condition" and "under the strictest discipline,"[32] adding that this was the requisite leadership for victory. Reid's criticism was usually couched in an urgent tug at the reader to recognize the army's efforts.

> If we are to win our independence, we must have a disciplined army and efficient and working officers to do it with. The sooner the people find this great fact out the better, and the greater our chances for ending this war. I can assure them, however, of one great fact, the men in our army have found it out, and many have learned, to their great sorrow, the difference between the capacity of the officer able to take his company, or regiment, through a holiday parade in the streets of a city and his total inefficiency in the field to perform his duties, attend to the wants, and secure the comfort and health of his men.[33]

It took six days for this dispatch to arrive at the *Picayune*. Such delays were not unusual, as several of his reports underscored the unreliability of wartime communications: "The trains are now so irregular, being detained by freight trains, both ways, that the mails seldom come through with any certainty, which will account for my letters being so long on the way."[34]

Reid, who was cited for bravery by the Texas Rangers for his service in the war with Mexico, had formed strong opinions about how the South might best position itself militarily to win. He did not hesitate to offer his opinions in his newspaper reports, which was one reason military officers who believed in censorship during wartime considered Reid troublesome. He fought attempts to censor his reports, emerging as a proponent of press freedom in the process. However, he also believed in press restrictions, especially with regard to revealing the location of armies.

"Great dissatisfaction is produced at headquarters by impudent correspondents and others, mentioning the movements of our Generals and other matters, thereby giving the cue to the enemy for obtaining information and our movements and designs," he wrote on April 6, 1862.[35] In addition to trying to keep rumors out of his own dispatches, Reid tried to correct those he heard from others. He added: "The boastful and knowingly exaggerated and false report of (Gen. Henry) Halleck, of the capture of Paris, Tenn., in his official communication to his government demands contradiction and denial for the vindication of truth."[36]

Reid's misfortunes as a roving correspondent made for entertaining material for readers at home. His vivid and biting commentary gave audiences a fascinating look at the traveler's journey into war. In an article in the *Picayune*, and "much fatigued" after a rough 10-mile journey on April 10, 1862, from Corinth to Monterey, Tennessee, Reid recalled the events of the day.

> I left Corinth this afternoon at 4 o'clock, in an ambulance of the 4th Louisiana, having been disappointed with the horse promised me, and it being impossible to gain another at any price . . . The road is very rough and hilly, with numerous mud holes and occasional swamps. To make the trip interesting and diversified, we had a miserable, wind-broken, balky, spavined C.S. horse which some speculating horse jockey had swindled the Government to pay no doubt $250 for. If the villain, and others of the same kidney, had thought for a moment that such a horse would be used for hauling wounded men from the battlefield, and knowing that he was unfit for service, his conscience would have been troubled with neuralgia. We broke down several times in the mud holes and swamps, and had every occasion to improvise a new set of harness, which consequently delayed us very much . . . There are no telegraph lines from here, and the news will have to be sent by couriers to Corinth.[37]

His dedication to truth-telling under adverse conditions showed Reid's devotion to accuracy and fact-finding. He fought to ensure that the public received information free from manipulation, speculation, or deceit. Factual and detached when reporting on the specifics of a given battle or on the movement of troops, Reid also used persuasive language to rally support from those readers who may have been questioning the South's presence in the war. His scenes of war often served as a sort of prelude to his opining. In Reid's view, surrender was not an option, and the cost of lives could not outweigh the need for vengeance against what he called a tyrannical foe.

> When the wearied soldier, at the tap of the drum, stretches himself at night upon his blanket on the tented field, it is but natural that he should ponder on the issues of the war which had induced him to take up arm's in his country's cause. When he reflects that the terrible resort to a bloody strife it forces upon us in defense of our national security and honor; for the preservation of our precious institutions; in the sacred cause of public security, which makes all wars defensive—then it is he becomes nerved for the conflict, and free in a firm reliance in the triumphant (sic) of its justice and holiness. Then it is he feels each morning's reveille is but the overture of our onward daily march toward the accomplishment of a glorious independence.[38]

His reports often contained strong opinions, whether about the battle he was covering or interjecting comments about the ineptness of Lincoln, again, much in the manner of a personal journal. Yet Reid also took pride in sending numbers, which if published, he reasoned, would encourage victory, as in this assessment, published on April 19, 1862, of the number of enemy troops present in the South. He wrote: "The enemy's forces in North Alabama and Middle Tennessee are distributed as follows, which may be considered reliable as to numbers: Gen. Roseneranix (sic) is at Tuscumbia with 20,000. Buel (sic) at Huntsville with 20,000. Rousseau at Decatur with 5,000. At Bridgeport 3,000; at Nashville 1,500; at Murfreesboro 1,500; and at Bull Nelson at McMinnville with 7,000, making in all 58,000 men."[39] Reid then encouraged readers to respond to his information by taking steps to rid the South of Northern forces.

> This army has to be dispatched of. How, a few days after this reaches, you will probably determine. It is in a critical situation, and a decisive blow struck at this moment must prove its ruin. With the homes of North Alabama and Middle Tennessee restored to our people, we cross the Cumberland and Nashville, and then Ho, for Louisville.[40]

It was during this time that Reid lost his newspaper voice in New Orleans, when Federal troops took over the city in April 1862. Reid's reports never missed a beat, however, in the other newspapers he was writing for, including the *Mobile Advertiser and Register.*

During Reid's time as a war correspondent, he angered Generals Braxton Bragg and P.G.T. Beauregard in a series of incidents that shed light on Reid's personal relationships with military leaders and on the relationship between the government and the press.[41] Reid had been supportive of Bragg, whose sternness made him an unpopular successor to Beauregard, who had been popular with the Confederate press.

Reid's problems with Beauregard stemmed from a different source, this one involving an information leak that eventually led to a restriction on the correspondents. The incident occurred after Reid sent a dispatch to the *Memphis Appeal* that resulted in a charge of breach of security. The controversial dispatch appeared on May 22, 1862, and as was customary in many such dispatches, it predicted an imminent battle. "A general engagement is expected tomorrow. Our troops marched out this evening," it read in part.[42] But Reid had likely angered Beauregard for another reason: his report referenced the general's failed advance earlier that month on John Pope's troops at Farmington, Mississippi, and Beauregard did not suffer such criticism well.[43]

Two days after the article appeared, Beauregard ordered all press correspondents to board a train and remain at least 25 miles outside of Corinth.[44] Reid denied the charges in a letter to the *Charleston Courier*, submitting evidence that the dispatch had been cleared for publication by the military beforehand. Reid even claimed that Bragg had ordered the journalists away, thus reinvigorating Bragg's anger with Reid for his reports on the Battle of Shiloh.[45] Since it was impossible for Reid to tell his stories without them, he included both Beauregard and Bragg in most of his accounts. "This movement of the enemy is for the purpose of flanking Chattanooga, and compelling General Bragg to abandon that almost impregnable position. Whether he will be successful or not, cannot yet be determined," Reid wrote.[46]

Reid's fallout with Bragg began after the Battle of Shiloh when he visited the general to get information about another recent battle. Bragg, who had recently read war accounts in other papers, felt that the press had been disrespectful to him by minimizing his presence in the battle reports. Infuriated by what he had read, Bragg refused to talk to Reid, who tried unsuccessfully to assure the general that his dispatches had indeed done him justice. There is evidence of Reid's support for Bragg. On the destruction of private property by Confederate soldiers during battle, Reid supported Bragg's order to punish those in the ranks guilty of destroying the property of the South's own citizens.

> We must . . . all rid ourselves of the army drones with which we are now inflicted. As an instance of this demoralizing effect of the elective system in our army, and the incompetentcy [sic] of officers to preserve a proper *esprit de corps* and discipline among the men of some of our regiments, I send you the following "orders" issued lately by Maj. Gen. Bragg, and approved by Gen. Beauregard, which should be read by every Soldier in the service.[47]

Bragg's order of March 16, 1862, "denounced acts of pillage, plunder, and destruction of private property of our own citizens, by a portion of the troops of this command, which will bring disgrace upon our arms, and if not checked, will assuredly entail disaster upon our cause."[48] Later, when Reid approached members of Bragg's staff who had promised him details for his report, he was informed that they had already forwarded all communication to the *Mobile Advertiser and Register*, leaving Reid empty-handed.[49]

The dispute between Bragg and the correspondent continued for months. In November 1862, Bragg's army was preparing to march into Kentucky, and Reid had sent a request asking permission to follow the troops. When he learned that his request had been refused and that he had been ordered to leave Chattanooga, Reid retaliated by writing a letter exposing Bragg's discrimination against him that appeared in the *Charleston Mercury* and the *Chattanooga Times*.[50] Reid's initial request to Bragg was reprinted verbatim.

> Sir: Learning that an order has been issued prohibiting all persons not properly associated with the army, from accompanying it, or remaining within its lines, I desire to ask the courtesy of being permitted to attend the army on its onward march, as correspondent of the Mobile Advertiser and Register.[51] If this

permission is granted, the General commanding may be fully assured that the strictest observance of all military rules and regulations will be complied with, and that any suggestions will be most cheerfully received and acquiesced in.[52]

Reid's outrage over the event illustrates both the passion he felt for freedom of the press and his unwillingness to be left out of a big story. He concluded:

And it has come to this, that all means of obtaining information for the people is to be stopped at the caprice of an officer, and that the press is to be silenced by corruption within, and gagged by force of arms without, and yet it shall be deemed *policy* not to utter a murmur of dissent or disapprobation? While I live, I will discharge what I consider to be the duty I owe my country in warning the people of their danger, and I shall never shirk the responsibility for their consequences, though I should perish as the victim of a malignant combination. It must not be forgotten that this is the people's war, and not a war of the making of any one man, or to be conducted by him. The people have paid for the support of this war themselves, not only with their money, but with their property and lives.[53]

Although Reid sometimes had to appease high-ranking military officials to get the story, he took pride in accuracy and in dispelling the "quantity of rumors in camp" that played on the emotions of the Southern troops.

For instance, it was a current report that our advance forces had captured yesterday at Monterey, ten miles from this place, six of the enemy's artillery pieces, and any quantity of mules—all of which was entirely false. Again, it was said the enemy had advanced last night with a force of 15,000 on Pea Ridge, on the road from Hamburg to this point, and that an engagement would take place today. To those who are posted, these rumors afford much amusement, in watching the thermometer of expectation rise and fall with our troops.[54]

Although Reid received permission from another general to enter Kentucky, his problems with Bragg were far from over. In January 1863, he received word that Bragg intended to arrest him the following day for traveling into Kentucky. Taking no chances, Reid left immediately for Tennessee. One report from Cumberland Gap and published in the *Mobile Advertiser and Register* shows the passion he felt covering this battle, and personifies Reid's reporting.

We are encamped on the Barboursville Road, one mile from the Gap, in a beautiful beech forest. I am writing to you with my back against a tree, and with my knees for a desk on which to rest my portfolio—a most tiresome and unpleasant position—and I hope your compositors for whom I have regard, will excuse my indistinct writing. I have been interrupted so often by camp duties since I commenced, that I feared I should never be able to give you any account of the Gap at all, and your readers must excuse this hurried sketch. I am finishing this by an inch candle.

The scene around, with the lights of different groups shining through the forest trees, looks like so many fairy bowers brilliantly illuminated. The courier leaves for Knoxville at daylight, and so I have got to arrange my sleeping bower. I must bid you good night. PS: There are rumors of the taking of Louisville, but nothing reliable yet. I think a big fight will take place before Louisville falls.[55]

Historians suggest that Bragg was probably more frustrated by the army's lack of confidence in him than he was with the reporter, since he made no attempt to pursue Reid. However, Bragg's hostility toward the press was well known.[56]

After Bragg's attempts to silence the reporter, Reid's dispatches became increasingly critical of the general. His *Memphis Daily Appeal* reports laid out his bitterness and willingness to criticize. "Little doubt can be entertained that the enemy have Chattanooga," Reid wrote. "That strong and important position was evacuated without a blow from Gen. Bragg; because it is said Rosecrans had again 'flanked' him, and he was compelled to make further retreat into Georgia, or fight in a position where complete victory alone could save his army from destruction or captivity."[57]

In fact, Reid was so negative that his editor at the *Mobile Advertiser and Register*, Colonel John Forsyth, a friend of Bragg's, insisted that all of his dispatches be screened before going to press. After one slipped past Forsyth, Reid was removed from Bragg's army and transferred to Charleston where he eventually quit the *Advertiser and Register* altogether. Soon after, he went to work for the *Mobile Daily Tribune*, where he felt his reports would no longer be censored.

Reid also approached some of the generals as though they were personal friends, and he referred to his interviews as though the two were neighbors catching up. In places, Reid's reports resembled society news, but in others, Reid lambasted government and army incompetence, voicing his opinion as a way to shed light not only on hypocrisy and especially on inefficiency and government waste. After a particularly unpleasant trip to Atlanta in June 1862, he criticized a government passport system that failed to protect the South from enemy infiltration.

> Our passport system is a perfect humbug. On leaving any of our cities for a train of cars, you find, generally, an ignorant, illiterate boy with a musket in hand stationed at the doors of the car, who asks you if you have a passport; on answering "yes," you are at once admitted, without the document being demanded for inspection. In my whole journey from Corinth to this place, I have not once shown my passports, and if I had, I doubt if the ignorant boys and men, detailed for this service, would have been able to read them![58]

With the future of the bountiful South hanging in the balance, Reid described what the South stood to lose. Even his battle scenes had additional context, revealing a region united in its own defense, as in this account of Federal General John G. Mitchell's attack on Chattanooga in June of 1862.

The frightful whizzing of the shell as they fell rapidly, near the dwellings of several families residing near the vicinity of the ferry, produced the greatest consternation among the women and children, who were seen running in every direction, from the river to the centre of the town in the wildest terror, while the most heartrending cries and screams of others in houses, frantically illustrated some of the horrors of war. Our batteries returned the enemy's fire, and one of the gunners of the Merrimac being there, did good execution at one of our guns, silencing two of the enemy's. Our sharpshooters did good work at the same time, killing a number of the enemy.[59]

Having written for seven different newspapers, Reid's love for the South, especially its geographic features, was abundant in his reporting. He devoted several passages to a discussion of variegated summer foliage and mountain pass vistas. At times, Reid sounded more like a travel writer than a war correspondent. Consider these directions he provided to a peaceful spot in the Tennessee hills on October 1, 1862.

From this point you come into full view of the House mountains, standing in a place by itself, and Copper Ridge, part of the chain of Clinch Mountains on the left, about seven miles distant—Following around the base of Copper Ridge, for two miles and passing trough a gorge, you come into Raccoon Valley, which is a perfect amphitheatre of rolling hills and well-cultivated farms presenting a most beautiful prospect.[60]

The transient nature of the work seems to have been a perfect fit for Reid's personality. Having already traveled extensively by the time he began corresponding, it was natural that he chose to do work that allowed him the freedom to roam. His adventurous spirit shone through in his dispatches, giving readers a glimpse of more than just a war and a land untrammeled by Federal armies. On October 16, 1862, he wrote, "After currying and feeding our horses, supper was announced which was done ample justice to, and then we spread our blankets on the ground, smoked our pipes, discussed the exquisite loveliness of the moonlight, and soon fell asleep to dream of home, friends and ambitious schemes."[61]

Through Reid's reports, readers in the South saw beyond their immediate locale, giving them a more panoramic South with concrete details and lush adjectives. One of his letters on October 3, 1862, told how enjoyable he found life as a reporter, empathizing with "cooped up" New Orleans residents while he basked in the "glorious autumnal" mountains of Tennessee, the "Switzerland of America," as Reid dubbed them.[62] In other reports, Reid described the hardships posed by the land. He provided vivid pictures of Confederate troops moving through harsh, enemy-filled terrain, as in this 1862 recounting of a Federal advance near Corinth, Mississippi, and published in the *New Orleans Picayune*. "Their advance is at Licking Creek, and our pickets could plainly hear the beat of their drums," he wrote. "The march was a very fatiguing one, as the roads are in a terrible state, a portion of the way being a swamp, and the men having to march at times in mud and water up to their knees."[63]

Events that impacted his daily life on the road were an integral part of Reid's reports to readers, and enlarged all they came to know of the war and of the surroundings in which it was fought.

> Among the incidents of the late battle of Farmington . . . was that of a young lad, of thirteen years of age, named Joe Mather Sloan, of the 9th Texas regiment, who had been regularly mustered into service, had his leg shot off during the battle. The gallant little fellow, as he looked down at his shattered limb, exclaimed: 'Well, I don't mind the loss of one leg much, but I can't get over the thought that I won't be able again to stand before the enemy, and get another shot!' I learn that Gen. Beauregard intends conferring on the young hero the order of the Southern Cross of Honor, who will be the first to receive this much-coveted badge of distinction.[64]

In addition to writing for the *Picayune* in 1862, Reid worked for two other papers, the *Mobile Daily Advertiser and Register* and the *Memphis Daily Appeal*. Although Reid stopped writing for the *Picayune* in 1862 after New Orleans fell to Federal troops, he increased his earnings from other newspapers.[65] His reports also appeared that year in the *Chattanooga Daily Rebel* and the *Montgomery Daily Advertiser*, which he left to write for the Mobile newspaper, and by the end of 1863 he was also reporting for the *Atlanta Daily Intelligencer*. According to Reid's diary, his wages for the first two and a half years were around $12,000, an impressive figure for that time period, especially since the compensation also included horse feed, today's equivalent of gas mileage.[66]

Reid not only worked for seven different newspapers; he wrote different versions for each story. Many of his fellow correspondents who sent reports to multiple newspapers usually sent the same piece. Clearly, Reid showed devotion to craft and to understanding how the expectations of his readers varied from region to region, as well as how to successfully market himself to those readers.

Reid's entrepreneurial skills gave him adequate resources and allowed him to reach more readers with the kind of reporting sought after by Confederate newspapers at the time. His reports also reveal the lengths journalists traveled to relay accurate and vital information during wartime. Banned in 1863 from covering the war in Kentucky by generals who labeled him as quarrelsome, Reid condemned what he considered censorship and the unfair treatment he had received simply because he was a member of the press.

> Great dissatisfaction is produced at headquarters by imprudent correspondents and others, mentioning the movements of our Generals and other matters, there-by giving the cue to the enemy for obtaining information of our movements and designs. It cannot be repeated too often, and should be kept before

the people, that in the present revolutionary struggle, every man of the Confederacy should act as if the whole responsibility of achieving our independence rested upon him. Let every one be governed by this principle, exert every means in his power to effect it, use reflection, prudence and caution, and keep up eternal vigilance.[67]

Reid prided himself in rooting out spies, among them women, as though they were land mines that once detected, made everyone safer. He was suspicious that the Yankees had "infiltrated" Atlanta, which had the "perceptible odor of Yankeedom."[68] Reid warned, "Too much rigor and strictness cannot be observed, and no passports should be granted without vouchers and security to persons of suspicious character."[69]

Hardly a pessimist, Reid's dispatches showed that he found his work enjoyable, even if at times the conditions were less than favorable. He relished being a correspondent and felt at home on the road. Many of his letters commented on the "glorious springs" and "rich foliage" and the effect that the countryside had on his spirit. Reid sounded poetic at times, as on January 4, 1863, when he described an evening after the rain: "At night it cleared off, and the young moon, in all her resplendent beauty, illuminated the surrounding scene with dazzling silver brilliancy."[70]

In some letters Reid quoted other newspapers and occasionally magazines as sources of relevant information when he could not see the war firsthand. He also cited opinions in the Northern press with which he disagreed or that he found of interest.[71] Reid noted on February 19, 1863, a *Cincinnati Gazette* report of a battle in which Confederate General John C. Breckinridge was involved: "If madness can be called bravery, then, indeed, were the rebels brave."[72]

Reid showed a romantic attachment to the South, playing upon the allegiances of residents by his loving descriptions. Many of the letters reflected the glamour of Southern society contrasted with the destruction of cities and towns. When he wasn't providing the particulars of a battle, Reid wrote of the civility and grandeur the South stood to lose. In February 1863, he reported attending a ball at Hibernian Hall in Charleston, South Carolina. Seeing the guests in their "fashion and elegance," Reid was reminded of New Orleans before the war when "glorious assemblages of beauty and fashion were wont to adorn the Opera House and Odd Fellows' Hall."[73] After contrasting the once peaceful evenings of New Orleans with the "dark, gloomy pictures of tyranny and desolation" that had since taken over, he urged citizens to reflect: "Let Charleston think of this, and let the last man die in the ditch before we shall give up Charleston to another Butler. As for peace, the time is not yet. We shall not be satisfied with peace until we have made the Northman feel the desolation, the wreck, and the tyranny of the despot's iron heel, which has trampled over our land."[74]

He connected to the land, giving readers an account of the weather in the regions he traveled, as in his description on March 9, 1863, of a tornado at Shelbyville, Tennessee.

> Chattanooga, March 9—There was a terrible hail storm here last evening. Outhouses were destroyed, trees blown down, and windowpanes generally broken. Saturday evening a tornado passed over Shelbyville. The depot and telegraph offices were blown down and the operator was badly injured. One man was killed. The cars were blown off the track and much damage was done.[75]

Reid understood that large portions of his audience depended on him for what they would know about the world around them. For most, the only information they would receive about the war was from the press, crowding around the newspaper and at telegraph offices awaiting the news. For this reason, Reid's reports were extremely detailed, addressing the concerns of most Southerners—soldiers and families alike. In a "Letter From Tennessee," Reid offered an update on the condition of New Orleans, specifically for those soldiers who were far from home: "For the benefit of our Louisiana boys, who have seldom a chance to hear from home, I make up a short summary of information received from New Orleans through Capt. J.H. Hughes, formerly a ship builder at Algiers."[76]

He also felt secure in the South's stance against Northern influence and wholeheartedly backed secession, urging citizens to stand together despite censure. He assured readers: "We want no recognition by foreign powers, and no intercourse with them unless they sue for it. We can live within ourselves; and if necessary, let us build a Japanese wall around our institution of slavery, and let in no one who will not acknowledge it."[77]

De-emphasizing the Confederate army's setbacks has led some historians to question Reid's accuracy. In his view, the Southern army never retreated but rather "fell back" or made a "retrograde movement." Delays in telegraphic communication contributed to this suggestion of inaccuracy. Facts changed as Reid's letters were delayed in telegraphic communication, prompting some to say that Reid had gotten it wrong, even if his facts came straight from the mouths of generals. His account of the Battle of Chickamuaga has been questioned for its accuracy, yet General Bragg provided many of the facts. Reid published a separate account in 1863 as *The Battle of Chickamauga, A Concise History of Events from the Evacuation of Chattanooga*. One way to address this concern is to think of Reid as striving for accuracy within an ideological framework. Simply put, he gave Confederate readers and editors the kind of writing they wanted, that is, the war from a Southern perspective. In early 1864, Reid finished writing *The Daring Raid of General John H. Morgan, in Ohio, his Capture and Wonderful Escape with Captain T. Henry Hines*, which was Reid's last book.

The age and experience that gave Reid an advantage at the start of the war worked against him in time. An attack of rheumatism in July 1864 forced him to retire from his army-reporting career. Illness was common among correspondents, and some younger men left the field after a much shorter time than Reid.

Although he was confined to bed for the remainder of that year, Reid recovered and resumed his law practice in 1865.[78] He married Josephine Bowen of Kentucky in 1866 and became the father of twins. True to his early interests in exploration, eight years later Reid established the Mississippi Valley and Brazil Steamship Company in St. Louis.[79]

Reid spent the later years of his life lecturing on "The Restoration of Southern Trade and Commerce" in principal cities of the South.[80] He died in Washington, D.C., on August 13, 1897.

14

William Wallace Screws: "Most Useful Citizen of His Day"

Amy Ransford Purvis and Bradley J. Hamm

WILLIAM WALLACE SCREWS WAS PRACTICING LAW IN ALABAMA AND actively opposing secession when the Civil War began, but he dropped everything to enlist in the Confederate army and head for the battlefront. Although he had no journalistic training, Screws began sending letters home to the *Montgomery Advertiser*, which, like many Southern newspapers, relied on soldiers who became correspondents.

Advertiser Editor Samuel G. Reid, who is not believed to have been related to Samuel Chester Reid, Jr., of the *New Orleans Picayune*, was so impressed with Screws' correspondence and political connections that Screws would become his partner and half-owner of the newspaper after the war. Screws would buy the rest of the newspaper in 1868 and become a major political and editorial influence in Alabama until his death in 1913.[1] Because a fire destroyed the newspaper archives,[2] much of his war correspondence is missing, but Screws wrote under several pen names that probably included "43."

Screws' main claim to Civil War fame, if it can be called that, was his arrest by a Confederate general. Editor Reid criticized the overly sensitive Confederate General Braxton Bragg in a July 9, 1862, newspaper article. The editor did not believe that Bragg was treating General P.G.T. Beauregard with enough respect and reminded Bragg that "Southern soldiers, as a class, are gentlemen, and, in a social and political point of view, are the equals of their commanders."[3] Reid argued that the troops were willing to obey orders and accept military discipline so long as they were treated fairly and with respect. However, Bragg had overstepped those bounds in his treatment of Beauregard, the editor wrote, and was setting a poor example of proper behavior for those under his command.

"[A] general who uniformly sets at defiance the laws of his country for the appointment and promotion of officers, and usurps all the powers of judge, jury and executioner in the treatment of his men, does not set a very commendable

William Wallace Screws. Courtesy of
Princeton University

example of soldierly conduct," Reid wrote.[4] "We hope, since General Bragg has
taken command of an army of volunteers, he feels the necessity of appealing
more to their principles as gentlemen, and less to mere arbitrary brute force, to
govern them."[5]

It is uncertain whether Screws knew the level of Bragg's anger at the time.
Three weeks after Reid's critical editorial, Screws wrote an article that contained "vague and uncertain reports about the movements of [Bragg's] troops,"
according to Reid.[6] The contents of Screws' article no longer exist in print, except one line: "It is reported that a portion of Bragg's men came in to-day, and
that large numbers are on the way."[7]

For Bragg, the article was not vague and uncertain. He ordered Screws arrested and imprisoned for publicizing the movement of troops. Reid quickly
protested and sent a note to Bragg: "Allow me to say the arrest of our correspondent, on the pretense of giving information to the enemy, can only be regarded
by all free-thinking men as another exhibition of that petty tyranny and vindic-
tiveness for which you have gained an unenviable notoriety." The information
provided by Screws, Reid argued, was less obvious than a telegraphic message
sent to Southern newspapers by General Bragg himself. In that telegram, the
general had declared, with some specifics, where, when, and how many of his
troops were moving.[8] Screws was released after 10 days, and on August 27, 1862,
Reid editorialized:

We think it due as well to the reputation of our correspondent W.W. Screws, Esq.,
as to his friends, to state that he has been unconditionally released, after a nominal

arrest of ten days. It may appear strange to the public that Mr. Screws should be thus treated after being charged by Gen. Bragg with the heinous offense of declaring to the enemy the movement of troops, but this singular result is easily explained. The simple truth is, Gen. Bragg sought an opportunity to injure this paper because he had seen a plain intimation in an editorial article from us that we had an insight into his usurpations and tyranny, and had not withheld the information from the public . . . We suppose Gen. Bragg at last found out, what we intimated in the beginning, that our correspondent had committed no offense, and at most was only guilty of an indiscretion for which he should not be punished.[9]

In an analysis of the Confederate press and public morale, historian J. Cutler Andrews concluded that "by its attacks on particular generals, [including Bragg] the press diminished public confidence in them and may have impaired their military usefulness as well."[10] Yet Bragg brought much criticism on himself through his questionable decisions as a military leader. He was criticized throughout the war by other important commanders and for his efforts to ban reporters from covering any action. Bragg even prevented the Press Association of the Confederate States of America, of which the *Advertiser* and most leading Southern newspapers were founding members, from reporting on battles.[11]

Screws served as a soldier during the war despite a medical condition that would have exempted him from enlistment.[12] He participated in action throughout the South, particularly in Florida, Kentucky, Tennessee, and Virginia. He was wounded in a battle at Drewry's Bluff along the James River in Virginia in May 1864 (where the Confederates held off the Union assault). The examining board of a hospital in Richmond granted Screws a 30-day leave of absence on May 19, 1864, because of a gunshot wound in his left shoulder. The certificate of disability notes that Screws had been suffering for 10 days from the effects of a ball passing through his deltoid muscle.[13]

After his leave, Screws returned to service, participating in the Virginia campaign near Petersburg, and was later captured at Sayler's Creek, now known as Sailor's Creek, on April 6, 1865, only days before General Robert E. Lee surrendered. The correspondent was sent to Johnson Island, Ohio, as a prisoner for several months before he was released on June 19, 1865.[14]

His battlefield experiences in Tennessee, Kentucky, and Virginia gave Screws a front-row seat on the death and destruction of war, but despite the horrors that he endured, the lawyer-turned-correspondent remained a believer in the cause, even after the war. "No matter what may have been the differences of opinion produced by the late conflict, no one can doubt the purity of the motives by which the Confederate soldier was actuated, nor the unparalleled heroism with which he contended so long as there was a ray of hope."[15]

Many historians indicate that Screws wrote frequently, but few mention his style or coverage, instead focusing on his political views and support of specific

Confederate lines outside of Petersburg, Virginia. Courtesy of Library of Congress

causes. Mystery surrounds exactly what Screws wrote during his time as a Civil War correspondent. When the city of Montgomery surrendered in April 1865, the *Advertiser* was not published for three months, and its files were destroyed by fire. Because of that destruction, there are significant gaps in remaining issues during key times when Screws was known to be writing. Specifically, only a few papers exist for the months before and after his arrest in 1862, and there is no record of the article that landed him in jail.

In addition to the loss of preserved papers, Screws' name is noticeably absent in the text of letters printed in the *Advertiser* that still exist. However, this is not unusual because most correspondents used pen names to conceal their identities. Screws would have likely followed this trend, especially after spending 10 days in jail for his wartime commentary. Screws' pen names are still unknown, with the probable exception of "43," a name that he most likely used in the late spring and summer of 1864 in an intriguing pattern of letters from Gracie's Brigade. On April 25, 1864, this correspondent, located at Camp Gracie's Brigade in Abingdon, Virginia, wrote about a foraging expedition into North Carolina. Subsequent letters from the Gracie's Brigade correspondent appear dated May 1, May 18, June 13, June 18, June 19, and June 30, all signed "43." From the text of these letters, it is clear that "43" is a soldier rather than a civilian correspondent. In his April 25 letter he wrote:

> Gen. (James) Longstreet and his troops have gone, "this deponent knoweth not whither;" Buckner is commanding this Department, and we settled down into our old humdrum life again. Unless things change greatly, we will spend the summer guarding mountain passes, railroad bridges, drilling, reviewing and some times chasing Yankee raiders, whom we will never catch, for the simple reason that horses can out travel infantry. [16]

And, in relaying events on the battlefield at Drewry's Bluff dated May 18, correspondent "43" wrote passionately about a Confederate victory after Federal forces made a "stubborn fight" of it.

> The battle on the 16th was a glorious victory to our arms. The attack was made first by Gen. (Archibald) Gracie's brigade on the extreme left, just at daylight, and quickly became general all along the lines. The enemy had built fortifications, fronting a large field through which our troops had to pass, and one protected by thick woods. They made a stubborn fight and the right of our brigade and two regiments of Kemper's, suffered severely. The left of the enemy was turned, their works taken, and Brig. Gen. (Charles) Heckman and four stands of colors captured. This ended the fight on the left. Next to us, (General Robert Frederick) Hoke's and (General Johnson) Hagood's brigade drove the enemy before them and captured five pieces of artillery.[17]

Correspondent "43" also expressed the weariness of the soldiers when he wrote on June 18 from battles in Petersburg, Virginia. "Longstreet's old corps is pouring into the city, and gladly do we welcome them, although we have held our own, yet we have been fighting six army corps with only two divisions. Gracie's brigade lost only five wounded in the 43rd, and a few in the 59th, I have not learned the exact number."[18]

Historian Andrews identified a number of key Civil War correspondents and their pen names, yet he did not identify "43," nor did he attribute any alternative names to Screws.[19] However, at the time that "43" was writing for the *Advertiser*, Screws was enlisted in Gracie's Brigade serving in Bushrod Johnson's division, which was in line with what the letters from "43" indicate. Geographically, Screws and his fellow soldiers of Gracie's Brigade were in Virginia and participated in various battles, including Drury's or Drewry's Bluff (both spellings appear in the *Advertiser*) where he was wounded. The pattern of letters from "43" follow this progression, including Drewry's Bluff in May, 1864, and battles in Petersburg, Virginia, in June and July of that year. No other identified *Advertiser* correspondents match the military assignment, timing, and geographic locations of "43" other than Screws.[20]

Confederate entrenchments outside of Petersburg, Virginia. Courtesy of Library of Congress

A noticeable gap in correspondence from "43" supports the theory that this could be Screws' pen name. Screws was hospitalized and was given a 30-day leave of absence May 19, 1864, in Richmond. Letters from "43" end on May 18, at Drewry's Bluff and pick up again on June 13, 1864, in Southside, Virginia.[21]

Finally, the writer "43" is seemingly educated, a proficient writer, and politically oriented, aligning with Screws' education and career as a lawyer and political disposition prior to the war. In his letter recounting the foraging expedition in North Carolina, "43" wrote:

I made it my business to inquire about North Carolina politics. Every where the people are true to our cause. I did not find a single supporter of (W.W.) Holden in the State. From every house a husband, brother or son is in the Confederate service. In every county is an organized "Home Guard" that apprehends deserters and keeps the Tennessee Tories in good behavior. It is encouraging to a soldier to find these poor mountain people as brave and so true.—How pitiful do such men as W. W. Holden, *par nobile fratrum*, appear when compared with the loyal patriots of the mountains![22]

Bold, passionate, and critical are key elements of Screws' writing style, as demonstrated by his editorial writings following the war. Those same elements are present in the letters by correspondent "43" and are highlighted in a June 19, 1864, letter describing engagements near Petersburg, Virginia, and his assessment of Ulysses S. Grant.

> Grant was on the field in person. Three corps were certainly engaged, and I have every reason to believe that three more were present. Gen. Beauregard had only two small divisions.—Mere weight of numbers would have crushed this force in a short time. But now the tables are turned, and Grant will have to slide off to the left again. He has courage, if indifference to loss of life can be so called, but unlike his ancient namesake, Grant does not possess any of the strategical *craft* of a great leader, nor has he the power of winning the admiration and love of his followers . . . His men are discouraged, and though they fight sometimes desperately, they do not do so willingly. I was told by a field officer of Hood's division, that in a fight which occurred near Howlett's house on last Friday, when the Yankees were drove back, that their own officers brought up a battery and tried to drive them into the fight with grape shot.[23]

As military activity in Petersburg intensified, correspondent "43's" June 30 letter indicated the constraints that he encountered in trying to get information to the press: "The enemy have done the city but little damage," he wrote. "Our troops are in excellent health and spirits: rations are excellent and plentiful. I send this letter by private conveyance to Stoney creek. I would write more fully but fear it may reach the Yankees instead of the Advertiser."[24]

Was Screws correspondent "43"? His military record, timing, location, and style fit with that of the Gracie's Brigade correspondent. There are no other known candidates who align with these factors. Unfortunately, the primary sources that could prove the identity of the *Advertiser*'s correspondent are not in known existence. It is likely that "43" was not the only pen name that Screws used when writing for the *Advertiser*. Although his work during the Civil War is not easily identified, his work following the war is well documented.

A known example of Screws' writing style and passion came a year after the war ended. Screws wrote of conflict between Southern women and occupying Federal soldiers over war memorials and Southern grave sites. "The heart must be dead to all the feelings of humanity that would object to the ladies of the South showing by this simple and touching act that they venerate the memory of their fathers, husbands, brothers and friends, who gave up their lives in a cause we all believe is just," Screws wrote.[25]

After the war, *Advertiser* Editor Reid recruited Screws to work for the newspaper when it was restarted in July 1865. Reid and a partner were able to fund the new paper, but, amazingly, the partner, a war veteran, died on the day of the first issue. When Reid sought another partner, he wound up selling half of the paper to Screws in November 1865. Reid posted a notice announcing Screws' new position.

> With this number of the ADVERTISER W. W. Screws, Esq., of this city, becomes joint editor and proprietor, with myself. Mr. Screws has been connected with me as associate editor since the re-establishment of this journal; was of the Old Line Whig School of politics antecedent to the war; served his term gallantly in the army of the Confederacy; and the readers of the Advertiser are indebted to his talents and industry for much of the information or entertainment its columns may have afforded them for several months.[26]

Newspapers changed owners frequently in the 1800s, and Reid subsequently sold a partial share to Screws' brother in 1867 before both sold the entire paper to Screws in 1868. On the journalism side, Screws and his brother were in charge of the reporting and editing, even after the sale of the paper. Screws owned and wrote for the paper, in one form or another, for the next 48 years, until his death. While information about Screws' war experience may vary from source to source, the details of his time at the *Advertiser* are fairly consistent—and likely benefit from his own work as a journalism historian later in life.[27]

Only the war had brought the opportunity for Screws to work in journalism, because early in life, he had other career goals. He was born on February 25, 1839, in Jernigan, Alabama. The records regularly list his name as W.W., as he often signed it, Wallace, as friends called him, and William or William Wallace, but clearly the designation he preferred was "Major" Screws, a title bestowed from the war.

As a young man, Screws prepared for college, but his father's business failed during an economic decline. He worked a few years before learning law in the office of Thomas Watts, a future governor of Alabama. According to several accounts, Screws was admitted to the bar even though he was not yet 21 years old. He considered returning to a law career before Reid persuaded him to try journalism as a full-time job after the war. After he bought the newspaper, Screws was married in 1867 to Emily Frances Holt, the daughter of a judge. They had four children: three sons and a daughter.[28]

In 1871, Screws bought part ownership of another Montgomery paper, the *Mail*, and the resulting publication was the *Advertiser and Mail*. The original owner of the *Mail* died a year later, and Screws purchased the company outright and returned the name of the paper again simply to the *Advertiser*. By 1885, Screws again sold half of the company to investors, and the newspaper remained in joint ownership, through the issue of stock to investors, until his death. Yet, the paper was identified with Screws for his entire life, regardless of the business makeup, and the other owners were not central figures in Alabama journalism history.[29]

In addition to changing ownership, the other constant at the newspaper was summarized by Screws in his 1893 history of Alabama journalism: "The *Advertiser* has supported the nominees of the democratic party, state and national, in every contest since its establishment in 1830, and is still vigorously advocating the measures of that party in the state and country."[30]

Combining the roles of political leader and editor was easy for Screws. When he ran for the office of secretary of state in 1878, Screws was described by a *New York Times* writer as publisher of the leading Democratic organ of the state—the *Montgomery Advertiser*. "His nomination was a reward for party services, and was perhaps the most popular that could have been made, as Republicans generally respect him, and because of personal considerations, some few of them may vote for him. His paper has been very bitter toward all Republicans, and especially Northerners."[31] Screws was elected in 1878 and again in 1880 as secretary of state.[32]

A scene in 1891 demonstrates Screws' influence and attitude. As a *New York Times* reporter interviewed Alabama Congressman Hilary Herbert about the presidential candidacy of Grover Cleveland, "Major Screws approached and contributed something as regards the situation in his state." The Republican *Times* article gives lengthy space to the views of both Herbert, who became secretary of the navy for President Cleveland in 1893, and Screws.[33]

Screws was also involved in local politics. The traditional Democratic party leaders in Alabama opposed the Farmer's Alliance in 1891, because of its stance on farming issues, railroads, and silver coinage. Screws was particularly incensed by the new political faction. "When, behind closed doors, and under the secret oath, they resolve to support one of their number for a public office, and to support no other person, then they become a threatening element in the field of politics," he wrote. Screws supported another congressman's statements "to declare open war and begin an aggressive fight instead of temporizing and making attempts to bring the Alliance leaders to the Democratic camp."[34]

That was Screws' style: blunt, combative, and attention-getting, yet some of his views were trapped in another era. While freed slaves gained the right to vote and were elected to political office after the Civil War, Screws argued for conservative positions that included advocating for white supremacy and battling postwar reforms. Governor Thomas Johnston, also a publisher and a Democrat, fought Screws and called his newspaper "Old Grandma" based on these conservative views.[35]

Screws criticized other newspapers, as was common at that time, and his targets included both Republicans and fellow Democrats. The *Advertiser*, through Screws, "excommunicates all who do not agree with it" and equates "independence and treason," wrote one editor in Alabama.[36] Screws served in other positions based on his political ties. He was named postmaster in Montgomery from 1893 to 1897. President Grover Cleveland also appointed him to a position with the Library of Congress.

One lasting tribute to Screws' statewide influence and organizational power is the Alabama Press Association. In March 1871, Screws invited all of the editors and publishers of Alabama newspapers to create a press association. Eight leaders joined him for the first informal meeting that year in Montgomery at his office at the *Advertiser*. Yet Screws could not find wide support for a convention, so in May 1871, he issued a statewide invitation through a newspaper editorial, and the responses soon followed.

A year later, the Alabama Press Association held its first convention in Montgomery. Thirty people joined the new group, and Screws was elected its first vice president. The group's role, as Screws envisioned it, was larger than simply a trade organization for state press. It was "to bring hither the representatives of the press from abroad [outside of Alabama]; to show them something of the capacities and undeveloped wealth of our great state," he wrote.[37] The state of Alabama needed reconstruction with money from the North. An example of this effort was the 1874 convention in Birmingham. New York editors were invited to attend, and many came to tour the state and industrial plants, coal mines, and iron ore deposits.[38]

Screws was elected president of the press association for four terms from 1878-1882 and remained a member for life. In 1905, an afternoon of the association meeting was devoted to speeches in praise of Screws. It was his 40th anniversary as a newspaper leader. "From the day the *Montgomery Advertiser* was resurrected from the ashes of a long and bloody war, July 20, 1865, to this hour, I have known no other field of labor than that afforded by its columns," Screws told the group.[39]

A few years before his death, Screws began work on a history of Alabama newspapers for presentation at the press association annual meeting. At the 1909 convention, he presented the report, a factual accounting that covers, in about 20 pages, the creation and development of a number of newspapers.[40]

Screws also wrote a more comprehensive history of Alabama newspapers in 1893 as part of a two-volume set. In the chapter, Screws lamented the lack of primary sources upon which to build the state's story and called his work an "unsatisfactory sketch": "Details are meager and the sources of information widely scattered,"[41] but Screws did produce a well-researched work that captures the details about many state newspapers. Screws died on August 7, 1913, at his second home in Coosada, near Montgomery.

One writer declared: "It is safe to say that no man in Alabama has done more to put the state upon the solid footing she now occupies than [Screws]."[42] Alabama Governor Thomas Jones agreed: "No man ever lived in Alabama who labored more unselfishly for the good of the state or set a finer example in his career of devotion to the things that make for the uplift of man." "Screws," the

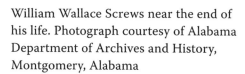

William Wallace Screws near the end of his life. Photograph courtesy of Alabama Department of Archives and History, Montgomery, Alabama

governor said, "felt that his position as the head of a great newspaper was a sacred trust, and not a mere personal possession."[43]

A scholar of Civil War reporting once wrote that Southern journalism was the most partisan of any in the country in the mid-1800s. "In an era when personal journalism was in its heyday, the editor as a man of consequence was admitted to the inner councils of his party and often became a powerful political force."[44] This description fit Screws perfectly. As a man of consequence through his journalistic activities, Screws led the *Advertiser* from 1865 until his death in 1913. Throughout his life, Screws wrote about, battled, and campaigned for causes both popular and unpopular, enlightened and unfortunate, self-rewarding and financially and personally costly. "The impartial verdict of history will be that while in the heat of conflict others won wider fame, Wallace Screws was the most useful citizen of his day," wrote Hilary Herbert, former Alabama congressman and U.S. secretary of the navy.[45]

15

William G. Shepardson:
Swashbuckling Journalist on the Chesapeake

Carol Wilcox

In today's journalistic world, William G. Shepardson would be labeled a consummate newshawk, an aggressive reporter who was in and out of trouble with military authorities for his coverage. He was always at the scene of intense action during the Civil War, even while doing his job as a Confederate surgeon and ministering to wounded soldiers and sailors of both sides. Shepardson began by covering the land war before joining the Confederate navy to participate in some of the historic actions at sea.

While Shepardson was on duty in Virginia, Confederate General Joseph E. Johnston was so furious at the correspondent for reporting the location of troops as the Army of the Potomac bivouacked for the winter of 1861-1862 that he ordered the correspondent's arrest for aiding and abetting the enemy. Shepardson fled, but Johnston was undeterred. Unable to apprehend Shepardson, Johnston ordered the expulsion of all newspaper correspondents from his army, a move that set the stage for more military censorship and alarmed the editors of Southern newspapers.

To avoid arrest, Shepardson fled from Virginia and was captured by Federal troops while covering the Battle of Roanoke Island in North Carolina. He was paroled and continued his work as a correspondent for the *Richmond Daily Dispatch* and the *Mobile Advertiser and Register* and as a surgeon for Confederate forces.

Shepardson reported the war from start to finish. He spent more than two years covering the war on land before joining the Confederate navy in 1863 and serving aboard the notorious cruiser *Tallahassee*, one of the most effective Confederate raiders of the war. His account of the *Tallahassee*'s seizure of 33 vessels between August 11 and 20, 1864, brought cheers from the embattled people of the South as the war neared its conclusion with a Union victory.

Shepardson was one of the most prolific and adventurous newspaper correspondents, a reporter who used trains, ships, and horses to take him to locales where he gathered news. His pseudonym was "Bohemian" for the *Daily Dispatch* and "Evelyn" for the *Advertiser and Register.* He witnessed and reported the battles at Manassas and Leesburg, Virginia, and at Roanoke Island, Drewry's Bluff, and Wilmington, North Carolina. He occasionally included poetry in his articles and edited a book of songs and verse, *War Songs of the South*, that included "Waiting,"[1] which may have been his, as well as "The Midnight Ride," which he translated from the German.[2]

Born in Alabama,[3] Shepardson was probably in his 30s when the Civil War began, judging from an 1861 story in which he told his readers that he was born on January 27 and was "on the sunny side of forty."[4] He lived in Germany as a youth, perhaps as a student, and was known to have visited Cuba and Bermuda. He traveled to Europe and spent some time in Paris in 1858, doing the social scene.[5] He was thoroughly familiar with European architecture and buildings, and thought a camp scene that he saw at Fairfax, Virginia, in October 1861 was similar to scenes that he remembered from Europe.

> I recollect to have seen—in the Belvidere at Weimar, I think—a picture of the occupation of a Polish town by the Austrian troops—The streets were full of soldiers and terrified citizens. Camp-fires were kindled in every direction, and through it all ran a vein of busy, excited life, that pleased me well—Ah! thought I, how much I should like to be a witness of such a scene. After years of wandering from that gallery which so delighted my boyhood, here, far across the Atlantic, was a picture as similar as one could wish.[6]

Shepardson smoked cigars, loved history, and appreciated Shakespeare. He understood some Latin, German, and French and occasionally included phrases in those languages in his dispatches. When the war began, he wholeheartedly joined the Confederate army as a physician and correspondent. Reporters of his time "put their lives at risk on the battlefield, and they took terrible chances in galloping across guerrilla-infested territory to get their stories published," he wrote. "They were often cold and hungry." His writings do not reveal that Bohemian was troubled by these hardships. Several times he wrote that he was willing to lay down his life for the Confederate cause.[7]

The correspondent covered the First Battle of Manassas, which would take its place in history as an astonishing Confederate strategy that forced the Union command to recognize the mettle of the Southern soldier. Afterward, the North would not question the tenacity of the Confederates. Shepardson was one of a small group of Southern reporters who gathered on a hilltop overlooking the Manassas battlefield July 21, 1861. While accounts from other reporters put him at the scene of the action, files of his *Montgomery Advertiser* covering the last half of 1861 were destroyed, and other correspondents attested to his presence at the scene of the historic battle.[8]

In addition to chronicling the early skirmishes and battles, Shepardson wrote about the culture of the South and day-to-day occurrences. One reporter described him as gentlemanly, and some of his writing showed that he had great respect for women. From Warrenton, Virginia, where he was caring for wounded soldiers, Shepardson wrote:

> I am now at this place, and have been for three weeks, in attendance upon some sick comrades, and I am free to declare that the poor fellows who have lain so long could not and would not have received more attention from the loving hand of mother, wife or sisters, at the cars, carry them home with them, provide every comfort for them, set up with them, nurse them, and when the icy hand of death fastens on them, they bestow a kiss for the poor soldier's loved ones at home, and attend him to his last earthly abode. [9]

Bohemian wrote about a night of amusement at Fairfax. The 1st Virginia Regiment band serenaded one of the generals. After the band had stopped, a tenor sang "a lone ditty under the window of a fair-faced girl." He sang song after song and ultimately sang lyrics from *The Bohemian Girl—Then you'll remember me,* "but the enchanting scene was interrupted when a soldier shouted, 'He's a married man! He's a married man!' and the romance that might have bloomed subsided. In popped the fair face; down crashed the window; the wicked soldier laughed all the way from his boots, and the mortified minstrel ended his tenor solo in basso curses," Shepardson wrote. Then Bohemian and his companions retired "to court the drowsy."[10]

He traveled around the countryside, often on horseback. "Your 'own' has a fine bay, on which, like a modern Atlas, he carries about with him, from place to place, in the process of dispensing and collecting news, the little world of intelligence which you daily see in the correspondence from the Army of the Potomac," he wrote.[11]

At a social gathering, Bohemian provided another glimpse of his news-gathering habits and his humor. "In a hotel parlor, gentlemen converse in one corner, and ladies in another. The reporter is taking notes at a center table. Finally, the work is completed, the notes go into a side pocket, the book is folded, pen wiped, and inkstand put away. Reporter prepares to leave the room by side entrance . . . but is intercepted by a woman who inquires if he is a spy." The reporter then claimed a relationship with Jefferson Davis and said he went to school with Pierre G.T. Beauregard and fought in the Battle of Bull Run. The woman smiled and all parties were satisfied."[12]

A few days later, Bohemian continued his saga about gathering news in the midst of curious spectators. When bystanders became a little too curious to suit him, he had the last laugh.

> There is a good story told of Gustave Planche, the celebrated French critic, who tried to conceal his residence to prevent the play-wrights and players, as well as bookmakers, from se[nding] bribes to his apartments. One evening a lady

endeavored to get the secret out of him, and asked abruptly, "M Planche where do you live?" "I live nowhere, Madame; I simply exist in Paris." "But where do you sleep?" persisted she. "I roost, Madame, Champ Elysies [*sic*], third tree on the left, going up." That night, so the story goes, a crowd collected to see the Bohemian go to roost. For fear some friend might call on me, or that somebody might attempt another serenade, or in case of general inquiries, I give present address in full, "in front of Hubball's hotel, first tree; right front door, lower limb."[13]

However, the grandest distraction of all for soldiers and townspeople, and one designed to boost morale early in the war, was a visit from Confederate President Jefferson Davis, who was escorted through Fairfax on October 1, 1861, by a troop of cavalry. Bystanders were amazed at his unannounced appearance. Shepardson wrote:

> Nothing could have been more gratifying than this timely visit; for both citizens and soldiers were chafing at delay, and somewhat anxious as to what was to be done with the Yankees, who were encroaching on us so steadily. Confidence seemed restored as soon as it was known the President was here, and people seemed to fancy him another St. George, who had come to give a personal battle to the great Dragon.[14]

The president was dressed in "deep-gray citizen's clothes" and wore a beaver hat, Bohemian wrote. "There were no vulgar crowds to stare at him like some wild beast, no toadyisms or foolish parades at his approach." Instead there was "a quiet look, a simple bow, or a military salute." As he passed by, three hearty cheers went up, and in return, "his Excellency raised his hat, and bowing gracefully, said: 'Gentlemen—I thank you heartily, and I hope that sooner or later you may have an opportunity of meeting the Yankees, and that you may return home with a good account of yourselves.'"[15]

Bohemian described the importance of newspapers at camp and in the settlements. "I believe that five hundred papers could be sold here every day, as easily as two hundred." On the days the *Richmond Daily Dispatch* was brought into Fairfax, "every copy sold in five minutes at a dime each," he wrote. "One night the stage drove up with the papers—a bundle containing about one hundred copies of the Dispatch and half as many of the Enquirer—and before I could elbow my way into the crowd every copy was sold."[16]

Shepardson delighted in reporting bizarre occurrences. At Fairfax, as he watched a battalion march through the streets, he saw a horse that had been spooked by drums charge through wagons and soldiers.

> . . . a horse became frightened at the drums, and throwing his rider heavily upon the ground, dashed off in a frightful manner. The street was filled with wagons and horses. Plunging through them, he knocked down a soldier, ran over several, and charged into the regiment. The men brought their bayonets to bear upon

him, whereupon the frightened animal leaped over a horse, and filling between two, became entangled in the harness. He was relieved and uninjured; but caused considerable excitement.[17]

When Shepardson rode to Centreville to a blacksmith who could repair his horse's loose shoe, "fancy led me into one of the bazaars that adorn the lively town." There, he found a dark room, so low he had to stoop to avoid hitting his head on the blackened beams above. Bohemian witnessed some soldiers being swindled. But he also took note of the sights and smells of the place and especially the array of goods for purchase.

> An odor, hardly as agreeable as Patchouly, caused by a combination of old clothes, new boots, ginger cakes, and tobacco pervaded the atmosphere. A few soldiers were leaning over the counter, behind which the honest shopkeeper kept an eye on . . . Every imaginable no-account article was spread out in a tempting manner. Buttons, pins, needles, tobacco, paper and envelopes, and beside them russet shoes, bright yellow shirts, bright red cravats, seal-skin caps, and blue bandannas. The prices were variable, but all four or five hundred per cent above an immense profit. Boots, worth ordinarily $3.50, cost $10.[18]

In one dispatch, Bohemian hinted to his readers how he came upon his pen name. In October 1861 at Centreville, he was struck by the image of Southerners abandoning Fairfax to Union forces. The words of a gypsy song rang in his ears: *"He who's no home to call his own Will find, will find a home somewhere."*[19] It was his habit to follow the war and establish himself wherever he anticipated action. At Fairfax, he witnessed action that moved him to tears.

> Whole families were seen walking by the wayside, carrying such articles as they could hastily gather in their arms. Old women, maidens, and little children tramped through the weary night to a home of safety beyond the reach of a vandal foe. With feelings of intense sorrow and pain, I rode by these unfortunate families, driven from their happy homes to seek shelter behind the line of our army. Leaning on the arm of an aged man the form of a sick girl, whose patient, pensive face comes to me more often than it ought, passed in the singular cortege. The sight was one that brought tears into eyes long unused to weeping. It was then I fully realized the sentiment of Queen Elizabeth's favorite, the chivalric and unhappy Essex, who said, 'Not for myself I smart, but I would I had in my heart the sorrow of all my friends.'[20]

Bohemian was on the scene at the Battle of Leesburg, or Ball's Bluff, in Virginia on October 21, 1861. Like First Manassas, the battle was a surprise for Union forces and a stunning victory for the Confederate army. About 4,000 Federals were assembled, including the 15th and 20th Massachusetts, the California, and the Tammany regiments "and three pieces of the Rhode Island battery."[21]

Confederate forces consisted of the 8th Virginia, the 17th and 18th Mississippi, with the 13th Mississippi regiment in reserve. The Union army, Shepardson wrote, "had upwards of 12,000 men on the opposite side of the river,"[22] but they could not cross the Potomac "in the face of the terrible fire that was opened upon every boat."[23]

At the climax of the battle, in a cleared field of six to eight acres, the Federals had assembled their artillery and planted two howitzers and a large rifled gun in a position to play upon the hill opposite. The Confederates came out of the woods, and a Colonel Featherstone cried out, "Mississippians, charge those Yankees; take their battery; drive them into the Potomac or into eternity."[24]

> With most terrific yells, the men charged up the hill, driving the Federals terrified before them. The Virginians took the two howitzers, and the Mississippians the rifle. The river was about one hundred yards from the battery, and between them was a steep precipice fully ninety feet high, and nearly perpendicular. Over this they were tumbled or impaled upon the bayonet. Perfectly conquered, they begged our men not to shoot, and surrendered themselves prisoners. The few who reached the river threw off their clothes and attempted to swim across, but the majority of them were drowned. The boats were crowded to their utmost, and were frequently so heavily loaded that they sunk [sic] under the weight of frightened human beings. One hundred and fifty were thus sunk with a single flat or raft. It was now very dark, and our men retired to Leesburg with their prisoners.[25]

Bohemian, using the "lightning" or telegraph to send his dispatches, first estimated 100 killed and 300 wounded.[26] "Our men fought like heroes, and succeeded in putting about five hundred hors du combat, in taking six cannon, six hundred prisoners, and a quantity of small arms. The rout of the enemy was complete." The exact number of Confederate soldiers killed and wounded was unknown on the evening of October 21, he added.[27]

Days after the *Daily Dispatch*'s initial report of casualty tallies, Bohemian estimated the enemy's losses. Including "killed, wounded, drowned and prisoners, I should say the loss would foot up to twelve hundred."[28] Shepardson told what happened to the prisoners.

> These were immediately put upon a large scow, or flat, and sent across the river, but they were overturned, and by this means quite three hundred were drowned. It is said that the river was black with floating bodies, and that the shrieks of the drowning was terrible. When night came it was found that we had about six hundred prisoners, all, or nearly all, of whom are now in Richmond.[29]

The soldiers were elated to find that so many Union troops had been captured. "The presence of the prisoners was quite cheering, and as good a show for the boys as a circus, or a horse race," he wrote. "The Yankees seemed to care little about being gazed at, and lounged around the grounds smiling and chatting with each other, or bartering their hats and fine overcoats to our men."[30] Shepardson found the shore thronged with men and boys gathering relics or fishing them from the water. "By wading into the stream excellent muskets could be found in great numbers."[31] Bohemian and a few Confederate soldiers seized the opportunity to take a small boat to an island on the Maryland side of the river. They cautiously entered an empty house and collected butter, flour, biscuits, corn starch, sugar, and salt. "An empty chloroform bottle and a sponge lay upon the table, just as they had been used by the physician in giving relief to some suffering piece of humanity," he noted in his dispatch.[32]

Bohemian detailed other spoils of war—a damaged topsail schooner "of some three hundred, or three hundred and fifty tons burthen, painted black, with clean spars and rigging." For the most part, the new sails were in good repair.

> On approaching the gang-way the marks of the shot were visible. The most important shot passed through the side, about midway the vessel, going through a heavy beam, tearing away a ring-bolt, and also through three bales of pressed hay, lodging in the fourth.—This shot was from the large sea-coast howitzer, and the ball was preserved; and we found it rolling about the cabin. The deck was in great confusion, caused by the labor of unseaman like hands in loading the cargo, but every thing gave evidence that ordinarily the vessel was kept in prime order.[33]

Residents of cities and smaller settlements had an insatiable thirst for information, Shepardson wrote. The people of Occoquan, a village southeast of Washington, depended on the newspapers for news. In late November 1861, the Saturday mail "produced quite a stir." A crowd surrounded the carrier and asked several questions simultaneously. "'Have you a Dispatch?' said a dozen voices, and as soon as it was ascertained he had the desired paper, there was no peace until one of the desired party had it in his hands."[34]

> The village miller was the fortunate person, and followed by an audience, went into the hotel to read "the news." Seating himself in a chair, he was soon surrounded by a circle of heads that pressed around him with listening ears. I sat in the corner and watched the proceedings, both interested and amused. The best part of all was the rustic comments made upon the various paragraphs as they were read.[35]

When soldiers were off duty, one form of amusement for some profit-minded males was buying provisions soldiers needed at low prices and selling them at a considerable gain. That was true in various locales until just before Christmas 1861, when General Joseph E. Johnston issued an order "closing every sutler shop in Manassas."[36] Although Shepardson believed some of the sutlers were "honest and fair in their dealings," some unscrupulous ones painted the whole lot with the reputation of swindlers.

"Sitting at dinner in the Warrenton Hotel," he wrote, " I overheard a short conversation between two men, in which one of them boasted that . . . he could

General Joseph E. Johnston. Courtesy of Library of
Congress

not make less than one hundred dollars a day off his contract to supply bread
to the army, and that he should be much disappointed if he did not clear two
hundred a day. Who the speculator was I am unable to say."[37]

While Bohemian avoided dealing with the sutlers, he secured some of his
needs through his readers. A female reader took pity on Shepardson because
he had written about ending a letter to the *Daily Dispatch* after his candle went
out. She sent him candles "packed very nicely in a small box." The correspondent confessed that he envied those who received boxes containing "nice things
from home," and in his sleep, he dreamed of "smoking caps, dressing gowns,
slippers, comforts, and all sorts of worsted things wrought by female hands."
But receiving the candle box had changed everything. ". . . when I get envious
and sad, I look at my little box of candles, and think that some one is interested
in me, or at least in the labor of my pen. My fair friend has ten thousand thanks
for her splendid gift," he wrote.[38]

Shepardson's military career took a sudden and dramatic turn on December 30, 1861, when he wrote an article for the *Daily Dispatch* describing the location of the Army of the Potomac's winter quarters.

MANASSAS, December 27

To-day our whole army is engaged in building log houses for winter quarters or in moving to sites already selected. Several brigades will remain where they now are, near the fortifications in Centreville, and the remainder will fall back a mile or two upon Bull Run. General Kirby Smith's brigade is at Camp Wigfall, to the right of the Orange and Alexandria road, near the run. Near by the whole of Van Dorn's division are making themselves comfortable in their little cottages, which rise rapidly day by day under diligent hands of the soldiers. A few brigades are scattered down towards the Occoquan [River], where wood and water is plenty, the farthest being by Davis' Ford. The artillery, with the exception of Walton's battalion, has already been located between Cub Run and Stone Bridge. The cavalry has fallen back a little and they are now building stables and houses near Centreville. General Stuart will remain in the advance. It is probable that General Johnston will occupy the Lewis House on the battle-field, and General Beauregard (in) Wier's, his old headquarters. Before the 18th and 21st, Longstreet's division will, if I am correctly informed, occupy the advanced position, and will remain near where it is at present. The artillerists detailed to man the guns in the battery will also remain by the fortifications. In case of an attack by the Yankees it will take about two hours to get the main strength of the army across Bull Run. Information of an approach would be given at least two hours before an enemy could come up, and in that time we could be well prepared to resist any force that can be brought up.[39]

The final sentences of the dispatch reveal the general feeling in the Confederate army in the vicinity, at least from Bohemian's point of view. He wrote that the soldiers would be ready for a Union attack when it came.

That is about the situation of affairs for the winter, and it remains to be seen whether our men are to have an opportunity of a brush with the Yankees or whether they will be allowed to enjoy their new houses in quietness. When I say all are ready for an attack, I express but feebly the feeling which pervades the enemy.[40]

Johnston was outraged that Shepardson had revealed in detail where the Confederate brigades could be found, where the artillery troops would wait, and what the cavalry was doing at the moment. Bohemian had even disclosed the location of three generals and speculated about what the Confederate strategy would be if the Union forces attacked and how much time the Confederates had to get ready for a Union assault.

Unable to locate Shepardson, Johnston wrote an angry letter to Secretary of War Judah P. Benjamin and enclosed a copy of the offending article.

I respectfully ask your attention to an article in the Richmond Dispatch of this morning, by 'Bohemian.' The information it contains would be very valuable to the enemy, such as he would pay for liberally. I cannot suppose it innocently published. The author's name is Shepardson or Shepherdson, styled Doctor. I respectfully suggest his arrest. He is now in Richmond . . . Could not the editor of the paper be included in the accusation?

Most respectfully, your obedient servant,
J. E. JOHNSTON, General.[41]

Shepardson's article also aroused the ire of the secretary of war, but Benjamin blamed Johnston for the breach of judgment, writing that the general had been too lenient toward newspaper reporters within his lines. Benjamin suggested that Johnston apprehend Shepardson and bring him to military trial as a spy.

I share your indignation at such an outrageous breach of duty of both the writer and publisher. I have anxiously sought for some means of punishing the offense, but the state of the law is such as to give no remedy for this wrong through the courts of justice, and I have appealed to the Military Committee of Congress for some legislation to protect the Army and the country against the great evils resulting from such publications . . . In this connection allow me to say that I think some of the mischief from this two-frequent offense arises from your own too lenient toleration of the presence of newspaper reporters within your lines. I will do all I can to help you, but the application of military regulations within the Army will be much more efficacious than any attempt at punishment by jury trial. I feel persuaded that this man Shepardson is a spy, and would be found guilty as such by a court-martial; and if he is caught again within your camp I trust you will bring him to prompt trial as a spy.[42]

Unable to find Shepardson to arrest him as a spy or to get satisfaction from the War Department, Johnston issued General Order No. 98, which called for the expulsion of all newspaper correspondents and reporters from his army. The action threatened newspapers with a news blackout from the army, a situation that alarmed Confederate editors. Johnston's edict would block all war information from Johnston's forces to the press except official army reports and occasional letters from soldiers who wrote down a few thoughts at their leisure.

Three weeks before he wrote the article that infuriated Johnston and Benjamin, Shepardson had noted that the December 6, 1861, *New York Herald* had published "a list of the number and name of the regiments and battalions now composing the Confederate Army . . ." Richmond officials were alarmed "for fear it was furnished by some spy in the War Department," but Bohemian thought otherwise.

If there be a clerk who acts the spy, who furnished the Herald with such a list, for God-sake do not disturb him. His many blunders and accuracies will do the other side more harm than ours, and he may be looked upon as a public benefactor rather than a traitor. The fact of the case is, this list is made up entirely from gleanings from the newspapers gathered here and there, and then summed up as any skillful and energetic editor knows well how to do.[43]

The now contrite Shepardson said he had depended on a trusted source when he gathered his information for his report about the winter quarters of the Confederate army. "But I have since learned from better authority that my publication was premature, and furthermore, that it was substantially incorrect," he wrote.[44]

> Ten thousand rumors upon the subject are floating on the current of public talk; but they are merely exaggerated reports upon a matter no one beyond our Generals can even predicates [sic] an opinion. In my college days I recollect to have read, I think in Terrence, the saying, 'Insita lomixibus libide sleadi de industria rumores'—men have in them a natural propensity for spreading rumors.[45]

As the storm gathered over the report he had written, Shepardson headed for Richmond to avoid being arrested. Remaining within the lines of the Army of the Potomac, he wrote with regret, "[M]y pen has been seldom idle. I have gathered many a sheaf of useful knowledge and experience, and only regret that I have scattered tares in the public highway. When first 'Bohemian' sat down to a quiet chat with his kind readers, he promised more than his poor abilities allowed him to accomplish."

> I ask the same dear readers to accompany me in further 'Bohemian' walks and talks in other ways. I presume I have looked my last upon the broad fields of Manassas plains, dotted with the white tents of our soldiers, and have done with the busy scenes of war on the line of the Potomac. Well, they will still cling to memory, and fancy can repaint them.[46]

Meanwhile, Southern newspaper editors, who attended an editorial conference in Atlanta in March 1862 to deal with the problems caused by Order No. 98, expressed alarm at the continuing mandates to quash the reporting of their correspondents. Their views were published in the convention minutes:

> A preamble and resolution was adopted expressing the desire that the order issued by Gen. Jos. E. Johnston, of the Army of the Potomac, excluding newspaper correspondents, as well as similar orders of other Generals, be rescinded, and that in lieu of peremptory prohibition, proper restrictions be employed to prevent correspondents from violating orders and the courtesies of the camp. [47]

Johnston and Benjamin were not alone in their frustration over newspaper correspondents who ignored the army's ultimatum. In a July 7, 1862, letter to then Secretary of War George W. Randolph,[48] General Robert E. Lee expressed his dismay about ". . . the great danger of publishing any movements of this army and anything exhibiting its strength in whole or part must be apparent to all. I thought it was understood that our papers were to be silent on all matters pertaining to the movements of the army, and I beg that you will take the necessary steps to prevent in future the giving of publicity in this way to our strength and position," Lee wrote.[49]

Military censorship increased steadily through the year, ending with General Braxton Bragg's issuance of an order that general headquarters must approve information planned for publication.

> Assistant Adjutant-General Geo. G. Garner issued General Orders No. 158 on December 21, 1862: The practice of subordinate officers . . . (providing information) . . . in newspapers is disapproved, and will be discontinued. Several instances recently have occurred where valuable information as to the position of our troops has been thus conveyed to the enemy. No such publications will be allowed unless approved at general headquarters. By command of General Bragg.[50]

Even if ordinary directives to silence the press failed, commanding officers who wished to keep pesky newspaper correspondents from disclosing military secrets had a powerful remedy in addition to General Order 98 and orders from Lee and Bragg. They could instruct the officers of telegraph companies not to send a message on the wire. Another order, No. 78, set limits when the message related to the movement of troops, when it related to the position of particular corps, and when it gave information from which the movements and strength of the armies of the Confederate states, or any portion of them, could be inferred."[51]

Bohemian left his censorship problems behind him, traveling to Norfolk on his way to North Carolina. There he wrote the *Daily Dispatch*, reminiscing about his visit six years earlier and reiterating his love for old books and records.

> I turn from the last words of this slight historical sketch to light a cigar, and listen to the rain beat against the window. One cannot always tramp for news, and stand at the street corners to catch the items of gossip which float on the current of public talk, and on such days, how better could "your own" employ himself than in reading up in the old time records.[52]

Shepardson traveled by steamer up the southern branch of the Elizabeth River and through the Albemarle and Chesapeake Canal on February 2,[53] arriving in time to cover the impending Battle of Roanoke Island, among the islands along the east coast of North Carolina. Roanoke Island, a marshy place 12 miles long, lay between Albemarle and Pamlico Sounds, about 50 miles from Cape Hatteras. "The swamp on the right was represented impassable, and the islanders said that a duck could hardly go through it with safety. The marsh on the left was protected by two companies of flankers," Bohemian wrote. The

Confederates had erected an 80-foot field fortification across the narrow 75 feet of solid ground. It had "three embrasures as large as barn doors, with three guns—one 24-pound howitzer, one 18, and one 6-pounder," but only 25 rounds of ammunition. The call went out for more ammunition, but none came.[54]

Shortly after noon, Union troops were seen "approaching on the right flank, wading waist deep through the morass pronounced Impassable. The place that could not be traversed by a duck was forded by a regiment." After the Union soldiers had gained a footing on the right, the Confederates were ordered to retreat.[55]

Casualties had been light, considering that some 7,500 Federal soldiers waded onto the island and that some 2,000 Confederates sought to safeguard it for the Confederacy. The *Daily Dispatch* declared that the combined total for the Union's killed and wounded was 1,000 and noted that "the infamous scoundrels have shelled and burnt the pleasant little town of Elizabeth City, and are threatening Edenton." The North's operations in the vicinity would be limited, the editors surmised, "and instead of depressing the spirits of our people, such acts of vandalism will serve to make them more determined, and rouse them to thrice vigorous resistance."[56]

Shepardson wrote that late at night he and other surgeons were in the nearby hospital tending to the wounded. Generally, the wounds were slight, he added. All the wounded were housed at Elizabeth City but would be moved north to Norfolk when transportation could be arranged. He asked for his readers' indulgence for the captives. "Do not judge any of us harshly until I have told the whole story, and then you may say what you please." The 60 Confederates who were captured kept nine full regiments at bay for four and a half hours, "until their guns were clogged and their ammunition exhausted."[57]

As morning drew near, "owing to frequent use of opiates and anodynes,[58] they [the patients] became easier, and I went down to the battery to see the result of the bombardment." The correspondent and surgeon recalled what he saw in these wee hours.

> The night was intensely dark and misty. The light of the burning huts reflected its red glare upon the ramparts of the fort, and showed us where the enemy's shots had taken effect. Just below us was the beach, up which the little waves washed musically, and far beyond the lanterns hung in the rigging of the ships indicating where they lay at anchor. We went through the work examining every embrasure, the magazine, parapet, gun carriage and traverse.[59]

Shepardson and others were taken prisoner on February 8.[60] Two days after the battle, his editors announced: "It is reported that 'Bohemian,' the special correspondent of the Richmond Dispatch, is a prisoner."[61] Another correspondent for the *Daily Dispatch* lamented Bohemian's incarceration, writing that he missed the correspondent's reports in the newspaper. The Savannah reporter expressed his regrets.

I heard with great regret that your adventurous correspondent, "Bohemian," than whom I knew no more pleasant and accomplished writer and acquaintance, qualifies me to add, no more whole-souled and generous gentleman has fallen, along with so many others worthy a better fate, into the hands of the enemy. I will miss his letters in the Dispatch, which have always repaid the careful reading I gave them.[62]

The *Dispatch*'s Bohemian did not say how he was treated or how he secured parole, but he was released and quickly returned to Richmond, where he wrote an account of the fight he had witnessed on the island. The *Daily Dispatch*'s editors expressed "unqualified pleasure" to welcome Shepardson back to their offices in late February. "He was captured by the enemy on Roanoke Island, while discharging the duties of a surgeon in the hospital; and during his sojourn 'abroad' has experienced some [vicissitudes] of war and added materially to his steek [*sic*] of adventures," his editors wrote.[63]

Bohemian said that the terms of his parole forbade him to report fully, but he offered to provide a list of killed and wounded soldiers. He counted 16 dead,[64] among them, Captain O. Jennings Wise of the 46th Virginia, who was "shot in several places."[65] According to the surgeon's count, 12 men were wounded.

Shepardson theorized about the odds against the Confederates in trying to hold Roanoke Island. "Taking all things into consideration, I believe that, had no force been landed upon Roanoke Island, it must have fallen inevitably in the course of a few days by cutting off communication with the main land . . . so soon as the Federal ships passed Roanoke it was literally in the hands of the enemy, and that the more men there were upon the island the sooner must it have capitulated."[66] Despite his misgivings about the Confederate chances of winning the battle, Bohemian said he would have paid the ultimate price to defend his country.

All fought like veterans and heroes, as they are. As the boats near the barges, the officers, amid a perfect shower of shot and shell, came out on the decks, and, swinging their hats, gave hearty cheers of encouragement to the soldiers. I do not remember a moment in the history of the Confederacy—not even when the "stars and bars" were first hauled upon the Capitol at Montgomery amid the enthusiastic shouts of an earnest people, when my heart has so swelled with emotion, and when I have been so willing to sacrifice my life, my all, in the defence of the right and my country.[67]

Shepardson also had strong views about the virtues of retreat. "Some have said that every man ought to have been sacrificed for the moral effect," he wrote. "I say, that when it was so well known the place would be finally captured, the men ought to have been preserved for future physical effect, instead of shooting them for a moral effect. But delay judgment until you hear the story out."[68]

Before Bohemian returned to writing after his capture, *Daily Dispatch* editors noted that "readers of the Dispatch in this latitude regret exceedingly the loss of your accomplished correspondent 'Bohemian.' His letters were always read with much satisfaction as being entertaining, instructive, and reliable. May he soon return to his pen."[69]

In reporting the Roanoke Island battle, Shepardson got himself into a bit of a controversy when he reported that the men of the 31st North Carolina ran to their quarters after the enemy had taken their battery. "I had no desire to impugn the courage of the 31st in saying they ran immediately to their quarters; for, after the enemy had taken the battery, what else could they have done?" Bohemian wrote. For this portion of his report, he had had "to depend entirely upon hearsay as to who they were."

The unit's commanding officer, Lieutenant Colonel Daniel G. Fowle, was incensed and wrote the *Dispatch* to complain. According to Fowle, "Eight companies of the 31st were on or near the battlefield" at the same moment. "This correspondent says they 'ran.' Mr. Editor, he must have been looking at some other men; for the forces under my command did not run, but walked. I walked a part of the way with them myself, and afterwards accompanied them on horseback . . ."[70]

Bohemian included the officer's statement in his correspondence that day and provided his insight about the duty of a newspaper correspondent in the 1860s. First-hand knowledge of the retreat was impossible, he said, "since I was principally in the hospitals."

> The duties of a newspaper correspondent are much more difficult and annoying than many are inclined to believe. He is obliged to know everything, hear everything, and do everything at the same time—in fact, he is expected to be ubiquitous. If anything escapes his eye, up jumps somebody and accuses him of a willful omission of facts to the prejudice of another; if he be led into error by the statements of others, he is accused of falsification; whether he blame severely, makes what he believes a plain statement of events, or praises but feebly, it is all the same. Somebody is dissatisfied. What wonder the band of young fellows who began with this war, and who wrote such pleasant, interesting, and gossipy letters for the Southern papers, has dwindled down to one or two?[71]

After his transfer to the navy as an assistant surgeon on May 1, 1863, Shepardson continued to cover land-based military activities for a time. The pay for assistant surgeons on duty at sea was $1,250, on other duty, $1,050, and on leave or waiting orders $800.[72] The Confederate Congress approved legislation on May 1, 1863, that provided for the transfer of army personnel to the Confederate navy, and so the timing of Shepardson's transfer was the earliest possible.[73]

Shepardson wrote about more than his exploits as a soldier and sailor. He revealed some information about himself when he hinted in his dispatches that he was single and had affection for children. He also wrote about civilians and was sensitive to the difficulties of supporting a family during wartime in Richmond, wondering how sewing women support themselves by making shirts at 25 cents each.

> There is many a poor clerk having a family to support at the above high prices that only gets $1,000 per year. It is only by walking upon the very verge of starvation they can get along. Rents are enormous. This is natural enough. When we consider the fact that there are one hundred and twenty thousand people here now, against forty thousand two years ago. I will mention that a 25 cents coffee pot costs $4. Living, as I do, in lodgings, getting my meals at the restaurants, I can hardly imagine how it is possible for a man with a family to support them on one, or even two, thousand per annum. But it is done.[74]

He also reported on other problems of civilians. In early summer, on June 5, Bohemian witnessed an attempt by Federal gunboats to destroy Southern crops. He detailed for readers how Union gunboats came up the Mattaponi River and landed men in the lower part of King William County. The object was to conduct a minor raid, steal slaves, burn houses and barns, and destroy the crops. "The Yankees said, some time ago, that they would not allow the planters of Gloucester, Matthews, King and Queen, King William, and other counties, to make their crops, and that they would desolate and lay waste the country. They have carried out the threat," Bohemian wrote.[75]

Military topics were frequent in the correspondent's dispatches. Like most Southerners, Shepardson had high regard for Lee's military savvy. The reporter first demolished the guesswork about the Confederates' next troop movements and then elaborated on the complexities of Lee's decisions and the difficulty many had in predicting what he would do next. "The secrecy with which Gen. Lee conducts his movements is perfectly wonderful," Shepardson wrote, "and yet he has never been guilty of the folly of sending newspaper correspondents outside his lines. He simply keeps his own counsel, and instructs his division commanders to do the same. He gives his orders to march to a designated place; there other orders will be found. 'Obey them.'"

> The public have speculated a great deal upon his plans, but he is too deep to be easily fathomed, and generally does just exactly contrary to what everybody expected. His reasons are always good, but time has to prove them so. He says nothing, makes no explanations, seeks for no momentary popularity, and is content with doing his duty. What a shining example for other officers to follow.[76]

Although Shepardson respected Lee's leadership, he found it difficult to determine where the general was at any given moment. "The movements of Lee's army are not very clear, and we have no idea where the main body now is. It is only known that the commanding General has his troops in motion, and all beyond that is mere speculation," he wrote. "Through it all—the awful uncertainty about what would come next from the enemy and the setbacks on the battlefield—the enemy was repulsed," and the Confederates celebrated another "glorious victory." [77]

Patriotism among Southerners manifested itself in various ways. Some contributed to a fund to raise a statue in tribute to General Stonewall Jackson who had died on May 10, 1863, after the amputation of his arm. "The gallant Stonewall was no more," were the words of a song.[78] The correspondent reported that Confederate citizens were rallying to this cause with contributions that "come in daily. The soldiers also subscribe liberally. This week Lee Mallory, proprietor of the entertainments at Metropolitan Hall, has given the proceeds of 1,000 tickets to the fund."[79]

Like others, Shepardson found himself speculating about the course of the war as days turned to months. He wrote about the demoralizing effect of the fall of Vicksburg and Port Hudson[80] on the Southerners. ". . . many gloomy faces are seen upon the streets to-day."[81] Fort Powhatan would be next, Bohemian predicted, and he described the scene even before the Federals informed Washington that the Confederate stronghold had been captured.

> The garrison of Fort Powhatan numbered about twenty men, and the place had been evacuated long before the Yankees got within firing distance. At any time, and with any force, the place was untenable. The enemy opened a heavy fire upon the deserted fort, and at the same time landed a force to carry the works by storm. This force charged upon them, and, with an immense amount of cheering, the "stars and stripes" were hoisted over the fort.[82]

By the middle of 1863, the journalist felt at home with predictions and analysis. After the capture of Fort Powhatan, the Federal forces headed up the James River toward Richmond. Within two days, Union troops were within 20 miles of Drewry's Bluff, just south of the Confederate capital.

> Here the river narrows, and the boats are much exposed from the shores. Thinking probably that danger threatened them higher up, they ran down to the river at night, and this morning [July 16], are below City Point again. Many were of opinion that another attack upon Drewry' [sic] Bluff was premeditated. I did not share that opinion; for an attack upon a place of its importance and strength, half a dozen of their best iron-clads would be necessary.[83]

Bohemian correctly surmised that the Union forces were merely engaged in a marauding expedition among James River plantations.[84] Other troops at Drewry's Bluff were also marauders. Soldiers had visited Shirley Plantation, taking 12 more slaves from the residence of Hill Carter. Sixty slaves had been taken in an earlier raid. So far, the plantation had been spared "on account of the females residing in the house, and it is fortunate for Virginia that they have the power of restraining the Yankee vandals."[85] The house and accompanying structures had been built of imported brick 173 years earlier. "The main house contains many valuable paintings, the family coat of arms, and a large portrait of Washington by Peale. It is sincerely hoped this relic of the early history of Virginia may be spared," Shepardson wrote.[86]

Bohemian's frustration about the enemy's next move and the interminable struggle between North and the South emerged in his reporting. The uncertainty was nearly unbearable, he wrote. After failed attempts to invade enemy territory on the opposite side of the Potomac River, the public "draws a long breath of relief" when the Confederates were encamped inside their own boundaries on the near side of the river.

> It is now conceded that our strength lies in the defensive; that our weakness becomes apparent when we attempt to invade the country of the enemy. Had our army been sufficiently strong to have won the battle of Gettysburg, no one can doubt but that peace would have been certain; as it is we see only a continuance of the struggle year after year, until the enemy sees the folly of his subjugating war. When that will be God only knows![87]

Shepardson correctly predicted the next move of General George G. Meade, commander of the North's Army of the Potomac. Meade would not "commit the folly of McClellan" and allow the Confederates to adhere to their established lines for two or three months. Instead, Bohemian predicted, the general "will immediately endeavor to seize the mountain passes on the Shenandoah," in hope of cutting off the Confederate army from communication with Richmond. However, Meade would fail because Lee had figured out his strategy, and "before Meade crosses the Potomac, the mountain gaps will be occupied by our troops." After that, "there will then be a race to Culpeper which will be won by Lee; then the enemy can establish his base wherever he thinks best, either by Manassas, Fredericksburg, or the Peninsula."[88]

An observer of military maneuvers, the social dynamic of Richmond, and the political scene, Shepardson noted the thousands of "idle characters now in the city of Richmond, who manage in some way to elude the conscript officers, and who ought to be in the army." He had little tolerance for officers whose tours of duty had ended and did not re-enlist. "It is hard to think there are those among us who, being willing to serve the country, *as officers*, are not willing to do so as privates, if required. Still they are daily seen in our midst."[89] Shepardson also had no use for the practice of paying a substitute to take a soldier's place in the army. He believed the system should be halted.

> Substitutes are beginning to command a large price. This morning a man offers to sell himself for $5,000, and another offers $4,500 for a man to take his place in an artillery company. This substitute system ought to be stopped, as it has already done much mischief in our army. From records kept in the Adjutant General's office, we learn that there have been received there *sixty thousand*

substitutes in the place of an equal number of able bodied men capable of bear-ing arms.[90]

Bohemian took his inside information a step further. Had those 60,000 sol-diers been with Lee at Gettysburg, as well as their substitutes, ". . . we should have had a treaty of peace in progress before this."[91]

The journalist's report was not confined to the normal news fodder about numbers of troops and substitutes. Shepardson's position as a surgeon gave him access to information about an unusual patient admitted to a hospital. He re-ported that "a large crane, measuring six feet from wing to wing, was captured on Shocco creek yesterday. He was wounded and had one of his legs amputated at a city hospital."[92]

Meanwhile, John Taylor Wood, who would be Shepardson's commanding of-ficer in the Confederate Navy, was planning raids on Federal ships in Chesa-peake Bay. Weeks earlier, in spring of 1863, Wood had begun assembling 11 officers and 71 seamen for an expedition to locate and destroy Federal ships in the bay's strategic waters, action that would take place in August.[93] Bohemian, writing from Port Royal, Virginia, acknowledged that the secretary of the Navy had not confided in him after he transferred from the army to the navy. "It may seem singular that when the secretary of the Navy gave me orders to join the party, he did not take me into his confidence, and I was therefore as ignorant about the matter as about the plans of Gen. Lee." But the journalist perked up when stories were "whispered into my buttonhole," and he "listened attentively to the recital of disasters about to befall me . . ."[94]

Wood's party of Confederate seamen, "armed to the teeth" and accompa-nied by "four splendid boats" loaded on wagons, left the city of Richmond on the Mechanicsville road on August 12, bound for the unknown. Shepardson was not with them on their departure, since his orders arrived when he was on liberty in the city, "enjoying the luxury of leisure and white linen." His orders directed him to start at daybreak to join the main party, but obtaining a pass-port was troublesome and he did not depart until midday of the next day. By that time he was 18 hours behind the main group of seamen.[95] Then, yet another obstacle plagued Shepardson.

> My command was some eighteen hours ahead of me, and I had to overtake them upon as sorry a piece of horseflesh as one could well imagine. That animal was nearly the death of me: He was somewhat rough and shook me until every joint in my body was loose and my teeth rattled in their sockets. Complaining did no good, and I determined to let no trials ruffle my good nature.[96]

At the end of the third day, after tracing the seamen across the Pamunkey and Mattaponi rivers, and riding through Essex County, Bohemian found his companions' trail. That night, August 16, the men bivouacked on the Paintbank

River, 25 miles from its mouth.[97] They lounged about and cooked their rations while they waited for Wood, the party's commander, to complete a reconnaissance. "Their destination was a matter of conjecture, and more than one anxious quid nunc puzzled his brain over the problem."[98] Wood returned the following evening, and the men began immediate preparation for departure. The purpose of their mission was finally revealed. They were to capture one of the Federal blockaders by boarding a ship in the night.[99]

In late afternoon, men were called to quarters, arms inspected, ammunition distributed, and a prayer offered by Wood. The crews took up their positions and quietly set off on their mission "with muffled oars rowed rapidly and silently down the stream, sending out no noise save the rippling of the waves around the cutters' bows as they ploughed their way through the water," Bohemian wrote.[100]

The group searched until a signal light showed them the gunboat's position. The sound of machinery told them she was in motion. The Confederates could only retreat and wait for a more favorable opportunity. They pulled 15 miles upriver and waited. At daybreak, an approaching steamer prompted Wood to send the Confederate boats high up a creek. He dispatched the main body of men to follow them on land. The Federals, alerted by a careless Confederate seaman, began firing on Wood, "shouting from boat to boat, 'Shoot him—kill him—don't let the d—d rebel get away,' firing their rifles rapidly and at random." Finally, the Federal vessel retreated down the river.[101]

The skirmish with the enemy forced Wood and his men to relocate to the Rappahannock River, arriving on August 19.[102] Good fortune awaited the raiding party when the crew spotted the gunboats USS *Satellite* and USS *Reliance* of the Federals' Potomac Flotilla and the *Currituck*, anchored near the mouth of the river. "One or all of these we were determined to have," Shepardson wrote.[103] The night was beautiful, dark on a calm river, beneath a starlit sky and crescent moon, he told his readers.

> Added to the picture was a line of black boats, filled with armed men, creeping snake-like over the water, prepared to spring upon the foe whenever he came in sight. Late in the night Lt. Wood called the boats alongside his own and gave instructions for the attack; then, after a fervent prayer, we pushed out into the bay. From pickets on the point we learned the steamers lay some three miles out towards Butler's, but after a careful search they were not to be found, and we were forced to return without accomplishing anything.[104]

Confederate Colonel T.L. Rosser arrived with his regiment on August 20 to help Wood, a welcome development, Shepardson noted. "His regiment, the 4th cavalry, was raised principally from the counties around, and knew every path and by-way in them." A storm kept the Confederates from an immediate attack, but when the enemy appeared a short distance away at Butler's Hole, "their

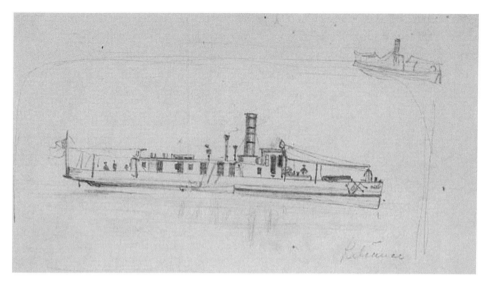

The Union gunboat *Reliance* was captured by Confederates after a bloody hand-to-hand battle aboard the ship in Chesapeake Bay in 1864. Shepardson, who was both a reporter and surgeon, attended to the wounds of both Union and Confederate commanders after they engaged in battle. Courtesy of Library of Congress

black hulls rising from the water, some two or three hundred yards apart," the Confederates, in four cutters, resolved to divide and conquer their prey:

> We pulled slowly and silently on. When within about fifty yards the sentinel on deck sang out his "boat ahoy." — Mr. Wood answered in some unintelligible words and then we gave way strong towards them. We had the starboard bow, Mr. Wood the port. It was a moment of anxiety—almost of misgiving. If the Yankees were aware of our approach, destruction was certain. There was no retreat now— Death lay in the silent guns ahead and in the mad waters around.[105]

The sea was furiously lashing itself, raising the Confederate cutters high into the air. The men used their entire strength at the oars. One cutter and the *Satellite* collided. After a few shots, "twenty of us were climbing over the netting onto her decks. The watch fired their rifles at us and gave the alarm, and immediately the Yankees came pouring from below, grasping cutlasses and side arms as they ran up the hatch." The *Satellite* defenders "fought well," but it was no use. The defenders surrendered, and the ship belonged to the Confederates.[106] Sharp firing on the decks of the nearby *Reliance* attracted the attention of Bohemian and his companions on the *Satellite* as he described the encounter.

> Captain Walters, of the Reliance was also a brave man, and did everything possible to save his ship. Upon the first alarm he sprang forward to slip the cable,

but was met by Lt. Hoge, who ran forward to encounter him, and was almost instantly shot through the body with a pistol. At the same time Lieut. Hoge received a dangerous wound through the neck, and fell beside the water tank. Although wounded, Captain Walters sprang to the pilot-house and blew the whistle to get help from the Satellite, but he was soon secured.[107]

Shepardson was summoned to attend to the wounds of Lieutenant Hoge and the Union officer, Captain Walters, on the *Reliance*. Both were "seriously hit and lying side by side in the cabin," Bohemian wrote. Meanwhile, a Confederate deserter lay dying on the deck, "and three or four Yankees and negroes had wounds from cutlass or pistol." On the *Satellite*, the wounded were more numerous, "but they were attended by the Surgeon's steward on the steamer. None of our men were hurt on board of her," Bohemian wrote.[108] The warships were taken to Urbanna.[109]

The wounded from both sides and the prisoners were removed from the ships. Bohemian noted the addition of sharpshooters after anticipating an encounter with the *Currituck*. "Col. Rosser had furnished from his regiment Capt. Clay's company of Sharpshooters, to assist in the engagement should we meet her."[110] The *Reliance* could not be pushed beyond two knots and lost steam as fast as could be gained, so the *Satellite* went on alone, with Shepardson on board. Wood and his crew reached the mouth of the river and ran out into the bay the night of August 23. Bohemian recalled the fruitless expedition.

> The sea was quite high, with a strong southeasterly wind, and every prospect of an approaching storm.—Having so little coal, it was impossible to go far; but Lt. Wood started boldly up the bay to see what there was afloat. The waves were every moment getting higher, and the Satellite creaked and groaned in every seam, and ran her head heavily against the sea, as if trying to commit suicide at the chagrin of capture . . . At two o'clock we turned back, and a little before day made Stingray Point . . . and we ran safely inside. [111]

Anchoring near Gray's Point, the men were exhausted after three consecutive nights on the bay, and when the anchor hit bottom, "nearly all dropped to sleep upon the deck. Having suffered severely with sea sickness during the night our cavalry were a forlorn looking set, and it was pitiful to see their pale, uneasy faces," Bohemian wrote.[112]

When sails appeared in the bay, the *Satellite* crew gave chase, capturing the Baltimore schooner, the *Golden Rod*, and Philadelphia's anchor-sweepers, the *Two Brothers* and the *Coquette*. The *Golden Rod*'s captain and crew "were the most surprised men I ever saw," Bohemian reported. The other two vessels had "a number of very fine anchors and cables on board. Taking the three in tow we ran up to Urbanna again, and let go anchors," Bohemian wrote. The *Golden Rod* was laden with coal, and the crew ran the *Satellite* alongside the schooner, taking the fuel on board. "The schooners were made ready for burning, and instructions left with Lieutenant Hudgins to take charge of them and apply the match should the enemy force us to retire."[113]

Shepardson went ashore the next day, August 25, "to carry the wounded some captured luxuries, taken from the prizes," and he reported on the condition of his patients. Hoge was progressing, despite a painful wound. Walters seemed to be losing ground, the deserter had died, and "an old boatswain beyond recovery . . . The ladies were assiduous in their endeavors to make all comfortable, and I am sure the wounded will ever cherish kindly recollections of their care."[114]

From Urbanna, the *Satellite* ran down the Rappahannock and waited two miles from the bay for something to happen. "The sea seemed to be higher than before, and we could see the white foam caps flash in the light, and the heavy breakers dash upon the beach with their continuous, saddening roar," Bohemian wrote. The Federal ship *Currituck* had arrived after calling for aid, and three large gunboats were visible in the distance. The Confederates retreated up the river toward Urbanna where the *Reliance* had arrived and was taking on coal. The two ships waited out the fury of the storm while "the wind shrieked around us as if all the sea-demons had been turned loose." The sharpshooters went ashore.[115]

The draft of the larger schooner, the *Golden Rod*, was too deep for the upper Rappahannock, so the ship was set afire at daybreak. In the midst of great suspense about where the Yankees would appear next, Bohemian paused long enough to take in his surroundings.

> I do not know of a more beautiful river in this country than the Rappahannock. The shores are high and slope from the hills behind gracefully down to the water. The Confederate flag was flying from the Satellite, and from some old bunting on board, the officers of the Reliance improvised a small flag of the new pattern—the white ground with battle-flag union. Our advance caused considerable excitement on the route: Some stared in mute astonishment, others thought it a trick of the Yankees, others then greeted us with enthusiastic cheers.[116]

The Confederates arrived on August 26 at Port Royal, where troops and a battery of artillery were stationed. The seamen were "very kindly greeted by all and promised every assistance in dismantling and getting ashore the cargo of the prize." Federal cavalry and infantry were camped only 15 miles away at King George Court House.

Women ashore, recognizing the gunboats from earlier Union raids to capture slaves and chickens, provided considerable attention. Arrangements were made to deliver the Richmond newspapers to the seamen, and Shepardson attended a dress parade in the evening and "listened for a sweet half hour to the rich tones of the organ in the village church."[117]

The *Richmond Sentinel* and other newspapers praised Wood's command of the Chesapeake raid, calling it the "exceedingly handsome operation by Lieutenant Wood whose name is now famous . . . Well done! Well done!"[118]

After Federal forces captured Roanoke Island in 1862, they moved southwest and occupied Newbern, North Carolina, a substantial community located at the junction of the Neuse and Trent rivers.[119] Fortifications were swiftly erected over a wide area, and most of the soldiers stationed there were "men from Massachusetts and New York, the blackest of Abolitionists, full of schemes and plans for negro emancipation, equalization and education," Bohemian reported.[120]

In a scenario similar to the one Shepardson experienced in the capture of the Union ships *Satellite* and *Reliance*, Confederate navy officials began planning another attack on Federal installations and ships in North Carolina in mid-1863. But instead of originating in Virginia, the "Newbern expedition" was launched from Wilmington, North Carolina, and aimed at Newbern to the north. The hush-hush plan was for General George E. Pickett's troops laying siege to Newbern from the south to create a diversion while Wood and a contingent of seamen captured the Union gunship *Underwriter* in the Neuse River north of the town.[121] Wood again selected Shepardson to accompany him as surgeon and correspondent.

The *Underwriter*, a large side-wheel vessel with 800-horsepower engines, had fired the first shots at the Battle of Roanoke Island. The vessel was one of several Union gunboats that cruised the Neuse River, terrorizing the Southerners living in the area. She had participated in most of the naval engagements along the North Carolina coast.[122]

Wood and his men left Wilmington with their boats on rail cars and reached Kinston on January 31, 1864, where they launched into the Neuse and silently followed the river to near Newbern. There, Wood explained the purpose of the expedition to his men. As night fell, ". . . Capt. Wood offered up fervent prayers for success, asking God to judge between us and our enemies, and once more we were winding down the Neuse."[123]

As Bohemian explained the plan, two Confederate brigades, led by General Pickett, would drive the Union troops back into the town. Meanwhile, General Seth M. Barton was sent up the Trent "to fall upon the town simultaneously with those in front," and a small force of infantry, a cavalry battalion and two pieces of artillery, had been dispatched across the Neuse to threaten Fort Anderson and deter Union reinforcements from Washington, North Carolina. Fort Anderson was a solid structure, 14 feet high, "mounting 11 guns of high caliber, with a ditch from 4 to 6 feet deep and 12 feet wide. The garrison, under Col. Anderson, was composed of 860 infantry, with some heavy artillery."[124]

While Pickett waited for aid from Barton, his nervous habits caught Shepardson's eye. "Gen. Pickett was standing under a tree, in full sight of the town and its fortifications, his staff lying upon the ground around him, looking anxiously towards the Trent, twirling his sword knot around his small white hand, or, as if in perplexity, fastidiously biting his finger nails." [125]

Within a mile and a half of Newbern, Pickett's troops met the Union forces at the Battle of Bechelor's Creek, routing the Union troops.With Pickett's men pressing close to the Federals, the Confederates poured shot into them, "whenever they endeavored to form," pressing them into a run to get under cover of the guns of the fort built around the town. Shepardson described the enemy on the run.

> Regiments became disorganized and scattered through the woods, and men and officers, with the shout of "sauve qui pent" [peut] threw away knapsack and rifle and ran for their lives. By three in the evening the enemy had taken shelter within the fortifications, and stood awaiting the anticipated attack upon the town; but straggling bands were found scattered through the woods, and were every moment being brought in by our men. [126]

In the aftermath, 100 Federals were reported killed or wounded and 13 officers and 280 troops captured. Pickett lost only 35 men killed or wounded.[127]

Meanwhile, Shepardson and his navy companions hunted for Union gunboats in the Neuse but found none. They retreated four or five miles up the Neuse and entered a small creek, where they could hear the fighting on the opposite shore.[128] To the call of "Boat ahoy! Boat ahoy!" Shepardson was roused from two hours' sleep early on February 2. As the Confederate vessel engaged the *Underwriter*, the journalist was bloodied by the first volley from aboard the ship. He described the tense moments.

> Hot and fast goes the firing; the Yankees, having all gotten on deck and armed, were pouring it into us with remarkable rapidity. The flashes came full in our faces, lighting them up with a deathly pallor, while the sulphurous of burning powder pervaded the air. Struck by a splinter the first fire, bringing a profusion of blood from my face and nose, I could scarcely see or comprehend all the rapid movements of our little fleet; but I knew our boat was first at the side, Capt. Wood's close after, then came Lieuts. Hoge, Kerr, Porcher, Gardner, Roby, and Wilkinson, while a short distance away, slackened up to prevent running down the other boats, was Gift with his launches.[129]

The fire was the most intense he had witnessed in three years' experience in the war, Shepardson wrote. He expected only half of the Confederates to emerge alive. While the Confederates were greeted with a volley of musketry as they boarded the *Underwriter*, a marine, shot through the heart "fell heavily upon me and crushed me down over the thwarts. Extricated from this I found the ship was ours." [130]

Under heavy fire from nearby Federal batteries, the Confederates were caught with no time to return fire and get up steam on the *Underwriter*. Instead, they placed the wounded and prisoners into smaller boats and set the vessel on fire. "In five minutes after our boats had left the side, the *Underwiter* was one mass of flame, burning up the dead bodies of the Yankees killed in action; also, three or four dead negroes in the coal bunkers." [131] The fight lasted only about 10 minutes, "but in that short time the enemy was overpowered, the decks in our possession, and the prisoners secured." In the process, disloyal Confederate soldiers, North Carolina "Buffaloes" who had deserted, were captured. " . . . the example of hanging them, after sentence of court martial, had a good effect upon the army and the people,"[132] Bohemian wrote.

Days after the naval battle, he recalled the steadfastness of the men and the danger the Confederates faced as they boarded the vessel.

> The steamer was boarded very handsomely. The enemy had sufficient notice to arm themselves, and the boarders had to fight their way upon the decks. Worst of all were the land batteries which turned their guns upon us. In the whole history of naval warfare, cutting a steamer from under land batteries has been considered the most daring and hazardous achievement that could be accomplished. The danger and risk is so great that such attempts have been few.[133]

His description of the night before the final effort is a portrait of a soldier's respite along the river. Bohemian's report to the *Daily Dispatch* offers a reporter's detail about the sounds and sights he remembered.

> . . . about 12 o'clock nearly all were in the land of dreams, and I sat down to have a comfortable pipe before retiring to the soft spot of ground picked out for a bed. We were upon a small bluff some fifty feet high. Below the river flowed smoothly on, shimmering in the light of the gibbous moon, while above it, just resting southward, was a dark line of woods, throwing a black shadow upon the water and sending out from every tree the night cry of the katy-did and sawyer. Disturbed watch-dogs in the neighboring farmyards barked to each other or the moon, and cows lowed in the meadows. But above all the sounds of the night was a single hootowl in the lonely branches crying, who shouted 'murder' to the Yankee foe beyond the river. [134]

Shepardson continued his naval adventures during the summer of 1864, when he joined Wood aboard the Confederate cruiser *Tallahassee* as she burned and scuttled Union ships along the northeast coast. The journalist kept a diary of the ship's expedition as a raider. His log began on August 6 and ended on August 31, adding rich description to the official record and challenging some of the reporting seen in the Northern press. "Only one side of the story has been told, and that, with all the exaggeration and falsehood of particular instances, is incomplete. In order to make known the true story . . . I cannot do better than transcribe the narrative from my diary, written from day to day during the cruise."[135]

CSS *Tallahassee*. Photograph from the U.S. Department of Navy, Naval Historical Center

The ship, a former blockade runner, was described as "an iron vessel of about 300 tons, manned by 125 men, with a double screw, very fast, and carrying three guns, viz, a 100, 20 and 12 pounder, respectively."[136] The vessel had been constructed on the Thames River in England in 1863 and purchased by the Confederates who turned it into a raider.[137]

A list of vessels captured by the *Tallahassee* totaled 33 in the 10 days between August 11 and August 20, 1864, the official record states.[138] "Some of the vessels, primarily schooners and pilot boats, were scuttled or burned. Seven were ransomed to clear her crowded decks of passengers and crews."[139] There may have been a discrepancy in the totals, however, because when the ship returned to its home port of Wilmington, Bohemian wrote that 35 ships had fallen victim to the dazzling bravado of the *Tallahassee*'s crew. Some of them were large and fine ships and barques, and others coasting vessels and fishermen.[140]

Wood and his crew had set out from Wilmington on August 6, a Saturday night. "He showed the blockaders a clean pair of heels; for that was the ship's main virtue, speed. . . ."[141] On the Sabbath, the second day of the voyage, the day of reflection could not go unheeded, and "Captain Wood read service on the quarter-deck to all hands. See large school of porpoises rolling and tumbling in the water. Three deserters from the fleet were found stowed away this morning. They were put in the coal bunkers to assist the firemen," Bohemian wrote.[142]

Five mornings after the cruiser's departure, "500 miles up the Atlantic Coast, *Tallahassee* encountered her first prize, the schooner *Sarah A. Boyce*, and before the day was over, she ran down six more Union merchant vessels, ransoming the last to put all prisoners ashore," historian Shelby Foote wrote. "Friday, off Long Island, she took six prizes, Saturday, two, and Sunday—as if by way of resting on the Sabbath—one. By now she was cruising the New England coast, rounding out a week that netted her thirty prizes, all burned or scuttled except seven."[143]

An account of the capture of the *Sarah A. Boyce* noted that the ship, bound for Philadelphia to take on coal, was "new and valuable. There are few provisions

Confederate Ram at Wilmington, North Carolina. *Harper's Weekly*, June 4, 1864
Courtesy of Rare Books and Special Collections, University of South Carolina
Libraries

on board, but these were removed, the captain and crew taken off, and the vessel
scuttled." The same day, a Northerner who had misunderstood the *Tallahassee*'s mission and wanted to offer himself as a pilot, boarded the cruiser from
the pilot boat, the *James Funck* or *Pilot BOAT 22*. "'What ship is this?' he asked
as he stepped upon the quarter-deck. Captain Wood then replied, 'The Confederate Cruiser *Tallahassee*'."[144]

The visitor was described as "a large, well-dressed man, with a heavy watch-
guard, a massive ring on his little finger, and the air of a genuine New York
butcher-boy. He was prepared to take us into port—having his clean shirt in a
bundle under his arm, and a few copies of the Herald and Times."[145] After he was
told that the ship belonged to the Confederates, color drained from the man's face.

> ... the fellow was frightened out of his wits. His face turned deathly pale, his
> knees shook violently, and drops of perspiration started from every pore. I never
> saw a more perfect picture of object misery than he presented when told his boat
> would be burned.[146]

Other ships that met their demise had names like *Carrie Estelle*, of Boston;
the *No. 22*; the *Carroll*, of East Machias, Maine; the *Atlantic*; and the *William*

Bell. It was difficult for Shepardson to come to terms with the destruction of the *William Bell,* or *Pilot Boat No. 24.* The ship was one of the finest vessels he had ever seen.

> Everything about her was fitted up in elegant style and in perfect order. Mahogany berths, rosewood panels, fine carpets, damask curtains, and broad lace trimmings on beds; silver, crockery, and . . . everything on board was of the best and costliest description. Built only three years ago, the "24" cost $16,000 in gold; and the fitting up, $1,000 more. We found two passengers on board, an old gentleman out for his health, and a New York drummer on a pleasure excursion.[147]

Bohemian wrote that he wanted to ensure that the owner, a Mr. Callahan, was comfortable, because his prisoner was so gracious. To that end, the correspondent helped the prisoner with his baggage, invited him to the ward-room table, and gave him blankets from his own bed for the night. "At night, while smoking our cigars, he spoke of the outrages committed by his own people, and condemned them in strong terms." But Shepardson had been deceived. When Callahan returned to his New York home, he told a *Herald* reporter he was "badly used, had his hat and boots taken from him; was kept without food, and had no place but the wet decks to lie at night," Bohemian wrote. Furthermore, Callahan told the *Herald* that Shepardson had confessed to being a Chesapeake pirate. Because of the experience, Bohemian vowed to keep his sympathies more in check and claimed that no prisoner taken aboard the *Tallahassee* was mistreated.

Union ships were not the only vessels at the mercy of the *Tallahassee.* The British ship, *Adriatic,* on a voyage from London to New York with 163 passengers, was destroyed, but nearly proved to be the *Tallahassee's* undoing. At 989 tons, the British vessel towered over the smaller ship, and in following orders from Wood to heave to, the ships collided, destroying the *Tallahassee's* mainmast and sweeping clear her decks. Bohemian wrote that the damage could have been worse. "Being a very large ship, towering high above us, she would have inevitably sunk us had she struck amidships." The passengers were transferred to the barque *22,* and Wood ordered the *Adriatic* burned.

> I shall never forget the scene, and yet it was a trifle compared to what I saw when the enemy took possession of the town of Fredericksburg. Women and children wept, screamed and prayed, while men cursed, laughed and got drunk. Two or three elderly females went into hysterias, while others were running here and there, with clasped hands, asking us to spare them. It was some time before they could comprehend that we did not intend burning them with the ship . . . They were allowed to take everything they desired . . . Three or four men were so drunk they had to be slung over the side.[148]

Many of the passengers traveled with "their all on board." Among their belongings were "broken pots and pans, jars, crockery, cracked vases, bird cages, cats,

The Confederate raider *Tallahassee* burned the English ship *Adriatic* after taking off its 163 passengers and crew. The *Adriatic* was bound from London to New York City. *Century Illustrated Monthly Magazine*, July 1898. Courtesy of Cornell University Library, Making of America Digital Collection

dogs, and other pets, brought with them from the Old World." And in a month's time, the able-bodied young men, who made up about half of the passengers, would seek their fortunes with the Army of Virginia, Bohemian predicted.[149]

The *Tallahassee* changed the destiny of more ships: the barque *Suliote,* bonded; the schooner of Maine, scuttled; the *Billow,* of Salem, Massachusetts, burned; the *Glenarvon,* a barque of Thomaston, Maine, scuttled. Passengers included the wife of the captain. Bohemian described her as "a perfect termagant, whose tongue was never idle, and her time about equally divided between abusing her husband, who bore it like a lamb, and distributing testaments and tracts among our men." After the Confederates obtained "mess stores, a few luxuries, some hams, a coop of chickens, and two pigs" from the *Glenarvon,* the ship was scuttled and Bohemian's sentimentality won out: "It seemed a pity to destroy such a noble craft, and I looked upon our work with sorrow."[150]

Because the *Tallahassee* had lost its mainmast and needed repairs to its engines, Wood looked for a port it could run into for a few days. Halifax was the leading candidate. En route, the cruiser eyed the *James L. Littlefield* of Bangor, Maine, hoping to take possession and confiscate its high-quality coal from Cardiff. But rough seas forced the crew to abandon such a fuel transfer.[151]

Further encounters expanded the *Tallahassee*'s reputation for capturing and sinking ships. It came upon the schooner *Mary A. Howes* of Chatham, Massachusetts; the Nova Scotia schooner *Sophy*, from Turk's Island; the schooner *Howard*, from Bridgeport, Connecticut; the fishing schooner *Restless*, returning from the Gulf of St. Lawrence; the schooner *Sarah B. Harris*, of Dorchester, Massachusetts, returning from the Gulf of Canse; and the *Etta Caroline*, a small fishing schooner from Portland, Maine, all on August 15.[152]

From the *Etta Caroline*, the *Tallahassee* crew got "some fine fresh fish—halibut, haddock and cod," ice, and other provisions. Shepardson described the exchange between Wood and the skipper of the smaller craft.

> The master, or skipper, as they are called, came over the side tremblingly, and walking up to Captain Wood, pulled his foretop and put his hat under his arm. Captain Wood said, "Well, captain, I must take charge of your schooner."
>
> "No!," said he inquiringly, "Oh! you wouldn't do that—I'm a poor fellow only a fisherman, sir."
>
> "But you are the very fellows we are after," was the reply.
>
> The poor devil looked ready to sink through the deck, but managed to get into his boat again, and pulled off after his dunnage. He was allowed to take everything he wanted—small boats, lines, &c., and then his craft was scuttled. The skipper and his three men were put into their small boats and towed down to the Sarah Harris and turned adrift. We saw him on board, and steamed away.[153]

Bohemian kept a detailed log of seized ships and their fate, and his pen captured for readers of the *Daily Dispatch* the beauty of the water, sky, and boats spread before him. The next day brought still more encounters with ships the *Tallahassee* could not ignore, such as the *P.C. Alexander* of Harpswell, Maine, and the schooners *Leopard, Pearl, Sarah Louise, Magnolia,* and *Sea Flower* of Cornwallis. Shepardson wrote that the men of the *Sea Flower* spoke in a peculiar Yankee twang, used strange idioms, and had an inclination to value their schooners over their wives.

> The males were much frightened when first taken; but when assured they would be well treated and soon returned, began to develop their Yankee traits; speaking in a very loud tone of voice, and with a nasal twang—cursing, using slang words, and very peculiar idioms, they cause us no little amusement. One expression was common to all, i.e., "to home,— they speak 'of going to home,' 'when I was to home,'" &c. They spoke of their wives as "the old woman," and the man who said he "would rather loose [sic] his wife than his schooner" was not the only one who showed singularity in his conjugal relations.[154]

The journalist had little sympathy for a skipper who lamented the loss of his schooner after five years of labor. "The boat was all I had in the world," said one, "and I've put five years hard work in it. Now it's all gone." Shepardson's response was terse: "Yes, I replied, and your people have destroyed not only what we have gained in our whole lives, but our ancestors for over a hundred years." He pointed out that Confederates on the *Tallahassee* placed no stock in the Northerners' assertions that they were Southern sympathizers. "All were opposed to the Government, to Lincoln, and the war, and a majority claimed to have been threatened with feathers and tar for their secession proclivities. I presume they thought we believed this gammon, and hoped to get better treatment by lying." In any case, their politics made no difference. ". . . one was treated as well as another, and all as prisoners of war."[155]

Other captures by the *Tallahassee*: the *North America*, a schooner from New London, Connecticut; the brig *Neva*, of East Machias, Maine; the schooner *Josiah Achom*, of Rockland, Maine; and two more schooners, the *D. Ellis* and the *Diadem*, of Harwick, Massachusetts, both returning from a fishing trip in the Bay of Chaleur. Shepardson did not try to contain his scorn.

> Such a pack of cowards I never saw—some were crying and asking if they were to be killed, or what was to be done with them. All disclaimed any connection with the war, and vowed they had always been opposed to Abolitionists and the Government. This information was volunteered, and, with Puritan solemnity and air, they called, with impious frequency, upon God to witness the truth of their declarations. They were Methodist Protestants, and boasted of their piety.[156]

At first Shepardson was unconvinced the prisoners were telling the truth. One of the men said, "I hope God may strike me dead if I ever had anything to do with the war." Bohemian protested. " 'But, said I, you carried a torch in that Black Republican procession in Harwick [Massachusetts]. How came that?' " At that point, the man admitted participating in the procession but added that he had not meant anything by it. Shepardson at last was convinced. The man was "too much confused" to be a liar, he decided.[157]

The next stop for the *Tallahassee* was Halifax. Although it was a neutral port, Halifax officials were suspicious about the vessel and its commander when they put into the city to take on coal. "I arrived on the 18th with only 40 tons on board," Wood said in an August 31 report to Secretary of the Navy Stephen Mallory. The next day Halifax officials expressed surprise that the ship was still in port and ordered Wood to leave, although he had received permission earlier to remain for two or three days.[158]

Lieutenant Governor Richard Graves MacDonnell, writing from the Government House, told Wood that he had been given only 24 hours in port. "As you have occupied the excess of time beyond that allowed to you in taking coal on board, I am obliged to request that you will immediately discharge all coal taken in since the lapse of the twenty-four hours allowed to you," he wrote. He reminded Wood that he was charged with adhering to strict neutrality that was "enjoined by Her Majesty's Government."[159]

Early in the evening of August 19, Shepardson wrote, ". . . without a word of warning several armed boats and launches were sent down to us with orders to go to sea at once, and forbidding us to take over one hundred tons of coal, enough, it was said, to take the vessel into the nearest Confederate port." About 9 o'clock, guards returned to the ship and reported 27 men missing, "evidently enticed away from the ship by Yankee emissaries." Because of the suspicion surrounding the *Tallahassee*, Wood thought it prudent to leave and steamed away from the city. A local doctor, W.J. Almon, had helped the crew locate a mast to replace the damaged one.[160]

Although the Halifax residents were largely sympathetic to the Confederacy, Shepardson wrote, "I learned that the Queen's counsel decided while we were there that the vessel of a belligerent power has the right to go into a neutral port and remain long enough to make all necessary repairs, take in coal, and [to remain] twenty-four hours afterwards."[161] Thirteen vessels were sent in pursuit of the prized *Tallahassee*, but Wood and his crew eluded them.

At sea the next day, the *Tallahassee* captured the schooner *Roan*, of Salisbury, Massachusetts, and outran Union gunboats that spotted the raider and gave chase. "In every instance the Yankees seemed perfectly astonished, and gave us a wide berth," Shepardson wrote.[162] Wood and his crew returned successfully to Wilmington.

Shepardson practiced surgery on a ship that earned a heroic reputation in the Confederacy and a reputation as a pirate ship to be sunk at all costs in the Union. In a message from October 26, 1864, Union Rear Admiral David D. Porter instructed U.S. Navy Lieutenant Commander Parker, "You will get under way without delay and go in pursuit of the *Tallahassee* . . . Keep a good lookout off the port of Halifax for her, and see that she does not get in. Sink her at all hazards . . ."[163]

After four years of reflection, Shepardson believed he understood the strengths and shortcomings of the Confederate military. "The country was full of gentlemen of education and those distinguished in civil life, but without military information. A few ideas gained from reading the campaigns of Wellington, Napoleon or Marlborough, was, perhaps, its greatest extent," he wrote. Generals were made and not born, Shepardson reasoned. The Confederacy had been misled. Educated gentlemen were thrust into a role for which they were not suited.

> When the time came for the people to arise these gentlemen must be officers, and, acting upon the popular but dogma "that generals are born and not made"—Nemo vir magnus sine afflutu aliquot divino unquam fuit—and the army was soon filled with general [sic] and other officers incapable of performing the solemn and important duties that devolved upon them. Thus the good of the nation was scarified [sic] to ambition, personal selfishness and nepotism; and disaster upon disaster has been the result. Many generals now in the field holding

responsible commands are ignorant of the evolutions of the line, and, to a great majority, grand tactics, strategy, and the other branches of the art, is a perfect mystery. It is in consequence of this want of professional information that so many battles have been fought without any great results.[164]

"Four years of experience in military matters has well taught us that no man can be fit to be a general who has not received a military education, or has not well studied the different branches of the science as a profession," he wrote.[165] An educated man, Shepardson epitomized the Confederate correspondent: dedicated to the Confederacy and to the responsibility for gathering the news and presenting it accurately to his newspaper readers.

Georgia

The burning of Atlanta, Georgia, in September 1864. *Harper's Weekly,* October 1, 1864. Courtesy of Rare Books and Special Collections, University of South Carolina Libraries

FIVE STATES, INCLUDING GEORGIA, SECEDED IN QUICK SUCCESSION IN January 1861, making Georgia the fifth state to leave the Union, but the role that Georgia played at the end of the war is engraved in public memory. No one can forget the images of Scarlett O'Hara fleeing from Atlanta with flames leaping to the sky or General William T. Sherman's devastating march to the sea. And at the end of the Confederacy's four-year existence, President Jefferson Davis' flight from Richmond led him to Washington, Georgia, where the Confederate government finally disbanded and where rumors still abound about the millions of dollars in Confederate gold that are buried somewhere in Georgia.

Peter W. Alexander, a Georgian who voted against the secession of Georgia, would be reputed after his death never to have had disunionist sentiments. However, when Confederates fired on Fort Sumter three months later in neighboring Charleston, South Carolina, he set aside his political objections to the war and signed on as a correspondent for the *Savannah Republican*, a newspaper that he had owned before the war. Writing under the pseudonym P.W.A., Alexander reported major battles in most of the Southern states and became one of the best correspondents for the South.

Alexander's editor at the *Republican* was James Roddy Sneed, whose correspondence during the war was limited to skirmishes and battles in South Carolina and Georgia. However, he was a significant advocate of high-quality, accurate reporting and helped establish the Press Association of the Confederate States of America. He also helped draft the letter of protest against military censorship when General Joseph Johnston ejected reporters from the army.

Faced with shortages of ink and paper, Georgia editors like Sneed continued publishing, although some were forced to flee or relocate. Georgia's newspapers were published in all shapes and sizes—half sheets; small sheets; on white, yellow, and brown paper; on wallpaper, and during one week the LaGrange (Georgia) *Reporter* was published in blue.

In addition to problems with paper and ink, editors were plagued with opinionated, redundant articles that frequently contained rumors. Exasperated editors like Sneed gathered in February 1863, in Augusta, Georgia, to organize the Press Association of the Confederate States of America. They hired John S. Thrasher as superintendent. One of his first and most significant actions was to copyright each news story sent out by the press association. Although neither he nor the association ever received much credit for taking this step, the action was a first in American journalism history, for it was the first time news had been recognized as worthy of copyright protection. He instigated strict new rules requiring that stories be free of unverified rumor or commentary. Thrasher required clarity, concise writing, and timeliness, and he fired reporters who did not adhere to his dictates. To those ends, he wrote and published a set of rules for reporters with instructions on how to write a news story that met his requirements for accuracy, fairness, and brevity.

16

Peter W. Alexander:
A Voice for the Foot Soldiers

Ford Risley

WHEN PETER W. ALEXANDER SAT DOWN TO WRITE FOR HIS NEWSPAPER on the evening of September 1, 1862, the Confederate war correspondent was troubled. The Army of Northern Virginia had just won its second victory at Manassas, Virginia, a smashing defeat of the far larger Union army. However, Alexander was concerned about what he saw after the battle. As weary Southern troops trudged away from the battlefield, many were hungry and ill-clothed. The Army of Northern Virginia had proven itself at Second Manassas to be one of the greatest fighting forces in history. But, as Alexander wrote, that meant little to the many men who for days had eaten nothing except what they could forage and who marched without shoes. In a letter to the *Savannah Republican*, he reported:

> [T]he army has not had a mouthful of bread for four days, and no food of any kind except a little green corn picked up in the roadside, for thirty-six hours. Many of them also are barefooted. I have seen scores of them to-day marching over the flinty turnpike with torn and blistered feet. They bear these hardships without murmuring . . . As for tents, they have not known what it was to sleep under one since last spring.[1]

Alexander's description of Confederate troops at Second Manassas was characteristic of his approach to reporting the Civil War. The Georgian was a skilled battlefield correspondent who covered many of the war's major battles and campaigns, including First and Second Manassas, Shiloh, Sharpsburg, Gettysburg, Fredericksburg, Chattanooga, Wilderness, and Petersburg.

In addition to his battle accounts, Alexander refused to be an idle observer when problems became apparent within the Confederate army, administration, and press. During an era when reporting and commentary often mixed, Alexander repeatedly condemned the Confederate government for its inability to

Peter W. Alexander. Courtesy of Peter Wellington
Alexander Papers, Rare Books and Manuscript Library,
Columbia University

provide proper food, clothing, and medical treatment for the troops. He also
criticized some Southern correspondents who he believed were ignoring the
facts when writing their stories.

Alexander was one of the most respected Southern war correspondents.
Clearly, he was a man of conscience and compassion. He made recurring pleas
for aid to Confederate soldiers in the field and tried to balance the public's right
to know with the military's need to operate to some degree in secrecy. He was
a staunch defender of press freedom and had little patience for officials restricting access to sources. His first thought was for the safety of his country's troops,
tempered with a commitment to the public's right to know.

Already known in Georgia newspaper circles when the war began, Alexander had become associate editor of Georgia's premier Whig journal, the *Savannah Republican,* in 1848. In 1853, Alexander purchased the paper and became editor-in-chief. He brought in a new assistant not long after purchasing the newspaper, James R. Sneed, who would also serve as an occasional correspondent for the newspaper during the war. Within a year of the Whig Party's collapse in 1856, Alexander sold his interest in the *Republican* to Sneed and F.W. Sims and moved to Thomaston in east-central Georgia to resume his law practice.[2]

Alexander was not a native of Thomaston or the surrounding area of Upson County. He had been born in the Elbert County community of Ruckersville on March 21, 1825, to Peter and Mary Marks Alexander. He graduated second in the University of Georgia's class of 1844; classmate Benjamin H. Hill beat out Alexander for top place. Hill would become a prominent Georgia political figure who served as a Georgia senator and congressman in both the U.S. and Confederate governments. However, Alexander did best Hill in one area: composition. Alexander achieved a reputation as a meticulous writer who honed his essays through multiple drafts before turning in his well-crafted work.[3]

After graduation, Alexander studied law and joined the state bar, a common path to a political career at that time, particularly in combination with journalistic work. The demise of the Whig Party in the late 1850s, however, put an end to any state or national political ambitions Alexander might have had and apparently prompted his move to Thomaston. He became involved in local issues after his move to Upson County, advocated the construction of the Thomaston and Barnesville Railroad, and worked on behalf of public education in the county. In 1858, he became an "examiner of teachers" for the county and, in 1860, he was named a county school commissioner.[4]

Alexander's political activities in his new hometown were sufficient to build trust in him among the local citizens. When the state of Georgia called for a convention of the people to decide the secession question in January 1861, Alexander was one of the delegates they chose to represent the county's views. He and other members of the Upson delegation initially voted against secession. However, when it became clear that the majority supported Georgia's withdrawal from the Union, Alexander and the other Upson delegates changed their votes so the convention could deliver a unanimous decision to the people of the state. Alexander put aside his personal views and signed the Georgia Ordinance of Secession. Once the war began, Alexander did not remain in Thomaston long. Within a few days of the secession vote, Georgia and the other seceded states sent delegates to Montgomery, Alabama, to form a government for their infant nation. Alexander attended the convention, although not as delegate. There is no evidence that he was serving as a newspaper correspondent at that time.[5]

Alexander began his career as a war correspondent in the spring of 1861 when he accepted appointments as a battlefield correspondent for the *Savannah*

Republican and the Atlanta *Southern Confederacy*.[6] Historian J. Cutler Andrews placed Alexander's entry into the ranks of war correspondents in early June, but tales from his adopted hometown of Thomaston indicate he was on the spot at least as an observer for many of the early events in the lead-up to war, including the assault on Fort Sumter.[7] Within a week of that attack, Alexander was back in Upson County to recruit a unit for Confederate service, although he did not serve in the unit. A few weeks later, Alexander left for Virginia. Nothing Alexander left behind indicates why he chose journalism rather than the military.[8]

Alexander arrived in Virginia in early June, and his first letter to the *Republican* dealt with the buildup for war. "The Old Dominion is one vast camp," he wrote. He reviewed states that had sent soldiers to Virginia, an enumeration that was reminiscent of Homer's listing in the *Iliad* of the ships that gathered in Aulis before sailing off to rescue the faithless Helen. Alexander's roster was even complete with poetic Homeric epithets for the seceded states.

> Not only have thousands of her own sons buckled on their armor, but tens of thousands of the very flower of chivalry of the South have rushed to her rescue. Not a train enters her borders from the West or the South that does not swell the gathering hosts. They come up from the wilds of Arkansas and Texas, from gallant Tennessee, Louisiana, Mississippi and Alabama, and foremost of all, from intrepid Georgia and South Carolina. But one spirit animates the moving legions, and that is to wash out the footprints of the invader with his own blood. There can be no such thing as peace so long as a single Abolitionist remains upon this soil.[9]

Although Alexander had worked for the *Republican* earlier, nothing during his career had prepared him for life as a war correspondent. Even before the war's first major battle near Manassas, Alexander had to fight a battle of his own—the battle to acquire a passport that would allow him to travel to the front. "I have just returned from the War Office where I went to get a pass or permit, to proceed to Manassas," he wrote. "Just think of a citizen of the Empire State of the South, 'Native, and to the manor born,' having to procure a ticket before he can be allowed to move about in the good Old Dominion, where the bones of his ancestors repose!" However, in his next sentence, Alexander relented and recognized the need for precautions, given the "large number of spies scattered throughout the State."[10]

As Alexander contemplated the passport that lay on the table in front of him, he tried to make light of what was to come with his move closer to the front lines, but the best he could manage was gallows humor. " . . . [M]y permit lies before me, and my landlady has filled my haversack with three days rations, and, like Gen. Beauregard, I shall proceed to extend my lines in the direction of the enemy," Alexander wrote. His story made it clear that Alexander was not enthusiastic about heading to the front. In fact, had he not made a tongue-in-cheek promise to friends, the correspondent might have been tempted to find a way to bow out. His story continued, "Having promised some of my friends a *scalp*, I must proceed to redeem the pledge. It may be that your correspondent will lose his own scalp in the undertaking. Well, a man should learn to give as well as take. So, here goes."[11]

Alexander put his passport to use three days later as he maneuvered toward the front to be in a better position when the anticipated battle began. He settled in at a location close to the fighting and then went directly to General P.G.T. Beauregard's headquarters at Manassas Junction. "A slight investigation satisfied me that the Junction was not the place for one to cast his tent who desired to witness a battle; and, therefore, following the example of the army, I advanced my lines to this place [Fairfax Courthouse], twelve miles nearer the enemy," he wrote. Alexander's location at Fairfax put him within six miles of the Union troops, close enough that "their drums can be distinctly heard from my window, as they beat their evening and morning calls. This letter is written, therefore, as it were, from the mouth of the enemy's guns."[12]

Without any actual fighting to write about yet, Alexander used the opportunity to indulge in some acerbic political rhetoric. "It sends the blood through the heart in a more tumultuous flow, when one reflects that he is separated from the hated despot who would blast his native land, by a space of only fifteen miles. How the patriot longs to clear the intervening distance by a bound and to throttle the tyrant upon his blood stained throne!" he declared. While Alexander insisted that Lincoln was president in name only, he believed the Republican president was "a despot, the violator of his country's laws, the usurper of its rights and liberties, and the base and beastly oppressor of the people" and that the position held by "the peerless Washington" had been sullied by the ascension of a fanatical, ignorant barbarian.[13]

When the war's first major battle, First Manassas, finally erupted in mid-July, Alexander quickly got a taste of the difficulties he would encounter in reporting the war.[14] After the battle, he was forced to walk the seven miles from the battlefield back to Manassas Junction. Arriving there about one o'clock in the morning, no doubt exhausted, he composed his account of the shocking Confederate victory. The report, served up with ample amounts of purple prose, began, "Yesterday, the 21st day of July, 1861, a great battle was fought and a great victory won by the Confederate troops. Heaven smiled upon his arms, and the God of Battles crowned our banners with the laurel of glory." Alexander, who had been on the battlefield during the assault, described the initial fighting.

The infantry were the first to open fire—precisely at 11 o'clock. By half-past 11, the infantry had engaged, and then it was the battle began to rage. The dusky columns which had thus far marked the approach of the two armies, now mingled with great clouds of smoke as it rose from the flashing guns below, and the two together shot upwards like a huge pyramid of red and blue . . . With what anxious hearts did we watch that pyramid of smoke and dust.

Concluding his account, Alexander patriotically claimed that First Manassas was "the greatest battle ever fought on this continent." Following the journalistic practice of the day, he signed his correspondence with a pen name: "P.W.A."[15]

Alexander followed up his account of the battle with a vivid description of the carnage left on the battlefield. There was a certain beauty to fighting, he wrote. "The long line of glittering bayonets, the roll of a thousand drums, the wheeling and rushing of squadrons, the huge columns of dust and smoke that shoot up like great pyramids from the plains below, the incessant roar of artillery and musketry, the great balls and shells that rush screaming through the airs like winged devils escaped from the regions of the damned." But afterward, the sight of the battlefield was repulsive. Alexander described the awful scene of dead soldiers awaiting burial.

> The enemy's dead still lay scattered in every direction, and the silent vultures had begun to circle above them. They were well clad, and were larger and stouter men than ours. Nearly all of them were lying on their backs, some of them with their legs and arms stretched out to the utmost . . . One poor fellow had died with his arms clasped around a small tree, and others with their hands clasped tightly around their muskets, or such twigs or roots as within their reach. One was found with his Bible open upon his breast. Some had their hands crossed and the whole body composed after the manner of a corpse.[16]

Alexander's description was skillfully constructed, but he recognized that he had plenty to learn about reporting on war. Responding to a letter from a reader, he admitted that "no full, fair, and satisfactory account" of the fighting at First Manassas had yet been written—and he included his story among those with shortcomings. In an example of the self-reflection that he would often practice, Alexander listed more than a dozen items that should have been included in his battle report, including "the brigade that first encountered the enemy. . . the position of the several batteries . . . [and] where the commanding generals were during the fight."[17]

Not only were Alexander's stories incomplete, they were slow in getting back to Savannah. However, he had a justification for tardiness in filing his stories; he became ill after a postbattle expedition to the site of the fighting. He had gone out early after eating very little for breakfast and ate nothing else that day except a cracker. Alexander spent the day walking around the battlefield under the hot July sun, traversing some 20 miles on foot. However, exhaustion and hunger were the least of his discomforts. The stench from the unburied bodies of soldiers and horses was "offensive and sickening."

Alexander wrote that he was grateful he had not become even more ill. There could have been another factor behind Alexander's illness: the stress of being so near the battle. The physician who tended Alexander told him that many of the men had succumbed to illness after the battle because of "the great mental and physical excitement under which they labored during the fight."[18]

Alexander also showed that he was not going to be a passive observer of the Confederate army and its operation. In a letter published a month after First Manassas, the correspondent criticized the practice of some soldiers to carry side arms and knives. He reported that drunken soldiers regularly got into fights and injured or killed one another with the weapons. In blunt language, Alexander suggested a cure for the problem. "A drunken soldier, with a revolver stuck in his belt on one side and bowie knife on the other is about as fit to go at large as an infuriated maniac," he wrote, "and the authorities ought to see to it that no more men be suffered to enter the service unless they leave all such weapons at home, where they may be needed."[19]

On his way back to Manassas, Alexander encountered a dying Union soldier. The Irishman begged Alexander for something to eat "for the love of the Holy St. Patrick." Alexander folded the coat of a dead soldier to make a pillow for the wounded man and walked back 400 yards to fill his canteen with water. "You may be sure he never ceased to ask the blessing of the holy Virgin upon me as long as I could hear him," Alexander wrote.[20]

First Manassas bloodied both Union and Confederate troops in the first major battle of the war, and while the following fall was punctuated with occasional skirmishes, neither army seemed anxious to re-engage. General Irvin McDowell's removal as commander of Union forces and replacement by General George B. McClellan may have accounted partly for the North's reluctance to wage full-scale war. General McClellan was brought in to train the green troops who had fled the field at Manassas, but he was a careful and meticulous general. His ideas of preparing soldiers for battle conflicted with the notions of those who urged quick, decisive, and aggressive forward movements—and that group included the Union commander-in-chief.

The South faced the same need to build soldiers out of the men who had volunteered for what they expected to be a short conflict. Consequently, military affairs moved sluggishly that fall, providing ample opportunity for editorialists to drone on in endless speculations about the "forward action" everyone thought was imminent. However, an incident occurred that wrenched public and press attention from the battlefield to the diplomatic front: the Trent affair. The incident gave Alexander an opportunity to report something specific.

On November 8, an American frigate, the USS *San Jacinto,* intercepted a British mail packet, the *Trent.* When *San Jacinto*'s Captain Charles Wilkes discovered two Confederate envoys to Europe, James Mason and John Slidell, aboard the British ship, he seized them. The incident resulted in British protest and demand for an apology from the United States. Confederates hoped the confrontation would push the United States and Great Britain into a war with one another, or at least so sufficiently strain relations that the British government would offer recognition to the Confederacy. When Alexander wrote about the affair, he confessed that no one had initially believed the story: "The arrest of Mr. (James) Mason and Mr. (John) Slidell is the most highhanded proceeding between nations at peace, as the United States and Great Britain are, of which I have ever heard or read. It is equivalent to a declaration of war followed up by immediate blow."

Alexander reported that Wilkes halted the British mail ship by firing a cannon shot across its bow, "and then boarded her, and violently arrested and brought away our Commissioners against their protests and that of the commander of the ship."[21] The Lincoln cabinet closed the incident on December 26 by agreeing to free Mason and Slidell, and the commissioners proceeded to London.[22]

As 1861 came to a close, it became apparent that the war would continue. The two great armies in Virginia settled into routine, so much so that Alexander no longer bothered to report each small incident of the war. "If I do not always inform you of the captures made by our pickets, it is because they have ceased to be of much interest on account of their frequency," Alexander wrote in the *Republican* in early December as Confederate troops were preparing for winter quarters.[23]

The need for proper shoes and clothing for Confederate troops during the cold months was not lost on Alexander, especially in light of recent orders to count the amount of baggage each soldier had, with an eye to reducing personal gear. Alexander saw this as a poor idea, especially if it meant taking blankets away from the men when their tents were too small to accommodate fires. "The blankets are small and the supply scant, but such as they are, if the men are to be stripped of them, much suffering and sickness will be the certain consequence," he predicted.[24] Stressing the need for shoes for soldiers, he wrote: "Men may fight with clubs, with bows, with stones, with their hands; but they cannot fight and march without shoes." Some of his harshest language was directed at the Confederate Medical Department for not getting necessary medicine to the troops. Alexander wrote:

> The supply of medicines is very meager, especially of certain important descriptions. And yet it is notorious that there are medicines enough in the towns and villages throughout the Confederacy to supply the army and the people. I allude to such standard articles as are necessary in the treatment of those diseases peculiar to the camp. A simple advertisement . . . would enable the Government to procure all it may desire. The efforts of the Medical Department, however, are limited to Richmond and a few other points where the prices are highest and the supply smallest. Meanwhile, the best and bravest men who ever drew a sword are dying for want of these medicines.[25]

Alexander also reported on what he clearly considered to be abuses of civilians by the quartermaster corps. Just before Christmas, he wrote that the quartermasters had decided to impress all the supplies and conveyances they could find in the countryside around Manassas. The result was that citizens had little left to supply their own needs and, worse, by taking wagons, horses, and crops, the army had made it impossible for people to produce new crops in the spring. "They have neither wagons to do the work of the farm nor horses to draw them, nor feed for such saddle horses and cattle as may have been left them," Alexander reported. "They have not even bread left for their families. Their fences have been destroyed, and their beef cattle killed and consumed." The result, he feared, would be that the army would not have a source of supplies in the next year. Alexander was indignant not because he was opposed to impressments of goods for military use but because he believed the foraging teams should have gone farther afield. He believed local supplies should have been left intact for use in case of an emergency. "If this had been done, there would have been no lack of the means to move the army just after the battle of Manassas," he wrote.[26]

The quartermasters compounded their mistake, Alexander believed, by failing to impress drivers with the wagons. Instead, soldiers were detailed from the army to drive the wagons—"young men who have no experience in driving, and who complain that they did not enlist to drive wagons. They are required to alternate, and thus every day or two there is a new driver, who is ignorant both of the ability and disposition of the horses, and who soon teaches them bad habits."[27] Not only were the soldiers incompetent drivers, Alexander added, they knew little about how to care for horses. "Sometimes, owing to the irregularity of the supply, the horses are fed for a week at a time on shelled corn alone; then on hay, or straw, and but seldom on hay and corn—and sometimes on nothing."[28]

There is no indication that Alexander's criticism of the Confederate war effort caused him problems in his reporting. As best as can be determined, he was never kicked out of the army for violating any military orders. This could be attributed to the fact that he was always careful not to reveal military secrets in his reports, at times telling readers that he had additional information he could have reported, but sound judgment prevented him from doing so. Alexander was also cautious in wording his criticism of Confederate officials, being careful not to be mean-spirited. His criticism was clearly intended to help, not hurt, the South's war effort.[29]

Alexander also balanced his criticisms with compliments to the Confederate government and military. In the fall of 1861, as some newspapers were calling for harsh treatment of Union prisoners of war, Alexander counseled judiciousness. "An eye for an eye, and a tooth for a tooth is their doctrine," Alexander wrote. "If the Federal authorities should cause a single one of our men to be executed, I should say, hang up ten of the enemy." However, Alexander believed the United States dared not take so drastic a step. "Let us do right ourselves, and we may well appeal alike to the judgment of men and heaven," he argued.[30]

In fact, Alexander was publicly critical of some Southern correspondents, who he saw as prone to constant fault-finding. In a letter to the *Republican*, he wrote that these newspaper critics "no longer speak of the mistakes of government and commanding officers as one friend should speak to another of his errors. They do not mean to be fractious, or to cripple or embarrass those in authority; yet such is the natural effect of their course." Alexander then suggested what seemed to be his approach: "By returning to its former patriotic policy . . . by abstaining alike from unmerited praise and well as undue censure, by criticizing with candor and justice . . . the Press may accomplish incalculable good."[31]

However, Alexander was not without faults as a journalist. He was guilty of making exaggerated statements that had no basis in fact and occasionally indulged in the kind of atrocity stories resorted to by other Southern correspondents. For example, he refused to acknowledge that Federal troops had fought courageously at Spotsylvania Court House, insisting that they had been well supplied with liquor before going into battle.[32] His reports sometimes lapsed into excessiveness. An example of the purple prose that appeared in his letters can be seen in his report of the Battle of Fort Donelson in Tennessee. In the account, Alexander noted what a critical loss the fort was for the Confederacy. But then he turned to invective as he wrote:

> The Federal "anaconda" begins to tighten his coil. The 'circle of fire' with which the South was to be surrounded, already illumines the horizon. A bitter foe—smarting under former defeat, jeered at by the world, even distrustful of his own courage—now thunders at our gates, a victorious and multitudinous host! . . . Fort Donelson has fallen. It is a great disaster, and has produced much pain and suffering here. The nation bows its head and smites its breast in bitter sorrow, but thank God! not in despair. The darkness is relieved by at least one cheering gleam—our men brought away "blood on their bayonets."[33]

During the early weeks of 1862, Alexander returned to Virginia after spending Christmas in Georgia. Although he generally did not report on political events, his early 1862 stories speculated (wrongly) that the Confederacy would receive the desired recognition by Great Britain and France within the next 40 days[34] and also reported on General Joseph Johnston's infamous "Order 98." Johnston's order expelled all correspondents with the Confederate Army of the Potomac in retaliation for a story by *Richmond Dispatch* correspondent William G. Shepardson that revealed the setup of Confederate troops' winter quarters. Alexander had spoken with some who believed the order was a good idea, but these were mostly people who had "some quarrel with the press" or who believed newspapers had not been quick enough to take notice of their contributions in politics or on the battlefield. Although he disagreed with these men, Alexander did not believe Johnston, a fellow Georgian, had been motivated by such petty concerns when he issued his censorship order. "I am unwilling to believe that Gen. Johnston was influenced by motives so unjust and unworthy," Alexander wrote.[35]

While Alexander defended press freedoms, he acknowledged that it would be inappropriate to have no restrictions on what could be reported and that those rules, as well as the standards reporters set for themselves, should be crafted to serve the "public good." He believed the majority of Confederate correspondents had been "prudent"—his word for responsible—in their reporting. "Many things have been withheld from publication out of a proper regard for the public service; and yet the next arrival by the underground railroad would bring us Northern papers containing the very information which had been withheld from the Southern people."[36] Consequently, he thought a better plan would be to allow only professional correspondents and reporters to be placed within the army and for those journalists to be held responsible individually for what they reported. Excluding reporters violated the press freedom guaranteed to citizens by the Constitution. Even the "despotic" French had not had enough gall to try such a thing, he argued, then he added, "To the Yankee government alone belongs the honor of an attempt to curtail the liberty of speech, and to suppress and suborn the press."[37]

Alexander believed the people had a right to know what was happening on the battlefield since they were supplying the soldiers and funding the cost of the war. "To whom does the country itself belong?" he asked, and then answered his question, "To the people." Without professional reporters to gather news, the quality of information available to citizens would decline, the correspondent warned. " . . . to satisfy their [the public's] demands, the press will be driven to the necessity of relying upon private letters written by volunteers to their families," volunteers who would have few opportunities to gather and verify information. "The result will be they will send home the numberless rumors, some of them the silliest and most contradictory, that find their way into camp," Alexander wrote. He also believed these amateur correspondents would "divulge a thousand things, unintentionally no doubt, that should be kept secret."[38]

Alexander had little choice but to retire back to Richmond. That move, however, put him in the proper place to file one of his rare political stories: the inauguration of President Jefferson Davis and Vice President Alexander H. Stephens on February 22, 1862. Despite heavy rain, a large crowd witnessed the event and received the two men with "hearty and prolonged cheers." Davis delivered the inaugural address "with great dignity and . . . much feeling and grace," Alexander wrote.

> It was a scene never to be forgotten. The lowering clouds above the gigantic statues of our revolutionary fathers, stern and motionless . . . the vast crowd spellbound and stillest, and the chosen Chief of a new born Republic, standing with uplifted eyes and hands, committing himself to the Ruler of Nations and of men,

and humbly invoking his blessing upon his country and his cause! There was not a heart in that great assembly which did not involuntarily respond to the invocation, amen!

However, the event was anticlimactic, Alexander reported. Stephens was encouraged to speak, but for unknown reasons he would not do so. The Georgian simply bowed to the crowd and returned to his seat.[39]

Later in the spring, Alexander went to Mississippi to cover his second major battle of the war, at Shiloh. He was delayed in Corinth until after the fighting started because he could not find a horse to rent. The next morning, he did find a conveyance: "a mule and a hard Mexican saddle without any padding in the seat."[40] He finally arrived at the battlefield about noon, some six hours after the fighting had begun. Although unable to estimate the number of troops killed and wounded, Alexander reported that the fighting the first day was "hot and close and raged with great violence and fury." He concluded, "[T]he roar of artillery and rattle of musketry fairly shook the earth."

Alexander was at General Beauregard's headquarters later that evening when a captured Federal commander, Brigadier General Benjamin M. Prentiss, was brought before Beauregard. Alexander reported that Prentiss opened the conversation by saying, "Well, sir, we have felt your power to-day, and have had to yield." Beauregard replied, "That is natural sir. You could not expect it to be otherwise. We are fighting for our wives and children, for generations to come after us, and for liberty itself. Why does your government thus war upon us, and seek us upon our own soil?" Prentiss responded that his fellow citizens could not allow the Union to be split apart. Beauregard said that the Union was already broken and maintained that the last man, woman, and child would willingly perish before allowing the South to give up its independence. That night Alexander slept in the tent of the quartermaster of the 53rd Ohio Regiment that had been captured in the day's fighting. He wrote his account on paper left behind by the quartermaster. With an eye for detail and description, he reported that the tent had been perforated by 21 musket balls.[41]

The next morning resumed "another day of battle and blood," Alexander reported. The Federal army, which had been reinforced the night before, fought "with great spirit and resolution." Alexander also felt compelled to report that the Confederate cause was hurt because many troops had spent the previous night enjoying the spoils left behind by Union soldiers, despite orders not to do so. Some soldiers resumed their search for items the next morning and were separated from their regiments when the battle resumed. Alexander correctly attributed this behavior to the fact that many of the troops were raw and too elated with the outcome of the previous day's fighting. Still, he wrote, "[T]here can be no excuse for the disgraceful proceedings . . . It is hoped that the experience of this day will not be thrown away either by our officers or soldiers."[42]

The casualties at Shiloh were nearly equal for both the Confederate and the Union armies in terms of killed and wounded, and the Union army's performance cost General Grant in reputation. However, the battle ultimately was a loss for the Confederates, for General Albert Sydney Johnston's army was unable to achieve its objective. Johnston had hoped to keep two Union armies from combining in Tennessee, but instead was forced to retreat, and an opportunity to turn the tide of the war was lost. Compounding the loss, Johnston, one of the South's best generals, was killed by a stray bullet.

Alexander spent the rest of April and most of May traveling between Memphis and the Army of the Mississippi. Correspondents had relatively free access to the army until the end of May, when Beauregard ordered all reporters away. The official justification offered for the order was that Samuel Chester Reid, "Sparta" for the *Memphis Appeal,* had revealed sensitive information in a story.[43] In fact, the reason for the order was that Beauregard and his new commanding officer, General William J. Hardee, had decided to evacuate Corinth. Alexander moved on to Mobile, Alabama, and while he was there, he learned that Beauregard had pulled his army out of Corinth. Alexander tried to send a report with the news, but the military superintendent supervising the telegraph office refused to approve it. Alexander appealed the decision to the military commander in Mobile, but he also refused to sanction the telegram.[44]

Alexander generally defended the work of Southern correspondents traveling with the army and he chaffed at official interference with the press when it seemed to have no strategic value.[45] However, he also recognized the faults of some members of the press corps who were not as truthful as they should be. In a letter to the *Republican,* Alexander wrote bluntly:

> The truth is, there are correspondents with the army who invariably magnify our successes and depreciate our losses, and who when there is a dearth of news, will draw upon their imaginations for their facts . . . The war abounds in more romantic incidents and thrilling adventure than poet ever imagined or novelist described; and it would be well if the writers of fiction from the army, who devote themselves to the marvelous and poetical aspects of affairs rather than to the stern realities of the campaign, would remember this fact.[46]

While Alexander was acknowledged as one of the South's premier war reporters, he did not always escape criticism. Some newspaper editors were apparently quick to condemn Alexander for his criticism of Beauregard after Shiloh and also for writing for more than one newspaper. By the time these stories appeared, Alexander was home in Thomaston, Georgia, recovering from an illness caused by polluted water at Corinth. Alexander was surprised by the newspaper criticism and unsure why his letters had created such a sensation. Some of Alexander's critics apparently accused him of becoming a correspondent for pecuniary reasons, for that was the focus of his response, conveyed through the pages of the *Savannah Republican.* Clearly miffed, he responded, "You well know that I have not been actuated, in my endeavors to serve the great cause in which we are engaged, by mercenary motives. I did not abandon my business, and give my time, and expose my life, either for the compensation which the Republican granted me, or for the purpose of pushing any scheme of my own, or of any other individual." In fact, Alexander wrote, the *Republican's* salary, while adequate, had not covered all of his expenses. He had picked up some of the costs himself, including doing what he could to relieve the needs of soldiers he encountered in his travels. "One finds it necessary, in his visits to the hospitals and travels over the railways, if he have any soul, to share not only his last crust, but his last dollar also, with the sick and needy solder," he wrote. However, in all his work, Alexander argued, his only objective had been "to serve the cause honestly and faithfully with the Pen, while others were doing it with the Sword."[47]

Alexander's correspondence had developed a certain consistency after the first year of the war. Although he usually sent telegraphic dispatches back to his newspaper after a major battle, most of his published correspondence was in the form of long reports in which he addressed a variety of subjects. In these he discussed additional details of a battle such as Shiloh, complained about the unsanitary conditions of Confederate camps, and praised the women of Tennessee for their attention to the sick and wounded.

Like all correspondents, Alexander worked under conditions that were far from ideal. He often wrote his correspondence quickly from wherever he could find a place to sit—whether it was under a tree or on top of a camp chest. After a battle, he frequently stayed up most of the night writing his letter, and at daybreak he galloped off on horseback or used a courier to get the letter in the hands of a telegraph operator or the postal service. Telegraph lines were frequently destroyed and the Confederate postal service was notoriously slow, so it was often a week or more before his stories appeared in the newspaper.

Travel conditions could be difficult, even harsh. While traveling to Mississippi in the spring of 1862, Alexander needed to take a train. However, the train was full, so the correspondent made the acquaintance of the engineer and fireman who agreed to let him ride in the tender if he would help keep the fire stoked. Later, he was soaked in a rainstorm and had to spend the night in the home of a one-legged man. The other guests, Alexander wrote, included "one idiot, two pigs, a man with a freshly broken arm, and a number of sick, weary soldiers."[48]

Travel problems also hampered Alexander's efforts to return to the Virginia battlefield later that summer. He missed the first day of fighting at the Second Battle of Manassas in August 1862. With no other way to get to the battlefield, he hopped a freight train in the town of Gordonsville the morning of August 29 and arrived at the terminus of the railroad at noon. There he found a horse, forded the Rapidan and Rappahannock rivers, and arrived in the town of

Warrenton at 1 o'clock the following day. After resting his horse, he traveled the 14 miles to the battlefield, arriving just as the fighting was drawing to a close. But he had his first-hand look at what the intense fighting of the summer had done to the proud, but suffering Confederate troops.[49]

Alexander was only one of several Confederate correspondents pointing out the sufferings of troops or criticizing the war policies of the government. At various times, other Southern journalists questioned the practices of the administration and government agencies in waging war with the North. But Alexander reported regularly and for the length of his time covering the war. Moreover, his elegant writing style, as well as his graphic description of medical atrocities and other hardships faced by the troops, gave his work particular impact.

Alexander's work on behalf of Confederate soldiers frequently extended to blistering descriptions of conditions in Confederate army field hospitals. He reported that many field surgeons performed their work sloppily, with seemingly little concern for the health of the soldiers. In blunt language, he accused field surgeons of drunkenness and of not caring about their patients. "While engaged at the amputation table, many of them feel it to be their solemn duty, every time they administer brandy to the patient, to take a drink themselves," he wrote. "This part of their work is performed with great unction and conscientiousness." He described the poor condition of hospitals in towns near the battlefields. Invariably, he wrote, the hospitals were located in "the most noisy, dusty and dirty part of the town," while officers occupied fine homes in quiet parts of towns. The wounds of soldiers were "seldom dressed" and the soldiers often had to lie "on a scant supply of straw, with a foul blanket over them." Alexander said it had become clear that government officials, officers, and surgeons had little concern for the lives of their troops.[50]

Alexander's criticisms of the Confederate administration and military, like those of other correspondents, were undertaken within the narrowly prescribed limits generally understood by experienced Southern journalists of the era. In this respect, it was permissible to criticize individuals, Congress, or government agencies for their policies in waging war with the North. However, to criticize slavery or the Confederate cause was to risk censure and was occasionally dangerous, just as advocating abolition had been during the antebellum period when Southern authorities even prohibited the distribution of abolitionist materials.[51]

None of that was on the mind of any Southerner after General Robert E. Lee's decisive victory at Second Manassas. Confederates were exhilarated by the showing of their troops, and that included the great general himself. In light of Second Manassas, Lee determined to alter the war effort from one of defense to one of offense. He believed the only way the South could win the war was by destroying the enemy's army in battle. Lee believed he had a better chance of doing this if he took the war to Maryland and Pennsylvania where he might force the Union to fight him on unfavorable terms. Further, if Lee could

Confederate troops ford the Potomac as they enter Maryland. Illustration
from *Harper's Weekly,* September 27, 1862. Courtesy of Rare Books and Special
Collections, University of South Carolina Libraries

reach Pennsylvania, he might be able to disrupt the flow of coal to the Northeastern cities, something he and Jackson would discuss prior to the Battle of
Chancellorsville.

Alexander was caught up in the euphoria of the moment. With the Confederate public and its armies, he expected great results from the invasion of Maryland. In one of his reports to the *Republican,* Alexander wrote about the feelings
of being with an invasion army, come to liberate a state that had "writhed in the
arms of the oppressor, like a weeping, trembling virgin who appeals in vain to
the mercy of her ravisher."[52] Alexander predicted a quick end to the war once
liberation occurred but he also observed, should the war be destined to continue, that "we are resolved, by the blessings of God, to maintain the stand we
have taken as long as there is a musket left and a hand to wield it."[53] Alexander's
next words would prove unfortunately prescient for the Southern cause: "We
can never quit Maryland except as conquerors, or a broken, ruined army."[54]

Upon reaching Frederick, Alexander rode into town with a Confederate general to see an old friend. As they were riding by, a young woman called out to
the correspondent and asked him if the officer with whom he was riding was
General Stonewall Jackson. When Alexander told her she was mistaken, the
woman exclaimed,

The Sharpsburg battlefield near Antietam Creek in Maryland. Photograph from the Library of Congress

"Oh! I shall go crazy if I don't see him."

"He is not much for good looks," Alexander replied, "but he fights like a lion."

"I know," she said, "and that is the reason I am dying to see him."[55]

Alexander told readers that before riding on, he entertained the woman with a story about Jackson. During one march, Jackson's officers wanted to know their destination, and finally a colonel said, "General, we are all desirous to know what our destination is—can't you tell us?" Jackson asked the officer, "Can you keep a secret?" "Oh, yes," said the colonel. "Well, so can I," Jackson replied. The young woman laughed at the anecdote.[56]

The army's welcome to Maryland was not always so accommodating, although Alexander appears to have mistaken the reason for that. As the army passed through Frederick, people—especially women and children—greeted the soldiers with a degree of warmth, but he noticed a reserve among them, too. Alexander attributed this to the need for caution among an oppressed people. "They say if they only knew we would not abandon the State, they would throw off every disguise and array themselves on our side at once, with arms in their hands," Alexander reported. By the same token, the army also found a good number of Unionists among the Marylanders they encountered.[57]

Witnessing the Battle of Sharpsburg, Alexander was impressed with the performance of the Federal army and wrote that it was the Confederate army's finest moment since Shiloh. He wrote his account of the battle from near an army hospital where he graphically described the carnage with its "amputated arms and legs, feet, fingers, and hands cut off, puddles of human gore and ghastly gaping wounds." Alexander concluded succinctly, "There is a smell of death in the air."[58] He reported the battle as "the fiercest and most hotly contested battle of the war."

> Whether we consider the numbers engaged, the fierceness of the assault, the dogged courage of the Confederates, or the almost unparalleled duration of the fight, it must be regarded as one of the most extraordinary battles of modern times. In no instance, since the revolution was inaugurated, has either party had engaged as many as 100,000 men at any one time. At Richmond, each side had, all counted, perhaps as many as 100,000; but in no one of the series of battles fought around that city was anything like that number engaged, either on the part of the Confederates or the Federals.[59]

Alexander provided an extensive narrative of the battle—virtually a blow-by-blow account, and it is a typical battle story that describes which units led and won which assaults, what artillery was used, and the number of casualties. But Alexander, the consummate storyteller, did his best writing in his conclusion when he offered an account of the death of a young soldier from his home county in Georgia.

> I turned aside yesterday in the midst of the battle to see how a true soldier can die. He was of twenty-two or three summers—clear of skin and mild blue eyes—John S. Hudson, of Elbert county, Ga. His thigh had been torn by a shell, and hung only by a thin piece of skin. He was calm and resigned, though his struggles were severe and protracted. Finally, as the dread hour of dissolution approached, he gathered up all his remaining strength, and turning to his brother, who hung over him in dumb agony, he said, "Tell mother I die rejoicing, and die a soldier's death." There was not a dry eye among the spectators who, strangely enough, had stopped to witness the last moment of the youthful hero.[60]

Despite the heroic effort by the army, Alexander ultimately judged the invasion of Maryland to have been a failure. While he had favored the Confederacy going on the offensive, he admitted that it had probably been a mistake. He based this view, in part, on the poor condition of the troops, a fifth of whom were barefooted, half of whom were in rags, and most of whom had little food. Alexander added, "Since we crossed into Maryland, and even before they frequently had to march all day and far into night for three and four days together, without food of any kind, except such apples and green corn as they could obtain along the way."[61]

Alexander became ill and traveled to Winchester, Virginia, to recuperate. While there, and with the poor condition of Confederate troops still on his mind, Alexander wrote a moving appeal on behalf of the soldiers. He described the hardships they had been enduring and appealed to citizens to come to their aid.

Confederates lie dead on the field at Sharpsburg after the Battle of Sharpsburg or the Battle of Antietam in Maryland in September 1862. Photograph from the Library of Congress

The men must have clothing and shoes this winter. They must have something to cover themselves with when sleeping and to protect themselves from the driving sleet and from storms when on duty. This must be done, though our friends at home should have to wear cotton and sit by the fire. The army in Virginia stands guard this day, and will stand guard this winter over every hearthstone in the South . . . Will you not clothe his nakedness then? Will you not put shoes and stockings on his feet? Is it not enough that he has written down his patriotism in crimson characters along that battle-road from the Rappahannock to the Potomac, and must his bleeding feet also impress their mark of fidelity up the snows of the coming winter?[62]

Alexander's plea for help, first published in the *Republican*, was reprinted by other Southern newspapers and earned widespread praise. The *Richmond Dispatch* noted, "This is true eloquence, coming from the heart of a man who not only sees what he describes, but is himself a participant." And in an editorial accompanying Alexander's letter, the *Athens* (Georgia) *Southern Banner* declared, "Our army must be clothed, and every one of us who remain at home must assist in the good work . . . Remember it is for your sons and brothers, and that necessity as well as patriotism demands that you act." Perhaps the most eloquent response came in a letter signed "An Old Soldier." The soldier believed the public owed Alexander a tremendous debt, one that could never be repaid. He wrote, "In my judgment he has done more for the army and the public in this war, than any other man in the Confederacy." The old soldier also wrote that he was one of 10 Savannah residents who had decided to contribute $100 each so as to raise $1,000 to buy a set of silver plates to thank Alexander for his service. In a private note to *Republican* Editor James R. Sneed, Alexander asked that the money be spent instead to purchase shoes for the soldiers he was writing about.[63]

Some questioned whether the situation was as desperate as Alexander made it sound. To answer the doubters, Sneed wrote to Confederate Secretary of War George Randolph asking if things were as Alexander described. Randolph replied that the government needed all the assistance that citizens could provide. By the following month, Alexander was able to report that thousands of pairs of shoes and dollars in cash had been donated to the army.[64]

While in Richmond, Alexander wrote a glowing profile of General Lee, who had been hailed as a hero since his victory at Second Manassas earlier in the year. A man of imposing appearance, he wrote, Lee did not care for the trappings of rank and was content to eat the same food as his soldiers. Although not blessed with the greatest intellect, Alexander claimed, Lee had "those qualities which are indispensable in the great leader and champion." Alexander concluded that Lee was "the peer of any living chieftain in the New World or the Old."[65]

The portrayal of Lee as a masterful general proved to be correct at the Battle of Fredericksburg, one of the worst Union defeats of the war. Alexander's growing skill as a battlefield reporter was evident in his account of the fighting. Initially denied a passport that would allow him to travel to the front, the correspondent did not reach the Virginia town until the battle was over. Nevertheless, his use of second-hand information and his own observations produced an engaging story.[66] He carefully described Frederickburg's commanding location overlooking the Rappahannock River. The Union army, he wrote, faced artillery that "poured a devouring fire into the ranks . . . Assault upon assault was made, each time with fresh columns and increased numbers. They never succeeded, however. . . ." The result of such savage fighting was a scene horrifying even for a war-hardened reporter like Alexander. He wrote, "I went over the ground this morning and the remaining dead, after two-thirds of them had been removed, lay twice as thick as upon any other battlefield I have ever seen." Alexander's eye for detail was evident in his description of a wooden fence and stone walls behind which soldiers fought and sought cover.

Some of the planks in this fence were literally shot away from the posts to which they were nailed, and one can hardly place his hand upon any part of them without covering a dozen bullet holes. Just at the foot of the stone wall behind which our men were posted, thousands of flattened musket balls may be picked up, whilst the hills behind it have been almost converted into a lead mine. [67]

Alexander described the destruction that took place in Fredericksburg. "There is hardly a structure in the place, however small that does not bear some of the marks of the conflict that rage through its streets and around its suburbs . . . ," he wrote. "The floors in some of the houses were covered with the blood of their wounded; and in some instances their dead still lay in the silent chambers, their leaden eyes staring wildly at the bare and blackened walls."[68]

Alexander spent most of the winter with the troops in Virginia, but in early March, he decided to make a trip to Charleston. Given the weather and conditions of the roads in Virginia, the spring campaign season would not begin there for at least two months, but Charleston harbor was under threat of imminent attack and Alexander hoped to be on the scene.[69] A Federal attack on the city had been rumored since the beginning of the year. The Union navy wanted to stop the blockade runners entering and leaving the harbor. Although he could find no signs of military activity, Alexander saw the impact the war was having on the city. In a story for the *Republican*, he described whole blocks of retail establishments that were closed because many of the men were away fighting.[70]

A fleet of Union ironclads sailed into the harbor on April 7 in an attempt to silence the Confederate shore batteries, but terrific fire from the Confederate guns forced the ironclads to withdraw after losing one vessel. To Alexander, the naval battle at the citadel of secession was a "magnificent spectacle" witnessed by thousands of residents at the city's battery and from rooftops. He wrote:

> The white puffs of smoke issuing from the portholes of the ironclads with a tongue of fire in the centre, the solemn waltz kept up by these huge monsters as they were led past the forts, the fantastic festoons of smoke that garlanded the heads of the fort and slowly floated off to the north . . . the silent city and the breathless multitude who crowded the housetops and promenade, made up a spectacle at once grand and imposing.[71]

Perhaps sensing that his report of the battle had more flowery language than real substance, Alexander sent another letter the following week describing the difficulties of covering naval operations. The correspondent wrote that damage inflicted on enemy warships, especially ironclads, was difficult to determine. "It is very different when the combatants meet on land where the line of battle is frequently several miles in extent, and where the beaten party leaves behind him dead and wounded to tell the tale of the disaster," he wrote.[72]

General James Longstreet's attack (left center) on the Union at the Battle of Gettysburg. The Blue Ridge is in the distance. *Harper's Weekly,* August 8, 1863. Courtesy
of Rare Books and Special Collections, University of South Carolina Libraries

By early May, Alexander was back in Virginia with Lee's army, arriving just
in time to report on General Stonewall Jackson's death following the Battle of
Chancellorsville. Alexander's source was one he considered impeccable, the
Central Presbyterian, "whose editor had peculiar means of obtaining correct
information." Whether Alexander copied the story or summarized it is unclear,
although he probably conveyed what the *Central Presbyterian* had published.
The story conveyed Jackson's last days as he lay dying from pneumonia contracted after having his arm amputated.[73]

Alexander had more success several weeks later when he reported Lee's next
invasion of the North, which culminated in the three-day Battle of Gettysburg.
His report of the pivotal battle, filed July 4, ran two and one-half full columns on
the front page of the *Republican,* making it one of his longest stories of the war.
The correspondent began his account succinctly as he wrote, "The bloodiest and
most desperate battle of this bloody and most desperate war has just been fought
here on the soil of Pennsylvania." Alexander set the scene of the fighting, describing the terrain and the field advantage held by the Union army. Meade had
chosen a battlefield that could hardly have been less favorable for Lee, Alexander
reported. The Confederate army was spread out from Gettysburg, Pennsylvania,
to Emmettsburg, Maryland, among timbered and rocky hills.[74]

Alexander's report included detailed accounts of the three days of fighting.
He noted the heavy losses that both sides suffered, including numerous officers

Harvest of death at Gettysburg. *Harper's Weekly,* July 22, 1865. Courtesy of Rare Books and Special Collections, University of South Carolina Libraries

from Lee's army. Alexander described in detail the various smaller fights that made up Gettysburg, giving readers a vivid picture of the battle. Of one assault by Confederate forces, he wrote, "The splendid divisions of [General John Bell] Hood and [General Lafayette] McLaws swept on to the charge in admirable style. An officer who was present said it was worth ten years of ordinary life to witness the manner in which McLaws' division rushed across the field and assaulted the almost impregnable position in front." Not surprisingly, Alexander focused on the valor shown by Confederate troops but he also credited the Union army as being a worthy foe. Perhaps weary from composing such a lengthy account of the battle, Alexander described the final Confederate assault by General George Pickett's troops simply: "Pickett's charge was made in excellent order and gallant style, and he succeeded in wresting a portion of the hill, and the guns in the quarter from the enemy; but the enfilading fires which were brought to bear upon him, and the failure of Pettigrew to get up simultaneously with himself, rendered it necessary for him to retire with great loss."[75]

The account of Gettysburg apparently was written under extreme deadline pressure because Alexander noted in the middle of it that the courier who would carry the dispatch "has saddled his horse and is ready to leave." He tried to put the best face on the Confederate loss, noting that both Confederate and Federal armies left the battlefield "worn, battle-scarred and severely punished." But Alexander recognized that some Confederate tactics during the three days of fighting were questionable. He raised questions about Lee's decision to fight at the time and place he did. He also questioned why Lee ordered an attack on the second day without proper reconnaissance.[76]

In late summer, Confederate General Braxton Bragg petitioned for reinforcements to help him hold the western theater's important transportation hub, Chattanooga, from a relentless assault by Union troops. Lee sent Longstreet's corps, and Alexander went with them to see first hand what was happening in the west. He arrived in time to report the last major Confederate victory of the war at Chickamauga.

However, Alexander arrived too late to witness the battle and had to rely on the statements of others. But unlike Fredericksburg, where he also arrived late but managed to write a compelling story, his account of Chickamauga lacked the telling details and graphic description of many of his other battle stories. He also lapsed into excessive language that bordered on the euphoric and made exaggerated statements.[77] Alexander called Chickamauga the "most important battle of the war, after that of First Manassas," and added:

> There is no longer an armed enemy on the soil of Georgia! Only the Federal dead, wounded and prisoners now remain. The multitudinous host, swelling with confidence and pride, who lately invaded that powerful State, threatening to overrun her territory and devastate her homes, has been defeated and forced to seek refuge behind barricades and breastworks along the banks of the Tennessee river. Let every heart in our suffering land give thanks to Almighty God for His great kindness—for this signal deliverance![78]

During the days leading up to the Battle of Chattanooga, Alexander continued to express his concern for the Confederate foot soldiers. He described men who performed guard duty in trenches half-filled with water as a result of heavy rains. Many of the troops did not have tents and were forced to sleep with only one blanket despite the cold November temperatures. In another story, he criticized the practice of some Confederate officers to have a large number of mounted escorts. Alexander expressed concern about the shortage of horses in the army, attributing the problem in part to the "scandalous exhibition of military vanity" by high-ranking officers who used the escorts. He reported that one officer had an escort of 40 mounted men and another officer had 125. Alexander's letter was reprinted by other Southern newspapers, and Confederate General Braxton Bragg eventually issued an order correcting the abuse.[79]

Alexander did not hesitate to criticize the conduct of Southern troops at Missionary Ridge, the turning point of the Battle of Chattanooga. At the height of the fighting, Confederate soldiers on top of Missionary Ridge broke and fled panic-stricken, despite holding the high ground. For the first time in the war, Alexander condemned the fighting spirit of Southern troops. "The Confederates have sustained the most ignominious defeat of the whole war—a defeat for which there is little excuse," he fumed. "For the first time during our struggle for national independence, our defeat is chargeable to the troops themselves and not to the blunders or incompetency of their leaders."[80]

After Bragg's disastrous losses in Tennessee, Alexander retired for the winter to Thomaston, Georgia. His pen was silent for much of that time, but in late December, he wrote to correct some rumors and to include a peevish complaint to his editor. The army was preparing to retreat to Atlanta, according to the rumor, and Alexander wrote that it was not true. He called on General William Hardee, who had been given command of Bragg's army in the wake of that general's failures, and Hardee told him he would not easily give up the ground between Dalton and Atlanta. He told the reporter that he would contest every inch of it.[81] Alexander's complaint was about the carelessness of the *Republican's* printers, and although the correspondent was no doubt serious in his comment, it does add a bit of comic relief at a grim moment in Confederate history.

> Your printer, who seems to take a malicious pleasure in perverting my letters, makes me say in the *Republican* of the 18th that our killed at Missionary Ridge was 800 instead of 300, as I wrote it. I would overlook this and other errors which occur in the publication of nearly all my letters but for the fact that I may not live to gather up the letter and correct these errors. I pray the future historian, therefore, should he design to consult your columns when he comes to write a history of this unholy war, not to visit his condemnation upon my head, but upon the fingers of those who will not print my letters as I wrote them.[82]

Early in 1864, heavy fighting occurred in Alexander's home state for the first time when General William T. Sherman launched his campaign to capture Atlanta. Rather than remain and cover the western front, Alexander returned to Lee's Army of Northern Virginia. In early May, the Confederate and Union armies collided in what would prove to be the beginning of a week of savage fighting. At Spotsylvania Court House, Alexander described fighting so close that at times opposing troops had little more than the length of their muskets between them. In the literary style that had come to characterize much of his work, he wrote:

> The battle was fully joined and for nine hours it roared and hissed and dashed over the bloody angle and along the bristling entrenchments like an angry sea beating and chafing along a rock bound coast. The artillery fire was the most sustained and continuous I have heard for so long a time, averaging thirty shot to the minute, or 1,800 to the hour, for six hours. The rattle of musketry was not less furious and incessant.[83]

However, Alexander's reporting of the fighting at the Wilderness later in May was not up to the standards he had established for himself. The correspondent admitted that his account of the Wilderness lacked details. But he said that was because of the difficulty of keeping track of the army in the heavily wooded area so thick with trees and brush that it was impossible "to distinguish a man . . . a distance of fifty paces."[84] Alexander was gratified to be able to write about this battle, even though he recognized it had not been a decisive victory for the Confederates, given that the enemy had not been routed. Nevertheless, he believed that the end of the war was near, and that made this battle all the more significant.[85]

Alexander reported Lee's last major victory, the futile Union assault at Cold Harbor, where this time his opponent was General Grant. Riding along the Confederate lines on the Sunday before the fighting began, Alexander observed the troops resting and observing the Sabbath. He wrote of the weary men who were reading their Bibles, while others were sleeping or sitting under trees listening to sermons, but all at rest. As Alexander observed "this vast machine, this great giant, this great, unmeasured, and immeasurable power, should be so terrible in battle," he wondered how it could be "so calm and gentle and devout in the hour of peace."[86]

In his account of Cold Harbor, Alexander described the repeated frontal assaults that Grant threw at the fortified Confederate line and the staggering losses that resulted. In one hour alone, an estimated 7,000 Federal troops were killed or wounded during a charge on June 3. Alexander also reported Grant's controversial decision to leave some of the Union casualties on the battlefield.[87]

Alexander remained in Virginia the entire summer to cover the long siege of Petersburg. He described the effect the hot, dry summer was having on the city and the surrounding area. With a fine eye for detail, the correspondent wrote:

> Everything partakes of the color of dust—the woods, the fields, the corn, the grass, the men, the horses, and the wagons. We breathe it, we sleep in it, and even move in it. It is thicker than the darkness that overspread Egypt in the days of the Pharaoh; so thick indeed, that Gen. Butler from his lofty lookout will be able to descry but little else except dusty. If there is no wind to blow it away, the dust raised by a solitary horseman is so great that it is impossible at the distance of a few paces to tell whether it is produced by a man, a horse, or a vehicle.[88]

Alexander clearly found the siege demoralizing, yet he, like so many Southerners, was not yet ready to give up on his cherished cause. Instead, he offered defiance. Alexander was convinced, wrongly, that Grant's army was too weak to mount an actual assault on Petersburg because of the loss of men to illness and expired enlistment terms. He believed the lack of men gave Grant only two options, neither of which would be attractive: to maintain the siege or to retire to the other side of the James River.[89] Grant, however, was perfectly content to hold out. He maintained his siege for the better part of a year, cutting off Lee's army from one of the Confederacy's most important railroad hubs. However, the siege would take its toll on Lee's army and on the *Republican*'s correspondent. In late

August, Alexander reported that he, like many in the army, was "on the sick list." They were all suffering from fever and "disorders of the bowels" brought on by the campaign, the recent drought, the hot weather, and the lack of healthy food.[90] Alexander added that the situation was made bearable only by the fact that Grant's men were suffering more than the Confederates.

Alexander was still in Virginia when Savannah fell to Sherman's troops in December 1864. As Union troops entered the city, *Republican* Editor Sneed fled with the Confederate army. One of Sherman's first acts was to take over the *Republican* offices and appoint a Northern newspaperman as editor. With his newspaper in the hands of an unfriendly journalist, Alexander apparently decided it was time to return to Georgia.[91]

He left on a month-long trip home, reporting along the way for the *Richmond Dispatch* and the *Mobile Advertiser and Register*. Traveling along the North Carolina coast, Alexander reported on the fighting at Fort Fisher near Wilmington. In several reports from the coast, he made exaggerated statements but also provided vivid details of the fighting. In one account, he wrote, "The bombardment of Fisher was the heaviest and fiercest to which any fort or town was ever subjected. The front forces of the fort are honeycombed from bottom to top, and the ground and rear is covered with shells and torn into great pits and gullies."[92]

The Civil War was over for Alexander, and it was the end of his sustained reporting. After the war, he was encouraged to collect his newspaper stories and publish them but he never did. He also declined requests from several publishers to write his reminiscences of the war.[93]

Instead, Alexander resumed his law practice, this time with a friend, James M. Smith. When Smith was elected governor of Georgia in 1872, Alexander was appointed his private secretary and served in that role for five years. Following Smith's governorship, Alexander became embroiled in a political controversy over the naming of commissioners to oversee the construction of a new state capital. The owner of the *Macon Telegraph and Messenger*, Major H.T. Hanson, wanted one of the appointments, but the recently elected governor sided with Hanson's political opposition and appointed someone else. Alexander got involved in the controversy by acting as Hanson's emissary to the governor. Despite his lack of success in acquiring the appointment for Hanson, the newspaper owner rewarded Alexander for his loyalty by naming him editor of the *Telegraph and Messenger*.[94]

Although Alexander was said to have been "of magnificent frame and courtly bearing . . . a splendid type of a Southerner," he did not marry until well after the war.[95] Alexander was a single lawyer living in the home of cotton merchant John E. Pleasant, along with the Shorter family.[96] He would find his wife in this household, Maria Teresa Shorter of Columbus, whose family had founded Georgia's Shorter College.[97] The couple had three children: Sarah, nicknamed

Sallie, who was born in 1873; George Shorter, who was born in 1875; and Paul Wellington, who was born in 1874. None of the three appear to have had children of their own.[98]

In 1877, Alexander and his family moved to Marietta, Georgia, and he worked as a cotton merchant.[99] Unable to get journalism out of his blood, Alexander purchased an interest in the *Macon Telegraph* in 1885 and became editor. But for unknown reasons, he soon sold his interest in the newspaper and returned to Marietta. He died there in 1886 at the age of 62.[100]

17

James Roddy Sneed: "There Can Be No Greater Tyranny Than a Muzzled Press"

Bruce Mallard

JAMES RODDY SNEED WAS A POET AT HEART WHO WROTE PROLIFICALLY about the Civil War in the *Savannah* (Georgia) *Republican* without wandering far from his hometown or his five motherless children.[1] He was a Unionist in principle and an outspoken advocate of good reporting and free speech who defended his beliefs in eloquent and angry editorials advocating an unfettered press. He also worked to protect free speech for newsmen by helping to organize Confederate editors to fight military censorship. He fought to improve the quality and quantity of news stories available to Southern newspapers, and helped create the Press Association of the Confederate States of America.[2]

Before the war began, Sneed was "anxious to avoid disunion," a position that wasn't shared by his competitor, the *Savannah Morning News*. However, "when secession came, all promised unity," he wrote, and devoted himself to the Confederate cause.[3] Although Sneed did not go far afield to cover battles and skirmishes, the war came close enough to Savannah to keep him busy. Most of his field reports were filed from nearby Charleston, beginning with the start of hostilities at Fort Sumter. As conflicts developed, he filed stories signed with "S" or "J.R.S." that were occasionally peppered with flowery prose, Latin quotations, and references to the Greeks. However, most of his Civil War work was published as editorials.

Like most 19th century editors, Sneed had ties through his newspaper work to politicians, who, according to a poem written by one of Sneed's political enemies, interceded to help the editor obtain his wartime appointment as collector of the port of Savannah.[4] This political appointment gave Sneed the authority to receive and pay out millions of dollars to the military department for the Confederate government.[5]

Born in Richmond County, Georgia, on December 3, 1818, Sneed was one of six children of Archibald Henderson Sneed of Granville, North Carolina, and Abigail Latham Roddy of Charleston, South Carolina.[6] Although Roddy is the most common spelling of his name, it is spelled Roddey on his tombstone, which is apparently an error. After Sneed married Anna Maria Hay of Washington, Georgia, on May 27, 1840, they had five children, Mary, Elizabeth "Lizzie" H., William Morgan, Gilbert H., and Francis G., all born between 1841 and 1850. Sneed's wife died after Francis' birth in 1850. She was 28 years old.

Sneed first became associated with the *Republican* a few years after his wife's death. The paper was then a leading Whig journal in the Empire State. Within two years of joining the staff, Sneed became part owner of the *Republican* when its former owner, Peter W. Alexander, sold the newspaper to Sneed and F.W. Sims. Alexander left the newspaper to practice law in Thomaston, Georgia, but when the war began, he returned to journalism and departed for the battlefield where he wrote under the pseudonym "P.W.A." for the *Republican*.

The historical record offers no information about what drew Sneed into the newspaper business, but it may well have been political aspirations; many young men spent time laboring at party newspapers as a sort of apprenticeship to moving on to higher offices. In any case, Sneed was well placed in 1860 to report and editorialize about the Civil War without ever traveling far from his hometown or his five children.

His first foray into war reporting came when he and William Tappan Thompson, editor of the competing *Savannah Daily Morning News*, traveled together to Charleston in April 1861 to cover the siege of Fort Sumter. Charleston would be the most distant spot from which Sneed would file reports. In between his brief visits outside Savannah, Sneed wrote short articles on the front page of the *Republican* along with extensive editorials inside. He never hesitated to offer a well-informed and sometimes blistering opinion on any subject.

Sneed's first big story recounted the bombardment of Fort Sumter and Charleston. He filed a lengthy article on April 13, 1861. With some flair, he datelined the story, "The Seat-of-War—Charleston." He wrote:

> Greek has met Greek, and we have had the "tug of war." That "Dies Free," so long feared and deprecated, and which all hoped would never come to pass, when Americans should meet Americans in deadly strife, has at last arrived. In all respects one of the most remarkable battles on record has been fought in the harbor of this city; and as it was our privilege to be an eye witness to its dreadful progress, or at least by far the most interesting portion of it, we propose to briefly sketch the event, as we, in company with thousands, saw it at a distance.[7]

Sneed wrote a detailed description of Fort Sumter, a powerful fortification in Charleston harbor located four miles from the city on the south side of the channel and surrounded by water. Major Robert Anderson and his small band of Federal troops, which Sneed estimated at between 60 and 90 men, had moved to the more defensible Fort Sumter from nearby Fort Moultrie soon after South Carolina's secession from the Union. Because Fort Sumter was only partially armed, Sneed wrote, Anderson's soldiers had mounted most of the guns on carriages constructed of boards and other loose materials found in the fortification, as well as bits of timber that were captured floating in the bay.

According to Sneed's story, the Confederate army was composed almost exclusively of South Carolinians, with the exception of General Pierre G.T. Beauregard, a Louisianian, and a few staff volunteers. Beauregard would become the darling of the Confederate people for his work in Charleston Harbor. Sneed told *Savannah Republican* readers that Beauregard dispatched members of his staff to Fort Sumter on April 11, with orders to demand the immediate evacuation of the works. Major Anderson replied that duty to his government and to his own honor as a soldier required that he should decline compliance with the demand.

> Nothing now remained but to enforce the evacuation by a resort to hostilities. Soon after day light, Friday morning, the contest was opened by two guns, fired in quick succession, from the battery at Fort Johnson. The sound was caught up by the other batteries, and in a few minutes a shower of iron hail poured in upon Sumter from nearly every point of the compass. Two hours and a quarter elapsed before Major Anderson returned the fire. All things ready, he finally opened his ports and turned his guns on Fort Moultrie and the Morris' Island battery, but chiefly on the former, nearly every ball taking effect. The engagement then became general, and the rapidity and accuracy with which Major Anderson returned the fire throughout the day, is highly complimented by the officers of the opposing army . . . The firing was kept up with but little intermission throughout the entire day, and though a fierce storm of rain was falling during a good portion of time, it did not cool the ardor of the combatants.[8]

According to Sneed, the cannon fire was steady throughout the early morning and into the day. Thousands of spectators gathered on the Charleston Battery to witness the display. "We will not attempt to describe that which baffles description," Sneed wrote. "The scene was grand beyond conception."[9] He reported that Saturday, April 13, dawned "a bright and lovely day" with the flags of both sides still flying in stately defiance, as the "deep mouthed cannon continued to belch forth their fiery thunder." However, because Anderson's men were slow to return Confederate fire, Sneed surmised that they were getting tired. About eight o'clock, smoke was seen issuing from the southern side of the fort, evidence that a shell or "hot shot" had begun burning the woodwork of the interior.

> The fire attracted no great attention at first, but the smoke continued to rise, until in the course of about two hours an explosion as of gunpowder, yet not loud

enough for a magazine, proved that the fort was on fire, and Anderson was blowing up his quarters to arrest the flames. A second explosion, but all to no effect.
In a few moments his entire barracks were on fire and the entire fort wrapped in
flames and smoke.[10]

Sneed wrote admiringly about the heroism of Anderson and his Union soldiers, saying that memories of the incident would "go down to the last syllable
of recorded time."[11]

During the course of an hour, Anderson's men succeeded in reducing the
flames, or rather, Sneed said, the fire went out for lack of fuel, it being understood that the officers' quarters were entirely destroyed. "Exhausted with labor,
and finding all chance of reinforcement hopeless, Major Anderson, about ten
o'clock, hung out a white flag from the parapet, his flag staff having previously
been felled by a ball from Fort Moultrie, and immediately all was silent and the
war at an end," he wrote.

> Boats went over immediately from Moultrie and Morris' Island, and it is said
> Major Anderson surrendered unconditionally, though of this there is some doubt.
> The terms are not yet arranged, though it is believed he will be allowed to come
> out with his side arms, and embark for New York in one of the Government steam-
> ers now lying off the bar. Throughout the long and tiresome engagement, the
> South Carolina troops—to whom, with their gallant commander Beauregard, all
> the honor of this great victory is due—conducted themselves with perfect order,
> the greatest enthusiasm, and with a courage that proved they were invincible.[12]

Sneed was astonished that no one had been killed during the battle, although
the forts, especially Sumter and Moultrie, were greatly damaged in what he
called an "unnatural struggle." He wrote that the battle lasted 32 hours with
hardly an intermission, "some fifty-odd tons of cannon balls were exchanged
between the belligerents, some eight tons of powder burnt; the weapons used
the most destructive known to modern warfare and skillful hands, and yet *on
neither side was there a solitary life lost.*"

> We may almost say, in the language of Lincoln, that "nobody is hurt"! We are
> credibly informed that . . . one is seriously wounded, and but a very few slightly.
> The forts though, especially Sumter and Moultrie, are greatly damaged.—There
> is nothing like this in the annals of the world, and verily it seems that Providence
> had interposed and resolved that Americans *should not* shed a brother's blood.[13]

Sneed would return frequently to Charleston during the war to look for
wounded Georgia soldiers in the hospitals and to report on the continuing
hostilities.

Even though Sneed was one of the Confederacy's first war correspondents,
he spent most of the war doing what editors do best: putting out the newspaper

and dealing with administrative headaches. Among the continual headaches Sneed dealt with during the war was military censorship. He addressed this problem directly on behalf of both his own newspaper and correspondents by working to organize Confederate editors to fight military censorship as a group.[14] Sneed's other big headache was finding enough materials to produce his newspaper—and means of transporting those materials to his plant. Sneed wrote a lighthearted note about the problem of finding enough paper, ink, and other printing supplies in October 1861.

> Something New. It is amusing—while it is at the same time a credit to their enterprise—to witness the shifts that some of our country exchanges have to resort to in order to combat the hard times and keep up a supply of paper. They come to us in all shapes and sizes, half sheets, small sheets, on white, yellow and brown paper, and this week the LaGrange *Reporter* caps the climax by coming out in a full dress of *blue*! We feel the hard times ourselves, and know how to sympathize with others.[15]

Problems with printing supplies escalated by the end of the year, and Sneed was not so lighthearted about his printing problems by January 1, 1862, when the *Republican* announced on the front page that it was starting the year in a smaller size because of shortages in supplies: "The *Republican* enters, to-day, on the sixty-first year of its existence—an old machine 'tis true, but we hope, with proper care and youthful engineers to run it, it may neither break down nor run off the track," he wrote.

Like most Confederate editors, Sneed was forced to increase subscription rates in June 1861 to cover the rising cost of paper, to absorb the loss of advertising, which had been greatly reduced, and to cover telegraphic expenses, which had nearly tripled.[16] Editors usually pleaded, cajoled, and begged people to pay for their subscriptions, but Sneed reprinted a curse upon the reader who wouldn't pay his bills.

> May he have sore eyes, and a chestnut burr for an eye stone. May every day of his life be more despotic than the Day of Algiers. May he never be permitted to kiss a handsome woman. May his boots leak, his gun hang fire, and his fishing lines break. May his coffee be sweetened with flies, and his soup seasoned with spiders. May his friend run with his wife, and his children take the whooping cough. May his cattle die of murrain, and his pigs destroy his garden. May a regiment of cats caterwaul under his window every night. May his cows give sour milk and rancid butter. In short, may his daughter marry a one-eyed editor, and his business go to ruin . . .[17]

Although Sneed wrote articles and editorials about conflicts near Savannah and surrounding areas, he reprinted articles from other newspapers and hired correspondents, including Peter W. Alexander, who had been editor of the *Republican* from 1853 to 1856. Alexander had left the newspaper to practice law, but when the war began, he returned to journalism as a war correspondent for the *Republican* and, eventually, several other Southern newspapers. Sneed also made arrangements for the South's other leading correspondent, Felix Gregory de Fontaine, "Personne" of South Carolina's *Charleston Courier*, to do some correspondence for the *Republican*. De Fontaine wrote as both Personne and "F.G. de F." for the *Republican*.

Sneed's perspective on the practice of newspapering was progressive for the time and certainly contributed to the professionalization of the journalistic craft. He was an adamant advocate of the reader's right to know "everything which transpires in the operations of the government, or the conduct of the war, that they might approve, support, condemn or rectify," though he maintained the same willingness other Southern editors and correspondents had to withhold military news when circumstances warranted.[18] Sneed also demanded accurate reports from his correspondents, and on at least one occasion, he issued a stern warning about the way the war was being covered.

> It is about time the press of the Confederate States should set its face against the practice of making mountains out of molehills, in telegraphic and other accounts of military affairs. We are falling into the habit of calling a skirmish a battle, and a battle a terrific engagement. Such bombast will make us the laughing stock of the world and as despicable as the Yankees. Let the Press denounce it at once.[19]

Sneed was equally quick to criticize military leaders for high-handedness in dealing with reporters who published innocuous information. He pounced on Confederate General Joseph E. Johnston in December 1861 for his reaction to a story by the *Richmond Daily Dispatch* correspondent "Bohemian" (Dr. William G. Shepardson). Bohemian wrote an article from Manassas that described in great detail the winter headquarters of the Army of the Potomac, even citing where Generals Johnston and Beauregard would be living.[20] Outraged by the extensive information in the article, Johnston sent the newspaper article to Secretary of War Judah P. Benjamin on December 30, 1861, along with a demand that Shepardson be arrested immediately.[21] Benjamin was equally outraged but he believed he had no power to address the matter. Neither state law nor the Confederate Congress' Military Committee gave him the authority to interfere with reporters. Benjamin wrote that he believed Shepardson was a spy and encouraged Johnston to detain him and try him at a court-martial.[22] Instead, Johnston ordered the expulsion of all newspaper correspondents and reporters from his army, an action that threatened newspapers with a total blackout of news from the Virginia army, with the exception of official army reports and letters from soldiers. Sneed and his fellow editors were alarmed.

When Johnston's order was followed with an effort by the Confederate Congress to restrict press freedom, Sneed lashed out with a fury. He quoted the

Confederate Constitution that stated: "Congress shall make no law respecting an establishment of religion, or prohibiting the free exercise thereof; or abridging the freedom of speech, or of the press . . ."[23] Writing sharply and critically, Sneed expressed disbelief that Congress was trying to restrict the liberty of the press. "Aside from the constitutional prohibition, there is no question that is approached with greater danger in a free republican government. There can be no greater tyranny than a muzzled Press, for the very idea involves the conclusion that there is some power in the State above public opinion and criticism."[24] Sneed and other Confederate editors spread the word about General Johnston's order.

> We are exceedingly grieved to read that Gen. Johnston has issued a general order expelling all newspaper correspondents and reporters from the lines of the army on the Potomac. This act is one without parallel in the present generation . . . the newspaper correspondent has been the aegis, the safeguard of the common soldier, the terror of inefficiency in office and of scoundrelism in the commissariat, the antidote to the poison of power so easily abused. A fine, fat time for army contractors and commissaries when none are there to report the condition and treatment of the private soldier.[25]

The editorial contained a lengthy personal and professional attack on General Johnston that was designed to rouse public sentiment against his decision.

> The general who plans his own movements and cannot keep them secret, but must blab them till they come to the watchful ears of a Grundy . . . is scarcely a general of great discretion. If a general's movements or strategy are so very vitrious that a mere newspaper writer can see through them, their opacity cannot be very great to the practical eye of (Union General George B.) McClellan.[26]

Some generals responded to such invective by growing increasingly wary of Confederate newspapers. At the end of January, General W.H.T. Walker wrote to Sneed from Camp Jackson saying: "I do not fancy having my name in the newspapers. I am not a public man. I am here to defend, as a Georgian and a gentleman, the glorious old State that I am proud to call my mother . . . (P)lease sir, leave Gen. Walker's name out when you write articles for the edification of the public."[27]

Sneed responded that the general was "too sensitive by half," but "as his request is a reasonable one, we shall certainly grant it, provided we can do so with justice to himself and the gallant men under his command."[28] With growing concern about military censorship as well as problems with telegraph transmission, Sneed and other newspaper editors called for a Southern editorial convention in Atlanta in March 1862, primarily to deal with the problems caused by Johnston's order.[29] The minutes stated:

> A preamble and resolution was adopted expressing the desire that the order issued by General Joseph E. Johnston, of the Army of the Potomac, excluding newspaper

Fort Pulaski, near Savannah, Georgia. *Harper's Weekly*, June 1, 1861. Courtesy of
Rare Books and Special Collections, University of South Carolina Libraries

correspondents, as well as similar orders of other Generals, be rescinded, and
that proper restrictions be employed to prevent correspondents from violating
orders and the courtesies of the camp.[30]

Sneed was one of three journalists who served on a committee with de Fontaine and J. Henly Smith, editor of the *Atlanta Southern Confederacy*, to draft a
series of resolutions critical of General Johnston's order to expel all newspaper
reporters from his army.[31] Although the editors would continue to fight for freedom of the press and against censorship and exclusion throughout the war, the
resolutions had little or no effect on Johnston or any of the other generals, including Bragg, Beauregard, and Jackson, each of whom expelled correspondents
from their armies at various times during the conflict.[32] Individual journalists,
especially those who also served as soldiers, were able to arrange access with
particular generals, but it would take a concerted effort by John S. Thrasher,
superintendent of the Press Association of the Confederate States of America,
in 1863 and 1864 to regain widespread access to military camps.

While Sneed was fighting for his profession's principles, the war moved into
his backyard when Fort Pulaski was attacked by Federals on April 10, 1862. The
massive, five-sided fort had been built to be impregnable—and it was, at the
time of its construction. By the time of the Civil War, however, weapons tech-
nology had advanced sufficiently that the fort was vulnerable. A young Lieutenant Robert E. Lee had selected and surveyed its site on his first assignment after

graduating from West Point. Pulaski guarded the sea approach to Savannah some 20 miles to the east. Sneed reported that "the most terrible bombardment of the siege commenced soon after daylight. The guns were louder and more rapid than at any time previous, and the windows of the city shook as if rocked by an earthquake; indeed the very earth trembled with the fierce cannonade."[33] The fort fell after only one day of bombardment.[34] Within six weeks of the surrender, most shipping in and out of Savannah ended, though daring blockade runners continued to slip past Federal vessels.

Soon after Fort Pulaski fell to the Union, Sneed married 21-year-old Leonora Cohen of St. Mary's, Georgia, on May 20, 1862, in Sandersville, Georgia.[35] Sneed, who had been a widower for 13 years, was 45 years old. Between 1863 and 1870 Sneed and his second wife had three children: Percival D., Nora V., and Anna Hay, who was named for Sneed's first wife, a common custom in the 19th century.[36]

When Sneed returned from his two-week honeymoon, he took up another editorial cause: what he perceived to be the incompetence of the South's initial wire service, the Southern Associated Press. Sneed had lost all patience with the quality of reporting from the service, which was a predecessor to the Press Association of the Confederate States of America, and he wrote a searing editorial.

> Whilst private individuals are telegraphing important information from Richmond concerning the late battles, we would be glad to know what that individual is doing who has set himself up at the capital as the agent of the Press and regularly comes forward with a bill for his services. He has been absorbed in a profound slumber, or swooned away into an equally profound indifference towards everything of interest to the Press and the public from the moment of his induction into office until now. A more shameful imposition was never attempted on anybody, and it is a mystery that his long suffering patrons should have borne with him so long. What are you at, Mr. (John) Grame, that everybody else can get important information, and you alone remain in the dark?[37]

Sneed complained with unforgiving bitterness about the quality and quantity of news stories that were arriving on his desk. He apparently had not tried privately to get the attention of Southern Associated Press Manager William H. Pritchard, Jr., and he wrote like an editor who had nothing to lose when he gave the press service a public whipping.

> If Mr. (Richard) Yeadon (editor of the *Charleston* (S.C.) *Courier*) and others could visit the battle field and find out who were killed and wounded, the forces engaged, by whom they were led, &c., &c., pray, why could you not do the same thing? For three whole days you have been burying the dead, without finding who they are, and watching with wonder and admiration the "quiet" that reigns "along the line"—is there nothing else you can do that would better interest the public

for whom you set yourself up as a caterer of news? We ask our editorial brethren: How long are we to submit to this state of things? Is there no remedy upon which we can unite and that will enable the Press to meet the just expectations of the public?[38]

Pritchard wasted no time striking back with an angry letter to F.W. Sims, the owner of the *Republican*. Pritchard defended his Virginia agent and told Sims that he planned to drop the newspaper from his list of subscribers and would do the same for all newspaper owners who made their press dispatches available to the *Republican*. Sneed published Pritchard's letter

> In your paper of this date, I find an attack upon my Agent at Richmond. Had a complaint from you been put in proper shape, and addressed to me at this place, I would have satisfied you (provided you can be satisfied by reason) that the fault does not lie with Mr. [John] Graeme. You propose to make other arrangements; I accede to your proposition. In three days from the date of this, your name shall be stricken from my list of subscribers. I do not wish any party to take any press reports against their will.[39]

Sneed followed Pritchard's letter with an angry editorial. His heated reaction was even stronger than before, and he was not intimidated by the threat of his newspaper being dropped from the news subscription list.

> As regards Mr. Pritchard's ability to satisfy us that his agent was not at fault, we wholly disagree and have only to refer to the Richmond papers of Monday and Tuesday last, for the proof that he has shamefully neglected the duties of his office, and imposed upon the Press. Had Mr. Graeme shut himself up in his room, omitted all effort to obtain information concerning the late battles, he might, at least have taken the Richmond gazettes of the days named, and with a small amount of labor compiled the intelligence for which every heart in the South was yearning most anxiously. But he did nothing; and now, because we dare to complain of this indifference to our interests by a regularly paid employee, why, forsooth, the Principal News Agent summarily strikes the *Republican* from the list of his subscribers.[40]

Sneed was certain that he would be joined in his complaints about the press association by other newspaper editors who were equally unhappy with the quality of the service. He had apparently decided that the Southern Associated Press was so bad that he would be better off without it, and he was confident that other editors felt the same way.

> We submit the case. For a brief period, at least, (Pritchard) has the power to subject us to a heavy extra expense, but he may rest assured it shall not be long. He has not a subscriber on his list that does not approve in his heart every word we said against his Richmond Agent, and who has not been chafing for weeks under a sense of imposition and wrong. We have the power to right ourselves in this

matter, and while we would not quarrel with Mr. Pritchard, we would assure him that we feel perfectly independent of him and would not turn on our heel to reverse his decision.[41]

Sneed was in a better position than other editors to launch the attack against the press association because he had two of the best and most prolific Southern correspondents on his payroll. He also recruited soldiers to write for the *Republican,* even going so far as to publish editorial guidelines for his soldier correspondents. The editor's instructions were so detailed that one of his soldier correspondents in the 13th Georgia in Virginia complained about difficulties he was having in meeting Sneed's specifications.

> Mr. Editor:—I know that it is against your rules for your correspondents to write upon both sides of the sheet, but circumstances alter cases, and I think this is one of the cases where I shall be compelled to violate your rules, and you will excuse me when I explain to you that paper is one dollar a quire, small sheets, and scarce at that. And besides that, the soldier, having as they say up here, to *pack* all he has on his back, and not knowing where to get more paper when the supply gives out, I think is a sufficient excuse.[42]

Sneed was right about gaining support from other editors in his conflict with the Southern Associated Press. In February 1863, Confederate editors met in Augusta, Georgia, to begin creating a new Southern wire service, the Press Association of the Confederate States of America. Sneed happily subscribed to the new service. The service would be managed by John S. Thrasher, a veteran journalist whose reporting standards required a high level of professional performance from his correspondents, including truthful, accurate reporting with no extraneous words.[43]

The war moved to Sneed's backyard again on February 17, 1863, when the Federal navy stepped up its operations along the Georgia and South Carolina coasts. General Beauregard ordered residents who could not help defend their homes in Savannah and Charleston to evacuate because of an expected Federal attack on one or both cities by land and sea. The general said he hoped "that this temporary separation of some of you from your homes will be made without alarm or undue haste—thus showing that the only feeling which animates you in the hour of supreme trial is the regret of being unable to participate in the defence of your homes, your altars, and the graves of your kindred."[44]

> Carolinians and Georgians! The hour is at hand to prove your devotion to your country's cause. Let all able-bodied men, from the seaboard to the mountains, rush to arms. Be not too exacting in the choice of weapons. Pikes and scythes will do for exterminating your enemies—spades and shovels for protecting your friends. To arms! fellow-citizens. Come to share with us our dangers, our brilliant success, or our glorious death. (Signed) G.T. Beauregard, General Commanding.[45]

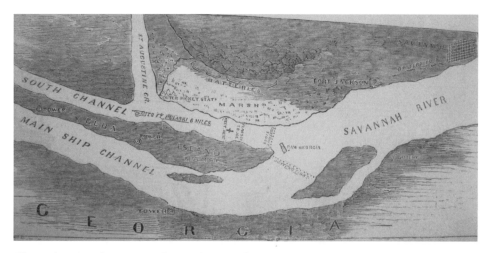

Chart showing the approaches to Savannah, Georgia. *Harper's Weekly* February 1863. Courtesy of Rare Books and Special Collections, University of South Carolina Libraries

Sneed wrote that the final preparations for the expected attack were being perfected and that the troops and people were confident and ready. He called on citizens to remain calm as they streamed out of the city.

> There is no just cause of excitement, much less of panic, and we hope to see all who can, depart quietly with the consoling reflection that those whom they leave behind will do all in human power to save their homes from the desolation of the invader and enable them soon to return to their peaceable enjoyment.[46]

Savannah was spared, but nine Federal ironclads would steam into Charleston Harbor to attack Fort Sumter later that spring. Although Charleston had been blockaded by Federal naval vessels since the beginning of the war, the attack marked the beginning of a siege that would not end until the city was abandoned by the Confederate Army in February 1865.[47] On July 13, 1863, Sneed headed for Charleston, where he reported the attack on Battery Wagner, located on Morris Island a little more than a mile from the city. "The ironclads took little or no part; at least they were not visible from eligible points in the city," he reported. "The fire on their side came chiefly from wooden gunboats and a new battery which they erected Friday and Saturday nights in front of Battery Wagner and a little more than a mile distant."

> I presume little or no damage has been sustained on our side, as up to dark the flags had made no report. One or two may have been killed and double that number wounded, a circumstance not considered now as worth telegraphing. How accustomed we are getting to the shedding of human blood![48]

According to Sneed, the Federals' primary target was Morris Island, a three-mile outer strip crowned on the north end with Cumming's Point Battery. He reported that they were "so devoutly aimed at by the enemy," because "it bears directly on Fort Sumter and the channel leading by it to the city."

But—and here comes the real trouble of the case—between Morris and James Islands lies Black Island, a small but densely wooded track of land, where almost any species of diabolical plots might be preparing against us without our knowledge, unless we went over at all hazards to see. A battery of long range guns erected on this island would effectually command our works at Secessionville on James island and also our channel of communication with Morris Island. This done, Sumter is doomed. Morris Island could be starved out and the strong position at its northern point gained without difficulty.[49]

Sneed also passed along stories about how Charlestonians were responding to the siege of their city. He was deeply impressed by a scene that he witnessed at 6 p.m. every day in front of the Charleston Hotel. He called it a "spectacle that should be photographed, as a lesson of patriotism for the generations to come. The living at the present day may also learn from it their duty."

It is The Old Men's Regiment, made up of exempts, and composed chiefly of the old men of the city. Most of their heads and chins are 'silvered o're with years,' and many with the infirmities incident to age upon them. A few foreigners are also among the number. All fired by patriotism and the duty they owe, while life itself lasts, to the noble State that gave them birth or protection, have come up in the day of her distress from their counting rooms, their studios, their workshops, and quiet retirement of the evening of their days, to stake their lives, if need be, in defence of Charleston. With a proud mien and resolute tread, they shoulder their muskets and respond to the work of command. It is a glorious and most affecting exhibition.[50]

Sneed was not as impressed with the way the battles were going, though he was quite impressed by the number and lethal qualities of the shells flying through the air. "The enemy has somewhat changed his programme to-day," he wrote. "There was occasional firing from their fleet, between the hours of 11 o'clock, at some object, real or imaginary, at the north end of Morris' Island."[51]

[A]t Battery Wagner, it was very bad gunmanship, for all the shell, except one or two, passed over and some distance beyond the battery, making it anything but comfortable to passers between the landing and the work. I happened to be one of the number, and at a time when the iron demons fell thickest and yelled most furiously, and consequently am prepared to confirm all that has been said and written of the infernal noise they make whilst screaming through the air on their wicked mission, the throwing up of mud and water or sand when they strike, and the irrepressible conviction on the mind of every one in hearing of the sound, that they are aimed and coming directly at himself. One soon becomes accustomed to them, however, and after a little safe experience pauses rather to admire than to dread the grandeur of the scene.[52]

When Sneed found that his prophecy about the danger on Black Island had come true, he began questioning the decisions made by the Confederate leaders. "I have good authority for saying that the enemy sent over a force to Black Island several days ago," he wrote. "What they are doing there, no body knows, but up to this time, it is understood no effort has been made to find out or to dislodge them. I cannot believe that so sagacious a man as Beauregard could overlook or be indifferent to so threatening a condition of things."[53]

Sneed was back in Charleston on August 26, 1863, hoping to visit Fort Sumter. As he approached the fortification, however, the "fire of the enemy became so tremendous that it would have been sheer foolhardiness to have ventured within its immediate vicinity." From the safety of nearby Fort Johnson, about a mile away, Sneed reported that the southern face of Fort Sumter was "one vast ruin."

A pile of rubbish—brick, mortar, stone, timber and guns—rises from the water and forms an inclined plain to the original parapet, some fifty feet in height. Many of the guns on this face are still in their carriages and pointing over the wreck. The interior of this, as well as the eastern side, was packed with sand bags, and for this reason, notwithstanding the walls have been battered down, there is no caving in, and but little diminution of the work. It also offers far more resistance to the shot of the enemy than the north or west side is capable of, and hence but little more damage can be inflicted from the Morris' Island batteries.[54]

Sneed continued to send reports to his newspaper on the Charleston situation and wrote that the Federals had opened fire upon the city from the Morris Island batteries.

The hissing demons are screaming through the air, and as my boarding house is directly in the line of fire, all the lodgers, including myself, have concluded to seek a safer refuge for the night higher up in the city. The streets are full of women and children, all moving forward with hurried steps and in the same direction. What a monstrous iniquity this is on the part of our unprincipled invaders![55]

Mindful of concerns about publishing military intelligence that would help the enemy, Sneed avoided reporting where the enemy shells reached so that the range of their guns couldn't be corrected. However, when he realized that the Charleston newspapers were publishing information, he too reported the location of the spots where the shells were landing.[56]

In Sneed's August 27 story, he reported that all the rifle pits in front of Battery Wagner on Morris Island had been captured on August 26 by an "overwhelming force" and that the Federals advanced to within 200 yards of the Confederate works. He gloomily reported that the island would eventually fall into the hands of the enemy "from their great superiority in all the appliances of war—guns, ammunition, working utensils, transportation, ships and men to waste."[57] Even before Morris Island fell, however, Sneed sadly speculated about the future: "Morris Island in their hands, and Sumter a wreck—for under the firing of a new three hundred pound Parrott gun her eastern or sea wall has been seriously damaged within the last two days—what then? Must Charleston fall?"[58]

When Sneed filed a story on August 28, 1863, on the continuing assault on Morris Island, he blamed all of the Federal victories on the lack of a Confederate navy.

> Whilst the enemy keep up so constant a fire from the island, they are also daily strengthening their position. They have now, probably, fifty guns and mortars in position between Craig's Hill and Battery Wagner, and a strong work is progressing within four hundred yards of the latter. It will be asked, what are our men doing that such things are allowed? With one well acquainted with the "situation" the answer is readily given. It is all explained by the fact that the enemy have a *navy*, while we have none. This has been the secret of nearly all their successes in the present war.[59]

The Federals continued to bombard Battery Wagner until September 6, when General Beauregard ordered the evacuation of the Confederate garrisons at batteries Wagner and Gregg after deciding that a Federal assault the next day would probably succeed.[60] Fort Sumter, which was a mass of rubble, and Charleston still held out. On July 8 Sneed reported that the "Yankees brought a force of negroes to attack our troops on James Island."[61] The soldiers that he described were members of the 54th Massachusetts Volunteer Regiment, which was one of the first all-black Federal units. Only its officers were white. The regiment was commemorated in the highly touted 1989 movie *Glory*. Following the battle, Sneed reported that 30 blacks were taken prisoner by the Confederates during the Union attacks. He expected lenient treatment for them.

> I have omitted to state in previous letters that the captured negroes, who were turned over to the State by the military authorities a few weeks ago, were brought up for trial under the laws of South Carolina on Monday. On motion of counsel on either side, the cases were postponed until next Tuesday week. Able counsel have been assigned the prisoners and other steps taken to secure them a fair and impartial trial. Public sentiment here is against a rigid execution of the law, and I shall not be surprised if a plea in defense that they were acting not of their free will, but under compulsion, should avail in securing a verdict of acquittal.[62]

Sneed's war experience vacillated between exciting moments like those reporting from the field and the more prosaic editorial worries of getting a newspaper published. As the Confederate industrial complex broke down under the pressure of the war, the problem of getting paper worsened, not always because of shortages. Sometimes, transportation was the issue. In October 1863, Sneed was obliged to suspend publication of the *Republican* for two days because he couldn't find a way of transporting paper from the mill to the newspaper offices.

> The Republican, like many other enterprises of its time, has had its share of the misfortunes of war—such as no human foresight could anticipate, and no effort prevent. For the first time in a career of over sixty years, for two days of the week just past no paper was issued from this office. This suspension was caused by the impossibility of procuring timely transportation for our paper from the Mills to Savannah, resulting, as we are informed, from the pressure of troops and government freight upon the trains . . . We make our re-appearance this morning, and we shall not have cause to lament a similar miscarriage for the future.[63]

Sneed took his concerns about shortages and business costs to the government. He wrote a letter to President Jefferson Davis asking for help in getting supplies to print the paper because "we are now reduced to the necessity of printing a paper which, half the time, nobody can read." He wrote:

> There being no foundry in the Confederacy from which we could renew our supplies, I have been striving for many months to procure a shipment of cotton through the blockade, the proceeds to be invested in such materials as will enable us to go on with our business, but thus far have failed. As, without relief, we shall be compelled to stop the paper at a time when we hope to make it of most service to the government and country, the laws of Congress and Department Orders from Richmond being published in its columns, as a last resort, I have determined to ask of you the privilege of shipping from Wilmington in some vessel which the Govt claims a certain position of the room, ten bales of cotton to the port of Nassau at Govt rates, with the pledge on my part that the proceeds shall be devoted exclusively to the purpose specified above.[64]

President Davis forwarded the request to Treasury Secretary George A. Trenholm, who denied Sneed's request, stating that other useful entities had made similar applications and that granting the request would "seriously embarrass" the operations of the Government.[65]

Sneed managed to keep the *Republican* in print and continued to work as collector of the Port and Confederate Treasury until December 1864 when Union General William T. Sherman captured Savannah and presented the city to President Lincoln as a Christmas present. As Sherman's troops approached Savannah and occupation appeared at hand, Sneed wrote his last editorial before fleeing.

Meldrim House, Sherman's Savannah headquarters. Courtesy of the Library of Congress

To the Citizens of Savannah: By the fortunes of war we pass today under the authority of the Federal military forces. The evacuation of Savannah by the Confederate army, which took place last night, left the gates to the city open, and Sherman, with his army will, no doubt, to-day take possession. The Mayor and Common Counsel leave under a flag of truce this morning, for the headquarters of Gen. Sherman, to offer the surrender of the city, and ask terms of capitulation by which private property and citizens may be respected. We desire to counsel obedience and all proper respect on the part of our citizens, and to express the belief that their property and persons will be respected by our military ruler. The

Confederate women leaving Savannah. *Harper's Weekly*, February 11, 1865. Courtesy of Rare Books and Special Collections, University of South Carolina Libraries

fear expressed by many that Gen. Sherman will repeat the order of expulsion from their homes which he enforced against the citizens of Atlanta, we think to be without foundation. He assigned his reason in that case as a military necessity, it was a question of food. He could not supply his army and the citizens with food, and he stated that he must have full and sole occupation. But in our case food can be abundantly supplied for both army and civilians . . . It behooves all to keep within their homes until Gen. Sherman shall have organized a provost system and such police as will insure safety in persons as well as property. Let our conduct be such as to win the admiration of a magnanimous foe, and give no ground for complaint or harsh treatment on the part of him who will for an indefinite period hold possession of our city.[66]

Although Sneed and *Daily Morning News* Editor Thompson had fought editorially during most of the conflict, they met the end of the war in Savannah just as they had the beginning: together on the Charleston train. Their departure coincided with the flight of General William Joseph Hardee and his disheartened Confederate soldiers.[67]

While [Sherman] was preparing on Christmas Eve to enter Savannah, the editors of the *Republican* and the *Morning News* were escaping with Hardee's Army into South Carolina. Thus two of the stoutest journals in the state became war casualties. Throughout the war they had quarreled consistently with each other,

After the fall of Savannah in December 1864, General William T. Sherman gave the *Savannah Republican* newsroom to Union correspondents traveling with his army. They published the *Loyal Georgian* from the newsroom for several days. *Harper's Weekly,* January 21, 1865. Courtesy of Rare Books and Special Collections, University of South Carolina Libraries

but until the last hour they had fought bravely against the dissenters within and the enemy without.[68]

Sneed remained in Charleston briefly before leaving with his clerks and records for Macon where he intended to establish his headquarters. When he discovered that Macon was not safe either, he moved after three months to the plantation of Dr. Thomas Parsons, about 25 miles southwest, where he remained until the end of the war.[69]

Neither the *Republican* nor the *Daily Morning News* published for several days after Sherman's occupation. Rather than leave the city without any newspaper, Sherman handpicked *New York Times* correspondent John E. Hayes to be editor of a new newspaper published out of the *Savannah Republican* newsroom but with decidedly Union sentiments. The new publication was titled the *Loyal Georgian*, but it was changed fairly quickly back to the *Savannah Republican*. The first issue under the new management appeared on December 29, 1864, with the new editor's greeting.

The common custom of presenting to the public an editorial salutation on the first appearance of a newspaper demands from the newly installed proprietor

of "The Savannah Republican" the brief statement of the objects of suddenly re-
suscitating from the ashes of rebellion one of the oldest journals in the state of
Georgia.

> The former editors of the 'Republican' having fled from this beautiful southern
> city, with its widespread live oaks, its noble magnolias and sycamores, shaded
> avenues, inviting parks, and refined society, to escape the wrath of an insulted
> army, whom they took special delight in vilifying, while safely ensconced in a city
> beyond range of their guns, it was deemed necessary to start a newspaper at once
> in order to furnish government with some ready vehicle by which the new order
> of things might speedily be conveyed to the army and the astonished citizens of
> Savannah. While sounding the sentiments of the people, we shall avoid, as far as
> possible, the shoals of intolerance and endeavor to show from our mast head in
> the darkest hours the light of magnanimity and justice.[70]

Hayes did not reflect so high a tone in the newspaper as he originally claimed
he would. While he was editor of the newspaper, he published a long derogatory
poem about "Roddy the Great," in which the former editor and other former
Confederate leaders were cruelly ridiculed. The poem was most likely written
by Hayes or one of his friends.[71]

The *Union* editor had briefly added "National" to the newspaper nameplate,
but he soon dropped it from the title and began publishing the paper again as
the *Savannah Republican*. However, Hayes began displaying very prominently
on the front page a loyalty oath to the Federal government: "[*The Savannah
Republican*] will maintain the Union, oppose Secession, and strive by argument
and persuasion to encourage that spirit of Loyalty to the Government, upon
which the future of Peace and Prosperity of the People must forever depend."[72]

Sneed, meanwhile, resumed his newspaper work in a new location: Macon.
While he was hiding there, the owners of the *Macon Daily Telegraph* asked him
to edit the paper, and he consented with the comment:

> Fanaticism still sits upon the throne, cruel and relentless. The South lies a bleed-
> ing, exhausted victim at its feet, with no weapon but the moral power of truth and
> the natural rights of man to save her from future harm. In this great battle for
> existence itself, she needs the aid of every faithful son. The undersigned does not
> feel at liberty to refuse his own, however feeble it may be, and especially when so
> few seem willing to protest against wrong and vindicate the right.[73]

Hayes published the *Republican* until he died in 1868. After his death, the
newspaper was sold at public auction on October 6, 1868, to Hiram Roberts,
who bought it for $11,515. Sneed returned from Macon to become publisher.[74]
The war and its aftermath had done little to calm Sneed's combativeness.
Within a year of returning to Savannah, he had taken on the Printer's Union
in an editorial. A letter to the editor on February 27, 1869, criticized Sneed for

stating that the "publishers of the newspaper should protect themselves against imposition and plunder of the Printer's Union."[75]

Charles Seton Hardee, Sneed's former Confederate Depository assistant deputy, became Sneed's partner on the newspaper; Sneed continued as part-owner of the *Republican* for about a year before he sold his interest and moved to Atlanta and then to Washington, D.C. The *Republican* was sold to the *Morning News*.[76] Sneed became postmaster of the U.S. Senate from 1882 to 1885 and was appointed the fourth auditor of the U.S. Treasury during the administration of President Grover C. Cleveland.

Sneed was also an occasional poet. His poems were colorful, and not brief, but noteworthy. His "Farewell to Savannah" refers to the city as the place "where Satan has placed his headquarters on earth," possibly related to Sherman's occupation and Sneed's eviction. On a lighter note, he called it a place "where the most approved tests of a gentleman are the taste of his wine and his Spanish segar."[77]

Always devoted to his family, Sneed expressed deep sadness in a letter to his sister-in-law, Maria Louisa Barnes Sneed, when his youngest brother, William A.H. Sneed of Forsyth, Georgia, died in 1889.[78] Shortly after his brother's death, Sneed's term of office as auditor of the treasury ended. He moved to Chicago in 1890 to live with his son Percival A., who was chief clerk to the general manager of the Baltimore and Ohio Railroad.

Sneed died of pneumonia on March 17, 1891, at age 73. His wartime nemesis, General Joseph Johnston, would die four days later in Washington, D.C., from heart failure.[79] Ironically, Johnston had moved to Savannah after the war and lived not too far from the offices of the old *Savannah Republican*.[80]

On the day Sneed's obituary ran in Savannah, the newspaper had grown from four pages during his tenure to 12 pages, at least on Sundays. His obituary ran in newspapers across the country, including the *New York Times*. In Chicago the *Daily Inter Ocean* described him as a man of "kindly nature and loveable disposition."[81] He is buried in Bonaventure Cemetery in Savannah, and his tombstone reads in Latin: *Antiqua homo virtute ac fide, homo multarum literarum.* It roughly translates, "A man of old-time virtue. A man of great, distinguished learning." His widow, Leonora C. Sneed, died on March 31, 1919, and was buried beside Sneed in the family plot.

18

John S. Thrasher:
Journalistic Revolutionary and Reformer

Janice Ruth Wood

JOHN S. THRASHER WAS A REVOLUTIONARY JOURNALIST LONG BEFORE HE took up a pen in support of the South's bid for independence in the American Civil War. As Cuba struggled for liberation from Spanish rule in the 1840s and 1850s, Thrasher ran an opposition newspaper in Havana. His deftness as a writer propelled him to a leadership position in the Cuban revolutionary movement— and to charges of treason that nearly sent him to prison in Africa for 10 years.

However, Thrasher's revolutionary ways extended beyond politics. As superintendent of the South's best-performing wire service, he also instituted revolutionary changes in journalistic practice during the Civil War that sped Southern newspapers' adoption of professional standards such as accuracy and exclusion of personal opinion in reports.

Even before Thrasher took the job as superintendent of the newly formed Press Association of the Confederate States of America in 1863, he was a dashing 19th century journalist, an expatriate, revolutionary, adventurer, and romantic who attracted the attention, and eventually the hand, of a landed woman who brought him money and notoriety. He would be sneered at publicly by Texas Governor Sam Houston for his conquest of that woman and berated by U.S. Secretary of State Daniel Webster for being "unreliable, unsafe, and unworthy."[1]

Webster's opinion grew out of Thrasher's work on behalf of Cuban revolutionaries who hoped to preserve slavery in Cuba and to annex the island nation to the United States. Thrasher's work for that group eventually resulted in his arrest by the Spanish, his trial as a co-conspirator, banishment from Cuba, and a sentence of 10 years hard labor in Africa. Despite the harshness of the sentence, Thrasher got off, essentially because of his claim of American citizenship. The Cuban leader of the revolution, Narciso Lopez, was executed by a firing squad.[2]

By the time of the American Civil War, Thrasher had developed excellent journalistic credentials for guiding the efforts of a wire service's reporters to cover a revolution. He also had new and revolutionary ideas about good jour-nalism that were significantly ahead of practices and standards of the political press that dominated Southern journalism at the time.

Thrasher set in motion advances in journalism that would carry far beyond the Civil War. One of his first and most significant actions was to copyright each news story sent out by the press association.[3] Although neither he nor as-sociation President Robert W. Gibbes ever received much credit for taking the step, the action was a first in American journalism because it was the first time news had been recognized as worthy of copyright protection.[4]

Thrasher is also credited with setting standards that survived the press asso-ciation's war reporting and inspired Southern journalism afterward. He worked to keep opinion out of news stories, insisting on using only facts, and he refused to allow unfounded rumors to be reported as news. He required clarity, concise writing, and timeliness, and he fired reporters who did not adhere to his dic-tates. While the writers he supervised failed at times to live up to his standards, their reporting served the needs of Southern newspapers far better than that of their predecessors and created a legacy for those who followed. Thrasher under-stood well the mission of the new press agency. He summarized its mission in a report to the board of governors.

> It has been left to our young Confederation to exhibit to the world the first in-stance of the entire press of a people combining in one body to prosecute the labors of its high mission; giving an adequate and worthy form to itself, and pre-senting to all a tangible representation of the fourth estate. What great power to procure the good, and to prevent the evil, resides in our association![5]

Although today's editors never give a nod of thanks to Thrasher, many of his basic rules are still used in newsrooms every day and would satisfy the most demanding editor in the 21st century.

Born in 1817 in Portland, Maine, Thrasher, whose mother was a Cuban na-tive, moved to Havana with his parents in his teenage years.[6] He worked as a merchant's clerk as a young man, but in 1849 he traded his apron for a pen when he purchased the *Faro Industrial* and used it to support the resistance move-ment to Spanish rule. Thrasher operated the newspaper until September 1851, when the latest insurrection failed. Spanish authorities retaliated by suppress-ing the paper and arresting Thrasher.[7] From a Havana jail cell, Thrasher wrote letters to American newspapers that explained how he had been arrested, tried, and convicted of treason. "I solemnly affirm that I have never had any connec-tions with the parties who invaded this land," he wrote. ". . . having been denied justice, I now ask at the hands of the American government, and the American people, that liberty of which I am so iniquitously deprived, all the horrors of the Spanish galleys are before me, and my only hopes are in the sympathies of my countrymen, and the prompt action of our National government."[8]

Newspapers, including the *Memphis Daily Appeal* and the *New York Times*, urged the American government to work for Thrasher's release.[9] In December 1851, the *Times* argued that Thrasher's case was more important than that of any of the others who had been arrested. The paper claimed that Thrasher was being persecuted because of his American citizenship "and because he interfered in behalf of the American prisoners."[10]

Secretary of State Webster was not anxious to take up Thrasher's cause because he believed the young journalist had willingly expatriated himself and had no plans to return to the United States. The secretary intimated that Thrasher was merely asking for the American government's help to avoid consequences he had brought on himself. Webster believed Thrasher would simply get into trouble again if he were released. The secretary was also troubled by the fact that Thrasher had not communicated directly with Webster or any other official after his arrest and conviction. Eventually, Webster asked the U.S. House of Representatives to determine whether Thrasher should be subject to Spanish law. The U.S. House responded with a resolution, sponsored by Virginia Congressman Thomas Henry Bayly, imploring President Millard Fillmore to negotiate for Thrasher's release based on his status as an American citizen.[11]

Even after his release, Thrasher's mind was focused on Cuba, albeit from a safe distance. He moved to New Orleans and established a Sunday journal called the *Beacon of Cuba*. From 1853 to 1855, he was part of a citizens' committee that backed military efforts against the Cuban government. The committee called upon General John A. Quitman of Mississippi to lead an expedition to liberate Cuba during that period, an expedition Thrasher fully intended to join—at least until U.S. officials intervened and halted the expedition. Thrasher relocated to New York City where he edited the *Noticioso de Nuevo York* and subsequently traveled in Mexico and South America for several years as a reporter for the *New York Herald*.[12]

He also launched a freelance career during this time, writing essays on Cuba for publications such as *De Bow's Review* and contributing a 95-page introduction to a book about Cuba that he translated from Spanish into English. The original author, Alexander Humboldt, claimed in a letter to American newspapers that Thrasher had altered his anti-slavery views and replaced them with Thrasher's own pro-slavery slant of advantages for slaves as well as masters.[13] Thrasher argued in one passage that the morals of slaves were improved by their exposure to their masters. He believed that when people associated with those of a better class, they learned more about how to function in the world around them.[14]

After those years as a roving reporter, Thrasher met and married Rebecca Mary Bass Menard, widow of Michel B. Menard. Menard was a noted Texas politician who had founded the coastal city of Galveston. He had been a signer of the Texas Declaration of Independence in 1836 and served in the Texas Congress from 1840 to 1842. Mrs. Menard's friends and family opposed the marriage because they considered Thrasher to be an adventurer. Texas Governor Sam Houston apparently shared the opinion, for at a campaign appearance during his last run for governor, Houston spotted Thrasher in the audience and referred to him as "the man wearing Mike Menard's clothes."[15]

Thrasher and his new wife settled on their plantation, Valverde, in Brazoria County, Texas, and apparently lived there quietly through the early part of the Civil War. In 1862, however, Mary's 11-year-old son from her first marriage, Menard Doswell Menard (sic), became ill, and the family moved to Macon, Georgia, in search of a better climate for the boy. That move put Thrasher in just the right spot a year later when Southern editors met in Augusta and organized the newest Southern wire service.

The South's editors had begun meeting regularly in January 1862 to try to resolve the problem of how to obtain telegraphic war news more efficiently. Six newspaper editors from three states gathered in Atlanta for that first meeting, and before long, the number of editors participating in the meetings, and the topics of discussion, expanded. Getting enough paper to continue publication was a perennial headache for Confederate editors, and postal laws made it expensive to mail newspapers. Editors believed they might find solutions to all these problems if they worked together. It would be early 1863, however, before they took the first step toward making the press association a reality.[16]

The association was the fourth to be established during the years of the Confederacy. William Pritchard, Sr., the Associated Press representative for Georgia, Alabama, and South Carolina and editor of the *Augusta Constitutionalist*, had established the South's first wire service in 1861, just after telegraph links between the North and South were shut down by the Union. Pritchard called his wire service the Southern Associated Press. When he died from diphtheria in 1863, his son, William Jr., took over the association, but the wire service was not a success under either Pritchard. It was expensive and slow, and so it lost subscribers.[17] The *Augusta Daily Chronicle and Sentinel* complained that the service was slow and its dispatches were irrelevant. The *Enquirer* of Columbus, Georgia, found the Pritchard service to be too expensive to continue membership.[18]

Two other news agencies appeared in Richmond in 1863. The first was the Mutual Benefit Association. Again, the *Chronicle and Sentinel* was unimpressed and warned other newspapers not to get duped into purchasing the service.[19] That service was not entirely successful either. The second Richmond agency, the Association of the Richmond Press, did attract subscribers outside the capital city,[20] but it also failed rather quickly. The men who were considering establishing the new Press Association of the Confederate States of America communicated with the second Richmond press association but apparently were unable to come to a satisfactory conclusion. The same day they heard from the Richmond agency, they voted to create their own service.[21]

Editors, or their proxies, from 15 newspapers gathered in Augusta, Georgia, in early February 1863. There is no record of Thrasher attending any of the early editorial meetings that resulted in the formation of the press association. However, he had been in Georgia for some time when the editors gathered, and he had a degree of notoriety as a result of his encounter with the Spanish courts, not to mention his later attempt to invade Cuba with John Quitman. Further, given the custom of the time, which called for traveling journalists to call on editors in the towns they visited, *Macon Telegraph* Editor Joseph Clisby and Thrasher were most likely well acquainted with one another by the 1863 meeting. Clisby may well have been responsible for Thrasher's appointment as superintendent of the new press association. Clisby was clearly influential among the editors who gathered to establish the new press association, for they elected him chair of the convention.[22]

Thrasher, then 46 years old, was hired some time between the February and May 1863 meetings, because it was at the May gathering that Thrasher gave his first superintendent's report. His 20-page report (with a similar number of appendix pages) was evidence that he had approached his new job with gusto and had already earned the $3,000 salary the board of directors had set aside for him (and would raise to $5,000 plus expenses before their meeting was completed).[23]

Thrasher's efforts in his early months with the press association showed that he and the organization would dramatically affect how journalism was practiced in the South.[24] The new wire service established its headquarters in Atlanta,[25] the geographic center of the South and eventually the center of a transformative effort that emphasized news and news-gathering rather than politics and political rhetoric.[26] This move from a political journalism model to a news-based model of journalistic practice had already begun prior to the existence of the association, but the standards and practices Thrasher set for the wire service hastened the transformation.

His first task after becoming superintendent was to find subscribers and correspondents to staff the wire service. Thrasher recruited all 31 newspapers that had subscribed to the Richmond wire service, and he also convinced every daily in the Confederacy to join the association.[27] Eventually, many of the weeklies would join. By April 6, 1864, the association was serving 44 newspapers.[28]

Thrasher began acquiring staff for the new agency by contacting the men who had worked for the defunct Association of the Richmond Press. When he was convinced they were doing their jobs well, he hired them to work for his agency. He hired 27 permanent and six occasional reporters, of whom only four received stated salaries. Reporters were paid by the story, and he said that he had not paid anyone in the field more than $25 a week by the time of his first report on March 13, 1863.[29] A reporter's job was secure so long as he was producing good work, but Thrasher was quick to dismiss any man not justifying his employment, and

View of Atlanta as it looked before Sherman's troops destroyed the city, which was home to the Press Association of the Confederate States of America. *Harper's Weekly,* November 26, 1864. Courtesy of Rare Books and Special Collections, University of South Carolina Libraries

that had included the correspondents in Petersburg, Lynchburg, and Gordonsville, Virginia, and Raleigh and Wilmington, North Carolina.

In those cases, Thrasher believed the needs of the association would be better served if member newspapers lived up to the requirements of Article No. 8 of the agency's Constitution: "It shall be the duty of members of the Association in localities where there are not Press Agents, to transmit all news of interest occurring in their vicinity to the nearest Agency, for distribution to all the other members of the Association."[30] He reminded newspaper editors in those cities where he had dismissed wire service reporters of their obligations to submit news to the press association. Thrasher tried to control costs by sharing a correspondent in Chattanooga with the *Macon Telegraph.* However, he admitted that the new arrangement was not working well. Thrasher assured the board of directors that he would not make such an arrangement again. "I have come to the conviction that the news reporters employed in the field by the press association must be its special agents, and subject to the entire control of your Superintendent," he wrote.[31]

However, the hiring of this correspondent spurred Thrasher to create a "code of instructions" intended to teach green reporters how to write a news story. That code of instructions laid out requirements for accuracy, fairness, and brevity.

Staffing was an issue in other places, too. Thrasher had to deal with reporters who resigned or were turning in sub-par work. "The Fredericksburg agent served during the month of March, when he was employed specifically by one of the Richmond journals, and our reports from there ceased. The news has since been served from Richmond. The Goldsboro reporter has sent us eighty-eight words since my advent, and one of the Raleigh journalists has sent a few reports of events in North Carolina, but our system in all that region is very incomplete and requires early attention."[32]

Thrasher also fired reporters who did not live up to the ethical standards he expected. He believed the dispatches and the conduct of his reporters had to be beyond reproach, and to accomplish those objectives, Thrasher established a strict set of professional standards. In 1863, one of his correspondents violated the service's code. Albert J. Street, who also wrote for the *Mobile Advertiser and Register* and the *Savannah Republican,* inserted news from Northern sources into a press report after the story had been cleared by censors. Because the story had been altered, it should have been sent back to the censors, which Street failed to do. Street also forged a censor's signature in order to get materials approved for telegraph transmission. These moves outraged Thrasher and led to the correspondent's dismissal from the wire service.[33]

Another of Thrasher's objectives was finding ways to save money on telegraphic transmissions. To accomplish this, he worked out plans with the Southern Telegraph Company to transmit news at affordable rates, and he set up a method of writing dispatches that would cut costs by limiting the number of characters transmitted in each story. Arrangements with Southern Telegraph limited the press association to 3,500 words a week, which was normally used at 500 words a day. Thrasher trained the staff of 20 reporters he had assembled in his travels through the South to leave out unimportant words that were, in his opinion, "seldom necessary to convey meanings, particularly if the language employed in treating every subject were divided into short sentences. On a careful study of the subject, I found that many words might be eliminated systematically from our reports, they being simply auxiliary words in our language. These were articles, pronouns, conjunctions, prepositions, adjectives and auxiliary verbs."[34] Thrasher pictured his system using two-fifths fewer words than normal writing and "that their absence would not be felt, as soon as senders and receivers had become practically accustomed to their abandonment."[35]

As he told that Chattanooga correspondent, Thrasher also required stories to be written clearly and concisely. Southern newspapers traditionally had received far more news than they originated, leaving many writers unfamiliar with standard formats.[36] Thrasher directed his reporters to write accurate accounts that were free of unverified rumor or commentary.[37] To those ends, he wrote and published the following set of rules for reporters:

GENERAL RULES FOR TELEGRAPHIC PRESS REPORTS

Correspondents by carefully adhering to these Rules, will greatly increase the value of their reports:

1. Keep within the maximum of words assigned to you as much as possible, without diminishing the interest of your reports for the public.
2. Write out your report of events in the form in which it should be given to the public.
3. Write every word clearly and use short sentences.
4. Avoid all unusual and ambiguous words and abbreviations.
5. Read every report over after writing it out; purge it of every word not necessary to convey your meaning and see where you can use one word to express what you have put in two or three.
6. Purge it of articles, pronouns, adjectives, conjunctions, prepositions and auxiliary verbs, whenever the plain sense of your meaning will not be lost.
7. Copy out carefully for the telegraph and mark boldly with equation marks, thus ==, every change of subjects in your reports in order that clearness in transmission may be attained.
8. Send no opinions or comments on events.
9. Be careful to sift reports, and see that you do not send unfounded rumors as news.
10. Put your reports in promptly and early.
11. When events of interest transpire, send a short report for the noon call for evening editions.
12. Do not wait for the call hour before you write out your reports, and then make them up hurriedly.
13. Do not repeat news.
14. Do not undertake to contradict local reports.
15. See that you are not beaten by special reporters for local journals.

J.S. Thrasher
Superintendent Press Association[38]

As he issued his general guidelines to correspondents, Thrasher's goal was to adopt a new style of reporting that would "result in a dead uniformity in its publication." He believed this could be accomplished if correspondents sent only "a nervous skeleton of the news" and editors used their "intelligence, tact and artistic skill" to reconstitute the language of agency dispatches.[39] Thrasher said he did not have any time to explain or give any advance warning to editors about his new system,[40] which was initiated by A.J. Wagner, the reporter in Jackson, Mississippi, who wrote the first abbreviated newspaper articles according to Thrasher's rules.

EVENING REPORT

Jackson 25. At 12 to-day enemy demanded surrender Enterprise—Loring arrived timely reinforcements—Enemy reported 500 1500 cavalry retreated without fight—About four hundred Yankee cavalry left Starkville about two days ago to-wards Bankston's mills—will take road by Grenada to Pittsboro—Burned on re-treat Female Institute and other hospital buildings Okalona—two trains burned Newton—Engines very slightly injured. WAGNER[41]

The abbreviated transmitted copy contained 54 words that editors were sup-posed to expand to 84 words by adding 30 auxiliary words for publication along with "such geographical information as is at hand to every editor in his Atlas, the List of Post-Offices and the Rail-Road Guide."[42] As an example, Thrasher rewrote and expanded Wagner's article and showed in italics auxiliary words that he added and the editorial additions in brackets to demonstrate how easily editors could add material to make the final edited version clear.

Evening Report *from Jackson.*

JACKSON, April 25—*At* 12 to-day *the* enemy demanded *the* surrender *of* Enter-prise, *[in Clark co., Miss., on the line of the Mobile and Ohio Rail-Road 14 miles South of Meridian.]* Gen. Loring arrived *with* timely reinforcements *and the* en-emy, *who are* reported *to be from* 500 *to* 1500 cavalry *strong*, retreated without *a* fight. About 400 Yankee cavalry left Starkville *[Octibeha co., Miss.,]* about two days ago, *taking the road west* towards Bankston's mills, *[Choctaw co.]* They will *probably* take *the* road by Tranada to Pittsboro, *[Calhoun co.]* The enemy burned on *their* retreat the Female institute and other hospital buildings *at* Okalona. Two trains *were* burned at Newton, *the* engines *being* very slightly injured.[43]

Some press association members complained that the system was incompre-hensible.[44] Defending his new style, while also admitting he had mishandled its introduction, Thrasher argued that his new system was "a complete revolution" in the way newspapers did business, and so he expected it to be unpopular with editors who were uncomfortable with change, especially since he had not had time to let them know the change was coming. In fact, he was pleased "the objec-tions to it have so soon subsided." He saw the fact that the complaints died down so quickly as evidence "that the system rests on solid and sure foundations."[45]

After partially incorporating the new system of telegraphic language, Thrasher was able to report that more news had been transmitted to the press in fewer words than had ever been sent before.[46] In spite of the initial criticism from some editors, Thrasher said he would continue to extend the practice of abbreviated reports "as a necessary measure of economy in behalf of the Press."[47]

He described the new system to the press association board of directors and showed samples of rewritten and revised stories. In arguing for his abbrevi-ated style of writing for the telegraph, Thrasher gave an example of a fight at

Birmingham that had been sent by three different reporters. The press association version was 12 words long while the others said the same thing but used 50 and 54 words each. "Apply this rule to all the news transmitted by telegraph, and we shall find that it will make a great difference in the substance of the 500 words daily to be sent from everywhere to Press," he wrote. "I hope this economy will yet be practiced by all our reporters, to the great individual advantages of each member of the Association."[48] The same rate of saving in words would allow the association to add 1,851 words to the weekly report without paying any extra telegraph charges, he said. "This saving is equal to $18 a week to some members, and $74 a week to others, according to their location."[49]

Thrasher's most unusual and demanding requirement dictated that press association stories should be free of opinion, rumor, and comment. Southern newspapers of the period were more closely aligned with the older partisan press than with the modern penny press. Therefore, many stories were more commentary than news, something Thrasher's rules seriously discouraged.[50] However, his directions to steer clear of opinion in favor of facts were not always followed. At times of severe defeats, such as Southerners suffered at Gettysburg, morale building would take precedence over news.[51]

Thrasher also required reporters to follow his General Instructions that included rules for transmitting reports, and requirements to visit sources twice a day. He urged caution in reporting the movements of troops and of commanding generals and said that the wishes and views of commanding or their adjutant generals must be consulted and respected. "As a general thing, it is better never to report changes of position of our forces or of commanders," he wrote.[52]

Press association reporters were directed to get the news first so that stories could be reported on a timely basis, because news about the war was so crucial to the folks back home. "See that you are not beaten by special reporters for particular journals," Thrasher wrote.[53]

However, a transformation in journalistic practice was not Thrasher's only objective. In those first two months of working for the press association, Thrasher was on the move building relationships with sources. He traveled to Charleston to meet with General Pierre G.T. Beauregard and arrange for reporters to cover that command. Beauregard agreed to cooperate with the new agency and also wrote letters to other Confederate commanders, suggesting that they might also cooperate with the press association. "I am gratified to report to you, that he assured me our reports in his department should have every facility for early access to intelligence compatible with the public interests, and proffered to me letters to friends of his commanding in other departments," Thrasher wrote. "This I accepted, and subsequently found them of service in advancing your interests."[54]

Thrasher continued his travels to Tullahoma, Tennessee, to meet with Generals Joseph Johnston and Braxton Bragg. "Both of these gentlemen received me with distinguished courtesy, and assured me of their willingness to advance your interests in the prosecution of my plans, and to afford every facility to our reporters for the early procuring of intelligence," he wrote. In return, Thrasher agreed to have copies of all press association reports telegraphed to Johnston at the same time they were sent to member newspapers. Later in his trip, he visited General John C. Pemberton in Jackson where he made arrangements to obtain news from his army in Mississippi. Pemberton gave him the same assurances.[55]

These efforts did not solve all the press association's censorship problems, and the assurances were short-lived. When General Bragg imposed strict censorship during his campaigns around Chattanooga in late 1863, he refused to give a press pass to Thrasher's reporter Will O. Woodson who asked to remain with the army in northern Georgia on an intended movement. Even after Woodson told Bragg that he would send nothing without his approval and did not desire to send anything that would be detrimental to the army, Bragg refused. As the army moved out from LaFayette, Woodson could not find transportation for the 26-mile trip to the nearest telegraph office in Resaca.

> [D]esiring to report the facts to you as early as possible, I started on foot, and after 12 hours hard traveling, reached the station, foot-worn and weary. It is but just to Gen. Bragg and Col. McKinstry, to state that the reason assigned for his course was the indiscretion of special correspondents in regard to army matters.[56]

With reliable information from the battlefront at a premium, it was inevitable that news stories contained errors. Inaccuracies and high costs created dissatisfaction among the press association's clients.[57] Thrasher tried to keep the editors updated about the problems the correspondents faced. "Owing to the anomalous condition of our country, orders have been issued, emanating respectively, as I understand, from the Secretary of War, military commanders, and the Postmaster General, under which numerous persons claim the right to exercise a censorship over the Press reports and to dictate what shall and what shall not be transmitted by telegraph," Thrasher wrote. "Whenever this censorship has been exercised in restricting the sending of information about the movement of our own forces, I have deemed it a just and necessary military measure, and have readily acquiesced in its exercise."[58]

He told the press association board that he had no problem with restrictions on the reporting of troop movements, but the implementation of censorship rules varied widely across the Confederacy. Censorship was being applied to information other than strategic military matters and had quickly expanded to include legitimate news stories. Thrasher said, "Persons have refused to permit news reports to be transmitted, because, as they alledge (sic) 'they were sensational;' and others, without assigning any reason, have stopped news reports in transit, after they had been partially transmitted to the Press."[59] Thrasher tried to deal with the problem of escalating censorship by asking his reporters to send him copies of any matter that was refused transmission over the wires with the reason and name and rank of the person stopping it. He contacted government officials, asking for copies of all orders issued by the postmaster general and officers concerning the transmission of matter by telegraph or mail to members of the press.[60] He also told the board of directors: "Meanwhile, should you not direct me to act otherwise, I shall vigilantly guard the rights of the Press from all invasion."[61]

Despite Thrasher's determined efforts to introduce new journalistic methods, news gathering during the Civil War was laden with problems. Editors continued to occasionally complain about opinionated and incomplete stories. Some military officials imposed strict censorship of telegraphic content that hindered the press association's efforts, and association directors encouraged their superintendent to use "all the means in his power" to oppose it.[62]

Thrasher also helped to successfully resist President Jefferson Davis' efforts to draft newspaper editors into the military. Like other Southern journalists, Thrasher feared the measure would be used to retaliate against newspapers that were critical of the military or the government. Congress eventually backed down.[63]

Thrasher also investigated complaints from Atlanta newspapers that they were not receiving association reports in a timely fashion. "This I found to arise from the peculiar manner of working the telegraph office at Macon," he told the directors. Press reports had to go through the Macon telegraph office to get to Montgomery, and it was only after the reports were copied by the newspapers there and retransmitted to Macon that they were forwarded to Atlanta.

"I endeavored to remedy this delay, by causing the Press at Macon to furnish the telegraph operator with paper to make manifold copies, I supplying him with carbonized sheets therefore, which, as they could not be purchased, I had manufactured for the purpose in Augusta," Thrasher's report stated. "I regret to say, that the old evil is not entirely broken up, and the subject requires still further attention from me."[64]

An unscrupulous wire service agent in Mobile who was selling association dispatches to "private clubs" constituted another of Thrasher's major problems early in his tenure. The agent was not only selling the dispatches to private individuals and pocketing the money, he was selling the stories at a lower rate than subscribing newspapers paid. Thrasher first realized that something was wrong when he asked for an accounting of monies collected by the agent from newspapers in Alabama, Tennessee, and Mississippi. He collected further evidence when he traveled to Jackson, Mississippi. Thrasher discovered similar arrangements in Tennessee and South Carolina. Not long before a director's meeting, he had received "an application to permit the establishment, or the continuance, I do not know which, of one in Virginia." In all, he uncovered a dozen such clubs and ordered the sale of dispatches to them terminated immediately.[65] The

Atlanta in ruins after the mayor surrendered on September 2, 1864.
Photograph from the Library of Congress

sale of the news dispatches led to the press association's inauguration of copy-righting the material.

As the war moved south from Tennessee into his back yard, Thrasher was forced to personally glean news of battles from soldiers returning to Atlanta and whatever other sources he could find, a process that led to unreliable news stories. In covering the campaigns for Chattanooga and Atlanta, Thrasher saw for himself how difficult it was to obtain accurate information, having to resort to whatever sources became available for even second-hand information, such as interviews with returning wounded soldiers.[66]

When Atlanta surrendered to Federal troops on September 2, 1864, Thrasher fled to Macon, where the news of the fall was transmitted to member newspapers

General William T. Sherman's Atlanta headquarters. Illustration from *Frank Leslie's Illustrated Newspaper,* October 29, 1864

two days later. Thrasher had been unable to get in touch with any reporters in Atlanta, all of whom had apparently left the city by then. Thrasher also packed his bags and left on September 5 for Texas, where he planned to reorganize from the Trans-Mississippi Region.[67]

In spite of optimistic reports distributed from Richmond by the press association, the end was in sight, and Thrasher never revived the association. Instead, he moved to New York where he edited *Frank Leslie's Ilustracion Americana* for several years.[68] He moved back to Galveston, Texas, in 1869, where he became one of the editors and owners of the *Galveston Civilian* newspaper. He was elected to the Board of Aldermen in 1871, and in that capacity would help entertain *New York Tribune* Editor Horace Greeley when he visited Galveston.

Thrasher died on November 10, 1879. He is buried in Galveston's Magnolia Grove Cemetery.[69]

Louisiana

A soldier rests in a Louisiana Swamp. *Harper's Weekly,* May 9, 1863. Courtesy of Rare Books and Special Collections, University of South Carolina Libraries

AFTER LOUISIANA JOINED THE CONFEDERACY ON JANUARY 26, HER citizens flocked to enlist and serve their new nation as it sought its freedom from the Union. One of the wealthiest states before the Civil War, Louisiana suffered grievously as one of the war's key battlegrounds. More than 500 battles and skirmishes were recorded as the state felt the effects of massive offensives by the Union, both on land and by sea.

The state lay prostate and devastated after the fall of New Orleans, the South's largest city, and the Federal takeover of the Mississippi River. By most estimates, the state lost much of her wealth by the time the South surrendered.

Louisiana correspondents who reported in such theaters of war as Pensacola, Florida, the Virginia battlefronts, and Vicksburg along the Mississippi lost their home newspaper bases when New Orleans fell by May 1, 1862. Newspapers such as the *New Orleans Daily Delta* and the *New Orleans Picayune* were taken over by the Union army, leaving Durant da Ponte, a correspondent for the *Delta* and an important political figure in the city, without a voice. Another New Orleans reporter, Henry Perry, also lost his voice at the *Picayune*. Both were covering the Confederate campaign in Virginia when New Orleans fell.

By the time da Ponte was 14 years old, he was working at the *Crescent* newspaper in New Orleans. Da Ponte clearly had a gift for writing and became an editor the next year at the *Daily Delta*.

Once the war started, da Ponte began identifying his reports to the *Daily Delta* under the pen name "D," offering a view of his strong secessionist views. *Daily Delta* newspaper files have been lost, and few of his writings survive. However, in a stroke of good fortune, a young New Orleans girl, Clara Solomon, kept a diary that reflected his whereabouts and writing activities through the early part of the war.

Da Ponte covered the war in Virginia through part of 1862. However, as the fall of New Orleans loomed, he returned to the city where he served as an adviser to the mayor. Da Ponte helped surrender the city to Union forces before he fled north to Virginia as a Confederate soldier.

Meanwhile, as the war began, Perry joined other Southern correspondents in Pensacola, awaiting the outcome of the standoff over the future of Fort Pickens, which guarded the entrance to Pensacola Bay. Writing under the pen name "H.P.," Perry often wrote multiple articles for the *Picayune*. His first reports appeared in the newspaper in May 1861 when he wrote from Pensacola about the Louisiana troops stationed there. Perry followed the Louisianans to Virginia, where he was embedded with the Louisiana troops and continued reporting for the *Picayune*. When New Orleans fell to Federal troops on May 1, 1862, Perry continued reporting for the *Memphis Daily Appeal*. He was a strong Confederate sympathizer who wrote for both newspapers in exaggerated and positive terms.

19

Durant da Ponte: Clara's Eyes and Ears on the War

Nancy McKenzie Dupont

LIKE OTHER SOUTHERN CORRESPONDENTS, DURANT DA PONTE OF THE *New Orleans Daily Delta* followed Confederate troops into the Civil War brimming with optimism. From the beginning of the war until the fall of New Orleans in 1862, he kept his readers informed of the battles and troop movements in Virginia. Although the Civil War was a significant chapter in da Ponte's life, it was far from the only one. He filled his 62 years with dramatic twists and turns, international intrigue, and unprecedented money-making, with only 14 months of formal education.

Although da Ponte did not report the most decisive battles of the war, his dispatches provided New Orleanians with first-hand descriptions of the skirmishes of the early war and with the increasingly discouraging news of Confederate failures. However, with the fall of New Orleans to the Union navy in May 1862, da Ponte lost his home newspaper base, and his readers lost their window on the war in Virginia.

Because da Ponte was a member of a prominent family, much is known of his life. Unfortunately, he left no papers or writing other than his newspaper reports. However, in a fortunate twist of fate, a treasure trove of information on da Ponte and his Civil War activities can be found in a diary kept by a teenager who was a devoted newspaper reader. Sixteen-year-old Clara Solomon began keeping a diary in April 1861, just before she watched New Orleans volunteers march off to Virginia to fight for the Confederacy. Clara was the second oldest of six daughters in a family of Sephardic Jews who considered themselves Southern aristocrats.[1] The Solomons kept their Jewish traditions but mixed with fellow aristocrats of all religions, ensuring that Clara's diary entries are based on observations of a wide spectrum of New Orleans 19th century life. She filled her diary with comments demonstrating that she was sociable and intelligent, gossipy as well as keenly analytical, fun-loving yet sensitive. Because

Durant da Ponte. Courtesy of Princeton
University Press

she interacted with other people so frequently and wrote of those interactions
with such detail, Clara provided a rich document of the daily concerns in the
Confederacy's largest city.

The diary's value to journalism historians is extraordinary. Clara and her
older sister, Alice, were voracious consumers of newspapers, and Clara wrote
frequently of their anticipation of obtaining daily papers by delivery and by purchase on the streets. Clara's diary indicates that she devoured the newspapers,
and she wrote extensively of their content and her reactions to them. The journalism historian, by reading the newspapers and Clara's responses, can observe
the full cycle of the mass communication process that existed in 19th century
life. It is only one person's reaction to the news, but it is detailed and thorough.

One detail of the origin of Clara's diary makes its story even more enticing
to the journalism historian. The diary was a gift from da Ponte, then an editor
for the *Daily Delta*. Da Ponte began his reports on the fighting in Virginia in
the same month Clara began writing in her dairy. She wrote to Philomen, the
name she gave to her diary, of da Ponte's dispatches from the front. Da Ponte
was back in New Orleans as the city fell to the Union in 1862. He became an
adviser to the mayor and possessed information that helped the Solomons stay
safe in dangerous days. Years later, da Ponte became a member of the Solomon
family through marriage, completing the circle historians are so fond of finding
in their research.[2]

Clara Solomon and Durant da Ponte were members of the Southern elite, and
da Ponte also numbered among his ancestors individuals who were both rich
(at times) and famous (and infamous at times). His grandfather was Lorenzo

Da Ponte, the librettist for Wolfgang Amadeus Mozart's three famous operas, *The Marriage of Figaro*, *Don Giovanni*, and *Cosi fan tutte*. Lorenzo was born Emanuele Conegliano in Ceneda, a small town north of Venice, in 1749. He was a Jew, but in 1763, his widowed father wanted to marry a Christian and his entire family was converted and given the surname Da Ponte by the presiding bishop.[3] Although the name was originally spelled Da Ponte, some members of the family, including Durant da Ponte, later lower-cased da Ponte. Lorenzo became a priest, but his debauchery and friendship with Casanova soon landed him in trouble with Rome, and he wandered away from a celibate life and, eventually, into a happy marriage.[4]

Lorenzo claimed that his childhood education was lacking,[5] but he used it as the foundation of a life filled with accomplishments. After his success with Mozart, Lorenzo fell on hard times and eventually immigrated to New York. He failed in business, but he met Clement Moore, author of the *Night Before Christmas*, in a New York bookstore. Moore encouraged Da Ponte to begin teaching Italian. He taught private lessons and later claimed in his *Memoirs* that the demand for his services soon overwhelmed him.[6] In 1825, he was appointed a professor of Italian at Columbia College, later Columbia University.[7] He died in New York in 1838.

Durant's father, who was Lorenzo's son, Lorenzo Luigi Da Ponte, died of consumption only two years later. He had been gravely ill since before his father's death. Lorenzo Luigi had been hired as a professor of Italian by Washington College in Chestertown, Maryland, in 1826. That same year, he married Cornelia Durant, a sister of the wealthy New Orleans lawyer Thomas J. Durant and a niece of President James Monroe.[8] A few months later, the college burned; Lorenzo Luigi went to Philadelphia and eventually returned to New York. On February 16, 1832,[9] Lorenzo and Cornelia had a baby, Durant, who would be their only child to survive to adulthood. One year later, Lorenzo wrote *A History of the Florentine Republic and of the Age of Rule of the Medici*. He also translated his father's operas into English and wrote an Italian grammar book and a dictionary.[10]

Sometime between his father's death and his own, Lorenzo Luigi took his wife and son to Kentucky and southern Illinois, where Durant attended school for 14 months.[11] The family then moved to New Orleans to the home of Cornelia's father and her brother, a well-established attorney.[12] In his early teens, Durant joined the staff of the *New Orleans Crescent*, where he probably met and worked with Walt Whitman.[13] Displaying a gift for writing, which his grandfather and father possessed, and a gift for business, which neither ancestor could claim, Durant da Ponte became an editor of the *Crescent* and then worked for the *New Orleans Daily Delta* during his teen years.

But the West was calling, and before he turned 15, Durant enlisted in the U.S. Army to fight in the Mexican War. He was among the troops that infiltrated

Monterrey after the city fell to the Americans in September 1846. On February 15, 1847, he began working for the *American Pioneer*, an English-language newspaper that had been set up by the occupation forces in Monterrey. Da Ponte was listed as publisher and associate editor.[14] When the war ended the next year, he returned to New Orleans and the *Daily Delta*.

On January 9, 1850, the *Daily Picayune* reported the marriage of Durant da Ponte and Sophia Brooke.[15] Although she may have never known it, "Sophie" da Ponte became the subject of gossip and intrigue in Clara Solomon's diary. And Clara certainly never imagined that, although Sophie would be the first Mrs. Durant da Ponte, Clara's sister, Rosa, only four years old at the outbreak of the Civil War, would become his second wife.

Durant da Ponte may have had limited formal schooling, but he brought intelligence to his position with the *Daily Delta*. He spoke seven languages, translated poetry, and was a talented watercolor artist. At the outbreak of the Civil War, da Ponte was considered worldly and scholarly with a keen understanding of politics. Because of the lack of bylines in pre-war newspapers, the historian has a difficult time pinpointing da Ponte's exact political views, but it is clear that the *Daily Delta* was strongly pro-secession.[16] Once the war began, da Ponte began identifying his reports and columns, giving historians solid evidence that he was strongly pro-South.

In June 1861, da Ponte set out for Virginia to join two other *Daily Delta* correspondents, D.C. Jenkins and Louis Montgomery.[17] Virginia had seceded in late May, and President Jefferson Davis had assembled troops there in anticipation of a Union attack.[18] The *Daily Delta* published da Ponte's first dispatch on June 8. In his first paragraph, da Ponte describes a beautiful woman he met during a 12-hour train change in Huntsville, Alabama. He also described troop movements he observed along the way and the enthusiasm for the Confederacy he observed in every city and town.

> From Huntsville to Lynchburg, all along the line of the road, you see the same enthusiasm that pervades the people farther South. Even in East Tennessee the flag of the Confederacy greets you at every station while after entering Virginia the people seem to be absolutely frantic with military ardor. From every house, as the cars pass along, men, women, and children, white and black, rush out and cheer the passing soldiers, and wave their hats and handkerchiefs—and such as possess neither of those articles have recourse to their coats.[19]

Da Ponte concluded by reassuring the people of New Orleans that the enemy's strength had been overestimated. Clara Solomon may not have read da Ponte's first dispatch. She complained to her diary on June 18 that her family wasn't receiving the *Daily Delta* and instead was reading its competition, the *Crescent*. She predicted the arrangement would be short-lived because she was attached to the *Daily Delta*, her "former friend."[20] And clearly she wanted to

Richmond, Virginia, was the seat of the Confederate government and bustled with commerce during the Civil War. Photo from the Library of Congress

read da Ponte's dispatches: "I wonder how 'Durant' is! I have scarcely bestowed a single thought on him since his departure. I wonder if in his journal, if he has ever kept any, I would see the same thing of us? I have not the slightest idea that I wouldn't. And that man's promises! Why, I regard them as 'trifles light as air.'"[21]

A week later, Clara again wrote playfully of da Ponte. A letter from correspondent Jenkins warned of an imminent battle near Winchester, Virginia. "The city (Richmond) has been thick with rumors this evening of brisk and continuous skirmishing."[22] Jenkins concluded with a plan to travel to Manassas Junction with "your Mr. DaP."[23] Clara took note and told Philomen, "What nice times they are having . . . They are enjoying themselves!"[24]

Clara may have been correct. If one can enjoy watching a war unfold, da Ponte had the opportunity to do it. He was in Virginia to report on the actions of the Confederate army. In his articles, he also defended the troops and

Southern citizens and attacked Northern journalists for their reporting on one battle.[25] "The *New York Herald*, with its usual mendacity, asserts that we had 30 rifle cannon in battery, and 168 12 pound howitzers and one rifle cannon. The fact is, we had but four pieces in front . . . ," he wrote.[26]

Da Ponte wrote of the kindness of a Virginia family he identified only as Crandell, who buried two Union soldiers whose bodies had been abandoned by their comrades. "A wounded man crept into an outhouse where he was found by Mrs. C., who supplied him with food and water, but her humane efforts were ineffectual to preserve his life. Before his death, he deplored the "insensate folly which had allured him to abandon his wife and children, and incited him to participate in a wicked assault upon a people who had never harmed either him or his country."[27] This was the beginning of a series of examples da Ponte would use to illustrate the Northern folly in fighting the South. The story, indeed all of da Ponte's letter, thrilled Clara.

> D's' letter was excellent to day. It was teeming with him. A superabundance of large words, for our benefit, I presume. In one part of it, I just imagined that I saw him, with his head resting upon his hands, studying about the rain.[28]

It is unusual in journalism history to find a reader imagining what a journalist was doing as he wrote a story, a story that was read and commented on in a diary.

Da Ponte's reporting contained a distinctly Southern bias designed to bolster the spirits of the readers back home. Still, although most of his reporting was of skirmishes rather than full battles, da Ponte had to report on Confederate defeats. He described the Southern defeat at Philippi, Virginia (now West Virginia), as "unaccompanied with any disgraceful features. Our men fought bravely, and although driven from their positions by overwhelming forces, turned at bay and repelled their assailants whenever the pursuit became close and threatening."[29]

For a few days, Clara seemed to become bored with the *Daily Delta*'s contents as she busied herself with household and social duties. Da Ponte had much to write about, however. The Confederate army had been defeated at Philippi, and da Ponte set about to bolster the spirits of his readers despite news of the loss. He wrote that the Confederate army would soon march through Union strongholds and overtake cities in the North. "If there has been for us a night of darkness it is succeeded by the dawning of a brilliant day," da Ponte wrote. He dismissed the defeat with a passage in Italian from *Dante's Inferno*, translated as: "Therefore we went out to see the stars once more."[30]

Da Ponte reported from Norfolk on June 29 that the enemy was concentrating troops at Fortress Monroe and that the Confederates were impatient for a fight. But no battle was predicted. "Our troops . . . are beginning to believe that, after all, there may be no contest in this vicinity, and that the end of the

Interior of Fortress Monroe at Old Point Comfort, Virginia. *Harper's Weekly,* February 9, 1861. Courtesy of Rare Books and Special Collections, University of South Carolina Libraries

campaign will find the two armies still watching each other from the opposite shores of Hampton Roads," da Ponte wrote. [31]

Clara told her diary she had a dream about da Ponte and called it "very confused" but made no other comment. Two days later, Clara made an equally confusing diary entry when she recounted Mrs. da Ponte's exit from New Orleans. Clara had been told by a friend that Mrs. da Ponte had gone to the "springs."[32] She also wrote that a woman named Julia Murray was divorced rather than widowed, as Clara had been told. "I was astounded, as I had always been told she was a widow.—She must be very wicked. I don't like her now. I wonder if she and Mr. da P. are as good friends. They are both very bad."[33] Equally confusing, on the following day, Clara told her diary of a friend's marriage. "Poor Mr. da Ponte. He will not witness the nuptials."[34] But Clara genuinely wanted to see the correspondent: "I am right anxious to behold his physiognomy."[35] On July 7, Clara imagined how pleasant it would be to have da Ponte to lunch; on July 11, she told her diary that she had dreamed of him again.

One might conclude from some of Clara's writing that she was expressing symptoms of a "crush" on da Ponte, but it should be pointed out that Clara writes of many people, her own age, older, and younger, and that not all of her written observations can be correctly analyzed from context. The readers of Clara's diary can only deduce that she wrote teasingly of many individuals and admiringly of many as well.

Clara noticed that da Ponte's letters were absent from the *Daily Delta*. On July 14, his report explained that his absence was because no changes had occurred in the military maneuvers in Virginia. He used his space on the first page of the newspaper to speculate on the possibilities of the Lincoln government recognizing the Confederate states, which he rejected as a solution unless the security of Maryland and Missouri are considered.

> We owe a duty to our friends in Maryland and Missouri, which we must discharge at all hazards. By their sympathy to our cause, by their efforts to afford us assistance by their generous attempts to relieve us by interposing between us and the invading armies of the enemy, they have drawn down on themselves the wrath and the power of the Lincoln Government. Their soil has been invaded, their sovereignty has been assailed, and their citizens arrested and imprisoned by armed bands of sanguinary mercenaries. We cannot make peace without providing for their security.[36]

Da Ponte again wrote of a lull in the action on July 17, when he described troop positions and the geographic landscape, but his letter contained no news of military action. However, the situation seemed likely to change; Clara told her dairy that she heard from a friend that da Ponte would not return to New Orleans for some time.[37]

Meanwhile, Clara's home life was changing rapidly. Her father was making his living as a sutler, a clothing and supply dealer who sells items to the military. "Pa," as she called him, wrote frequently from Richmond. The Solomon family remained in New Orleans and was in dire need of cash. At one point, Clara ran out of space in her diary and was delayed in buying a new, blank one.[38] Worse yet, New Orleans began to suffer under the naval blockade of Southern ports ordered by Lincoln five months earlier. Da Ponte apparently took a break from writing letters to the *Daily Delta*, because the next time his writing appears in a legible extant edition of the newspaper, the First Battle of Manassas had been fought and the two armies were again in a standoff in Virginia. Da Ponte appeared to have been in New Orleans before his letters from Virginia appeared again.[39]

> For some time after the battle of Manassas, I, with others, was induced to believe that an aggressive military policy was about to be adopted by the Confederate military authorities. But circumstances, which have since come to light, show that an offensive movement, following up the victory, was utterly impracticable at the time when it could have been effective, on account of the lack of subsistence and transportation.[40]

In a published letter badly smeared before microfilming, da Ponte wrote on September 24 to analyze Confederate military strategy by comparing it with that of Napoleon Bonaparte. Although there may be no accurate account of what da Ponte wrote that day, we do have a record of what one of his readers thought of his writing: "This morning I read the paper, and tried to wade through a letter of 'D's,'" Clara wrote.

The *Daily Delta* published letters from da Ponte on September 25 and 28, but both issues of the newspaper are almost illegible. Of the lines that can be deciphered, da Ponte's concerns appeared to be the difficulty of getting accurate information in Virginia and the despair over the lack of progress by the Confederate army. "Our brilliant anticipations of speedy ascendancy . . . have been grievously disappointed. We have indulged the hope that, long before this time, the armies of the enemy would have been either captured or driven from the State," da Ponte lamented.[41] He saw depression in Richmond, too, and wrote to the *Daily Delta*:

> The Marylanders now in Richmond have been very much depressed in spirits lately, and seem to have lost confidence in a speedy redemption of their State from the tyranny of the Lincoln Government. I sincerely hope they may be mistaken and misinformed.[42]

Da Ponte's report continued with elaborate explanations for the lack of an advancing attack after the First Battle of Manassas, and his writing was earning Confederate approval. On November 4, Clara received a letter from her father who had spent time with da Ponte in Richmond. The elder Solomon described a letter to da Ponte from General P.G.T. Beauregard that complimented him on his reporting on Manassas. The letter claimed that da Ponte was serving as a volunteer, unpaid aide to General Earl Van Dorn,[43] justifying da Ponte's use of the courtesy title "Captain" by which he was known the rest of his life.

Da Ponte's letters for the remainder of 1861 are concerned with the reorganization of the Confederate army in Virginia, the weather, the constant rumors of movements that proved to be untrue, and, oddly enough, food. On November 12, da Ponte listed an entire bill of fare that he enjoyed under a tent with Louisiana officers and guests. The meal included lamb, beef, and oyster dishes, with fresh fruits and an assortment of nuts for dessert.[44] At the same time, Clara often complained of the lack of good food available in the markets of New Orleans because of the blockade. Of one dinner she wrote, "The fare was not very epicurean, for I believe the cow had reached a mature age."[45] Although Clara wrote about reading the newspaper almost daily, she did not mention da Ponte during this period.

As General George B. McClellan built up forces in his Army of the Potomac, da Ponte spent the Christmas season assuring New Orleans readers that the enemy would not succeed. He had learned, he wrote, not to believe everything he heard in the seat of the war. "I have been so often plunged into a state of profitless agitation and frantic bewilderment by reports of impending battle, that it is hard now to disturb the calm equilibrium of my skeptical equipoise," he wrote.[46]

Before the new year, da Ponte moved to Norfolk to better receive news from the North; by the middle of January, the outlook for the South had changed dramatically. Da Ponte reported the defeat of the Confederate army in Fishing Creek, Kentucky, on January 30. "We have learned that no people, however valiant they may be, however just their cause, are exempt from the changes and calamities of war," he wrote.[47] For Clara, those calamities were the constant worry about her father, waiting for his letters, and the lack of paper on which to continue her diary. Her last entry of 1861 was on November 30; she would not have a notebook again until March of 1862. By that time, Da Ponte had written his last Civil War letter to the *Daily Delta*.

Da Ponte's report of February 11, 1862, written in Richmond, was full of bad news for the Confederacy. Federal forces had overrun Roanoke Island, North Carolina, despite a gallant defense by an outnumbered Confederate force holding the island north of Cape Hatteras. "Many a Richmond household has been desolated, and grief carried to many a heart among the citizens of this city," da Ponte wrote.[48]

Da Ponte also wrote sadly of Captain O. Jennings Wise, who was mortally wounded in the small Confederate force's gallant defense of Roanoke Island. Wise was the son of the Roanoke commander, Brigadier General Henry A. Wise.

> Capt. Wise, who was wounded, and it is feared mortally, fell while combating the foe with unparalleled bravery. He was engaged in personal recontre with a number of assailants, and until his sword broke in his hand, when he prostrated one of the enemy by inflicting a blow with the hilt. The manner in which these brave men resisted the attack of overwhelming numbers reflects glory upon Virginia. Her sons have perished nobly upon the field; and if they have not secured victory, they have deserved it.[49]

The Union capture of Roanoke Island and defeat of the Confederate troops shocked the Richmond community. da Ponte wrote: "It would be idle to deny that in this city much depression has been caused by the intelligence of these events."

> Many a Richmond household has been desolated, and grief carried to many a heart among the citizens of this city. The company of Richmond Blues is stated to have been almost totally annihilated in the unequal conflict. This company was composed of young men of position in this city, and almost all of them had hosts of relations and friends here.[50]

Da Ponte reported that General Wise had protested that his troops were being sent to Roanoke on the ground that the position was indefensible against the powerful Union naval armament and the large military force with which the Union was about to assail it. "But we can all be prophets after the fact," he wrote. "It is easy or ought now to say that the Island could not be maintained, or that a far more powerful force ought to have been sent there; but it is unreasonable to anticipate continual success . . ."[51]

> It is understood today that the whole of Commodore Lynch's fleet of gunboats was captured at Elizabeth City, and that that town was burnt by the inhabitants on the approach. Capt. Lynch is a splendid officer, and did all with his vessels that they were capable of effecting . . . Nevertheless, it is impossible to dispute the fact the enemy will now have full sweep for his gunboats in the spacious sounds of the North Carolina coast, and that he will be able to destroy towns with impunity, desolate the country along the shore, and subject the inhabitants to much distress.[52]

Da Ponte wrote depressing news about the intentions of the Union army, predicting that the Federals would attack Weldon to try to sever Confederate railroad communication with the South by that route.

> This danger, combined with that which apparently menaces the other great line, where the enemy have made a demonstration caused an uneasy feeling in the public mind. It seems to be the design of the enemy to shut up our army in Virginia and to gain a victory over it by the inglorious process of starvation.[53]

Da Ponte's activities became difficult to pinpoint after mid-February. On March 14, Clara told her diary that Mr. and Mrs. da Ponte had visited the Solomon home while she was at school. But, as usual, Clara recorded detail and emotion. "A (her sister Alice) is impressed with the idea that she (Mrs. da Ponte) is affected, and consequently does not admire her as much as formerly," she wrote to her diary Philemon. She also wrote that the Confederate regiment would return to New Orleans in a few days. Clara was nothing if not confident in Southern success.[54]

A few weeks later, da Ponte again visited the Solomon home, this time alone and "very ill." His exact illness wasn't recorded, although Clara said he was complaining of a headache and was carrying ammonium carbonate. Despite his malady, da Ponte came with news for the Solomons, and it was the worst the family could possibly imagine: The Yankees were coming and could have control of New Orleans within a few weeks. Clara was panicked, and confided her fears to her diary.

> Then what a miserable state of existence to be governed by Yankee devils. Oh! God! It is too terrible to contemplate . . . And the women—they will have to protect themselves. Oh! we are in the midst of dangerous times. Will it ever come, when the Federal flag will be waving in our city. Oh! God, avert such a calamity.[55]

The Battle of New Orleans. Courtesy Library of Congress

Two days later, Admiral David Farragut sailed up the Mississippi River toward New Orleans in command of 11 Union vessels. Confederate forces fired on the vessels for about 30 minutes, but as Farragut described it, it was a "dash and a victory."[56] Unknown New Orleanians set fire to the port, and Farragut found it all—ships, cargo, and docks—engulfed in flames. Following an afternoon rainstorm, Farragut ordered one of his officers to find city officials and demand surrender.[57]

Da Ponte was already closeted with Mayor John T. Monroe, preparing a response.[58] All or part or none of the mayor's official statement may have been written by da Ponte. The only certainty is that the words displayed da Ponte's firm resolve against the enemy.

> I beg you to understand that the people of New Orleans, while unable at this
> moment to prevent you from occupying this city, do not transfer their allegiance
> from the government of their choice to one which they have deliberately repudi
> ated, and that they yield simply that obedience which the conqueror is enabled to
> extort from the occupied.[59]

Days of confusion, violence, and anger followed before Union General Benjamin "Beast" Butler arrived in New Orleans and, with General David Port,

New Orleans Market. *Harper's Weekly*, January 24, 1863. Courtesy of Rare Books and Special Collections, University of South Carolina Libraries

secured the city for the conquerors.[60] Meanwhile, da Ponte spent at least part of his time helping the Solomon family assure their own safety.

Clara found herself in the middle of the chaos and wrote of her family's indecision about what to do as they sought advice from neighbors and friends. "You can imagine the state of downtown. They had seen different people, went different places, and had been advised differently, by some to remain, by others to leave the city," she wrote.[61] She indicated that the *Daily Delta* had advised evacuation. Da Ponte had procured a "transport" for Mrs. Solomon and told her to leave the city with her children and join her husband in Virginia. The Solomons had several other visits from da Ponte, who informed them that Farragut had given women and children 48 hours to leave the city.

The Solomons stayed in New Orleans, but da Ponte decided to leave. Clara wrote, "He was so despondent, so sad. He gave us an account of the events of the day and the tears in the eyes of men, as our flag was lowered. He held the consultation with the Fed. Officers. I pitied him for I knew his feelings."[62] The following day, Clara and da Ponte said good-bye, with the reporter promising to find Clara's father to convince him to return to New Orleans.

Da Ponte's only plan was to get to Jefferson Davis, even though he didn't know where he was. Clara confided to her diary her gratitude to da Ponte. "I must not here fail to express our thanks to him for his kind attention during our late struggles," she wrote. "But for his kindness we would have been isolated, deserted, and we appreciate it. Oh! so highly, and hope at some future time to repay it but under more pleasant circumstances."[63]

Two weeks earlier, da Ponte's beloved *Daily Delta* was shut down by the Union forces in New Orleans. Clara was indignant and copied the order from headquarters into her diary: "The office of that paper will be taken possession of and its business conducted under direction of the U.S. authorities." For the young Confederate, the war was far from over. She wrote, "The taking of this city and the burning of our cotton will be the making of our Confederacy, for it will show the foreign nationals that we are in earnest and willing to make any sacrifices."[64] Although there would be further sacrifices, there would be no victory for the cause of da Ponte and the young diarist.

Da Ponte returned to the seat of the war in Virginia, but his exact activities at this point are unclear. His obituary reported that he was severely injured at the Battle of Seven Pines on May 31–June 1, 1862. He was taken to Richmond but escaped as McClellan's army advanced toward the city.[65]

After he recovered from his injuries, on October 2, 1862, da Ponte volunteered for the Confederate army and was assigned to serve as captain and assistant quartermaster to General John B. Magruder. Late in 1863, da Ponte was ordered to Cuba to buy munitions; he was chosen for the job because he was fluent in both French and Spanish. Da Ponte bought an unknown quantity of arms and put them on two ships bound for Texas. Near the mouth of the Rio Grande, French forces seized the ships. Da Ponte was then ordered to Mexico to try to negotiate their release. He returned to Cuba with the arms and gave them to Major Charles Helm. Whether they reached the Confederacy isn't known, but it is unlikely since da Ponte found himself stranded in Cuba, unable to get back to General Magruder because Union forces were occupying the river bank along the Rio Grande. Da Ponte requested and was given orders to report to Richmond.[66]

Da Ponte returned to the fighting with General Lee's Army of Northern Virginia. He is believed to have fought in some of the final battles of the war, one of which was probably the Battle of Sayler's Creek, which led Lee to the conclusion that the Confederacy must surrender. It is not known whether da Ponte was present or nearby on April 9, 1865, when Lee surrendered at Appomattox Courthouse, Virginia. But in a twist of either coincidence or luck, da Ponte was able to translate a long friendship with General Ulysses S. Grant into a personal pardon from the U.S. government.[67]

Clara Solomon married shortly after the end of the Civil War, although she would be widowed by 1867. She was remarried to Dr. George Lawrence in 1872 and had four daughters.[68] The family spent time in New Orleans and Hot Springs, Arkansas; but Clara was living with her children in New Orleans at the time of her death in 1907.

Da Ponte's wife Sophie died, and at the age of 50, he remarried a much younger woman: Rosa Solomon, age 23, Clara's younger sister. Da Ponte left the newspaper business, made a fortune selling stocks and real estate, and built a

Durant da Ponte near the end of his
life, Pen and Ink drawing from the *New
Orleans Picayune*, August 8, 1894

mansion called Roselawn on St. Charles Avenue. The house featured an entire
theater where Rosa starred in plays. Rosa da Ponte was the toast of New Orleans society, and she and her husband traveled extensively. In a bizarre event,
Rosa was kidnapped while the couple was in Cairo, Egypt, but she was released
with the assistance of the American consul. Da Ponte was so taken with Rosa's
beauty that he named some of his land on St. Charles Avenue "Rosa Park." To-
day, it is a private street, lined with mansions.

Da Ponte died at his summer residence in Alameda, California, at age 62.
His obituary appeared in the *Daily Picayune* on August 8, 1894; the news was
conveyed to New Orleans by telegraph. His family, including his sons by Sophie
and Rosa's sister Clara, gathered at Roselawn to share their grief.[69]

Da Ponte's son Harry became a cotton merchant in New Orleans and had
at least five children. One child, William Graham, lived only six months, and
is buried in Lafayette Cemetery in New Orleans with a tombstone that reads
"our baby." Another son, Harry Jr., worked for Adler Export Company in New
Orleans. Yet another of Harry's sons, the second Durant Da Ponte, became a
professor of English literature at the University of Tennessee and was killed in
a United Airlines plane crash in 1964 when he was 45 years old. His daughter,
Graham, became an attorney practicing in New Orleans. The first of Durant's

sons with Rosa, Thomas Serrill da Ponte, extended the family tradition by becoming a New Orleans newspaper reporter.

Durant da Ponte is one of the 157 names inscribed on the Civil War Correspondents monument at Gathland Park, Maryland, but his coverage of the war does not include any of the decisive battles that dashed all Confederate hopes later in the war. However, his writing does provide graphic accounts of Louisiana troops who marched into battle when hopes of a Confederate victory were high and when the first realities of war were introduced to the young secessionists.

Da Ponte's writing, together with Clara's diary, gives Civil War historians a picture of the war rarely seen: descriptions of battles and the reaction of the reader. It is this picture of battlefront and home front that moves Americans closer to understanding the role played by newspapers in the South's unsuccessful effort to secede from the Union.

20

Henry H. Perry:
Confederate Apologist and Reporter

Jinx Coleman Broussard and Skye Chance Cooley

Readers knew him primarily as "H.P." as they began reading his stories in May 1861 in the *New Orleans Daily Picayune*. It is difficult to definitively identify the Major Henry H. Perry who signed stories only with his initials, for he was like many full-time Civil War correspondents who used pen names or cryptic acronyms to mask their identities in case of capture.[1] It is clear that the man using the abbreviation H.P. had knowledge of New Orleans and Louisiana and was well acquainted with Louisiana troops, constantly referring to regiments from the state as "our boys."[2]

In one of his earlier dispatches following the skirmishes at Fort Pickens in Pensacola, Florida, en route to report on the Louisiana 6th, 7th, and 8th regiments heading to Virginia, Perry demonstrated his knowledge of Louisiana's military advancements leading up to the war when he favorably compared the troop movements of North Carolinians following secession to that of Louisiana's early troop movements. "Like ourselves," he wrote, "they seized every fort and stronghold on the coast, and prudently went to work to put out every approach by sea in a perfect state of defence [sic], so that now an invasion from that quarter is believed to be impossible. They also (like Louisiana and the Washington Artillery) seized upon the well fed arsenal."[3]

Major Henry H. Perry saw the war firsthand while embedded with frontline troops, and he had some access to high-ranking military officials for the first half of the war: 1861-1862. Yet little is known of his movements or activities during the latter half of the war. Perry's accounts for the *Daily Picayune* and later the *Memphis Daily Appeal* have brought historians to consider him a significant correspondent, yet it is difficult to know him beyond his writings.

Military service records available at libraries, archives, and special collections in Louisiana do not have a certified death or pension record for a Major Henry H. Perry that would be consistent with the years in which Perry lived.

Perry followed the Louisiana regiments into Virginia after the skirmishes at Fort Pickens, Florida. *Harper's Weekly*, April 20, 1861. Courtesy of Rare Books and Special Collections, University of South Carolina Libraries

The Soldier and Sailor Civil War Database and U.S. Armed Forces records for both Union and Confederate soldiers during and after the war do not list Perry.

The elusive Perry may not have hailed from Louisiana, since no birth, marriage, or death records in the Louisiana State Archives, or at churches and synagogues in the state, show any supporting evidence of a Major Henry H. Perry, Henry H. Perry, Major H. Perry, H.H. Perry, or Henry Perry who lived during the time frame and had the work skills necessary to be H.P. Other evidence did not link anyone bearing a similar name to the H.P. who wrote for the *Picayune*. Most records for the *Picayune* prior to 1878 were turned over to Tulane University and subsequently destroyed during Hurricane Katrina, complicating the search for Perry's background. Hence, Perry is only known through the newspaper.

Before New Orleans fell to the Union and into late April 1862, the *Daily Picayune* often ran multiple articles by Perry in each issue. After that event and the subsequent loss of the Confederate-run newspaper, Perry began writing for the *Memphis Daily Appeal* and continued until after the paper moved to Grenada, Mississippi, on June 6, 1862. Research revealed no articles by H.P. following the *Appeal*'s move to Jackson, Mississippi.

Perry was indisputably a Confederate sympathizer and, one could argue, a propagandist who described virtually everything Confederate in positive and exaggerated terms. His first report about the war appeared on May 12, 1861, when he commented on the health and spirit of Louisiana troops in Pensacola during their movements under General Braxton Bragg. Perry praised the "great souls of our brave men who have accomplished so much."[4]

However, Union occupation of Fort Pickens continued to frustrate Bragg's Confederate forces, and the prospect of a major battle began to loom on the horizon for the state of Virginia. Perry joined the Louisiana regiments traveling north. Along the way, he filed reports filled with his romantic notions of war, the beauty of the Southern landscape, and the heroics of all people from all the states within the newly formed Confederate borders. His dispatch from Weldon, North Carolina, in the early days of the war is an example of how Perry constructed an optimistic view of the military superiority and genius of the Confederacy. He wrote:

> Of all the States through which I have passed from the banks of the Mississippi here, the good "old North State" seems best prepared for the great struggle before us. Never before have I seen so much military enthusiasm among any people; never, withal, a people who manifested a spirit so calm, so firm, and so determined. From the mountains to the seashore the whole State is in arms . . .[5]

Another letter in the May 28, 1861 issue of the *Daily Picayune* found Perry offering encouragement as Union and Confederate armies gathered in Virginia. The prospect of battle increased daily, with Northern troops aggressively invading the South in response to the Confederate attack on Fort Sumter. A number of smaller skirmishes[6] were preludes to what was to come, and Perry, like many Confederate generals and sympathizers, hoped that the Washington Artillery of New Orleans would arrive before any major engagement began. "It is to be hoped that the Washington Artillery will be in time," Perry wrote. "It would again baptize the arms of Louisiana in eternal baptism to turn the tide of battle in this, the first field of our new war of independence."[7]

Perry's pride in "our boys" from Louisiana conveyed a desire to reassure distant readers and families how the soldiers were faring. Leading up to the First Battle of Manassas, Perry described the 6th, 7th, and 8th regiments of Louisiana troops as being "in excellent spirits and health" and confident of victory.[8] One reason for the bountiful spring of Louisiana pride is that Louisiana was highly represented in the Confederacy, accounting for more than 23,000 enlisted troops, or 14 percent of Confederate troops, in November 1861.[9] Perry described the numbers of Louisiana troops in Virginia by calling for even more volunteers.

> Therefore I say send forward the troops in such numbers as can be spared, and as rapidly as possible. It is having a great moral effect. I know what Louisiana has already done. In proportion to her population she has already more men in the field than any other State. And yet she can do more, and more is expected of her. In particular our famous battalion of artillery is looked for with breathless interest.[10]

Evidence suggests that Perry's accounts of what transpired during the war, especially on the battlefield, were often inaccurate or, at the very least, misleading.

In fact, there was quite a distinction between the way he reported on battlefield events and that of other, more cautious and objective journalists. While correspondents such as Durant da Ponte of the *New Orleans Delta* warned readers not to put much stock in the outcome of small-scale skirmishes, Perry made completely contrasting statements following such events.[11] He declared on one occasion: "I do not believe. . .that on a fair field our men can be whipped by double their number. They cannot be whipped at all. They certainly have not been yet."[12]

By June 1, 1861, Perry was reporting from Richmond and, true to his customary style, he had great things to say about the arrival of the Washington Artillery: "They have had a long and tedious journey, but every man of them looks well (over) fifty percent better than when I saw them at over two weeks ago. Their journey was a perfect ovation all the way."[13]

Although the journey of the Washington Artillery was described in other accounts as joyous, the company was certainly not "well over fifty percent better" than when Perry had seen them a week earlier. According to an account by one of the Washington Artillery soldiers, two soldiers identified as "Lane and Carl" died of heat exhaustion during the march out of Baton Rouge, and soldiers complained about delays and poor transportation and lodging throughout much of the journey to Virginia.[14]

Because all of Perry's correspondence came in the first half of the war, his sentiments of optimism, joy, and pride reflected early Confederate success and were thereby more warranted, especially after the decisive Confederate victory in the first major battle at Manassas Junction. He was an eyewitness to the action in that campaign.[15] Confederate troops were invariably successful in battle, according to Perry, and generals were "handsome" and "brilliant."[16] Reporting after the First Battle of Manassas, Perry characterized it as an "important victory" and "the first step in a movement which will result in the expulsion of the invaders from the sacred soil of Virginia. Our army is in a most splendid condition and equal to almost anything."[17] The victory at Manassas would remain Perry's constant reference point for all future battles.

Although Manassas was a decisive Confederate victory, general reports from the battlefield agreed upon missteps, blunders, and some disorganization on the side of the Confederate forces that could have been costly in terms of the battle outcome or Confederate lives lost. H.P. took exception to any error on the part of what he termed "brilliant" Confederate leaders, and he went to great lengths to disprove any report to the contrary. "I notice there are still many misapprehensions abroad concerning the great and memorable battle of the [July] 21," he wrote, and Perry protested that some people asserted that the Confederacy was "fairly whipped."

> There is not a word of truth in this. The misapprehension, however, to many is natural, especially to such as might have belonged to regiments which were

temporarily beaten back or for various reasons were ordered to fall back, during the long and hard fought engagement with an enemy vastly our superior in numbers. Such persons saw only a portion of that bloody day's work, that in which they themselves were engaged, and their misapprehension is natural. To the general observer, also, who was not personally acquainted with the latest movements of the enemy and the plans of Gen. Beauregard, which were from necessity constantly being changed—were even changed on the field of battle, there were many movements which seemed unusual. To explain these I must impress upon the reader's mind, as I have sought to do so before, the fact that our line of defence, from the opening to the end of the battle, extended over a space of at least fifteen miles on Bull's Run, taking in all its windings.[18]

From his perch in Richmond, Perry characterized as "fugitives"[19] the mounting enemy forces and the volunteers from the North who came together in units such as the Maryland Guard. They were incompetent and weak, according to the correspondent. Keeping up a steady verbal attack on the Union soldier, Perry, reporting from Yorktown, observed that nothing was to be feared of the Union soldier, for he was "doubly a coward who is driven by fear of losing caste at home, to engage in a war which his better feelings cannot approve."[20]

Perry sought to reassure his readers, pointing out that most of the Union soldiers had returned home "disgusted" and had been replaced "by real mercenaries, who, having no interest whatever in the war," had "sold themselves for plunder on a mere soldiers pay. Very many of them are un-naturalized foreigners, and all of them the worst rabble that prey upon the North."[21]

Perry's reports remained positive as he covered events that included the movement of the Confederates to Centreville where the soldiers cut trees for fires and built earthworks for winter encampment. Union troops were becoming more organized as the volunteer and draftee forces became better trained. In addition, the Confederate troops were poorly equipped for a Virginia winter, without enough clothes or supplies, and the work ahead of securing fortifications was an unpleasant one. Confederate General Joseph E. Johnston retreated to Centreville where it was easier to construct and defend a fort and offered a defendable position from both the enemy and the cold. A member of the 7th Virginia Infantry described the bitter process of constructing the new defense positions.

> . . . the Army of Northern Virginia soon made Centreville what Fairfax Courthouse had been and the fields around were converted into drill grounds for thousands of Confederate soldiers. Engineers were soon at work; forts, breastworks, rifle pits and batteries, marked the high points around. Regular details from every regiment in the army were daily made for ditching and digging, and the adjacent country for miles around became alive with men. The big balloon of the enemy appeared often in the direction of the Courthouse, and, no doubt, its occupants

took the Southern army for a large body of sappers and miners, as men and officers for days and weeks were in the [ditch].[22]

In retreating, Johnston had given up ground to the Union. Despite this outcome, the difficult process of moving, and the dreary task of rebuilding fortifications ahead, Perry described the withdrawal by noting the "excitement of the townspeople" in receiving the incoming soldiers and the "picturesque movements of the midnight march" of October 15–16.[23] One of Perry's first dispatches following the retreat to Centreville came on February 2, 1862, from Petersburg, Virginia.

Despite the retreat only a few months prior, a cold and unforgiving winter, and a mounting Union army, Perry tried to maintain good spirits and put minds at ease, pointing out that it was very quiet at Roanoke Island and that Burnside and his army of 30,000 men were "evidently at a loss which way to move and the commander does not appear to see his way clear to any point, either to the rear of Norfolk direct or to the seaboard road by the nearest route."[24]

Ever the optimist, Perry concluded: "It is probable therefore, that this expedition like that of Butler to Hatteras will ultimately come to naught."[25] A few days later, on February 6, 1862, Perry again echoed the sentiments of reassurance, yet with a tinge of caution rarely present in his writings. He explained that the Union had sent all available resources in the country to the West, making it "the real seat of the war." As if seeking to add reassurance, he wrote:

> If our new lines are maintained there, I see no danger ahead: and that they will be the spirit in the Southwest and the presence of Gen. Beauregard are, to me, ample security. They must indeed be maintained. Everything depends upon it. There is no such word as 'fail.' The forcing of our lines there would be such a disaster as would prolong the war indefinitely.[26]

Unfortunately for Perry and the other Confederates, the following day, February 7, 1862, Burnside landed 7,500 men on the southwestern side of Roanoke Island in an amphibious operation launched from Fort Monroe. The following morning, supported by gunboats, Federals assaulted the Confederate forts on the narrow end of the island, driving back and outmaneuvering General Henry A. Wise's outnumbered command. After losing fewer than 100 men, the Confederate commander on the field, Colonel H.M. Shaw, surrendered about 2,500 soldiers and 32 guns. Burnside had secured an important outpost on the Atlantic coast, tightening the blockade. After lamenting briefly the loss of the island as a tragedy, Perry attempted to put the best face on the blow in his February 14, 1862, dispatch.

> From a personal examination of the position, the loss of Roanoke Island does not appear to be so great. The greatness of the calamity consists in the loss of so many men taken captive. Nevertheless, the time and labor spent in defending it, if spent

Perry was reporting from Memphis, Tennessee in March 1862. *Harper's Weekly*, June 28, 1862. Courtesy of Rare Books and Special Collections, University of South Carolina Libraries

on the neighboring coast, would have before now placed it beyond the power of the enemy to do us further serious damage. As it is they can only move up to some undefined position shall it land a few men.[27]

Following the capture of Roanoke Island, Perry made his way to Memphis. One of his first reports from there came on March 19, 1862. He wrote about the state of affairs of the Confederate army, the movements of Union General Burnside, and the impending gunboat battles for control of the islands along the Mississippi River. In his *Daily Picayune* report of March 21, Perry seemed less interested in romanticism and more concerned with actually winning the war. Discussing the removal of Federal troops and gunboats from the Mississippi River Valley, he lambasted Confederate notions of European protection in a fit of anger and called for action against the enemy entirely centered from the South. This was a turning point in Perry's reporting.

And then for 200,000 men to drive the enemy out of the Mississippi Valley. It is useless to say that they cannot be had or armed. The cotton States have not yet put forth half their strength; not a fourth of it. No more has any other State of the Confederacy. Up to the present time we have been juggling the delusive hopes, either that our enemy would break down in their avowed attempt to subjugate us—that England and France would intercede in our behalf, or that something else equally improbable would turn up. It is high time that we rid ourselves of these delusions and went to work to conquer our independence for ourselves with our own strong arms at once. Half a dozen gunboats on the Mississippi, and 200,000 men on the Memphis and Charleston Railroad, would sweep the enemy from the river and the valley and roll back the tide of war, where it should have been in the beginning, to the region beyond the Ohio. And they can be had, if our authorities and people bestir themselves.[28]

Perry was equally optimistic at the Battle of Shiloh in southwestern Tennessee on April 6 and 7, 1862. He wrote that it was impossible to predict the outcome of the battle "as both sides are fighting desperately, though it is believed that the Confederate will triumph."[29]

The night closed upon us yesterday before we could secure the full fruits of our victory, allowing a portion of the enemy to gain their river works and gunboats from which they threw balls all night. The Confederates slept in the enemy's encampment during the night. The enemy's transport went down the river to Cramps Landing and brought a new division of 7,000 men. This morning they reappeared with reinforcements and vigorously attacked our whole line. The firing was returned with spirit and for an hour the cannonading and musketry were terrific, but the enemy have been repulsed all along the line and are now falling back towards the river . . .[30]

As the war continued, Perry began to paint a more objective picture for his New Orleans audience, as it became more and more difficult to put a good face on every decision made by the Confederacy. Following the Confederate loss at Shiloh, Perry seemed less enthusiastic about the Confederate generals, the Confederate soldiers, and even the people in surrounding towns the following week.

We have met with another reverse; another disgraceful disaster has befallen our arms. Monday morning the enemy who were known to have been for several days moving down Hickman in the direction of Union City, suddenly appeared before that place, captured our pickets, took them all prisoners, drove out the garrison and captured the town. If the reports be true, it was a most disgraceful affair and calls for the most rigid security and condign [well deserved] punishment. The pickets surprised and captured, it appears had some time the night before deserted their post, the punishment for which is death . . .

Not a man escaped to convey news to the town, or give warning of the enemy approach! Is it not disgraceful? Where is recorded a baser crime? Is it not worthy the punishment from time immemorial, affixed to desertion or sleeping upon a post? And then for the sequel! A patriotic citizen of the neighborhood did manage to make his way to town with the news, but as we might have expected, he was too late . . .[31]

Yet even in his dismay, Perry could not end his report on a sour note, nor leave his beloved Confederacy without hope of victory. He asserted that the war was continuing "with the most favorable auspices," and he wrote that the Army of the Shenandoah was experiencing success near Winchester and had secured the line of the Rappahannock on the Potomac side of the mountains. "In no direction, therefore, can the enemy move upon us, then without the certainty of defeat and disaster."[32]

By mid-1862, Perry found himself in the town of Corinth, Mississippi, which had become one of the South's most strategic strongholds. The Mobile and Ohio Railroad crossed the Memphis and Charleston Railroad at Corinth, creating a crucial nexus for the transport of supplies, materiel, and men throughout the western Confederacy. The First Battle of Corinth (better known as the Siege of Corinth) began April 29, 1862.[33] Marching from Tennessee toward Corinth, the Federal Army under General Henry Halleck was preparing to attack the Confederates, who had retreated to Corinth after Shiloh. After brief skirmishing, General Beauregard ordered his troops to retreat to Tupelo, Mississippi, leaving Corinth under Federal control. After the retreat, Perry headed north, where he would eventually cover the gunboat battle that resulted in the capture of the city of Memphis.[34]

Not all of Perry's reporting was firsthand. He sometimes relied on information from Union deserters and prisoners to supply his readers with news of enemy morale and troop movements. Most soldiers and later scholars regarded the practice as extremely unreliable, because men of such character or in such positions simply said anything to lessen their chances of being killed or having to return to battle.[35]

In a dispatch from Virginia, Perry had described the movement of Union troops in one of the early skirmishes leading up to the First Battle of Manassas as "absurd" and noted that when they left the main path, because of a series of wrong turns, "they exposed themselves to a cross fire, and if they had succeeded in passing beyond us, it would have only been to be entrapped in a morass." Perry boasted in a report to the *Daily Picayune:*

> There was not a single movement of the enemy therefore that exhibited any generalship whatever, and I am not surprised to learn that the prisoners complain bitterly of the incompetence of their officers. It is openly charged, indeed, that many of them, including the renowned Major Gen. Butler, were intoxicated.[36]

The prisoners captured during the Battle of Bethel Church in Tabb and Hampton, Virginia, were "a sorry looking set of fellows," who could not provide a satisfactory explanation for enlisting. Perry added that "most of them were unemployed and accepted this for want of better."[37]

Perhaps Perry used criticism of the Union army by defected Union soldiers, as well as other secondhand information, to bolster his readers' confidence about the South. He may have been seeking to create an air of credibility when he reported three days into 1862, "A very intelligent gentleman" who had just returned from traveling extensively in the North, had assured Perry that a "very large number of the people were opposed to the continuance of the war, and that they had never freely and voluntarily joined the war effort."[38]

In a report from Memphis, only a few days before the attack on New Orleans that ended Perry's work at the *Daily Picayune*, he wrote that Union soldiers throughout Memphis complained of Southern soldier superiority: "Loud complaints to this effect have already been made, especially by Sherman," he wrote. "Everywhere, especially after a repulse, the cry is 'the rebels outnumbered us' and more men must be had."[39]

A few days before filing that account, Perry wrote with specificity from Memphis that "a gentleman from Nashville says the Federal loss was 21,000,"[40] and the correspondent repeated that the man told him four regiments from Wisconsin and Kentucky had mutinied. "The Kentuckians stacked their arms and went home saying that they won't fight for Lincoln's abolition programme [sic]."[41]

Perry's love of adventure and war was evident in his writing. In early 1862, his dispatches revealed his desire to find "the real seat of the war"[42] and a "desire to be where our own city and State were more particularly threatened."[43] Even after witnessing gruesome and horrible deaths (roughly 2,950 for the Union and 1,750 for the Confederates in the First Battle of Manassas alone),[44] as well as human suffering, Perry traveled from Virginia to Shiloh and Corinth, and on to Memphis in search of war and imagined glories.

He filled the time between troop movements, relocation, and battles reporting general news or his critiques of it. He criticized newspaper reporting on the constant picket fighting between Union and Confederate troops on the front lines, which Perry considered exaggerated. Picket fighting, the practice of firing random shots at unsuspecting troops of the opposing army, was characterized as a murderous and largely frowned upon act. Perry maintained that commanding officers had "strict orders never to fire unless it may be in self defense, or necessary to maintain a post, and so far as I have seen, the men are inclined of themselves to obey these instructions."[45]

As the war progressed and the Confederacy was not faring well, Perry continued to rely on secondary information to suggest that the South would eventually prevail. He painted a picture that recognition of the Confederacy was imminent and aid was forthcoming. Frequent dispatches in early 1862 professed that all of Europe would rally to the Confederate cause.

Taking the slightest bit of news from Europe and characterizing it as "of an equally important character," Perry wrote in one article that "everything now argues the speedy recognition of our Confederacy."[46] England was preparing for war, according to Perry, and the French people and government had denounced "this unholy and barbarous war our enemies, regardless of every law, human and divine, are waging upon us, to the destruction of commerce of the world and in violence of every sentiment of our common humanity."[47]

It is clear that Perry knew the dynamics of the relationship between European countries and the South. Both England and France received cotton and other primary manufacturing goods, as well as other agricultural products from the South, and both nations benefited from the cheap products Southern slave labor afforded them. Arguably, neither nation could afford recognizing the Confederacy and risking possible war with the United States or the loss of U.S. corn in the European market.[48] It was also obvious that neither country could rationalize supporting a nation that upheld the institution of slavery.

In addition to suggesting European involvement in the war, Perry's other secondhand reports addressed economic news about foreign markets and their negative impact on the North, which he referred to as "Lincolndom." Perry's dispatch on January 3, 1862, indicated that the steamer *Asia* had arrived from England with news that Europe was gearing up for war. Optimistically, he reported:

> The war preparations in England still continue, the outside popular pressure being intense. The Gibraltar fleet has been ordered to America. More troops have been sent to Canada, and the Admiralty have taken steps to protect shipping in the India and China seas. All Europe is outraged at the action of the Federal authorities in sending the stone fleet to blockade the Southern ports. The English Ministerial press has assumed a more decided tone. The French press believed war to be inevitable, and are urging England to accept it. Europe everywhere expects war.[49]

A little more than a month later, he reported on the increase in the gold and silver exchanges and stated that the "Northern Government is in a hopeless condition."[50] As if to give credibility to his pieces, Perry often wrote at the beginning of the dispatch that the news came by way of reputable sources. One such source was the steamer, *Flag of Truce*. Examples included: "The flag of truce arrived with news of . . . ," or "The flag of truce brought news to-day . . ." In April 1862, the steamer brought news of "six thousand heavy failures in New York," leading Perry to conclude, "The shipping merchants have become quite panic struck for fear of the Confederate steamer Nashville."[51]

News of troops, battles, and economic ramifications for the North were only some of the topics Perry addressed. He also wrote about the health of Confederate President Jefferson Davis, when he made public appearances.[52] Some of Perry's dispatches included multiple topics. Along with news about treasury bills and the reason for the resignation of the secretary of war, a *Daily Picayune* dispatch brought news that Monrovia had defeated Grenada, that Austria agreed with England on the Trent affair, and that Mexico was resisting "foreign occupation" by France.[53]

There was a significant absence of Perry's articles, particularly war correspondence, after his move from Richmond to Shiloh. This was largely a result of

Perry's attachment to Louisiana soldiers under the command of General Pierre G.T. Beauregard, a Louisiana native.[54] The unit's lack of major military engagements following the Battle of Manassas until the Battle of Shiloh also accounts for the decrease in correspondence.[55] Perry followed Beauregard's troops from Manassas to Shiloh and Corinth before leaving Beauregard's army and heading to Memphis, presumably at the behest of the *Memphis Appeal* for which he was writing at the time.

Only a few weeks after the Battle of Shiloh, New Orleans fell to the Union, and Perry was forced to find employment elsewhere. Eventually gaining employment at the "refugee paper," the *Memphis Daily Appeal*, Perry went on to cover the Corinth campaign and the Memphis gunboat battle before once again heading back into obscurity.[56]

It is debatable whether Perry actually believed what he was writing. He witnessed enough Confederate losses to realize all was not as "glorious" as he described it, and several other correspondents described the same events in far less glowing terms. Perhaps Perry saw himself as one of the defenders of the South who wielded a pen instead of picking up a musket in order to spin stories in defense of a sacred homeland in the face of invaders from the North. Perhaps his belief in the cause blinded him to the harsh reality surrounding him. Perhaps he simply saw himself as a recruiter of support or counterbalance to the more "pessimistic" correspondents. Regardless of the reasons, H.P.'s style served only to misinform and ultimately mislead.

Texas

Reporter William Doran was in New Orleans when he learned that Union forces were about to depart for the Sabine Pass to invade Texas. He alerted Confederate authorities who fortified the pass and defeated Union attackers September 8–9, 1863. *Harper's Weekly,* October 10, 1863. Courtesy of Rare Books and Special Collections, University of South Carolina Libraries

Despite the Lone Star State's location on the periphery of the Confederacy, more than 70,000 Texans donned uniforms and earned reputations as fierce and brave fighters in such important battles as Gettysburg, Shiloh, Chickamauga, the Wilderness, and Second Manassas. They also fought in battles closer to home, including the Red River Campaign, the invasion of New Mexico, and the defense of Texas itself.

Even in their remote location, Texans clamored for news, and editors faced great difficulties in delivering this precious commodity to readers. The state had only 350 miles of railroad lines; the telegraph connected only Houston and Galveston; roads were poor; and rivers often flooded.

The April 1861 Federal blockade of Confederate ports and the occupation of New Orleans a year later only exacerbated editors' news-gathering problems. Texas editors found themselves largely without paper, ink, and lead to produce type, as well as access to news itself. Within a few months of the war's outbreak, newspapers began suspending operations for indefinite periods or outright closed for the duration of the war. Edward Cushing, editor of the influential *Houston Telegraph*, was reduced to writing General John B. Magruder in December 1862 to beg for out-of-state papers from which to crib news. Most of the existing publications within the state, including the *Austin State Gazette*, copied much of their news directly from Cushing's publication or Willard Richardson's *Galveston News*.

Obtaining permanent, trustworthy correspondents to ensure more accurate news was a need that few publishers could afford. Cushing and Richardson shared the services of William P. Doran, a former soldier, who wrote under the pen name of "Sioux." Cushing also hired another former soldier, R.R. Gilbert, who served as a correspondent and news editor and also wrote humor columns. Some editors who enlisted, including the *Tyler Reporter*'s James P. Douglas, who served as an artillery officer, and Charles DeMorse of the *Clarksville Standard*, who served mostly in Indian Territory and Arkansas, sent regular reports back to their publications.

How many other correspondents actually served Texas' newspapers is difficult to tell. Other editors, including J.B. Reilly of the *Kaufman Democrat* and John Lancaster of the *Texas Ranger*, also served, but no copies of their newspapers from the war years exist and they left no memoirs. The only newspaper with several correspondents was the *Houston Telegraph*, whose editor claimed eight individuals provided news from within and outside of Texas during the war years. Aside from Doran and Gilbert, who wrote under the name "High Private," most of the other correspondents were periodic letter writers. Only one individual, who went by the initials "H.A.," appeared to be a regular, bylined correspondent. H.A. did not do original correspondent work but sent regular columns of news containing short items gleaned from newspapers throughout the South. The four Texas correspondents who could be identified and who did original reporting—DeMorse, Doran, Douglas, and Gilbert—served readers a much-needed diet of news that kept them abreast of the war, as scant as it was at the time.

21

Charles DeMorse:
Reporting from the Indian Territories

Mary M. Cronin

Ten months into the Civil War, Charles DeMorse, the long-time editor of the *Clarksville Standard* in northeast Texas, announced in his newspaper that if there were no "speedy cessation" to the war, he would take a leave of absence, raise a cavalry regiment, and go to war.

"The undersigned," he wrote on February 8, 1862, ". . . feels unsatisfied to see others offering their persons to the shock of battle, and the far more dangerous ordeal of camp diseases resulting from privation and exposure, while he attends to his private interests." DeMorse was looking for recruits with like backgrounds—older, settled, with families and established business interests, but who would sacrifice themselves "upon the altar of Patriotism in support of Texas and the nascent Confederacy."[1]

While DeMorse's declaration was infused with the same nationalist and religious rhetoric used by other Texas journalists before they went off to war, the *Standard* editor differed from his fellow editors in uniform.[2] DeMorse was 46 years of age—more than a decade older than the requirement for Confederate service. Furthermore, he had been publishing his journal in a small community for 20 years, an almost unheard-of success story on the frontier.[3]

The Confederate Conscription Act of 1862 exempted editors from the draft; therefore, DeMorse did not have to volunteer.[4] Several of his younger colleagues, including outspoken Confederate nationalists Edward Hopkins Cushing of the *Houston Tri-Weekly Telegraph,* John Osterhout of the *Bellville Countryman,* and Robert Loughery of the *Marshall Republican,* chose to remain in Texas and continue their fight in the columns of their newspapers, rather than engage in actual combat.[5]

Determined to go to war, but on his own terms, DeMorse received approval from Confederate Secretary of War George W. Randolph to establish the 29th Texas Cavalry and was appointed the regiment's colonel.[6] He would fight in

Charles DeMorse. Photograph courtesy the
Texas State Library and Archives

three battles (and a few skirmishes), all in the Trans-Mississippi West. His cavalry bore the brunt of the fighting in its first engagement at the Battle of Elk
Creek (also known as Honey Springs) in July 1863 and was soundly defeated.
DeMorse was badly wounded in the arm. The resulting Union victory gave Federal forces control of Indian Territory north of the Arkansas River.[7]

DeMorse would make up for this humiliating loss in his final two battles—at
Poison Spring in April 1864, when Confederate troops and their Indian allies
attacked a Union foraging party and captured 198 wagons filled with much-
needed corn, and at Cabin Creek five months later in September 1864. The
Cabin Creek battle proved to be a morale-booster and a crucial victory. Hungry and ragged Confederate and Indian troops again attacked a Union supply
train—one of the largest in the war—and took 205 military wagons, 91 sutler
wagons, 4 ambulances, and more than 720 mules. These latter battles would
become noted for their massacres of black troops from the 1st Kansas Colored
and of black teamsters. Neither the Texans nor their Indian allies would give the
black troops any quarter after those troops helped Union forces drive Confederate Indians from their homes earlier in the war.[8]

Battle of Elk Creek. *Frank Leslie's Illustrated Newspaper,* August 29, 1863

DeMorse would serve double duty during the war as an officer and correspondent. His battle reports published in his newspaper by Acting Editor John Woolridge undoubtedly drew avid readers. Not only were the battles fought relatively close to home, but many Texans, frightened by the possibility of a Federal invasion of their state by Union troops from Kansas to the Indian Territory, sought out news from that region. DeMorse was one of the few journalists to report on these battles. Many of his subscribers would also read the accounts with interest because his men hailed from his newspaper's circulation area.[9]

DeMorse sent more than 20 multi-topic letters to the *Standard,* beginning with his trip to Richmond to obtain supplies and ending with his final battle at Cabin Creek in Indian Territory. His accounts usually provided a chronology of a day's or week's events. Clarksville lacked both railroad lines and telegraph facilities to quickly get news to readers. Consequently, reports regularly filled two to three full columns in the *Standard* and were often published three to four weeks after they were written. DeMorse included news of camp life in the Trans-Mississippi West, detailed accounts of the troops' maneuvers during battle, and observations about the relationship between white Confederate soldiers and their Indian allies. It was intriguing information for Texans, many of whom had faced repeated raids by hostile Indians before and during the war and whose trust in their native allies was tentative at best.[10]

For reasons unknown, DeMorse deviated from the accepted practice of the time and signed letters under three different names—his own and two pen

Fort Arbuckle, Texas. *Harper's Weekly,* March 16, 1861. Courtesy of Rare Books and Special Collections, University of South Carolina Libraries

names. Using his full name with some letters was an unusual practice, since most journalists used their initials or a pen name. DeMorse signed some of his letters with the name "Private," in reference to the military rank, while other letters were signed "A Soldier of the Twenty-Ninth."[11] The style of writing and consistent punctuation errors clearly suggest that regardless of signature, the reports were all written by DeMorse.[12]

His personality and personal interests infused his war correspondence. A well-educated man whose home contained extensive gardens and a library filled with works on science, especially botany, history, and religion, DeMorse wrote letters that read like those of a gentleman scholar.[13] His reports of camp life in Indian Territory and Arkansas were replete with descriptions of the flora, fauna, and geology of the regions and often read more like camping trips taken by a naturalist than by a man awaiting battle with his troops. Upon arrival at the Indian Territory's Fort Arbuckle in late March 1863, DeMorse described the region.

> The prairies were gemmed with myriads of little white flowers, and the little chickasaw Plum bushes were frequent. I looked for cactus, but found only a few of the common Prickly Pear. Arbuckle is a beautiful locality. High ground with mountains in the distance; sandy around the Fort, but in the bottom near by splendid mulatto soil, resembling Old Caney.

He described the clear stream and its fish, as well as the geological features near the outpost.[14] The subtext of his letter was clear—the land was worth fighting for.

Although his accounts were written in a straightforward, matter-of-fact style, largely devoid of opinion, DeMorse on occasion dipped into the patriotic rhetoric common to Confederate nationalists. His early calls for volunteers were framed around duty and sacrifice to Texas and the Confederacy and protection of homes and families. DeMorse's letters rarely were tinged with the religious rhetoric commonly used by both sides as a means of legitimizing the struggle.[15] His accounts before the war and during the battles occasionally used pejorative terms and common stereotypes, referring, for example, to Union troops as mercenaries.[16] During the Battle of Cabin Creek, DeMorse claimed that Union troops fought in a drunken rage. Like other reporters of the time, he regularly puffed his superiors, citing their gallantry.[17] The nation's newspapers and magazines played important roles in upholding morale and subsequently took on an ideological cast as they served the broader patriotic culture that developed during the war years.[18]

Despite his use of stereotyped terms and patriotic rhetorical devices, DeMorse's reports offered a measure of objectivity and accuracy. With the exception of one report from Virginia in 1862 when he toured three battlefields with a Confederate general as guide, DeMorse's accounts of fighting were based on personal observations. He did not dip into the speculation common at the time, and the bulk of his information, including casualty figures, was essentially accurate.

Even before DeMorse enlisted, his desire for accuracy led him to exercise a high degree of editorial caution in determining which battlefield letters from soldiers and reprints from other publications would run in his newspaper. Although as eager as any Confederate citizen for victory, DeMorse explained that separating rumors from truth was a battle in and of itself. "So little reliance can be placed in the reports we get from Telegraphic Despatches that but little credence is given," DeMorse wrote in a May 12, 1862, editorial.[19]

Yet when DeMorse finally went to war, his loyalty toward the Confederate cause, his understanding of the morale-boosting role of the press, and perhaps his own self-interest in how he wished his leadership to be perceived by his readers led him to make occasional editorial omissions in his reports.[20] For example, his descriptions of camp conditions in Indian Territory largely omitted the extent of material shortages and hardships that eventually led to increasing numbers of desertions by his men during the winter of 1863-1864.[21] Notices of $30 rewards for deserters from his regiment published in the *Standard* bore public witness to the hardships that existed on the frontier. DeMorse's letters largely did not reflect that.

A rare admission of need came in a report following the Battle of Cabin Creek. DeMorse acknowledged the Confederates' relief upon seizing a huge

Union wagon train loaded with military supplies, foodstuffs, and sutlers' goods. The massive amounts of clothing, boots, shoes, and food were immediately used by troops "that were suffering for them," he wrote. He cryptically attributed the troops' lack of clothes and equipment to "much uncertainty about a supply through the Agents of the Government," but provided no further explanation.[22]

None of his letters revealed the ongoing feud DeMorse was having with his superior officer, General Richard Gano, caused by his belief that he—rather than Gano—should command the territory's white soldiers.[23] Instead, De-Morse's battle reports from Poison Spring and Cabin Creek referred to Gano as "gallant."

However, DeMorse was far from alone in engaging in such practices. Historian James McPherson wrote that such distortions and credibility issues were common in Civil War reports, in large measure because "the temptation is powerful to put the best face on one's motives and behavior, to highlight noble and courageous actions and to gloss over the ignoble and cowardly."[24]

DeMorse's service as an officer and a war correspondent was typical of a frontier editor. He was the *Clarksville Standard*'s editorial staff. The newness of his state coupled with its rural conditions and thinly populated communities meant that Texas publishers frequently served in all capacities—as publisher, editor, reporter, business manager, and, in some cases, printer.[25] While large, better-funded Northern newspapers could afford to send reporters to the battlefield, most Southern journals were severely handicapped by small circulation and lack of capital.[26]

The Texas journalists who went off to war usually relied on themselves to send both eyewitness battlefield and camp reports, as well as any copies of other newspapers back to their own publications.[27] And despite the inclusion of patriotic rhetoric in their reports, Texas journalist-soldiers, including DeMorse and his contemporaries William Doran of the *Houston Tri-Weekly Telegraph* and James P. Douglas of the *Tyler Reporter,* often provided better-quality news than other soldier correspondents. In the words of one historian, those correspondents offered "little more than boastful propaganda proclaiming the superiority of their side's cause and the bravery of troops."[28]

Despite his devotion to the Confederate cause, DeMorse was a northerner. Born in Leicester, Massachusetts, he was educated in Connecticut and New York, eventually becoming an attorney. As a young lawyer itching for adventure, and perhaps looking to advance his station in a less-populated region of the country, DeMorse left New York in 1835 with a group of volunteers organized by Major Edwin Morehouse to aid in Texas' battle for independence.[29] He accepted a commission as a first lieutenant in the Marines in the Texas Navy in March 1836 and served coastal duty aboard the schooner *Independence.* Part of that duty involved transporting the heads of the Texas government and their Mexican prisoners of war, including General Santa Anna, to Velasco following the Texans' victory at San Jacinto. When DeMorse heard rumors of a possible second Mexican invasion of Texas in July of that year, he left the navy for the army, believing he would see military action and enhance his career.[30]

The future editor of the *Clarksville Standard* served with General Albert Sidney Johnston, assisting Johnston by organizing and drilling the army while stationed near Lavaca Bay and at Navidad. Discharged in May 1837, DeMorse moved to Matagorda in 1838 and was admitted to the Texas bar. He met and married Lodiska Wooldridge, daughter of Colonel Thomas Wooldridge of Spartanburg, South Carolina, a wealthy planter and the first American consul to Matagorda. DeMorse and his pregnant wife moved to Austin in August 1839 where he worked as a state government stock commissioner. During the 1841-1842 legislative session, he also served as a reporter for the House of Representatives and edited a small daily paper.[31]

Newspaper work apparently agreed with DeMorse. Reporting and editing brought him attention and numerous job offers, including the editorship of the *Austin City Gazette* and editorship of a proposed newspaper in San Antonio. But members of the state legislature from communities along the Red River enticed DeMorse with their offer to cover all of his expenses if the lawyer-turned-journalist would establish a newspaper in Clarksville, a hamlet 135 miles northeast of Dallas. He accepted the Clarksville position, believing it presented the best job opportunity and a chance to wield a powerful political influence in a growing region.[32]

From the first issue, the *Standard* was solidly Democratic in tone. DeMorse advocated development of the state's infrastructure, including transportation and education, but he also supported the state's Southern institutions—slavery and cotton.[33]

The political, social, and economic issues of the 1850s posed continual challenges. Ever a pragmatist, DeMorse cautioned moderation in the decade before the Civil War. As the U.S. Congress wrestled with the issues of slavery and Texas boundaries in 1850, DeMorse supported the Pearce Compromise Bill, which eventually established his state's boundaries, but he worried whether the Union would survive if Northern politicians nullified the law. Although he was a slave owner, DeMorse also struck a moderate tone on the South's "peculiar institution," opposing the reopening of the slave trade, believing that as the South grew economically, the need for slavery would eventually end.[34]

Behind DeMorse's moderation was his firm belief that Texas' economic progress would best be achieved by remaining in the Union.[35] Secession would slow both the creation of a transcontinental railroad, as well as the development of rail transportation throughout Texas, he wrote.[36] Equally important, DeMorse believed secession would be a blow to free government and to liberal institutions and result in war. "We scorn the humbug cant about peaceful secession, for there can be no such thing," he wrote in a January 4, 1850, editorial.[37]

The possible repeal of the Fugitive Slave Law also weighed heavily on his mind. DeMorse warned in editorials that any attempt by Northern politicians to repeal, alter, or fail to carry out the terms of the fugitive slave law would spell the end of the Union.[38] But he was no alarmist. During the controversy over the Missouri Compromise, DeMorse again expressed his belief that Texas should remain in the Union. He reminded members of the Federal government that Southerners wanted a government "that would respect their dignity and institutions as well as their belief in state rights."[39] During the campaign of 1856, DeMorse reiterated that the Federal government must be cognizant of and accede to voters' demands. He cautioned readers to exercise their voting rights and he warned that if a Republican were elected president, the slave-holding states would secede immediately.[40]

Despite the seemingly inevitable move toward secession and war by 1859, DeMorse continued to assert that rational decision-making might preserve the Union and leave the South's cotton culture and slave institution alone. In an April 1859 editorial, titled "Democracy and Disunion," he voiced his belief that all of the Southern states would act together should dissolution of the Union be necessary. But he cautioned that the time was not right for Texans to make any such move. ". . . to our view, Texas has no greater reason now, than she had at the time of annexation, to desire a separate national existence." In DeMorse's opinion, individuals who were calling for secession were "in advance of the times."[41]

In his editorial quest to keep the Union together, DeMorse announced his support for John Breckinridge of Kentucky for president, writing in his newspaper that Breckinridge was the best hope for both maintaining the Union, while assuring Southerners of their rights and dignity.

> We believe our political rights and prosperity best preserved within the Union as recognized by the Constitution, and we shall adhere to this until we are forced to a different course by a positive outrage of legislation . . . we believe in the plainly intended non-interventionist principles of the Utah, New Mexico, and Kansas bills.[42]

By September 1860, when the election of Lincoln seemed a certainty, DeMorse warned in editorials that Southerners would not tolerate a nation led by a "Black Republican" president.[43] He held out hope that the Union could be saved, arguing that if any states were to secede, it should be the New England states. DeMorse's pragmatic streak forced him to realize that Texas' economic fate so matched that of the other Southern states that it was necessary for Texans to act in concert with their fellow Southerners.[44]

By January 1861, DeMorse felt that secession was a foregone conclusion. "The Union is going into fragments," he wrote on January 19. "He who cannot see it is blindly political. It is past hope."[45] Despite his misgivings, DeMorse acceded to the public's will when the Texas convention voted to secede on January 28,

1861, and voters ratified the decision on February 23. He sadly noted that Texas must "go out of the Union" and take part with her "natural associates." By the end of the month, DeMorse had accepted the fact of belonging to a new nation: "We can do well in a Southern Confederacy. We shall mourn (the passing of the Union), even though we approve severance as a stern necessity," he wrote in a February 23 editorial.[46]

In spite of DeMorse's claims to support the Confederacy, Texas newspaper historian Marilyn McAdams Sibley wrote that he took a gloomy view of events, conceding the necessity of secession but at first making no effort to remove the U.S. flag from his nameplate or to change his motto, "The Constitution and the Union—the Union Under the Constitution."[47] Perhaps in response to critics, the editor wrote that his loyalty remained with Texas and the Confederacy.

> Everybody who reads the *Standard* knows that we are not extremist or disunionist. We have not yet abandoned the hope that the glories and benefits of the Union are to be perpetuated. Yet, so hoping, we give this day our vote "For Secession."[48]

A few weeks later, DeMorse replaced the engraving of the Union Flag on his front page with the Lone Star flag. He announced on March 11, 1861, "There can be no propriety in the continuing of the *Standard* of the late Union at our editorial head . . . It is not with pleasure that we unfurl the old flag although we have done it before." He added that he used the Lone Star engraving because he couldn't get a woodcut of the Confederate flag.[49]

When war finally came, DeMorse, like many Americans, believed the conflict would be brief.[50] He asserted that Northern soldiers would quickly see that they were not putting down a "fractious rebellion" but instead, were oppressing "a whole people, and those people their brethren."[51] As news of the firing upon Fort Sumter trickled back to Texas, DeMorse encouraged men to enlist, framing the issue in Confederate public rhetorical terms. The war, he said, was a fight for personal liberty and home. God, he said, was on the side of the Confederacy because Southerners had a just and moral cause, while the Union did not.

> We do not fear the result, conscious that we are contending for the RIGHT. Armed in a holy and just cause, we can but appeal to the God of battles with pure conscience, and the victory He will give us. It may cost blood, it may cost treasure. Be it so! If only at the point of the bayonet, we can force them into an acknowledgment of our independence, and obtain our rights no other way, let it come in all its horrid realities . . . We are fighting to accomplish no mercenary aim, and actuated by no motives of aggrandizement—simply defending our own firesides, household goods, the love of liberty, and the inherent right of self-government, transmitted by a patriotic ancestry to a no less worthy posterity.[52]

Once the war began, DeMorse encouraged readers to enlist. The pace of that editorial encouragement increased after he made his February 8, 1862, announcement that he was going to war. DeMorse exhorted men to join his cavalry regiment, saying they were needed. Fighting, he said, would be fierce in the spring when muddy roads dried, allowing men and artillery to move. He used the cause of liberty as both a fear appeal and as a rallying cry. Northern subjugation, he said, must be stopped.

> We have all at stake and must prepare to defend it or we must be trampled into a servitude, compared with which the servitude of the negroes is paradisaical; [paradise] for our sensibilities, as well as our political rights would be outraged beyond endurance, if we could be overcome. We cannot be overcome![53]

DeMorse left Clarksville on March 2 on a recruiting tour through northeast Texas. He carefully studied the regiments being raised to determine whether the men he wanted, older and established Texans, were available for his cavalry regiment.[54] He continued to use the *Standard* and public meetings to encourage enlistment. In his pitches to sign up volunteers, DeMorse emphasized that he was the only man currently in northeast Texas with authority to raise a cavalry regiment. He wrote in a March 29 editorial what most Texans already knew—that they preferred to be in cavalry rather than infantry.[55]

"We do not wish to dissuade anyone from the Infantry service, which is a service exceedingly valuable to the army, but we are aware that there are many who are quite unwilling to go as infantry; and for these the opportunity is unquestionable," he wrote.[56] He called for 10 companies to begin training as soon as possible.

As late winter turned to spring, DeMorse framed his pitch for volunteers around four common Confederate themes and issues: the need to end the war quickly, the defense of Texas, an appeal to manhood, and the reality that the conscription law of May 15, 1862, meant Texans would no longer have a choice about their military service. Nor would they be able to receive a bounty.[57] In a May 5 editorial addressed to the men who lived in the counties along the Red River, DeMorse wrote:

> . . . let's not defer the contest longer. If we all turn out we can beat off the oppressor. This war is too *lengthy and too tardy* . . . The want of men is our deficiency. Texas can do more—she has done well. The field is before us and invites us to action. Are we men? Now is the time to show it.[58]

The Union's capture and occupation of New Orleans on April 28, 1862, was a stunning blow to the South and taught DeMorse an important lesson: An army cannot fight a war against a well-equipped foe without equal equipment and supplies to level the field. Morale, solid military strategy, and a sense of righteousness in their cause would not be enough for the Southerners to prevail. DeMorse attributed the capture of New Orleans to the Union's superior preparation, expenditures, and materials.

"We have been defeated by Capital and not by warlike qualities, whenever defeated at all," he said in trying to preserve the public's morale. "It is money which has massed men against us and supplied them with superior equipments, with longer range weapons, and with more appliances for the preservation of health and comfort than we have," DeMorse wrote.[59]

He was determined that his cavalry regiment would enter the war prepared. Although he told volunteers to bring a double-barreled shotgun, two six-shot pistols, and a hatchet with a 14-inch handle, DeMorse insisted that self-sufficiency would not rule.[60] He headed to Richmond to appeal directly to President Jefferson Davis, the secretary of war, and Texas legislative representatives to obtain the needed supplies. DeMorse arrived in Richmond in early August 1862 as the Peninsula Campaign was ending and General Robert E. Lee was turning his troops north toward Washington, D.C., to face General John Pope's troops, which would culminate in the Union's defeat at Second Manassas August 29-30.[61]

DeMorse had journeyed to Richmond with high hopes the Confederate government would provide for his regiment, yet provide they did not. Although he wasn't naive about the slow nature of political bureaucracy—his work with the Texas legislature two decades earlier taught him as much—his letters from Richmond reflected impatience with the Confederate bureaucracy and surprise at the shortage of supplies available in the capital.[62]

In a letter written on August 24 and published three weeks later on September 13, DeMorse vented his frustrations: "We have been here nearly two weeks though time passes without much note, except the daily feeling that it is passing without bringing adequate results.[63] There are continued obstacles to progress if one wants much done; and I have determined to get every thing desirable done this time, and not to running to and fro." He placed the blame on the quartermaster, rather than the South's lack of industry and preparedness. Like other Confederate correspondents, DeMorse was not afraid to criticize government and military officials when he believed their actions were harming the Confederacy.[64]

I find the President sensible, affable, and disposed to assist; the Secretary the same; but our Quarter-Master finds continual difficulties in the way of getting all we want for the regiment, and I have to remove those obstacles by appeals to the Sec'r of War, and the President, and this takes time. I am determined to have all we are entitled to, and more than most get, before we return home. I have been engaged for two days past in a fruitless effort to coax some Revolvers out of the Navy Department, assisted by a letter from the President, RECOMMENDING it, and the friendly concurrence of the Naval Ordnance officer, but I have failed, and shall to-morrow make a requisition for the money to purchase, which the President has told me I shall have. The army in the field in this State is without tents, but I think I can get some on the way home. I shall have to hunt up my shot guns in the Southern Arsenals—there are none here.[65]

DeMorse also directed his personal ire at officials who were critical of Texans and the Trans-Mississippi region. During his search for supplies, he found some members of the Confederate government who believed that Texans were not doing their fair share in providing men and materials for the war. He responded to these complaints with a degree of anti-semitism that was not uncommon for the time.

> The Secretary of War stands well, and is certainly an intelligent and most agree-able public Agent. Mr. Mallory, the Secretary of the Navy is not especially popular or influential; and Mr. Memminger, the Secretary of Treasury is most decidedly unpopular, and I think probable [sic] deservedly so.[66] He seems to have an especial pique at Texas, and will be apt to get some hard rubs before long. He frequently says that Texas has done less, and claimed and received more than any other State in the Confederacy. As this is simply untrue, he will be likely to hear more of it. I think that he, and another Jewish functionary here, have very little favor for the Southwest. Col. Myers the Quartermaster General seriously informed our Quartermaster yesterday, that he would not give an order for anything to go west of the Mississippi. This was in answer to our requisition for tents, accompanied by a request for an order on Columbus. But whenever this Hebrew gentleman gets in our way, I intend to put him out of it by a little leverage from Headquarters.[67]

Despite his initial gloom, the rest of his letter mixed praise and disap-pointment at the paradoxes of the Confederacy. DeMorse touted Richmond's manufacturing capabilities, particularly its arms and munitions operations, as patriotic contributions to nationalist self-sufficiency, despite the fact he was un-able to procure his arms and munitions needs there.

"We make nearly everything here important to service," he noted with ad-miration. "The manufacture of Percussion Caps, for small arms and cannon, is quite ingenious and interesting." Adding further reassurance, he wrote that Union troops were on the run following the Seven Days Battles, in large mea-sure because Confederate officers exhibited superior military strategies.

> We have been expecting here daily the news of battle, but the enemy has fallen back by the strategy of our Generals, however, we have got the blackguard Pope encircled, and if we do not bag his whole force, he will be lucky. Two lines of our army are between him and McClellan, the latter having abandoned James River altogether. Pope is already backing out of his intended outrages upon our peace-ful citizens; he does not like the reprisals we have commenced.[68]

DeMorse also denounced what Southerners generally perceived to be one of the worst failings of the Confederacy—the wartime development of greed and inflationary prices, what Southerners termed "extortion" throughout the war. From the first rationalizations of secession in the winter of 1860–1861, southerners had been citing the growing materialism of America, and especially northern society as a fundamental justification for Confederate independence, according to historian Drew Gilpin Faust. "The seemingly unbounded prosperity of the American nation had corrupted the republican virtues of its politics, while 'Mammon-worship' had undermined the spiritual foundations of religious life."[69] Secession, its supporters argued, would free Southerners' natural spiritualism and generosity and end the "moral degeneration" associated with such prosperity. The argument belied the fact that high cotton prices and tremendous economic growth throughout the South during the 1850s were putting the agrarian region on the road to commercial expansion. But perhaps more significantly, economic growth was "posing significant challenges" to the traditionalism that imbued the Southern social and economic order.[70]

Buttressing his case, DeMorse put forth a lengthy list of items commanding "fabulous" prices for foodstuffs and the huge prices charged by hotels. "Flour is worth $12 per barrel," he wrote in disbelief. But he tried to temper the extortion in the Confederacy's capital by writing with unbridled pride that this same flour was "manufactured here by mills which are, I believe, unsurpassed in the world, in capacity, and quality of manufacture."[71]

The Texan appeared overwhelmed by the throngs of people after his years of living in comparatively rural Clarksville. He also expressed surprise that despite the proximity of battles to the city, Richmond's night life was thriving, theaters were full every night, and money was flowing freely to support such unwarlike activities.[72]

While waiting for the supplies, the dogged Texan determined to make good use of his trip east. He began discussing battlefield tactics with officers who had recently participated in the first encounters that were part of the Seven Days Battles. The massive engagements, which took place during the last week of June 1862, near Richmond, involved more than 200,000 troops and culminated in the Peninsula Campaign.[73] DeMorse described the difficult terrain and hard fighting that took place, with a detailed account of the battles' military maneuvers. He took a moment from his recounting of the first three fights to explain that even the South's slaves believed the North was wrong to invade.

> Right here it is proper to mention the information which our negro driver gave us. He fully participated in all the feelings which the sight of the ground called up, and thought it strange that the enemy should come to drive people from their own homes.[74]

DeMorse demonstrated some of his finest writing of the war, as well as a sense of his own humanity, in one passage that graphically described the remains of a fallen Union soldier. He provided a detailed description of the horrors of war, which had yet to reach northeast Texas, a degree of sympathy for an unknown soldier caught up in the conflict.

> In a gully on the hill side where a body had been buried to avoid much digging, the rain had washed it bare. There was the scull [sic]; then the frame work of the breast with the federal uniform, with the belt across the breast, the cartridge box, the cap pouch; and the bayonet sheath. By the side, were some fleshless fingers. There was a little space between the waist line of the coat as though something might have severed the parts of the body, and then came the light blue soldier pantaloons, showing the outline of the hip bones, and the legs, and the fleshless bones terminating the figure of what had once been a federal soldier, and for all we know, one in whom had centered many joys and hopes of a fond house hold, lying there an object of contemptuous hate in a strange land, a victim, possibly, not of his own inclination, but of the malignant fanaticism of a low spirited government.[75]

The Seven Days campaign were notable for the active participation of troops from Texas, as well as the death of one of the most prominent Texas editors to enlist—Colonel John Marshall, the ardently secessionist editor of the *Texas State Gazette*.[76] DeMorse detailed how brigades from three other Southern states had been trying to seize a key hill at the Battle of Gaines Mill on June 27, 1862, only to fail before men from the 1st, 4th, and 5th Texas Infantry Regiments succeeded. The men faced murderous and incessant gunfire and artillery while they maneuvered down a ravine, climbed over ditches and through streams, finally charging a hill through a timbered area. De Morse wrote proudly of their accomplishment.

> The Texans charged with a terrific yell, reserved their fire until it would all tell; with a run and continued it clear over the field. If they had marched up slowly they would have been annihilated. There was no pause, from the commencement to the conclusion of the charge. The whole affair was the enthusiastic dash of men who started to go through, who knew they could go through, and did not look upon failure as a possibility.[77]

Leaving Richmond, DeMorse continued his search for supplies, deciding to visit Atlanta before heading home. He made a brief stop in Lynchburg, Virginia, in mid-September to see a relative, commented on the beauty of the Blue Ridge Mountains, and reminisced about his boyhood memories of New England's mountains and ocean.[78] His letter also highlighted attempts at Confederate self-sufficiency with a description of a rural salt-making operation that was producing 3,000 bushels daily and distributing it through the Southern states.

"The works in their origin were private property, but the government controls them now," DeMorse wrote, adding, "I see that the Government of Georgia has already commenced to distribute a little *giving* to each wife or widow, or

widowed mother of a soldier in service, half a bushel, and giving them a preference over other purchasers for more."[79]

DeMorse reached Georgia in hopes of obtaining clothing for his men at a textile mill. His expectations for supplies fell short in quality, quantity, and price,
proof of the South's need for Texas wool and cotton, he wrote.

> Had from Atlanta, Col. Cumby, of Greer's old regiment for a travelling companion.
> Leaving, we detached a friend to Augusta, and I went to Columbus, (Ga.) to try
> the market for clothes etc. At Augusta our friend found nothing for sale that mili-
> tary men wanted. At Columbus I found little—that little mostly from Richmond,
> greatly increased in price. I had heard a great deal about Georgia cloth manufac-
> ture, and Columbus has two mills, but none of the products that I could find or
> hear of, were half as good as our home made Jeans, with plenty of wool in it. The
> Eagle mills are working strictly for the Government, but the product is poor in
> every respect, and nearly all cotton. The truth is wool is very scarce east of the Mis-
> sissippi, and the Texas wool deposited at Jefferson and Shreveport much needed.[80]

DeMorse said he expected to receive clothing and blankets from Louisville,
Cincinnati, and Baltimore, after obtaining only a small amount in Georgia. He
said that what he obtained was better than that available in Richmond.[81]

DeMorse was happy to report on October 4, 1862, that enough supplies and
ordnance had been obtained to equip his cavalry regiment. Writing from Monroe, Louisiana, he listed ordnance stores, tents, and arms, but was trying to arrange transportation to get his purchases home to Clarksville.[82]

The regiment began training at Camp Jeff Davis near Clarksville and Camp
Sidney Johnson near Paris in October and remained in Texas until March 1863
to protect settlements from Indian attacks and against an anticipated Federal
invasion of the state.[83] DeMorse and his men were ordered into Indian Territory
in March to take part in a daring plan to drive Federal troops from the territory
and to reopen the Arkansas River to Confederate commerce.[84]

Once seen as a barren wasteland suitable only for natives, the Indian Territory became both a strategic and a defensive priority for the Union and the
Confederacy.[85] The region already had several Union forts that were connected
to Kansas by military and mail roads. The Arkansas River allowed whoever
controlled the region to ship supplies by water, and under the prairie soil, lead
deposits were available for ammunition. The territory could serve either as a
buffer to stop a Union attack on Texas or it could become a staging area for
Confederate forces seeking to launch raids into Federal territory.[86]

DeMorse wrote on March 30 that his regiment had arrived safely at Fort Arbuckle near the Washita River in Indian Territory. The letter was not published
until almost a month later, on April 25. He described the former Union facility
as a series of buildings—officers' quarters, soldiers' barracks, a hospital, and
family residences, but lacking any perimeter defenses, including fencing.[87] "The

buildings here are commodious and extensive, but were never quite as good as at Washita, and have been more abused. All the post furniture has been carried off, except one large double desk, and a few iron bedsteads," he wrote.[88]

DeMorse's biggest concern in Indian Territory was the trustworthiness of the Confederates' Indian allies. He did not view them as equal partners. His racial belief in the superiority of whites, coupled with his inherent distrust of Native Americans following years of frontier Indian attacks, left DeMorse unsettled. His realization that his pragmatic commanding officer, General Samuel Bell Maxey, was willing to treat Indians fairly and promote those under his command when they distinguished themselves did not sit well with DeMorse. Confederate law was on Maxey's side—no color distinction between Indian and white troops was recognized. The *Standard*'s editor bitterly protested Maxey's decision to promote Indians to officer ranks. Worried that white officers, including himself, might become subordinate in rank to their native allies, De-Morse asked to be relieved of duty immediately and transferred away from Indian Territory. Although he eventually relented when he decided that Maxey had no intention of having Indian officers command white troops, DeMorse never conveyed any of his concerns to the *Standard*.[89]

DeMorse wrote in his April 25 letter that he would accompany Colonel Richard Gano to an important conference with the leaders of seven tribes to solicit their cooperation in the coming battles to end Federal control of the Indian Territory. The meeting, he noted, would prove equally important for the natives because several of the tribes had split between supporting the Union and the Confederacy. The Indians, DeMorse wrote, "have long awaited his coming, having been informed that he would bring a force sufficiently imposing for protection."[90]

DeMorse said one of the Indian leaders, a Tonkaway who called himself Jeff Davis, appeared unexpectedly at Fort Arbuckle and presented Colonel Gano with a homemade rope in exchange for rations for his family. DeMorse described Davis as a "shrewd man" with a "decidedly sensible cast of countenance—rather intellectual." He then launched into a description of Davis' wife and daughter.

> His old squaw was large, fat, and as a matter of unusual delicacy, had a clean cotton handkerchief over her breast. The younger one (I suppose) looked old in the face, but was thought to be a daughter. Both wore Buckskin pantalettes, and had a much saver [sic] way of riding on horseback than the feminines on our side of the creek. These ladies in the graceful style of their tribe, held their feet down on both sides of their horses; I believe it looks better, because more natural, than the way of disposing of one's entire bulk, on *one* side of the horse, to say nothing of the natural position.[91]

DeMorse's attendance at what turned into a series of meetings with tribal leaders was an eye-opening experience for the Texan who may never have been among natives before. His lengthy letter opened with a stereotypical account of the Confederates' potential allies: Some of the chiefs, he wrote, were "fat good natured looking men" and one had "a decidedly sensible expression." Another tribal leader did not appear that intelligent-looking to DeMorse, yet the editor acknowledged his impressions might be deceiving. "He is considered quite a sensible old fellow matter of fact business like Indian." DeMorse wrote that he was particularly taken by Seminole Colonel John Jumper's appearance. The six-foot, three-inch officer had a "dark expressive countenance, serious" with a stout frame and looked impressive in his Confederate uniform, replete with the cape of a cavalry officer. DeMorse wrote that Jumper "had a semi-savage and imposing look" but conceded that the officer's bearing and style of speech were impressive.

DeMorse described the Indians' camp with his reporter's eye for detail, telling about nearly every square inch of the lodge in which the officers and chiefs met, including the robes and blankets upon which they sat, as well as the impressive tall grass and good water nearby. He said Gano's discussion with the Indians was lengthy—a fact that surprised DeMorse, who had assumed natives were impulsive, battle-ready individuals. The tribal leaders asked many questions and were cautious about going to war, apparently an unexpected turn of events for the white officers who ended the meeting "expecting not much from them."

DeMorse also conveyed his surprise at the number of horses the Indians possessed, at first believing many were stolen. A tribal leader assured him that the horses belonged to the tribe and that many more had been stolen by Kiowas. "Geo. Washington [one of the chiefs] told us he had eleven young men trying to recover horses stolen from them by wild Indians," DeMorse wrote. "Not a few of us thought they might be out stealing themselves; especially as it was said they had been out 30 days, and the tribe was getting anxious about them. But we did them injustice," he admitted, acknowledging that despite his reservations about the Indians, at least some of his impressions were wrong. Shortly after his discussion with Chief Washington, the 11 young Indians returned home with 53 ponies. The Kiowas, DeMorse wrote, would not relinquish 36 other horses.[92]

Apparently satisfied with the terms and conditions of military service, the Indians enrolled their names for battle. DeMorse described the camp scene that evening. The enlisted men were ordered to their barracks to keep them away from the Indians, but the white soldiers peered out of the windows watching a war dance in fascination. The bored soldiers eventually opened the windows and, against orders, offered their new Indian allies tobacco in exchange for a demonstration of their prowess with their bows and arrows. DeMorse was impressed with their accuracy. He had assumed the Indians would be dour and silent and was surprised at how talkative and happy they seemed.

Fort Arbuckle would serve as an important center for the tribal people to receive rations of salt, flour, and beef, De Morse wrote, omitting the fact that repeated warfare had devastated much of the Territory, making it largely uninhabitable. He was concerned by the heavily armed Indians arriving with guns, hatchets, and knives on their persons. Their need for such arms while traveling from their respective camps to the fort was a necessity, he later learned. The complicated Union and Confederate alliances meant many tribes were fighting among themselves. The Tonkaway in particular, he wrote, were at war with some of their tribal neighbors and had lost more than 70 members of their tribe in battles. "Now they have only 50 warriors left of them, 20 are with our companies across the river," DeMorse wrote.

He ended his letter on a sentimental note, saying he had visited the post's graveyard and found it in a dilapidated condition. "These graves have a neglected and deserted appearance which says as plainly as inanimate things can say, that they are rapidly on the road to desolation and forgetfulness." Perhaps sensing his own mortality on the eve of going into battle, he ruminated on how the dead should be remembered and buried.

> It matters little where we lie at last except that in a well managed ground within the circle of active life, surrounded and cared for by the posterity of our selves or our friends, the chain of kindly association seems to be preserved after death; in the memory of those who know us and loved us in life, and in the knowledge imparted to their children. But on one of these remote hills where nobody goes, a slab, with an inscription is a mockery of memory frigid and wholly unsatisfactory.[93]

DeMorse reported on May 12 that his regiment had moved to Camp Butler in the Creek Nation along with Gano and three companies. The letter described several days of travel, and DeMorse, probably in violation of military censorship rules, provided a detailed description of the various companies and their exact complements that were to arrive within the next three days. Knowing that readers would be concerned about their loved ones, DeMorse said his men were in good health because the march from Fort Arbuckle was not an arduous one.

As DeMorse and his men arrived within 14 miles of their objective, the Union-held Fort Gibson, the editor witnessed but did not participate in his first battle. Federal troops, he reported, were making largely unsuccessful attempts to convince Indians allied with the Confederacy to switch sides. "The Feds have a mixed force of whites, Indians, and negroes at Gibson, and their commander Col. Phillips has been scattering proclamations among the Creeks on this side, to induce them to abandon the Confederacy. Their success has not been flattering," he wrote, adding that a group of Confederate-affiliated Creek Indians lured a boatload of Union soldiers across the river, pretending to switch sides, but with the intention of killing the Federal troops. The Indians opened fire prematurely and killed some men, he wrote, while others jumped overboard and were presumed drowned. "The current setting to the opposite shore, the boat drifted back, and the Creeks lost their prizes. I do not know whether the Feds will bank much on the Creeks, after that specimen of allegiance," he wrote.[94]

Almost three weeks passed before DeMorse put pen to paper again. He launched into a lengthy account of a week's worth of skirmishes. The fighting he described was largely confined to pickets sniping at each other at several river crossings, along with small groups of soldiers on both sides testing each other's forces. During these skirmishes, DeMorse learned some important lessons. The enemy, he discovered, was better equipped, possessing long-range rifles that carried across the river. The Confederate guns were largely ineffective at long range.[95]

Putting the best face on the situation, DeMorse said his men's bravery under fire more than made up for the shortcomings of their weapons. Union troops, he said, frequently retreated during the skirmishes, despite having a heavily armed fort with reinforcements nearby, while the Confederate troops stood their ground. "They fired upon us at each exposure of a man's person on the bank of the river, and we returned the fire with our largest range guns. We tried them at two fords, and made them run back to their covers at each," he said with satisfaction. A few days later, when his men captured an ambulance, DeMorse proudly proclaimed an enemy escort of 100 men abandoned the wagon, despite the fact that they outnumbered the Confederates. "Our boys were greatly elated by the running away of the foe, so near their stronghold with its 3,000 men, but did not incline to stay a great while longer, lest they might be surrounded."[96]

DeMorse learned another important lesson on May 26 when he accompanied Gano's men and the Indian troops in a show of force, marching the men in a circle three times by a river crossing in plain view of the enemy. As the Union troop's shots "flew thick and unceasingly," he discovered that some troops and their horses became unnerved during their first actual combat. "Horses first under fire were hard to manage, and now and then some amiable rider seemed disposed to keep on the safe side of a tree," he said in acknowledging that some men shirked their duty.[97]

Prisoners, both Indian and white, were captured several times during the week. DeMorse admitted confusion reigned over whether the captured Indians were friend or foe. One day his men found a Creek Indian who promptly claimed to be one of Confederate Colonel David McIntosh's men. Uncertain as to whether he was telling the truth, DeMorse sent the prisoner to his commanding officer, General Douglas Cooper. DeMorse noted: "He was a hostile. How he was disposed of, I do not know." A few days later, DeMorse's racial beliefs about Indians led him to assume that two captured Osage soldiers had to have been enemy troops because of their perceived fierceness. Although one man smiled at DeMorse and his men, the other had "the most villainous expression" he had ever seen. He was not alone in his beliefs.

"Would not the sight of those devils frighten any body?" one of his men said about the tall natives with their Mohawk-style haircuts, earrings, and red war paint. DeMorse agreed with the nameless soldier. He learned later that both men were in General Cooper's service.[98]

The confusion caused by both sides employing native troops nearly led Confederate Creek troops to open fire on DeMorse and part of his regiment as they returned one evening to their camp. White rebel pickets shouted in alarm as he and his men rode up a riverbank, although they had announced themselves. Only Colonel David McIntosh's order that DeMorse and his men halt until he could send word to the Indians that Confederate troops were about to enter camp kept them from being attacked.[99]

Although DeMorse gave Indian General Stand Watie and his men credit for a successful raid that netted the Confederate troops 500 horses and mules, he remained uncertain of the abilities and dedication of his Indian allies. Writing in the *Standard*, he blamed the Indians for failing to stop and seize a Union wagon train filled with supplies in May 1863. The Creeks had spotted the train of 160 wagons bound for Fort Gibson one moonlit night and had themselves been spotted by the train's armed escort. DeMorse wrote that the Creeks decided to delay attacking until morning. He did not indicate the size of the Union escort, nor did he indicate how many Indian troops had spotted the train. He also omitted a crucial fact that, if known, might have reduced his stature in the eyes of his readers: DeMorse himself, and not the Indians, was given the task of intercepting any supply train from reinforcing Fort Gibson. Instead, he wrote a partial truth—that Union troops had made a daring night march and had gotten to the safety of the fort, eluding the Confederates without saying which commander was responsible.[100]

In a morale-building conclusion to his letter, DeMorse said that Union troops were hungry, demoralized, and wanted to go home; information he claimed to have obtained during a truce of sorts between Confederate and Union pickets. "The opposite pickets at Niven's ferry got amiable yesterday, concluding that they were doing no good, firing at each other long distance, laid down their arms, and went down to the water's edge, and had a talk," he wrote. The Union soldiers asked about the wheat crop in Texas, telling the Confederates that the fort had little flour for baking bread. The soldiers also said they were short on tobacco and were tired of fighting. Their Creek Indian allies, the men said, "would not fight at all."[101]

DeMorse and his men experienced their first real battle at Elk Creek on July 17, 1863, during the Battle of Honey Springs about 15 miles south of Fort Gibson. The Confederate troops had moved away from the fort to await reinforcements from Arkansas before renewing their offensive. The Union commander, General James G. Blunt, correctly predicted why the rebel troops had left and launched an attack before the Arkansas troops arrived. Blunt's force numbered 3,000 men, including whites, Indians, and black troops from the 1st Kansas Colored. Following a skirmish in the morning after a rainstorm, a pitched battle erupted in the afternoon. The battle proved disastrous for the Confederates, but especially for DeMorse, who at one point tried to press the Confederate advantage when he thought Union troops were retreating. He had misunderstood a Union commander's call for his own Indian troops to move out of the line of fire. When DeMorse ordered his men to charge, soldiers from the 1st Kansas Colored delivered two volleys into his men from just 40 feet away. The first rank of the 29th Regiment fell in the first volley, while the second volley brought down more men. By the third volley, DeMorse's men began a disorganized retreat.[102]

Making matters worse, the Confederates, including DeMorse's men, discovered that their already poor-grade powder had gotten wet, leaving their weapons misfiring. Equally alarming to the Confederates: the men of the 1st Kansas Colored fought with intensity. The Texans had believed that they could merely march up to the black soldiers and capture them.[103] When rain began falling again in the afternoon, the Confederate commander, General Douglas Cooper, ordered his troops to fall back to get more ammunition. He discovered that the Union was about to turn his left flank, and the Confederate retreat began. Several rebel counterattacks took place, but all failed and the Confederate troops fled, ending their attempt to take Fort Gibson and leaving Union forces in control north of the Arkansas River. The rout was not only total, but the Confederate casualties were disproportionate to those of the Union troops. Only 79 Union troops were killed or wounded, while the rebels lost 637 men.[104]

The battle was an embarrassing defeat for the Confederates, and DeMorse had received a severe arm wound. He wrote to General Cooper—and sent a copy to his newspaper—to straighten out reports Cooper had already received claiming the 29th Texas Cavalry did not take part in the battle. "Reports of the fight have gone out, in which the regiment is not recognized as having been in it, when in fact its participation was not secondary to that of any of the forces engaged," DeMorse wrote. After he was wounded, his second in command, Lieutenant Colonel O.G. Welch, held his ground until all other forces had withdrawn. He had then marched his men back to a ravine to regroup for another assault. Realizing that Union troops were closing in on the men of the 29th from two directions, DeMorse's men retreated.

DeMorse was developing a level of respect for the Confederates' Indian allies, although he would never view Native Americans as equals. "The Choctaws were notably prompt and gallant not merely in the portion of the action, which they sustained, but subsequently, when other actions were expected, showed promptness and alacrity," he wrote.[105] His newspaper report, as well as his official report, turned a hard-fought, humiliating loss into testaments of bravery.

DeMorse's men would retreat again at Perryville near the Canadian River. He left the hospital still suffering from the effects of his arm wound and returned to his men, discovering them in full retreat on the evening of August 25. Assuming command, DeMorse led his troops and a number of Indian families, complete with their household goods and animals.[106] Although the two retreats proved emotionally and physically difficult for DeMorse and his men, the soldiers were far more sorely tested by the winter weather. Food was lacking and many soldiers were poorly clad. Desertions began occurring in substantial numbers, since many of the soldiers had homes on the south side of the Red River. Food, shelter, and a chance to harvest their crops awaited them in Texas, and many deserted, despite the potential consequences.

DeMorse stopped writing during the winter months. However, the men's presence back at their homes would have alerted citizens to the increasing number of desertions, as well as regular advertisements in the *Standard* offering a $30 reward for deserters. The advertisements contained the names and physical descriptions of men from the 29th Cavalry and the 2nd Texas Brigade.[107]

Recognizing the tenuous nature of holding out during the frigid winter months, DeMorse requested permission to move his regiment back to northeast Texas. His camp was under-provisioned, his men were freezing, and he could not beat back a Federal attack, should one occur. DeMorse assured General Maxey that such a move would prompt the deserters from his regiment to return because they would be defending their homes from potential invasion. His request was refused; Maxey responded that their Indian allies would abandon the Confederate cause should DeMorse's men leave the territory. If any fighting were to occur, Maxey wanted it to be in Indian Territory, rather than risk battles near Clarksville and the surrounding wheat and corn-growing region of north Texas.[108]

DeMorse would see battle again in the spring of 1864 as part of the Red River campaign in Arkansas. His cavalry regiment was transferred from Indian Territory to assist in the Confederate effort to stop the expected Federal invasion of Texas via the Red River. DeMorse and his men finally achieved a victory on April 18, 1864, at Poison Spring, Arkansas, at a tremendous cost to the enemy. DeMorse's cavalry, as part of General Maxey's forces, attacked and captured a foraging party sent by Union General Fred Steele to gather corn. The Federal troops, many of whom were black, were returning to Camden when Maxey's forces met them about 15 miles from town at Lee Plantation and attacked the party in the front and the rear. "Raising the well known Texas yell, we dashed at them, and met with a warm reception," DeMorse declared proudly in a report to the *Standard* four days later.

> The whole force of the enemy outnumbered us by four to one, aided by four pieces of artillery, was brought to bear against us. The enemy had burnt the woods in their front and the thick smoke between us, prevented us from getting a fair view, but the command to "shoot low" was well obeyed, and afterwards showed with

what deadly effect. Their artillery rained showers of canister shot but luckily most all passed too high.[109]

The Confederate's return fire forced the Union troops to retreat north to Camden. The foraging party lost 198 wagons of corn and equipment and suffered 301 deaths, 182 of whom were from the 1st Kansas Colored, while the Confederates lost far fewer, with estimates ranging from 95 to 114. The rebels also captured 4 cannons and 1,200 mules. While the battle was one of the greatest Confederate successes of the war in Arkansas, the fight was forever marked by the massacre of members of the 1st Kansas Colored—the same troops who had met the rebels the previous year at Honey Springs.[110] DeMorse, flush with success, wrote of the battle with pride, praising his men and the Choctaw who fought in the vicinity of the 29th Cavalry.

> This engagement lasted some 45 minutes, and during this time, the musketry was exceedingly heavy, and upon our part effective. The enemy made no stand of any importance afterwards. To the troops of the Indian District, it was a proud day. We were fighting with the same enemy with whom we had contended last year in a series of unsuccessful engagements, with numbers always against us, and with arms that were almost useless. This time we were better armed more equally matched, and I am glad to say done their whole duty, fighting through the whole engagement, with a valor unsurpassed by any troops, and gave to the enemy such a severe whipping at the start, that he never recovered from it during the day.
>
> Individual acts of heroism by men in the ranks of the Texas brigade were numerous—Our Choctaw allies stood nobly by us to a man and burning with wrongs, and insults heaped upon their defenceless women, and children, by the enemy in his invasion of their country last fall, wreaked tenfold their vengeance.
>
> General Maxey fully sustained his reputation as a prudent General and successful fighter, both by his gallantry upon the field, and his ingenuity in attacking, gaining the entire confidence of all engaged, and the confidence of the Indians to a greater extent than any man who has heretofore commanded them.[111]

DeMorse made no attempt to stop the Indians' massacre of the men from the 1st Kansas Colored. He most likely knew that he could not have stopped the natives' desire for revenge even if he had tried.[112] The hungry and ill-clothed Choctaw and Chickasaw troops despised the black soldiers, viewing them as "the ravagers of their country, the despoilers of their homes, and the murderers of their women and children."[113]

Following their victory at Poison Spring, the 29th Cavalry was ordered to return to Indian Territory. DeMorse and his men would participate in just one more battle, at Cabin Creek, in September 1864. The battle again would be noted for the massacre of black soldiers who were part of a hay-gathering party at the Cabin Creek crossing on the Fort Scott-Fort Gibson military road. In a

September 29 report to his newspaper, DeMorse said that he and his men were part of a force of 1,200 men (700 of whom were from the 1st Indian Brigade) that accompanied Generals Watie and Gano on a 14-day march that covered 400 miles to seize a Union supply train loaded with winter supplies. The expedition would prove to be the last successful Confederate expedition north of the Arkansas River.

Capturing the wagon train's supplies was a necessity for the hungry and ill-clad Southern troops and their Indian allies. Ensuring its safe delivery to Fort Gibson was equally important for Union troops. Two years of warfare in Indian Territory had caused a near scorched-earth policy. Homes were burned, crops destroyed, livestock taken or scattered, and families divided between their Union and Confederate allegiances. Although many Union supporters had moved to Kansas, Indian families attempted to return home following the Battle of Elk Creek. The Indians allied themselves—some on Union and others on Confederate sides. Federal troops had to supply not only Fort Gibson but also their Indian allies, thousands of whom died of starvation and exposure.[114]

The Confederacy's Indian allies who served under General Watie also wished to return home and sought to drive the Federal troops out of the region. Gano, commander of the 5th Texas Cavalry Brigade, and Watie met on September 13 at Camp Pike in the Choctaw Nation to develop their battle plans. The two generals coordinated their attack plan together, but remained in charge of their own men. Under Gano, DeMorse's men camped at Prairie Springs on September 14, crossed the Arkansas River the next day, and camped at Camp Pleasant in the Creek Nation within a few miles of Fort Gibson. The Confederates were soon detected, and both sides realized that speed was of the essence. For the Confederates, this meant accomplishing their objective of seizing the wagon train. For Union troops, gaining reinforcements for that train became imperative. Watie's men viewed these scouting encounters as a chance to "even the score" with their "traitorous" brothers in the Union army.

The Confederate troops did not have to wait long for battle. Watie, Gano, and their men crossed the Verdigris River on September 16 and came across Federal troops cutting and gathering hay 15 miles northwest of Fort Gibson. Their commander, Captain E.A. Barker, rode out with a scouting party and was promptly met by an advance rebel force of some 200 men. After fighting his way back to his troops, Barker discovered that the rebel troops had attacked the haying party from five different directions. The Union troops held out for half an hour before Barker and 65 of his men led a desperate charge to break through the rebel lines. The Confederate forces attacked and slaughtered the men of the 1st Kansas Colored, captured all the haying machines and several hundred tons of hay. Gano's report of the engagement was effusive: "The sun witnessed our complete success and its last lingering rays rested upon a field of Blood."[115]

DeMorse's report to the *Standard* described the Confederate troops' maneuvers, noting that the "surprise was complete . . . and the cavalry portion [i.e., Captain Barker's men] were flying in every direction, endeavoring to make their escape." He recounted the attack on the 1st Kansas Colored infantrymen who ran 200 yards toward a creek, halted behind trees to regroup, and attempted to open fire on the Confederates and their Indian allies before they were killed. His description of the slaughter was matter-of-fact. DeMorse accepted that killing was an expected outcome of battle.

> An immediate demand for surrender was made [by the rebels to the black soldiers], with the assumption that their lives would be spared. This they refused to do, and fired upon the officer who bore the flag. A few rounds were exchanged with them, by the scattered men from the various commands. Failing to dislodge them, Howell's Battery was ordered to open. One shot thrown in their midst, had the desired effect: they scattered in all directions along the creek . . . The vengeance of the red man was not thus to be appeased, and his natural sagacity suggested that in the creek, and under the tall grass and bushes overhanging the banks, the "*contrabands*" might be found. A search proved the supposition to be correct, for there sure enough, with noses protruding from under the water, the foe had secreted himself. Call to memory the Choctaws at Poison Springs, and you have the remainder of the fight described.[116]

The rebels, DeMorse wrote, captured weapons, wagons, mowing machines, and 90 prisoners. Confederate troops burned all of the hay, which DeMorse estimated at 3,000 tons. The prisoners, he wrote, told their captors that the wagon train was due any day, and the rebels headed to intercept it.[117]

Two days later on September 18, the Confederates seized the wagon train in a daring evening raid at Cabin Creek. The commander of the train, Major Henry Hopkins of the 2nd Kansas Cavalry, knowing that Confederate troops were set on attacking the train, had warned the Union army posts between Fort Scott and Fort Gibson that the enemy was in the area. He had picked up reinforcements, and patrols spotted the Confederates three miles away.[118]

DeMorse's account of the battle rang with patriotism and demonstrated his growing respect for the Confederates' Indian allies, as well as his willingness to stereotype the enemy: "We retained our position until dark, when we withdrew to a better one, farther back to our rear, to await the arrival of Watie. This gallant officer, ever prompt, arrived at 12 o'clock, and the whole line was moved forward, and a partial investment of the place was made. The enemy by this time infuriated with whiskey, would ride within a short distance of our lines, and defy us to move up, and give battle."

DeMorse had previously avoided extensive purple prose, but finally burst forth in reporting the successful seizure of the wagon train.

Whilst in this position the rumbling of wagons, and the confusion incident to the gearing of mules, gave evidence that the enemy under cover of night, were endeavoring to run off the train. Instantly the command of column forward ringing upon the midnight air, aroused the hitherto impatient attacking party, and upon ground already historic from Watie's defeat last year, by the bright light of the moon, through the tall wet grass, destined to be the final resting place of a few, our column with a shout, rushed gallantly forward. The bright flashes of musketry along both lines, the white smoke of the bursting bombs, the whistle of the minnie ball, accompanied by the guttural sound of Howell's artillery as it belched forth its iron messengers of death, at the hour of midnight, under the brilliant lustre of the moon and stars, upon both parties engaged in the death struggle, rendered the scene sublime.[119]

After an hour's hotly contested battle, the troops were withdrawn to secure positions to await morning, DeMorse added. Then he puffed the officers involved, crediting them for their "daring and gallantry," including Colonel John Jumper, the Seminole commander, whose towering form "was always to be seen in the thickest of the contest, a conspicuous mark for the enemy, as he mingled among his braves, encouraging them, and setting for them a noble example." His report also praised his commander Gano and Indian commander Watie for their "indomitable energy . . . They were everywhere in the hottest of the action." DeMorse reserved his highest praise for Captain Sylvanus Howell, commander of the six-gun artillery brigade that accompanied Gano's men, claiming that Howell's well directed fire had helped win the battle.[120]

The Confederate troops recovered 140 wagons "rich in plunder." It would be DeMorse's final battle and the only successful foray north of the Arkansas River. He and his men were sent to Marshall, Texas, during the winter of 1864-1865 to await a rumored Federal invasion of Texas. The spring of 1865 saw DeMorse and his men ordered to Galveston and then Houston, again to protect the state against an expected invasion. The news of General Lee's surrender, followed by the surrender of the Trans-Mississippi Department of the Confederacy on May 26, ended DeMorse's career as a war correspondent.

He returned to Clarksville and resumed his editorship of the *Standard*, encouraging readers in his first editorial to help restore order and civil law to Texas and work for the development of the state.[121] He spent the last 22 years of his life promoting economic and agricultural development, while railing against radical Republican control. Although he encouraged citizens to take the oath of allegiance to the Union, DeMorse hoped that some form of modified slavery could be continued in the state. He would hold his white supremacist views for the remainder of his life.

Although he had little interest in political office, DeMorse took a prominent role in shaping the Texas Constitution of 1876. He also helped organize the Texas Veterans Association in 1873, was active in the state Grange, and served on the board of directors for the Agricultural and Mechanical College of Texas (now known as Texas A & M). In 1873, he was elected president of the Texas Press and Editorial Association, but he spent most of his postwar years in Clarksville editing the *Standard*. DeMorse retired in 1874, shutting down his newspaper's operation. Several years later, upon friends' insistence, he purchased another press and restarted the *Standard*. The editor died on October 25, 1887, and was buried in the Clarksville Cemetery. His daughter continued the paper for most of a year, but the journal's character and tone had always been DeMorse's. When he died, in essence, so did his publication.

22

William P. Doran: A Texas Hero Takes Up His Pen

Mary M. Cronin

Tired but patient, Texas war correspondent William F. Doran bumped along on a slow-moving mule behind Confederate cavalry brigades headed for Lafayette, Texas, in July 1863. The Texas troops were marching to engage Federal forces in Louisiana to stop a rumored invasion of their home state.[1]

After the Texans drove Union troops out of Thibodeauxville, Doran found an abandoned hayloft and fell asleep. When he awoke, he was surprised to find that the troops from the 47th Massachusetts Regiment had regrouped during the night and recaptured the town. Although Doran was a civilian, he was taken with the troops to New Orleans and jailed.[2]

Doran wrote for two newspapers, the *Houston Tri-Weekly Telegraph* and the *Galveston News,* and his reputation as a war correspondent saved him from being indefinitely confined. Union General William H. Emory learned of the reporter's presence in New Orleans and ordered him brought to his headquarters. Emory wanted to question Doran about the health and well-being of his long-time West Point classmate and now-adversary, General John Magruder, whose forces had retaken Galveston in a daring New Year's Day attack.[3] When Doran was brought to Emory's office, the correspondent waited in an antechamber until the general finished conferring with New Orleans Union commander General Nathaniel Banks. The men were discussing obtaining more shallow draft gunboats to navigate the Sabine Pass bar so that the Union invasion of Texas could go forward.

Emory, who was nearly deaf, spoke loudly with Banks, which allowed Doran to hear the entire conversation. As the correspondent listened, he realized Banks was planning to capture Houston and Galveston if his troops could take the fort at Sabine Pass. Doran kept this knowledge to himself and had a polite meeting with Emory. Afterward, the correspondent was taken to the city's customhouse, which was serving as a makeshift prison. Because of his civilian status, Federal officials agreed to release Doran on his promise that he would book passage to Matamoras, Mexico.

William P. Doran. Illustration from *Galveston Daily News*, February 22, 1896

As Doran was boarding the English schooner *Gleaner* for four days at sea, he learned that thousands of Federal troops, flush with success from the Vicksburg campaign, were waiting with their caissons and mules to board transports to begin an invasion. It would catch Texas by surprise unless Doran could relay the news to Confederate commanders back home.

When the schooner entered the Matamoras harbor, passengers were transferred to a small boat for the trip to shore. High waves almost capsized the boat and nearly drowned the passengers. The waterlogged correspondent caught a carriage for the 30-mile trip to Brownsville, Texas, where he told General Hamilton Bee, the commander of the Rio Grande district, of the Union's invasion plans. With no telegraph or railroad lines at his disposal, the general gave Doran and a cavalry soldier letters of instruction to Magruder in Houston. The two men undertook a nine-day, 250-mile ride, getting fresh mounts at Confederate camps along the way. Doran finally arrived on September 3 and delivered his letter. Magruder sent word of the impending invasion to his engineers at Sabine Pass and ordered them to fortify the community.

More than 4,000 Union troops aboard several transport vessels and four gunboats tried to storm the seaport on September 8, only to be repelled by members of the Davis Guards who unleashed an artillery barrage on the invading Federal forces. The Confederate troops captured 300 prisoners and two gunboats. The rest of the Union troops retreated back to New Orleans, ending immediate hopes of capturing Texas.[4]

Doran's devotion to the Confederate cause led to his Paul Revere-like efforts. His willingness to go beyond the standard duties expected of a correspondent during the Civil War helped seal his status as a Texas legend. His actions also demonstrated that Doran, like other correspondents from both North and South, believed he had a duty to serve both editors and the military.[5]

He again displayed his heroism and devotion to the Confederate cause in February 1865 while visiting the blockade runner, the *Wren*, in Galveston harbor. His boat capsized, sending Doran and four other men, including three officers, into the water. Although Doran was thrown a rope, he insisted that two officers—one who was pinned under the boat when it capsized and another suffering from a gunshot wound—be rescued first. A witness to the accident wrote a letter to the *Houston Tri-Weekly Telegraph* describing the correspondent's heroism.[6] In his newspaper account of the sinking, Doran said nothing of his actions, only hinting at the dangers without providing any details: "I have been in some tight places before, since the war began, but this adventure was the most unpleasant of all."[6]

Doran was a prolific correspondent, frequently sending letters more than once a week. His war reporting began two months before the first shots were fired on Fort Sumter in April 1861, when he covered the seizure of Federal forts along the Rio Grande River by volunteer Texas troops. He continued writing for the *Galveston News* and the *Houston Tri-Weekly Telegraph* until the end of the war. He covered a number of major battles, including Shiloh and Corinth, the Federal blockade and seizure of Galveston and the city's subsequent recapture by Texas troops, and the Union's disastrous Red River campaign. The newspaper exchange system embellished his fame across Texas, although readers only knew him by his pen name of "Sioux."

Doran's correspondence strikes no single overall tone. Although he does not appear to have had any newspaper experience prior to the war's outbreak, he demonstrated a strong reporter's instinct for finding newsworthy items. Like other Confederate correspondents, he frequently mixed fact and editorial commentary and demonstrated a willingness to question and even criticize military decisions when he felt they were wrong. His reports often had strong human interest angles. In August 1864, Doran wrote from Galveston addressing the possible executions of two men for desertion. Although the majority of Texans served the Confederacy with honor, the 33rd Texas Cavalry (as well as other regiments) spent much of the last two years of the war rounding up deserters.

Letters from home describing food shortages and hardships along with harsh camp conditions led a number of men to desert.[7] Although Doran had little use for shirkers and deserters, he wrote that these two men might not be guilty and should not be executed.

> One is a Lieutenant in Waul's Legion. The charge is desertion, for not reporting to his command when ordered, after being declared exchanged. There are many extenuating circumstances in this case and [I] trust that mercy will be extended to the condemned until President Davis can learn the facts. Neither of them have been trying to join the enemy. They are no more guilty than many others have been, and the Lieutenant has been promoted from the ranks for gallantry, and served through all the terrible campaign which ended in the surrender of Vicksburg. They have always, heretofore, been good soldiers and I sincerely trust that the mantle of charity will be thrown around these wretched men, and believing that the Confederacy will thereby gain two gallant and brave soldiers.[8]

Doran was also known for addressing Texans' concerns about the security, health, and well-being of their relatives in uniform. Virtually all of his battle reports contained news of the troops' health, while noting that spirits remained high.[9] Similarly, after Confederate soldiers were paroled by Federal troops in May 1863 at Franklin, Louisiana, Doran sought to ease readers' concerns by telling them that the soldiers were receiving the best care by the citizens of Franklin.[10]

Although he often said he strove for accuracy in his work, Doran's writing at times dipped into the boastful and bombastic propaganda and purple prose common among war reporters of the time.[11] In a letter dated April 4, 1862, from Alexandria, Louisiana, he reported that the city's women met the newly arrived Texas troops with flowers as a sign of their gratitude.

> The flowers will fade, but the noble aspirations in the hearts of the Texians who have been the recipients of them, will endure until the flag of a rescued nation, from the galling thraldom of a covetous grasping and robbing band of usurpers, shall wave in triumph through the length and breadth of our Sunny South.[12]

Patriotism in particular colored his reports. Doran, like many Southern correspondents, promoted the Southern cause and saw his job, in part, as one of boosting morale.[13] He was prone to exaggerate and use pejorative labeling tactics in his reports. In a November 1861 report on the defense of Galveston, Doran noted the island's preparedness, writing: "nearly every county in our State has sent forth her valiant sons to drive back the haughty invaders."[14]

When the Confederate Army of the West began its move from camps in Arkansas to Memphis in early spring of 1862, Doran engaged in boastful rhetoric, referring to the men as "as brave an army as was ever marshaled on the field of battle." He also exaggerated the importance of the impending battle for

Memphis, saying that it would probably be "one of the largest and most decisive battles ever fought on this continent."[15]

Doran also highlighted problems within Union ranks, including Federal casualties, knowing that such news would cheer Texans. Following battles at Fort Bisland, Louisiana, on April 12 and 13, and Franklin the next day, he wrote that Federal deserters were pouring into Confederate lines.

> The federal soldiers hate the idea of serving with negroes, and great disatisfaction and demoralization exists in the army. Thousands are ready to desert at the first chance. Our officers and men in Louisiana are all in good spirits, and confident of success.[16]

To keep up civilian and military morale alike, however, Doran failed to note that the fighting of April 12 through 14 resulted in a Union victory and a subsequent rebel retreat toward Opelousas. In the aftermath of Confederate defeats at Shiloh and Corinth, his reports remained optimistic and filled with patriotic rhetoric. In May 1862 he acknowledged that Confederate ranks were thinning but said the dead were martyrs to liberty as well as to the defense of their homes. Mixing extravagant prose and bravado, the correspondent said the depleted units "shall still be found in the battle's van, and will still uphold the fame of our state. We shall strike the last blow for Southern Liberty, firmly placing our trust in the Almighty that victory will come of our efforts. Our late reverses have nerved us to greater exertions."[17]

Doran's fellow Texans avidly read his reports. Although Texas was often viewed by other Southerners as a backwater of the Confederacy, more than 70,000 men donned uniforms.[18] Civilians clamored for any news about their relatives, and Doran complied with news of the Texans' bravery and their health and well-being in camps. The correspondent referred to the state's civilians and soldiers alike as predominantly brave, virtuous, courteous, sociable, of good character, and honorable. A typical report filed before the Battle of Shiloh noted: "The boys are as enthusiastic as ever. Many have blistered feet, but so anxious are they to push forward that many who are on the sick list talk of nothing but 'Let's press onward.'" Promoting the commonly held stereotype of Texan bravery, Doran added, "wherever their destiny may be cast, your readers may rest assured that the name and fame of the Texian character will still be maintained."[19]

When he felt that injustice or unethical actions were undertaken, however, Doran was willing to criticize soldiers, officers, or government officials. He couched his criticism broadly, rarely pinning the blame on specific individuals. He preferred to publicize the wrongdoing and call for authorities—civilian or military—to take the appropriate actions. He frequently acknowledged that Confederate soldiers often were inadequately fed, clothed, and housed—conditions that sometimes led to looting. In February 1865, Doran angrily criticized Confederate soldiers on Galveston Island, writing they were doing more damage destroying buildings to obtain firewood than the hated Yankee invaders ever did.

> On every side we see the work of destruction going on—residences and outhouses are ruthlessly destroyed for fuel, as though they were the confiscated property of pirates, and there seems to be no protection to property from the authorities. The troops are allowed to tear down and destroy thousands of dollars of property belonging to the citizens.[20]

However, Doran laid no specific blame for the destruction: "Somebody is surely to blame if the troops fail to be supplied with wood, and I trust that General Walker will stir up the party who is to blame, with a long and sharp stick." Although he rebuked the troops, he was certain the city would not fall again to Union forces. "I am confident that this city will be defended to the last, should the enemy see fit to attack it," he wrote. "The garrison is composed of veteran troops. The old heroes of Shiloh, Vicksburg, Glorietta, and Val Verde are here."[21] Patriot that he was, Doran did not mention the dispirited soldiers who were increasingly deserting to Federal blockade forces.[22]

Despite his patriotic rhetoric, Doran was a Northerner by birth. He was born in Rochester, New York, on March 3, 1838. His obituary, published on November 26, 1901, and a biographical sketch he wrote in 1896 for the *Galveston Daily News,* provide the barest of details of his life prior to his arrival in Texas. Doran migrated west in 1853 when he was 15, spending some time in Chicago before moving to Kansas. He tasted battle prior to the Civil War when he fought the Pawnee, Cheyenne, and Sioux while leading 26 wagons and driving oxen from Leavenworth, Kansas, to Fort Laramie, Wyoming, for a government contractor.

Doran moved to Texas in 1860, at age 22, and settled in Harris County. Despite his New York upbringing, his ideology and sympathies were clearly Southern. He wrote several letters to the Rochester newspaper after his arrival in Texas, supporting slavery, telling upstate New Yorkers that the institution was not bad and that Northerners had the wrong impression of slaveholders. In reply, the editor of the newspaper said of Doran: "He is not sound on the grand question."[23]

Abolitionists were campaigning against slavery in the state when Doran arrived in Texas, and his suspicious neighbors initially viewed him as an abolitionist. The claim almost led him to be hanged, demonstrating the tensions that existed in Texas after Abraham Lincoln was nominated for president in 1860. A farmer who had rented land to Doran expelled him when the young man's corn crop was ready for harvest, then spread rumors that he was an abolitionist after Doran brought suit for $100 against the farmer to regain the profits from the sale of the corn.

He moved to a new job as a cook at $15 a month for the supervisors of the Texas and New Orleans Railroad. As Doran recalled, he heard the rumor that he was "a damned Yankee and proposed to get a gang of slaves together and run them off to Mexico." Shortly thereafter, a number of "half-drunk" men visited the San Jacinto Bridge where Doran was working, seeking to hang the "damned abolitionist." His boss, Hal G. Runnels, who hailed from a large slave-holding family, gave the young man his horse, telling him to clear out of the area for a few days. Runnels' parting words to Doran were: "If you are innocent of this charge, I will protect you, and if you are guilty, I will hang you."[24]

The transplanted Texan soon switched careers again, taking a correspondent's position with the *Galveston News*. He received his first taste of war reporting two months before the first shots were fired at Fort Sumter when he enlisted in the Galveston Rifles Company led by Captain A.C. McKeen. The Texas Committee of Public Safety—an organization appointed by the Secession Convention—had issued a statewide call for volunteers to take over all Federal forts and munitions.[25] As part of the Galveston Rifles Company, Doran went to Brazos Santiago, Texas, where the troops met no resistance.

His first few letters of correspondence were brief affairs and were heady with the expectation of fighting the retreating Federal troops—an opportunity that never materialized for the Galveston Rifles. Doran's reports noted little more than the health of the troops, their abiding patriotism, and the able leadership of their commanding officers.[26] Like many correspondents, he had to write quickly and post his material when the opportunity presented itself. He sometimes wrote that reports would be short at times, promising more information would follow in later letters. He often said they could obtain further accounts from soldiers and civilians whose accounts editors usually published. When Doran was dashing off an account of Texans' seizure of Federal forts and property along the Rio Grande River a month before the war's outbreak, he wrote:

> In the hurry of leaving our late encampment at Brazos Santiago, I shall have to neglect many matters that have transpired since my letter to you of the 7th inst. The passengers by the steamer Rusk will, however, supply this deficiency.[27]

After the expeditionary troops secured Brazos Santiago, many of the men returned to Galveston. Doran remained, deciding he had a joint duty to continue to help rid his state of Union troops as well as to report back home. He joined Company C, a battery of light artillery that marched 30 miles to Brownsville to ensure that retreating Federal troops left the state.[28]

The health and well-being of the troops were always at the top of Doran's priorities. Writing from the camp of Captain John R. Waller's Texas Rangers on the banks of the Rio Grande near Brownsville, Doran reported in March 1861 that "all of the men were healthy and in the best of spirits."[29] However, when yellow fever broke out among the Confederate defenders at Sabine Pass in October

The Confederates evacuating Brownsville, Texas, *Harper's Weekly,* February 13, 1864. Courtesy of Rare Books and Special Collections, University of South Carolina Libraries

1862, he acknowledged the spreading illness and claimed it was the sickness more than the rebel defenders that kept Federal troops from invading.[30]

From his early reports on the Rio Grande to war's end, Doran also engaged in a common journalistic practice—name-dropping. He frequently puffed officers and occasionally enlisted men who performed admirably in Sioux's view. In a letter dated March 19, 1861, from Brownsville, Doran wrote that the troops were in a high state of readiness: "Capt. Waller is an old frontiersman, and knows how to select a reliable body of men," he wrote. "His company numbers 104 picked men—and mostly Southern born. The other officers of the company have been selected with great care."[31]

Beyond Doran's puffery lay an unspoken, yet publicly known concern: not all Texans supported the Southern cause. Only 77 percent of the state's voters cast ballots in favor of secession on February 23, 1861.[32] While some pro-Union Texans fled the Lone Star state, others remained, particularly in the Texas hill country.[33] Historians estimate that as many as one third of all Texans had pro-Union sentiments, although the war cowed many voices.[34] Captain Waller, therefore, had to pick his men carefully. Doran acknowledged the fact in a September 1861 report from Fort Brown, Texas. "We are in as much danger from traitors at home as from the invasion of enemies," he wrote.[35]

Recruiting calls were numerous in many of his reports in 1861 and 1862. He intoned the memory of the freedom fighters at the battles at San Jacinto and the Alamo to remind the state's citizens that their liberty from Mexico had been hard fought. Writing from Velasco, Doran invoked these near-sacred battles to instill in the younger generation that fighting was often a necessity when freedom was threatened. Paraphrasing part of H.L. Flash's patriotic poem, "The Lone Star Flag," he wrote: "Nearly every person capable of doing military duty in this district now stands ready to march to any point that might be invaded and the men of Old Brazoria will rally under that star which shone so bright, when it braved the battle of San Jacinto's fight."[36]

He appealed to merchants and civilians to provide for soldiers when the government and military could not, writing that it was their civic duty to help outfit and feed the troops defending their land and freedom. Reporting from Velasco, he wrote that the soldiers of Colonel Bates' regiment were protecting the state from Yankee invaders, despite the personal cost. "They have furnished their own arms, and as yet have had no clothing found them by the government." He added that coffee and tea, staples of the Texas dinner table, were nonexistent for the soldiers. "I trust those merchants who have such large stocks on hand will not forget the soldiers on this coast."[37]

Doran finally reported on a major battle—Shiloh, in April 1862. Until then, he sought to make his letters rise above the mundane stories of camp life by reporting on unusual events and human interest stories. A letter from Galveston dated January 10, 1862, noted that the city was quiet; the blockading fleet was still anchored in the harbor. Then he launched into the heart of his letter, saying that "considerable excitement" occurred at the provost marshal's prison when a detainee named Charles Brown, who was facing charges of treason, was found to have committed suicide. Doran wrote: "He was arrested by scouts belonging to Col. Bates' Regiment, near Velasco, a few weeks since. He was found with a sail-boat on the shore of the gulf and could not give a clear account of himself." Brown was arrested for giving "contradictory statements" about working for the Union blockading fleet. Doran reported that Brown "has had a bad reputation among his neighbors, who charged him with having been in the habit of harboring runaway negroes." The report closed with his usual patriotic rhetoric and a smattering of bravado: "There is considerable talk among the troops, as to marching to the border States when spring comes; and if the President would accept of a few regiments it would please the Texas boys. They are tired of inaction and wish to practice shooting at invaders."[38]

Doran soon got that chance. The following spring, with the war well under way, *Galveston News* Editor Willard Richardson and *Houston Tri-Weekly Telegraph* Editor Edward Cushing made arrangements for him to accompany the 2nd Texas Infantry on its long journey from Beaumont to Corinth, Mississippi.

The Texans were to join the army of General Albert Sidney Johnston. Doran provided his two newspapers with detailed accounts of the journey, which included a march, a trip by steamer from Alexandria, Louisiana, to Memphis, and an all-night train trip to Corinth.

His letters from the trip read in part like travelogues. Doran extolled the virtues of the communities in which the troops passed, a not-so-subtle reminder of what Southerners were fighting to protect. Reaching Memphis, Doran wrote: "Memphis is a beautiful city; situated upon a series of red bluffs, it commands a view of the river in both directions."[39] Always mindful of his readers' concerns for their relatives in uniform, he discussed the troops' health during their march through Arkansas and Mississippi on the way to Memphis.

"The health of the men is as a general thing, as good as could be expected, taking into consideration the sudden changes of climate endured," he wrote. "Many are suffering with bad colds." In a nod to patriotism, he added: "but all are in the best of spirits and anxious to meet the foe."[40] Doran also dipped into a mix of invective and fear tactics in his letters to encourage Texans to enlist. In a March 1862 report from Louisiana, he rallied Texans to fight the Union army before the invaders made their way to Texas.

> We are aware of the purpose of our unprincipled enemy. For years they have coveted the plantations of the South to divide among their people. It is not a war to preserve the Union, as they say, but a war to filch from the Southern people the homesteads where they were reared. A war to emancipate the negroes of the South and render the most beautiful part of America a vast scene of desolation, and a graveyard for themselves, who will expect to people your plantations.[41]

He concluded by adding a recruiting call, again drawing upon history to establish a parallel between Federal troops and German mercenaries who fought with British troops against Americans during the Revolutionary War: "And, people of Texas, are you prepared to bow to the oppressor? Then, if not, at once enroll yourselves under your country's banner and assist in driving the cowardly Hessians from the soil of your country!"[42]

Although Doran arrived safely, he nearly missed the Battle of Shiloh. Confederate commanders issued an order for all nonmilitary personnel to leave the camp and cut off rations for all civilians, including Doran, to ensure they would leave. He had to enlist in order to cover the battle for the *News* and the *Telegraph*: "Pleading my case as a newspaperman did no good, and I was forced to enlist in Co. A of Capt. Christian. I then put on the uniform and became a soldier bold," he recalled after the war.[43]

Shiloh was Doran's first taste of war, and the bloody conflict led him to pen an introspective picture of the scale of bloodshed and the depth of human tragedy that occurred during wartime.

Reader, did you ever see a battle? Did you ever see two powerfull armies, each furnished with the most improved implements for each other's destruction, approach each other? If not, then you can form no idea what a battle is; there you see a whole line of humanity, eagerly eyeing the other. The order to fire is given, and the ground is covered with the dying, dead, and wounded.[44]

Doran also reported in the same letter that Confederate troops suffered from hunger and exposure. As usual, he laid no particular blame—either on the government or military officials—for not providing proper food, blankets, and tents for the men before the Battle of Shiloh.

The health of the men is somewhat better, and all are fast recovering from the exposures of the great battle. For three nights prior to the battle, our men slept without blankets, and had only crackers to eat. Two of these nights were rainy, and we suffered terribly, both with hunger and cold! We had expected the battle to take place much sooner.[45]

Shiloh would weigh heavily on Doran. The correspondent discovered that the so-called cowardly oppressors fought harder than he expected. He acknowledged this fact in a report from Corinth dated May 6 in explaining his role as one of 22 men picked to act as skirmishers during the siege of Corinth. Posted in the woods, the small number of troops soon found themselves overrun by Union troops, much to Doran's embarrassment.

We were concealed behind logs, trees and brush. The Yankee cavalry came sweeping down on the two sides of us in overwhelming numbers, and our only chance was to escape the best way we could by the rear road. Down they came on us, and I will be honest and say it—we did run like wild cats, our gallant Captain (old Joe Smith) bringing up the rear. The scene was ludicrous. There we were imitating the Yankees at foot races, and we Texians too.[46]

Doran sent another frank account of the Battle of Corinth the following month that included an admission of fatal mistakes made by Confederate troops.

Our regiment has been into the Corith [sic] fight and I am happy to report that we have none killed or wounded, or missing. The men were ordered to report to Gen. Van Dorn on the 9th inst., and he immediately led us out to attack the enemy's advance guard, who had Farmington, at some four miles to the east of Corinth. Our plans were somewhat frustrated by a sad mistake of his Arkansas regiments mistaking each other for enemies. They fired on each other, killing and wounding 6. Gen. Price's army made a forced march on the left wing of theirs, and attacked them. They resisted stubbornly for a while, but soon broke and run, leaving much property behind. Our loss I learn is some 16 killed and 28 wounded. That of the enemy killed, wounded, and prisoners, is from 500 to 800, besides a brass battery. The battle raged awfully for a few hours, and the federals suffered terribly. Our regiments were near exhausted by our long exposure, but they won from Van Dorn and Price, high praises for their good order in line.

The correspondent ended his letter, as was his style, on a positive and patriotic note: "The health of the men is improving slowly, and all are ready for the next fight."[47] Doran was shot in his heel during the battle, a wound that eventually led to his discharge.[48]

Despite his injury, Doran remained in Company A and sent compelling accounts on the city's siege and the Confederate troops' subsequent retreat. He tried to frame the retreat from Corinth in early June 1862 under General P.G.T. Beauregard as orderly and somewhat of a victory, rather than the defeat that it was. "Our retreat from Corinth is in order," he wrote. "No hustle or bustle. It will prove one of the greatest strategic movements of the war eventually."[49] Doran failed to mention that exhausted Union troops did not pursue the retreating rebel soldiers. Nor did he speak of the psychological damage inflicted by the Union army on Confederate troops' morale following their forced retreats from both Shiloh and Corinth. Instead, he painted a picture of brave and determined troops who lived up to the stereotypes readers expected.

> In every instance when the Texians charged, the federals ran. This has been so ever since I have been here. This is no more than could be expected of Texians. Of the other troops here, I will say of them, they are indeed brave, and in no wise behind Texians in deeds of bravery and valor.[50]

As he did in many of his reports, Doran also reassured the folks back home that the troops were physically well. He noted a few cases of measles among the troops but ended on an optimistic note: "We are getting acclimated now, and the worst I think is past."[51]

Doran's enthusiastic assessment of the troops following twin defeats was printed on the same page as an editorial by *Telegraph* Editor Cushing somberly admitting the fall of Memphis and Fort Pillow as General Beauregard "retired" with his army toward Mobile. "The movement left the Memphis and Charleston road in possession of the Federals, and put it out of our power to save any point on the Mississippi river," Cushing wrote with an air of despair. Like Doran, Cushing's devotion to the Confederate cause and belief in the superiority of the South's military minds led him to say that he had no doubt that Beauregard would eventually "ensnare" Union Major General Henry Halleck and that daily skirmishes were "considerable."[52]

The injury suffered by Doran resulted in an honorable discharge following the retreat from Corinth. He began the long trip back to Texas, crossing the Mississippi to Vicksburg, then walking across much of Louisiana to Shreveport where he paid a $25 stage fare to Navasota, Texas. His two editors sent him to the Union-occupied and blockaded city of Galveston where Doran again did

Confederate forces recaptured the city of Galveston New Year's Day 1863 by forcing the 43rd Massachusetts volunteers off a pier into Galveston Bay. Union forces had captured Galveston in an 1862 battle. *Harper's Weekly,* January 31, 1863. Courtesy of Rare Books and Special Collections, University of South Carolina Libraries

double duty—as a reporter and as a civilian scout for the military. Recounting his exploits after the war, he wrote: "To get proper information, I had to slip into Galveston at night, and would foot it to the city five miles, and generally managed to get one or more Yankee newspapers, for which I often had to pay a silver dollar for each."[53]

After the war, Doran admitted he opposed the daring land and sea operation to regain Galveston on January 1, 1863, believing the plan reckless and unprincipled since civilians remained on the island. "I never advised General Magruder to make the desperate move against the powerful fleet armed with the best kind of modern artillery, but did the reverse, because I considered it wrong to fight behind breastworks of men, women, and children then occupying the city."

True to form, however, Doran praised Magruder, Major P.C. Tucker, and other officers for their valor in regaining the city for the Confederacy, while portraying the Union occupying fleet as cowards who "fled the harbor under their white flag." It was an act, he said, that "violated one of the most sacred customs of civilized nations."[54]

Although Doran's lengthy account praised many officers and men as heroes and repeatedly used such terms as "gallant," he admitted three decades after the war that his account of Texan bravery and Yankee cowardice reflected the

Confederate point of view rather than the reality of the situation. From his vantage point near the Galveston post office, Doran watched a number of troops break and run from their posts when Union troops attacked, crying out, "We're whipped! We're whipped! I don't want the Yanks to take me to New Orleans!" Later in the day, as the tide turned in the rebels' favor, he witnessed many of the same men run past him, exuberantly proclaiming, "We've whipped 'em!" A number of enlisted men and officers who previously fled from the enemy, recognizing the value of publicity, asked Doran to mention them favorably in his battle account.[55] As he noted in his postwar recollections:

> Many men who run like scared turkeys when Yankee bullets began to fly or got sick when the smell of gunpowder filled the air were generally the first to call on war correspondents to put in a good lick for them in the newspapers.[56]

Doran spent much of the rest of the war in Texas, covering coastal skirmishes, the effects of the war on the state's cities and towns, and the state of Union prisoners of war held at Camp Groce, two miles east of Hempstead. He took a realistic approach to the state's prisoners, encouraging Confederate authorities in October 1863 to exchange the troops quickly for captured Confederate officers, stating the cost of feeding and housing them was more than the Confederacy could afford. He also praised the leadership of the camp commander, Colonel John Sales, for keeping a clean, sanitary, and healthy facility.[57]

In the spring of 1864, Doran's editors sent him to cover the Red River campaign. The correspondent accompanied General Dick Taylor who was to confront General Nathaniel P. Banks in what turned into a disastrous attempt by Federal forces to plant the Union flag in Texas.[58] Doran followed Confederate forces, reporting on the battles at Mansfield and Pleasant Hill. He discovered that his fame as a reporter would not protect him after he was threatened by a Confederate cavalry unit and was ordered to keep his distance for "not doing them justice" in print.[59]

After filing a final report from Alexandria about prisoner exchanges from the Pleasant Hill and Mansfield campaigns in June 1864, Doran returned to Texas, where he spent the remainder of the war traversing the state on horseback as a roving state news reporter.[60] His reports from such towns as Gonzalez, Huntsville, Palestine, Austin, Waco, and Bastrop read like a modern-day road trip. Doran described the towns' buildings, the surrounding farmland, and what each town was known for—in some cases a military academy, in others a prison or rich farmland.

The reports appeared designed to generate a sense of normalcy and encourage morale-building as the war headed to a conclusion. Although the war had ravaged the economies of other Southern states, the conflict had a less marked effect in Texas. The state's agriculture and manufacturing were healthy, and the war had encouraged greater self-sufficiency. Furthermore, children remained

The Union flotilla during the Red River expedition. *Harper's Weekly,* April 30, 1864. Courtesy of Rare Books and Special Collections, University of South Carolina Libraries

in schools and their parents' morale remained high. A November 14, 1864, account was representative of Doran's reports.

> After leaving Columbus we pass through a beautiful farming country, the lands are rolling prairies, and present a pretty landscape. We soon come to Fayetteville, a pretty little rural village, surrounded by well cultivated farms and presenting the appearance of prosperity on every hand.[61]

Another report from Round Rock in Williamson County also presented a picture of prosperity in times of conflict: "Here there is quite a large settlement. A steam wool carding machine is in full operation. There seems to be considerable wool raised in the neighborhood. The land is very rocky in this vicinity, and the sheep seem to thrive well."[62] When Doran passed through Waco in December 1864, he wrote that Baylor University was flourishing with many students hard at work.[63]

But by the end of 1864, he was acknowledging the war was affecting the state's citizens and their homes. During a late November 1864 visit to Austin, Doran discovered the lack of hard currency was putting a burden on the state's legislators. True to Southern ingenuity, however, a number of members of the legislature learned to successfully employ the barter system. "Many of the members [of the legislature] have been destitute of specie since their arrival, and they find it very inconvenient in this country where nothing but specie is taken," Sioux wrote. "But a few of the more knowing ones brought along some articles that were scarce here for the purpose of exchange. One man brought some tobacco; another a keg of nails. All of these articles proved to be a good legal tender."[64]

Some of Doran's final reports were critical but, true to form, he never blamed specific individuals and instead called for government intervention to remedy the perceived problems.

In a dispatch from Austin in November 1864, he praised the beauty of the growing city but despaired at the lack of attention paid to military graves.

> I visited the graves of General McCullough, Scurry and McLeod yesterday. They are built upon a hill about one half mile from the city. The graves have been sadly neglected, not even their names are inscribed upon the headboards. This is a shame—these gallant men have sealed their devotion to their State with their lives, and it is a great wrong to see their [g]raves so sadly neglected. I hope the proper authorities will make some move to remedy this evil.[65]

By 1865, an increasing number of cracks were appearing in Doran's reports of normalcy. He began noting that a number of families were suffering for want of food and clothing while their men were in the army, that soldiers were tearing apart private homes in Galveston for firewood, and that pockets of crime were occurring. Patriot that he was, he laid no specific blame and called on authorities to remedy the situations. In a letter dated January 2, 1865, to the *Houston Daily Telegraph,* Doran called for more fund-raising concerts.

> There is not a more holy and nobler object than the relief of the suffering poor. The cold and chilly blasts of winter are upon them—many of these families are those of our soldiers whose protectors are in the army away from home, and it is our duty to see that they are well provided for.[66]

The correspondent's concerns for the poor extended to threadbare returning soldiers. He wrote that many men who fought in Louisiana were returning to Texas and, although in good spirits, were barefoot and ragged: "I saw these same men in one of the bloodiest battles fought during the eventful campaign of 1864 . . . and now I am to be told that these men are barefooted and suffering for clothing? I cannot, nor will I believe it."[67]

Doran also acknowledged that crime was on the increase in Texas and attributed the banditry to the fact that most men were serving in the military and unable to protect their homes and communities. In a March 1865 report, he wrote that a gang of deserters and robbers was creating panic in the community of Georgetown. One man was brutally robbed and a furloughed soldier was hanged. The correspondent wrote that authorities were pursuing the gang. Doran called on officials to allow enough furloughed soldiers to remain at home until the troubles ceased, to protect their families.[68]

As the war wound down, Doran established his own newspaper, *The Free-man's Champion*. Willard Richardson, the editor of the *Galveston Weekly News*, praised his correspondent's foray into the publishing world, stating that Doran is an honest champion of good causes.

> When he sees a wrong perpetrated, or a public duty neglected, he is not afraid to speak of it. He declares himself the soldier's friend, and we hope and believe he will be able to render the soldier essential service, as, in fact, he has done on many occasions through the columns of other papers. We predict that the "Freeman's Champion," under his management, will be a valuable journal. Sioux is opposed to a military man for Governor. In this, we think, the soldiers will not agree with him. We would also prefer a civilian, if equally well qualified, because we do not want to take a valuable man from the army when such men are now so much needed. We hope Sioux will bring out the right man for the time.[69]

As one of the few correspondents to cover the entire conflict, Doran's career as war reporter ended in fitting fashion—with a final report from Galveston on the surrender of Texas Confederate troops on June 2, 1865.[70] He remained in journalism after the war, publishing newspapers in several Texas communities. Doran also served as the first special local editor on the *Houston Telegraph* and later was elected city marshal of Brenham serving two terms, beginning in 1880. He married Sallie M. Linsicum in December 1865 in Long Point, Texas, and had three sons, W.R., C.B., and Frank. A biographical sketch of Doran published in the *Galveston Daily News* at the time of his death in 1901 stated that Doran never wavered from his Democratic beliefs.[71]

Late in life, Doran referred to the Civil War as "a great and awful struggle."[72] Like many reporters of the time, Doran's correspondence was far more descriptive than analytical. He demonstrated no great ability to comprehend the military strategies that were unfolding around him. Although his loyalty to the Confederate cause led him to frequently fill his reports with the invectives, exaggerated statements, and stereotypes common among war correspondents, Doran's writing was marked by a desire to frame the war as a noble and gallant fight for freedom from the perceived tyranny of the Federal government. Doran became the trusted eyes and ears of Texas citizens during wartime.

23

James P. Douglas:
Fighting for the South with Pen and Sword

Mary M. Cronin

Cᴏɴꜰᴇᴅᴇʀᴀᴛᴇ Lɪᴇᴜᴛᴇɴᴀɴᴛ Jᴀᴍᴇs Pᴏsᴛᴇʟʟ Dᴏᴜɢʟᴀs ᴋɴᴇᴡ ᴛʜᴇ ꜰᴏʟᴋs back home in Texas would relish the story about the Union spy caught inside their battery camp on July 18, 1861, so he added the information in his report for the *Tyler Reporter.*

> On last evening a man claiming to be a messenger from McCulloch arrived in camps. He said he was sent with dispatches to Gen. Childs, who was authorized to raise a regiment. His story and the circumstances contributed to throwing suspicion on him, and he has been taken prisoner . . . The prisoner may be honest; if so he can demonstrate it at Fort Smith. If he fails to do so, he will be shot as a spy.[1]

Douglas' story from Boggy Depot in the Cherokee Nation, in the area that would become Oklahoma, was one of dozens that he would write during the war for the *Reporter*, where he had been co-editor before the war began. Texans relied on editor-correspondents like Douglas to provide them with news. The state's location on the periphery of the Confederacy, coupled with Texas' few railroad and telegraph lines, meant news was often slow in reaching citizens who felt cut off from the rest of the Confederacy.[2]

Yet news was as vital a commodity for Texas residents as it was for other Southerners. More than 70,000 Texans went to war, distinguishing themselves in some of the conflict's most important battles, including Shiloh; Chickamauga; Pea Ridge; Vicksburg; the Wilderness; Gettysburg; Second Manassas; Franklin, Tennessee; and the Red River campaign, among others.

Editors desperate for news sought information wherever they could get it, including other Confederate and Union newspapers, soldiers, and travelers, as well as editors and reporters in uniform.[3] Not surprisingly, rumors often trumped real news. Many officers declared dead by the press lived to old age,

James P. Douglas. Courtesy Smith County Historical
Society, Tyler, Texas

enemy casualty figures often were wildly inflated, and victories were claimed
when defeats actually occurred.[4]

Douglas acknowledged in a June 1864 letter that Texas newspapers were doing a poor job providing accurate news. Writing from Marietta, Georgia, he told
his fiancé, Sally White, to ignore what she was reading. "You need pay but little
regard to the accounts which appear under telegraphic head in our newspapers.
They are full of errors, as the press depend on gathering of scraps of news from
stragglers, etc., who never tell the truth."[5]

Douglas and other Texas editors who donned uniforms, including William
Doran, of the *Houston Tri-Weekly Telegraph* and the *Galveston News*, and Editor
Charles DeMorse of the *Clarksville Standard*, tried to compensate by sending
what they perceived as accurate news of battles and military life back to their
newspapers. These men had the reporting experience and an understanding
of what constituted news, especially to their hometown readers. In hindsight,
their highly detailed stories have to be taken for what they were: eyewitness
accounts by Southern patriots who were devoted to the Confederate cause.
Like his counterparts, Douglas did not provide the broader perspective of the

significance of the battles in which he fought. Instead, he wrote of his experiences and observations from his vantage point as an artillery officer, adding occasional facts gleaned from other soldiers and officers. Furthermore, Douglas' Southern and Texan loyalties led him to minimize Confederate losses and not criticize the decisions made by his military superiors.[6]

Douglas' letters home to his wife and his co-editor, Hanse Van Hamilton, suggest that he sent regular reports from the battlefield for publication in the *Reporter*. How prolific a correspondent he was will never be known, however, since most issues of the *Reporter* were destroyed in a fire following the war. Only about a dozen issues from the war years still exist in libraries. Of those, only one issue—from July 19, 1861—contains a letter from Douglas. One other letter that was published in the *Reporter* also exists, a lengthy, detailed account of the Battle of Elkhorn Tavern in March 1862, which was reprinted in the *Telegraph*. The loss of most of Douglas' war reports is tragic since Douglas and his men went on to fight in all the major battles with the Army of Tennessee, including Chattanooga, Chickamauga, Murfreesboro, the battles for Atlanta, and John Bell Hood's Tennessee Campaign of 1864. His compiled letters suggest he sent a number of news reports to his co-editor.[7]

Unlike many Confederate editors who originally hailed from Northeastern states, Douglas had roots in the South. He was born near Lancaster, South Carolina, on January 7, 1836, in the home of his maternal grandfather. His family moved to Talladega, Alabama, when he was 2 years old and to Texas in 1847 when he was 11. The family settled the next year in the small village of Tyler, where Douglas would remain for the rest of his life.

Like many children on the Texas frontier, Douglas' education was a patchwork of private tutoring and occasional schooling for brief periods of time. Douglas became a school teacher and the family breadwinner at 17, when his father died suddenly. His younger brothers, Eli and John, were among his students. Douglas also read law and eventually was licensed to practice law, which served him well following the Civil War when he was elected to the 12th Texas Senate. Despite his legal studies, he was drawn toward newspapers and he purchased the *Tyler Reporter* in the late 1850s in partnership with Van Hamilton.[8] A staunch Southern patriot, Douglas supported secession, slavery, and state rights.[9]

When the war broke out, Douglas, then 25, received orders from Colonel Elkanah Greer of Marshall to assemble 50 men from Tyler for a 100-man field artillery battery (the other men were recruited from the Dallas area) for Greer's regiment. Although Douglas' artillery unit is listed in Confederate records as the 1st Texas Battery, it was more commonly referred to as the Douglas Battery. Douglas was commissioned as a first lieutenant and later promoted to captain after the Battle of Elkhorn Tavern.[10]

Douglas found himself commanding men from various professions and occupations, including other newspapermen. Former private James Lunsford said the battery included: "three editors, several printers, several lawyers and law students, some medical students, some farmers' boys, merchants' sons and clerks, and some who had been Texas Rangers."[11] Seventy percent of the battery's men were under age 22 and 90 percent were under age 25. Only four men were older than 30. All served for the duration of the war.[12]

Because the initial Confederate conscription laws exempted editors and printers from military service, Douglas did not have to go to war. His strong Confederate nationalism beliefs led him to volunteer.[13] He was one of many Texas editors and printers who donned a uniform. The staff of the LaGrange-based *States Rights Democrat* enlisted en masse in September 1861. Editor J.G. Wheeler summed up the feelings of many Texas editors who enlisted, stating: "All hands; editors and printers, have considered it their duty to go to war, and none of us are likely to return before our independence is acknowledged."[14] Editors, publishers, and printers from the *Dallas Herald*, the *Houston Telegraph*, the *Austin State Gazette*, the *San Antonio Herald*, the *Texas Ranger*, the *Clarksville Standard*, the *Henderson Times*, the *Kaufman Democrat*, and the *Nacogdoches Chronicle*, among others, also served.[15]

Douglas' artillery unit was formally organized in Dallas on June 15, 1861. The editor-turned-officer quickly came to public attention for his leadership abilities on the field, as well as his ways with Dallas women when off duty. The *Dallas Herald* noted in June 1861 that Douglas "is a general favorite" among his men. The article's author then rakishly added: "He will be in good hands while he stays in Dallas, as we have heard it whispered—so gently—that the gallant lieutenant is as invincible in the parlor as he will be on the field."[16]

Once trained, Douglas and his men marched into Indian Territory where he sent the first of his surviving reports to the *Reporter* in July 1861. In a relatively brief report, Douglas showed excitement at the prospect of facing the enemy and included news of the Confederate army's Indian allies, including the military's wariness in mixing its white soldiers with native soldiers, and the reason why certain tribes decided to tie their fate to that of the Confederacy.

> The Chocktaws and Chickasaws are full of the war spirit. A war-dance is on hand at this place to-night. The soldiers are anxious to see it, but it is thought imprudent for them to attend. A regiment of 700 Chocktaws, under Col. Cooper, left this place for Fort Smith on the 10th inst. All the tribes of the Nation have concluded a treaty with the Confederate State, except the Cherokees. It is doubtful what they will do. There is a disposition on the part of the Indians to enter the Confederacy as States. They think they can sustain their rights under our States Rights Constitution.[17]

Shortly after penning this article, Douglas and his battery received orders to march to Fort Smith, Arkansas, about the first of August. His men, along with other Confederate regiments, then moved into Missouri, but missed the

Battle of Oak Hill. They eventually returned to Arkansas, at Camp Jackson near Bentonville, and spent the time drilling. They returned to Missouri in the fall in anticipation of engaging Union forces, but an expected battle against General John Fremont's troops never occurred. The battery left Missouri in late December and spent the remainder of a frigid winter near Fayetteville, Arkansas.[18]

The battery finally saw action on March 7 and 8, 1862, with its first engagement at the Battle of Elkhorn Tavern (Pea Ridge), Arkansas. Although the battle has failed to gain as much attention as those fought in other Confederate states, it was pivotal. The engagement was a Union victory that decided the fate of Missouri, keeping that state in the Union. The battle also ended the Confederacy's hopes of gaining dominance in the Trans-Mississippi region.[19]

The battle at Elkhorn Tavern was also notable for the poor leadership shown by General Earl Van Dorn whose decisions cost the Confederacy a crucial victory. Van Dorn led 16,000 Confederate soldiers against General Samuel R. Curtis' 10,250 Union troops. Although he had a strong numerical advantage, Van Dorn had marched his ill-clad, undershod, and underfed troops on a nine-day frigid, forced march to meet Curtis' forces. Convinced of victory and desirous of speed, Van Dorn left his supply wagons behind and only allowed the soldiers to carry three days' rations, their weapons, 40 rounds of ammunition, and one blanket each. Many of the men marched without adequate clothing, and a number were barefoot. The Confederate general, confident of victory, counted on capturing the enemy's supply wagons to further feed and equip his army but ultimately failed in this objective.[20]

The forced march proved disastrous for the Confederate troops. Men dropped from exhaustion during the march after running out of food and encountering an unexpected blizzard. Barefoot soldiers left bloody footprints in the snow and ice. Despite pleas on March 6 from Generals Benjamin McCulloch and Albert Pike to let the men rest for the night, Van Dorn continued the march, forcing his troops to march all night to meet Federal forces by morning. The overconfident general's plan failed as thousands of his men collapsed, destroying his numerical advantage. Federal patrols also had discovered the rebels' movement, destroying Van Dorn's plans for a surprise attack.[21]

Douglas mentioned nothing about the exhausting march in his account of the battle. Instead, his story reflects what he was: a patriotic officer who would not criticize command decisions, even when those decisions put troops' lives at stake. His letter opened with a brief mention of the march being forced but he provided no details of the brutal march. He then detailed the first day's fight, in which Confederate troops came across 600 men under the command of General Franz Siegel who had lingered behind in Bentonville to have breakfast before continuing on to rendezvous with Curtis' troops in an impregnable position at Little Sugar Creek near Elkhorn Tavern. Douglas' account is notable for increasing the number of enemy five-fold.

On the morning of the 3d of March, Gen. Van Dorn ordered us on a force[d] march to the vicinity of Curtis' army, in Benton county. Accordingly we moved, and on the 6th our cavalry encountered 3000 Federals near Bentonville, surprising them, capturing their foragers, and engaging the main body and killing 30 or 40 of them, and losing four or five. We were in hearing of Siegel's cannon, as he fired retreating; but did not reach the scene until he was gone. Greer's regiment did good service in the engagement.[22]

Douglas' report of the battle was limited to his personal experiences. He was a soldier first and a journalist second for the duration of the war. Yet, despite the patriotism interwoven in his narrative, his account of the two-day battle at Elkhorn Tavern provided a vivid portrayal of what he and his men experienced. And unlike many other editor-officers who made disparaging claims about the enemy's abilities to buoy the morale of civilians and soldiers alike, Douglas acknowledged that he faced a determined and deadly foe during the first day.

We opened on a fine battery in our front, and at a distance of 400 yards, and for an hour I paid but little attention to the progress of the battle generally, as the belching mouths of the enemy's big guns refused to be silent. But at the end of that time, with my entire approbation, our antagonists limbered to the rear and hurried away, leaving the field to us, together with 17 dead Federals—the captain among the number. Our loss was four men wounded and three or four horses killed. It seems strange that no more damage was done us in this deal, as the shot and shell fell in showers around us; besides the enemy had two rifled guns, whose fire was so accurate as to compel us several times to move our guns out of their range. During our engagement, McCulloch had led the infantry forward to our left, and inch by inch had driven back the enemy around the slope of the mountain near half a mile.[23]

While Douglas' men were unleashing their artillery barrage, General McCulloch was killed by members of the 36th Illinois who fired a thunderous volley en masse when they saw the Confederate general leading his men toward them. McCulloch, who was struck down by a bullet through his heart, had been trying to lead an infantry assault against an unexpected force of Federal troops who were positioned much further north than he had been told. The charge, historians have noted, was a reckless one because McCulloch led it himself, a habit he had acquired prewar while serving with the Texas Rangers.

Douglas acknowledged the general's death in his report, as well as the death of General James M. McIntosh, who had ridden quickly through trees and brush toward the enemy and was just as quickly cut down by another company of the 36th Illinois. Following the two generals' deaths, McCulloch's men were left in disarray.[24] Although historians have referred to the two men's actions leading up to their deaths as reckless, Douglas portrayed both generals as noble patriots who gallantly led their men against an unexpected and hidden enemy force.

> Soon I heard a tremendous roar of musketry to our left, of which I learned that Gen. McCulloch had led the old 3d Louisiana and some other regiments in person to a charge, which proved to be a very dangerous one. The enemy being driven back several hundred yards, concentrated on that wing and resisted him with a three-fold force—also opening a masked battery on him. The infantry promptly drove back the superior numbers, and took the battery; but in the moment of victory, the noble patriot, McCulloch, fell! Almost simultaneous with him fell the gallant Gen. McIntosh, Col. Hebert commanding 2d Brigade, was, about the same time, cut off and captured; also Maj. Tanerd, commanding 3d Louisiana. Our troops, not aware of the misfortunes of their leaders, fell back and formed and awaited orders.[25]

Douglas also wrote that McCulloch's former soldiers, who included Douglas' battery, quickly organized to await orders when the reality was that many of the leaderless Confederate soldiers refused to accept General Pike's attempts to assume command. Half of the Confederate troops, including Douglas' battery, eventually followed Pike away from Leetown and toward Elkhorn Tavern, while the remainder dispersed with some remaining behind and others heading away from the battle and toward nearby Little Sugar Creek.[26]

Despite the generals' deaths, Douglas portrayed the first day as a success and credited General Van Dorn's leadership with the results. The general, he said, "had surmounted hill after hill, until he had reached and driven the enemy from the commanding summit, where is situated the Elkhorn tavern—had captured one fine battery, and the enemy's commissary and quartermaster's stores, with extensive supplies. The day seemed ours without a doubt."[27]

Although Confederate troops did overwhelm Union troops and capture Elkhorn Tavern, Douglas' account did not include what happened next, a twilight charge that proved disastrous for the Confederate forces. From his encampment, Douglas may not have known about Van Dorn's decision to continue the battle into the dusk. The general, smelling victory and convinced that he could rout all the Federal troops, ordered his soldiers to engage the retreating Federal forces who were regrouping east of the Tavern on Telegraph Road to make another stand. As night fell, yelling and cheering Confederate troops poured into Benjamin Ruddick's cornfield and charged toward the enemy. Their exposed position allowed masses of rebels to be mowed down by the Federal forces' artillery. The surviving Confederates were forced to retreat toward the tavern.

Union General Samuel R. Curtis used the cover of darkness to consolidate his troops, moving scattered Federal forces from Leetown and Little Sugar Creek to meet up with the rest of his forces on Telegraph Road. Rebel forces also were on the march all night, but to their dismay, when they reached Elkhorn

Tavern, the expected bounty of food from the sutlers' wagons and abandoned Federal haversacks that Douglas boasted about in his report turned out to be a meager supply. Making matters worse, rebel troops also found themselves unprepared to go into battle at dawn. In the confusion of the day's fighting, the Confederate ammunition train had been left 12 miles to the rear at Little Sugar Creek.[28]

When dawn broke on March 8, Curtis expected to see Van Dorn's army resume its attack. When the Confederate general failed to do so, Curtis surmised that the Federals now had the upper hand and ordered his artillery to open fire. For two hours, 27 Union cannons poured "a continual thunder" upon the Confederates. A charge by more than 10,000 Federal soldiers followed at 10 a.m., forcing Van Dorn to realize the battle was lost. The general ordered his troops to withdraw and also ordered Douglas' battery and two other batteries to provide cover fire until they ran out of ammunition. Casualties mounted among Douglas' men throughout the morning, but the editor framed the scene in patriotic rhetoric, stressing the bravery and sense of duty inherent in his men, while lapsing into purple prose to discuss a young gunner's death.

> Our boys manned the guns with coolness and great rapidity. Soon many of them were wounded and finally Charlie Erwin, the brave boy, fell nobly by his gun; our numbers being finally diminished to about one half the proper number of cannoneers, I took my position at gun No. 2, as gunner Lieuts. Boren and Davis also acted as gunners. We stood their fire for an hour and a half, when the 12 pounders' ammunition failed, which we reported and were ordered to fall back. Capt. Harts' battery took our place. We moved back to replenish our ammunition chests.[29]

Douglas and his men joined a general retreat ordered by Van Dorn. Historians have noted the Confederate retreat from Pea Ridge was "as disastrous as the advance and the battle." Thousands of frozen, famished soldiers, including the men of Douglas' battery, marched for a week through sparsely populated countryside, traveling along poor roads and almost impassable trails, unable to find enough food to feed themselves and their animals. Hundreds of men wandered off in search of food and never returned. The remaining stragglers eventually crossed the Boston Mountains and spent time recuperating near Van Buren by the Arkansas River, recognizing that their loss at Elkhorn Tavern meant Missouri remained in Union hands.[30]

Douglas' account of the retreat largely lacks details, reflecting little of the chaos or hardship endured by the Confederate soldiers. Although he admitted that Union infantry supported by cavalry "broke our centre," forcing a retreat, Douglas said the majority of Confederate troops did so "in perfect order, and were marched away to the Southeast—save our battery, which, with 3 pieces of Price's artillery, one regiment of infantry and one company of cavalry and some stragglers, failed to get the order, and moved down the Springfield road."[31]

Although Douglas acknowledged the difficulty of his battery's four-day march, this section of his account lacked detail, giving little sense of the actual harshness of the late-winter retreat. It concluded on a victorious note.

> We were pursued by the Cavalry about one mile. The infantry formed once and drove them back. Our battery and Capt. Teel's [illegible] from the field, took a dim road over the mountains to our right, while the other batteries moved up to Keetsville, and turned to the right. We marched hard, all day almost without a road, and the evening shades found us fifteen miles away in the White River mountains; and, by marching all night and the next day, we succeeded in out-flanking the enemy, and making our escape. We continued our march over an almost impassable road, and on the 4th day were met by Greer's regiment as an escort, the presence of which made us feel quite agreeable. All the artillery got out safely—besides, we brought away three fine pieces of the enemy's.[32]

Knowing that concerned readers would want to know about casualties, Douglas wrote that "not more than 200 Confederate soldiers were killed," while the enemy lost at least 600 men. Douglas badly underestimated casualties on both sides of the conflict. Union troops actually suffered 1,384 casualties: 203 killed, 980 wounded, and 201 missing. By contrast, Confederate troops are estimated by historians to have suffered at least 2,000 casualties. The actual figure was never known because Van Dorn lied about his losses in his reports to superiors in order to disguise the enormity of his defeat.[33]

Perhaps because of the magnitude of the defeat or possibly because of Douglas' patriotism and devotion to his cause, he portrayed the Battle of Elkhorn Tavern as predominantly a victory for Confederate forces, noting: "All in all it was a most lucky engagement on our side, and although we left the field, I think we have taught the Feds a lesson they won't forget soon."[34]

His narrative of the battle also reflected a level of romanticism about war that can be attributed to the editor's lack of combat experience, his patriotism, and his assumptions about the nature of war. He wrote, for example, that the opening artillery salvos on March 8 were "ceaseless and sublime." Similarly, toward the end of his account, Douglas romanticized the battle as a whole, writing: "The grandeur of the battle is indescribable, as we had 65 guns and the enemy a greater number." [35] Two years later, a battle-hardened Douglas was more circumspect about war. "I am weary of the business myself and wish from my heart it was over," he told his wife in a letter sent from Georgia.[36]

Following their defeat at Pea Ridge, Douglas and his men fought in many of the war's major engagements, including battles at Farmington, Mississippi; Richmond, Kentucky; and Murfreesboro, Tennessee, in 1862. The battery spent much of the rest of the war fighting with the Army of Tennessee, with battles in 1863 at Liberty Gap, Elk River, Chickamauga, and Missionary Ridge in Tennessee.

Douglas was reporting from Tennessee when Orchard Knob was captured by the Federals during the Battle of Missionary Ridge in Chattanooga, Tennessee. *Harper's Weekly*, December 19, 1863. Courtesy of Rare Books and Special Collections, University of South Carolina Libraries

Douglas and his men saw their heaviest fighting in 1864, beginning in May in Georgia with battles at Resaca, New Hope Church, Lost Mountain, Mount Zion Church, Kennesaw Mountain, Peach Tree Creek, and the Atlanta Campaign, followed by fighting in Alabama at Shoal Creek. As winter began, the battery returned to Tennessee for incursions at Columbia, Franklin, Nashville, and Spring Hill. Its final military service was performed during February and March 1865 during the siege of Mobile.

He and his men were under fire for more than 100 days in 1864 while covering the withdrawal of General Joseph E. Johnston from Chattanooga to Atlanta. They also covered the December 16, 1864, retreat of General John Bell Hood's army when the battery lost its guns after they became stuck in muddy roads. Several of his men were captured by General Philip Sheridan's troops while attempting to rescue their artillery. Douglas barely made his escape on horseback.[37]

After a furlough to Tyler in March 1865, Douglas was heading for Mobile to rejoin his battery when he learned that General Johnston had surrendered to General William Sherman. He returned to Tyler and threw himself into rebuilding Texas and establishing himself in various businesses following the war.

Although he remained in his position of co-editor for several years, Douglas also served as a member of the 12th Senate of Texas, where he "had a strong

The Confederate fort near Atlanta. Courtesy of the Library of Congress

influence in ousting the carpetbaggers," according to his daughter Rutherford Douglas, who recalled that her father "was never a man for political office."[38]

Douglas also helped improve the state's transportation system by organizing and serving as the first president of the Texas Branch of the Cotton Belt Railroad, called the Tyler Tap, which was later sold to Jay Gould. His daughter wrote that his interest in transportation "no doubt developed as he rode the lonely trails of East Texas" as a young man prior to the war.[39] While that may be true, Douglas also had more pragmatic reasons. He was one of East Texas' more prominent planters and was credited with growing the first peach orchards in East Texas. He also owned a chain of canning factories.

Douglas when he was older. Courtesy of Smith County Historical Society, Tyler, Texas

Douglas married twice. On March 24, 1864, in Canton (later called Omen) he married Sallie Susan White with whom he had four children. She died on August 22, 1872. He was remarried on July 7, 1874, to Alice Earle Smith, a planter's daughter from Corinth, Mississippi, whose family plantation was destroyed during the Battle of Shiloh. Douglas had six more children with his second wife. He died on November 27, 1901, and is buried in Tyler's Oakwood Cemetery.[40]

24

R.R. Gilbert: A Texas Humorist Goes to War

Mary M. Cronin

A LOAD OF BLANKETS FOR CONFEDERATE SOLDIERS FINALLY ARRIVED IN Alexandria, Louisiana, on a frosty day in December 1863. The soldiers' hopes for warmth were quickly dashed, however, when officers took all of the blankets, leaving the soldiers, who slept outdoors, to continue suffering the effects of a chilly winter. The officers were quickly condemned in a scathing report to the *Houston Tri-Weekly Telegraph* by their correspondent Rensalear[1] Reed Gilbert, who wrote:

> A lot of Mexican blankets arrived here, which were placed in the Quartermaster's Department. Forthwith several picayune officers, who happen to be lying here on furlough or for other reasons, and several detailed men in the different departments here, all of whom sleep in comfortable quarters, go tout their "requisitions" and drew these blankets, while the poor blanketless soldier, who is compelled to sleep in the open air, with the thermometer down to within 20 degrees of zero, as it was last night, could not draw one! A captain told me yesterday that he applied for some of these blankets for his men, who have none, or shoes for their feet, and he was told that there was none to spare!

The Texas reporter was outraged and let loose with a tirade against the officials responsible for mistreating the Confederate troops who were sleeping out in the freezing weather.

> To use a mild expression, I consider this a damnable outrage. And, yet, you will hear these very men, who have robbed the exposed soldier of these blankets say, "We are bound to succeed in this contest, because God is on our side." If we ever do succeed it will be in spite of innumerable acts of injustice, such as every generous heart turns from in disgust . . . My soul is sick of such acts of injustice, for they have long been familiar to my eyes, not only here but elsewhere.[2]

Gilbert's blend of news and editorial commentary was typical of reporters of the time, and the combination would prove to be his greatest strength.[3] It

R. R. Gilbert. *Houston Post,* October 7, 1899

allowed him to be part of the growing group of professional reporters who were willing to criticize military and government officials while exposing problems that threatened the young Confederate nation, its soldiers, and its people.[4] He was anything but one of the "thoughtless scribblers" or "sentimental chroniclers" so denounced by Confederate correspondent Peter W. Alexander.[5] Gilbert's belief that reporters should be watchdogs was not an unpatriotic stand. He had chosen as an adult to move to Texas and had a vested interest in shaping the policies of his home state and emerging nation.

Gilbert was hired as the *Telegraph*'s correspondent because of his writing ability, but he also was proficient with a telegraph key.[6] He made the acquaintance of *Telegraph* Editor Edward Cushing after Cushing had read Gilbert's humorous sketches of army life published in the *Victoria Advocate.* In more than 15 letters that the *Telegraph* also published, Gilbert billed himself as a "raw recruit" in the 6th Texas Infantry at Camp Henry McCulloch near Victoria.

Signing his columns "High Private," Gilbert lampooned army life and cast a critical eye on social issues that brought both levity and criticism to the war.[7]

Cushing, who edited one of the most influential newspapers in Texas, encouraged the humorist to leave the military for a position as a war correspondent for the *Telegraph*, a job offer that may have saved Gilbert's life. Gilbert found the offer too good to turn down, and so, despite his devotion to the Confederate cause, he left his unit at Camp McCulloch and headed to Houston. While he was on his way to start his new position in May 1862, his regiment was transferred to Arkansas, a move that would be costly for the men of the 6th Texas Infantry. Come January, many of the men Gilbert had served with would be captured, wounded, or killed in the Battle of Arkansas Post.[8]

Even after Gilbert began his civilian reporting in May 1862, he continued to send occasional comic sketches to the *Telegraph* during the war years. His comic letters did not incorporate dialect or misspellings commonly used by some 19th century funny men to provoke laughter.[9] Instead, Gilbert's descriptions of situations, as well as his linguistic wordplay, were amusing. Several of his letters made light of the extensive and elaborate drills that the 6th Infantry's commander, Colonel Robert R. Garland, taught the recruits, Gilbert included. One of those recruits, Jim Turner, said of Garland:

> Our Colonel was an old army officer and having spent twenty-five years of his life in the regular army, was a perfect martinet and everything had to be done in strict accordance with military rules. He kept us hard at work drilling and converting the regiment into a machine which would move with clock-like precision.[10]

Gilbert lampooned the incessant drilling with his creation of a sage but merry prankster persona—"High Private." A January 1862 letter to the *Telegraph* discussing an accident that occurred while Gilbert was drilling is representative of his humor writing.

> Soon after being enlisted I was put in an "awkward squad," myself and a corporal being the only members. In attempting to perform a difficult evolution denominated "right wheel," I came in collision with the corporal with such violence that he "ground arms" and I collapsed three paces in the rear. A court-martial was the result, where it was decided that had I *spoken* in time the *hub*-bub might have been avoided; and that henceforth when drilling en-*tire*-ly alone, I must avoid getting in a bad *box*, or be *lynch-pinned*. *Wag*-on, said I, and again *rolled* to duty.[11]

Like his more famous comic counterparts, Gilbert recognized the psychological value of humor in times of conflict. Humor, he believed, was not an end in itself but an important vehicle for social criticism.[12] Historian Alice Fahs said humor is notable among the various genres of U.S. Civil War literature because of its ability to provide a critical distance from the conflict, a distance, she said, that was not possible for writers of sentimental and patriotic war literature.[13] Gilbert applied this same perspective to his war reporting.

Houston Telegraph readers only knew Gilbert by his pen name of High Private or by the initials H.P. throughout the war. His dedication to Texas and the Confederacy was such that many would have been surprised to learn that this private was far from the typical recruit.[14] At 41, Gilbert was older than the average Confederate volunteer. He was a physician who hailed from Vermont, but little else is known about his life prior to 1861. He left no private papers and wrote only a short two-page biographical sketch, which was included in a collected volume of his humor writing. He died before lengthy obituaries that recounted individuals' accomplishments were commonplace.[15]

Gilbert hinted at a life of travel prior to his arrival in Texas, noting in an April 15, 1862, letter to the *Telegraph* that he had "taken my chances in every zone, except the north frigid."[16] Federal and state census records list him as having been born in the state of New York in 1821. His obituary, presumably provided by his family to the *Houston Post,* lists his birth a year earlier, in 1820, in Enosburg, Vermont.[17]

Gilbert was equally circumspect about why he settled in Texas before the war. He noted in a postwar collection of his war writing that he arrived shortly before the war began. "I remained in the South during the war from choice," he said. "I was not 'caught' here and compelled to remain; for after the State seceded, all who did not want to remain in it were given three months to leave it, and their safety while doing so was guaranteed."[18] Although biographical information is scant, Gilbert apparently had relatives in the north because he wrote a column for the *Telegraph* on February 20, 1862; it was a mock letter to Northern relatives concerning the war and unusual for its angry tone. The letter demonstrates his Southern sympathies and his anger toward Northern relatives.

> What in the devil are you banging and popping away at me for? Have I ever done you any more harm than to ask you to let me alone? Did I ever eat any of your molasses candy or swing on your gate without paying for it? Did I ever refuse to pay my share of the bill? Did? When? Have I ever failed to help sustain my share of what was a Union? Never. And if you cannot sustain your share without my aid, why not sell out to one who can; Old England, for instance? You want to free my negroes? What do you want of my negroes? You have more white people than you can sustain as well as my negroes are supported; besides, you are making laws every day to get rid of what you already have. (See late proceedings in Ohio and elsewhere).
>
> You say you want to tie the bonds of brotherhood that are snapped. Well, I don't, and if I did, I don't think you would do much toward it by shooting at me every time you can 'sight' me. Bonds are not usually tied in that way.[19]

Although the correspondent's whereabouts during the first 40 years of his life are largely unknown, the lack of public information may have been intentional.

Texas may have served as a fresh start for Gilbert. Perhaps in a demonstration of loyalty to his newly adopted home, Gilbert joined the Victoria Company, also known as Company B, of the 6th Texas Infantry in the fall of 1861.[20] He began submitting his comic letters to the *Victoria Advocate*, the closest publication to Camp Henry McCulloch, almost immediately upon his arrival.[21] *Telegraph* Editor Cushing soon followed suit, printing the first of Gilbert's correspondence in January 1862. Cushing clearly found a kindred soul in Gilbert, and the two men had much in common. Both hailed from the Northeast, were well educated, came to Texas as adults, embraced the South's institutions, supported the South's development, and were ardent Confederate patriots.[22]

Gilbert's initial humor writing was so popular that readers frequently commented on his articles, and visiting editors were disappointed if Gilbert was not in Houston when they were in town.[23] He was asked to entertain from time to time, and in January 1863, during a brief break from his correspondent's duties in Louisiana, Gilbert performed an original, sarcastic but humorous, song, "The Yankee President," at a banquet to benefit the 8th Texas Cavalry, popularly known as Terry's Rangers. The song depicted President Lincoln and members of his cabinet sailing upon the seas of abolitionism until they crashed upon the shore of the Confederacy where they were soundly defeated in Galveston. Two stanzas of the song read:

> He next selected from his friends an Abolition crew,
> To help him sail the ship of State, according to his view;
> And then instructed one and all to put her thro' and thro'
> And never leave a sail unfurl'd "while slavery wore a keel!"

> With Seward's compass as a guide, he soon did run ashore,
> And dashed his ship upon some rocks, he never knew before,
> And when he found what he had done, he rav'd and foam'd and swore,
> That he would mend the cussed thing, or fight forevermore.[24]

The morale boosting song praised General John B. Magruder's daring New Year's Eve raid in 1863 that resulted in the successful recapture of Galveston from Union forces.[25] Gilbert also used satirical poetry in his newspaper articles to lampoon individuals and wartime conditions, paralleling the work of his comic contemporaries, including satirical poet David Ross Locke, who used the pen name "Petroleum V. Nasby." Songs, poetry, and oratory aimed at boosting morale filled Northern and Southern newspapers and magazines during the war.[26]

In recognition of the role the popular press played, Gilbert denounced the December 1864 issue of *Harper's* in one of his news articles to the *Telegraph*, calling it a "reliable budget of lies, beautifully illustrated." Gilbert's ire was raised by an article, "Heroic Deeds of Heroic Men," by popular historian John S.C. Abbott. The article described the capture of Roanoke Island by General

Ambrose Burnside on February 8, 1862. Gilbert castigated Abbott, calling him "the man who sacrifices truth on all occasions for a rhetorical flourish, and for ten cents a line,' [and who] undertakes to do his share of lying for the Prince of Humbug publications."[27]

The popularity of Gilbert's comic letters undoubtedly led readers to seek out his news columns when he made the transition to war correspondent. From the time he was honorably mustered out of the 6th Regiment "on a surgeon's certificate" in May 1862 until the end of the war, Gilbert wore two editorial hats—that of reporter and humorist.[28] He provided news to the *Telegraph* first from New Orleans in 1862, then moved north, reporting from General Richard Taylor's headquarters in Alexandria during 1863. By 1864, Gilbert had moved to Shreveport, reporting from General Kirby Smith's headquarters for seven months. He then made a final move near the end of the war, reporting from Camden, Arkansas, near General John B. Magruder's command when the telegraph line was extended.[29]

Gilbert was a prolific correspondent. He usually sent the *Telegraph* two to three full columns of material every 24 to 48 hours. Uneven mail deliveries, coupled with frequent river floods, meant that Gilbert's reports from Louisiana and Arkansas were sometimes late in arriving to Editor Cushing. If Cushing received two packets of reports from his correspondent, he ran the most recent on the front page and the earlier ones on page two. When the Mississippi River experienced one of its frequent floods in February 1865, Gilbert wrote that mail, and thus news, would be delayed.

> There is no longer any stage connection between here [Shreveport] and Washington or Camden, Ark. Stage line being drawn off, mail to be carried on horse. It is impossible to reach the Mississippi river now, except in boats, the whole country being overflowed.[30]

Gilbert also found it difficult to get back to Houston for periodic visits once he was posted. An attempt to return for Christmas in 1863 resulted in failure. He sent the *Telegraph* a letter with the address listed as "Upon the High Seas," writing that the Yankee blockade made it impossible to leave Alexandria.[31]

The lack of news reaching the Trans-Mississippi region, as well as its often incomplete nature, led to shortened reports at times, a reality Gilbert acknowledged and accepted. At the end of one four-paragraph report from Shreveport in April 1864, the correspondent wrote:

> There are conflicting opinions among military men, about our being able to bag Steel's force in Arkansas. Some contend that he will escape, others that this is impossible. The matter will be decided in a very short time. I have nothing new or novel, sour or stale, in the way of news to send on to-day. News, like the wind at this season of the year, come in fitful gusts, and this does not happen to be one of the "fit" days . . . So wait for the morrow.[32]

Gilbert was not a battlefield correspondent. His reports consisted of separate paragraphs of news he gleaned at regimental headquarters, as well as carefully selected information taken from various Northern and Southern publications with a dose of editorial opinion when he felt it necessary.[33] For example, at the end of an August 1, 1863, article describing the Richmond newspapers' views of the fall of Vicksburg, Gilbert warned readers of the implications of the Federal victory, telling them that an invasion of Texas could well be forthcoming.

> What is most to be feared as the immediate result of the fall of Vicksburg, is the conversion of the great army under Grant from a stationary to a moving force. From its organization, almost it has been confined to the work of taking that city. It is now free to operate elsewhere. This is the evil against which the government is now called to take the most energetic preparation. It is not difficult to imagine in what direction Grant will move nor to estimate the effect of so powerful an army coming upon the field, with no corresponding accession to our side. This is the danger that presents the most serious grounds for alarm. It would be blindness not to see it and imbecility not to put forth the most strenuous exertions to guard against it.[34]

Similarly, a dispatch written near the end of the war, in February 1865, included the following news and commentary: "Breckinridge has entered on his duties as Secretary of War. General Beauregard will soon take charge of Hood's army in person. If we hear that our peace commissioners only reach Fortress Monroe, and then returned to Richmond, by reason of Lincoln's reply to them, we need not be disappointed."[35]

Although Gilbert did not cover battles, his role as a compiler of information was a necessity for the *Telegraph*. Although the journal was one of the largest and most influential in Texas, constant increases in the price of paper and ink meant Editor Cushing could ill afford to pay a stable of war correspondents. Small circulation and lack of reporters meant most Confederate publications, including the *Telegraph*, received most of their war news from clipping and reprinting articles from other newspapers.[36] The *Telegraph* did have one war correspondent, William Doran, who also wrote for the *Galveston News*. The *Telegraph* also had other correspondents—some civilian and some in uniform—who sent regular reports, known only by their pen names. "Local" sent news of Houston; "H.A." reported from Louisiana; and "Amicus" and "Tom Anchorite" sent regular articles from their units. However, Gilbert sent the largest volume of news on a regular basis.[37]

Gilbert prided himself on his accuracy, doing his best to obtain official reports and telegrams to verify facts, rewriting carefully and trying to exclude rumors or innuendo. "I furnished Texas with the bulk of reliable news that was received from the enemy during three years of the war," he asserted in 1890, recollecting his war reporting.[38] Yet, his faith in the accuracy of those official reports meant his news material contained the typical, inflated enemy casualty figures, as well as some major errors. They included a claim that General George McClellan had been captured in Virginia with 36,000 of his men during the Peninsula Campaign when, in fact, he had retreated down the James River.[39]

An October 1863 report from Alexandria exemplified Gilbert's concerns about accuracy. Before presenting news about General William Rosecran's Union defeat at Chickamauga September 19-20, 1863, he wrote:

> During the last six days, the following information has daily reached here through different channels. At first I did not heed the reports, but as each succeeding day fresh rumors seem to confirm previous ones, I am induced to send them forward though they need confirmation.[40]

Gilbert began a mid-January 1864 report from Alexandria in similar fashion: "There are glorious rumors here and some of them at least may be confirmed in two or three days—I wait for the documents," he wrote.[41] He delivered that news a week later, saying that three rumors of major Confederate victories surfaced: that General Robert E. Lee had "whipped" General George Mead; that General James Longstreet had driven Union forces out of Knoxville; and that General Ulysses S. Grant had fallen back from Nashville. Gilbert cautioned his editor not to publish the information. The rumors were "too good to be true," he said. "I wait with great anxiety, but will not embody these rumors in my letter as I must have the documents before sending such intelligence."[42]

Unlike some correspondents who turned rumor into fact, Gilbert was "bitterly opposed to the promulgation of rumors, favorable or unfavorable" because of the psychological damage they posed during wartime.[43] Taking a verbal swipe at inaccurate journals and reporters, he wrote:

> If you elevate a people with "good news" which subsequently proves to be false, the reaction which follows leaves a depression which would not otherwise have existed; and if "bad news" be circulating which has no foundation in fact, a gloom and despondency is produced from which it is difficult to recover.[44]

Toward the end of the war, however, the correspondent admitted that providing bad news, especially casualty figures, was wearing heavily on his psyche. "Since I have been a correspondent of the *Telegraph* I have frequently sat down to write with a gloomy heart," he acknowledged in a January 1865 report from Washington, Arkansas.[45]

Gilbert's reputation for accuracy led *Huntsville* (Texas) *Item* Editor George Robinson to praise the correspondent in poetic form in July 1863.

> High Private is a truthful man,
> Which none will deny;
> He told us when Vicksburg fell,
> And never told a lie!

We believe High Private as certain a reporter
as there is in the Confederacy.[46]

The doctor-turned-correspondent also opposed press censorship. He criti-cized the Confederate government's willingness to muzzle the press, believing that a democracy couldn't flourish without a well-informed public. "We have always advocated the policy of placing before the people all news, good or bad, not contraband, when there no longer existed any doubt of its authenticity; for the reason that the people should look the `situation' square in the face, and govern themselves accordingly," he wrote. "They should know how they stand at home and abroad at all times. In fact, our form of government can only be main-tained by continually disseminating correct information through its length or breadth."[47]

Gilbert was willing to acknowledge Southern losses and retreats at a time when many of his colleagues were not, choosing instead to refer to "backward move-ments" or "retrograde maneuvers."[48] In an October 27, 1863, report of Union ac-tivity in Louisiana, he wrote: "Reports came in last evening and to-day that the enemy has been heavily reinforced and is not advancing in this direction," he said, referring to Alexandria. "They were last reported at Opelousas. Our forces are falling back. If the enemy keeps advancing, look out for blue blazes."[49]

Despite Gilbert's devotion to the Confederacy, he was sufficiently pragmatic and honest to caution readers that their beliefs in the glory of the Confederacy and the bravery of their troops were not enough to win the war. In a March 1862 article written while he was still in the service of the 6th Infantry, Gilbert wrote the truth as he saw it: the fight would be long and hard since the North's popu-lation was larger and its soldiers were better armed and equipped. The South, he said, needed all men to volunteer. Shirking duty and postponing enlistment were not only shameful, the South's men had to do their duty if the Confederacy was to survive.

All of you who have asserted that one Southern man can, all things being equal, whip ten Yankees, and who acting on this supposition refuse to engage in the strife now raging, 'because there are men enough already in the field,' must dis-abuse yourselves of this gross error. I am as well acquainted with the people of the North as I am with those of the South, and I tell you the Northern people are not cowards. A man is not necessarily brave because he lives south of Mason and Dixon's line, neither is he a coward because he lives north of it.[50]

Soldiers occasionally found themselves the subject of Gilbert's criticism. His medical training was put to use in one column when he denounced drunken-ness, both in the army and in society, claiming alcohol was one of the chief causes of problems in the military and at home. In a strongly worded temper-ance report, the correspondent wrote that drinking caused more than problems within regiments; it also lowered the standard of morality in society.[51]

Gilbert's support of openness only went so far. Boosting morale at home was a necessity most correspondents accepted, and many Southern reporters believed that loyalty to the Confederacy superseded any emerging professional ethical norms, including adherence to truth or accuracy.[52] Although Gilbert didn't appear to knowingly lie, he did omit important details that might damage morale. In his report about the outcome of fighting at Chickamauga, for example, he acknowledged that Federal forces were "completely cut up" during the two days of brutal combat. Yet he left out a key fact: Confederate General Braxton Bragg lost more than 20,000 men, a loss of such staggering proportions that Gilbert may have been concerned about the report's effect on his readers' state of mind.[53]

Gilbert also continued to submit occasional humorous, morale-boosting letters to the *Telegraph*. A November 29, 1863, letter from Alexandria lampooned the Union army's inability to recruit soldiers and Louisiana editors' willingness to issue newspapers even when little news had occurred.

> For two long weeks we have looked for an arrival from the other side, but as Lincoln looks for conscripts, so we have looked—in vain. Not a stranger has arrived here to tell us of the "situation" and nary paper later than the 14th has come to land ... Unless something turns up soon, I shall be obliged to adopt the plan in vogue among the Shreveporters—get out an Extra anyhow.[54]

Gilbert's return to civilian life and new editorial duties did not mean an end to his humor writing. The correspondent instead turned his attention to issues that civilians and soldiers alike faced. A May 1862 report from Houston castigated the rich for creating hardships by inflating the prices for goods for their own material gain. He tied the city's growth to the rise in prices, lampooning the greed and ego pervading Southern society.[55]

> I actually saw in Main street yesterday, buildings so high that I had to look three times before I could see the top of them! My hair stood on end as I gazed upward and calculated the height of man's aspirations. I have discovered a remarkable coincidence in this city. To be brief, the higher the buildings grow, the higher the prices of goods climb! If I were a Christian in good standing, I would pray that the scenes of Babel might be enacted over again; and that all those who attempt to build *high* buildings might have their "tongues" confused and their ambition cuppled[56] [sic], if so by doing prices would diminish and justice become reinstated.[57]

A March 1863 letter from Alexandria, Louisiana, lampooned the promises made by gubernatorial candidates at election time. Gilbert, through his persona of High Private, said he was throwing his hat into the ring and made a two-paragraph campaign pledge that undoubtedly resonated with his readers.

> ... if elected Governor I will never call an extra session of the Legislature without some object in view; I will see that rain falls in dry places; that the sun shines in

wet places . . . I will destroy all shinplasters, hang all extortionists and execute all depreciators of Confederate money. I will look after all the wives of soldiers. I will raise all the corn I can and give it to the poor. I will stay all correspondence with newspapers until paper becomes cheaper. I will give the devil his due on all occasions . . . I will not allow the cars to run off any railroad track in the state, especially the Central. I will make all the rivers navigable and all the old maidens marriageable.[58]

Even after Gilbert became a correspondent based in Louisiana, and later in Arkansas, his columns offered glimpses of humor, usually toward the end of his correspondence or at the beginning. Following a report on New Year's Day 1864 on the latest war news from Northern and Southern newspapers, Gilbert wrote in his inimitable way that not much was happening in Alexandria, Louisiana, while taking a verbal jab at the high retail prices that Confederate citizens faced. "Everything very dull here except the shopkeepers—they are still sharp enough."[59]

Searching for an ending to his column a week later, and not finding one, he again took a tall-tales approach to provide a sense of levity in difficult times: "I have read of a country where it was so cold that every word uttered in the open air was frozen as soon as articulated. It has been colder than that here for the last two days; for my thoughts, during the last forty eight hours were chilled before they could be uttered. If that is not a good reason for closing this letter, I'll offer a better when thawed."[60]

Most of Gilbert's correspondence from Louisiana was serious in tone. In an October 1863 report from Alexandria, he wrote about the prisoner exchange. Engaging in his usual mix of facts and editorial commentary, he wrapped the exchange in the mantle of Confederate nationalism.

Four hundred and seventy-four Yankee prisoners left here this morning on foot for Shreveport. The nights are now very cool, and the prisoners have no blankets. Of course they will be obliged to shiver it out until they reach their place of destination. As the road is a long one, Especially if they are obliged to go to Hempstead, Texas, they will have plenty of time to ask themselves what they are here for, and no doubt they will frequently wish they had stayed at home where they belong.[61]

Gilbert took a break to marry Louella Lyon on January 26, 1865, in Houston. Upon hearing the news, the *Tyler Journal* produced a tongue-in-cheek marriage announcement imitating Gilbert's style.

The painful news has reached us that our esteemed friend, Rennessaiaer Reed Gilbert, alias H.P., alias High Private, whilst walking the streets of Houston, unsuspicious of lurking danger, was, on the morning of the 26th of January, suddenly seized by a female Lion, which had been petted and domesticated in that city, and carried off into the forest. We are informed that some of his friends were immediately informed of the mishap, and started in pursuit of the captor and captured, toward Courtney, but they entertained no hope of being able to rescue our friend alive. Alas, poor Gilbert! He was a man of many parts; wrote reliable news to the Houston Telegraph, and was at times fond of cracking jokes.[62]

"But we rejoice," the *Journal* added, "that Gilbert still lives, although captured and carried off by a Lyon, it was a beautiful and harmless one. We have just received the following announcement, which explains itself: MARRIED—In this city on the 26th inst, by the Rev. J.M. Curtis, Mr. Rennesalaer[63] Reed Gilbert to Miss Louella Lyon, all of Houston." Over time, the couple had seven children: Hattie, Jeff, Edward, Kate, Allen, Lavenia, and Annie May.[64] Tragedy struck R.R. and Louella in 1883 when Annie May died on December 4 when she was two years old. The Gilberts buried her in Palestine in the East Hill Cemetery.[65]

As the war neared its conclusion, Gilbert continued to blend news and editorial commentary. In April 1865, he called on the Confederate government to appropriate money for maimed soldiers who needed artificial limbs. Gilbert noted the U.S. Congress had passed an act for Northern soldiers to receive such help and he exhorted the Confederate Congress to do the same. He also urged the establishment of a Trans-Mississippi Association for Maimed Soldier Relief and urged it to raise private funds to aid soldiers.[66]

By war's end, Gilbert had become reflective about the Confederacy's failures. He wrote that in his opinion the government tried to do too much too fast.

> It did wrong in adopting a Constitution at the very outset, instead of creeping before it attempted to walk. To act on the supposition that cotton is king. To spend so much on fortifications within range of Union gunboats. To not make provisions for paying troops regularly and promptly. For Davis removing General Johnston at the time his services [were] needed. If conditions and planning had been different, the end result (would have) brought this war to a fortunate termination.[67]

His commentary should not be read as pro-Union, however. Gilbert remained devoted to Texas and Southern views. A May 1865 article used word play sarcastically to assess the Federal government: "A Yankee paper says the crocusses [sic] are in bloom in Washington. So are many other cusses in that s[t]ink of iniquity."[68] He was more circumspect a month later. His newspaper, which had been based in Houston, appears to have failed and he returned to the *Telegraph* as that journal's Galveston correspondent. As Federal troops began arriving in Texas, Gilbert expressed his anger and dismay at the Confederacy's loss, yet ended on a hopeful note for readers facing the uncertainties of reconstruction.

> The revolution which has just been brought to a close, was conceived in error, conducted with unparalleled corruption and weakness and disgracefully abandoned, especially by the Trans-Mississippi Department. Error characterized every step

taken by the Confederate Government from its beginning to its close, and our ruin followed as a certain result... We must make the best of a bad job. We appealed to arms and have been defeated. Our duty and policy require that we submit to the decision effected by the sword. It is a bitter pill to swallow, but let us behave like men, and endure what we have not the power to resist. We tried our hand at separation and failed. Let us now atone by pursuing a *wiser* course.[69]

He amended this statement two days later to note: "I said that the rebellion was conceived in error. I should have said planned in error. This would have explained my meaning exactly."[70]

Gilbert said that he considered Galveston his adopted home and sent regular reports throughout the summer and into early fall of the arrival of Federal troops, the return of Confederate soldiers, the pardon process, development of new railroad lines, Galveston city news, and items of interest from Mexico. His articles reflected postwar uncertainties, although true to mid-19th century humorist form, he sprinkled comic relief through his reports, while also taking jabs at the Federal occupation troops. His June 16, 1865, letter noted that the port city was jammed with people waiting to be transported from Texas to Louisiana.

At least three hundred people, big and little, are waiting here to be transported to New Orleans, or some other penal colony . . . Among the latest arrivals I notice Gen. Drayton and Col. Lawler. They are also outward bound, but it is to-day generally believed that Capt. Sands will permit no more departures of "rebels" until the troops and their commanders arrive. This causes no little uneasiness for various reasons—the principal of which is a large proportion of those waiting for permission to leave are dead broke. The hotels are more than full, so much so that a very large proportion of those in transit are compelled to sojourn most of the time in whisky shops and lager beer palaces . . . It is astonishing how closely live humans can be packed without salt, for several days in hot weather, without spoiling. It can only be accounted for on the supposition that innate sweetness is proof against external influences of a putrifying character.[71]

In one of his final columns for the *Telegraph* in October 1865, Gilbert ruminated on the "negro question," stating that, in his opinion, Texas' labor problems could only be solved by encouraging immigration, preferably from Germany. He said the state should devise a plan to give land, housing, food, and sufficient wages to German immigrants, whom Gilbert viewed as reliable and trustworthy workers, for at least two years to help them get established. He accepted that slavery was over but adhered to the common belief of the time that newly freed slaves were not as reliable as whites: "Without the power to compel the negro to work, would not the weeds continue to grow? I am one of those who think that without compulsion, there is no reliability, so far as those of African descent are concerned."[72]

In his postwar years, Gilbert and his family lived as rolling stones, returning to old employers, establishing new publications, and working for others. His travels even brought him back to the medical profession for a brief time. In April 1865, Gilbert established his own publication, the *Texas Weekly Record*, in Houston. The *Galveston Weekly News* took notice of Gilbert's prospectus, stating:

> We call attention to Dr. Gilbert's Prospectus for a new weekly paper in this city. Dr. Gilbert has been extensively and favorably known to the public by his valuable contributions to the Telegraph, over the signature of "H.P." or "High Private." Our readers will at once infer from the Prospectus, that the "Texas Weekly Record" will not be a mere transcript of the general news, but will be a "peculiar" and original paper and as such will serve to give an agreeable variety to the very limited journalism of the State.[73]

The *Austin State Gazette* was similar in its praise. "Dr. Gilbert's well known ability as a correspondent is a good earnest that he will publish an interesting paper," the *Gazette*'s editor wrote. Gilbert promised to run an original story in the first issue that he would later publish in book form. The new paper would cost $3 a year, but the *Gazette* asserted the story alone would be worth the price of the subscription.[74]

The *Texas Weekly Record* was a neatly printed, double-sided single sheet. The journal embodied Gilbert's ideals of honesty, integrity, and community concern. He offered a mix of general news, articles focused on health and education, letters to the editor, literature and poetry, and a column of jokes. His serialized original story, called "Philanthropos," told the tale of a boy, his dog, a kindly uncle, and a cruel teacher called "Old Hickory." Gilbert wrote that the story was a morality tale but said he was leaving it up to readers to figure out the moral to the story.

The literary aspect of his publication was particularly important to Gilbert and, he proclaimed, such a publication was particularly necessary because of the times. "As we are now shut in from the outer world, and may be for a long time to come," readers could not always gain access to recent works by the best authors, he wrote, pledging to put accuracy first in news gathering. "Great care and caution" will be observed "and all rumors will undergo thorough scrutiny before being ventilated. The good of society demands this."[75]

Gilbert hoped to expand the publication and create a true literary journal. He wrote in the April 21, 1865, issue that he eagerly wanted to begin serializing Victor Hugo's monumental work, *Les Miserables*, but was forced to wait until he had more subscribers so that he could increase the size of the journal.[76] Only a few copies of the *Texas Weekly Record* exist, but it is likely the journal suffered the fate of other western newspapers and died quickly, since Gilbert soon returned to the *Telegraph* and was assigned to cover Galveston. He remained through October 1865. His correspondent's pay was probably insufficient for his family, so he announced on July 15, 1865, that "Gilbert and Company," a new advertising agency in Galveston, would take advertisements from Galveston firms for placement in the state's newspapers.

It is unclear how long Gilbert continued to work for the *Telegraph*, but by November 1869, he had moved to Crockett, Texas, where he published a newspaper alternately called the *Central Journal* and the *Crockett Journal* by the *Dallas Herald*, which tracked Gilbert's postwar career.[77] The *Herald* noted that Gilbert sold the paper less than five months later.[78] Gilbert moved to Bryan, where he was offered "a more lucrative position" editing the tri-weekly *Brazos Eagle*. He said his newspaper would be "adapted to the local wants of the community." The *Dallas Herald* said of the new venture: "The doctor can and no doubt will, make an excellent paper."[79]

Within two years, Gilbert was on the move again, this time to Dallas where he left journalism, briefly returning to his medical practice. An advertisement in the August 10, 1872, *Dallas Herald* announced that the doctor was taking patients who had "rheumatic affections, chronic and acute rheumatism, neuralgia, paralysis, sciatica, lumbago, and etc." He announced that his charges were moderate and that patients could find his office at H.C. Hoskins and Co. Drug Store.[80]

The lure of journalism, or perhaps the lack of patients, forced Gilbert's return to newspapers. By 1876 he was in Palestine as the proprietor of the *Palestine News*.[81] His family lived in a boarding house on Maple Street. In Palestine, Gilbert was one of more than 90 citizens who petitioned the Brazos County commissioners in August 1871 to order a special election to increase property taxes to raise $22,000 to establish Texas A & M University, the first public college in Texas.[82]

Gilbert sold the *Palestine News* in March 1881 to Edwin E. Overall, a New Yorker, and the *Galveston News* reported that Gilbert was retiring from the newspaper business,[83] a retirement that did not last long. It is unclear what work Gilbert did in the early 1880s, but he returned to his humor roots, freelancing at least one article to the humor journal, *Texas Siftings*, in June 1881. The article about Texas hotels is reminiscent of his Civil War columns.

> The average Texas hotel makes up in price what it lacks in quantity and quality. Those who have traveled much in Texas have learned by experience to expect a big bill when the fare is poor, and a reasonable one when the fare and accommodations are satisfactory.

Gilbert cracked jokes about the food and the rooms and provided 10 rules for travelers, including: "Rule 4—Travelers are at liberty to use the hotel mosquitoes and bed bugs, but these counter-irritants must not be enticed away from the hotel."[84]

Gilbert returned to journalism full time in 1885, editing the *West Texas Star*.[85] By 1887, he had moved to Austin, trying his hand at editing his own newspaper again. He called his new journal *Texas Tidings*, but the paper did not last long, and Gilbert again took a job, this time as an editor at the *Austin Statesman* in the late 1880s.[86]

As he approached age 70, Gilbert collected his humor columns for the *Houston Telegraph* and republished them as a short book in 1890. The aging editor maintained his sense of humor, referring to the Civil War as the "war of 1861-2-3-4-5."[87] He reprinted the work in 1894, adding more letters and an essay titled, "The Secrets of Success: Or Business Advice to the Young Men of the South."

By 1892 or 1893 he had changed jobs again, working as an exchange editor for the *Galveston News*. Within two years he had founded one last newspaper in Austin, an immigrant's guide to Texas called the *New South*.[88] Gilbert may have left Austin in 1897, for the Austin City Directory lists his wife living alone in Austin, and the two may have separated. The humorist died in October 1899 at his daughter's home in Houston, where he was buried. His wife and two of their sons are buried in Austin.[89]

Gilbert and his humor were products of the 19th century. It is perhaps fitting that he died as the century closed. A decade before his death, Gilbert noted how he wanted to be remembered.

> When we finally pass in our pencil and go to join those who have gone before us, all that we ask is that some friend will inscribe on our headboard these words: "Here lie the remains of one whom adversity could not cower, and who did as well through life as the best among us would do if surrounded by like circumstances."[90]

During the Civil War and occasionally afterward, Gilbert provided comic relief and relatively reliable news for an anxious population. He also served as a watchdog—criticizing political and military decisions when he felt that they were warranted. The strength and value of his work lay in his ability to blend criticism and humor in addressing the issues that concerned Texas readers.

Virginia

An Alabama regiment marches through Capitol Square in Richmond on the way to join the Confederate forces under General Beauregard. *Harper's Weekly,* October 19, 1861. Courtesy of Rare Books and Special Collections, University of South Carolina Libraries

Virginia was fashionably late arriving at the secession party but, once there, proved to be the belle of the ball as the new capital of the infant Confederacy. By the time Virginia seceded on April 17, 1861, seven Southern states had preceded her, beginning with South Carolina on December 20, 1860. However, Virginia would not be the last to secede. That honor was reserved for Tennessee.

By May 29, 1861, the newly formed Confederate government was relocated to Richmond from Montgomery, Alabama, and the South began gearing up for the conflict. The major Confederate victory at Manassas on July 21 set the stage for four years of war, which concluded in Virginia by the Confederate burning of Richmond as troops fled the capital in 1865. Reporters from all over the Confederacy, including far-off Texas, converged on Virginia to watch the battles and tramp the battlefields following the bitter struggles. Some of the best reporting of the war came out of this coverage and from those who covered political activity in Richmond itself.

James B. Sener, a "hometown boy" from Fredericksburg, literally covered the war from his home in one of the most hotly contested cities in the Confederacy. Sener was never more than 100 miles from his home town when he was embedded with General Robert E. Lee's Army of Northern Virginia.

Another "hometown boy" covering the war was John R. Thompson in nearby Richmond. Thompson was a prominent journalist whose poetry was widely read. When war erupted, he switched to reporting and joined the staff of the *Memphis Daily Appeal*. Thompson's accounts of life in the capital city and his colorful writing as "Dixie" made him a popular figure in the pages of the *Appeal*. Thompson wrote about Union prisoners of war, the activities of President Jefferson Davis and other political figures, and the ravages of war in the Virginia countryside.

Dr. George W. Bagby, Jr., was the Richmond correspondent for the *Charleston Mercury* in South Carolina. Some readers considered him the worst sort of "croaker," an irritating dissident who was fearless in his criticism of Confederate generals, even Robert E. Lee, and who never hesitated to attack anyone in government, including President Jefferson Davis. To other readers, Bagby was an attack dog of a reporter, refusing to be silenced in his denunciations of government corruption and waste. His criticism hit so hard that the editors of the fire-eating *Mercury* attempted to soften his rhetoric. Bagby remained in Richmond until the end, fleeing as Union troops converged on the city in 1865.

One of the war's few women correspondents reported from Virginia. Calling herself "Virginia," she wrote to the *Mobile Advertiser and Register* from Norfolk, where she followed the activities of troops from Alabama and Mobile. She had attracted the attention of her editors with her feisty defense of the people of Norfolk against charges that they were unenthusiastic about Confederate secession. Virginia's letters resonated with Alabama readers, and she offered a woman's view of the war, responding to Mobile readers' concerns for news of their hometown boys.

25

George William Bagby, Jr.: Confederate "Croaker"

Debra Reddin van Tuyll

To many, the *Charleston Mercury*'s Richmond correspondent "Hermes" was the worst sort of croaker—an irritating dissident whose impassioned prose put everything the Confederacy was fighting for at risk. To others, he was a fearless writer who had no compunction about reporting the truth, even when it included the blunders, missteps, and corruption of the Confederate government and its president, Jefferson Davis.

Hermes, whose real name was George W. Bagby, Jr., was scathing in his rhetorical attacks on Davis and his policies, which expanded the power and size of the government while simultaneously stripping citizens of cherished civil liberties. Bagby could—and did—take on anyone, even General Robert E. Lee, when he believed their actions were counter to Confederate interests. One of the correspondent's diatribes landed him in front of a tribunal, essentially a 19th century press council charged with adjudicating an officer's complaint against him. Bagby was unfazed, however. He was committed to the ideal of Southern independence, he had specific ideas about how it could be achieved, and he was not shy about complaining whenever Confederate leaders, military or civilian, deviated from what he considered to be the proper path.

A surviving photograph of Bagby, taken after the Civil War, is deceiving.[1] It shows a frail man in late middle age with a goatee and mustache, and a full head of snowy hair combed to one side across a high forehead. His face and shoulders are thin and narrow and his dark eyes are sad. He bears little resemblance to the man with rakish, sultry, and confident eyes peering back from an earlier portrait of the much younger Bagby, who seems to view the world with a slight touch of disdain and a certain haughtiness.[2] Or perhaps a bit of arrogance. The younger Bagby has the defiant look of a man who could—and did—take on the president and leading generals of his country. He had the look of a man who would question their war strategies, condemn their politics, and ultimately play

A young George W. Bagby, Jr.
Courtesy of the Virginia
Historical Society

a role in shattering public confidence in their ability to win a devilish war for independence.[3]

That man easily could be Hermes, the *Charleston Mercury*'s political correspondent in Richmond who wrote fearlessly frank letters about politics and war. The two portraits of this editor, lecturer, essayist, and war correspondent exemplify the seeming dichotomy of George Bagby: the stormy, passionate, sometimes unpleasantly shrill political commentator for whom only perfection was good enough and the doe-eyed soul who seemed to have learned in later life, through his own suffering, to love and cherish others.

For most people, the *Mercury*'s correspondent would not have been an easy man to be around most of the time, though he could be kind and, especially with his family. He treated them with tenderness, kindness, and affection— sometimes to the point of silliness. A letter to his wife, for example, written while visiting Georgia in 1864, began, "Dear Old Oman," and concluded, "Your huzzy." His family had equally warm feelings for Bagby. In March 1862, when Bagby apparently considered returning to the Confederate army, his nephew, William B. Matthews, wrote to plead with him to reconsider: "... please let me entreat you not to go. I know if you get into an engagement you will almost certainly get killed," the young Matthews wrote. Matthews himself had plans to join the army, and he was anxious to do so. But his concern for his uncle took precedence, both with Matthews and with his mother, Bagby's only sister, Ellen.

The city of Richmond, Virginia. *Harper's Weekly*, May 31, 1862. Courtesy of Rare Books and Special Collections, University of South Carolina Libraries

Charleston, South Carolina during the Civil War. The street to the far left is Broad Street. The *Mercury's* office was at the top of the street, near the Custom House. *Harper's Weekly,* January 26, 1861. Courtesy of Rare Books and Special Collections, University of South Carolina Libraries

After telling Bagby of his own plans to join, Matthews added, "If you want Ma's oil cover you shall have it at the risk of my life because Ma told me so."[4]

However, Bagby did not always evoke such positive feelings from those he encountered. He could be hurtfully strident, sarcastic, and melancholy, a tendency that was due perhaps to life-long ill health brought about by the chronic dyspepsia that would eventually claim his life.[5]

Bagby could also be peevish and biting when annoyed, which was often during the war. He could be nasty when he believed he was right and the subject of his venom was wrong, frequently the case in his political reporting. It was this side of Bagby that catapulted him to fame during the war—not as George William Bagby, Jr., but as the bombastic Hermes, whose snarling correspondence could give little old ladies the vapors—literally, according to *Mercury* Editor Robert B. Rhett, Jr. The editor wrote to his correspondent that "many old ladies, I understand, have a cold shiver whenever the *Mercury* containing a letter from that terrible character arrives. They're asking 'Who in the name of God is Hermes?'"[6]

Despite other qualities, Bagby was a romantic. A 1927 literary biography referred to him as "a poetic young writer" whose prose was characterized by "tenderness and pathos, the gentle grace" of a true man of letters.[7] His prose—journalistic and creative—waxed lyrically about the romance of war, the chivalry of officers, and the courage of the troops. Ironically, the correspondent's fondness for all of this did not produce a willingness to suffer its hardships, but Bagby found another way to serve the interests of his country. After a few months as an unsuccessful soldier, he became a newspaper correspondent again, an activity he had pursued for several years before the war. He would cover the war until the end when he fled Richmond with President Davis' entourage.

Bagby was born on August 13, 1828, in Lynchburg, Virginia. His parents were George W. Bagby and his frail wife, Virginia Young Evans Bagby. Bagby's father was a merchant and a descendant of one of the first Virginia settlers at Jamestown, and his mother was the daughter of a Revolutionary War veteran. Bagby's father was "not very successful in business, and exceedingly pious." His mother was ill for as long as Bagby knew her. She had been in the first stages of consumption at the time she married, and her health had worsened with the births of her son and daughter, Ellen. Mrs. Bagby's health was so poor that she had to leave her children with relatives when they were very young while she spent time in the mountains trying to improve her health. Even those measures did little to help; Mrs. Bagby died by the time her son was eight years old.[8]

Most of Bagby's childhood was spent with his aunt, Elizabeth Hobson, on her plantation, deep in the hinterlands of Cumberland County, Virginia. He once quipped that his aunt lived in such a remote area that she resorted to eating just to relieve the boredom.[9] The well-prepared and abundant food made a strong impression on Bagby. Later in life, he would remember that his aunt always "had more good things to eat than anybody he had ever heard of."[10] The varieties of breads on her table made a particular impression: rolls, biscuits, waffles, battercakes, muffins, pone, ashcake, hoe-cake, salt-risen bread, apple bread, and "cracklen" bread, but Bagby's real favorite, he recalled, was pigskins.[11]

Bagby's education began in a local "Old Field School," but by the time he was 10, he had enrolled at Edgehill School in Princeton, New Jersey. The length of Bagby's studies at Edgehill is unknown, but in November 1843, he was enrolled at Delaware College, where he studied for two years. Bagby's college adventures seem to have been typical. He joined the Athenian Literary Society, took up pipe smoking, and had several "desperate love affairs" with local girls. One winter while skating, Bagby fell through the ice but was unharmed other than being seriously wet and cold. One of Bagby's more intriguing adventures was his membership in "The Knock-kneed, Bowlegged, Pidgeon-toed, Hyena Club." The activities of that club, unfortunately, were never recorded, but one can imagine.[12]

At the end of his sophomore year, Bagby left Delaware College, although he would return at least once to give an address in 1854 commemorating the Athenian Society's anniversary. At age 18, he enrolled in medical school at the University of Pennsylvania.[13] He completed that degree in 1849 and returned home to Lynchburg via canal boat, "the happy owner of a diploma in a green tin case and the utterly miserable possessor of a dyspepsia" that would dog him throughout his life.[14]

Lynchburg in 1849 offered good opportunities for a young man with a college education. It was a relatively large manufacturing and tobacco city of 8,000 residents in the Virginia piedmont. Bagby made a half-hearted attempt to set up a medical practice after completing medical school, but he would soon gravitate to what would become his life's work: writing. Lynchburg's newspapers offered fertile ground for a would-be writer. Its newspapers had historically served as training grounds for some of Virginia's best journalists, including John Hampden Pleasants who founded the *Richmond Whig*, a paper that would be edited almost exclusively by Lynchburg men throughout its history. Bagby would eventually be employed there as well.[15]

His first foray into journalism began at a relatively new Lynchburg newspaper, the *Express*, which he edited with a boyhood friend, G. Woodville Latham, the son of a Lynchburg physician. The paper had been established in the early 1850s by Hudson Garland. Bagby and Latham purchased it a few years later. Many years later, Bagby recalled that he and Latham earned little money or reputation with the paper, but they had an enormous amount of fun. Because of the inexperience of its two proprietors and because Latham had something of an aversion to work, the paper was not a great success.[16]

During the three years that he and Latham edited the *Express*, Bagby began building his writing career. He wrote essays for a variety of newspapers and national magazines, including the competing *Lynchburg Daily Virginian*, *Harper's*, and the *Atlantic Monthly*. He also began writing humorous sketches for publications such as the *New Orleans Sunday Delta* and the *Southern Literary Messenger*, the magazine Edgar Allen Poe edited when he lived in Richmond.[17] Bagby was on his way to building a national reputation as a writer.

After Bagby and Latham closed the *Express*, Bagby retired to a maternal uncle's plantation, Mountain View, to recuperate and restore his health. His chronic stomach ailments had become more serious during the *Express* years, although his illness did not exempt Bagby from the demands of the Southern Code of Honor during his sojourn at Mountain View. In December 1856, Bagby enraged a fellow editor with a supposedly humorous *Harper's* essay titled, "The Virginia Editor." The sketch characterized the typical Virginia newspaper editor as being "an imperial gallon" that "cannot be contained in a quart pot," a man who "is not a very good citizen because he wants to be a better editor." The Virginia editor, according to Bagby, was . . .

> . . . a young, unmarried, intemperate, pugnacious, gambling gentleman. Between drink and dueling pistols he is generally escorted to a premature grave. If he so far withstands the ravages of brandy and gunpowder as to reach the period of gray hairs and cautiousness, he is disposed to make room for a youth who hates his life with an utter hatred, and who can't keep drunk more than a week at a time . . . His first waking moments in the morning are saturated with a number of power cocktails, to cure a headache, "brought over," as an accountant would say, from the previous midnight. Cocktailed past the point of nervousness and remorse, he dresses himself, and wends his way to barber shop to get shaved, if he shaves at all . . .[18]

The Virginia editor at least had a room to himself, probably in a hotel or boarding house, according to Bagby, and while it may well have been quite comfortable when the journalist first moved in, before long, it would become so messy, he could no longer sleep there. The young writer explained:

> He has a room of his own, originally furnished with some taste and care, but has a mortal antipathy to sleeping in it. Nor is this aversion to be wondered at. Through a puddle of newspapers, congressional speeches, tobacco juice, cigar stump, broken spit-boxes, and pipestems, he wanders to a bed whose sheets bid adieu to the washerwoman at a period too remote to be recalled, and whose counterpane secrets its primitive tints under a sweet and greasy scum of spermaceti and spilled brandy toddies . . . Upon the window-sill, near the foot of the bed, stands marshaled a platoon of various-sized bottles, from the grenadier champagne to the squatty porter and the slab-sided tickler . . . The odor of this apartment is not inviting. The door is always open, night and day, and it is the common dormitory of all belated roysterers. Anyone may sleep here who chooses . . . Habits which would outlaw any other man enable him to ride rough-shod over the inviolable law of custom . . . He loves to talk, and his great theme, after politics, is himself . . . The Virginia editor is not a profoundly learned man . . . His specialty is politics;

Washington Monument at the Virginia Capital. Courtesy of the Library of Congress

and his tastes not less than his occupation conspire to prevent his acquiring any other knowledge.[19]

The sketch was a caricature but it was also fairly close to a truthful descrip-tion of a typical 19th century editor. Bagby's story hit too close to home for one Virginia editor who believed it was a not-so-cleverly disguised description of himself, and he challenged Bagby to a duel over the unflattering portrait. Bagby met his nemesis at the famous Bladensburg dueling ground. The opponents took their positions and readied themselves for the signal. At the last moment, the combat was averted by the arrival of Virginia Congressman Thomas S. Bocock, a friend of both parties who had heard of the duel and rushed to the site to stop it.[20]

After a year of "work in moderation, a good country bill of fare, and a diverting association with friends and relatives," not to mention the excitement of the duel, Bagby's health was sufficiently restored that he could return to Lynchburg. Before long, he received a job offer from another newspaper. William M. Semple, an old friend and another Lynchburg native who had taken up the journalist's pen, was resigning as the Washington, D.C., correspondent for the *New Orleans Crescent*. He recommended Bagby as his replacement.[21]

The George Bagby who took the *Crescent*'s Washington job was very different from the medical school graduate who had come home to Virginia almost a decade earlier. He had several years of newspaper experience at four Lynchburg newspapers, and he had become a contributor to distinguished magazines like *Harper's* and the *Southern Literary Messenger*. Bagby moved to Washington and took up residence at a boarding house that Semple jokingly referred to as the "Hotel de Riley."[22] Bagby's work for the *Crescent* left him ample time to accept correspondence assignments from other newspapers, including the *Memphis Eagle and Enquirer*, the *Charleston Mercury*, and the *Richmond Whig*.

Bagby would work for two of those newspapers, the *Mercury* and the *Whig*, off and on for many years, and he would remain loyal to the Charleston paper, despite its stingy fees.[23] Beginning with his first article for the *Mercury* in January 1858, and consistently thereafter, Bagby asked to be paid $5 a letter, the fee he was paid by the other newspapers. Just as consistently, the *Mercury* editors offered, and Bagby always eventually accepted, an alternate figure of $3. This fee was even lower than the $4.37 per story he received from the *Whig*. *Mercury* Editor Robert Barnwell Rhett, Jr., explained that he had received brilliant Washington correspondence in the past and never paid more than $3 per letter. He would not budge from that figure.[24]

At first, Bagby had some trouble adjusting to life in Washington. He was lonely and initially had some difficulties developing sources. He also was not confident about his writing and reporting abilities. "In my new vocation, I shall achieve but little—at least that is my feeling," he wrote to a friend. "I write letters, but not brilliant ones."[25] Bagby would also be troubled by depression brought on by illness. In January 1859, he wrote to a friend that his health was so bad that he did not expect to live very long.[26]

His years in Washington were more valuable than Bagby realized. He developed a good knowledge of political affairs and built important relationships with leading politicians that would prove useful in the coming war. However, being a first-hand witness to the political machinations of the growing sectional conflict was profoundly depressing for Bagby. In a February 1859 letter to the

Crescent, he lamented the lack of strong political leaders and wondered what would ever become of the country.[27] Still, just over a year later, Bagby would put his knowledge and his Washington connections to work for a cause he passionately believed in, Southern independence.

By 1859, Bagby was obliged to write at least five letters each week, two for the *Crescent* and three for the *Eagle and Enquirer*. That left sufficient time to expand a new literary project Bagby had begun the previous year: a series of humorous stories for the *Southern Literary Messenger*. The stories were in the form of letters from a backwoodsman, Mozis Addums, a fictitious character based on people Bagby had known in Lynchburg. Like so much mid-19th century humor writing, the Addums stories were in dialect, an immensely popular genre of that day. Many of the Mozis Addums stories were written in the form of letters that recounted the protagonist's adventures. His first letter describes a train trip taken by Addums. It includes language and imagery that might be offensive to some contemporary readers.[28]

> Seagar in mouth I retide to the smoking car, and seeing uv a weakly-lookinge yung man on the bench behine me, I detummind to put my afferbul in pracktis on him. I offud him a lite to his seagar. He ackseptid with thanks. We struck up a talk on the wether, in the cose uv which he let fall he wus frum South Carroliny. Being Suthun to the bac-boan, I were delitid to meet him, sayinge:
>
> ADDUMS—"Sir, I'me rejoyst to incountur you. Next to my oan beluvd Vurginyer, I esteam South Carroliny abuv all the Suthun Staits."
>
> WEAKLY MAN—"Haow?"
>
> I repeetid my obzervashun.
>
> WEAKLY MAN—"Wal, it is a kinder nice plais. I calkerlatid to do a smart spec o' bizniss doun Saowth, but the ager took a holt onto me, and I had to leave."
>
> I begun to smelle uv a ratt.
>
> ADDUMS—"Whar're you going to, now?"
>
> WEAKLY MAN—"Goinge hum to Vummaount Stait, quick as steem will taik me."
>
> "Full bluddid Yanky, by jing!" I ixclaimd intunnily, and abandund my afferbul ixperrymint on the spot, shut up my fly-trap, and nuvver utterly a werde untel I got to Fedricksbug, whar I stept on the flatform, sent my luv to Ellick Masin by a nigger, reterned to the car, and smoaked in perfoun silunce tel I got to the steembote at Putomuck Creak.[29]

The Addums stories catapulted Bagby into the position of Virginia's first prominent humorist. Bagby and *Messenger* Editor John R. Thompson were surprised at the success of the stories. In the preface to his collected works, Bagby wrote that Thompson printed the first Addums story "not without misgivings, and its success amazed both of us … I literally 'woke up and found myself famous . . .'" Bagby recalled that he had probably earned more from his Mozis Addums stories than from all his other writings put together, but he eventually came to regret creating the character.[30] He wrote in 1878 that even his best work had not gained the attention of those silly stories in dialect. "My best exertions have still left me plain 'Mozis Addums,' a name that for many years made me a little sick when I heard it."[31]

By March 1859, Bagby decided he needed a break from Washington.[32] He left the city as a well-connected journalist whose intimate knowledge of contemporary politics had given him definite opinions about the South and its place in the Union, even if he was dismayed about its future. He also left with a growing reputation as a newsman and as a literati.[33]

However, Bagby's respite from the rigors of journalism did not last long. By late 1859, he had moved to Richmond to take up his pen again and to try several new projects. He found employment as a librarian at the state Historical Society, and he also gave the lecture circuit a whirl.[34] His first lecture in Richmond was titled, "An Apology for Fools." One of the gimmicks used to build interest in the lecture was the ticket itself. Three words appeared on the ticket: "Fools: Admit One."[35]

The evening did not go smoothly. On the advice of Thompson, Bagby drank a strong cup of tea before beginning his lecture, and his mouth became so dry that he could scarcely speak. He also had to deal with an overly affectionate dog and a drunk who "meandered slowly up to the stand, looked me full in the face, said in a thick growling voice but loud enough to be heard by half the house, 'Damn fool yourself!' and slowly wandered out again."[36] Bagby might have given up lecturing after that night, but the monetary rewards and encouragement of friends convinced him to continue to lecture around Virginia. Bagby earned enough money—usually around $20 a lecture—to pay for a summer in Canada, New England, and New York.[37]

In mid-1860, Bagby took on yet another job: editor of the *Southern Literary Messenger*. Thompson was leaving to become editor of *Southern Field and Fireside* in Augusta, Georgia, and he arranged for Bagby to take over the Richmond literary magazine. Bagby's salary was $300 a year, approximately $7,106.70 in 2008 money, plus all the books, newspapers, and magazines that came to the magazine's office.[38]

The editorship came with certain liabilities, one of which was persistent purveyors of pencil sketches seeking publishing possibilities. They included a young man named Blanchard, who became a frequent visitor at the *Messenger* office shortly after Bagby became editor.

"Bothered by a young fellow named Blanchard of this city, who is of the opinion he has an original talent as a pencil sketcher," Bagby noted in his diary. "Also has dyspepsia horribly and a very active tongue."[39] Young Blanchard apparently returned the following day, much to Bagby's annoyance. "Another visit from Blanchard," he wrote. "Made me so mad I hardly knew what to do with him or myself. He must be deranged."[40] Overall, with the exception of a few annoyances here and there, the job of editor was not onerous. It gave Bagby the opportunity to dream of what he would like to do with one of the South's most prominent literary magazines, and one of those dreams was to include illustrations. He was aiming higher than local talent for the magazine, for presumably, Blanchard's work did not measure up to Bagby's expectations.[41]

Bagby's efforts at the *Messenger* built his reputation as a man of letters. One of his early biographers went so far as to refer to him as "Virginia's Nineteenth Century Literary Giant."[42] However, that biographer's conclusions may have been somewhat exaggerated. An article in an 1865 edition of the *Boston Daily Advertiser* did not give the impression that Bagby was a nationally noted literary figure. In fact, in the *Advertiser*'s opinion, literature produced by any Southerner, Bagby included, was of virtually no importance. The paper pontificated: "The deprivation (of Southern literature) was not one to be taken to heart, and we fancy neither publishers nor public missed very seriously the loss of the contributions of the communities in rebellion to the literature of the day."[43]

But the *Advertiser*'s editors grudgingly listed the pantheon of contemporary Southern writers, and Bagby's name appeared on that list, fourth behind William Gilmore Simms of South Carolina and two other Virginians: John R. Thompson who, like Bagby, was an editor, poet, and journalist; and John Esten Cooke, also a poet. Although the *Advertiser*'s editors did not believe any of these men produced anything noteworthy, they did put their work leagues ahead of other well-known Southern writers of the day, including Henry Timrod, who became the Confederacy's poet laureate; Paul Hamilton Hayne, also a poet; and Henry Lynden Flash, another poet-journalist who edited the *Macon Telegraph and Confederate*. Despite the Boston newspaper's condescension, Bagby would be included in any "thorough examination of the literary conditions in the South from 1830 to 1880."[44]

Although Bagby enjoyed some stature as a writer and lecturer, his importance as a journalist was neglected. His earlier biographers generally noted that he worked as a Civil War correspondent for multiple newspapers, but they focused almost exclusively on his work as a literary figure and humor writer. None turned a careful eye to the nature and influence of Bagby's journalism. His first biographer did not comment on this part of Bagby's life except to note that Bagby was a correspondent for "various newspapers in town and country."[45] In the writer's opinion, Bagby's letters to newspapers "furnish a good commentary on the turbulent political life of the time, but, of course, deserve no lengthy treatment as literature."[46]

Bagby figured prominently in J. Cutler Andrews' history of Southern war correspondence, but even in that volume, Bagby plays third fiddle to Peter W. Alexander of the *Savannah Republican* and Felix G. de Fontaine of the *Charleston*

Courier. Both were traditional field reporters who tramped around army camps and battlefields with the troops. Bagby's work was less relevant to Andrews because of its political nature. Hermes was on the periphery of actual battlefield war reporting but he was on the front lines of reporting the political battles of the war, even before the fighting began.

After South Carolina seceded in December 1860, Bagby returned to Washington. The *Mercury*'s editor was looking for a correspondent there, and Rhett had been impressed by the work of the *Richmond Dispatch*'s capital city reporter. When he realized that the reporter was his former correspondent, Rhett immediately tried to recruit his old employee. As part of their negotiations, Rhett sent Bagby a description of his requirements. The correspondent was to write terse letters, like those he provided the *Dispatch*. Rhett's caution was ironically curt: "My space at this time is too valuable."[47] Once again, Bagby's salary was to be $3 per letter—"all that I have ever paid for 1/2 to 3/4 columns," the editor noted. Should Bagby decide to accept the offer, he would be expected to send all letters to W.A. Courtenay, a Charleston merchant who would also serve as a correspondent for the paper.[48] The newspaper's correspondence was being intercepted in New York and Washington, according to Rhett, and this measure circumvented those interceptors. Bagby became the *Mercury*'s correspondent in mid-January 1861.

One of Rhett's early letters to Bagby addressed the issue of correspondent anonymity. Bagby had apparently written to Rhett to discuss the need for him to remain anonymous, a common practice among antebellum journalists. Bagby's need for secrecy would have been even more compelling. As a representative of a newspaper from a state in rebellion against the nation, he risked being considered a spy himself. Were he known to be the *Mercury*'s correspondent, he could have been arrested as a traitor. Rhett replied, "We agree with you that it will be best that you should not be known as the *Mercury*'s correspondent. No one will know it from us."[49] The editor returned to that topic in a second letter a few days later when he addressed a disagreement with Bagby over what should be done regarding the Union occupation of Fort Sumter. Rhett wrote that he and Bagby needed to come to an understanding of "one another in regard to the correspondence for the *Mercury*."[50]

Rhett laid down additional rules. The first was anonymity. "I consider your connection with the Washington correspondence strictly confidential," Rhett wrote. "No one in South Carolina, out of the *Mercury* office, knows your name; and if you will be as discrete as I will, no one ever shall know." Rhett wrote that the usefulness of Bagby's correspondence would depend entirely upon his anonymity. "If you are known, it is impossible to criticize and use names as you otherwise can do, to the great benefit of the Southern cause."[51]

Rhett pointed out that the *Mercury*'s previous Washington correspondent, someone he referred to only as "Crandall," had been particularly good at "exposing the intrigues of sundry would-be fire-eaters . . . until, through his own imprudence," he allowed his identity to be ferreted out. The same thing happened to a man named Jones, the *Mercury*'s New York correspondent, who was revealed either "through his own indiscretion or the treachery of some telegraph operator."[52]

Rhett's letter contained another important point: a claim of editorial privilege over Bagby's work. "I shall sometimes strike out of your letters what I do not like, and add *arguments* (emphasis his) such as I desire to come out in the shape of correspondence instead of editorially." Rhett claimed this privilege because he wanted to goad South Carolina Governor Francis Pickens into taking the proper action with regard to Fort Sumter but, he wrote, he did not want to demoralize the governor by doing so editorially. Pickens was perceived in South Carolina as an inept governor, one who needed help running the newly seceded state. State leaders were sufficiently concerned about Pickens' soundness that they created an Executive Council to assist in the administration of the state government.

Had the *Mercury* attacked Pickens head-on in an editorial, the governor would have been both embarrassed and weakened, and the editorial would have given lie to the claims of unity among the ardent secessionists of the Palmetto State. However, remaining indecisive about whether to attack the fort meant Pickens was "trifling with the honor of the state and the cause of the Southern Confederacy" in Rhett's eyes. Having a correspondent criticize the governor's inactivity instead gave Rhett and the *Mercury* a degree of deniability. The paper could argue that the criticism was not the official policy of the official organ of the secessionists; it was merely the opinion of some Washington pundit. Rhett added that he knew he would be compelled to "assail" the governor if he did not act soon, but manipulating Bagby's correspondence bought him some time.[53]

Bagby's stint as a Washington correspondent lasted only a few weeks. By mid-April, following the Confederate occupation of Fort Sumter, Bagby went home to join a volunteer unit from Lynchburg. His beloved Virginia had not yet seceded—a fact that pained him to the bone—but the war had started, and it was time to take up arms. Bagby enlisted as a private in the Lynchburg Rifle Grays, a unit that would eventually be renamed Company A of the 11th Virginia Volunteers, and headed to Camp Lee, better known before the war as the Richmond fairgrounds.[54] While shivering through cold nights and huddled under a blanket, Bagby received another summons from the *Mercury*. This time, Rhett asked him to report from Richmond so the paper could keep up with the military activity there.[55]

The 33-year-old Bagby had too many other obligations to continue reporting for the newspaper, including his military ones to the "fat little cadet—young enough to be my son," who oversaw the training of newly enlisted men. However, he found a solution for the *Mercury:* he recruited his father to write temporarily for the paper.[56] The elder Bagby, a merchant, may not have been a satisfactory correspondent, for by late April Rhett was again asking Bagby to send telegraphic accounts "daily of facts at Richmond concerning Virginia, Washington, Baltimore and Norfolk."[57] By May, Rhett was seeking daily letters, and Bagby sent them for awhile.[58] When his unit left for the front, it appears that his work for the *Mercury* ended but again only temporarily.

Bagby was clearly not cut out to be a foot soldier, for he found much to dislike about his military experience. The food, the cold water for drinking and washing, the early rising, his whole military experience "indeed, was misery."[59] He had a stroke of luck, however, when his unit reached the Virginia front, near the village of Manassas. He met up with Thomas Jordan, General P.G.T. Beauregard's adjutant, whom Bagby had known in Washington. Jordan recruited Bagby for the headquarters staff as an orderly on the graveyard shift, serving from midnight until 6 a.m. Because of his assignment, Bagby was off duty and asleep at headquarters during much of the early skirmishing that preceded the First Battle of Manassas.[60]

On the day of the battle, Bagby remained at headquarters to guard Beauregard's important papers. His orders were: If headquarters were threatened by the Union army, get the papers on a train that would whisk them to safety. Throughout the day, Bagby fretted about what was happening at the front. Restless and anxious, he could not sit patiently with the records, so he made a visit to a nearby house and listened while the lone occupant, a woman, stormed about what would happen to "herself, her house, her everything."[61] Finally, Bagby could bear the suspense no longer and made his way to the battlefield. He arrived in time to hear the Confederate victory shouts.[62]

Like so many other Southerners, Bagby expected an immediate forward movement after Manassas and, like all those others, he was disappointed. The Confederate victory at Manassas had been as much the result of good fortune as anything. The Southern army was not strong enough, trained enough, nor confident enough to capitalize on its victory by pursuing the Union army back to Washington. Bagby's growing frustration with the military's inactivity mirrored the flow of the hot, steamy days of July 1861 toward the even hotter, steamier dog days of August. He chaffed at what he perceived to be the incompetence and cowardice of both military and civilian leaders.

Finally, later in August, Bagby was assigned to accompany the body of a Confederate officer to Richmond. While there, he managed to obtain a medical discharge. In an essay about his military service, Bagby joked about his undistinguished career in the army. "A discharge was granted me after my arrival in Richmond," he wrote, "and thus ended the record of an unrenowned warrior."[63]

Back in Richmond, Bagby was poised to begin a career as a political correspondent in earnest, a career that would span the war years and contribute to the disintegration of civilian morale that some historians have identified as one of the reasons why the South lost the war.[64] Once he was free of the army, Bagby wrote the *Mercury* about his availability. By the end of September, he was back on the newspaper's payroll, presumably at $3 a story once again.

Bagby's first official letter from Richmond, written on September 29, appeared in the *Mercury* on October 2. He had received a telegram from Managing Editor Bartholemew Riordan instructing him to: "Begin correspondence today. We want your first letter for Monday's paper." Bagby would not write exclusively for the *Mercury* for long. He continued or established relationships with several newspapers during the war, including the *Nashville Union and American*, the *Richmond Whig*, and the *Mobile Advertiser and Register*. His diary from early November 1861 indicated that he was already writing letters for the *Union and American*, which paid considerably better than the *Mercury*. Bagby noted in his diary that he had been paid $60 for writing 12 letters for the Nashville paper. He had finally achieved that magical $5 per story.[65]

In terms of content, Riordan's instructions were to include both news and gossip, provided they hadn't appeared in the Richmond newspapers. Richmond newspapers arrived in Charleston faster than letters, so if Bagby copied items from the newspaper—a common practice in that day—they were old by the time they reached the *Mercury* office. "Your letters would be much more valuable to us if they consisted of intelligence of which the papers give nothing—or only partial mention," Riordan instructed.[66] At times when Northern newspapers did not travel South so easily, Riordan would also ask Bagby's help in acquiring them.[67]

Bagby took the instructions to heart. He supplied the official news from Richmond but he also included snippets of what life was like in the city and, on occasion, in other parts of Virginia. These items were generally appended to the ends of his letters and addressed topics such as the state of enrollment at the University of Virginia and the fact that city gas had been turned off in Charlottesville. Residents of the college town were struggling to find enough tallow candles to light their homes, and Bagby predicted, "People will have to go back to lightwood knots." He also occasionally included an assessment of how Richmond was faring as the major staging point for the army—in his assessment, not well, for the city was rapidly sinking into degeneration due to the proliferation of tobacco shops and barrooms.[68] He also sent small items of news, reporting, for example, in November 1862 on the sale of a well-known Richmond hotel and the appearance of illness in the town.

> The Exchange Hotel was sold yesterday for $101,000. It was bought by a company of gentlemen who have distinguished themselves of late for their extensive purchase of real estate. It was stated in the meeting of the Common Council yesterday, that there were seventy-five cases of small pox in the city, and the number of deaths showed the disease to be of a virulent type.[69]

The *Mercury*'s editors also asked for Bagby's help on another matter: providing daily telegraphic reports about events in Virginia, Washington, Baltimore, and Norfolk. Rhett asked him to take on the second job because "the truth is hard to get." There is no evidence that Bagby took on this additional job. The *Mercury* collected telegraphic correspondence throughout the war, but for much of the period, various Confederate wire services sent telegraphic dispatches from Richmond to subscribers. What is interesting about Rhett's instructions is that he singled out Bagby to help the paper collect not just accounts but what he called *truthful* accounts. The implication was that the *Mercury* was not interested in publishing inaccurate stories. It wanted a telegraphic correspondent who could get sound information. Rhett's letter spoke not only to the esteem in which he held Bagby but also to his commitment to sorting out the truth, at least as much as possible in wartime.[70]

Bagby's correspondence for the *Mercury* was prolific, although the frequency varied throughout the war, depending in part on the instructions he received from the editors. During paper shortages, he was told to cut back to only three letters a week. "We're in a bad fix about paper," Riordan once wrote. "Can't get enough for a full sheet and can't get our advertising in a half sheet." Because of the paper shortage, Riordan reported, none of Bagby's letters had been printed for the past week. They were all set in type, waiting to go, but they were being crowded out by advertising.[71]

Bagby wrote with greater frequency early in the war. In his first full month of correspondence for the *Mercury*, Bagby filed 24 letters.[72] In 1864, his production was about half what it had been in 1862. By 1864, however, Bagby was writing for a number of other newspapers, and he was also working for the *Richmond Whig*. He had given up the editorship of the *Southern Literary Messenger* in 1863, but the demands of corresponding for four or five newspapers, plus working for a Richmond newspaper, would have been enough to explain the decline in correspondence even without the addition of new personal responsibilities acquired in 1863 and 1864: a wife and a baby.

Recognition for the Confederacy by European powers, particularly Great Britain and France, was also a consistent theme in Bagby's correspondence. Recognition would have given the fledgling country official status as one of the world's sovereign nations, and it could have brought financial and perhaps military assistance from other countries. Confederate leaders believed their cotton production would be the key to European recognition, especially Great Britain, which depended on Southern cotton to keep its textile mills running and thousands of workers employed. But Confederate leaders miscalculated the value of "King Cotton."

Great Britain and France, the two nations the South looked to most fervently for recognition, were less concerned with the economic impact of losing Southern cotton supplies than they were with the legal and political implications of getting involved in a conflict that was not a clear-cut war between sovereign nations. President Lincoln claimed the conflict was an insurrection, but the blockade of Southern ports complicated that claim because they are tactics used by one sovereign nation to force its will on another. Given this conflict between rhetoric and action, Britain and France remained neutral.

In the early stages of the war, Bagby was convinced a cotton famine could bring recognition if Confederates would put their greed aside and refuse to send the product to market. He fully recognized the political complexities of recognition for England and France—both domestically and internationally—but he could not, until much later in the war, believe recognition would be withheld entirely.

Early in the war, he wrote about an article from the *New York Times* by a writer in Manchester, England. The writer, according to Bagby, believed the world was dependent on Southern cotton and that its lack of availability spelled doom for the textile factories in his city. "With such facts before them, how can Southern people send their cotton to market?" Bagby demanded. So long as no Southern cotton reached the market, the pressure would mount on European factories, he believed. But cotton was the main cash-producing crop for many Southerners, and the temptation was great to smuggle cotton through the blockade and to market. Two years later, Bagby realized that "American affairs have ceased to be of much interest in England. Out of the whole number of magazines and reviews there is but one that continues an article relating to American affairs, and that is adverse to the Confederacy."[73]

Other common themes in Bagby's stories included life in Richmond; domestic, foreign, and military politics; women and their role in the war effort; and the sense and sensibilities of Southern people. Perhaps because he was writing for a South Carolina audience, he credited citizens of the Palmetto State with having greater valor, patriotism, and common sense than their countrymen.

Weather was also an important element in Bagby's dispatches. The poetics, not to mention the dogged consistency, of his weather reports gave them an endearing quality. In virtually every story he wrote for the *Mercury*, Bagby either began or concluded with an assessment of the weather in Richmond. His weather reports, be they brief descriptions or longer, more lyrical considerations of the emotions evoked by the climatic conditions, offer a momentary escape from the grave matters he most often wrote about.

Weather became a big story when it interfered with the war, as it did in spring 1862 when early rains made the roads around Richmond impassable, delaying the spring campaign. In April, Bagby reported that rain had been steadily falling since the previous day. "Bad for military operations," he wrote, "very bad for boys who have no tents."[74] While it is somewhat jarring to go from a denunciation of the president as a despot who has abandoned even the appearance of adhering to Southern principles to a report that it is snowing or raining, his weather reports have a sort of charm to them, as well as a touch of normalcy amid the chaos and horror of civil war.

Bagby's weather reports could turn downright lyrical when the conditions touched his romantic side. One fall day early in the war, Bagby led his story with a simple weather description, the beginning of which read almost like a Japanese haiku: "A leaden sky, from which pours down a cold, slow rain, sloppy streets, wet housetops, soaked people and streaming horses—such is Richmond, as seen today through the dabbled window-panes." [75]

Bagby's imagination often took him beyond the fortifications and entrenchments around Richmond, out into the camps among the Virginia front lines, where soldiers were enduring the cold rain with few comforts, thanks, in his opinion, to the Confederate government's tentativeness in prosecuting the war. Bagby could not resist stepping outside of his serene narrator's voice with a subtle dig at President Davis' administration.

> 'Tis a sorry sight. I think of the brave boys away yonder in the bleak mountains, and at Manassas, Yorktown, Norfolk, and on the coast. I see the great Southern army, stretched all along Mason and Dixon's line, waiting, waiting, waiting in this cold rain. Cruel winter is close at had, and they must wait, wait, wait. Ah, me![76]

Bagby often used weather reports as a foundation for admonishing Confederate citizens to take better care of their soldiers. In February 1863, he wrote, "A southwest wind, a dazzling clear sky, and a rapid melting snow, which must be very deep in localities further north. This is the sort of weather that tells severely on our soldiers, fills our hospitals and calls for renewed efforts in behalf of the health and comfort of our brave defenders."[77] His articles often reflected concern for the well-being of the troops. "The soft, golden, hazy days, selected in years of peace for the Agricultural Fairs, have come," he wrote in the fall of 1862. "The nights are cold; musquitos are gone. Supplies, though costly, are abundant; the river water is again drinkable, and all is well with us in the city, who can sleep in warm beds. How is it with the poor fellows who lay out in the front, with naked feet, and without blankets?"[78] He returned to that subject a week later.

> We little expected to find the house-tops covered with snow this morning, and the air filled with the white shower blown about by the gusts. But such is the case. Winter has come upon us at a bound. The snow is still falling, but melting almost as rapidly as it falls. There has been a furious storm on the Northern lakes, and this feathery precipitation is caused by the contact of the Boreal with the southern air saturated with moisture. As we look out upon the frigid scenery, our thoughts go back to the good old days of peace and hot apple toddy, but quickly return to the ill-clad army of the Potomac, fighting its way towards the Rappahannock—fighting and marching all day, and sleeping in icy slush at

night. Let us not be content with saying, "God help the poor fellows!" but put out
our hands to the work and help them ourselves. Though the wind is tempered to
the shorn lamb, human charity, forethought, energy, and self-denial is needed
to supply shoes, underclothes, socks, over-coats and blankets. These never fall
from the wintry skies, for the frost is merciless, and will freeze a thousand men
as readily as an apple.[79]

While Bagby devoted a good deal of space to the welfare of soldiers, he almost never offered first-hand accounts of soldiers in battle, even when the fighting came within mere miles of Richmond. His reporting actually had more in
common with 21st century television commentators or pundits. When it came
to reporting on military actions, Bagby's output included color stories, descriptions of what it was like when the troops massed in the streets of Richmond,
and assessments of how they were faring. As the spring 1862 campaign went
into full swing, Bagby wrote about the street scene that preceded departure of a
division of Georgia soldiers for the front.

> Some of the regiments were admirably drilled, and the officers of all the regi-
> ments were as gallant looking fellows as you would see in a summer's day. The
> lower part of Main street for many squares, was perfectly lined with soldiers,
> sitting on the curb stones as contentedly as if they were in rocking chairs, smok-
> ing, talking, laughing and hurrahing at every stray dog that came along, just as
> though they were not going to, perhaps, the deadliest of all the battles of the war.
> It was amusing to see some of them eating raw fat bacon as if it were cheese.

Bagby's description did not neglect the unit's commander, the flamboyant
Georgia lawyer and former Confederate secretary of state, Robert Toombs.
Bagby reported that Toombs "rode a grey horse, and wore a big high crown
black slouch hat and a long red worsted comfort around his neck."[80]

His correspondence also covered the war through another prism: politics.
The main focus of Bagby's stories, as directed by *Mercury* management, was
goings-on in Richmond and the Confederate government. His stories tended to
vacillate between thunderous when he was incensed by what he saw as Jefferson
Davis' latest outrage, despondent when the tide of war turned against the South,
and hyper-enthusiastic when he could report a Confederate victory. In mid-
October 1861, a clearly frustrated Bagby lamented the Confederacy's seeming
disinclination to prosecute the war. The passion with which Bagby wrote, coupled with its often daily frequency, kept his view of Confederate politics and
military situations very much in the public eye. In one article, he wrote:

> Poor Lee! Rosecrans has fooled him again. The great Southern General digs dirt
> at Camp Defiance and waits for reinforcements; they come, and still Lee digs
> dirt and waits; and lo! The morning comes, Rosecrans with his army is sixteen
> miles away! and "the roads are so bad that we can't pursue him!" Are the roads

any worse for Lee than Rosecrans? The people are getting mighty sick of this dilly dally dirt digging, scientific warfare; so much so, that they will demand that the Great Entrencher be brought back and permitted to pay court to the ladies. Meantime Rosecrans will come back upon Jackson and cut him to pieces. Then we will give up Western Virginia, and set our big Generals to playing marbles or "mumblepeg," instead of "hop-scotch" and "prisoner's base," of which we have had plenty.[81]

When Bagby did write about the war and the battles, his sources were almost always either official War Department dispatches, rumors, soldiers, or citizens who were passing through Richmond, or the nabobs down at the Spotswood Hotel. He also cultivated a stable of political sources.[82] His two years as a Washington correspondent had allowed him to build relationships with leading political men, including many who transferred their allegiance to the fledgling Southern nation. Occasionally, Bagby would refer to his political sources by name, but more often they would simply be called "Reliable," an unnamed source who was passing along information for his readers.[83]

Political reporting was Bagby's specialty, and he was one of the few Richmond correspondents who specialized in it. There were other sources of political news, such as the Richmond newspapers themselves and the wire service those newspapers established to feed news to other media but whose offerings were considered inferior by most editors. Bagby served as an additional vehicle that could help spread information into the far reaches of the Confederacy.

He was also devoted to the cause of Southern independence. When the *Mercury* editor began searching for someone "owning the strict states rights faith," he could not have found anyone to fit that bill better than Bagby. However, the correspondent's ardent devotion to the ideologies of Southern rights and Southern independence was tempered somewhat by his libertarian perspective. Bagby wanted Southern independence, but he wanted it without limitations on individual rights or without any growth in the size or power of government.[84] That perspective made it seem imperative to Bagby that he alert Confederate citizens of any moves by the Southern leadership that might violate libertarian ideals. That made him an outspoken critic of many measures non-libertarians like Davis believed were necessary to win the war.

Early on, Bagby warned readers about an encroaching government lurching toward corruption. He wrote in October 1861, "Already we find the General Government exercising other than police functions, conferring favor for puffs in the paper, and starting on the highway to centralization and corruption." He offered a specific example by describing the case of a "worthy gentleman" who had been seeking employment in Richmond for some months. That man had not found a position, yet "clerk after clerk sneaked out of Washington and got a place," Bagby reported with disdain. The gentleman finally got a government job after he wrote three articles for a daily newspaper that puffed up the administration.[85]

Bagby's tendency to criticize actions and policies that did not square with his principles was magnified by the fact that he fell into that camp of Southerners who objected to what they perceived as President Davis' tentativeness in prosecuting the war. The president's cold remoteness and his efforts to build a strong, centralized state were other views this group of Southerners shared. Bagby often veiled his criticism in sarcasm. He attacked the president's tentativeness in moving the war to Kentucky this way:

> Breckinridge, Preston, and Humphrey Marshall are urging the Administration to prosecute the war in Kentucky with the utmost vigor. They want large, well-appointed army, and all the means necessary to drive the Lincolnites over the Ohio in double-quick time. The administration does not seem inclined to grant their 'offensive' request. This decision adds to the already abundant evidence in favor of the Mercury's strictures upon the government policy. In a word, there is too much reason to believe that the people, unless they approve of dilly-dally and a Yankee league, will have to take the war into their own hands and drive the Administration as well as the Yankees.[86]

Bagby's critiques of the president remained consistent throughout the war. He nagged Davis for ignoring public sentiment and accused the president of inertia with regard to military affairs, interfering with military affairs, conceit, squeamishness about retaliation, and lack of leadership.[87] Bagby was particularly incensed by Davis' mercy on deserters.

> Here in Virginia, we have never had a disciplinarian, except Jackson. Lee does his best; but how is it possible for a general to do his duty where the mistaken clemency of the Executive almost sets a premium upon desertion, and the War Department relies on the moral suasion of public opinion to cure straggling, instead of holding officers of all grades to the sternest accountability . . . That General Jackson fears [too much mercy] is evident from the excitement he exhibited not many days after the late battles when, in speaking of the delay of the government, he said, holding out his wrists, "If this folly is to be repeated, then let them manacle us at once." While this inaction is telling upon the spirit of troops and exciting uneasiness in the people, the President appears smiling and cheerful to a degree unknown before.[88]

President Davis had other detractors, but Bagby's commentary differed significantly from other press dissenters in signaling his displeasure. A number of editors, including men such as William W. Holden of the *Raleigh Standard* and Nathan Morse of the *Augusta Chronicle and Sentinel*, worked from different motives. Like Bagby, those editors wanted Confederate independence but they equally desired peace. By the summer of 1863, Holden had concluded that the South would not be able to win the war decisively and he began to agitate for peace on the best terms possible. Holden's support—or, as some of his contemporaries and some historians have argued, his leadership—of the North Carolina peace movement resulted in his newspaper being mobbed by a band of angry soldiers from Georgia.[89] Morse argued from a similar perspective and worked with Confederate Vice President Alexander H. Stephens and a handful of other Georgia journalists to hammer away for a negotiated peace.

Bagby never flirted with the peace movement, although some of his letters must have aided that cause. However, he was no dove; his primary complaint about Davis and his government, particularly early in the war, was their reluctance to engage the Union army in battle. One of his favorite diatribes against the president was to accuse him of inaction and hesitancy in prosecuting the war. Bagby returned to this theme over and over during the four years of the conflict. He was especially concerned, ironically, that military inaction would lead to demoralization of Confederate citizens. In one of his diatribes, Bagby wrote:

> Meantime, where do we stand? An enormous army in the field. The mock blockade permitted. Commissioners are not recalled. The Confederacy has not been recognized by the Powers whose good we have so obsequiously sought. Winter is near at hand, as the brown trees and falling leaves attest. Our soldiers are pining from inaction. The sick are pouring into this city at the rate of 150 a day. We are losing more men by supine delay, than we would lose in battle. The people are discouraged. They are losing confidence in the "five-year's war" Administration.[90]

Bagby was also convinced that the Confederate president's ego and ambition knew no bounds. Once, early in the war, when rumors were current in Richmond that President Davis had decided to lead the coming offensive as field commander of the Confederate army, Bagby wrote, "This looks as though there were some truth in the oft-repeated allegation that the President wanted all the glory for himself." In fairness to Bagby, he cautioned readers that rumors were not reliable, but this article made his sentiments about the president perfectly clear.[91]

He would also take exception to some of Davis' stands on legislation and his decisions about military appointments. In 1861, he accused the president of proposing false economies. In reporting Davis' veto of a bill[92] calling for the appointment of assistant surgeons for each regiment, Bagby demanded to know, "What kind of economy is it to equip, drill and pay soldiers and then bury them, for the want of proper attention?"[93] Bagby periodically accused the president of manipulating military appointments to benefit his friends and of petty jealousies. He argued that the list of Davis' abuses should be published, except that it would be too upsetting to Southern citizens in a time of war.[94] Of course, he had been publishing those kinds of accusations for most of the war, and he would continue to do so for the duration.

Bagby seemed to be aware that his letters often consisted of litanies of complaints, but he offered a strong—and very modern—rationale for publishing bad news: government corruption and evils cannot be fixed if they are not reported.

> This is croaking. This is looking at the dark side of the future only. But the dark side ought to be looked at. These things are; they are facts; concealment will not dissipate them into thin air . . . For my part, I think we have played ostrich, hid our heads in the sand, and thought "all's right—no danger" long enough. I intend to keep on croaking.[95]

The *Mercury* correspondent knew he was presenting the bleakest possible picture, but he did so for a reason: to counteract those unrealistic attitudes of so many Southerners, those who believed that the perceived "rightness" of their cause meant they could not lose. Bagby had another reason for his criticism, and that was to motivate Confederate citizens to get behind the cause and put their all into fighting for their independence. He was an ardent Confederate sympathizer who longed for independence from the Northern yoke—despite once during the war flirting with the idea of fleeing to Nassau or Bermuda.[96]

Bagby's critiques of the Confederate government and its leaders were unrelenting in the early days of the war, but as time passed, his diatribes declined precipitously, although they never entirely ceased. As early as spring 1862, Bagby's more vicious attacks had become intermittent and far less venomous, although certain cataclysmic events, such as the failed invasion of Maryland in September 1862, would briefly stimulate more flamboyant denunciations of Davis and other Confederate leaders.[97]

The newspaper in which his letters appeared made Bagby's correspondence more effective. The *Mercury* had long been influential because of its connection to the secessionist movement, but its circulation in the antebellum period had been decreasing steadily. The senior Rhett's oldest son, Robert Barnwell Rhett, Jr., a Phi Beta Kappa graduate of Harvard University, had taken the reigns of the paper in 1857.[98] To increase circulation, the senior Rhett bought the *Charleston Southern Standard*, owned by Leonidas W. Spratt, who would become one of their correspondents during the war. Spratt's newspaper had grown in the preceding four years to 1,200 subscribers with $17,000 in annual revenue.[99] When he sold it in 1857 for $800, the purchase in effect tripled the *Mercury*'s circulation.[100] Although Spratt continued writing and editing for the Rhetts, he was never the editor of the *Mercury*.[101]

Rhett, Jr., continued to guide the paper's editorial policy by his famous father's political philosophy: individual liberties and states' rights. During the Civil War, that would make the *Mercury* a prima facie adversary for Jefferson Davis and, to some degree, the Confederate government. For example, secret Congressional sessions became one of the *Mercury*'s pet issues. The newspaper's editors believed the people had a right to know what government was doing, even though secret sessions had been common practice, even before the war began. An article the *Mercury* reprinted from the Columbus, Mississippi, *Southern Republic* condemned closed sessions of Congress as inimical to liberty. The article contended, "Secret sessions of Congress are in the highest degree dangerous to the liberties and interests of the people, and it becomes them to frown indignantly upon a practice which, though thus far, perhaps, attended with no great evil, may lead to disastrous consequences."[102] Bagby also targeted Postmaster General John Reagan for the inefficiency of his department,[103] although not to the extent he attacked the president.

Bagby's vitriol against Davis would become so fierce that even the *Mercury* editors were appalled. In late November 1861, Rhett ordered the correspondent to cease his constant diatribes against the president. The editor explained that he had not been able to run Bagby's last three letters because of their "despondent and fault-finding tone." A gap in Bagby's correspondence in the *Mercury* confirms this. He had been writing almost daily since beginning his work for the paper earlier that fall, but no letters appeared between November 23 (written November 17) and December 3 (written November 29).

Rhett added: The *"Mercury* is clearly right," but they—the paper and its correspondent—must leave the president alone for now. The Confederate people were "weak," Rhett wrote. "People cannot always stand too much truth." The editor clearly feared his correspondent's accounts could lead to citizen despondency and loss of circulation. He instructed Bagby, "Please try and shape your correspondence with these views: the truth, but not all the truth for now."[104]

Half a year later, Rhett once again would rip apart some of Bagby's stories to remove what to him read like personal assaults on Davis. Rhett wrote that he would never resort to attacking the president on personal matters. Public issues were another thing, so long as the *Mercury* was in possession of "infallible proof." He continued, "People will not tolerate the expression of mere opinions derogatory to this great head of a great country. Many already abuse the *Mercury*, and all victories strengthen Davis."[105] Bagby kept a watchful eye on the president's missteps because he hoped to stimulate policy changes that were more in keeping with the libertarian ideals he and the *Mercury* believed were the heart of Confederate political ideology.

The *Southern Literary Messenger* was another important vehicle through which Bagby could shape public opinion. Its most recent previous editors, Edgar Allen Poe and John R. Thompson, had kept the magazine entirely literary in nature, and Bagby promised to do likewise in his editorial in June 1860.[106] He pledged to use his authority as editor to encourage production of a uniquely Southern literature. "We wish its pages to reflect the spirit of the South as something separate if not superior to that of all other climes and countries whatsoever," he wrote.[107] The brewing war, however, and Bagby's close attention to politics made it impossible for him to keep silent on the topic. He could not resist the lure of using the *Messenger* as a platform for his beliefs.

One of Bagby's initial political stories was Virginia secession. He used the literary magazine's "Editor's Table" section to goad Virginia toward action as war fever spread in the months following Lincoln's election and secessionist sentiment escalated. The December 1860 issue of the magazine was fulsome in its praise for South Carolina's decision to secede, and Bagby pined for his home state to do the same thing.[108] "By the life Virginia gave me, I know and I swear that our noble Mother will not be recreant to her fair fame, to her unsullied honour. Never, never, never, will she consent to the shame, the infamy, the everlasting disgrace of joining the Abolitionists," he wrote.[109]

Whether in his newspaper correspondence or his *Messenger* editorials, one of Bagby's favorite topics was military politics: who was getting promoted, who was not, who was "in," who was "out," and why. Even Robert E. Lee was not exempt from his critiques. He challenged Lee's strategic planning and his West Point training. In an indignant assessment of Lee's engineering skills, Bagby wrote:

> The country between Richmond and the battlefields presents some notable features. Until you reach the scene of operations, the roads are the worst in the world; then comes a strip of neutral ground, where the roads are grown over with grass, and then fine roads built in all directions by the Yankees. On our side, the roads were in such a condition that for days nothing but flour was served out to the army, so difficult was transportation—while in Richmond, only six miles off, the Government storehouses were crammed with provisions; on the Yankee side, every road was traversable in the worst weather—new roads and fine bridges were made wherever needed. McClellen's bridge over the Chickahominy, built in four days and during high water, is a magnificent structure, which will last for ages. It is not a little singular that both at Cheat Mountain and at Richmond Gen. Lee, whose reputation was based upon his talents as an engineer, should have neglected the roads by which his supplies came.[110]

Almost a year later, Bagby turned his critique to Lee's generalship when, in October 1863, the Confederate commander thought he saw an opportunity to cut Meade's Army of the Potomac to pieces with a multi-pronged attack near Briscoe Station. Two of Lee's subcommanders, A.P. Hill and Richard Ewell, whose troops outnumbered those of the opposing Union units, should have had an easy time annihilating the enemy, but they failed to do so. Bagby called the battle "an unexplained blunder." He was correct but only to a point. While it was true that Lee's Army of Northern Virginia did not destroy the Army of the Potomac as he had hoped, the Confederates did push the Union troops back nearly 40 miles, which was no small accomplishment for a one-day battle.[111]

Earlier in 1863, his assessment of two other Southern generals had been more discerning. In the January 1863 issue of the *Messenger*, Bagby provided readers with an analysis of Union General Ambrose E. Burnside's defeat in December 1862 at Fredericksburg, citing Lee's uncanny ability to predict Burnside's next move, and Confederate General Braxton Bragg's blunderings in Tennessee.[112] Of Bragg's campaign, Bagby wrote: "One thing is certain—the campaign in Tennessee has failed . . . Bragg has had two fair trials. He has failed in both."

But Bagby predicted the general would not "be deserted by his friend in Richmond."[113] That friend was President Davis, a stalwart and loyal supporter of Bragg, even after the general lost all of Tennessee for the Confederacy in November 1863, a loss that would open Georgia for Sherman's Atlanta campaign and march to the sea. "Do what he [Bragg] will, that friend is bound to sustain him," Bagby wrote. "And we are bound to believe that while General Bragg is a brave soldier and a good disciplinarian, [but] he has not the intellect to plan a campaign, or a great battle. As a Division commander, he will do well; beyond that his capacity does not reach."[114] President Davis did not immediately heed Bagby's analysis. Bragg's troops revolted against continuing to serve under him after the disastrous Tennessee battles in late 1863. The situation disintegrated so thoroughly that Davis traveled to Tennessee to sort it out himself. The end result was that General Joseph Johnston was put in command and Bragg was transferred to Virginia to serve as a military adviser to the president.

Bagby was just as vicious in the gossip he shared about another general who would ultimately fail at his assignment: George Pemberton, commander at Vicksburg during Ulysses S. Grant's siege of that city in 1863. Vicksburg would not fall until the summer, but in January, Bagby had decided that Pemberton, the Confederate commander there, was not up to the task. He wrote: "At Vicksburg, a gallant defense has been made by Pemberton, who, with the assistance and advice of Joseph E. Johnston, will, it is hoped, yet assert some just claim to his extraordinary promotion to the rank of Lieutenant-General."[115]

This piece was chatty, light, and accurate in its assessment of both Bragg and Pemberton. He recognized the likely outcome of Bragg's errors in Tennessee in the fall of 1862, and he made his gloomy predictions only days after the first reports of Bragg's defeat at Murfreesboro reached Richmond. Either Bagby had an amazing grasp of military tactics and strategies or an excellent source was explaining the strategic importance of these battles to him. Bagby could have discerned some of what he wrote just from looking at a map, but his observations show a keen insight into military strategy and politics and also into the characters of the generals themselves.

Bagby's penchant for military gossip eventually got him in trouble. In late 1863, he sent a letter to the *Mobile Advertiser and Register*, a paper for which he wrote under the pseudonym, "Gamma." The story was based on a rumor about a quartermaster who had allegedly defaulted on $5 million.[116] Bagby did not name the quartermaster, but Major Alfred M. Barbour, then stationed in Mississippi, believed the story was about him and demanded a retraction. When it was not immediately forthcoming, Barbour determined that Bagby was Gamma and sought leave to go to Virginia and demand satisfaction. Barbour's commanders would not grant him the leave, so he sent a friend, Captain Carey, to the *Advertiser and Register* office to place an ad denouncing the story.[117]

Meanwhile, Bagby had discovered that the rumor was false and rushed to telegraph his editors not to publish the story. He followed the telegram with a letter explaining what had happened, but the initial story had already been published. Bagby's explanatory letter arrived at the *Advertiser and Register* office about the same time as Captain Carey.[118] Editor W.G. Clarke showed him Bagby's explanation, and Carey decided that Barbour would not have sent the inflammatory ad if he had seen Bagby's explanation of what happened. The ad was uncompromising in its denunciation of Bagby. It read, in part: "I do therefore publicly denounce Dr. George W. Bagby of Richmond City, Va., a COWARDLY SLANDERER, a BASE CALUMNIATOR, a POLTROON, and a CONTEMPTIBLE PUPPY—unfit to be associated with or countenanced by gentlemen."[119]

Clarke and Carey agreed that Carey should return to Meridian, where Barbour was stationed, with a copy of Bagby's letter. Both hoped Barbour would agree to withdraw the statement, but the major was too incensed to consider a compromise. The letter, Barbour thundered, only made matters worse because the journalist admitted using information Bagby had not known for certain was accurate. Barbour refused to straighten out the matter publicly and under his own name.[120]

Because so much time had passed, the *Advertiser and Register* decided not to publish Bagby's letter or the telegram exonerating Barbour. The ad was published, however, causing one to wonder whether Barbour's intransigence had anything to do with the paper's decision to withhold the information that would clear him of suspicion.[121]

A tribunal consisting of war correspondent Peter W. Alexander of the *Savannah Republican* and a Confederate officer and congressman from Virginia, Brigadier General Williams C. Wickham, was asked to review the controversy and advise how the situation should be rectified.[122] The tribunal was an early example of a press council reviewing an incident of journalistic malfeasance. Alexander and Wickham concluded that several actions should be taken: First, Bagby's report and explanatory letter should be published in the *Advertiser and Register*. Second, Bagby should publicly express regret for the initial article. Third, Major Barbour should withdraw his statement. The record does not indicate whether the recommendations were followed.

Bagby's wartime contributions to journalism extended beyond the *Mercury*. In 1863, he gave up editing the *Messenger* for financial reasons to become editor

The Confederate Custom House, foreground, and Capitol, in the distance, following the fall of Richmond in 1865. Courtesy of the Library of Congress

of the *Richmond Daily Whig*.[123] Bagby also wrote occasionally for the *Richmond Examiner* and for the *Southern Illustrated News,* the South's answer to *Harper's.*

Bagby's career as a war correspondent ended on April 2, 1865, the day Lee sent word for Jefferson Davis and his government to flee Richmond. Bagby fled with the Confederate troops, leaving behind his ill wife and infant daughter. He recalled the parting in an unpublished biography of his daughter, writing that he departed at the urging of his wife. While she packed his valise, he went into the kitchen to say goodbye to his daughter. "She sat in her night gown in her nurse's lap, eating her simple supper of bread and milk—an angel to my eyes," he recalled. "As I knelt to kiss her, the little thing for the first time in her life of her own accord threw her arms around my neck and hugged me tight. What I felt at that moment and afterwards as I walked through the darkness over to the depot, I can never tell. Death only will efface the memory."[124]

Ruins on Main Street in Richmond at the end of the war. *Harper's Weekly,* April 22, 1865. Courtesy of Rare Books and Special Collections, University of South Carolina Libraries

Within a month, Bagby was back in ruined Richmond facing a shattered career, a shattered city, and a shattered dream. The years following the war were difficult ones for him, but they were among his most productive. He continued to work as a writer and newspaper correspondent, although the latter was no longer lucrative. Many newspapers were too poor to pay correspondents at all after the war.[125] Bagby completed some of his most famous and enduring work after the war, including "The Old Virginia Gentleman," a nostalgic essay about Virginia before the Civil War. Between the end of the war and his death in 1883, he started a new newspaper in Orange County, the *Native Virginian.* He inquired about starting a new paper in Alexandria and considered returning to Washington as a newspaper correspondent. He became assistant secretary of state for Virginia and state librarian in order to support a growing family that eventually included eight children.[126]

Bagby also returned to the lecture trail. One of his most remembered postwar lectures, "Bacon and Greens," became a source of ribbing among his acquaintances. In 1866, when Bagby was considering lecture sites, he wrote another former correspondent, Felix Gregory de Fontaine—"Personne" of the *Charleston Courier*—to check the prospects in the South Carolina capital. The jocular de

Fontaine, then owner and editor of the *Columbia Daily South Carolinian,* began his response with the salutation, "Dear Bacon and Greens." De Fontaine assessed Bagby's chances of drawing a big crowd in Columbia as poorer than in Charleston or Virginia but he did promise to provide food, shelter, and good newspaper publicity should Bagby decide to make the trip south. De Fontaine wrote that he was "poor as thunder, but can give you some straw by night, like that which easeth my bones, and something more substantial to the inner man than your bacon and greens" (emphasis his).[127]

Bagby's later years were plagued by dyspepsia and failing eyesight. He gave his last public lecture on December 18, 1882, in Trenton, New Jersey. Titled "Yorktown and Appomattox: A Plea for the Union," Bagby argued that Yorktown and Appomattox were preordained steps in the progress of American democracy. He returned home to Richmond after that lecture and remained there in declining health for 11 months until his death at age 55 on Thanksgiving Day, November 29, 1883. He is buried in Shockoe Hill Cemetery in Richmond.[128] One of Virginia's most famous poets, John Esten Cooke, eulogized Bagby in a poem, as the "True Virginian of Virginians."

> He was easily our master
> In the great art of the pen:
> Never in Virginia letters
> Shall we see his like again.[129]

26

James B. Sener: Covering the War from His Hometown

Debra Reddin van Tuyll

For most of the South's correspondents, covering the Civil War meant packing up and traveling hundreds of miles from home to Virginia or Mississippi or Tennessee. Not so for James Beverley Sener. The Civil War was literally a hometown story for him.

Sener was a native of Fredericksburg, Virginia, one of the most hotly contested cities in the Eastern theater. All roads to Richmond seemed to run through Fredericksburg, a convenient ford on the Rappahannock River halfway between the Confederate capital and the Union capital in Washington, D.C. Unlike so many of his brothers of the quill, Sener was not covering hometown boys fighting in some far-off place. He was covering boys from far-off places fighting in his hometown. Even during the months Sener was embedded in Lee's Army of Northern Virginia, his own bed was never more than 100 miles away. In a word, Sener was "Johnny-on-the-spot" in covering the "bloodiest landscape in America" during America's bloodiest war.[1] That gave his writing enormous power, insight, and restrained passion.

Fredericksburg was a city where the Union presence was both real and surreal, especially through 1862 and early 1863, when long periods of friendly, even cordial, relations between soldiers from both armies existed. They traded good-natured taunts across the river and met to exchange newspapers, coffee, and tobacco. These periods of détente were punctuated by occasional desperate, fearsome, and bloody fights for control of the city.[2]

Because Sener was writing about his hometown, where he held the office of sheriff, he was able to obtain stories that eluded other correspondents and he could tailor his correspondence accordingly. When the Union army advanced on Fredericksburg for the first time in November 1862, Mayor Montgomery Slaughter gave Sener access to all the correspondence between himself and General E.V. Sumner, the Union officer who demanded the city's surrender.

James Beverley Sener. Photograph courtesy of the Wyoming State Archives

Sener included each of the letters in his story for the *Richmond Dispatch*, one of his several employers during the war.[3]

In a story for the *Richmond Enquirer* about an attack on Fredericksburg that would occur the following month, Sener was able to interpret damage to the town, even from a distance, because he knew where steeples and buildings were supposed to be. He wrote:

> To the friends of the old "Burg" I may say, that being within sight of it to-day, I think that not over one-tenth of the town is seriously injured. The squares containing the Post Office and the Virginia Bank were certainly destroyed. The church and the Court House steeples are all standing and we could see no gaps on the hill.[4]

Only someone familiar with the city could get "within sight" of a town and understand enough about what he was seeing to offer such an estimate, although later, when he had returned home, Sener's assessment of the damage would change.

Sener was a young man of 24 when the Civil War broke out. He was born in Fredericksburg in 1837 to Joseph W. and Mary A. Sener. His father was a merchant whose business was listed in both the 1860 census and the Fredericksburg City Directory as plumbing and tinning. The elder Sener became superintendent of the Fredericksburg Water Works later in life.[5] Several sources list the younger Sener as having an interest in the *Fredericksburg Democratic Recorder* in 1850, but this is unlikely as he would have been only 13 at the time.[6]

City of Fredericksburg. *Harper's Weekly*, April 26, 1862. Courtesy of Rare Books and Special Collections, University of South Carolina Libraries

Sener began his studies at the University of Virginia in 1855, according to the university's matriculation book for 1855-1856. He completed his under-graduate degree in 1859 after he took courses in mathematics, chemistry, and something abbreviated AL. He also took courses in Latin, Greek, constitutional law, and a subject abbreviated as ML. In signing the matriculation book, Sener pledged that he had read the university's laws and wished to "reap the benefits of its instructions . . . with a determined resolution."[7] In 1859, he began legal studies at Washington College (today, Washington and Lee University) with the renowned Virginia Judge John Brockenbrough. The judge is remembered as the man who would offer Robert E. Lee the presidency of Washington and Lee University after the war. Upon completion of his studies, Sener returned home to Fredericksburg and took up the dual careers of law and journalism.[8]

When Sener began working as a correspondent is unclear. As early as De-cember 1860, someone using the pseudonym "X," Sener's journalistic handle, was writing occasionally for the *Richmond Dispatch*. Correspondent "X" cov-ered news items from the University of Virginia, including campus preparations for what to do if a war broke out in the aftermath of South Carolina's seces-sion. "The McKennie Rifles fell in to a man," X reported, "and several rounds, in honor of the event, were fired. Great enthusiasm was shown by Carolinian students." It is unclear whether Sener was X in this case, but he was then in law school at nearby Washington College. A correspondent X even showed up in Charleston, South Carolina, in early 1861 to cover a horse race for the *Dispatch*; another in Hanover County, Virginia, in April 1861, covering a citizen's meeting to organize a home guard. Yet another appeared in Annapolis, Maryland, in May 1861 to report on the occupation of the Naval Academy by the 13th Brooklyn Regiment, made up of "mostly clerks from the city of Brooklyn—genteel young fellows of good address, short wind and impassible legs."[9] No evidence exists to determine whether these stories were written by Sener, some other correspondent, or several different correspondents.

By the fall of 1862, however, Sener was writing for the Richmond Press Association, one of several wire services that would be formed in the Confederacy. A story he wrote for the press service about negotiations between the Fredericksburg city fathers and the Union army appeared in the *Dispatch* on November 25, 1862, complete with full copies of the foreboding correspondence passed between Mayor Slaughter and General Sumner, who was commanding the advance corps that preceded the first of several attempts to occupy the city.[10] The mayor was desperately trying to persuade Sumner not to attack, and the officer, annoyed that shots had been fired at his troops across the Rappahannock, grudgingly agreed not to start the attack as soon as originally planned.

The attack would come, however. Union General Ambrose Burnside had planned to strike across the Rappahannock since becoming commander of the Army of the Potomac. His goal had been to cross the river before Robert E. Lee could move to oppose him. If successful, Burnside could turn one of the greatest barriers to the Union's southward advance with little fighting. His plan was not to be. Although Burnside was ready by mid-November, problems with the delivery of the army's pontoon bridges held him up almost an entire month. Finally, around midnight on December 12, Burnside's army crossed the river.

By then, Sener was writing for the *Richmond Enquirer*, but like most residents, he fled in the face of the Union invasion. When the train on which Sener was fleeing stopped briefly in Summit, he took the opportunity to write about what was happening in his hometown. "In the brief interval I have to write you that the old 'burg,' so long the seat of all that is refined and ennobling, has fallen victim to Yankee deviltry," Sener informed his editors.[11] The town, he wrote, had been left in ruins. "It is also said that the square just above on Main street, commencing with the Virginia bank, and extending to Warren's corner is a heap of ruins. . . Indeed, in the language of a gentleman who came from near there, late yesterday evening, there is scarcely a house in town which is not more or less injured." He added that he had heard about six civilians being killed. Sener correctly predicted that the big battle would come on the next day, December 13.

After the fighting stopped, Sener settled in at an army camp to write his description of the first day's battle for Fredericksburg from an army camp. He had gotten within a mile of the city's outskirts to gather information about the

The Bombardment of Fredericksburg. *Harper's Weekly*, December 27, 1862. Courtesy of Rare Books and Special Collections, University of South Carolina Libraries

fighting, which he conveyed in detail. He gave a vivid description of the Union army's contested crossing on December 10 to 12.

> We are here near the great line of battle, and will briefly recapitulate what we have seen and heard. The enemy attempted the passage of the Rappahannock by laying down their pontoons at 1 o'clock of Thursday morning. They were permitted to get their bridges half finished before our men fired upon them. About dawn, however, the 17th and 18th Mississippi, a part of Barksdale's Brigade, opened fire upon them, killing and wounding a large number. These regiments were armed with Springfield rifles, and for a while drove the pontooniers from their work. Then it was that the Yankees opened upon the town with shot, shell and grape, to the destruction of the houses and the terror of its panic stricken and flying inhabitants, two-thirds of which were women; but doing little or no harm to the gallant band of Mississippians who were there to dispute their entrance.[12]

The Union guns shelled the city for four hours, according to Sener's report, "with batteries placed close together over a space of nearly two miles." The shelling completely destroyed two squares on the north side of Main Street, including the Virginia Bank and Post Office. Sener portrayed the Union assault on the city as an unprovoked attack, but that was a naïve assessment of what had actually happened. As the Union army was laying its pontoons, Barksdale's

Mississippians opened fire on them. The Union artillery attack was in response to the Confederate fire.

Many, including one slave, James Rollins, barely escaped. According to Sener, Rollins "had his hat knocked off and his hair singed." Sener estimated that only about a tenth of the city was in ruins, and that Fredericksburg, like the Phoenix, would rise again from the ashes.[13] However, in none of his stories did Sener write about the fighting for Marye's Heights, which was where the main part of the fighting took place.

Other destruction included the home of Mary Washington, George Washington's mother. The Washington house was almost completely destroyed, Sener reported, and a slave had sworn to him that the Union troops intentionally selected it as a target. "Master," the slave was quoted as saying, "those devils picked the house, for the frame tenement just adjoining is unhurt."[14] Following the attack, Sener learned, the Union troops were celebrating their victory by "destroying and plundering all that lies in their way . . . It is reported that they have sacked and burned the elegant dwelling of J. Warren Slaughter, better known as Hazel Hill, in the lower part of the town."[15] Even the normally "most charitable" cursed the enemy soldiers, he wrote.[16] Later in the same story, Sener observed that the suffering of Fredericksburg citizens was heartbreaking.

> The picture which meets the eye at every farm house, cabin and hut—fugitives from burning homes and desolated hearthstones, clustered in melancholy groups in the houses and about the yards watching the clouds hovering over the fated city and listening to the steady roar of the artillery, whose every volley adds to the already terrible scene of destruction—is enough to affect the stoutest heart.[17]

The attack had surprised residents, who had not realized the Federal army was merely waiting. Instead, the men and women of Fredericksburg assumed the enemy force was content to occupy the far bank of the river. They had been lulled into a false sense of security by the weeks-long inaction of the Union soldiers. The assault "startled [residents] from their dream of security by the hissing shell through the bed chamber, the rattling of grape in the street and the solid shot opening with murderous crash its way through roof and floor, even of Churches, and plowing up the very bones of their ancestors in the churchyards," Sener wrote. The cries of the terrified women and children who had been forced from their homes would appall even "a Yankee's heart," he added. Some citizens had thought to take refuge in their cellars but were soon driven outside by "blazing rafters and steaming timbers overhead." That any escaped was a miracle, he concluded.[18]

The whole area was enshrouded with smoke, some from the burning city, some from the cannonading, and some from the soldiers' campfires that were gleaming on every hill, Sener wrote. The soldiers he was watching were engaged in what would have been homely activities like cooking, except that the men were preparing rations to sustain them through the next day's fighting. The South's soldiers, the correspondent observed, displayed a "careless confidence, for they know we have the men and the generals . . . equal to the coming trial."[19]

By the third day of fighting, December 14, Sener's thoughts turned to casualty reports, but he had a difficult time acquiring them—or much news of any kind. Desultory fighting continued, but that made it difficult to get accurate information of any sort. After riding the entire length of the army's rear lines, Sener estimated that the Yankees had fared far worse, an estimated 3,000 Union casualties to 1,000 Confederate casualties. The actual losses on both sides were much higher, but Sener was correct on the main point—Union losses were at least double those of the rebels. Union "dead and wounded literally line the ground as far as the eye can reach," he wrote. Sener concluded that "[t]he enemy fought well. Our forces did better," especially the forces under Stonewall Jackson and A.P. Hill. Sener believed General Lee had every reason to be pleased with the day's outcome. "The enemy have been baffled and checked," he crowed. "Our brave troops . . . will yet make them rue the day they crossed the Rappahannock." The armies bedded down near one another that night, and soldiers on both sides slept on their arms, Sener reported.[20]

By December 16, the immediate danger to Fredericksburg had passed. A truce to bury the dead had been negotiated, the Confederate cavalry had reclaimed Fredericksburg, and Burnside had withdrawn his troops across the Rappahannock. "The work of 'evacuation,' 'skedaddling,' or 'change of base,' which ever it may be, was commenced last night about sundown, and was concluded this morning at which time they took up their pontoons and once again achieved a great victory by falling backwards," Sener wrote.[21]

Roads on the southern side of the river were thronged with ambulances and wagons conveying wounded soldiers to Richmond where, Sener suggested, they could be better cared for by "fair and gentle women" than by the surgeons in camp hospitals. Sener continued to try to get casualty reports, and he had some success with Dr. J.C. Herndon, "the polite surgeon on Gen. Lee's staff." The surgeon estimated Federal losses at between 5,000 and 8,000 (in actuality, they were closer to 13,000). The Union prisoners that Sener had spoken with "all agree that our army gave them a decent drubbing."[22]

Sener's letter to the *Enquirer* written from his home on December 17 included a first-hand account of what he found when he returned to Fredericksburg after the evacuation and battle.

Had Satan, in the councils of Hell, called together the worst spirits of the damned, and charged them to pour out upon this people the concentrated vials of their wrath, I honestly believe less mischief would have been done by them than the "Union restoring Yankees." Not a single dwelling, office or out-house, in the town, escaped their search, use and abuse. Where families remained, it was only to be insulted by the ruffianly mob, whose incentive to action, if not battle cry, was "booty and destruction." [23]

The correspondent used the power of his pen to lobby for aid for the citizens of Fredericksburg who had lost everything in the battle for the city. Advocacy stories were not uncommon, but generally the appeal was for soldiers' rather than citizens' needs. However, Sener focused attention on citizen suffering, and aid rolled in, even from the soldiers themselves. He reported on all the contributions because he had access to the details through Mayor Slaughter.

On the last day of December 1862, Sener reported that Longstreet's corps had collected $688 to aid the people of Fredericksburg. The letter that accompanied the contribution commended the city's residents "who, by their forgetfulness of selfish interest, and heroic disregard of danger, have taught our common enemy that though they may destroy, they cannot possess."

Other brigades also made donations, according to Sener's letter to the *Enquirer*. Four regiments in Cooke's brigade, the North Carolina 15th, 27th, 46th, and 48th, had sent $2,071, less a $10 counterfeit bill; the Washington Artillery Battalion of New Orleans contributed $1,391. The Infantry Battalion and Troup Artillery of Cobb's Georgia Legion contributed $543. General Garnett's Brigade sent $1,117.75. Major Chichester and his 16th Georgia Regiment sent $224; General Anderson's Division sent $4,865. Total soldier donations amounted to $15,636.[24]

The Battle of Fredericksburg marked the end of the campaign season for 1862. As the army settled into winter quarters, Sener continued to write for the *Enquirer*. That winter, his letters often noted that all was quiet around Fredericksburg, and he assured readers that army morale was high. One of Sener's biggest concerns that winter was the spiritual well-being of the troops, and he often made reference to religious services that he had observed.[25]

During the winter, he built relationships with the soldiers and officers of the Army of Northern Virginia. When a military man was especially helpful, Sener would mention him favorably in a dispatch. Sener singled out General William Barksdale and Colonel W.A. Luce of the 18th Mississippi Cavalry as particularly helpful, as well as mail carriers. As one of Mississippi's most prominent newspapermen, Barksdale may have been sensitive to a reporter's need for information.[26]

Sener also singled out Dr. C.A. Jones, "that faithful and capable physician" who had been in Fredericksburg for 10 or more weeks. "He's not too lazy or ashamed to do what's needed, even serving as nurse and commissary."[27]

When General Joseph Hooker was chosen to replace General Burnside as commander of the Union Army of the Potomac, Sener thoughtfully commented, "Joe Hooker means to fight and at once. He is a man of dash, energy and determination. Let us not underrate him. His army may be demoralized, but we should prepare for him under a different impression. Because Pope and Burnside have shown their incapacity for wielding large armies and fighting pitched battles, it is by no means a fair deduction that Hooker lacks the elements of a great or successful General." [28] Sener noted that Hooker was placed in command when the Federals felt hopeless. "He can but lose—he may gain; hence he is prepared to resort to desperate expedients to bolster his sinking cause."[29]

By early April 1863, all signs pointed to the two great armies preparing for a new campaign season. Both armies were anxious to get back to the business at hand, Sener wrote. He wondered what the effect of renewed fighting would be

> Will the groans of the dying, the shrieks of the wounded or the mangled corpses of the dead appeal more eloquently or successfully from the coming battlefields than those which have gone up from the hundreds which have been fought during the war? If the memories of Manassas, Shiloh, Corinth, Murfreesboro, Sharpsburg and Fredericksburg are unavailing, why hope we that another conflict will cool the passions, instruct the reasons or guide the judgments of men to right conclusions, when all the pointing and teaching of the hour tells us that "Ephraim is joined to his idols?" I confess that, for one, the hour to me is dark and gloomy enough. I see around me the ruin which the sword and the sacking have wrought. I look back for encouragement, but I cannot look forward with hope of but one thing, that alone sustains me, viz., our final triumph. How long we are to journey through the wilderness, Heaven only knows.[30]

Before the end of April 1863, the Union and Confederate armies would meet in the Battle of Chancellorsville, one of the most important Confederate victories of the war. The win was significant enough to tempt Lee to try a second invasion of the North, and it was in this meeting of the two armies that Lee's most important officer, Stonewall Jackson, was mortally wounded by friendly fire. The battle lasted the better part of a week, April 30 to May 6, and cost the two armies combined more than 25,000 men—a figure Sener wrongly put closer to 30,000: 5,000 Confederates and 25,000 Federals. Actually, 9,500 men were lost for the Confederates, 14,000 for the Union.

The battle began when Union forces crossed the Rapidan and Rappahannock rivers to the northwest of Fredericksburg with some 90,000 men and the forces met at Chancellorsville, a farmstead in the Virginia wilderness. Hooker was essentially trying to do the same things as Burnside but by going in the opposite direction. While Burnside had moved south to Fredericksburg to make a surprise crossing, Hooker went north along the river and actually did make a successful surprise crossing. The result was a complex, multifront battle. Sener raced on horseback between troops all across the front during the struggle, trying to "sift the grains of truth from the mass of false reports in circulation." His first story, published on the second day of the battle, reported that one Confederate position was successfully captured by Union troops because their captain

Stonewall Jackson's attack at the Battle of Chancellorsville. *Harper's Weekly,* May 23, 1863. Courtesy of Rare Books and Special Collections, University of South Carolina Libraries

paid no attention to the noises he was hearing through the fog. Although the Confederates heard what sounded like enemy troops approaching, they did nothing to defend their position and were captured with their guns unloaded, according to Sener's account.[31]

This was Sener's only published report until after the battle, when he claimed a "glorious victory" for the Confederates in both parts of the battle—at Chancellorsville and on Marye's Heights, closer to Fredericksburg. His reporting on the main fight at Chancellorsville was reasonably accurate. After a relatively quiet day, he reported that "Stonewall" Jackson launched a late (5 p.m.) attack, which succeeded in pushing the Union forces well back. "The sound of artillery and small arms was well nigh deafening," until about midnight, as Jackson pressed the enemy for a night fight, Sener wrote. "Our boys drove the Yankees who stoutly held their ground until near day." By 11 the following morning, the conflict had died down. "The Yankees had been badly whipped near Chancellorsville and were in full retreat," he added. However, his descriptions of Union General John Sedgwick's storming of Marye's Heights above Fredericksburg and the following battle as Lee attempted to destroy Sedgwick were completely inaccurate. Sener portrayed the Union attack as successful only because of weak Confederate defenses and the Confederate counterattack as a great success leading to chaos and disorder on the Union side. In fact, Sedgwick had carried the Heights against significant opposition and successfully parried Lee's counterattack. Also, contrary to Sener's suggestion, Sedgwick never contemplated an advance on Richmond with his single corps. It is also doubtful that the Federals "celebrated" their capture of Marye's Heights. Sener's assessment of the battle:

> Hooker expected success. He had planned well; but General Lee has proved himself more than a match for him, and his splendid army now lies a part dead on the south side of the Rappahannock, a part wounded on its north bank, and some

here, too, and a large part of the advance is already near your city . . . The bravery, fortitude and endurance of our men in all of these regiments cannot be too highly praised or too gratefully remembered by the country. [32]

By May 9, Sener and the *Enquirer* were reporting that all the Federals had recrossed the river, the old picket lines had been reestablished, and Confederate soldiers were resting in their camps.[33]

Like many Confederate correspondents, Sener underestimated the Union fighting man. Because Sener spent most of the war covering Lee's defensive battles, he never had the opportunity to observe how difficult it was to wage an offensive during the Civil War. Sener was a conscientious correspondent who was reporting what he was being told by his sources, and doing it well, but accurately reporting what his sources told him did not always equate to accurately reporting what had happened. For example, Sener's interpretation of Hooker's actions was logical but inaccurate because Sener could not have known why the Union general crossed the river and then stopped. It was not a strategic decision, as Sener assumed. It was because General Hooker lost his nerve. Sener was not in a position to fully describe and interpret the battle more accurately. No one, including the generals themselves, had an accurate picture during or immediately after the fighting.

The Union army's offensive in this eight-day battle did contain fatal blunders, but the same could be said about Lee's two offensive campaigns, Antietam and Gettysburg. Offensive warfare was more difficult than defensive warfare because Americans had no previous experience with armies as large as those that fought the Civil War. Further, this was the first war in which railroads and telegraph played a major role, and the Virginia terrain favored the defenders to a significant degree.

Sener's stories were not always accurate, nor were they always complete. One of his stories about the Battle of Chancellorsville contained one conspicuous absence: Thomas "Stonewall" Jackson's death from pneumonia a week after he was wounded by friendly fire. Sener delayed sending the details of the general's death until a week after the Union army retreated across the river. When Sener did write, his story was impeccably sourced. He had interviewed the only man in Jackson's escort who survived the attack, his signal officer Captain Richard Eggleston Wilbourne of Mississippi, who described in detail what had happened. According to the captain, Jackson had ridden out with several members of his staff and that of General A.P. Hill to survey the results of the fighting on May 2. Near dusk, Jackson and his party headed back to camp but were intercepted by a North Carolina unit that mistook the general and his escort for Union troops. The soldiers fired before ascertaining exactly who they were shooting at. Everyone in the party was killed or wounded, with the exception of Wilbourne and perhaps one other person, Sener reported.[34] The story continued:

The messenger who carried Gen. Lee the intelligence of this severe misfortune tells me that he found the General on a bed of straw, about four o'clock in the morning and that when told of what had occurred, his words were these: "Thank God it is no worse; God be praised that he is still alive"; and that he further said: "Any victory is a dear one that deprives us of the services of Jackson, even for a short time." Upon the informant mentioning that he believed it was General Jackson's intention to have pressed them on Sunday, had he not fallen,[35]

General Lee hastily dressed and "partaking of his simple fare of ham and cracker, he sallied forth, I hear unattended, and made such dispositions as rendered that Sabbath a blessed day for our cause, even though a Jackson had fallen among its leaders," Sener wrote, knowing that every incident connected with Jackson and Lee would interest his readers. Citing his sources, the correspondent added: "I will mention, as quite current, that when General Jackson received the letter which General Lee sent him on Sunday morning, bursting into tears, he said, 'far better for the Confederacy that ten Jacksons should have fallen than one Lee . . .'

> . . . Of Jackson it may be said what can be affirmed of but few men that have lived in this great struggle, that he has fulfilled a great purpose in history, wrought out the mission for which he was ordained of Providence, and that, "dying, he has left no stain which, living, he would wish to blot." His example, let us hope and believe, will survive him, and in the coming fight let Jackson's men show to the world that "a dead Jackson shall win the field."[36]

Sener concluded his story with a lament for his hometown. Fredericksburg had survived, he reported, although some houses were charred. "This poor old town, too, battered, and in some instances, demolished, is just now smiling in the gay robes of rich, ripe verdure with which spring has bedecked her. She is far from finished, and will yet live in history an undying memorial of the brutality of our foe, and an imperishable monument of sacrificing patriotism."[37]

Despite the inaccuracies, Sener's Chancellorsville stories were beautifully written and well sourced. They reflected the situation as the generals and soldiers understood it at the moment, which is all a journalist can hope to do. His stories were sufficiently well done that one historian assessed the coverage in the *Richmond Examiner* by Sener and another correspondent (possibly J.W. Albertson) as the best battle accounts of Chancellorsville in the Confederate press.[38]

Lee used the momentum from his Chancellorsville victory to propel his army on its second invasion of the North, but Sener did not follow immediately.[39] Instead, he reported from Fredericksburg until early July when the *Enquirer* moved him from freelancer to regular staff correspondent and sent him to join Lee's army as it retreated from the disaster at Gettysburg.[40]

Sketch of Confederate pickets killed during the skirmishing at Fredericksburg. In the background, the hotly contested Federal pontoon bridge. Courtesy of the Library of Congress

Sener reached Winchester by July 13 but was unable to continue forward to meet Lee's columns at Williamsport, Maryland, where they were crossing the Potomac back into Virginia. Not only was Sener too ill to continue, it was not safe to get any closer to the army, he wrote. He noted that Martinsburg, Virginia, was nearer Lee's troops than Winchester, but he had decided not to venture closer because that town lacked the mail and telegraph facilities that made Winchester a good vantage point for him.[41]

Although Sener did not actually witness the fighting at Gettysburg, he was able to piece together information from the wounded who were still being brought from the front. Some had walked the whole way with few comforts. These evacuations were complicated by harassment from Union forces. "The Yankee cavalry attacked our trains on Sunday near Greencastle, Pa., but were driven off after a short fight," he wrote. The Federals had burned the pontoons the Confederates were using to build bridges across the Potomac at Williamsport, but the Confederates had gotten their licks in, too, Sener reported. Southern troops had destroyed abolitionist Thaddeus Stevens' iron works in their invasion.[42] Sener got himself in trouble with Winchester women with one story, intimating that few of them were showing up to volunteer for nursing duty with the wounded.[43]

Finally, by mid-July, Sener was able to begin moving toward the front. He did so with something of a heavy heart, for he had learned enough about the invasion and the fighting in Winchester that he did not expect "grand results" from this invasion of Maryland and Pennsylvania. He believed the people there had grown complacent. He was especially concerned about Maryland. Sener wrote, "She has been so long held down and so long exempted from the ravages of war, that I believe the impulse of patriotism will be merged in the reflections of expediency and drowned in the calculation of interest and necessity. Had Virginia so reasoned, her manhood would have been long since destroyed and her fame unenviable."[44]

Within only a few days of leaving Winchester, Sener arrived at the headquarters of the 3rd Army Corps. He made an uneasy crossing of the Potomac, but it was still high from the recent rains and the army was still busy building pontoons.[45] He continued toward Martinsburg, but once there got the feeling that he was not in Virginia any more, but rather in "Yankee doodledom." The people there were unionists in their politics, he wrote, and they were not pleasant to the Confederate soldiers who came through. "I learn that our soldiers are scowled at and jeered as they pass through, and that, per contra, the Yankee prisoners are always cheered, the women here calling them 'our soldiers,' and begging permission not infrequently to be permitted to serve them such delicacies as they have." However, there were exceptions. Sener stayed one night with "a true Southern man" who treated him well and whose daughters "are true Southern women."[46]

Sener also faced professional concerns on his trip to the front. One of those was unequal treatment by the army of the correspondent for the *London Times* and correspondents for Southern newspapers. He wrote:

> The correspondents of the Richmond papers—without whose recognition this war would have been a failure—are snubbed, and its readers, the men who are giving the best blood of their off-spring and the substance of their wealth, must not expect to get the battle in detail until it is written here by a foreign eye and is read by a distant people. [William Howard] Russell was not permitted to enter Yankee army lines. The South admits foreign correspondents and recognizes them, even though sent by a people refusing to recognize us, but she taboos those who write for her own people. Is this a military necessity, or are we disposed to lick the hand that would smite us?[47]

Sener was overlooking two important points when he wrote this diatribe. Because the *London Times* stories were written by a foreign eye and read by distant people, they were less dangerous than stories published in Confederate newspapers that circulated freely to the North. And second, the Confederacy was desperately trying to gain official recognition by either Great Britain or France. Currying favor with English reporters might result in kind treatment by their newspapers, which might translate into improved chances for diplomatic recognition.

Sener did not remain long at the front. By July 22, he was back in a quiet Winchester. He filed another story upon his return that quibbled with the *New York Herald*'s claim that the Union army had annihilated Lee's force and the rebellion was over. The army, Sener argued, was getting stronger daily. He believed it would be back to its regular fighting trim within a week. "The country can rely upon the army of Northern Virginia, and Robt. E. Lee, its chosen General," he declared.[48]

Following the army to Culpeper Court House, Sener settled in for the dog days of August. Most fighting was confined to cavalry, but the soldiers were not idle. Drills and inspections were occurring daily, but more important, from the troops' perspective: paymasters were in the camps, settling salaries through July 1. The only problem was that the Confederate money was worth so little, Sener observed, adding that Congress should consider raising soldier pay.[49]

The correspondent himself had a rough time that month. He was always careful not to reveal information that would be useful to the enemy, so when previously cooperative authorities cut the spigot to any information, Sener became annoyed. Information had dried up as the result of a controversy over a correspondent who wrote as "A." Sener was incensed at the treatment he was receiving and huffily reported that he had arranged to get information from other officers.

> I am not "A," as any man with three grains of sense ought to know, nor do I care about the merits of "A's" controversy; but this I do know, that certain gentlemen with "stars and stripes" endeavor to extend the "usual incivilities of their office to the press," with the expectation that a lack of brains and politeness can be made up by a bold display of rudeness and a coarse attempt at ignoring and belittling the importance of the press, which at once reflects the incompetency and stamps the character of those who thus reason and act. A few, however, seem to appreciate the value of the press, and extend its representatives those decent courtesies which are due it between gentlemen. For the former I beg to express, and here take leave to record, my unbounded contempt. It is gratifying, however, to know that among those who have kindly consented to furnish meas [sic] your representative with information proper to be made public in regard to the achievements of the army, as Lieut. General Longstreet, whose claims to the admiration of his countrymen for genius and bravery will not be outshone by his disposition to serve those who are serving the public . . .

Sener predicted that he would soon have from Longstreet "all the facilities the distinguished officer can give in aiding me to present accurate reportings of the doings of our brave soldiers in the field." He expected similar courtesies from Generals Ewell and Hill, "and I hope I shall not be disappointed." Sener concluded:

There is no antagonism between those who are with the army to record its history and those who are making history. On the contrary, every interest is in common, and nothing but narrow and contracted views can prevent the hearty cooperation of those who are doing the fighting with those who are trying to do the writing correctly.[50]

Sener did not hint who "A" might be, but historian J. Cutler Andrews thought he might be J.W. Albertson. Also, Georgian Peter W. Alexander, widely known as the *Savannah Republican*'s P.W.A., wrote under that pseudonym. He also corresponded as "A" for the *Mobile Advertiser and Register*. Alexander and several other correspondents had been involved in a controversy over criticism of cavalry commander J.E.B. Stuart over the way he disciplined his troopers.[51]

A month later, the camps near Culpeper Court House were dealing with two other issues. The Federals had recrossed the Rappahannock near Brandy Station, along with units of black soldiers, and the Army of Northern Virginia was preparing for multiple executions of men convicted of desertion. The pickets for the Union and Confederate armies were also close enough to talk and exchange newspapers, Sener reported. "Indeed, everything is so much like the situation at Fredericksburg last winter that one is sometimes induced to think that hostilities have ceased," he wrote. "This is not the case, however, as the capture of some fifteen prisoners and a three bushel mail-bag, near Stevensburg, yesterday evening, will readily assure us." The main body of the Federal army was entrenched outside Centreville, and Sener predicted that they would remain there unless General Lee went on the offensive.[52]

While waiting in Culpeper with the army, Sener witnessed a first for General Lee: public execution of soldiers for desertion. The 10 deserters had compounded their crime by murdering the officer sent to return them to the army. The men were from Co. H. of the 3rd North Carolina, Stuart's Brigade, Johnson's Division, and Ewell's Corps, and their old units had the duty of seeing to the executions. His first-person description rendered the grim ceremony in stark detail.

On my arrival at the spot selected for this dreadful, though necessary work, which was in an open field surrounded on all sides by woods, I found the whole of Johnson's division drawn up without arms in three sides of a square, with faces fronting inwards and toward the stakes, which were placed on the line of the fourth side, and at intervals of about twenty feet apart. After a short interval, Gen. Johnson and staff made their appearance and took a position by the side of the camp colors which were planted about the center of the square. Another interval of 15 or 20 minutes, and the sound of slow and sullen music heard. Turning my eyes in the direction whence the sound proceeded and there could be seen the doomed men marching slowly to the spot where they were to yield up their lives. On they come with measured and solemn tread—first the music, the condemned, and next and lastly, the guard and executioners, with their bright guns and bayonets glistening in the splendid light of a declining September sun. One side of the square is parted, and this grim procession centers and moves to the fatal stakes, which being reached, the column is halted and then the reverend clergyman (Mr. Patterson) offers up a feeling prayer. This concluded, and each prisoner is taken in charge by two men and led to the stake at which he is to be executed where he is fixed in a kneeling posture, his back against the stake and his arms pinioned behind him to a plank board. The bandages are next adjusted over the eyes and their hats placed over these bandages. Thus pinioned and placed with their faces to the executioners and not their backs as is commonly supposed, these condemned men are left.[53]

Sener reported the utterances by the condemned men, "such expressions as 'Lord, have mercy,' 'Oh, my poor mother' and 'Oh, save me, save me!'" The executioners were quickly divided into squads of 10 men each, 5 with loaded muskets and 5 with unloaded muskets. Sener wrote that the executioners took their respective positions, each squad just 14 feet from the man at whom they were to fire.

A moment more and Major Wood, of the 37th Virginia, field officer of the day, gives the commands, "ready," "aim," and then, at the word fire, an irregular volley salutes the ear with its harsh, grating sound, and as the smoke clears away, it is discovered that all of the condemned have not been killed—some are only wounded, and the most revolting part of the whole affair transpires. The reserves, of which there were two to each squad, are ordered up and they have to kill those whom the volley has only wounded. Some six or eight successive shots are fired in this way, showing that probably some one at least had to be fired at probably as often as three times. At length the work is done, and ten dead bodies, with motionless heads hanging lifeless over and upon bosoms that cease to throb, are all that remains of the ten living creatures who but a few moments before walked up to those stakes. The penalty is paid, the law is avenged, and a crowd of witnesses have been to see it well done.[54]

Sener stayed with the troops, but he wrote little for the *Enquirer* the rest of the summer, and in the fall he took a month off for an undisclosed reason. When he returned in November 1863 to report again from Lee's army, Sener had a new employer: the *Richmond Dispatch*. He would write for that newspaper for a year. His first report upon his return was written as if nothing had changed. It began: "After an absence of four weeks from the Army of Northern Virginia, I find upon my return that its health, spirits, and morals is in every respect up to the highest standard of military requirements, and that the troops are ready and willing to give the enemy battle, and only await his advance."[55]

Rejoining Lee's army at his headquarters in Orange Court House, Sener wrote for the *Dispatch* that the Confederate troops were in good spirits but in need of blankets, shoes, and socks for the coming winter, a fact that he would continue to remind readers about.[56] Many soldiers had no shoes, blankets, or overcoats to protect them from the cold weather. To demonstrate his point, he offered particulars: "In Hays's Louisiana brigade, for example—and it is by no means singular in its unsupplied wants—there are 239 men who have no blankets or bedding of any description. There are two hundred and twenty-one who have neither blankets nor overcoats, and there are 482 who are without overcoats."[57]

One brigade had taken it upon itself to supply its need for at least one item: shoes. Brigadier General William Mahone's command had set up a shoe-manufacturing facility in its winter quarters, complete with facilities for cutting, sewing, and soling new shoes, as well as for repairing old shoes. So far, Sener wrote, the shop had repaired 500 pairs of shoes that would have been thrown away otherwise.[58]

Sener's first *Dispatch* story also reported that Union General George Meade was still fumbling about but had not yet made any real advances. Sener predicted that no further significant fighting would occur until spring. President Davis and his staff had recently spent two days in camp with the troops, he reported. Most of Lee's officers had come by headquarters to pay their respects to "Uncle Jeff," and "Marse Robert." Lee had given Davis a tour of the front. "But for inclement weather the President would have reviewed the whole army," he added. During the visit, Davis and Lee attended Sunday services at the Episcopalian Church in Orange Courthouse.[59]

Sener was correct in his assessment that the camps' locations were "permanent—at least for awhile."[60] The army settled into a routine of occasional skirmishes and artillery demonstrations that accomplished little for either side.[61] Of Meade's tentative demonstrations across the Rapidan in late November, probably intended to frighten Lee into moving back toward Richmond,[62] Sener wrote, "A mountain in labor, and behold at parturition a mouse is brought forth. Meade has marched up the hill and then marched down again. Perhaps he reasoned after wise, 'That he who fights and runs away may live to fight another day.'"[63] The correspondent added that he fully expected "some of your hot-house military critics in Richmond who have 'never smell gunpowder'" would criticize Lee for not having engaged Meade. Sener explained that the general's reticence was due to disagreements with his subordinates as to the wisdom of an assault.[64] Perhaps some caution was called for: the fall 1863 engagements had cost Lee far more than Meade, and the only attacks Lee launched in this period had been failures.

A few days later, Sener offered an end-of-the-year wrap-up of the state of affairs in Virginia.

The campaign of 1863 may now be said to be over. The troops are doubtless in their winter quarters, and the condition of the weather to-day leads us to believe that all warlike operations are now at an end until the vernal suns of 1864 shall bring a more favorable season for military movements. The enemy is in Culpeper county, with the bulk of his infantry, consisting of four corps, lying around the Court-House and Brandy Station, and with his cavalry pickets reaching out to and beyond Mitchell's Station. One corps is beyond the Rappahannock, for the purpose of guarding the railroad. It is not true that the enemy have ever destroyed any part of the railroad, or that they intend to change their base of operations. On the contrary, as soon as spring opens, Meade will either push for Richmond, or be forced back to Washington.[65]

Many of Sener's letters to the *Dispatch* through the winter of 1863–1864 dealt with camp life, like the ones he had written the previous winter. In one story, Sener reported that the Army of Northern Virginia had established a post office for its men. Some 10,000 letters were received, and a similar amount sent out, from the army post office each day. Captain John L. Eubank, formerly commander of an artillery battery and "secretary of the last Va. Convention," was serving as postmaster. Eight postal clerks worked "from early morn until long past midnight of each day." The clerks were encountering letters sent to soldiers without postage—a common practice; the receiver was expected to pay the postage, but the problem was that individual soldiers did not come to the post office to collect their mail. Instead, each brigade sent one mail carrier to collect the letters for all the men in the unit, and those mail carriers would not advance postage out of their own pockets for unpaid letters and packages. Sener encouraged Southern newspapers to spread word that unpaid letters were not getting to soldiers.[66]

Sener also reported on promotions of officers, road repairs, supply shipments, highway robberies of soldiers (dealt with by stationing sharpshooters along the road), the brisk business being done by sutlers with the army in winter quarters, and, one of his perennially favorite topics, the "state of religious feeling throughout the army."[67] Sener believed this was the foundation of the Army of Northern Virginia's "great successes," and he feared the lack of religious sentiment among Bragg's Army of Tennessee was the reason for its recent defeats.[68] However, that religious feeling did not pervade all of Lee's army. A few days after his story extolling the spiritual state of the Army of Northern Virginia, Stener reported that a mob of soldiers had robbed the settlers located near the train depot in Orange Court House. The men took "everything valuable," including "some $20,000 in Confederate money, $500 in gold, and some eight or ten gold and silver watches." The guard had captured only five or six of the robbers, and they had been turned over to the army for courts-martial.[69]

When no other topic presented itself, Sener wrote letters reviewing the campaigns of 1863 or foreshadowing what might happen when campaigning season opened in the spring.[70] For much of the winter, "no sound of artillery or discharge of small arms [would break] the quiet which has reigned supreme along the waters of the swift flowing river, as its name Rapidan implies," Sener wrote in late winter 1864. However, that quiet would soon be broken, he predicted, and the two armies facing one another across the river "will again seek each other in deadly conflict, to determine the great questions presented in the issue of Union and subjugation, or the South and independence secured."[71] By early March, the Union army came out of winter hibernation with a feint toward Charlottesville, days before General Grant took supreme command of all Union armies. It would be two months before the campaign season started in earnest.[72]

As the 1864 campaign began, the Confederacy faced other problems. Morale, both civilian and military, would be a major issue in the fourth year of the war. Desertion was already a problem in the army, and civilian support for the war had flagged in the previous summer. The decline in civilian support for the war was particularly acute in places like North Carolina where prominent newspaperman William W. Holden was waging his own campaign for peace, and eastern Tennessee where Union sentiment had prevailed for most of the war. The Army of Northern Virginia's spirits were still running high that spring, however, and soldiers were confident of victory, Sener reported. To support that claim, he included a letter from the 15th Virginia Cavalry in one of his dispatches. Unit members wrote that they looked . . .

> . . . with profound contempt upon the craven hearted croakers in or out of the service, who would skulk from duty or hesitate to fly to the rescue of their country in the hour of need and remain to defend her soil and honor, without limit of time or proviso of circumstances, do hereby offer themselves to the authorities of the Confederate States without reserve as to time, arm of service, or other restrictions during this war; while we might prefer cavalry service, and under officers of our own selection, we consider our duty first to our country—waive all personal considerations and bind ourselves to fight mounted or on foot, in cavalry, artillery, infantry, or anywhere—on land or water—on full or half rations, or such as the country can furnish—well clad or not—so long as we can wield a weapon of any sort, and one of the vile horde can be found to raise a hand against our flag or dispute our right to freedom and separate nationality.[73]

By early May, Grant's army had made the first move of its Overland Campaign, a relentless and costly effort to grind Lee's army down. Sener announced Grant's opening gambit with restrained anticipation.

> The armies of Northern Virginia and of the Potomac are no longer in hybernis, with pickets walking dull and monotonous beats. Everything is life, animation and activity. Burnside, after a long season of preparation, has quit Annapolis, and is once more about to essay the fortunes of war with the ill-fated Army of

the Potomac. Hooker has also come to help Grant out of or into a difficulty, most probably the latter.[74]

Sener was certain Grant's campaign would fail because, for the first time, the Army of the Potomac was fielding black soldiers. Even the white soldiers were only fighting "in obedience to the behest of power," he reported. Sener mistakenly believed this would make the Union troops easier to defeat. He predicted that Grant's army had little chance of victory, while Lee's army "is hopeful and buoyant, and will no doubt add another to their many and well earned victories."[75]

The first engagement of that campaign was the Battle of the Wilderness, fought in the same area as the Battle of Chancellorsville. The choice of battle-grounds was fortunate for Lee. His army of 60,000 men was vastly outnumbered by Grant's 100,000 troops, but the terrain helped equalize the two armies. The battle raged May 5 and 6, then on May 7, the day after the fighting ceased, Sener sat down to write what he knew. He included two dispatches from Lee to James A. Seddon, Confederate secretary of war, which (overoptimistically) reported successful maneuvers to push Grant back toward the river. In a multiple-deck headlined story, Sener reported, "I have been in the saddle for the last twenty-four hours, and have been unremittingly active during the time endeavoring to sift the true from the false." Sener described the action surprisingly accurately for a story written so soon after a battle. He reported Grant's crossing of the river at several places Tuesday night and Wednesday morning. On Thursday, the Union troops began their forward movement. That night, General Richard S. Ewell's forces clashed with Union forces near Germanna ford.[76] Sener reported desperate fighting in heavy skirmishes. "During the attack on Battle's brigade, and just at a time it was being rapidly forced back, Gordon's brigade was ordered forward, and made one of the grandest charges of the war, forcing the enemy back at all points," he wrote. Union troops later assaulted Confederate lines and were "terribly cut to pieces."[77]

The fighting resumed the next day, and although the Confederate troops made progress against the Union forces, the Southerners suffered a devastating blow: corps commander James Longstreet was badly wounded by friendly fire only a few miles from where Stonewall Jackson had been killed almost exactly a year earlier. Ultimately, the outcome of those two days of fighting was inconclusive. Lee inflicted massive losses on the Union army, but Grant was not so badly hurt that he disengaged. He was pushed back but continued the campaign. Lee's army was not unscathed either. Sener suggested some 6,000 casualties on the Southern side, but the real number would be much higher.[78]

No sooner had the fighting in the Wilderness been resolved than Grant returned to fight near Spotsylvania. Sener described the fighting as beyond any that had previously engaged the armies of Northern Virginia and the Potomac. "For ten mortal hours the contest raged with unabated fury, and so deadly and destructive was the fire of musketry that trees were cut down," he wrote. "Again and again did the enemy, inspirited by the little success of the morning, their whiskey rations, and Grant's braggadocio and lying, assault our line of works; each time did they waver, and give back, until finally, at nightfall, the Yankee wounded and dead strewed the field 'thick as autumnal leaves in Vallambross' . . ." In Sener's opinion, the Union soldiers "fought with a courage and devotion worthy of a better cause; whilst our men, safe behind breastworks, rejoiced in their ability to deal death to the accursed foe with such slight loss." The fighting continued into the night, resulting in hand-to-hand fighting in some places. Even past midnight, pickets continued fighting and artillery fire rumbled.[79] Losses on that first day of fighting were 3,500 wounded and 500 killed, according to Sener's estimate. Actual losses for the two-week battle were closer to 12,000 for the Confederates, compared to 18,000 for the Union.

Two days after filing his first story, Sener had the opportunity to tour the battlefield. What he saw must have reminded him, being the religious man that he was, of the apocalypse.

> To-day I rode over the battlefield in front of field's front and found a large number of dead Yankees scattered everywhere about over the field. As usual, their clothing had been stripped from them, and they lay with their swollen forms stretched at full length upon that soil which they had come to desecrate and have desolate, and with their faces upturned towards that Heaven whose religion they have mocked and whose God they have defied. Their punishment was swift and sure. Would to God that their misguided companions in arms may be profited by the sad scene through which they are called to pass.[80]

Sener's stories for most of May focused on the skirmishing that continued after the stalemates at Wilderness and Spotsylvania.[81] The litany of battles that month was long: Yellow Tavern (May 11), Meadow Bridge (May 12), Wilson's Wharf (May 24), North Anna (May 23-26), Totopotomy Creek (May 28-30), Old Church (May 30), culminating in the bloody Battle of Cold Harbor.

The fighting began at Cold Harbor on May 31 when Union General Phil Sheridan's cavalry seized an important crossroads. The Confederate cavalry attacked the next day, and within the next two days, both cavalries were reinforced with infantry. Fighting continued along a seven-mile front that stretched from Bethesda Church to the Chickahominy River. The battlefield must have been an eerie place for the soldiers, for it was the same ground as the battles of Gaines Mill and Seven Days in 1862. As the soldiers were digging trenches, they unearthed remains of men who had fallen during that earlier fighting.

The Confederates were outnumbered, just as they had been in 1862. Grant had almost a two-to-one advantage over Lee in the number of troops, but many Union soldiers were raw recruits, brought in to replace the nearly 50,000 Federal soldiers who had been lost in the Overland Campaign. The two armies waged nine days of wretched trench warfare at Cold Harbor. In some locations, those trenches were only yards apart. Men could almost reach out and touch those they were about to slaughter. Thousands of wounded languished in the no-mans-land between the trenches, none more terribly than those abandoned for two days while Grant dithered over whether to ask for a flag of truce to attend the wounded. Grant believed that asking for a truce would signal that he had lost the battle. In fact, his first request for a truce was sent under the signature of a corps commander, General Gordon, who asked to be allowed to tend the wounded troops for "motives of humanity." Lee, realizing what Grant was trying to do, sent a message that he would deal only with the commanding general. The next day, Grant acquiesced and sent a request of his own.[82]

Cold Harbor was Lee's last victory. The campaign had been costly for both sides. Grant's losses totaled some 55,000 for the month of May, compared to Lee's 30,000. At Cold Harbor, however, the casualty figures clearly favored the rebels. Sener's early stories about the fighting at Cold Harbor did not capture the cataclysmic nature of the two-week battle. In fact, his reporting glossed over engagements among the troops. His first story, written on June 2, claimed that only irregular but sharp skirmishing was occurring. "The enemy tried their old game, massing heavy columns and pushing them against a single point in our line, but as usual, failed to accomplish anything more than a temporary success," he reported. The Union troops paid dearly for that success. According to Sener, "The enemy in their flight left their dead unburied, broke up three ambulances, threw away their arms, and left in haste generally. We also captured some three hundred horses." He believed the skirmishing was nothing more than delaying tactics by Grant as he waited for reinforcements.[83]

Sener was not able to piece together an entirely accurate picture of the importance of the skirmishing that continued in the aftermath of the Cold Harbor blood bath.[84] On June 6, he wrote, "Since my last communication nothing of special interest has occurred in the fighting line."[85] His report was not entirely accurate. On June 3, Union commander Hancock's troops broke through Breckinridge's lines, and the fighting devolved into hand-to-hand combat. At one point, the Confederate fire was so intense that Union soldiers, caught between the lines, began entrenching, using anything they could find to dig, including cups and bayonets, and when those were unavailable, using the bodies of their dead comrades as improvised earthworks.

As the battle raged, Sener's stories grew shorter. His dispatch written on June 14 at 5 p.m. was only three paragraphs long. In it, he reported that Grant was still on the move, probably intending to cross the James River.[86] In fact, Grant had slipped away from Cold Harbor, intending to approach Richmond from the south via Petersburg. When Sener wrote again, nearly a week later, he was in Petersburg and, this time, he got his story partly right: The fight now would be for the Confederate capital. "The battles for the possession of Petersburg have been fought and won," he wrote. "Henceforth the engagements on this line will be for the capture of Richmond."[87] He also got it partly wrong: "That Grant has now no show of success it is scarcely necessary for me to say. The time of our peril has passed, and the hour for congratulation and felicitation is now."[88] Sener did not understand Grant's strategy—but neither did Lee. Grant was not particularly interested in Petersburg, or even Richmond. Instead, Grant wanted to use the Confederate capital as an anvil against which to crush Lee. While Lee successfully held Petersburg, he was in check. He could not yield the city because it was the most important remaining supply route from further south. Abandoning it meant abandoning Richmond. Lee was not defeated but he was trapped.

The two armies had fought and slogged their way to Petersburg over the course of five days, and each army had achieved some success. The first severe fighting occurred on Thursday, Sener reported. Since then, the fighting had been continuous, with some success for each army. On Friday morning, Confederates faced overwhelming numbers of Union troops "near the Baxter road and near Avery's road." Outnumbered, the Confederates could not mount an adequate defense. The fighting around Petersburg would eventually settle into a "sort of siege" that would last almost to the end of the war.

The operations around Petersburg have generally been referred to as a siege, but they were actually less siege and more trench warfare on three sides of the city. Almost daily battles or skirmishes ensued for much of the summer, and Sener was in the thick of things. In late June, he wrote to the *Dispatch*, "Events succeed each other in such rapid succession that a correspondent has no leisure, and little time to do more than merely chronicle results, without indulging speculations or entering much into details."[89] As the summer passed, Sener grew more frustrated with the Confederate army's ineffective attempts to stop the Union cavalry. "Though our cavalry have been 'routing' the Yankee cavalry for the last two months, still the Yankee cavalry manage to turn up wherever and whenever they can do us most harm."[90]

Few major battles took place during July, much to Sener's displeasure. The waiting had become interminable, and the correspondent lashed out against Grant in frustration. "Heat and dust, shells and Minnie balls, mangled and dying soldiers, fugitive women, decrepit old men, and children, make up the summary of news which daily goes forth to the world from the point of the compass in irrefutable proof of the brutal cowardice and insane persistence of the God forsaken wretches whom we are forced to meet in honorable warfare,"[91] he wrote. He found the Union army's July 4 observance particularly vexing. He believed the day would have been more productive had it been spent killing Yankee soldiers in battle.

Yesterday was the anniversary of the Declaration of independence. The prince of humbugs, Grant, "availed himself of this occasion" to hang out his dirty dish-rag flag at every ten steps on his works and to keep his horn tooters busy all day.

Whiskey is said to have circulated freely. U.S. and the army were doubtless all on a bender. The grand charge did not take place, and consequently, we have to mourn the loss of a number of Yankees whose bodies would be manuring the soil of Prince George had they have essayed to carry our works yesterday.[92]

Despite Grant's success in investing the city, Sener remained unrealistically defiant and convinced of Confederate victory.

Everybody wants to know what Grant is likely to do, and I suppose that is just what Grant himself would like to know. It is almost superfluous for me to say that if Grant could not take Petersburg with his whole army when it was defended by Beauregard in hastily constructed defenses, with a mere handful of men, that he has no shot of capturing it . . . He is a worse humbug and a greater braggart with less pretensions than even poor Pope.[93]

The Confederate army was in fine shape, Sener reported more optimistically than perhaps warranted, with "nothing diminished as to morale and discipline." The men believed Grant had gone almost as far as he was able and that his efforts around Petersburg would fail within the next few days.[94] Sener and his sources were both wrong. Grant would hang on, slowly tightening the noose around Lee's army for the next eight months.

Sener's letters became shorter and less frequent in this period, for often there was little news to convey. In late July, he wrote to the *Dispatch*, "I have not written you for upwards of a week, simply because I had nothing worth recording. There is no change in the situation . . ."[95] In early August, it was much the same. "There is a profound quiet at this writing on this front, and the heat and dust are both intolerable," he wrote. "The troops in the trenches have many improvised comforts which persons at distance little dream of—though, of course, soldiering is not the most pleasant business in the world, even under the most favorable circumstances."[96]

However, within days Sener would have plenty to write about when the Union army tried an atrocious scheme to break the siege: digging a mine shaft under the Confederate positions and filling it with explosives that could create a hole in the Southern defenses. Miners in Burnside's command dug a shaft and filled it with explosives; black soldiers were trained to rush the Confederate position. At the last minute, they were replaced by untrained white soldiers. Concerns had been raised about the political repercussions in the North if black soldiers were needlessly sacrificed. This was a volatile time in politics since the presidential election was only a few weeks away. Lincoln's chances for re-election were not looking good, and Grant believed he needed to be cautious about any potential fallout from military matters. Unnecessary deaths of black soldiers could be just what Lincoln's opponent, George McClellan, needed to snatch victory from the incumbent. Despite Grant's caution, the substitution of untrained men turned the surprise attack into a disaster. The black soldiers had been briefed on what to expect when the explosion occurred and how to maneuver around the resulting crater. The substitute troops had not been briefed, and in rushing forward, the troops fell into the crater that measured some 170 feet long, 70 feet wide, and 30 feet deep. They were like fish in a barrel, and the Confederates responded by shooting them. More than 5,000 Union troops were lost.

Sener sent a letter on the day of the attack and followed it a few days later with more details, primarily casualty estimates.[97] He also reported on the burial parties that met in the area between the two armies on the day after the explosion.

> At the hour named, or just about sunrise, three gaily-dressed, flashy-looking officers raised an elegant white flag, mounted on a handsome staff, and advanced from their line of works. Simultaneously two shabbily dressed but brave Confederates, mounting a dirty pocket handkerchief on a ramrod, proceeded to meet them. A brief parley ensued, civilities were exchanged, and then the details came to do the work of the truce—the burial of the dead. For five hours the work went vigorously forward. The Yankees brought details of negroes, and we carried their negroes out under guard to help them in their work. Over seven hundred Yankees, whites and negroes, were buried. A.P. Hill was there, with long gauntlets, slouch hat, and round jacket. Mahone, dressed in little-boy-fashion cut of clothes, made from old Yankee tent cloth, was beside him. The gallant Harris, of the Mississippi brigade, and the gallant, intrepid Sanders, who but forty eight hours before had so successfully retaken those works—the best looking and best dressed Confederate officer present—was sauntering leisurely about, having a general superintendence over the whole affair. On the Yankee side there was any number of nice young men, dressed jauntily, carelessly smoking cigars and proffering whiskey, wine, and brandy of the best labels, and of sufficient age to warrant its flavor. More than one Confederate took a smile. Some took two, and one told me that finding the liquor of the "peace" order, he went it seven times.

Sener wrote that the Yankees talked freely, said their loss would be five thousand, that the whites blamed the negroes, and the negroes in turn charged the disasters of the day upon the whites. "They all agreed that Burnside was just an hour and a half behind time, and that he was the greatest of modern butchers, as Marye's hill and Griffiths farm would abundantly attest."

> Whilst the truce lasted, the Yankees and the "Johnny Rebs," in countless number, flocked to the neutral grounds and spent the time in chatting and sight-seeing. The stench, however, was quite strong, and it required a good nose and a better stomach to carry one through the ordeal. About nine o'clock, the burial being completed, the officers sent the men back to the trenches, on each side. The officers bade each other adieu and returned to their respective lines.[98]

The *Dispatch* did not publish another letter from Sener until near the end of August, and that one reported bad news. "To-day, for the first time in the history of the campaign of the Army of Northern Virginia, the Confederate arms have suffered a check and repulse," the correspondent reported.[99] The cause: a brigade that lost its nerve and refused to rally in heavy fighting. When one unit balked, "The contagion spreads; other troops give away, and soon the whole mass comes rushing back pell-mell, exposed to as murderous a fire in retreat as that to which they were subjected whilst advancing," he wrote. However, one unit did come through, Hagood's South Carolinians, according to Sener. An aide had surrendered Hagood's troops without consulting the general. When Hagood found out what his junior officer had done, he "ordered the men to fire and then to save themselves, his supports on the right and left having both long since fallen back." Sener added that "General H. himself escaped, though two horses were killed under him whilst retreating."[100]

Fighting continued into September 1864, with Grant making slow but steady progress tightening his hold on Petersburg.[101] Sener vacillated between believing that Grant was getting nowhere in his campaign and recognizing that Lee was not profiting.

> We have entered upon the fifth month of this terrible campaign. General Grant could not have supposed the obstacles first met after crossing the Rapid Ann [Rapidan] would so long have resisted his powerful blows. He avoided them on one side to meet them vis-à-vis tomorrow. Commanders of more feeling and less determination would have despaired of overcoming difficulties which seemed insurmountable, and gone to protect Washington, or have the causes for the failure of their late campaign investigated.
>
> If Grant was deceived in regard to the magnitude of his task, Lee was astonished that his was not more easily performed . . . Lee is the great sufferer in these under-estimates. Grant loses time, and men, and money; Lee loses the Confederacy and his immortal past reputation. To be mistaken in your foe and then conquered is a great trial. Deceived in an enemy—and defeated by an expected easy prey. This is the Great Chieftan's (sic) fate, and a hard one it must be to so successful a general.[102]

Still, Sener thought that if Lee could hold on for the next three months, the Confederacy had a chance to win the war. He conjectured again that Grant was getting desperate. "In place of the former cool, cunning calculations made to insure our self-destruction, signs of restlessness appear," he wrote. "Little more is required than to hold this situation firmly . . . "[103] His next letter painted the situation as dire. He wrote, "Atlanta has fallen; Forts Powell, Morgan and Gaines have been surrendered into the hands of the enemy, and Jack Morgan is dead. Truly, misfortunes never come alone. But super-add to these reverses the rejoicing which rescind throughout the entire North, and bear in mind that the enemy announce large accretions to their military numbers, and you have the military situation."[104]

Ruins of Fredericksburg. Courtesy of the Library of Congress

If more men were found to serve in the Army of Northern Virginia, Sener believed the situation could be reversed. Men detailed to jobs in the quartermaster, commissary, medical, and ordnance services should be sent to the front. He called for negroes and disabled men to take those positions. Without those new troops, the war could be lost, Sener predicted. "Shall General Lee be reinforced by men, or shall this army, worn with the fatigue and exhaustion of a long and bloody conflict, be forced, in the hour of its triumph, to lose the price of victory for a lack of men?" he demanded.[105]

Sener did not write again until early November when he filed two dispatches before his stories suddenly disappeared from the *Dispatch*'s columns. His last two stories focused on the occasional skirmishing around Petersburg and the preparations for winter quarters. "The campaign of sixty-four, in my opinion, has ended," he wrote. "There may be a few more 'reconnaissances,' a dash or a sally, but the stubborn fighting is over." The soldiers were not wanting for food, shelter, or clothing, Sener reported, and the horses had forage. "The Government seems to be doing better than ever before," he wrote.[106]

One historian suggests that Sener was one of the more significant correspondents for the Confederacy, and that assessment seems to fit.[107] Sener was not in the field the entire war, and much of his correspondence was written from his home, but his proximity to all the important events in the war in the Eastern theater gave him a front-row seat from which to witness the desperate fighting and devastation. He reported what he observed and experienced with grace, dignity, and, for the most part, a commitment to truth and accuracy.

Sener rarely took the time in his dispatches to indulge in reflection, but one exception addresses what Sener saw as the role of the war correspondent. In mid-August 1863, as he was covering the return of Lee's army from its failed invasion of Maryland and Pennsylvania, he shared with his readers the value of war correspondents to Confederate society. He wrote that the utility of war correspondents is "not so much to give a great amount of news as to give accurate news." There were, he speculated (wrongly), only four paid correspondents with the Army: Peter W. Alexander who wrote primarily for the *Savannah Republican*; "S" of the *Atlanta Southern Confederacy* (probably its editor, James Henly Smith); "Y" of the *Dispatch*, whose identity is unknown; and himself. "The letters of these gentlemen, of course excluding myself, are valuable, not because they fill their respective papers with rumors, speculations, and suggestions; but because they approximate to accurate recitals of actual events, which ought to be known. It is better to have one truthful fact than five hundred reports from reliable gentlemen."[108]

For the most part, Sener declined to publish rumor, and he was diligent about checking facts, as best he could, given the confusion and chaos of war. Journalism appears to have been a good career for Sener, and he prospered during the time he worked in the newspaper industry. According to the Fredericksburg tax records for 1860 and 1867, Sener's estate increased across those years from a value of $30 to nearly $900. During the postwar years included in that span, Sener managed the *Fredericksburg Ledger*, a postwar revival of the city's former newspaper. He associated the newspaper with the Republican Party and ran it from 1865 until 1872.[109]

Sener served as a delegate to the Republican National Convention in 1872, the same year he was elected to Congress.[110] He served a two-year term but was defeated for re-election by Beverly B. Douglas of the Conservative Party. During his term, Sener served as chair of the Justice Department's Expenditure Committee and led an unsuccessful effort to get Congress to pay for the monument on the grave of Mary Washington, the mother of George Washington.[111]

In 1879, President Rutherford B. Hayes nominated Sener to be chief justice of the Wyoming Territorial Supreme Court. The *Decatur* (Illinois) *Daily Republican* commented that Sener's "nomination occasions some surprise."[112] The paper did not explain this statement, but perhaps it was because Sener was not from Wyoming and had never been a judge. The Senate approved his nomination within a few days, and Sener held the office for five years.[113] In 1884, a group of ranchers petitioned President Chester A. Arthur to remove Sener, who had returned an unpopular decision in a lawsuit favoring Wyoming farmers over ranchers. The *New York Times* reported that Virginia's senators "were not pleased with the displacement of Judge Sener, whose retention had been promised to them."[114] The *Times* had published a story the previous week and argued that Sener was a good judge who ought to retain his office.[115]

After President Arthur removed him from office, Sener returned home and took up law practice in Washington, D.C. He never married and lived quietly for the rest of his life. In an ironic twist, Sener was appointed in 1899 as an honorary member of the Society of the Army of the Potomac, the Union army commanded by Ulysses S. Grant, and the army that Sener had covered for the *Dispatch*. He died in 1903 and is buried in the Fredericksburg City Cemetery.

27

John R. Thompson:
A Poet Makes His Impact as "Dixie"

Janice Ruth Wood

"Could you conquer us, Men of the North?" John R. Thompson asked in one of his poems that appeared in the *Raleigh* (North Carolina) *Daily Register* as the Civil War got under way in May 1861.

> Could you bring desolation and death on our homes as a flood—
> Can you hope the pure lily, Affection, will spring
> From ashes all reeking and sodden with blood?[1]

With its timeliness and motifs in current events and, more specifically, the Civil War, verses such as this led a biographer of Thompson to describe him as "a poet in journalism and something of a journalist in poetry."[2] He has been portrayed as slight in frame with blue eyes, chestnut hair, brown beard and mustache, and a distinctive manner of dress called "elegant" and "fastidious." Terms used to describe his penchant for silk handkerchiefs scented with cologne and fashionable pantaloons include "dandy" and "a tendency toward foppery."[3] He was called personable with a highly social nature.[4]

Thompson's dual careers as journalist and poet blossomed in Southern newspapers during the war. In regular correspondence that he contributed to the *Memphis Daily Appeal* and poems that appeared periodically in various publications, he focused on war-related issues, events, and personalities surrounding the swirl of his social life in Richmond, Virginia.

The Confederate capital city remained Thompson's favorite place throughout his life. He regretted having to leave his home state of Virginia and city of Richmond, where he served as the city's poet laureate. He loved the city all the more for the losses it suffered during the war. Born there on October 23, 1823, he was named John Reuben by parents who originally came from New York and New Hampshire.[5] Happiest when working in Richmond, he ventured out only when

John R. Thompson, correspondent for several
Virginia newspapers and the Press Association of
the Confederate States of America. Courtesy of the
Virginia Historical Society

compelled for employment or for warmer climates to treat the tuberculosis that
eventually claimed his life in 1873. Fittingly, he was laid to rest in Richmond.

Much of what is known today about Thompson comes from the University
of Virginia, where he wrote for a literary journal as a student and earned a law
degree in 1845. Thompson's poetry, counted among the best of the school's literary graduates, was compiled in 1920 by librarian John S. Patton, who added
a comprehensive biographical sketch. In 1979, Gerald Garmon produced a biography,[6] and other researchers added more insights into his life and work.
Sources covering Thompson's multifaceted career include encyclopedias of
prominent Southern writers (Hubbell,[7] Link,[8] Manly,[9] and Flora and Vogel[10]),
a book on Southern war correspondents (Andrews[11]), the history of the *New
York Post* where Thompson worked as a literary editor and critic (Nevins[12]), and

a history of the *Memphis Daily Appeal*, the newspaper that carried his stories during the Civil War (Ellis[13]).

When Thompson began work as a correspondent for the *Appeal* in 1861, he had already distinguished himself in literary circles as the editor of the *Southern Literary Messenger* in Richmond and *Southern Field and Fireside* in Augusta, Georgia. He had been practicing law for two years in Richmond when he purchased the *Southern Literary Messenger* in 1847. Although he hoped to combine his two interests, the magazine eventually demanded his full attention and he abandoned the law. For 13 years, Thompson filled the *Messenger* with poetry, including his own, and other fiction that established his reputation as an influential editor and critic. At the *Messenger*'s helm, he groomed Southern poets Henry Timrod and Paul Hamilton Hayne and associated with popular writers in New York literary circles and the South. Thompson contributed poetry to other magazines, such as *Harper's* and the *Knickerbocker*, and broadened his contacts in 1854 when he spent six months in London and other European cities, sending travel articles and poetry to the *Messenger*.[14] In *A Souvenir of Zurich*, some of the world's most scenic views paled alongside the enticing woman at the center of the poem.

> Away in the distance, the Alps in the glow
> Of morning, lay shiningly crested with snow;
> But the lake how insipid, the landscape how flat,
> Compared with the object which vis-à-vis sat![15]

Established in Richmond by Thomas W. White in August 1834, the *Messenger* emerged as a major voice of the South, with its stature elevated by the presence of a previous editor, Edgar Allan Poe.[16] Thompson continued to publish Poe's work in the *Messenger*, working closely with him. Later in life, Thompson drew on the relationship for a lecture he presented around the country, titled "The Genius and Character of Edgar Allan Poe" and for a biography of Poe.[17]

Kindred spirits, Poe and Thompson shared a vision of the *Messenger* becoming a national rather than merely Southern publication and a hope of steering it away from political debate despite growing tensions leading up to the war. In his column, dubbed the "Editor's Table," Thompson wrote: "We have endeavoured [sic] to cultivate kindly feelings between the two divisions of the country, believing that in the Republic of Letters at least there should be no strifes and bickerings."[18]

Yet Thompson remained sensitive to the image of the South portrayed for Northern audiences. He condemned Harriet Beecher Stowe's classic novel *Uncle Tom's Cabin* as a vicious attack on the Southern way of life he so admired. But Thompson never defended slavery. He wrote, "Never before have the forces of fanaticism been so banded together to compass the destruction of Southern interests."[19]

Aware of the *Messenger*'s responsibility to represent the South, Thompson also recognized the toll it was taking on his life. In his own words, the *Messenger* "proved to be a dead loss to me" with all the time and money he had invested.[20]

> I have sunk so far $5,000 in endeavoring to give the Southern people a magazine worthy of their fame and their intellectual standing . . . I think it merits a better fate than bankruptcy, while thousands of dollars are spent by Southern men to pay Northern magazines to abuse them . . . Shall it die, to the shame of the Southern people? The *Messenger* is almost gone. I look into the future to see nothing but disaster. My affairs are really so much embarrassment that the sale of my library hangs over me like an impending doom . . .[21]

Reluctant as always to leave Richmond and his close circle of friends, Thompson sold the *Messenger* in 1860 and accepted the editorship of *Southern Field and Fireside*, based in Augusta, Georgia, on conditional terms. For a salary of $2,000, he would edit the periodical that combined the concerns of a farm and home journal with a literary magazine for one year unless a better opportunity arose. Finding the Georgia heat oppressive, he survived on "uniformly temperate habits and daily use of the cold bath," as he wrote to a friend.[22] The arrangement ended later the same year.

Back in Richmond, Thompson found work close to home. He turned down a suggestion by the *Baltimore American* that he serve the Commonwealth of Virginia as assistant secretary and state librarian. His precarious health kept him out of military service.[23] However, the war had transformed Richmond into a major news center for the South, and newspapers across the Confederacy clamored for information.

Thompson turned to reporting and wrote and edited for a number of publications, including the *Southern Illustrated News* and the *Richmond Record.* But he earned a broader reputation as a correspondent for the *Memphis Daily Appeal,*[24] today called the *Commercial Appeal.* He ranked among the best correspondents in the South, matching the finest reporters in the Washington press corps.[25] Exactly how or why Thompson became affiliated with the *Appeal* is open to speculation, but the partnership produced mutual benefits. Thompson found employment that kept him in the city he loved while the newspaper acquired the dependable services of a seasoned writer and editor well-connected to members of the Confederacy's administration. An *Appeal* editor considered Thompson a "well-informed gentleman of talent and extended political information."[26]

Established in 1841 at the western end of Tennessee on the Mississippi River, the *Appeal* took seriously the challenge of covering the Civil War. Its editors, John McClanahan and husband and wife Benjamin and America Dill, helped organize the Press Association of the Confederate States of America but also sought the exclusive services of its own reporters. Not even the Union occupation of Memphis from 1862 to 1865 stilled its pro-Confederacy voice. Editors moved the operations and continued publishing from other locations: first Grenada, Mississippi; later the Mississippi towns of Jackson and Vicksburg; Montgomery, Alabama; Atlanta; and, lastly, Macon, Georgia, and back in Montgomery, Alabama.[27] Thompson saluted the newspaper's persistence in an 1863 column.

> The indomitable energy manifested by you, Messrs. Editors, in maintaining the publication of the *Appeal*, in the face of all the difficulties and discouragements which have beset you since your departure from Memphis has called forth the admiration of your brethren of the press here, and must satisfy the Southern public that your paper is an institution, exempt from the ordinary mutations of time and circumstances. Like the king, in the contemplation of law, the *Appeal* never dies, from Memphis to Grenada, and from Grenada to Jackson, and last of all from Jackson to Atlanta, out of Tennessee into Mississippi and out of Mississippi into Georgia your migrations have been unexempted in the American history of newspaperdom.[28]

One of the *Appeal*'s most widely read columnists was "Dixie," the pen name that Thompson used. Other correspondents aspired to his success.[29] Thompson began submitting letters from Richmond in mid-1861 and continued through mid-1864. He first tested another pen name, "Virginius," but abandoned it, possibly because it could be ridiculed.[30] In fact, letters from Virginius appeared in the *Appeal* about a month before Dixie replaced it. The columns commonly ran on the paper's second page under the heading "From the Seat of War in Virginia" but occasionally appeared elsewhere.[31]

Thompson's letters were susceptible to the same mishaps that befell all newspaper columns. It took up to three weeks for some of Thompson's letters to arrive in the mail from Richmond, tending the contents more toward observations and features than so-called breaking news from the battle zones.[32] The design of the newspaper was so poor that one of the "Dixie" letters ran as a single paragraph that filled three columns of the paper.[33] On another occasion, Thompson complained that a typo had altered his meaning. He had intended a line to read as "O, for a *Juvenal* to satirize the vices of the day!" and was horrified when it ran as "O, for a *journal* to satirize the vices of the day!" [emphases added].[34]

Thompson's descriptive language was easy to spot in the *Appeal*. The vices of the day that he observed among members of the military and the public drew his attention and the descriptive power of his pen. Known as a teetotaler, Thompson wrote that Confederate legislators in Richmond would be distraught that the price of brandy had risen to $150 a gallon. He warned that the "chain-lightning, blue-ruin, liquefied fire" found in Confederate camps would doom the South to losing the war. However, Confederate troops held no monopoly on whiskey. Thompson wrote that battle was being waged by "two great armies largely made up of drunken soldiers, led by reeling generals."[35]

He also warned about the demoralizing effect of gambling—a "curse as intolerable as bad money," using Washington, D.C., as an example. Gambling had increased near Capitol Hill while Congress was in session, especially since Lincoln had become president. "[F]or the sake of the purity of the Confederate government, of good morals, and of national decency, let us hope that stringent measures will be adopted for the suppression of this vice at *our* Capital," he wrote.[36]

Imagery was just as important in Thompson's journalism as in his poetry. In reports to the *Appeal*, he created mental pictures for his readers of the sights, sounds, tactile experiences, and internal sensations of everyday life in Richmond, where key decisions were being made for the Confederacy. He reported on the intense summer heat.

> Since August came in, the sun has been increasing his rays with every reappearance, and is now blazing down upon us as if he were about to take matters to himself and kill all the armies in the field with the terrific power of his noontide ray. It is in vain that the Virginians suggest that the oppressive warmth of our current August is only a meteorological expression of the ardent sympathy of the Old Dominion, with the cotton states of the Confederacy.[37]

Thompson also noted the effects of heavy rainfall: "Weeping skies and muddy streets, encampments drenched with water and roads absolutely impassable to the army trains. [It will be some time] before our war dogs can shake off the moisture from their hides, rush again to the fight."[38]

On the streets of war-torn Richmond, a sense of anticipation was palpable at times, which influenced how news was reported and later recorded in history, as Thompson wrote:

> It is well for us, perhaps, that we have had two or three dull days, for had the intense excitement of the earlier part of the week been kept up by the news of further operations in the field, brain fevers might have prevailed to an alarming extent. As it is, an opportunity has been affording the public mind to calm down into a healthy condition.[39]

Thompson described the "immense mass of facts" that had been accumulated by reporters covering the battles, "from which it will be the duty of the historian to write out an intelligible narrative of events of the day. The official account would be read by thousands, with the greatest interest, but it has not yet been presented to the world, and for reasons satisfactory to the War Department at least may not be for some time."[40]

On one of those occasions when facts were hard to come by, Thompson acknowledged that rumors were easier to compile than facts: "We have no news. In the lack of this, a spurious kind is manufactured and supplied in any quantity

Skeletons lie abandoned in the woods in the Federal lines on the north side of the Orange Plank Road. The site was part of the Wilderness battlefield. Courtesy of the Library of Congress

to suit the credulous at every street corner. Sensation items, such as would make the fortune of an unscrupulous press in a large city, are in everybody's mouth."[41]

Thompson's professional and personal associations with Confederate leaders gave him insights into their activities and character, insights that he folded into his reports and verses. Written in London, his poem, "Lee to the Rear," commemorated the general during the 1864 Battle of the Wilderness.

> Not far off in the saddle there sat,
> A grey-bearded man in a black slouched hat;
> Not much moved by the fire was he,
> Calm and resolute Robert Lee.[42]

Thompson also wrote admiringly of Lee for the *Appeal*. The correspondent was impressed with Lee's ability to keep his thoughts and plans to himself.

His life, since he assumed the chief command of the Virginia forces, has been a model of soldierly patience and energy and watchfulness. Six o'clock in the morning has seen him regularly enter his office, which with rare exceptions, he has not left, save at meal times, till eleven at night. A man of few words, of unvarying courtesy, but of a singularly cold and distant manner, he has kept his own counsels with more than the impenetrable secrecy of Louis Napoleon, and no one has dared to trifle with his time upon unimportant or frivolous missions. If the visitor had business, he was requested to state it in the briefest or most direct way; if he came through sheer curiosity to see the man, or converse with him idly about public affairs, Gen. Lee excused himself so promptly and coolly that he never ventured to call again.[43]

Confederate officer J.E.B. Stuart developed a friendship with Thompson, but the personal alliance did not prevent Dixie from criticizing Stuart in print. On one occasion, he blamed Stuart when his soldiers were "disgracefully surprised" because his head had been turned by feminine admirers and flattering press accounts.[44]

However, he rose to Stuart's defense in another report: "He gave the Yankee cavalry a very heavy check and undoubtedly prevented their advance . . . where they might have inflicted upon us grievous injury."[45] When Stuart died in 1864, Thompson honored him with a poem, published in the *Richmond Examiner*.

And thus our Stuart at this moment seems,
To ride out of our dark and troubled story,
Into the region of romance and dreams,
A realm of light and glory.[46]

He fed his readers' hunger for news about their leaders, including Confederate President Jefferson Davis. Thompson socialized with Davis, recording an entry in his diary about a dinner with the leader in 1864.[47] Nonetheless, Thompson wrote about the Confederacy's growing dissatisfaction with Davis in one of his *Appeal* reports.

Strange to say, there has been no popular demonstration of welcome since his arrival. Whether it be because the people of Richmond are so cold and undemonstrative by nature, or because they are not in the best humor with his Excellency . . . your correspondent will not hazard conjecture.[48]

In a column reporting a rumor that Davis himself had made propositions for peace to the "reigning despotism at Washington," Thompson complimented the president's restraint at putting on a public show when the Confederacy moved its leader into a new home in Richmond in 1861.[49] Thompson contrasted the presidential styles of the Southern and Northern chief executives: "No announcement has yet been made of special events set apart, and I trust there will be none. While the war lasts, this pomp and ceremony may be left to his apeship in the White house at Washington,"[50] an apparent criticism of Lincoln, also calling him an "insensate, vulgar tyrant in Washington whose stolidity has brought sorrow and desolation upon the land."[51]

Thompson also invoked the name of Andrew Jackson, another former president, and one of particular interest to his readers in Tennessee. Known as "Old Hickory," the military hero of the War of 1812 lay buried at his home in Nashville. Reports had surfaced in 1861 that a Confederate cabinet position would soon be opening, and Thompson suggested to his readers that Jackson's home state deserved a prominent voice in the administration of Southern government.[52] Residents of the Volunteer State may have needed bolstering, for Tennessee had seceded from the Union just one month earlier, as Thompson noted.[53]

Thompson's accounts of Richmond life for readers still demonstrate the war's drastic impact and the colorful style of his writing. "Except for wagons and the occasional movements of troops our streets are as dull as the broad dusty road that leads through a county court house, and the bustling, active capital of three weeks ago seems, by some spell, to have been provincialized."[54] Thompson observed:

> . . . groups of excited men at every corner; dense crowds before the bulletin boards of the newspaper offices; long lines of army wagons rattling over the clamorous pavements; here and there, an officer in a smart, fresh uniform, in strange juxtaposition and contrast with a knot of pallid, ragged soldiers whom the bright sun had tempted to stroll out of the hated hospital; couriers, covered with the dust of the road, on broken down horses in feeble gallop towards the War Department.[55]

Richmond residents found their lifestyle changing with the scenery around them. Thompson reported on shortages in housing and other basic necessities. "The scanty supply of coal has already deprived us of gaslight in the streets and thoroughfares, and the dearth of provisions is attested in the almost fabulous prices of all articles of daily consumption," he wrote in 1862.[56]

Government activities complicated everyday life. Thompson told the story of local women staging a "somewhat senseless panic" in April of 1863 after the secretary of war seized all barrels of flour for army use. It took an appearance by Jefferson Davis himself, who threatened gunfire from the militia, to quiet the protesters demanding food. When Thompson filed a news story on the resulting bread riot, the War Department stopped the unflattering portrayal from being transmitted.[57] Additionally, railroad travel was suspended in 1864 as troops moved through the area, and privately owned horses and vehicles were pressed into use for military purposes.[58]

As public morale sagged in Richmond, Thompson expressed contempt for "craven souls" who frightened residents with thoughts of their own soldiers abandoning them to Yankees about to enter the city. Outside Richmond, he

Confederate winter quarters at Centreville, Virginia, in 1862. Courtesy of the
Library of Congress

reported, vandals "committed the most wanton outrages wherever they went."[59]
Richmond public passages displayed incongruous sights: "One or two stabbings
in the streets and numerous little evening parties have marked the Christmas
week, which will be set down as altogether the dullest within memory."[60]

Witnessing the devastation of battle and relaying it to readers of the *Appeal* became even more challenging in 1862 when Confederate General Joseph
Johnston issued an order banishing reporters from the lines of the Army of the
Potomac.[61] However, descriptions of the battlefields in the aftermath of war remained unrestricted, and Thompson wrote about a field that lay quiet afterward
"as if [Union Gen. George] McClellan had carried off his troops to the moon."[62]
Prisoners of war arriving from the battlefield after the Battle of Fair Oaks in
early June 1862 "bore themselves with no little insolence, and despite their bedraggled and soiled condition made no mean appearance," he wrote.[63]

Visiting Centreville, a town near Richmond that stood in the path of war
during both battles of Manassas, Thompson saw:

> . . . a long struggling street with dilapidated houses at considerable intervals, the
> roadway very much obstructed by rocks . . . camps all around, horses hitched to
> every rail of the tumble-down fences . . . small specimens of "peculiar institu-
> tion," other "contraband of war" peddling chickens and chestnuts . . . Never was

a picture of war so peaceful—never was a region which seemed like a dream of peace so full of warlike images and suggestions.[64]

Thompson had traveled to Centreville in October 1861 for a presentation of flags to the Virginia regiments in the Army of the Potomac after the Federal retreat of First Manassas, a ceremony and location that stirred his inner bard: "The air was balmy, the sky a tender blue, the sunshine just that rich golden flood which, like the imagination of the poet, converts all it rests upon into splendor."[65]

Thompson expressed concern that Southern soldiers and the Confederate cause were being jeopardized on the battlefield by confusion over flags. Especially at Manassas, the Confederate flag not only resembled the Union flag too closely, he wrote, but had been duplicated by Northern soldiers as a hoax. The solution, Thompson thought, was to fly regimental flags, which were more individualized and harder to copy.[66]

Readers in Tennessee craved news about troops from the Volunteer State, so Thompson worked exhaustively to compile the names of 174 casualties from the 14th Tennessee known to be among more than 900 soldiers buried in mass graves. He endured hospital scenes so gruesome and toiled so diligently to help identify the bodies that he briefly passed out, according to a history of the *Memphis Daily Appeal*. Yet his health rallied sufficiently for him to report Lee's efforts to drive Federal troops away from Richmond in the Seven Day Campaign. He recovered to write: "Nothing could exceed the desolation of the country. Fences torn down, wheat fields trodden under foot, farm houses and comfortable dwellings abandoned."[67]

Needs were dire among soldiers for better food, clothing, and pay, especially as harsh winter weather rapidly approached, and in 1861 Thompson urged relief efforts with patriotic fervor.

> Now there is no danger that too large a supply of clothing will be furnished. Let us, therefore, all go to work to give something. There is not a homestead in the South which cannot furnish two pairs of warm yarn socks. Few families cannot afford to provide a serviceable blanket. Coats and overcoats can also be made of excellent quality at the domestic fireside. The great and distressing want will be shoes . . .
>
> Our fathers at Valley Forge crimsoned the snows of the revolution with the blood of their lacerated feet, and the sons of the South are not so degenerate that they would not march unshod over ice to fight the enemies of their country, if the worst should come, but the worst must not come.[68]

Thompson expressed concern again for the material needs of Confederate troops when he told a lighter story in 1862. "Folly and extravagance have not ceased with the war," he wrote. "I heard of a young Richmond belle, yesterday, just about to be married, who paid $85 for one bonnet, $50 for a second, and $45 for a third, for her nuptials. This is none of Dixie's business, but the young bride had far better have given two-thirds of the money to cover the feet of the soldiers than her own pretty head."[69]

As the war sputtered to a close late in 1864, so did the need for news coverage in Richmond. Employment possibilities turned sour again for Thompson, whose health was feeble. He was replaced at the *Appeal* by George W. Bagby, Jr., who was a correspondent for a number of southern newspapers, including the *Charleston Mercury*. Tapping into pro-Confederate sentiment in England, Thompson decided to pursue employment across the Atlantic. He slipped through the Federal blockade at Wilmington, North Carolina, and sailed to England to join the staff of *The Index*, a newspaper produced in London by the Confederacy. Thompson worked there for two years.[70] His contributions to London magazines, including *Punch*, brought him into contact with literary notables such as Thomas Carlyle, William Thackeray, and Alfred Lord Tennyson.[71] While in Europe, Thompson corresponded briefly for the *Louisville Journal* and the *New Orleans Picayune*. Thompson's location in England would have made it easier for him to write for newspapers like those, which were in Federally-held territory. The London years brought happiness, but nothing kept his mind off his homeland. Tellingly, he recorded in a diary, "I envy everyone going home. I long to see old Virginia. I love her deeper for her impoverishment."[72] Thompson's home state again came to mind when he entered his thoughts on April 26, 1865, upon hearing the news of John Wilkes Booth's assassination of President Lincoln.

> I fear the mind of Europe will be easily persuaded that Booth was prompted to commit the horrible crime by Confederates. I was especially pained to learn that he profaned the motto of Virginia, "Sic Semper Tyrannis," by shouting it from the stage just before making his escape.[73]

Back in the United States in 1867, Thompson turned northward to New York, where he worked for the *Albion*, a pro-British weekly for a colony of 25,000 transplanted Southerners.[74] Thompson acquired his last major position as literary critic for the *New York Post*, edited by William Cullen Bryant. Allan Nevins, who wrote a history of the *Post*, ascribed to Bryant an understanding of Thompson, noting that the editor assigned his critic no books that insulted his Southern sentiments. Nevins described Thompson as one of the most likable members of the *Post* staff who received many male visitors from Virginia. Although he often visited in Bryant's home, Thompson made no lasting impact on the newspaper. His rapidly failing health and liberal doses of whiskey prescribed by his doctor frequently kept him out of the office.[75]

Thompson suffered serious disappointments in attempts to publish books of his work. The first setback came in the 1850s when fire at a publishing house destroyed a travel book he had written. Later, war conditions prevented Thompson and another writer from following through on plans to produce an anthology titled *Poets and Poetry of the South*. Next, a joint poetry collection that he and Henry Timrod compiled mysteriously disappeared on its way to a London publisher during the war. The final blow struck shortly before his death, when an associate misplaced another set of Thompson's poetry marked for publication.

One of Thompson's best-known poems, "Ashby," was written for a friend's funeral. The hero, like the poet, remained a loyal son of Virginia all his life and was laid to rest beneath his home state's soil. The poem, which ran in a Little Rock, Arkansas, newspaper in 1866,[76] might well have been included in the services for Thompson seven years later.

> Be strong, my friend, these days of doom
> Are but the threads of darkest hue
> That daily enter to renew
> The warp of the eternal loom.
> And when to us it shall be given
> In joy to see the other side,
> These threads the brights shall abide
> In the fair tapestries of heaven.
> There, throughout the coming ages,
> When his sword is rust,
> And his deeds in classic pages,
> Mindful of her trust,
> Shall Virginia, bending lowly,
> Still a ceaseless vigil holy,
> Keep above his dust.

Thompson escaped harsh New York winters with visits to Cuba, Mexico, and the Bahamas. He was returning from Colorado when he suffered his final bout of illness. He made it back to New York City before dying on April 30, 1873.[77] After a well-attended service there, the body was returned to Richmond where a committee of the Virginia press, bar, and University of Virginia alumni associations planned tributes. They held a final service for Thompson at St. Paul's Church, where the poet and journalist had worshipped with the likes of Robert E. Lee and Jefferson Davis. He was buried in Hollywood Cemetery near the grave of his friend, J.E.B Stuart. In granite, Thompson is praised as "the graceful poet, the brilliant writer, the steadfast friend, the loyal Virginian, the earnest and consistent Christian."[78]

Aside from his struggle with tuberculosis, little information has been recorded about Thompson's personal life.[79]

28

Virginia: "From a Lady Correspondent"

Debra Reddin van Tuyll

Like most Civil War correspondents, "Virginia" of the *Mobile Advertiser and Register* wrote under a pseudonym to protect her identity. Unlike most of her fellow chroniclers, however, there is some question as to whether she actually meant to become a correspondent. The answer hinges on whether Virginia-the-war-correspondent was the author of a letter that appeared in the August 17, 1861, *Mobile Advertiser and Register* under the signature, Virginia.

The letter was specifically written to address rumors then circulating in Mobile that wrongly accused Norfolk and its citizens of being unenthusiastic about the Southern revolution. "I have been very much grieved [unreadable word] to hear a number of unjust charges brought against my native State—especially the city of Norfolk," the writer complained.

"If you will allow me the space in your paper, I should like to state a few facts bearing upon these charges."[1] The letter decisively addressed charges that two-thirds of Norfolk's residents were abolitionist in sentiment, that men from that city were not volunteering for military service, and that citizens had voted against secession. Virginia contended that none of that was true and argued that the vast majority of residents of her city favored secession and that Norfolk citizens had cast only three votes against the secession referendum. Two of those ballots had been cast by persons who left the city in the course of the next 24 hours and the third by a man 80 years old, deaf, and almost blind, and "a man remarkable from his youth for 'always being on the other side,' in every manner."[2] Further, the author argued, more Norfolk residents were serving in the Confederate military than was the case for many other places. Virginia offered the following statistics to document her contention:

> Norfolk has now about 15,000 inhabitants. Of these, 5,000 at the least are connected with the service of the Confederacy, in the Navy, or Navy Yard, where they cannot be spared. From the remaining 10,000, after fitting out four or five privateers manned principally from Norfolk—forming a home guard of their old

Norfolk, Virginia. *Harper's Weekly*, April 19, 1862. Courtesy of Rare Books and Special Collections, University of South Carolina Libraries

men, and furnishing an extra police force—they have furnished and fitted out eleven volunteer companies for the war. Had the whole South furnished as large a proportion of its population for our army, it would this day number fully 800,000 men, instead of 200,000 or 300,000, as it really does.[3]

The author continued: "From her very situation, Virginia must be the battle-field on which the common rights of the South are to be defended and our common liberties won; and when the war is ended, history will show, I doubt not, that no State in the South has done more or suffered as much in the common cause as Virginia."[4]

This letter seems very much to be one written with a single purpose in mind: to challenge imputations upon the honor and character of the citizens of Virginia. The gender of its author is ambiguous, despite the pseudonym selected, and this is an important point to consider when examining war correspondence by a female writer during this period. There is no doubt about the gender of the Virginia who reported on Alabama troops in Norfolk for the Mobile newspaper. She was female, and a letter published in the paper on August 18 makes it clear that the female war correspondent Virginia did not volunteer for her assignment. She was recruited by the newspaper. Her letter published that day states that she is accepting a proposal from the editors to supply correspondence.

Entering the city of Norfolk. *Harper's Weekly*, May 24,
1862. Courtesy of Rare Books and Special Collections,
University of South Carolina Libraries

While this question of whether there was one Virginia or two may at first
seem frivolous speculation, it really is not, for it goes to the bigger issue of the
changing role and status of Southern women during the Civil War. A Southern
woman might well have written to a newspaper in a fit of indignation over perceived slights to her city. The Confederacy's other female war correspondent,
Joan, certainly contributed her own diatribes frequently enough. But would a
Virginia woman have stepped so far out of her assigned social place as to offer
to be a war correspondent? Again, Joan did, but Joan was unusual by many standards of the time. The author of the Virginia letters seems more like a woman
who lived by the conventions of the day. It seems likely then that she might, if
asked by an editor, agree to write an occasional letter about the Alabama boys

occupying her hometown, especially if the editor had used his best diplomatic skills to persuade her that she would be doing a service to his readers who were longing for news of their menfolk so far away in Virginia.

An earlier writer has rejected the idea that the August 17 letter was written by a woman. He attributed the letter to "one Norfolk citizen, unidentified" and used the pronoun "he" to refer to the writer.[5] However, elements of the last two paragraphs of the letter strongly hint that the author must have been a woman rather than a man. If the writer was a woman who signed herself "Virginia," it would make sense that the author of the future "Virginia" letters was most likely the same person.

In the next to the last paragraph of the letter, Virginia speculated that the "difficulties that have occurred between members of the 3d Alabama Regiment and citizens of Norfolk" were the result of an all-too-common cause: demon whisky, "that common disturber of the peace."[6] The Alabama soldiers had among their ranks, the August 17 Virginia observed, that certain type of man who existed everywhere: "In every regiment of soldiers, and in every city, there are to be found men who will drink to intoxication when they get the means and opportunity."[7] Nevertheless, the author added, "It is no more fair to judge of the body by the conduct of such members in the one case than in the other,"[8] and this was probably especially true in the case of the 3rd Alabama, which had a reputation for good behavior.[9]

The key element in this paragraph that increases the probability it was written by a woman was the reference to whisky as the source of male misbehavior. True, temperance spirit extended to both men and women in this period, but it was by and large a movement fueled and sustained by women. Further, the inclusion of a qualifier—"but, this doesn't mean all men are drunks"—seems like something a woman would write rather than a man.

Even more telling is the final paragraph of the letter. The writer asks, "I hope I may be excused the attempt to defend the fair name of my native State. A State offering so much in the common cause should be shielded from reproach by all true southern people."[10] The patriarchal nature of antebellum Southern society taught men that they were masters.[11] Someone steeped in that mindset would never have apologized for defending his state. He probably would not apologize for much of anything else, either.

It is understandable why one might think the two Virginias were different writers. For one thing, the letters appeared only a day apart. It would make sense that some time ought to separate letters written several days apart. However, for a variety of reasons, newspapers did not always publish correspondence as soon as it was received. That could easily explain why two letters written by the same person would have been published so close together. It could be, too, that the *Advertiser and Register* waited to publish Virginia's first letter until they had gotten her agreement that her correspondence could be published at all. There was little question that the August 17 letter was intended for publication, but if the paper's editor, former diplomat John Forsyth, wanted to court her as a potential correspondent, he might well have delayed publication of that initial communication.

If the August 17 letter is Virginia's first to the *Advertiser and Register*, she clearly wrote for only one purpose: to defend her home state. There was no overt, nor any *sotto voce*, attempt to garner a correspondence assignment expressed in that letter. The earlier historian who believed there were two Virginias conjectured that there would have been an initial letter from Virginia-the-correspondent offering her services, and it would have been that letter that triggered the letter from the newspaper editor to which Virginia referred in her August 18 letter when she wrote, "Dear Sirs," yours of the 4th inst. came to hand last evening, and I have to thank you for your courteous reply to my communication, for your kind appreciation of my projects, and to express satisfaction respecting your proposal."[12]

Virginia's proximity to troops from Alabama and Mobile would have been one reason the editors asked her to continue writing, but her feisty defense of principles may also have resonated with true Southern partisans like Forsyth and his staff. Whatever their reasons, the request for continued correspondence was made and accepted, and a brief professional relationship began that lasted from August 1861 until early 1862.

Virginia's correspondence has garnered little scholarly attention. J. Cutler Andrews noted her existence in a footnote in his study of Confederate war correspondence, *The South Reports the Civil War*.[13] In the mid-1980s, two Alabama historians compiled Virginia's letters into a published collection.It was this collection that speculated about the existence of two Virginias and also suggested a possible identity for Virginia: Virginia Gordon, daughter of Norfolk banker John D. Gordon.[14] These authors admitted that this identification is entirely speculative. There is no evidence to support the argument other than an unsubstantiated reference in a history of Norfolk.

Whoever she was, Virginia's letters offer a look at who she was as a person. Virginia's anonymity has effectively cloaked her identity, and it has proven impossible thus far to find an actual name for her. However, like any author, her writing reveals as much about her as it does her subject. Consequently, while these words will be speculative, that speculation will be based on the solid evidence provided by Virginia's letters.

Virginia, like another woman correspondent from the South, Joan, offered a uniquely female perspective on the war and the men who fought it, not only because that was her gender but because her sex restricted her vision of the war to what she could see from her front gate. Virginia's letters focused not on battlefield events but on preparations for naval battles and garrisoned troops whose presence was more static than dynamic. She could observe and write about both from that most protected of domains: home. A male correspondent for a Confederate newspaper would have been either a soldier or a professional journalist. In either case, he most commonly would have left home to cover armies in the field and report on frontline actions, the sort of news that readers anxiously awaited. Only one of the known male correspondents, James B. Sener, also a Virginian, had the luxury of sleeping in his own bed for much of the time he covered the Army of Northern Virginia.

However, readers were anxious for another sort of news: how their home-town boys were faring, including those whose duties involved enduring the monotony of camp life, enlivened by the occasional amusement of tying a canteen to an unsuspecting dog's tail or preparing for a Glee Club concert.[15] These were the kinds of cozy war stories most women would encounter, if they encountered camp life at all. Their closest encounter with the actual fighting and horrors would more likely come through the experience of nursing wounded soldiers than from direct battlefield experience. So, Virginia's correspondence, while homely and pedestrian, offers an excellent example of how city women would have experienced the early days of the war.

Although her experiences were similar to those of Joan, another of the Confederacy's women war correspondents, Virginia's manner of expression—and, to some degree, her attitudes—set her apart from Joan. Virginia appears to have fallen into journalistic work by accident, while Joan intentionally approached the *Charleston Courier* about becoming a correspondent in Richmond to help defray her expenses of living away from her South Carolina home.[16] Virginia had other reasons for writing to the Mobile newspaper: She was defending the honor of her state and of her city.

Another difference was that Joan was a devoted, even radical, supporter of the Confederacy who wrote with the intensity, urgency, and fire of an ardent evangelist. Virginia's approach was calmer and more rational, although she, too, supported secession and Southern independence. Virginia was more a journalist and was more likely to observe what was happening around her and convey it dispassionately to her readers. On the other hand, Joan could—and did—fly off into diatribes without ever really paying attention to what was going on around her. Virginia's sentiments, both religious and patriotic (and often intermingled), were every bit as strong as Joan's but she expressed them in a more measured manner.

> God and our Southern cause seem to be the watchword of all among us who feel properly upon the things concerning the times . . . The deep bell in the grey old tower of St. Paul's Church stirs the evening air on Thursdays and Fridays, with the call to pray for those who have gone forth at the call of their country to preserve our rights and privileges and to protect us in our property and homes. The congregation seem fraught with the solemnity of the time, and they seat themselves, and here and there among them we see the varied uniforms of the different

companies of our vicinity. There are some from Lynchburg, some from the several companies of the neighboring low country counties, some from our gallant little cockade city, some from our Metropolis—Still they come—these brave soldiers—groups of them from "the land of sun and flowers." The Empire State of the South sends her sons—Glorious Alabama!—from the ranks of the W.L.D.s, the G.C.G.s, the Cadets and others, hither they come with respectful tread, to join us in the house of God to give thanks for the glorious day of Manassas, to pray for the further success of our armies. North Carolina, too, our Sister State! Her hearts are never wanting for our altars, her arms for our defense![17]

Unfortunately, Virginia revealed even less personal information about herself in her letters than Joan. One of the few possible keys to identifying her is that she wrote that her home was on the same street where Edgar Allen Poe was born. Another was that she attended St. Paul's Episcopal Church.[18] These clues have been insufficient to establish an identification.

Virginia was religious but not so zealously Christian that she denied the existence of all other faith traditions. She was sufficiently open-minded and well-educated to mention pagan religions and Stonehenge in describing the camp.[19] The unit, she wrote, had been wise in its choice of locations: "The camp fires for cooking the evening meal were burning brightly as our party entered, and as the moon rose over the scene, I might, perhaps, have fancied the assemblage sacred to some ancient Druid rites, and attuned my ears to catch the 'Casta Diva' of the fated Norma, but alas for my sentimentality!"[20]

Virginia also had a social conscience and was devoted to the Southern cause. In one of her letters, she praised John R. Hathaway, editor of the *Norfolk Day Book*, for his decision to hire women to work at the newspaper. The paper, she wrote, always hired women instead of men whenever possible for "type-setting and other light work, thus affording means of subsistence to many young girls who, in these troublous times might be wandering homeless and it may be *breadless* [emphasis hers] too, in the streets."[21]

In another letter, she demonstrated her devotion to the South with two anecdotes, one about the removal of the "last relic of Unionism in Norfolk," the removal of a "Bell and Everett flag pole that occupied a conspicuous stand in front of the Custom House," and the other about "A Mrs. _____ of this city, who married here from the North some year or two since." The woman left Norfolk and her husband for a "more congenial atmosphere" but had recently been "returned under escort from Fortress Monroe to some post down the river by four of Lincoln's Lieutenants, one of whom, by the way, is reported to have congratulated her on coming to Norfolk—*the safest place she could find* [emphasis hers]." According to Virginia, Norfolk residents were indignant "that Yankee women should be allowed to go hither and thither in this unrestrained fashion, and I doubt not it will be brought to a full stop here."[22]

In another expression of Southern nationalism, Virginia encouraged Southerners to support their native literary arts. She wrote, "The 'Southern Literary Messenger' for August, has come to us with the usual complement of pleasing matter. The Magazine has peculiar claims upon the people of our Confederacy." The magazine had suffered, though, for its support of the Southern cause, Virginia stated. "Always loyal, nay almost enthusiastic in the advocacy of everything Southern, it *lost ground* [emphasis hers] as far as its subscription list may be considered, by the anticipating position assumed in contemplation of the present crisis, and it now behooves our people—from Maryland to Texas—to place it by their patronage upon a firmer basis than it has ever yet occupied." Virginia encouraged the *Advertiser and Register*'s readers to support the magazine and Southern literary endeavors in general. "Even amid warring armies and cannon's flash we must read, or else we accord the enemy a mighty, gratuitous advantage," she wrote. "They may degrade us more by destroying our literary and educational facilities than by felling our men like forest trees."[23]

Virginia also had a finely tuned sense of humor. She revealed this when she related a story about how the "soldier boys hereabout" plot to get away from camp into town to see the pretty girls.

> At the Artillery camps where horses are employed they say they go to attend to *them* [emphases hers] at night, one branch of which attention is, so themselves report, to take off the *shoes*, so that the next day they can be brought to the blacksmith in the city to have the shoeing done over again. Mr. H. of the Mobile Cadets, (he is French, I think, or rather, of French descent) told me that he could only come to town once in *forty days*, unless he *ran away*. Why! You never try that? I exclaimed. "Yes, indeed!" was the reply, "frequently if not oftener." On the next day, I saw him pass on the street opposite our window, and bow, looking somewhat quizzical. A gentleman from our vicinity visited the Alabamians that afternoon and found Monsieur in the *guard tent*, not saying *pretty words* either.[24]

Despite the incident, Virginia vowed that these "gentlemen of the South" were behaving quite well. She conveyed another humorous story about the work of Norfolk women on behalf of the soldiers encamped there.

> The manufacture of socks for the soldiers is engrossing the attention of our ladies, or such of them as have learned the art of knitting, and can get the material for the work. I believe it has been agreed that every lady in the city shall manufacture one pair—if this is to be the limit, Jack Frost will have a nip to somebody's toes![25]

The main purpose of Virginia's correspondence, however, was to keep Mobile readers informed about the state and experiences of the soldiers they had sent to defend the Old Dominion, and she also revealed something of her kind, compassionate nature in these stories. Virginia went to great lengths to offer reassurances about both the physical and spiritual well-being of the Alabama troops. In several of her early letters, she reported on who had preached most recently in the 3rd Alabama camp and who would be coming to preach and included descriptions of religious services that the men had attended.[26]

Throughout her correspondence, however, Virginia showed true interest and concern over the physical well-being of the troops. In one of her early letters, she described the camp of the 3rd Alabama to give the newspaper's readers a sense of the circumstances in which their soldiers were living. "The Third Alabama Regiment is camped at a distance of about four miles from the city, and about half a mile from Broad Creek," she wrote. "They are located in a beautiful grove, and occupy, certainly, not less than fifty acres of ground." The camp, she added, was on ground that the government had cleared and leveled. There were drainage ditches and wells. The tents were all raised off the ground and had plank floors, many of which were covered with carpets. Further, of the 1,094 (her estimate) men in the unit, only some 25 were in the Norfolk Naval Hospital, but they were doing well "enjoying the salubrious air."[27]

After another visit to the field hospital, Virginia sent an even more encouraging description of the facilities, the layout of the hospital, and the efficiency of the manager. She reported that she "was more than ever impressed with the beautiful adaptation of all its appliances to the wants of the frail in health, and especially the invalid stranger." The hospital had previously been the home of an heiress, Miss Ann Heron. It was spacious and elegant with . . .

> . . . velvety deep green turf, the magnificent oak and horse chestnut trees with their overspreading foliage, and the flower bordered walks—what more delightful spot for a convalescent to indulge in that *dolce far niente* [emphasis hers] that delightful essential to a convalescent state. I happened in while the inmates were taking supper, and the table was set in the marble-tiled hall, with the whitest of cloths, the yellowest and brightest of butter, and the freshest and lightest looking of bread, and Sister Bernard, the presiding genius of the place; well, it is enough to make a sick man well only to see how gently she moves about in her quiet labors of love. There are coming in few patients, comparatively, so Sister B. tells me. A few from the Alabama and Carolina regiments, each, make up the present sum of inmates.[28]

In another story, she reported that the Alabama camp had become "a place of resort for our city people" because of the "courtesy and affability with which they are met by the gallant Alabama boys."[29] Trips to the camp were so popular, in fact, that a steamer made three trips daily there and back.[30]

Virginia wrote especially enthusiastically after a fund-raising concert by the Regimental Glee Club: "Hurrah for the 'Alabama boys' in general and the 3d Regiment especial! They paid over to the ladies of the 'Soldier's Aid' Society, the sum of $512.62, as the proceeds of their concert, to which Hon. J. Gill Shorter, Governor elect of your State, added a donation of $20," she reported. The concert had also encouraged "some other of the young sons of Mars" to offer a concert themselves. "These performances and the preparation for them, afford an agreeable variety from the monotony of camp life, they are some recreation for our anxious non-belligerent citizen, and, if last mentioned, not least in importance, they will result in the accomplishment of many an act of sweet charity." [31]

Virginia also wrote about individual soldiers. She reported, for example, that Private Cleveland[32] of the Mobile Rifles, 3d Regiment, had been sent to a company at Manassas because he was "suffering from the effects of measles."[33] Sometimes, however, Virginia had much sadder information to report, and on those occasions, she did so with great compassion. She chose her words for the comfort they would bring readers, as in the paragraph she wrote about a soldier's death.

> Private John O'Connor of the Tuskegee Light Infantry, breathed his last on Tuesday at the Hospital of St. Vincent de Paul. Though the severe character of his disease gave no encouragement to home for his recovery, everything which could administer to the comfort of dying man was performed for him by those in charge. The Sisters are indefatigable in their labors for those committed to them. O'Connor was a young man, only twenty-five years of age, and seemed to cling, with all youth's tenacity to the hope of life; and with a soldier's desire to the thought of performing some act of chivalry in his country's behalf.[34]

From time to time, Virginia reported on general news from the Norfolk area, even if that news was that nothing was happening: "Everything is dull in Norfolk at present, Messrs. Editors," she wrote in mid-September, "except that the city and surrounds look refreshed and revived by the recent rains, in fact on Sunday we had almost a flood."[35]

Her correspondence for the *Advertiser and Register* matured across the months Virginia corresponded for the newspaper. Throughout her tenure, her writing focused primarily on matters within a woman's sphere: the physical and religious well-being of others, the experiences of other women, her devotion to national ideals. However, as she gained more experience, and greater confidence, as evidenced by an occasional reference to herself as "your correspondent,"[36] Virginia's subject matter expanded a bit to include tentative forays into military affairs but never to the point of revealing everything she knew. "We must not write everything, however, especially that of an anticipatory nature," she wrote. "Still I should not be surprised at an occasion to write you a news letter very hurriedly on some day ere long."[37] After the Union captured Cape Hatteras, North Carolina, Virginia declined to pass along rumors she was hearing about the military action there. "Reports are promulgated with so little regard to truth in these times of excitement, that it were worse than idle to detail all we hear," she wrote.[38] Joan, too, was a newcomer, but she blithely reported rumor as readily as she reported fact.

When Virginia turned to a military topic, it dealt often with the naval aspects of the war, which distinguished her letters from those of other correspondents who focused primarily on land battles. On one occasion, she described a gun battle between a newly acquired Confederate gunboat and a Union sloop. The gunboat *Patrick Henry* came upon the Union's sloop, the *Savannah*. According to Virginia, each ship fired enthusiastically at the other. She had spoken with a witness to the battle, and he claimed that the *Patrick Henry* had fired 14 shots, all but one of which hit the *Savannah*. The Federals fired back not only from the sloop but also from the shore. The battle would have continued, Virginia speculated, except for the coming of nighttime.[39]

As this passage illustrates, Virginia's writing style changed over the months she worked for the Mobile newspaper. Her efforts at description and scene-setting became more acute and also, in keeping with the tastes of the day, more romanticized. Her description of a ceremony at which the women of Norfolk awarded a flag to the Regiment[40] even dared to make use of the editorial "we," which gave the article a far-fetched and contrived tone.

> The gold-blue haze of the Indian summer is upon us, enveloping trees and house tops, and glorifying with its half cloud, half halo, the spire of St. Mary's and the gray old tower of "Old St. Paul's." The air is balmy as a May breeze, and we hold in strange contrast with this scene of peace the "circumstances of war" about us. The tread of armies and the beat of drum are upon our ear as we write, and the fields about us—far as the eye can reach are bestarred with the white tents of our gallant Southern crusaders. God bless and seed them, one and all—for why should *they* cry "peace! Peace!" when there is no peace!
>
> Today the drum-beat which salutes our ear heralds the movement of your own gallant sons upon our soil—not, God be thanked! To the red field of fight—but younder, (sic) where the green sword welcomes each footfall as the long lines of the military pass into the Academy grounds, they gather to receive the testimonials which woman has prepared to evince her appreciation of their chivalry. I cannot choose but follow! Rest here pen younder is the sword, and I must, at least look—and listen.
>
> Age! They were there—thick as trees in the old primeval forests! Mobile Cadets, Mobile Rifles, Montgomery True Blues, Washington Light Infantry—hosts of others—and an imposing sight they presented.[41]

It is impossible to know much about Virginia as an individual, but even if her name and circumstances were knowable, they would do little to increase the value of her work. Still, her correspondence ought not be dismissed as valueless or consigned to a footnote. She may not have been writing the poignant stories about brave soldiers desperately fighting for an ideal, but Virginia's stories had

Ruins of Norfolk, Virginia Navy Yard. *Harper's Weekly*, April 8, 1865. Courtesy of Rare Books and Special Collections, University of South Carolina Libraries

their own poignancy. Her chronicles of daily life among the 3rd Alabama distinctly portray the monotony of camp life, the lengths to which soldiers would go to relieve the unrelenting boredom of garrison duty, the compelling religious sentiments of the day, and the devotion of so many to so futile, and even unwise, a cause.

Like Joan, Virginia's correspondence was relatively short-lived and, in the greater scope of things, did not compare with the work of the more important male correspondents in keeping readers aware of the progress of the war. By the same token, her stories about the experiences of the 3rd Alabama provided sought-after information. Clearly, if a grandfather shared a letter from his soldier grandson with the *Advertiser and Register*, there was a desire for information from the unit and a willingness to share it. Sociologist Benedict Anderson has theorized that news is one of the primary elements for binding desperate individuals together into a nation. If that is true, Virginia's patriotism and devotion to the Southern cause would also have been a mechanism for forging connections between citizens of the far-flung Confederacy.

Ultimately, those connections were not strong enough to sustain the effort to create a separate Southern union but, as Virginia's correspondence indicates, it was not for lack of devotion and commitment by many to the ideal of a separate Southern nation. It is possible to read Virginia's correspondence as nothing new or different, as being very similar to what one might read in Mary Chesnut's diary or in the letters of other pro-Confederate women. There is one distinction, however—Virginia wrote her letters for publication, and she was persuaded to do so by the exigencies of the time. She was not a woman who would have written for publication in other circumstances.

Her correspondence stands as testimony to the ways in which the Civil War changed social roles for Southern women. Dozens of books have been published on this subject, and, in that way, Virginia is nothing new. By the same token, despite the changing roles for women, few turned to journalism as their chosen way of serving. That means Virginia, a "lady correspondent," was unusual among a very unusual set of women.

Tennessee

Battle of Lookout Mountain. *Harper's Weekly,* November 17, 1863. Courtesy of Rare Books and Special Collections, University of South Carolina Libraries

On the eve of the Civil War, Tennessee was a state divided against itself. The East opposed secession, but the West was firmly in favor. The deciding vote came on June 8, 1861, when middle Tennessee tipped the scales in favor of secession, making it the 11th and last state to secede from the Union.

As the war began, editors and correspondents faced major problems beyond the usual shortages of paper and ink. Since more battles were fought in Tennessee than any other state except Virginia, some editors became nomads who were forced to move from place to place to keep Federals from taking over or destroying their newspapers. The *Memphis Appeal* moved so often to evade Federal troops that it became known as the *Moving Appeal*. The newspaper lost its home base when Federal troops captured Memphis in June 1862, but it steadfastly continued publishing from all over the South.

The *Chattanooga Rebel*, one of the most popular newspapers with Confederate troops, lost its home base when the Federals captured Chattanooga in late 1863. Like the *Appeal*, the *Rebel* moved south with Southern troops as the

Northerners pushed them toward Atlanta just in front of the military assault of General William T. Sherman, whose troops would eventually capture that city.

Henry Watterson, who would become one of the best-known journalists in America after the war, was editor of the *Chattanooga Rebel*, one of the most widely read army newspapers, with a circulation of more than 8,000. When the city was attacked in 1863, Watterson shipped the printing facilities of the *Rebel* into Georgia. He remained with a skeleton crew and published under fire until the city fell, and Watterson and his staff were forced to flee.

Watterson was also one of the many editors and correspondents who ran afoul of Confederate General Braxton Bragg. After Watterson published a steady barrage of criticism and inadvertently confronted him face-to-face at a social gathering, Bragg threatened to exclude the newspaper from the camps and to confiscate copies if Watterson continued as editor. The threat of lost circulation cost Watterson his job, but the *Rebel* continued to publish on the move. It would be published in three states, five towns, and one boxcar traveling with the Confederate armies. Federal troops finally caught up with the newspaper in Alabama where the *Rebel* printing equipment was destroyed in Selma in April 1865.

Watterson continued writing as a correspondent named "Shadow," who wrote for the *Appeal*, but that identity was not discovered until 1996, when computer-assisted analysis offered evidence that he was the mysterious reporter. Of all the correspondents who wrote for the South during the Civil War, Watterson would become the most famous postwar journalist. In the late 19th century and into the 20th century, he became one of the most prominent and influential journalists in the country as editor of the Louisville *Courier-Journal*. By the time of his death in 1921, he had earned a reputation as one of the last great personal journalists.

29

Henry Watterson: Reconstructed Rebel with Many Causes

Patricia G. McNeely

As the four-year-old son of an influential Tennessee congressman, Henry Watterson was "dandled on the lap" of Andrew Jackson.[1] When he was eight years old, Watterson tearfully rushed to the side of his friend John Quincy Adams as the former president lay dying on the floor of the House of Representatives, and as a 21-year-old reporter for the Associated Press, Watterson stood beside Abraham Lincoln when he delivered his inaugural address in March 1861.[2] By the time Watterson died in 1921, he had met and quarreled with almost every president from John Quincy Adams to Franklin D. Roosevelt and he was personally acquainted with dozens of nationally and internationally known celebrities and politicians.

When Watterson became an editor and reporter during the Civil War, he developed a writing style that would be described in later years as personal journalism. His was a voice "crying aloud in the wilderness" of print that reached the hearts of the "boys in the trenches," as well as ordinary readers everywhere, his admirers said.[3] Although he also joined the Confederate Army, Watterson was never destined to be a great soldier. He was not quite five feet tall and weighed only 80 pounds.[4] He was blind in his right eye from a childhood accident and had poor vision in the other from a severe case of scarlet fever.[5] He had also lost part of a thumb in a childhood accident. One of his officers said he often felt Watterson was committing suicide every time he was sent out on a raid.[6] Yet, he was a staff officer at different times for Generals Leonidas Polk and Nathan Bedford Forrest, chief of scouts for General Joseph E. Johnston, and an aide to General John Bell Hood.[7]

Like other war correspondents, Watterson reported anonymously from the field to keep from being shot or imprisoned if captured by the enemy. Although he was captured twice during the war, he was not identified as a reporter and managed to persuade the Federals to release him almost immediately. He

Henry Watterson. Photograph from the Library of Congress

wrote as "Grape" for the *Mobile* (Alabama) *Daily Advertiser and Register* and the *Augusta* (Georgia) *Daily Constitutionalist.* Computer-assisted analysis offered evidence in 1996 of what historians had always suspected: Watterson was very likely the mysterious "Shadow"[8] who wrote sporadically for the *Memphis* (Tennessee) *Daily Appeal.*[9] He may also have used the pen name "Waverly" in some of his work for the *Advertiser and Register.* In addition to his war correspondence, Watterson edited four newspapers at different times during the war, including the *Chattanooga Rebel,* which became a popular and well-read army newspaper. He also edited the *Nashville Banner,* the *Atlanta Southern Confederacy,* and the *Montgomery Mail.*[10]

When the war ended, Watterson made his home in Louisville, Kentucky, where he wasted no time forcing a merger between the *Journal,* which he partly owned, and the rival *Courier.* Riding on the widespread appeal of his strong editorials in the *Louisville Courier-Journal,* he became one of the best-known and most influential journalists in America. He wrote for national publications that included the *Saturday Evening Post, Harper's Monthly, Collier's Weekly,*

Cosmopolitan, and *American Magazine.* During a poker game, the mayor of Louisville started calling him "Marse Henry,"[11] a title Watterson used for two autobiographies that he wrote near the end of his life. After becoming a national celebrity, he was regularly lampooned in editorial cartoons[12] as an old Rebel who played cards, smoked tobacco, played the banjo, brandished pistols, bet on horses, cut shady backroom political deals, and generally continued "to raise hell."[13] He was so well known that a variety of businesses borrowed his name. His fans could belly up to the bar and ask for a shot of Henry Watterson whiskey with a Henry Watterson cigar and could spend the night in the Henry Watterson Hotel in Louisville.[14]

With Henry Grady at the *Atlanta Constitution,* Watterson became a New South editor who supported economic development free from radicalism, and he liked to say that he straddled the journalistic eras between editors defending themselves in duels and defending themselves in libel suits.[15] His half-century reign as one of America's most prominent and powerful journalists overshadowed his war correspondence and the almost forgotten newspapers that he edited in his early 20s. After his death, flags flew at half mast during his funeral in 1922 in Louisville, and the *New York Times* called him the "dean of American journalists."[16]

A son of privilege, Watterson was born on February 16, 1840, next door to a Washington, D.C., print shop during the first congressional term of his father, Harvey Magee Watterson, whose immediate fear was for his son's political future. It was "a bad year for Democrats," he said, and he worried that "the boy will grow up to be a Whig."[17] The family was financially and politically well off because of young Watterson's grandfather, who had amassed a fortune building railroads, and was an early friend and comrade of General Andrew Jackson.[18] In 1843, President John Tyler sent the congressman on a two-year mission to Buenos Aires. Young Henry and his mother, Tabitha Black Watterson, remained in McMinnville, Tennessee, until her husband returned home and reentered politics. In 1845, Watterson was elected to the Tennessee Senate where he served as speaker.[19]

The elder Watterson bought the *Nashville Union* in 1848, a Democratic newspaper that had once been an Andrew Jackson organ. Eight-year-old Henry Watterson received his first taste of journalism hanging around the newspaper office. His father returned to Washington in 1851 as assistant editor of the *Washington Union.* An only child who was often an invalid,[20] Watterson was tutored by his mother until he was 12 years old. He had only four years of formal education at the Academy of the Protestant Episcopal Church in Philadelphia, which he left when he was 16 years old. While he was there, he was editor of the school newspaper for all four years.[21]

The family returned to Tennessee where his father began practicing law. Instead of going to college, the young Watterson was privately tutored because of his poor eyesight. When his father gave him a printing press in the summer of 1856, Watterson started the *New Era*, a single-page broadsheet. He was elated when his first editorial was picked up by the *Nashville American*, the *Washington Union*, and other newspapers on the east coast.[22]

As a teenager, Watterson wrote fiction and poetry under pen names. "Though I wrote verses for the early issues of Harper's Weekly—happily no one can now prove them on me, for even at that jejune period I had the prudence to use an anonym—the Harpers, luckily for me, declined to publish a volume of my poems," he wrote.[23] An accomplished pianist, he briefly found work as a free-lance entertainment critic for the *New York Times*.[24] "In my early life—as it were, my salad days—I aspired to becoming what old Simon Cameron[25] called 'one of those damned literary fellows' and Thomas Carlyle[26] less profanely described as 'a leeterary celeebrity,'" he wrote.[27] Moderately successful but unhappy in New York, he returned to Washington where he moved back into his childhood home in the Willard Hotel and found a job with the *Daily States*.[28] "Finally I gave up fiction and resigned myself to the humble category of the crushed tragi-comedians of literature, who inevitably drift into journalism," he wrote.[29]

In the final countdown toward the Civil War, Watterson also became the Washington correspondent for the *Philadelphia Press* and interviewed John Brown in his prison cell after the raid at Harpers Ferry.[30] After Watterson left the cell, he could not conceal his disgust for Brown and agreed with Lieutenant Jeb Stuart that the prisoner was crazy.[31] Still not believing that war would come, Watterson thought that the repudiation of the Harpers Ferry violence by both sections of the country would allay any threat to the Union.[32]

In the winter of 1860, the need to help support his parents, who by then had lost the family fortune, led Watterson to take on a third job, a position in the Interior Department. Washington was both "stormy and nebulous," he wrote. "Parties were at sea. The Northerners in Congress had learned the trick of bul-lying from the Southerners . . . All of them, more or less, were playing a game. If sectional war, which was incessantly threatened by the two extremes, had been keenly realized and seriously considered, it might have been averted. Very few people believed that it would come to actual war."[33]

When Watterson reported on the convention of border state representatives in Washington, presided over by ex-President John Tyler, he wrote, "It might as well have been held at the North Pole. Moderate men were brushed aside, their counsels whistled down the wind."[34]

In addition to his correspondence for two newspapers and his full-time job with the Interior Department, Watterson was hired by the Associated Press to help cover the March 4, 1861, inauguration of the new president.[35] Lincoln was also staying in an apartment in the Willard Hotel when Watterson called on him to get a copy of the speech. "The President that was about to be seemed entirely self-possessed; not a sign of nervousness and very obliging," Watterson wrote. He accompanied the presidential party from the Senate chamber to the east portico where Lincoln removed his hat to face the vast throng of people in front and below.[36]

> I extended my hand to take [the hat], but Judge Douglas, just behind me, reached over my outstretched arm and received it, holding it during the delivery of the address. I stood just near enough the speaker's elbow not to obstruct any gestures he might make, though he made but few; and then I began to get a suspicion of the power of the man.[37]

When Lincoln finished his inaugural address and the crowd on the east portico began to disperse, Watterson went back into the rotunda with some old friends of his family from Tennessee. "For a little we sat upon a bench, they discussing the speech we had heard," he wrote. "Both were sure there would be no war. All would be well, they thought, each speaking kindly of Mr. Lincoln." However, by then Watterson had changed his mind about the coming conflict. "They were among the most eminent men of the time, I a boy of twenty-one; but to me war seeming a certainty."[38]

A few days after the inauguration, Watterson was offered a job as private secretary to the secretary of war with the rank of lieutenant colonel. Watterson believed the high-ranking officials making the offer were crooks who planned to rob the government and wanted him to be the "confidential middle man." After a sleepless night, he decided to skip his appointment about the job offer and return to Tennessee.[39] "I would go back to my books and my literary ambitions and let the storm blow over," he wrote. "It could not last very long; the odds against the South were too great."[40] He resigned his secure post with the Interior Department, closed his accounts, and made plans to turn his back on Washington and find adventure elsewhere.[41]

When South Carolina left the Union, Watterson did not wholly believe in extreme[42] political positions. He called himself a Constitutional Nationalist and believed all his life in "first the nation and then the state."[43] Soon after Watterson reached Nashville, shots were fired at Fort Sumter in South Carolina in April 1861. Although he never intended to join either army, he was swept up in war fever.

> As well expect a chip on the surface of the ocean to lie quiet as a lad of twenty-one in those days to keep out of one or the other camp. On reaching home I found myself alone. The boys were all gone to the front. The girls were—well, they were all crazy. My native country was about to be invaded. Propinquity. Sympathy. So, casting opinions to the winds, I went on feeling. And that is how I became a rebel, a case of "first endure and then embrace," because I soon got to be a pretty good rebel and went the limit, changing my coat as it were, though not my better judgment, for with a gray jacket on my back and ready to do or die, I retained my

Watterson passed the winter of 1861 and 1862 in what he described as "desultory newspaper work" as editor of the *Nashville Banner* until the city of Nashville fell to the Federals in February 1862. Courtesy of the Library of Congress

belief that secession was treason, that disunion was the height of folly and that the South was bound to go down in the unequal strife.[44]

Watterson found himself joining the Confederate army while still "an un-doubting Union boy," he wrote. "Neither then nor afterward could I be fairly classified as a Secessionist. Circumstance rather than conviction or predilection threw me into the Confederate service, and, being in, I went through with it."[45]

Although he had no military experience, his first assignment was on the staff of General Leonidas Polk, who was making an expedition into western Kentucky. After a few weeks with the army, illness drove him back to Nashville in late September. He passed the winter of 1861 and 1862 in what he described as "desultory newspaper work"[46] as editor of the *Nashville Banner* until the city fell in February 1862. As Watterson fled from Nashville, he caught up with the regiment of Colonel Nathan Forrest.[47]

"I was making my way out of town afoot and trudging the Murfreesboro pike," he wrote. "Forrest, with his squadron just escaped from Fort Donelson, came thundering by, and I leaped into an empty saddle." A few days later, Forrest, who by then had been promoted to brigadier general, attached Watterson to his staff.[48] Forrest's cavalry was making quick raids across Tennessee and Alabama. It was the kind of fighting Watterson enjoyed: no long days in muddy bivouacs and good hot food:[49] "and the next six months it was mainly guerilla service, very much to my liking," Watterson wrote.[50]

Watterson was captured by the Federals a few months later. "Forrest took it into his inexperienced fighting head to make a cavalry attack upon a Federal stockade, and, repulsed with considerable loss, the command had to disperse—there were not more than two hundred of us—in order to escape capture by the newly-arrived reinforcements that swarmed about," Watterson wrote.[51] They were supposed to rendezvous later at a certain point, but having some time to spare and being near the family homestead at Beech Grove, he decided to visit there.

It was midnight when Watterson reached his destination. He had been erroneously informed that the Union Army was retreating, "quite gone from the neighborhood; and next day, believing the coast was clear, I donned a summer suit and with a neighbor boy who had been wounded at Shiloh and invalided home, rode over to visit some young ladies. We had scarcely been welcomed and were taking a glass of wine when, looking across the lawn, we saw that the place was being surrounded by a body of blue-coats. The story of their departure had been a mistake. They were not all gone."[52]

There was no chance for escape, and they were marched across country into camp. "Before we got there I had ascertained that they were Indianians, and I was further led rightly to surmise what we called in 1860 Douglas Democrats," he wrote. "My companion, a husky fellow, who looked and was every inch a soldier, was first questioned by the colonel in command. His examination was brief. He said he was as good a rebel as lived, that he was only waiting for his wound to heal to get back into the Confederate Army, and that if they wanted to hang him for a spy to go ahead."[53] Watterson was horrified to hear his companion speaking so recklessly.

I was aghast. It was not he that was in danger of hanging, but myself, a soldier in citizen's apparel within the enemy's lines. The colonel turned to me. With what I took for a sneer he said, "I suppose you are a good Union man?" This offered me a chance.

"That depends upon what you call a good Union man," I answered. "I used to be a very good Union man—a Douglas Democrat—and I am not conscious of having changed my political opinions." That softened him and we had an old-fashioned, friendly talk about the situation, in which I kept the Douglas Democratic end of it well to the fore. He, too, had been a Douglas Democrat. I soon saw that it was my companion and not myself whom they were after. Presently Colonel Shook, that being the commandant's name, went into the adjacent stockade and the boys about began to be hearty and sympathetic. I made them a regular Douglas Democratic speech. They brought some "red licker" and I asked for some sugar for a toddy, not failing to cite the familiar Sut Lovingood saying that "there were about seventeen round the door who said they'd take sugar in their'n."[54]

Watterson said, "The drink warmed me to my work, making me quicker, if not bolder, in invention." When the colonel did not quickly reappear, Watterson went to him.

"Colonel Shook," I said, "you need not bother about this friend of mine. He has no real idea of returning to the Confederate service. He is teaching school over here at Beech Grove and engaged to be married to one of the—girls. If you carry him off a prisoner, he will be exchanged back into the fighting line, and we make nothing by it. There is a hot luncheon waiting for us at the—'s. Leave him to me and I will be answerable." Then I left him. Directly he came out and said: "I may be doing wrong, and don't feel entirely sure of my ground, but I am going to let you gentlemen go."[55]

Watterson thanked him and made off amid the cheery good-byes of the assembled blue-coats. "No lunch for us," he wrote. "We got to our horses, rode away, and that night I was at our rendezvous to tell the tale to those of my comrades who had arrived before me."[56]

After six months with Forrest, "Fate, if not Nature," decided that Watterson was a better writer than fighter, Watterson wrote, so he was sent to Chattanooga to edit a newspaper that had been bought by the Bank of Tennessee. The *Chattanooga Advocate* and the *Chattanooga Advertiser* had been merged to form the *Chattanooga Gazette*. When the *Gazette* failed, the Bank of Tennessee bought the run-down newspaper plant and turned it over to Francis M. Paul, who was clerk of the state Senate.[57] Paul contacted Watterson in July while he was accompanying Forrest on a successful raid on Murfreesboro and persuaded the General that his aide "could do more for the Southern cause on the tripod than in the saddle," Watterson wrote.[58] "I was sent there to edit *The Rebel*—my own naming[59]—established as the organ of the Tennessee state government. I made it the organ of the army."[60]

The first issue of the *Rebel*—a four-column, four-page, 14 × 20 inch newspaper—appeared in August 1862, with the masthead showing that the newspaper was published by Paul. Watterson was never listed on the masthead as editor. The *Rebel* would become one of the most widely read Army newspapers, with a circulation of more than 8,000.[61]

Describing himself as a "born insurrecto," Watterson began developing his distinctive personal journalism style on the *Rebel*. After receiving complaints

from his readers about the conduct of Confederate soldiers in Middle Tennessee, Watterson rode out into the countryside to take a look at the desolation and
destruction.[62]

> We were enabled to see ourselves visibly the truth of many of these statements
> and to discover that the disregard of the rights, comforts and protection of inof-
> fensive private citizens has but too frequently marked the course of some of our
> mounted troops. Fences, for example, have been thoughtlessly burned, provisions
> illegally pressed and other acts perpetrated, with little color of authority and very
> far from any color of right.[63]

Watterson said it was his duty to "remonstrate upon behalf of our suffering
citizens, first with the soldiers themselves, most of whom have not been guilty,
we sincerely believe, of any willful intent to do harm, and secondly with commanding officers, whose business it is to guard against such indiscretions."[64] He
described the pitiful conditions that he found.

> The people of Middle Tennessee are poor. They are loyal, patriotic, generous, self-
> sacrificing. They have been preyed upon in the vilest manner by the enemy. Their
> homes invaded, themselves either driven thence into exile, or borne to Northern
> prison houses, their property destroyed, their crops squandered, and in many
> instances, their premises put to the torch of the vandal, these brave men and
> women have endured, have resisted, have toiled, patiently, courageously.[65]

He chastised the soldiers for their carelessness and begged the Confederate
cavalry to leave the citizens in peace. Offended by the horrendous condition of
the Tennessee countryside, Watterson became increasingly critical of governments on both sides of the war. From that day, whether it was Confederate or
Federal, Democrat or Republican, he never found a government that he liked.[66]
He launched an attack against President Jefferson Davis and the Confederate
Cabinet, calling them a "plurality of black sheep, ignorant politicians and blatant demagogues."[67]

Watterson's editorial knife cut both ways, and three days later, he was attacking Lincoln, calling him a "vulgar knave, fool and poltroon, Abraham the
First."[68] Although Watterson in later years would express admiration for Lincoln and call him the greatest figure in American history, his wartime rhetoric
against the Federal president became increasingly vicious during 1863. In an
unsigned editorial, Watterson called Lincoln a "man without mind or manners—as limbless in intellect as ungraceful in person—a rude, vulgar, obscure
backwoods pettifogger."[69]

> He is raw-boned, shambled-gaited, bow-legged, knock kneed, pigeon-toed, swob-
> sided, a shapeless skeleton in a very tough, very dirty, unwholesome skin. His hair
> is, or was black and shaggy, his eyes dark and fireless, like a coal grate in winter

time. His lips are large and protrude beyond the natural level of the face, but are pale and smeared with tobacco juice. His teeth are filthy. [70]

"[H]is voice is coarse, untutored, harsh, the voice of one who has no intellect and less moral nature. His manners are low in the extreme, and where his talk is not obscene, it is senseless," Watterson wrote. "In a word, Lincoln, born and bred a rail-splitter, is a rail-splitter still . . . [A]nd this is the man, who incapable of a stronger or higher inspiration than that of revenge, aspires to be master of the free South, as he is of the enslaved and slavish North."[71] Ironically, Watterson would become known after the war as "the most attractive lecturer on Abraham Lincoln on the circuits," and his most successful lecture would be "Lincoln," which was reprinted in several books.[72]

When Watterson became increasingly concerned about the role the press was playing in helping the enemy, he launched an attack on "indiscretions of the press."

> Many of our contemporaries, and their . . . representatives, innocently perhaps, . . . in their zeal to furnish reliable articles to their readers give the minutest particulars of every thing occurring in the vicinity of the Army; the movement of troops; the transfer of commanders; the number of fortifications and their character and positions, etc. This is decidedly improper.[73]

It was also improper, he said, to write that certain officers were unpopular with the troops.[74] Watterson saw this sort of unnecessary criticism of commanders as abuse of the privileges of the professional press and special correspondents. "The fostering protection of the Press, by our government; the implicit confidence reposed in its representative, in the sanctum and in the field by the military authorities, and the freedom of the lines, the camp and the headquarters to the representatives, are permitted, but to embarrass the plans of our commanders, nor to anticipate the movements of our troops" is wrong, he wrote,[75] and continued:

> . . . [The] Confederacy today rejoices in a free press, conducted by well meaning, patriotic and conscientious and honorable men. Its only fault is its indiscretion. Not one journal of the South is entirely free from this fault. It should be the duty of the whole Press to remedy it.[76]

Although Watterson was an advocate of a free press, he also believed that critical military information should not be published. "Better far to advance the interests of our cause now, than to win the applause of the few for bold independence of criticism, where criticism is useless," he wrote. "There is certain information the public have no right to hear. We best serve the public interests by protecting the armies of the people and by withholding all information calculated to assist the enemy in his schemes for our destruction."[77]

Confederate battery on top of Lookout Mountain. *Harper's Weekly,* December 26, 1863. Courtesy of Rare Books and Special Collections, University of South Carolina Libraries

Oddly, after his impassioned warnings to the press about providing information to the enemy, Watterson described in detail in another news column on the same day the importance of defending the mountains of east Tennessee. He was "glad to see the fitful flashes of fire among the hills and passes" as he accurately predicted conditions that could, and eventually did, lead to the downfall of the Confederacy.[78]

> The mountains of East Tennessee—to use the illustration of one of our ablest generals—form a breast plate to the Confederacy. Pass them and the problem of the enemy at once reaches the guts of the South. Therefore is East Tennessee to be defended at every hazard. Lose it, and Georgia—the Egypt in the country — is lost. Lose it, and where goes the capitol? What becomes of Richmond? This river is our surest base. It rolls in front of the enemy, like a passless guerdon. It coils at our feet, like a lasso, which we may wind about the loins of the foe. We can never see it go from us.[79]

"[W]ith the new recruits, who are beginning to pour in—with the renewed spirit which the responsibility resting upon them is animating our army—we shall hold the stream, and all that it embraces," he wrote. "If we can defeat Rose-crans at this distance from the base, farewell to him forever."[80]

However, in less than two weeks, General Rosecrans was leading the Army of the Cumberland toward the Tennessee River west of Chattanooga, and more Federal troops were arriving in Covington, Kentucky, for the impending attacks on East Tennessee.[81] In spite of the growing Federal threat, Watterson was hap-pily courting his future wife, Rebecca Ewing, whom he had met during the winter of 1862. She was the beautiful, elegant daughter of former Congressman Andrew Ewing from Nashville.

The first indication of the attack on Chattanooga came on August 21, 1863, when Federals fired a few shots from a ridge. "The warning which awoke the army and the town . . . was not neglected for a moment," he wrote. "All men seemed to understand, by that tacit intuition which sometimes moves large masses of people as in single impulse, that a battle was impending, and citizen and soldier at once began to prepare for it."[82] A few days later Federals lobbed a few shots at the offices of the *Rebel*, but the shells smashed into the nearby Chattanooga Presbyterian Church where Watterson and his future bride were attending a service.

> She had a fine contralto voice and led the church choir. Doctor Palmer, of New Orleans, was on a certain Sunday well into the long prayer of the Presbyterian service. Bragg's army was still in middle Tennessee. There was no thought of an attack. Bang! Bang! Then the bursting of a shell too close for comfort. Bang! Bang! Then the rattle of shell fragments on the roof. On the other side of the river the Yankees were upon us.
>
> The man of God gave no sign that anything unusual was happening. He did not hurry. He did not vary the tones of his voice. He kept on praying. Nor was there panic in the congregation, which did not budge.
>
> That was the longest long prayer I ever heard. When it was finally ended, and still without changing a note the preacher delivered the benediction, the crowded church in the most orderly manner moved to the several doorways.
>
> I was quick to go for my girl. By the time we reached the street the firing had become general. We had to traverse quite half a mile of it before attaining a place of safety.[83]

Watterson's fiancée left town during the general exodus that followed, and they would not see each other again until the war ended nearly two years later.[84] "By dusk on Sunday evening private families had retired beyond the range of danger, in the event either of a direct assault upon the city or other perils incident to active operations in its vicinity," he wrote. "The military has-tened heavy baggage to the rear, and the several commands received orders, which suddenly electrified them from the torpor of camp life to the animation of the field."[85]

Watterson reported that the "heavy baggage" of presses and type of the *Rebel* was packed into railroad boxcars and shipped to Marietta, Georgia, but Watterson and Albert ("John Happy") Roberts stayed in Chattanooga with enough material and typographical equipment to print a daily war bulletin.[86] Although Watterson knew how to set type and make up a paper, a printer, probably Louis L. Parham, had remained with the editors.[87]

"Whilst we are penning these lines, shells from the enemy's batteries are falling within our rear premises and exploding in the street in front," Watterson wrote. Pledging to stay until the last hour, he said, "Chattanooga may be burnt to the ground, but the position will not be lost; and so long as our army is here to defend it, we shall share whatever befalls its gallant soldiers, most of whom are fellow comrades of ours in past campaigns, and nearly all of whom are our friends and patrons."[88]

Chattanooga had been evacuated so rapidly that the *Rebel* was "about the only public institution left in the almost deserted, and once proud martial city of Chattanooga," he wrote. "Every other is on the wing, and probably still fancy that the shells are hot after them. We are left alone in our glory. Alone with our types . . ."[89]

With only minor opposition, General Rosecrans' Army of the Cumberland crossed the Tennessee River in early September to prepare for the attack on Chattanooga and General Bragg's Army of Tennessee. At the same time, Knoxville, Tennessee, fell to General A.E. Burnside's troops who destroyed the railroad link between Chattanooga and Virginia as part of a plan to help Rosecrans in his attack on Chattanooga.[90]

Watterson, Roberts, and the printer continued to publish to the "distant ring of rifle or rattle of musketry."[91] When word spread about the flight of the *Rebel*, several newspapers, including the *Montgomery Advertiser* and the *Atlanta Southern Confederacy*, ran notices that the *Rebel* had been suspended. Quick to let people know the newspaper was still alive, Watterson published a notice on August 30, 1863, saying, "The publication of the *Rebel* has never been suspended. Will our Southern contemporaries oblige us by the correction?"[92] As the shelling continued in Chattanooga, Watterson and Roberts and the "solitary printer with his 'case' and composing stick" moved to the basement of the Bank of Tennessee, which was located next door to a tavern operated by a man named Haskell. In spite of their dire circumstances, the editors laughed over the plight of a "dry" soldier who arrived at the tavern in desperate search of a drink.

> Excited individual next door can be heard frantically imploring our neighbor Haskell to open his door. The voice is evidently that of a "dry" soldier. At least we judge so from the huskiness of his throat. Possibly wants a drink. Probably won't get it, as Haskell has retired to his earthworks.
>
> Boom! Whiz-z-z!! goes another and another angry shell.

"Oh, Mr. Haskell!" goes voice outside.

Boo room-BOOM! Ker-gip!

"Haskell! Open the door!"

Crash came a shell over the roof, struck a Chattanooga hog in the side and sent him squealing to the happy hunting grounds.

Soldier couldn't stand it any longer. He broke. We can hear the retreating echoes of his footsteps. Haskell has at length opened the door and calls after him. "What do you want?"

Reply in the dim distance: "Oh, d—n it, you're too late. 'Spect a man to have nine lives like a cat, and get murdered for one drink?"

Drama closes. Scene shifts! Suthin' rumbles! Exeunt, at a double quick.[93]

Watterson continued to criticize General Bragg and was waging a campaign to have him replaced by General Joseph E. Johnston. After publishing one of his most scathing editorials, Watterson was thrown in the company of General Bragg, although neither knew nor recognized the other. The story of their odd confrontation was remembered in 1890 by Louis L. Parham, a printer on the *Rebel*.[94]

It happened this way: While in Chattanooga one day before the Rebel left there, Mr. Watterson was accidentally thrown in company with Gen. Bragg—unknown to each other, however. The conversation turned upon the war very naturally. The editor very vigorously, but courteously, criticized Gen. Bragg. The latter promptly defended the commanding general. One word brought on another, when the general, straightening up suddenly, asked the editor if he knew who he was: the latter professed his ignorance on that point. Nothing daunted, though somewhat astonished, Mr. Watterson stoutly maintained his previous suggestions and ideas. The controversy was abruptly terminated.[95]

The next day, Watterson, Roberts, and their printer packed what was left of the *Rebel* and headed for their main newspaper operation near Atlanta. They escaped shortly before General Bragg abandoned Chattanooga on September 9, 1863, and withdrew into LaFayette,[96] Georgia. Federal and Confederate forces soon converged at Chickamauga Creek, Georgia, 12 miles south of Chattanooga, where Confederates claimed victory in heavy fighting on September 18–20. The Federals retreated to Chattanooga while the Confederates held the surrounding heights, including Lookout Mountain and Missionary Ridge, but Bragg was criticized for not destroying the Army of the Cumberland as it retreated from Chickamauga. President Davis responded to the criticism by leaving Bragg in command and calling for "harmonious co-operation,"[97] but Watterson stepped up his criticism in the *Rebel*.

The personal incident in Chattanooga along with Watterson's continuing complaints in the *Rebel* infuriated Bragg, who issued orders excluding the *Rebel*

Confederate prisoners at the Chattanooga railroad depot. Courtesy of the Library of Congress

from his army camps and confiscating any copies that were found. Faced with the sudden loss of circulation of the *Rebel*, Paul was forced to ask Watterson to resign, and Bragg lifted his ban.[98] With a less interesting, less exciting editor, the *Rebel* continued its nomadic travels. Several unauthorized editions were published in Atlanta before the *Rebel* parked in Griffin, Georgia, but the newspaper moved on to Alabama where Federal cavalry finally destroyed the *Rebel* in Selma in April 1865.[99] Before the end, it would be published in three states, five towns, and one boxcar while traveling with the Confederate armies.[100]

After losing his job with the *Rebel*, Watterson moved into Atlanta with Roberts in the fall and early winter of 1863, where they took editorial jobs at the *Atlanta Southern Confederacy*.[101] While they were working there, the Federals and Confederates clashed in battles at Lookout Mountain and Missionary Ridge on November 24-26, resulting in major victories for the Federals and opening a path into the heart of the Confederacy.[102] Bragg retreated to Dalton, Georgia, where he wired Davis on November 28 to inform him of the defeat and asking to be relieved of duty. Two days later, Davis accepted Bragg's resignation and asked him to transfer his command to General William J. Hardee. Watterson's editorial wishes had come true.[103]

Unhappy with his position at the *Confederacy,* Watterson resigned and re-joined the army where he became chief of scouts on the staff of General Johnston and was assigned to watch the Union army moving from Chattanooga toward Atlanta.[104] He also became a correspondent for the *Daily Constitutionalist* in Augusta, Georgia, and began signing his letters as Grape.[105] Watterson and his companions made frequent scouting expeditions through the hills north of Dalton, Georgia, to watch for General William T. Sherman's army gathering south of Chattanooga.

Although Johnston had retreated steadily along the railroad line from Chattanooga to Atlanta, the Federals attacked Hood's troops on May 15, 1864, at Resaca, a small town 45 miles southeast of Chattanooga. Watterson had transferred to the staff of his old friend General Polk, who invited him to join him one day for lunch on the battlefield. Concerned about the safety of the location that Polk had chosen, Watterson suggested a safer place. After moving into a ravine, they spread their feast under an oak tree and were just sitting down when shrapnel smashed into the tree over their heads. When the general picked himself up from the debris, he said, "You're a pretty fellow for selecting covers! Come! We may as well take ourselves back to the front."[106]

In addition to writing for the *Constitutionalist* and the *Confederacy,* Watterson also was filing stories under his pen name Shadow for the *Mobile Advertiser and Register* and the *Memphis Appeal.* As he watched battles and skirmishes almost daily in north Georgia, he wrote passionately about the refugees who were forced to flee. Writing from Marietta on May 24, 1864, under his pen name Shadow, Watterson described the exodus in the *Register and Advertiser.*

> One of the saddest aspects of the retreat from the North of Georgia is the crowd of refugees it has pressed upon the lowlands. These unfortunate people are flying in every direction and by every conceivable mode of conveyance, panic-stricken and heart-sick. Many of them have left their homes in such haste that they have brought nothing with them, and have not only the bleak prospect of exile before them, but that worse promise of absolute want. Their appearance is pitiable. For the most part they are irresolute and uninformed, the women in tears and the men in fearful perplexity.[107]

He described them on the highways moving along in a hopeless manner, in search of a hiding place at the little stations along the railroad, or huddled together in box cars. "Here a handsome mirror, there a pot or kettle, a divan, a milk pail, a family picture, a coop of chickens, a watch dog lying upon a Brussels rug, a cat on an ottoman, a crock of butter and basket of eggs amid a profusion of broken china, parlor curiosities and pantry niceties, nice no longer," he wrote. "Doleful, inexpressibly doleful. Let the grim picture pass on."[108]

Watterson filed more stories about the refugees under his Shadow byline for the *Mobile Register* as he watched the caravan of refugees fleeing from the enemy on May 26.

General Polk. *Harper's Weekly,* October 25, 1862. Courtesy of Rare Books and Special Collections, University of South Carolina Libraries

Alas, poor souls! The procession moves slowly by my window. See the pater familias, haggard, hopeless of aspect, but resolute as a martyr, riding on a bay filly, and keeping the cows and sheep in line; in the vehicle (it is very unfashionable, truly, . . . but still it has four wheels, is drawn by two beasts, and does move); in this vehicle, there is the good dame, very lugubrious, shrill and irritable, yet full of pluck; a pair of shy girls, peeping out of sun-bonnets; three little toddlekins, curious and excited, and any number of baskets, buckets and tin pans, hung upon strings, or heaped in the bottom of the carriage.[109]

As uncomfortable as everybody else, the family dog leaned his head wishfully through the spokes of a spinning wheel as two or three carts and a farm wagon followed, Watterson wrote. "And thus they pass along the dusty highway, en route for _____. Aye, for where?" he asked. "Do they know? Perhaps they do, but many of them are without compass or purpose, trusting to God's good mercy and providence to shelter them from the storm, now that they are out of reach of the Yankee. It is a dolorous pageant. You may smile at it, but take care your dimples do not catch a tear."[110]

Before the Atlanta campaign opened, Watterson left with Tennessee's Confederate former Governor Isham Harris,[111] on a tour of the army to build morale. General Johnston had asked the governor to "go around among the boys and stir 'em up a bit."[112]

> Together we visited every sector in the army. Threading the woods of North Georgia on this round, if I heard it once I heard it fifty times shouted from a distant clearing: "Here comes Gov-ner Harris, fellows; g'wine to be a fight." His appearance at the front had always preceded and been long ago taken as a signal for battle.[113]

Watterson was even more horrified by the scenes he saw in north Georgia on May 27, 1864. "The populace are in the wildest confusion," he wrote. "Men, women and children are flying in panic before the advance of the enemy, like flocks of sheep. Farms have been abandoned, homes deserted, and even personal apparel sacrificed to the terror-stricken haste which has impelled many of these unfortunate refugees. They may be seen encamped on the road side in the most abject despair, knowing and caring little as to their destination, so that they are able, with the remnant of their means, to evade the Yankee."[114] As Watterson approached Atlanta, the military operations crowding the scene made it more tumultuous.

> The heavy wagons lumbering along, the trains of ordinance and artillery, the troops of escort, the staff officers, the couriers, all mingle in the strange din and disturb the vision. No wonder that some of the more ignorant fancy the world is coming to an end. Atlanta is like to nothing that can be conceived. The streets filled with wagons, its side walks with excited men and women, its trenches with soldiers. Trade has ceased. The city is now a camp.[115]

Watterson was at the front outside of Atlanta in early June as Federals plunged deeper into Georgia and Sherman's troops moved cautiously toward Johnston's new position near the mountains northwest of Marietta.[116] "In regard to the change, it can only be said to have arisen out of the necessity, which compels us to move with the enemy," he reported.[117] Moving again, he was south of Atlanta at Pine Mountain a week later when General Polk was killed on June 14.[118] Writing under his Shadow byline, Watterson grieved over his old friend, calling him "my Bishop, my General and my friend." Perhaps remembering their lunch under the old oak tree, Shadow wrote, "I always fancied somehow that there was

The evacuation of Atlanta. *Harper's Weekly,* October 15, 1864. Courtesy of Rare Books and Special Collections, University of South Carolina Libraries

safety within the magic circle of his presence."[119] Along with his grief-stricken words was a mournful prediction that Atlanta would fall within the next two months.[120]

Little time could be spared to grieve over fallen friends as the Federal infantry attacked the entrenched Confederates from three directions with a thunderous show of artillery fire. Watterson was dug in with Johnston's army on the slopes of Kennesaw Mountain near Marietta when Sherman attacked on June 27.[121] It would be one of the few Confederate victories during the Atlanta campaign. "The silence along the lines today proclaimed the bloody character of the repulse," Watterson wrote. "They have been engaged burying the dead . . . Among the Yankee prisoners captured was a girl in the disguise of a soldier of comely appearance and rather modest mien."[122]

Undeterred, the Federals continued the bombardment, and Sherman's troops entered Marietta on the Fourth of July. "They found the village very nearly deserted," Watterson wrote. "Three-fourths of the resident population and all of the rebels vanished—a mere skeleton of what it was remained of Marietta."[123] Shadow's prediction in early June that Atlanta would fall within the next two months had raised a stir of protest among some of the Confederate editors. As Sherman's troops circled closer, Shadow jabbed a little "I told you so" at the editors as he reiterated his prediction of doom and described the flight of news-papers out of Atlanta.

> When I wrote you a month ago that Atlanta would fall, yourself, and numbers of my friends of the Atlanta press, were somewhat violent in your dissent, and yet the latter have packed their traps and are now branching out in search of new places of refuge. The Confederacy goes to Macon. The Register to Augusta. The Intelligencer to Milledgeville. And the Appeal, which is considered a bird of ill omen, is pluming its wings to descend like a raven upon the unoffending capital of Alabama.[124]

President Davis was so unhappy with Johnston's continued delaying tactics in fighting the Federal army that, as Johnston was preparing for the Battle of Peachtree Creek, Davis replaced him with General John Bell Hood.[125] Watterson was transferred to Hood's staff to serve as a military aide.[126] While waiting with Hood's troops for Sherman's attack, Watterson wrote on July 19 about the agony of waiting: "Suspense, the most depressing of human senses, holds possession of the popular mind, and anxious care is written in every line of the popular countenance. There is not a sound but startles the expectant ear. The roll of distant carriage wheels is mistaken for artillery, and the clatter of wagons over the stones of the street for the rattle of musketry.—The fall of any heavy body, as a bale or a box, often startles one as though it were a shell fallen in that part of the town . . . Not an hour in the day but additions are made to the lies of the dawn; and you lie down at night to dream of loud alarums, and neighing steed and bursting rockets and bombs and guns. Such a city is Atlanta."[127] He said the streets were full of the rude trappings of an army and no place was quiet or uninvaded by the stir of war.

> Seek those silent walks which but a month ago echoed only with the tones of musical instruments or happy voices, and rolling wagon wheel and coarse language dins the ear. The little portico, where you saw a group watching the set of the sun, is deserted, the doors and windows barred, the inmates gone. You may not meet a cheerful face. Care sits in the eyes of the citizen, defiant courage overcasts the hard visage of the soldier.[128]

Regardless of what might happen in the battle that was to follow, Watterson considered Atlanta a broken city. "The place is a perfect shell," he wrote. "The Yankees will gain little if they do gain it. All private and public property of value has been removed, and the decks are cleared for a fair fight. Will we get it? I do not know. I rather believe we will not. Sherman has what he considers a flanking force. He will fortify in our front, leave a third of his army to occupy and advance on Stone Mountain."[129] The attack, which came the next day on July 20, was a staggering defeat for the Confederates, who counted 4,796 killed, wounded, and injured compared to only 1,779 Federal casualties.[130] When the

Federals turned their guns on Atlanta, the city would become a smoking funeral pyre during the next six weeks.

> As near as I can estimate, about five hundred shells have fallen within our line of fortifications, and many of them into the streets. A number of houses have been struck, but the casualties in the city comparatively insignificant. Several members of a family up town were wounded by fragments of an exploded shell, and one little child was killed.[131]

Watterson heard the constant clatter of muskets night and day around the city's circle of fortifications, with a running heavy bass accompaniment of 12 and 24 pounders. "The scene at night is singularly picturesque and startling in effect," Watterson wrote under his Grape byline. "The rocket's red glare and bombs bursting in the air, with the flash of guns, like heat-lightning on the horizon, presents a panorama at once exciting and wildly beautiful to the uninitiated in war."[132]

As shells continued to rain on Atlanta, Watterson watched the scene "from a pleasant window in a deserted dwelling, just in rear of the eastern fortifications—the window of a room once occupied by the cruel mistress of the heart of a poor young friend of mine." Heartsick for the falling Atlanta, he described the mangled shade trees and flower beds and "topsy-turvy summer houses"[133] as refugees continued to pour out of the almost deserted city.

> The very streets stare at you mournfully and spectrally...The breezes, that "pause and die in the woodlands," roam up and down the broad, bare avenues like unhappy ghosts.—The sunshine pours its lonely rays upon deserted pavements. They vainly seek the giddy throng that whilom floated in fanciful mazes the promenades of Marietta and Peachtree.[134]

At night, Watterson watched the stars interspersed with exploding night lights. "I watch the range of the shells out of amusement partly, and partly out of discretion, which is after all the better part of valor...I trace the meteoric bivouacs that blaze through the sky, and those less mysterious camp fires which flicker up from the gleaming...and flash around the horizon like a circle of warlike fire flies; and I crawl down again about midnight, weary and bewildered."[135]

Although Watterson had earlier predicted that Atlanta would fall, he still saw one ray of hope in the "confusion and the destruction, the loneliness and the weariness" that surrounded the city. "There rises one inspiring figure," he wrote. "Early or late, or by the branding camp-fire or the sun's first ray, may be seen a tall spare form, with a single arm and a single leg, a youthful face and a beaming eye in the line of the front. It is Hood...Look cheerily upon the campaign as it moves onward, and never cease to hope. We are resolved to conquer or to die in these ditches."[136]

Atlanta had once teemed with journalists and newspaper offices, but the war had taken its toll. The editors and correspondents left town one by one as their offices were destroyed by the continuous explosion of 40-pound spherical case balls.[137]

> The offices of the old establishment are pretty thoroughly "done for." The Regis-ter office is represented by a pile of blackened brick. It was burnt to the ground a month ago. The Confederacy had its flag staff cut away by a shell, and several tokens of attention through its front. The Intelligencer is thoroughly used up, powder stained and bullet riddled. The Appeal building is also shot through and through. Indeed the press of Atlanta has suffered as severely, if not more so, as any other institution of the city.[138]

Watterson was one of the few journalists remaining in Atlanta who contin-ued to write "in the trenches" with the troops as he did on August 23. As he watched the constant attacks on Atlanta, he resorted to poetry.

> Shells all night, shells all day, shells for breakfast, dinner and tea, shells—
> "For all hours and all sort of weather"
> so that I am tempted to exclaim with one of our older bards a little altered—
> Tell me ye winged winds,
> That round my pathway roar—
> Is there not
> Some favored spot
> Where Yankees shell no more.[139]

He described the destruction of a large cotton warehouse containing more than 500 bales of cotton and a nearby wooden dwelling. "These conflagrations are very beautiful," he wrote. "They mingle uniquely with the explosion of the shells. The fire brigade works manfully under a raking cannonade."[140] Watterson bitterly described the continuing attacks on August 26 as fires raged through the almost deserted city.

> The vandals in front of us having failed to take the city by fair means, and in open combat are resorting to the last expedient of a baffled, unprincipled and dis-consolate bully—that of its destruction by fire. Within the past four and twenty hours as many as nine buildings have touched the ground, and are now visible only in smouldering walls and charred ruins. During these conflagrations the Yankee batteries played vigorously among the fire battalion. They obtained the range by the clouds of smoke and flame and had nothing more noble to do than to drop their shells in among the humane non-combatants at their work of charity, and the frightened and houseless women and children fleeing from the wrath of the two fierce and consuming enemies.[141]

Sherman settled into a siege of Atlanta, shelling the city and sending raids south and west to cut Hood's last supply lines into the city. When the Federals captured the railroad track in Jonesborough on August 31, General Hood feared a direct attack and began pulling his troops out of Atlanta, destroying supply depots as they left to prevent them from falling into enemy hands.[142] As an aide to Hood, Watterson had shared "the beginning of the chapter of disasters that befell that gallant soldier and his army."[143] However, as the general began reorganizing for future attacks, Watterson believed that Atlanta and the Confederacy were doomed.[144]

"I had an affectionate regard for General Hood," he wrote, "but it was my belief that neither he nor any other soldier could save the day, and being out of commission and having no mind for what I conceived aimless campaigning through another winter—especially an advance into Tennessee upon Nashville—I wrote an old friend who owned the Montgomery Mail, asking for a job."[145] When his Alabama friend offered him the editorship and half ownership of the newspaper,[146] the proposal was so opportune and tempting that Watterson decided to leave the next day for Montgomery.[147] By happenstance, his old friend Colonel George W. Adair, who had been editor and owner of the *Southern Confederacy* until 1863, was on his way out of town in an old tobacco peddler's wagon. As Watterson and "John Happy" Roberts jumped aboard, they could see blazing fires from the old rolling mills and 400 bales of cotton. Powder kegs and artillery shells were exploding all around. "The flames were so high that I could count the hairs in the horse's tail by its light," Adair said later. The threesome drove through the night toward Montgomery, reaching the capital of Alabama 48 hours later.[148] Atlanta Mayor James Calhoun surrendered on September 2, and Sherman sent a telegram to Washington saying, "Atlanta is ours and fairly won."[149] He remained in Atlanta for two months before ordering the remaining civilian population to evacuate. What little was left of Atlanta was burned to the ground a few days before Sherman began his destructive march to the sea on November 15. He left behind a smoldering city lying in ruins under a pall of black smoke.

When Watterson moved to Alabama to edit the *Montgomery Mail*, he was spared "the last and worst" of the fall of the Confederacy. However, he didn't hesitate when a Confederate official offered him the opportunity to go to Liverpool, England, to sell about 100,000 bales of cotton for the Confederate government.

> The initial step was to get out of the country. But how? That was the question. To run the blockade had been easy enough a few months earlier. All our ports were now sealed by Federal cruisers and gunboats. There was nothing for it but to slip through the North and to get either a New York or a Canadian boat. This involved chances and disguises.[150]

Watterson headed for west Tennessee near Memphis, with the plan of getting on a Mississippi steamer, but his efforts were foiled when he was captured trying to get through the Union lines to the Ohio River. He pretended to be a relative of the family of the Federal commanding officer and was taken to General

N.B. Dana, who saw through his disguise but invited him to dinner anyway and gave him a pass to the North. However, Watterson's dream of wealth through a commission on the Confederate cotton was shattered and his mission aborted when he found that the cotton had been burned.[151]

Not wishing to return to Montgomery, he moved in with relatives in Glendale, near Cincinnati, where in the early spring of 1865 he became editor of the *Cincinnati Evening Times*.[152] He did not intend to remain. "My objective was Nashville, where the young woman who was to become my wife, and whom I had not seen for nearly two years, was living with her family," he wrote.[153]

About that time, his two friends and "bunkies" from the *Southern Confederacy*, Roberts and George Purvis, passed by on their way to Nashville, where Roberts' father owned the *Republican Banner*, which had been dormant for four years. Roberts planned to revive the newspaper with Purvis as business manager and Roberts and Watterson as editors.

> Less than a week later saw us back at home winnowing the town for subscribers and advertising. The way we boys hustled was a sight to see. But the way the community warmed to us was another. When the familiar headline, The Republican Banner, made its appearance there was a popular hallelujah, albeit there were five other dailies ahead of us. A year later there was only one, and it was nowise a competitor.[154]

The three editors had left their sweethearts behind during the war, but by New Year's Eve, all three were married "and comfortably settled, with funds galore, for the paper had thrived consumingly."[155] Watterson was soon called to Louisville where friends on the *Journal* and the suspended *Courier* separately offered him part ownership and sole editorship of both newspapers.[156]

> This I could not accept, but proposed as an alternative the consolidation of the two on an equal basis. He (the owner of the Courier) was willing enough for the consolidation, but not on equal terms. There was nothing for it but a fight. I took the Journal and began to hammer the Courier . . . I had discovered that the field, no matter how worked, was not big enough to support two rival dailies.[157]

Watterson won the newspaper battle, and in mid-November, a "double-headed stranger calling itself the *Courier-Journal*" appeared on the doorsteps of the city.[158] "Our exclusive possession of the field thus acquired lasted two years," he wrote. "At the end of these we found that at least the appearance of competition was indispensable and willingly accepted an offer from a proposed Republican organ for a division of the Press dispatches which we controlled. Then and there the real prosperity of the *Courier-Journal* began, the paper having made no money out of its monopoly."[159]

During his tenure as editor, Watterson served in the 44th Congress[160] from 1876 to 1877 and was a five-time delegate to the National Democratic

Henry Watterson near the end of his life. Courtesy of Library of Congress

Convention, where he received a few votes for the vice presidential nomination in 1892. He became widely known as a lecturer and orator, particularly on the subject of Abraham Lincoln.

Writing colorful and controversial editorials on many subjects, Watterson was considered "the last of the great personal journalists."[161] He won the Pulitzer Prize in 1918 for two editorials supporting the United States entry into World War I and remained editor of the *Courier-Journal* until 1919 when he retired after an editorial dispute over the League of Nations with Robert Worth Bingham, who bought the newspaper in 1918.[162] Watterson's publications include *History of the Spanish-American War* (1899), *The Compromises of Life* (1902), and *'Marse Henry:' An Autobiography*, volumes one and two (1919).

Watterson died while visiting in Jacksonville, Florida, on December 22, 1921. He was buried with honors three months later on April 4, 1922, at Cave Hill

Cemetery in Louisville, Kentucky. In the eulogy, his minister said, "He leaves no successor for only Ulysses can wield the bow of Ulysses."[163] In later years, Vice President Alben W. Barkley wrote: "No one will deny that Henry Watterson was the last of his tribe; the last great personal editor, whose very language and syntax were so distinct as to make it easy to realize that Henry Watterson was writing."[164]

Epilogue to
Knights of the Quill

When co-authors Patricia G. McNeely, Debra Reddin van Tuyll, and Henry H. Schulte conceived *Knights of the Quill* late in 2005, they had more in mind than writing dozens of chapter drafts and spending hundreds, if not thousands, of hours on research and editing.

In fact, the three had a list of expectations and goals:

They wanted to produce a book about the Civil War that would explore previously visited, but uncharted, places and issues.

They wanted to preserve the memories of the men and women who wrote anonymously about the horrors of America's bloodiest war, and they hoped to correct some of the errors currently contained in the literature about the 19th century Southern press.

They were looking for evidence to substantiate academic arguments about the quality of Southern journalists' work during the Civil War.

The authors decided they might be dealing with pundits, but they never dreamed they would be producing a book about pirates, poets, and pedants. However, that is the nature of such a project as this. It can lead to surprises.

Perhaps the greatest surprise of all has been the depth of characterization these biographies of Civil War reporters have achieved. They are no longer faded black-and-white-turned-brown-with-age caricatures. They are real men and women who loved to eat baked goods at Auntie's house like George Bagby, whose publicly stiff neck masked a passionate nature and devoted social conscience. Or like Peter Alexander, whose sensitivity to soldiers without shoes gave the people of the South a new reason to give of themselves. Or like Joan, the Confederacy's original citizen-journalist. Or like that Homeric teller of tales, Felix Gregory de Fontaine, whose books are still being reprinted in the 21st century. Or like William G. Shepardson, who was so touched when a young woman cared enough to send him a box of precious candles. Shepardson's story about the gift, coming soon after he had expressed jealousy over soldiers who received packages from home, was enough to break a reader's heart. Add in his swashbuckling adventures on the high seas off the Northern coast, and readers have a romantic hero fashioned for the pages of a Peter O'Brien *Master and Commander* novel.

As these men and women were rendered more real by these biographies, some explanations began to suggest themselves for the way they wrote about the war—what some have claimed was propaganda and others have dismissed as lacking much value because of the taint of slavery. The idea suggested in the preface has been confirmed: the majority of these correspondents were from the elite of Southern culture. Their demographics placed them with the social class of those who had vested interests to protect.

Other explanations have arisen for the correspondents' devotion to the cause of Southern independence, even when they despised civilian leadership and fought military censorship. Civil War historian Gary Gallagher has suggested that the ideological engine that informed the North's martial spirit was an idea not much in vogue in the 21st century: the abstract idea of Union.[1] Similarly, the South's ideological inspiration, scholars agree, was slavery. However, the South's soldiers had an additional motivation that Northern soldiers lacked: they were also fighting for the very practical reasons of protecting home and family. Those motivations also existed for the South's correspondents. Imagine James B. Sener, standing on a hill above Fredericksburg on a cold December day, looking down on the devastation wrought upon his hometown by the Union army's assault on his city. The Southern press, like the region's soldiers and citizens, was caught in the crucible of war, and that created more strident, shrill, and sharp critics of any infringements on individual liberties, even when those infractions might have aided the cause. Through it all, however, they were patriotic and loyal to that most ironic of causes: freedom, but only for a certain class of Southerner.

While some historians have argued that Southern reporters were propagandists for the power structure in the fledgling country, that argument does not hold up when examined closely. Propaganda implies an intent to manipulate, and one cannot read the work of most of the subjects of this book and come away believing they were out to manipulate their readers. When these journalists put a positive spin on a battle that had been lost, they were often writing only what they had been told by generals who themselves often had no clear view of what had actually happened. At other times, the reporters were writing what they believed out of conviction or because that was how their backgrounds had taught them to interpret events.

Probably the most satisfying products of this study are the facts that underscore the revolutionary changes in journalistic practice during the Civil War that sped Southern newspapers' adoption of professional standards such as accuracy and exclusion of personal opinion. This book has produced new knowledge about the Confederate press and its contributions to modern journalism.

The Confederate press set new standards that survived the war and inspired Southern journalism afterward. A news industry that created what was essentially a press council and persuaded Congress to establish copyright protection for dispatches sent by telegraph and sufficiently valued press freedom to take on powerful generals does not fit the notion of archaic. Nor does it support the notion that Southern newsmen were under the thumbs of some sort of ruling junta of elite planters who suppressed any dissenting voices.

Ultimately, the authors found that social and professional differences existed between Southern and Northern reporters that affected their war reporting. While the differences existed, they were not in all ways profound. Southern correspondents felt freer to add their own interpretations, but, by and large, they were committed to similar basic journalistic principles: accuracy, truth, and separating rumor from fact. Southern reporters and their editors were also committed to fighting for access to information and for few military restrictions on news-gathering and publishing. As a whole, there was one major difference between Southern and Northern war correspondence: resources.

The *New York Herald* spent some $500,000 to cover the Civil War.[2] The South's newspapers did not have the resources to match, so they were limited in the number of professional correspondents they could put in the field. That story remains the same today. Different media have different available resources. Despite the lack of resources, historians agree that the work of the South's correspondents easily was as good as that of the North's.

Like all scholarly projects, this one took on a life of its own and told its own stories. However, the editors and authors have done what they set out to do: add to the record and build the argument that the Southern press was relevant, despite the limitations it faced because of lack of resources.

Appendix

Correspondents[1]

Name	Age	Slaves	Wealth In Dollars	Married	No. children	College/ Prof.	Profession
Charleston Mercury							
George W. Bagby, Jr.	32	1	0	no	0	yes	physician
John Dickson Bruns	24	0	unk	yes	1	yes	physician
William A. Courtenay	29	5	9,500	yes	0	no	businessman
Leonidas W. Spratt	42	unk	10,100	widowed	1	yes	lawyer
Henry Timrod	32	0	unk	no	0	yes	teacher/poet
Charleston Courier							
Felix G. de Fontaine	26	0	unk	no	0	no	journalist
Joan	unk	unk	unk	unk	1	no	unk
Pensacola Observer							
L.H. Mathews	30	0	unk	no	1	no	teacher
Mobile Advertiser & Register							
Virginia	unk	unk	unk	unk	unk	unk	unk
John Forsyth	48	2	47,000	yes	2	law	lawyer
Henry Hotze	27	0	0	no	0	unk	journalist
Ben Lane Posey	31	1	500	no	0	law	lawyer
William G. Sheperdson	unk	unk	unk	unk	unk	yes	physician
Mobile Tribune							
Samuel C. Reid	42	unk	unk	no	0	law	lawyer

Montgomery Advertiser							
William W. Screws	21	0	unk	no	0	law	lawyer
Atlanta Southern Confederacy							
J.N. Bass	50	8	66,855	no	0	unk	farmer
George E. Purvis	25	0	0	no	0	unk	11
Athens Southern Banner							
James B. Sledge	30	2	11,000	yes	2	unk	journalist
Savannah Republican							
Richard T. Davis	35	6	11,500	yes	2	law	lawyer
James R. Sneed	42	6[2]	6,000	widowed	4[3]	unk	journalist
Peter W. Alexander	35	8	19,080	no	0	yes	lawyer
Confederate Press Association							
John E. Hatcher	27	6	4,595	yes	2	unk	unk
John S. Thrasher	43	10[4]	60,000	yes	1 stepson	no	journalist
Robert W. Gibbes, Jr.	51	39	60,000	yes	6	yes	physician
Bartholomew Riordan	21	unk	unk	unk	unk	unk	journalist
Jonathan Albertson	33	5	1,500	yes	3	yes	lawyer
New Orleans Daily Delta							
Durant da Ponte	24	unk	unk	unk	unk	unk	journalist
Donelson Caffery Jenkins	35	0	0	no	0	0	journalist
New Orleans Picayune							
Francis F. de Gournay	29	0	100	yes	0	unk	journalist
H.H. Perry	unk	unk	unk	unk	unk	unk	unk

(continued)

Name	Age	Slaves	Wealth In Dollars	Married	No. children	College/ Prof.	Profession
New Orleans Delta Durant da Ponte	24	unk	unk	unk	unk	unk	journalist
Charlotte Bulletin E.H. Britton	43	1	5,000	no	5	unk	journalist
Houston Telegraph William Doran	22	unk	unk	unk	unk	law	lawyer
Clarksville Standard Charles DeMorse	unk	unk	unk	unk	unk	unk	unk
Galveston News R.R. Gilbert	29	unk	unk	unk	unk	yes	physician
San Antonio Herald Robert Franklin Bunting	22	0	6,000	yes	0	unk	minister
Tyler Reporter James P. Douglas	24	unk	1,000	no	9	no	journalist
Richmond Dispatch John Bell Pinkney	25	0	500	yes	0	unk	journalist
Richmond Enquirer James B. Sener	23	unk	unk	no	0	yes	lawyer
Richmond Daily Examiner George Henry Clay Rowe	30	3	33,000	yes	4	law	lawyer

	Age		Wealth	Married				Occupation
Richmond Whig								
John Esten Cooke	30	1	unk	unk	unk	unk	unk	unk
Memphis Appeal								
J.G. Flournoy	40	7	27,000	widowed (?)	7	unk	unk	10
W.B. Galbreath	29	11	65,000	yes	1	unk	yes	priest/lawyer
John H. Lindbaugh	47	unk	unk	yes	unk	yes	yes	poet/editor
John R. Thompson	37	unk	unk	no	0	0	yes	8
William D. Barr	27	unk	unk	yes	0	0	unk	unk
Nashville Republican Banner								
Albert Roberts	25	0	unk	no	0	0	unk	journalist
Chattanooga Rebel								
Theodoric Carter[5]	21	29	67,000	no	0	0	unk	unk
Charles D. Kirk	27	1	unk	unk	unk	unk	unk	unk
Henry Watterson	20	unk	unk	no	0	0	no	journalist

Note: All data based on 1860 information.

[1] Includes all correspondents for whom information could be found, not just those profiled in this book. Most information is from the 1860 U.S. Manuscript Census. Wealth figures result from combining the real property and personal property figures from the census. If a correspondent is listed with 0 in any category, he was listed in the census, but no wealth figures were given. If he is listed as unk in any category, that means he was not listed in the census.

[2] He is listed as James R. Snead in the census slave schedule.

[3] Sneed had five children by 1850, but one could have moved out or died by 1860.

[4] Thrasher did not own the slaves himself, nor was the listed wealth his, per se. His wife, Rebecca, brought both the slaves and the wealth to the family when the couple married. However, in this period, it was common for a man to take possession of his wife's property upon marriage; in any case, the slaves and the wealth would have been available to Thrasher to some degree by virtue of his marriage.

[5] Carter still lived at home with his father and siblings; wealth and slave-owning figures refer to numbers listed under his father's name.

Source Notes

Preface

1. *Richmond Enquirer,* February 6, 1863; *Richmond Dispatch,* July 1, 1862.

2. J. Cutler Andrews, *The South Reports the Civil War* (Princeton, N.J.: Princeton University Press, 1970), 516.

3. *Ibid.,* 507–542.

4. David Manning White, "The 'Gate Keeper': A Case Study in the Selection of News," *Journalism Quarterly* 27:4 (Fall 1950), 383–390; Pamela J. Shoemaker, *Gatekeeping* (Newbury Park, Calif.: Sage Publications, 1991); Erving Goffman, *Frame Analysis: An Essay on the Organization of Experience* (London: Harper and Row, 1974); K. Johnson-Cartee, *News Narrative and News Framing: Constructing Political Reality,* (Lanham, Md.: Rowman & Littlefield, 2005); Stephen D. Reese, Oscar H. Gandy, and August E. Grant, *Framing Public Life: Perspectives on Media and Our Understanding of the Social World* (Maywah, N.J.: Lawrence Erlbaum, 2001).

5. James M. Perry, *A Bohemian Brigade: the Civil War Correspondents, Mostly Rough, Sometimes Ready* (New York: Wiley, 2001); Louis M. Starr, *Reporting the Civil War: the Bohemian Brigade in Action, 1861–65* (New York: Collier, 1962); Louis M. Starr, *Bohemian Brigade: Civil War Newsmen in Action* (New York: Knopf, 1954); J. Cutler Andrews, *The North Reports the Civil War* (Pittsburgh: University of Pittsburgh Press, 1955); Bernard A. Weisberger, *Reporters for the Union* (Boston: Little and Brown, 1953); Emmett Crozier, *Yankee Reporters, 1861–1865* (New York: Oxford University, 1956); John F. Marszalek, *Sherman's Other War: the General and the Civil War Press* (Memphis, Tenn.: Memphis State University Press, 1981); Harry J. Maihafer, *War of Words: Abraham Lincoln and the Civil War Press* (Washington, D.C.: Brassey's, 2001); Harry J. Maihafer, *The General and the Journalists: Ulysses S. Grant, Horace Greeley, and Charles Dana* (Washington, D.C.: Brassey's, 1998).

6. William S. Powell, ed., "Hinton Rowan Helper, December 27, 1829–March 9, 1909," *Dictionary of North Carolina Biography* (Chapel Hill: University of North Carolina Press, 1979–1996), available from http://docsouth.unc.edu/browse/bios/pn0000711_bio.html (accessed December 8, 2007).

7. Hinton R. Helper, *The Impending Crisis of the South: How to Meet It* (New York: Burdick Brothers, 1857), 404, available from Documenting the American South, http://docsouth.unc.edu/browse/bios/pn0000711_bio.html (accessed December 12, 2007).

8. *Ibid.*

9. *Ibid.,* 387–389.

10. Lorman A. Ratner and Dwight L. Teeter, Jr., *Fanatics and Fire-eaters: Newspapers and the Coming of the Civil War* (Urbana: University of Illinois Press, 2003), 118; Carl R. Osthaus, *Partisans of the Southern Press: Editorial Spokesmen of the Nineteenth Century* (Lexington: University of Kentucky Press, 1994), 10.

11. Stephanie McCurry, *Masters of Small Worlds: Yeoman Households, Gender Relations, and the Political Culture of the Antebellum South Carolina Low Country* (New York: Oxford University Press, 1995), 7, 19, 240; Babcock, 1–5.

12. See, for example, J. Mills Thornton, III, *Politics and Power in a Slave State: Alabama, 1800–1860* (Baton Rouge: Louisiana State University Press, 1978), 128–129.

13. *Ibid.*, 28.

14. William J. Thorn, "Hudson's History of Journalism Criticized by His Contemporaries," *Journalism Quarterly* 57 (1980), 99–106.

15. George Henry Payne, *The History of Journalism in the United States* (New York: D. Appleton and Company, 1920).

16. Helper, 300–301; Payne, 300.

17. Payne, 295–299.

18. Havilah Babcock, "The Press and the Civil War," *Journalism Quarterly* 6:1 (March 1929), 1–5.

19. James W. Carey, "The Problem of Journalism History," *Journalism History* 1 (Spring 1974), 4.

Chapter 1, The Press in the Crucible of War

1. Peter Arnett, *Live from the Battlefield: From Vietnam to Baghdad, 35 Years in the World's War Zones* (New York: Simon and Schuster, 1994), 368.

2. Philip Knightley, *The First Casualty: From the Crimea to Vietnam: The War Correspondent as Hero, Propagandist, and Myth Maker* (New York: Harcourt Brace Jovanovich, 1975), title page, 3.

3. Fred Fedler, *Lessons from the Past: Journalists' Lives and Work, 1850–1950* (Prospect Heights, Ill.: Waveland Press, Inc., 2000), 13.

4. Bernard A. Weisberger, *Reporters for the Union* (Westport, Conn.: Greenwood Press, 1977); George E. Stephens and David Yacovone, *A Voice of Thunder: A Black Soldier's Civil War* (Urbana: University of Illinois Press, 1998); Emmet Crozier, *Yankee Reporters, 1861–1865* (New York: Oxford University Press, 1956); Brayton Harris, *Blue and Gray in Black and White: Newspapers in the Civil War* (Washington, D.C.: Brassey's, 1999); James M. Perry, *A Bohemian Brigade: the Civil War Correspondents, Mostly Rough, Sometimes Ready* (New York: Wiley, 2001); Louis M. Starr, *Reporting the Civil War: the Bohemian Brigade in Action, 1861–65* (New York: Collier, 1962); Louis M. Starr, *Bohemian Brigade: Civil War Newsmen in Action* (New York: Knopf, 1954).

5. John B. Boles, *The South Through Time: A History of an American Region*, 3rd ed., vol. 1 (Upper Saddle River, N.J.: Prentice Hall, 2004), 218. Statistics regarding the demographics and slave-holding rates of Southern journalists come from unpublished databases created by Debra Reddin van Tuyll. The information was gathered primarily from the 1860 U.S. Manuscript Census and the 1860 U.S. Manuscript Census Slave Schedule.

6. Debra Reddin van Tuyll, "Necessity and the Invention of a Newspaper: What it Took to Start a Newspaper in Civil War North Carolina," *Journalism History* 34 (Summer

2008), 87–97; "Grey Ladies of the Confederacy: Newspaper Culture in the Old South" (Unpublished Ph.D. dissertation, University of South Carolina, 2000); Thomas D. Clark, "The Country Newspaper: A Factor in Southern Opinion, 1865–1930," *Journal of Southern History* XIV (1), 3-4; Othaus, 7.

7. Jeffrey L. Pasley, *"The Tyranny of Printers": Newspaper Politics in the Early American Republic* (Charlottesville: University of Virginia Press, 2001), 19, 158.

8. J. Cutler Andrews, *The South Reports the Civil War* (Princeton, N.J.: Princeton University Press, 1970), 50.

9. *Richmond Dispatch*, July 11, 1861.

10. *Richmond Enquirer*, February 6, 1863; *Richmond Dispatch*, July 1, 1862.

11. Knightley, 25.

12. Carey, 5.

13. Susan Thompson, *The Penny Press: The Origins of the Modern News Media, 1833–1861* (Northport, Ala.: Vision Press, 2004), 2.

14. W. Joseph Campbell, *The Year that Defined American Journalism: 1897 and the Clash of Paradigms* (New York: Routledge, 2006), 6.

15. *The Press Association of the Confederate States of America* (Griffin, Ga.: Hill and Swayze's Printing House, 1863), 56. These were printed minutes for the Press Association's board of directors.

16. *Memphis Appeal*, November 6, 1863.

17. *Savannah Republican*, March 17, 1862; William Herbert Wilken, "As the Telegraph Saw It: A Study of the Editorial Policy of the Macon Telegraph (And Confederate), 1860–1865," (unpublished master's thesis, Emory University, 1964), 12–13.

18. Wilson, "Confederate Press Association: A Pioneer News Agency," 160; Andrews, *The South Reports the Civil War*, 55–56; Tucker, "The Press Association of the Confederate States of America in Georgia," 2; Risley, "Georgia's Civil War Newspapers: Partisan, Sanguine, Enterprising," 114; Louis Turner Griffith and John Erwin Talmadge, *Georgia Journalism 1763–1950* (Athens: University of Georgia Press, 1951), 73.

19. *The Press Association of the Confederate States of America*, 21, 23, 25; *Minutes of the Board of Directors*, 28.

20. *Augusta Chronicle and Sentinel*, August 8, 1863; *Minutes of the Board of Directors of the Press Association*, 14.

21. Knightley, 24.

22. *Minutes of the Board of Directors of the Press Association*, 28.

23. Andrews, 94–95.

24. Patricia G. McNeely, *Fighting Words: The History of the Media in South Carolina* (Columbia: South Carolina Press Association, 1998), 30; *Abbeville* (S.C.) *Press*, October 2, 1863.

25. J. Ford Risley, "Dear Courier": The Civil War Experiences of Melvin Dwinell (paper presented at the annual meeting of the American Journalism Historians Association, Billings, Montana, October 2003).

26. *Anderson Intelligencer*, February 2, 1865.

27. Risley, "Bombastic Yet Insightful: Georgia's Civil War Soldier Correspondents," *Journalism History*, 24:3 (Autumn 1998), 104.

28. Risley, 106, 109.

29. *Memphis Appeal*, April 8, 1862.

30. *Macon Telegraph,* January 2, 1863.

31. *Ibid.*

32. *Ibid.*

33. Knightley, 22; Risley, "Bombastic Yet Insightful," 104.

34. Bagby Diary, Bagby Family Papers, George William Bagby file, Virginia Historical Society, Richmond, Va.; George W. Bagby to Robert Ridgeway, March 31, 1858, Brock Collection, Huntington Library, Pasadena, California; Andrews, 49; Robert Barnwell Rhett, Jr., to George W. Bagby, Jr., January 27, 1858, Virginia Historical Society.

35. Bagby Diary, Bagby Family Papers, George William Bagby file, November 6, 9, 1861, Virginia Historical Society.

36. *The Press Association of the Confederate States of America,* 19–20; *The First Annual Meeting of the Press Association: Minutes of the Board of Directors,* 28, 33.

37. Inflation calculator available at Homepage of S. Morgan Friedman, http://www.westegg.com/inflation/ (accessed February 15, 2009); information on Confederate inflation and currency value available at "Confederate Inflation Rates," Inflation.com, Financial Trend Forecaster newsletter on-line, http://inflationdata.com/Inflation/Inflation_Rate/ConfederateInflation.asp (accessed February 15, 2009).

38. *First Annual Meeting of the Press Association,* 25.

39. *Journal of the Confederate Congress,* vol. 4 (Washington: Government Printing Office, 1904), 207; *Proceedings of the Second Confederate Congress, First Session and Second Session in Part,* Frank E. Vandiver, ed. (Southern Historical Society Papers, New Series No. 13; Whole No. 51, 1958), 100, 136, 234; *The First Annual Meeting of the Press Association: Minutes of the Board of Directors,* 25.

40. Andrews, 18, 21; *Charleston Mercury,* July 27, 1861; *Memphis Appeal,* April 30, 1862.

41. Risley, "Georgia's Civil War Newspapers: Partisan, Sanguine, Enterprising," (Unpublished Ph.D. dissertation, University of Florida, 1996), 96–97.

42. James M. Matthews, *The Statutes at Large of the Confederate States of America, 1st Congress, 3rd Session* (Richmond: R.M. Smith, Printer to Congress, 1863), 106.

43. Richard B. Kielbowicz, "The Telegraph, Censorship and Politics at the Outset of the Civil War," *Civil War History* 40 (1940), 95.

44. Ruby Florence Tucker, "The Press Association of the Confederate States of America in Georgia," (Unpublished master's thesis, University of Georgia, 1950), 83.

45. Robert N. Mathis, "Freedom of the Press in the Confederacy: A Reality," *The Historian,* 37:4 (August, 1975), 634.

46. Jefferson Davis, Second Inaugural Address, February 22, 1862, The Jefferson Davis Papers, Rice University, Houston, Texas, http://cohesion.rice.edu/humanities/pjdavis/resources.cfm?doc_id=1514 (accessed August 13, 2008).

47. *Savannah Republican,* September 8, 1864.

48. Mark Neely, Jr., *Southern Rights: Political Prisoners and the Myth of Confederate Constitutionalism* (Charlottesville: University of Virginia Press, 2005).

49. *Nebraska Press Association v. Stuart,* 427 U.S. 539 (1976).

50. *Savannah Republican,* September 8, 1864; Jefferson Davis to Braxton Bragg, August 5, 1862 (cited in Seitz, *Braxton Bragg, General of the Confederacy* (Columbia: The State Co., 1924).

51. *Savannah Republican,* June 2, 1862.

52. *Savannah Republican*, June 2, 1862.

53. Knightley, 22.

54. *Charleston Mercury*, July 6, 1861.

55. Albert Rhett to Edmund Rhett, October 12, 1861, Robert Barnwell Rhett Collection, Southern Historical Society, University of North Carolina.

56. T. Conn Bryan, *Confederate Georgia* (Athens: University of Georgia Press, 1953), 207; Patricia Towery, "Censorship of South Carolina Newspapers, 1861–1865," in James B. Meriweather, ed., *South Carolina Journals and Journalism* (Spartanburg, S.C.: The Reprint Co. Publishers, 1975), 50.

57. General Order No. 98, OR, Series II, Vol. 51, Pt. 2, 428.

58. Joseph J. Matthews, *Reporting the Wars* (Minneapolis: The University of Minnesota Press, 1957), 80, 95.

59. Jefferson Davis to Braxton Bragg, August 5, 1862, cited in Don C. Seitz, *Braxton Bragg, General of the Confederacy* (Columbia: The State Co., 1924), 155.

60. OR, Series I, Vol. 11, Pt. 3, 636.

61. *Journal of the Congress of the Confederate States of America, First Congress, Second Session,* Volume 5 (Washington, D. C.: Government Printing Office, 1904).

62. OR, Series 1, Vol. 15, 772.

63. OR, Series I, Vol. 15, 771–72; Donna Lee Dickerson, *The Course of Tolerance: Freedom of the Press in Nineteenth-Century America* (Westport, Conn.: Greenwood Press, 1990), 195–96; *Proceedings of the First Confederate Congress, Second Session*, Southern Historical Society Papers (New Series No. 7; Whole No. 45, 1925), 225–227; Robert N. Mathis, "Freedom of the Press in the Confederacy: A Reality," *The Historian*, 37:4 (August, 1975); John Paul Jones, "The Confederate Press and the Government," *Americana* (January 1943), 14–15.

64. *First Annual Meeting of the Press Association,* 29, 54–55.

65. Andrews, *The South Reports the Civil War,* 530.

66. L. Edward Carter, "The Revolution in Journalism During the Civil War," *Lincoln Herald* 73 (Winter 1971), 235.

67. *Augusta Chronicle and Sentinel,* August 26, 1863.

68. *Charleston Mercury,* July 16, 1861.

69. *Charleston Mercury,* August 26, 1862

70. OR, Series 1, Vol. 15, 772.

71. *Charleston Mercury,* August 26, 1862.

72. Catherine Patricia Oliver, "Problems of South Carolina Editors who Reported the Civil War," (master's thesis, University of South Carolina, 1970), 33–34; *Sandersville Central Georgian,* January 8, 1862.

73. *Athens Southern Banner,* November 30, 1864.

74. Risley, "Georgia Newspapers in the Civil War," 32.

75. Knightley, 24–28.

76. Hodding Carter, *Their Words Were Bullets: The Southern Press in War, Reconstruction and Peace* (Mercer University Lamar Memorial Lectures No. 12, Athens: University of Georgia Press, 1969), 31; Andrews, 48, 536.

77. Andrews, 536.

78. Knightley, 33; Joseph J. Mathews, *Reporting the Wars* (Minneapolis: University of Minnesota Press, 1957), 95; *Charleston Mercury,* October 15, 1861.

79. *Savannah Republican*, October 4, 1862.

80. *Savannah Republican*, October 20, 1862; *Rome* (Georgia) *Southerner*, October 10, 1862; *Savannah Republican*, November 5, 1862.

81. *Savannah Republican*, November 11, 1862.

82. Felix de Fontaine, *History of Abolition; its Four Great Epochs, Embracing Narratives of the Ordinance of 1787, Compromise of 1820, Annexation of Texas, Mexican War, Wilmot Proviso, Negro Insurrections, Abolition Riots, Slave Rescues, Compromise of 1850, Kansas Bill of 1854, John Brown Insurrection, l859, Valuable Statistics, &c., &c., &c.; Together With a History of the Southern Confederacy* (New York: D. Appleton, 1861). The articles were published in the *New York Herald* on February 2, 1861. Felix G. de Fontaine, *Army Letters*, vol. 1 (Columbia, S.C.: War Record Publishing Company, 1896), 3–69; Felix G. de Fontaine "The First Day of Real War," *The Southern Bivouac*, 2:2 (July 1886), 73–79; and Felix G. de Fontaine, "The Second Day of Real War," *The Southern Bivouac*, 2:4 (September 1886), 201–207.

83. *New York Times*, May 16, 1866.

84. *Ibid.*

85. This was the short-lived initial name of the Army of Northern Virginia. It fought only the First Battle of Manassas as the Army of the Potomac.

86. Mathews, 95; *Charleston Courier*, October 28, 1861.

87. *Charleston Mercury*, July 25, 1861.

88. Reprinted in the *Augusta Constitutionalist*, January 1, 1861.

89. *Constitutionalist*, January 1, 1861; Henry T. Malone, "The Weekly Atlanta Intelligencer as a Secessionist [sic] Journal," *Georgia Historical Quarterly* 37 (1952), 282; *Augusta Chronicle and Sentinel*, November 29, 1864.

90. *Gainesville* (Fla.) *Cotton States*, reprinted in the *Charleston Mercury*, July 10, 1863.

91. Risley, "Bombastic Yet Insightful: Georgia's Civil War Soldier Correspondents," *Journalism History* 24:3 (Autumn, 1998), 104.

92. *Chronicle and Sentinel*, December 15, 1861.

93. *Western Democrat*, March 28, 1865.

94. *Athens Southern Watchman*, November 2, 1864.

95. *Charleston Mercury*, April 18, 1861.

96. Cornelia Phillips Spencer, *The Last Ninety Days of the War in North Carolina* (New York: Watchman Publishing Co., 1866). Reprinted by Broadfoot Publishing Co., Wilmington, N.C., 1993, 244.

97. Benedict Anderson, *Imagined Communities: Reflections on the Origin and Spread of Nationalism* (New York: Verson, 1983); Talcott Williams, "The Press and Public Opinion: Abstract," *Proceedings of the American Political Science Association*, vol. 9, Ninth Annual Meeting (1912), 201–203.

98. *Charleston Courier*, August 9, 1861.

Chapter 2, William A. Courtenay

1. *Charleston Mercury*, November 6, 1861.

2. Courtenay to Gibbes, August 21, 1865, Confederate Imprints, 1861–1865, reel 83, no. 2564.

3. James Calvin Hemphill, *Men of Mark in South Carolina*, Vol. 1 (Washington, D.C.: Men of Mark Publishing Company. 1907), 78.1880 U.S. Manuscript Census for South Carolina.

4. *Ibid.*

5. "Fifty Years a Washington Light Infantry," Tuesday, April 30, 1901, unidentified Charleston newspaper, William Ashmead Courtenay Scrapbook, South Carolina Archives; P900170; also, Gail Moore Morrison, "I Shall Not Pass This Way Again: The Contributions of William Ashmead Courtenay," http://192.220.96.192/thisway.htm (accessed August 2, 2008); also, "Washington Light Infantry, Charleston," Confederate Veteran, VIII, No. 2, (Nashville, Tennessee, 1900), 76.

6. William L King, *The Newspaper Press* (Manchester, N.H.: Ayer Company Publishers, 1872), 155, 156.

7. *Charleston Mercury,* October 18, 1861.

8. *Ibid.*

9. *Ibid.*

10. *Ibid.*

11. *Charleston Mercury,* November 6, 1861. This article was written by Barnwell Rhett, Jr., who was paraphrasing Courtenay.

12. *Charleston Mercury,* November 1, 1861.

13. *Ibid.*

14. *Ibid.*

15. *Charleston Mercury,* November 4, 1861.

16. *Ibid.*

17. *Ibid.*

18. *Ibid.*

19. *Charleston Mercury,* November 5, 1861.

20. *Ibid.*

21. *Ibid.*

22. *Ibid.*

23. *Ibid.*

24. *Ibid.*

25. *Ibid.*

26. *Charleston Mercury,* November 6, 1861.

27. *Ibid.*

28. *Ibid.*

29. *Ibid.*

30. J. Cutler Andrews, *The South Reports the Civil War* (Pittsburgh: University of Pittsburgh Press, 1970), 185. (Footnote: *Charleston Mercury,* November 6, 1861; *Richmond Daily Dispatch*, November 23, 1861; *Memphis Daily Appeal*, November 29, 1861; G.B. Cuthbert to R.B. Rhett Jr., March, 7, 10, 14, 1862; R.B. Rhett, Jr., to G.B. Cuthbert, March 10, 13, 1862, Robert Barnwell Rhett Papers, Huntsville, Alabama.)

31. *Charleston Mercury,* December 6, 1861.

32. *Charleston Mercury,* December 3, 1861.

33. Courtenay's war record is presented differently by Richard B. McCaslin, *Portraits of Conflict: A Photographic History of South Carolina in the Civil War*

(Fayetteville: The University of Arkansas Press, 1994), 223, 224, 308. Apparently, the war record of W.A. Courtney of Old Store, South Carolina, was interpreted as the war record of William A. Courtenay of Charleston. Courtenay is listed in the 1860 census as living in Charleston, while Courtney is listed as living in Old Store, a district of Chesterfield County on the North Carolina border. Courtenay was 29 years old in 1860 and Courtney was 24. The Old Store Courtney was a prisoner of war at Johnson's Island, Ohio, from September 13, 1864, until June 16, 1865, but the Charleston Courtenay was writing letters from Hardeeville, South Carolina, during that period. The document showing the release of the Old Store Courtney from the Union prison is in Confederate Records, Microcopy 267, Roll 229, South Carolina Archives. The Charleston Courtenay letters showing Courtenay in Hardeeville during that period are in Correspondence, Confederate Imprints, 1861–1865, reel 83, no. 2564, Cooper Library, University of South Carolina.

34. William A. Courtenay, "Heroes of Honey Hill," vol. 26, *Southern Historical Society Papers* (Richmond: Southern Historical Society, 1898), 238.

35. Courtenay correspondence to DePass, Hardeeville, South Carolina, October 1, 1864, Microfilm, New Haven, Connecticut, Research Publications (1974), Confederate Imprints, 1861–1865, Reel 83, No. 2564, Cooper Library, University of South Carolina.

36. Thomas W. Salmond to Stuart Gibbes, Camden, South Carolina, November 24, 1864, Hardeeville, October 1, 1864, Correspondence, Confederate Imprints.

37. Courtenay, "Fragments of War History Relating to The Coast Defence of South Carolina, 1861–1865, and the Hasty Preparations for the Battle of Honey Hill, November 30, 1864," vol. 26, *Southern Historical Society Papers* (Richmond: Southern Historical Society), 62–87.

38. *Ibid.*

39. *Ibid.*

40. *Ibid.*

41. *Ibid.*

42. Courtenay, "Heroes of Honey Hill, 237.

43. Courtenay, "Coast Defence," 73.

44. *Ibid.*, 78.

45. Courtenay, "Heroes of Honey Hill," 232.

46. Courtenay, "Coast Defence," 26 (August 1898): 86.

47. E.B. Long, with Barbara Long, *The Civil War Day by Day* (Garden City, N.Y.: Doubleday, 1971), 614.

48. Dede Norungolo, *Daily* (S.C.) *Journal Messenger*, March 2005 (no day listed), Courtenay Scrapbook.

49. Courtenay to Gibbes, August, 21, 1865, Confederate imprints, 1861–1865, reel 83, No. 2564.

50. Courtenay to Gibbes, August, 21, 1865, Correspondence.

51. Hemphill, 78.

52. Rob Salzman, E-Familytree.net: http://www.efamilytree.net/F216/F216350.htm.

   1. Edith Courtenay: Born: March 18, 1867: Died: January 12,1949: Married: John Michael Bateman.

2. Campbell Courtenay: Born: 1868: Died: 10 Nov 1930.

3. Carlisle Courtenay: Born: July 4,1869: Died: December 14, 1952 at Columbia, South Carolina; Wife: Laura Elmore Davant.

4. Ashmead Courtenay: Born: November 2, 1870: Died: February 1,1952 at Columbia, South Carolina.

5. Julia Courtenay: Born: July 18 1875: Died: December 5,1960: Married: Louis Morgan Barnwell.

6. St. John Courtenay: Born: June 19, 1877 at Charleston, South Carolina: Died: December 22, 1932 at Columbia, South Carolina: married: Margaret Hayne Beattie.

7. Arthur Courtenay: Born: c. 1879: Died: c. 1879.

8. Edward Courtenay: Born: c.1881: Died: c. 1881.

9. Elizabeth Courtenay: Born: c. 1883: Died: c. 1883.

10. Edward C. Courtenay: Born: c. 1885: Died: c. 1885.

53. Morrison.

54. *Ibid.*

55. Most references call this a hurricane.

56. "A Memorial of Public Service 1879–88," 11, Courtenay Scrapbook.

57. *The Chester Bulletin* and the *Rock Hill Herald*, undated copies, Courtenay Scrapbook.

58. Hemphill, 78.

59. No author listed, *Textile Excelsior* (Charlotte, N.C.: John Cuthbertson & Co., August 28, 1897), Courtenay Scrapbook.

60. "The Timrod Revival," *The Saturday Review*, no author listed, New York, Mrs. Emma Moffett Tyng, New York editor, 1899, Courtenay Scrapbook.

61. "A Memorial for Henry Timrod," *The Literary News*, February 1899, Courtenay Scrapbook.

62. Unnamed magazine article, *Home Journal*, New York, Wednesday, March 1, 1899, Courtenay Scrapbook.

63. "The Timrod Revival," Courtenay Scrapbook.

64. "The Life and Genius of Timrod," *Charleston Sunday News*, April 30, 1899, Courtenay Scrapbook.

65. Morrison.

66. *Keowee Courier*, June 14, 1900, Courtenay Scrapbook.

67. Wedding invitation for the November wedding of Julia Courtenay and Louis Morgan Barnwell, circa 1899, Courtenay Scrapbook.

Chapter 3, Felix G. de Fontaine

1. Felix Gregory de Fontaine, *Army Letters, No. 1* (Columbia, S.C.: War Record Publishing Company, 1895), 27–32.

2. Louis Morris Starr, *Bohemian Brigade* (Madison: University of Wisconsin Press, 1987, c1954), 28–29.

3. *New York Herald*, April 13, 1861.

4. Starr, 28–29.

5. Jess Stein, *The Random House Dictionary of the English Language* (New York: Random House, 1967), 254.

6. Family records of Tony and Maryjane Islan of Summerville, South Carolina. Islan is a direct descendent of de Fontaine.

7. *Ibid.*

8. *The State*, Columbia, S.C., December 13, 1896.

9. Felix Gregory de Fontaine, *De Fontaine's Condensed Long-Hand and Rapid-Writer's Companion, a system of condensed long-hand, whereby with but little study, one is enabled to greatly increase the rapidity of his hand-writing,* (New York: American News Co., 1886).

10. Mary C. Simms Oliphant, et al. eds., *Letters of William Gilmore Simms* (Columbia: University of South Carolina Press, 1952–1982), 543.

11. Edwin A. Perry, *The Boston Herald and Its History* (Boston: *The Herald*, 1878), 34–35.

12. *Ibid.*, 34.

13. *American Mercury*, LXVI (February 1948), 228–233.

14. Felix de Fontaine, and Daniel Edgar Sickles, *Trial of the Hon. David E. Sickles for Shooting Philip Barton Key. February 27th, 1859,* (New York: R.M. DeWitt, 1859).

15. August Kohn, *Charleston News and Courier*, December 12, 1896.

16. Felix de Fontaine, *A History of Abolition from 1787 to 1861: a History of American Abolitionism its Four Great Epochs, Embracing Narratives of the Ordinance of 1787, Compromise of 1820, Annexation of Texas, Mexican war, Wilmot Proviso, Negro Insurrections, Abolition Riots, Slave Rescues, Compromise of 1850, Kansas Bill of 1854, John Brown Insurrection, 1859, Valuable Statistics, &c., &c., &c.; Together With a History of the Southern Confederacy.*(New York: D. Appleton, 1861). The articles were originally published in the *New York Herald* on February 2, 1861.

17. *Ibid.*

18. Felix G. de Fontaine, "Marginalia; or, Gleanings from an army note-book." By "Personne" [i.e. Felix Gregory De Fontaine], Steam Power-Press of F.G. de Fontaine (Columbia, S.C., 1864).

19. N.G. Osteen, untitled and undated article in the *Sumter Watchman and Southern*, Sumter, S.C., responding to an editorial in the *Columbia Record* of Tuesday, February 21, 1911, de Fontaine papers, University of South Caroliniana Library, Columbia.

20. Felix Gregory de Fontaine, *Army Letters*, Vol. 1, No. 1 (Columbia, S.C.: War Record Publishing Company, 1895), 3–21.

21. *Charleston Daily Courier*, April 25, 1861.

22. J. Cutler Andrews, *The North Reports the Civil War* (Pittsburgh, Pa.: University of Pittsburgh Press, 1955), 14, 77.

23. Herbert Ravenel Sass, *Outspoken: 150 years of the News and Courier* (Columbia: University of South Carolina Press, 1953), 117.

24. *Charleston News and Courier*, December 12, 1896, also J. Cutler Andrews, *The South Reports the Civil War* (Pittsburgh, Pa.: University of Pittsburgh Press, 1985), 52.

25. Timrod Papers, Henry Timrod's letter to his sister Emily on April 11, 1862, University of South Caroliniana Library, Columbia.

26. Andrews, *The South Reports the Civil War*, 548, 549.

27. *New York Times*, May 16, 1866.

28. *Richmond Daily Dispatch*, July 25, 1861.

29. *Charleston Daily Courier*, July 23, 1861.

30. *Charleston Daily Courier*, July 30, 1861.

31. *Ibid.*

32. *Charleston Daily Courier*, July 23, 1861.

33. *Charleston Daily Courier*, July 27, 1861; *Richmond Daily Dispatch*, July 25, 1861.

34. *Charleston Daily Courier*, July 29, 1861.

35. *Ibid.*

36. Andrews, 97–98.

37. W.H. Pritchard to Hon. L.P. Walker, Secretary of War, Sept. 2, 1861, Office of Confederate Secretary of War, 1861–1865, letters received, 3966-1861, National Archives.

38. *Charleston Daily Courier*, August 15, 1861.

39. *Charleston Daily Courier*, September 7, 1861.

40. *Charleston Daily Courier*, October 9, 1861.

41. *Ibid.*

42. *Ibid.*

43. *Ibid.*

44. *Ibid.*

45. *Charleston Daily Courier*, October 24, 1861.

46. *Ibid.*

47. *Charleston Daily Courier*, October 28, 1861.

48. *Ibid.*

49. *Ibid.*

50. E.B. Long, with Barbara Long, *The Civil War Day by Day* (Garden City, N.Y.: Doubleday, 1971), 129.

51. *Charleston Daily Courier*, November 8, 1861.

52. *Ibid.*

53. *Ibid.*

54. *Charleston Daily Courier*, October 24, 1861.

55. General Orders, 1861–1863, No. 78, issued by the Adjutant and Inspector General's Office from Richmond, October 28, 1862, Special Collections, Library of Virginia, Richmond.

56. *Charleston Daily Courier*, October 28, 1861.

57. *Charleston Daily Courier*, November 17, 1861.

58. *Charleston Daily Courier*, November 27, 1861.

59. *Charleston Daily Courier*, December 3, 1861.

60. *Charleston Daily Courier*, November 29, 1861.

61. *Charleston Daily Courier*, January 4, 1861.

62. *Ibid.*

63. John S. Bowman, *The Civil War* (North Dighton, Mass.: World Publications Group, 2006), 51.

64. *Charleston Daily Courier*, January 27, 1862.

65. *Ibid.*

66. *Charleston Daily Courier*, February 24, 1862.

67. *Ibid.*

68. *Ibid.*

69. Long, 175.

70. *Charleston Daily Courier*, February 24, 1862.

71. *Charleston Daily Courier*, April 23, 1862.

72. *Charleston Daily Courier*, April 22, 1862.

73. *Ibid.*

74. *Charleston Daily Courier*, April 15, 1862.

75. *Charleston Daily Courier*, April 22, 1862.

76. *Charleston Daily Courier*, April 15, 1862.

77. *Charleston Daily Courier*, April 22, 23, 1862

78. *Charleston Daily Courier*, May 8, 1862.

79. *Charleston Daily Courier*, April 25, 1862.

80. *Charleston Daily Courier*, April 22, 23, 1862.

81. *Charleston Daily Courier*, April 23, 1862.

82. *Ibid.*

83. *Ibid.*

84. *Charleston Daily Courier*, May 20, 1862.

85. *Charleston Daily Courier*, May 15, 1862.

86. *Charleston Daily Courier*, May 20, 1862.

87. *Charleston Daily Courier*, May 29, 1862.

88. *Ibid.*

89. *Charleston Daily Courier*, June 9, 1862.

90. *Charleston Daily Courier*, May 28, 1862.

91. *Charleston Daily Courier*, June 17, 1862.

92. *Ibid.*

93. *Ibid.*

94. *Charleston Daily Courier*, June 21, 1862.

95. *Ibid.*

96. *Charleston Daily Courier*, June 26, 1862.

97. *Ibid.*

98. *Ibid.*

99. Walter Brian Cisco, *Henry Timrod, A Biography* (Cranbury, N.J.: Associated University Presses, 2004), 81.

100. *Charleston Daily Courier*, July 23, 1862.

101. *Charleston Daily Courier*, July 18, 1862.

102. *Charleston Daily Courier*, July 24, 1862.

103. *Charleston Daily Courier*, July 28, 1862.

104. *Ibid.*

105. *Charleston Daily Courier*, July 24, 1862.

106. *Charleston Daily Courier*, August 8, 1862.

107. *Ibid.*

108. *Ibid.*

109. *Charleston Daily Courier*, August 14, 1862.

110. *Charleston Daily Courier*, August 9, 1862.

111. *Ibid.*

112. *Charleston Daily Courier*, August 30, 1862.

113. *Ibid.*

114. *Ibid.*

115. *Ibid.*

116. *Charleston Daily Courier*, September 3, 1862.

117. *Ibid.*

118. *Charleston Daily Courier*, September 25, 1862.

119. *Charleston Daily Courier*, September 3, 1862.

120. *Ibid.*

121. *Charleston Daily Courier*, September 11, 1862.

122. *Ibid.*

123. *Charleston Daily Courier*, September 23, 1862.

124. Mark M. Boatner, III, *The Civil War Dictionary* (New York: Vintage Books, 1991), 17.

125. *Charleston Daily Courier*, September 29, 1862.

126. *Ibid.*

127. *Charleston Daily Courier*, September 29, 1862.

128. *Ibid.*

129. *Ibid.*

130. *Charleston Daily Courier*, October 3, 1862.

131. *Charleston Daily Courier*, October 23, 1862; also *Daily South Carolinian*, October 23, 1862.

132. *Charleston Daily Courier*, January 5, 1862.

133. *Charleston Daily Courier*, January 20, 1863.

134. *Charleston Daily Courier*, January 23, 1863.

135. *Charleston Daily Courier*, February 5, 1863.

136. *Ibid.*

137. *Charleston Daily Courier*, January 31, 1863.

138. *Ibid*

139. Andrews, "South," 55–56.

140. The number of newspapers that belonged to the Press Association fluctuated during the war.

141. William H. Johnson, Jr., "Dr. Robert Wilson Gibbes: Southern Editor and Publisher, 1852–1864," (master's thesis, Columbia: University of South Carolina, 1969), 101.

142. *Ibid.*, 102.

143. Minutes of the Board of Directors of the Press Association embracing the Quarterly Reports of the Superintendent Fourth Session, Atlanta, October 14, 1863, and Fifth Session, Augusta, January 14, 1864, Atlanta, Georgia (Franklin Steam Publishing House, J.J. Toon & Co., Proprietors, 1864), 54–56.

144. *Charleston Daily Courier*, April 2, 1863.

145. *Ibid.*

146. *Charleston Daily Courier*, April 11, 1863.

147. *Charleston Daily Courier*, September 7, 1861.

148. *Savannah Republican,* July 14, 1863.

149. Mrs. Georgia Moore de Fontaine, *Confederate Veteran,* 5:2 (October 1897), 585.

150. The *New York Times,* October 18, 1897.

151. The *State,* December 13, 1896.

152. de Fontaine papers, *Personal letter from Georgia Moore de Fontaine to Mrs. C.C. Pinckney,* Charleston (struck out and replaced with Salkehatchee), South Carolina, 1891, Caroliniana Library, University of South Carolina, Columbia.

153. Long, 405.

154. *Charleston Daily Courier,* October 12, 1863.

155. *Ibid.*

156. Long, 412.

157. *Charleston Daily Courier,* October 12, 1863.

158. *Charleston Daily Courier,* October 20, 1863.

159. *Charleston Daily Courier,* October 22, 1863.

160. *Ibid.*

161. *Charleston Daily Courier,* November 5, 1863.

162. *Charleston Daily Courier,* November 7, 1863.

163. *Charleston Daily Courier,* December 11, 1863.

164. *Charleston Daily Courier,* December 23, 1863.

165. Johnson, 109; Minutes of the Board of Directors of the Press Association, Atlanta, Ga., Franklin Steam Publishing House, 1864, 37.

166. The *Daily Carolinian, Charleston Daily Courier,* July 2, 1864.

167. de Fontaine letter, Scrapbook, Atlanta, July 8, 1864, Caroliniana Library, University of South Carolina, Columbia.

168. *Ibid.*

169. The *Daily Carolinian,* July 22, 1864.

170. Andrews, *The South Reports the Civil War,* 455, 456.

171. *Savannah Republican,* July 27, 1864.

172. 1900 U.S. Manuscript Census entry for Georgia A. de Fontaine Schuyler; Felix G. de Fontaine, "Marginalia; or, Gleanings from an army note-book." By "Personne" [i.e. Felix Gregory De Fontaine], Steam Power-Press of F.G. de Fontaine (Columbia, S.C., 1864).

173. *Daily South Carolinian,* November 23, 1864.

174. Robert N. Rosen, *A Short History of Charleston* (San Francisco: Lexikos, 1982), 151.

175. *South Carolinian,* reprinted in *Charleston Daily Courier,* November 26, 1864.

176. Osteen.

177. Julian A. Selby (b. 1833), *Memorabilia and Anecdotal Reminiscences of Columbia, S.C., and Incidents Connected Therewith* (Columbia, S.C.: R.L. Bryan Company, 1905, reprinted 1970), 101.

178. Selby, 194.

179. *Ibid.*

180. John Hammond Moore, *South Carolina Newspapers* (Columbia: University of South Carolina Press, 1988), 202; *Daily South Carolinian,* April 19, 1865.

181. Dallas D. Irvine, "The Fate of Confederate Archives: Executive Office," *The American Historical Review,* 44:4 (July 1939): 823–824.

182. *Ibid.*, 831, 832.

183. James A Hoyt, "The Confederate Archives and Felix G. de Fontaine," *South Carolina Historical Magazine*, South Carolina Historical Society, 57 (Charleston, S.C., 1957), 199–200.

184. *Ibid.*

185. *New York Times*, August 20, 1865.

186. Publication had been resumed by November 17, 1865.

187. Oliphant, 552.

188. 1880 U.S. Census; Wade Hampton de Fontaine's passport, U.S. Passport Applications, available from ancestry.com.

189. *New York Times*, May 26, 1866.

190. *Ibid.*

191. Douglas J. Robillard, "Henry Timrod, John R. Thompson and the Ladies of Richmond," *S.C. Historical Magazine*, 62, 129, 1961.

192. Wagener, who had been a Confederate colonel in the German Artillery battalion, became mayor of Charleston in 1871.

193. "Mrs. Georgia Moore de Fontaine," *Confederate Veteran* 5 (Nashville, Tenn., 1897), 585.

194. Kohn, *Charleston News and Courier*, December 12, 1896.

195. 1880 U.S. Census.

196. De Fontaine's books and major magazine articles included:

De Fontaine and Sickles, Daniel Edgar, *Trial of the Hon. David E. Sickles for Shooting Philip Barton Key . . . February 27th, 1859* (New York: R.M. DeWitt, 1859).

De Fontaine, *A History of Abolition from 1787 to 1861: a History of American abolitionism its four great epochs, embracing narratives of the ordinance of 1787, compromise of 1820, annexation of Texas, Mexican war, Wilmot Proviso, Negro insurrections, abolition riots, slave rescues, Compromise of 1850, Kansas bill of 1854, John Brown insurrection, l859, valuable statistics, &c., &c., &c.; together with a history of the Southern Confederacy* (New York: D. Appleton, 1861). The articles were originally written for the *New York Herald* before the war.

De Fontaine, *Marginalia or Gleanings from an Army Note-book* (Steam Power-Press of F.G. de Fontaine & Co., Columbia, S.C., 1864, reprinted by Thomson Gale 2006).

De Fontaine, "The state ex relatione the attorney-general of South Carolina, vs. the president and directors of the bank of the state of South Carolina. Mandamus - writ of error." Thursday, January 14, 1869; South Carolina, Supreme Court, Charleston: Walker, Evans & Cogswell, Printers, 1869.

De Fontaine, "Shoulder to Shoulder: Reminiscences of Confederate Camps and Fields," *XIX Century*, vol. 1–2, 1869, 35–42, 85–91, 226–234, 381–388, 439–450, 611–617, June 1869–January 1870.

De Fontaine, "Shoulder to Shoulder," *Century Magazine*, Vol. XIX, September, 1889.

De Fontaine and Hall, Charles Bryan Hall, "Chas. B. Hall and his collection of war time portraits; he is the only man who has made this a specialty, and he has 20,000 photographs of men who were engaged in the Civil War by Fontaine"; Charles Bryan Hall, publication date unknown.

De Fontaine, "The Burning of Columbia," publication date unknown.

De Fontaine, "The Story of the Great Eastern," publication date unknown.

De Fontaine, ed., "Birds of a Feather, or, Talks with Sothern," (New York: G.W. Carleton, 1878).

De Fontaine, *The Fireside Dickens: A Cyclopaedia of the Best Thoughts of Charles Dickens,* (New York, G.W. Carleton, 1883), 600 pages, and in its ninth edition at his death, reprinted December 2004.

De Fontaine, *The Hoffman House: C.H. Read and E.S. Stokes, proprietors; its attractions* (Photo-Engraving Co.: New York, 1885).

De Fontaine, "The First Day of Real War," *The Southern Bivouac,* Vol. II, July 1886, No. 2, 73–79.

De Fontaine, "The Second Day of Real War," *The Southern Bivouac,* Vol. II, September 1886, No. 4, 201–207.

De Fontaine, "The Life and Doings of Lord Dundreary," publisher, publication date unknown.

De Fontaine, "A Popular History of America," publisher, publication date unknown.

De Fontaine, "De Fontaine's Condensed Long-Hand and Rapid-Writer's Companion, a system of "condensed long-hand, whereby with but little study, one is enabled to greatly increase the rapidity of his hand-writing," (New York: American News Co., 1886).

De Fontaine, "Personal reminiscences of secession," publisher unknown, Philadelphia, 1893.

De Fontaine, Felix Gregory, "Army Letters," No. 1 and No. 2, (Columbia, S.C.: War Record Publishing Company, 1895).

197. De Fontaine, "Army Letters," No. 1, 1.

198. Although de Fontaine's obituary in the *State*, Columbia, S.C., on December 14, 1896, said he was "interred within a few hundred yards of the Confederate enclosure" at Elmwood Cemetery, his grave site has not been located.

199. *State*, December 13, 1896.

200. *Confederate Veteran*, 5:10 (Nashville, Tenn.), 585.

201. *New York Times*, October 18, 1897.

202. *Confederate Veteran*, Vol. 5, No. 10, 585.

203. *New York Times*, October 18, 1897, 7.

Chapter 4, Robert W. Gibbes

1. *United States' Telegraph*, August 10, 1835; Arney R. Childs, "Robert Wilson Gibbes, 1809–1866," *Bulletin of the University of South Carolina*. October 1925, 210, 28, 34, 35; William H. Johnson, Jr., "Dr. Robert Wilson Gibbes: Southern Editor and Publisher, 1852–1864." (Unpublished master's thesis, University of South Carolina, 1969), 2, 34; J.L. Hatch, *Rights of Corporators and Reporters: Being a Report of the Case*

of R. W. Gibbes, Editor of the South Carolinian, vs. E. J. Arthur, Mayor of Columbia, S.C, and John Burdell, Chief of Police (Columbia, S.C.: Steam-Power Press of R. W. Gibbes, 1857), 10–11.

2. *Frank Leslie's Illustrated Newspaper,* September 5, 1857, 213.

3. *Ibid.*

4. Childs, 2, 7.

5. *Ibid.,* 5, 8.

6. Simms to M.C.M. Hammond, November 1, 1849, Oliphant, Mary C. Simms, *The Letters of William Gilmore Simms,* vol. II (Columbia: University of South Carolina Press, 1956), 567.

7. Simms, William Gilmore Simms, *Sack and Destruction of the City of Columbia, S.C.* (Columbia, S.C.: Power Press of the Daily Phoenix, 1865), 36.

8. Nell S. Graydon, *Tales of Columbia* (Columbia, S.C.: R.L. Bryan Company, 1905), 44.

9. Hatch, 93.

10. *Ibid.,* 88.

11. *Ibid.,* 90–91.

12. *Ibid.,* 90–91.

13. Inscription is from the goblet of Columbia, S.C.

14. *Frank Leslie's Illustrated Newspaper,* September 5, 1857, 213.

15. *The Press Association of the Confederate States of America* (Griffin, Ga.: Hill & Swayze's Printing House, 1863), 7.

16. *Ibid.,* 2.

17. *Ibid.*

18. *Charleston Courier,* March 3, 1858.

19. *Ibid.*

20. *First Annual Meeting of the Press Association* (Montgomery, Ala.: Memphis Appeal Job Printing Establishment, 1864), 4.

21. *Ibid.,* 5.

22. *Ibid.*

23. Johnson, 66.

24. Childs, 20; Johnson, 7, 17, 18, 24, 25, 78, 88.

25. Letter from Gibbes to "your Excellency," February 28, 1865, Robert W. Gibbes Collection, South Caroliniana Library, University of South Carolina, Columbia.

26. Childs, 41.

Chapter 5, Joan

1. Elizabeth Fox-Genovese, *Within the Plantation Household: Black and White Women of the Old South* (Chapel Hill: University of North Carolina Press, 1988), 61.

2. *Ibid.,* 15.

3. Sylvia D. Hoffert, *Jane Gray Swisshelm: An Unconventional Life, 1815–1884* (Chapel Hill: University of North Carolina Press, 2004), 106.

4. Fox-Genovese, 244–245.

5. See, for example, L.S.M, "Uncle Tom's Cabin," *Southern Quarterly Review* (January 1853) http://quod.lib.umich.edu/m/moajrnl/browse.journals/squa.html (accessed

June 21, 2007) or A South Carolinian, "Slavery and Political Economy," *DeBow's Review* (October and November 1856) http://quod.lib.umich.edu/m/moajrnl/browse.journals/ debo.html (accessed June, 21 2007).

6. Lee Ann Whites, *The Civil War as a Crisis in Gender: Augusta, Georgia, 1860–1890* (Athens: University of Georgia Press, 1995), 5.

7. Whites, 87.

8. See, for example, *Charleston Courier,* November 18, 1861.

9. *Charleston Courier,* September 28, 1861, November 18, 1861.

10. J. Cutler Andrews, *The South Reports the Civil War* (Princeton: Princeton University Press, 1970), 94–95.

11. *Richmond Enquirer,* July 19, 1861 (reprint of story from the *Charleston Courier*).

12. *Our Women in the War: The Lives They Lived, the Deaths They Died* (Charleston, S.C.: News and Courier Presses, 1885), vii.

13. *Ibid.*

14. *Richmond Enquirer,* July 19, 1861; *Charleston Courier,* September 24, 1861.

15. *Richmond Enquirer,* July 19, 1861.

16. *Charleston Courier,* August 31, 1861.

17. *Charleston Courier,* August 31, 1861.

18. McCurry, 48.

19. Stephen Hahn, *Roots of Southern Populism* (New York: Oxford University Press, 1983), 27–33.

20. *Charleston Courier,* August 31, 1861.

21. *Charleston Courier,* August 14, 1861.

22. Stephanie McCurry, *Masters of Small Worlds: Yeoman Households, Gender Relations, and the Political Culture of the Antebellum South Carolina Low Country* (New York: Oxford University Press, 1995), 7.

23. *Charleston Courier,* October 17, 1861.

24. *Charleston Courier,* August 31, 1861.

25. *Ibid.,* 242.

26. Whites, 51.

27. Fox-Genovese, 47.

28. Fox-Genovese, 245; Richard S. Lounsbury, ed., *Louisa S. McCord: Selected Writings* (Charlottesville: University Press of Virginia, 1997).

29. *Charleston Courier,* July 25, 1861.

30. *Charleston Courier,* August 3, 1861.

31. *Charleston Courier,* August 9, 1861.

32. *Charleston Courier,* September 11, 1861.

33. *Charleston Courier,* August 17, 1861.

34. *Charleston Courier,* August 5, 1861. Scripture is from 1 Kings 12:14.

35. *Charleston Courier,* August 3, 1861.

36. *Charleston Courier,* August 10, 1861.

37. Mark E. Neely, Jr., *Southern Rights: Political Prisoners and the Myth of Confederate Constitutionalism* (Charlottesville: University Press of Virginia), 21, 95.

38. *Charleston Courier,* August 3, 1861.

39. *Charleston Courier,* October 1, 1861.

40. *Charleston Courier,* August 9, 1861.

41. *Charleston Courier,* August 15, 1861.

42. *Charleston Courier,* August 5, 1861.

43. *Charleston Courier,* August 14, 1861; R. Ernest Dupuy and Trevor N. Dupuy, *Encyclopedia of Military History* (New York: Harper and Row Publishers, 1977), 872.

44. *Charleston Courier,* October 7, 1861.

45. *Charleston Courier,* August 3, 1861.

46. Dupuy, 872.

47. *Charleston Courier,* August 3, 1861.

48. *Charleston Courier,* August 24, 1861. The scripture quoted in this passage is from Psalm 46:1.

49. *Ibid.* The scripture, although Joan placed it in quotation marks, is actually a paraphrase of 1 Samuel 17:47 and 2 Chronicles 20:15.

50. Steven A. Channing, *Crisis of Fear: Secession in South Carolina* (New York: W.W. Norton & Co., 1974), 20.

51. *Charleston Courier,* August 5, 1861.

52. *Charleston Courier,* August 30, 1861.

53. *Charleston Courier,* October 7, 1861.

54. *Charleston Courier,* September 24, 1861.

55. *Ibid.*

56. *Charleston Courier,* September 28, 1861.

57. *Ibid.*

58. *Charleston Courier,* September 24, 1861.

59. *Ibid.*

60. *Ibid.*

61. *Charleston Courier,* October 7, 1861.

62. *Charleston Courier,* September 24, 1861.

63. *Ibid.*

64. *Charleston Courier,* October 1, 1861.

65. *Charleston Courier,* September 3, 1861.

66. *Ibid.*

67. *Charleston Courier,* November 12, 1861.

68. *Ibid.*

69. *Charleston Courier,* August 28, 1861.

70. *Charleston Courier,* September 3, 1861.

71. *Charleston Courier,* August 27, 1861, October 1, 1861.

72. *Charleston Courier,* September 14, 1861.

73. *Charleston Courier,* November 12, 1861.

74. *Charleston Courier,* September 24, 1861.

75. *Charleston Courier,* September 28, 1861.

76. *Charleston Courier,* August 17, 1861.

77. *Ibid.*

78. *Charleston Courier,* September 12, 1861.

79. *Charleston Courier,* November 23, 1861.

80. *Ibid.*

81. *Charleston Courier,* August 3, 1861.

82. *Charleston Courier,* August 14, 1861.

83. *Charleston Courier,* August 23, 1861.

84. *Charleston Courier,* August 5, 1861.

85. *Charleston Courier,* September 7, 1861.

86. *Charleston Courier,* August 12, 1861.

87. *Charleston Courier,* August 27, 1861.

88. *Charleston Courier,* August 15, 1861.

89. *Charleston Courier,* August 30, 1861.

90. Whites, 4.

91. *Charleston Courier,* August 9, 1861.

92. *Charleston Courier,* August 5, 1861, September 5, 1861.

93. *Charleston Courier,* August 27, 1861.

94. *Charleston Courier,* September 5, 7, 1861.

95. *Charleston Courier,* August 30, 1861.

96. Richard E. Beringer, Herman Hattaway, Archer Jones, and William N. Still, Jr., *Why the South Lost the Civil War* (Athens: University of Georgia Press, 1986).

97. *Charleston Courier,* August 30, 1861.

98. *Ibid.*

99. *Charleston Courier,* September 12, 1861.

100. *Charleston Courier,* August 9, 1861.

101. *Ibid.*

102. *Charleston Courier,* September 24, 1861.

103. *Ibid.*

104. *Charleston Courier,* August 9, 1861.

105. *Ibid.*

106. *Charleston Courier,* August 9, 1861.

107. *Charleston Courier,* August 19, 1861.

108. *Charleston Courier,* August 9, 1861.

109. Whites, 135.

Chapter 6, Bartholomew Riordan

1. *Charleston Mercury,* May 4, 1861.

2. *New York Times,* March 22, 1897.

3. Randall's Capital Letter, March 27, 1897, "Death of B.R. Riordan—Friend after Friend Departs," Washington, D.C. March 24 dateline, *Augusta (Georgia) Chronicle,* William Ashmead Courtenay Scrapbook, P900170; South Carolina Archives. Also, J. Cutler Andrews, *The South Reports the Civil War* (Pittsburgh, Pa..: University of Pittsburgh Press, 1985), 64, 65.

4. Randall's Capital Letter. Randall said he "coquetted with figures in a ship brokers office."

5. Andrews, 64, 65

6. Randall's Capital Letter.

7. *Ibid.*

8. *Ibid.*

9. W.L. King, *The Newspaper Press of Charleston* (Charleston, S.C., 1872), 180; *Charleston* (S.C.) *News and Courier,* 150th Anniversary Edition, January 11, 1953.

10. *Richmond Daily Examiner,* October 21, 1861; *Savannah Republican,* September 23, 1863; *New York Daily Tribune,* March 22, 1897.

11. *Charleston Mercury,* April 30, 1861.

12. *Ibid.*

13. *Ibid.*

14. *Charleston Mercury,* May 3, 1861.

15. *Ibid.*

16. *Ibid.*

17. *Ibid.*

18. *Ibid.*

19. *Charleston Mercury,* May 4, 1861.

20. *Ibid.*

21. *Ibid.*

22. *Ibid.*

23. *Ibid.*

24. George W. Bagby, Jr., Papers, Virginia Historical Society, Richmond, Va.

25. *The Press Association of the Confederate States of America* (Griffin, Ga.: Hill & Swayzes Printing House, 1863), 20.

26. Robert N. Rosen, *Confederate Charleston: An Illustrated History of the City and the People during the Civil War* (Columbia: University of South Carolina Press, 1994), 100–105.

27. *Richmond Daily Dispatch,* October 30, 1863.

28. *Ibid.*

29. *Minutes of the Board of Directors of the Press Association,* October and January; Fourth Session–Atlanta, October 14, 1863, Fifth Session–Augusta, January 14, 1864 (Atlanta, Ga.: Franklin Steam Publishing House, J.J. Toon & Co., Proprietors, 1864), 10.

30. *Richmond Daily Dispatch,* October 30, 1863.

31. *Ibid.*

32. E.B. Long with Barbara Long, *The Civil War Day by Day* (New York: Da Capo Press, 1971), 429.

33. Charles R. Rowe, *Pages of History: 200 Years of the Post and Courier* (Charleston, S.C,: Evening Post Publishing Co., 2003), 52–54.

34. Unidentified Charleston, S.C., newspaper, dateline Monday, March 22, 1897, Courtenay papers.

35. Rowe, 52–54; also, unidentified Charleston, S.C., newspaper, dateline Monday, March 22, 1897, Courtenay papers.

36. *Ibid.*

37. *Ibid.*

38. Randall's Capital Letter.

39. *Ibid.*

40. *New York Times,* March 22, 1897.

41. Randall's Capital Letter.

42. *Ibid.*

43. Unidentified Charleston, S.C., newspaper, March 22, 1897, Courtenay papers.

44. *Ibid.*

45. William Watts Ball, *The State that Forgot: South Carolina's Surrender to Democracy* (Indianapolis: Bobbs-Merrill, 1932), 173. McDow confessed to killing Dawson, but was found not guilty by reason of self-defense on June 24, 1889, even though Dawson had for 23 years publicly written and demonstrated that he never carried concealed weapons.

46. Randall's Capital Letter.

Chapter 7, Leonidas W. Spratt

1. *Richmond Daily Dispatch*, May 4, 1861.

2. John Amasa May and Joan Reynolds Faunt, *South Carolina Secedes* (Columbia: University of South Carolina Press, 1960), 213.

3. *Ibid.* Also, *Thomas Dryden Spratt's Recollections of his Family*, Spratt Family, Manuscripts, Vol. 1, 1875, Manuscripts, South Caroliniana Library, University of South Carolina, Columbia, 44; and A.W. Cockrell, Jr., *Descendants of Thomas "Kanawha" Spratt*, 1908, Spratt Family, Vol. 2, Manuscripts, South Caroliniana Library, University of South Carolina, Columbia.

4. Congressman John Spratt (D-S.C.), who is the great-great nephew of Leonidas Spratt, said Spratt men could generally be spotted in any picture because they are usually "tall and spare with angular faces," telephone interview, June 30, 2008. Leonidas' son, James, also fits the description of a tall, spare man in C.E. Johnston Affidavit about J.W. Spratt, U.S. District Court, Jacksonville, Fla., April 14, 1919, State of Florida, County of Duval, 33.

5. Susan Bradford, who was a 15-year-old eyewitness at the Florida secession convention, described Spratt on January 7, 1861, in "Florida Passes the Ordinance of Secession," Katherine M. Jones, *Heroines of Dixie: Confederate Women Tell their Story of the War* (Westport, Conn.: Greenwood Press, 1973), 7.

6. May and Faunt, 213; Dew, 42.

7. May and Faunt, 213; also Thomas Dryden Spratt, 44, and Cockrell, 26.

8. The younger Spratt became an attorney and teacher who died in Augusta, Georgia in 1892. Cockrell, p. 26.

9. Charles B. Dew, *Apostles of Disunion: Southern Secession* (Charlottesville: University of Virginia Press, 2001), 42.

10. John Ashworth, *Slavery, Capitalism and Politics in the Antebellum Republic*, Vol., 1, (London: Cambridge University Press, 1995), 114.

11. Leonidas W. Spratt, "The Foreign Slave Trade: The Source of Political Power and of Material Progress, of Social Integrity, and Social Emancipation to the South," (Charleston: Walter Evans & Co., 1858), 8, 23; *De Bow's Review*, xvii (New Orleans, La.: J.D.B. DeBow,1854), 612.

12. Spratt, Speech upon the Foreign Slave Trade, Before the Legislature of South Carolina (Charleston, South Carolina, 1858), 9; also Ashworth, 266.

13. Ronald T. Takaki, *Pro-Slavery Crusade* (New York: The Free Press; London-Collier-MacMillan Ltd., 1971) 28–30; Spratt, *Foreign Slave Trade Source of Political Power*, 28–29; Ashworth, 267.

14. The *Charleston Southern Standard* was owned by Spratt and E.H. Britton from 1853 to 1858. John Hammond Moore, *South Carolina Newspapers* (Columbia: University of South Carolina Press, 1988), 39.

15. William C. Davis, *Rhett: The Turbulent Life and Times of a Fire-Eater* (Columbia: University of South Carolina Press, 2001), 364, 365.

16. Spratt was incorrectly listed as the editor of the *Charleston Mercury* on February 13, 1861, in "The Philosophy of Secession: A Southern View, Presented in a Letter addressed to the Hon. Mr. Perkins of Louisiana, in criticism on the Provisional Constitution adopted by the Southern Congress at Montgomery, Alabama," February 13, 1861, Documenting the American South (Chapel Hill: University of North Carolina at Chapel Hill, 2001), http://docsouth.unc.edu/imls/secession/secession.html.

17. Dew, 42; Davis, 365.

18. Davis, 371.

19. Barton J. Bernstein, Southern Politics and Attempts to Reopen the African Slave Trade, *The Journal of Negro History*, 51, 1 (Washington, D.C.: Association for the Study of African-American Life and History, January 1966), 16–35, http://www.jstor.org/stable/2716374 (accessed June 28, 2008).

20. Clifford Berry, "Ordinance of Secession and the Signers," *Confederate Veteran*, 26:1 (January 1918), 8; Dew, 42.

21. Dew, 44.

22. *Richmond Dispatch*, January 2, 1861.

23. Bradford, 7.

24. F.W. Pickens letter to L.W. Spratt, January 12, 1861, *Confederate Veteran*, 37:4 (April 1931), 130.

25. Spratt, "The Philosophy of Secession: a Southern View."

26. Dew, 44.

27. Spratt, "The Philosophy of Secession."

28. *Charleston Mercury*, February 16, 1861.

29. *Ibid.*

30. *Charleston Mercury*, May 10, 1861.

31. *Charleston Mercury*, May 16, 1861.

32. *Charleston Mercury*, May 23, 1861.

33. *Ibid.*

34. *Charleston Mercury*, May 22, 1861.

35. *Ibid.*

36. *Charleston Mercury*, May 23, 1861.

37. *Charleston Mercury*, May 24, 1861.

38. *Ibid.*

39. *Charleston Mercury*, May 27, 1861.

40. *Charleston Mercury*, May 25, 1861.

41. *Charleston Mercury*, June 7, 1861.

42. *Charleston Mercury*, June 10, 1861, published June 15, 1861.

43. *Ibid.*

44. *Charleston Mercury*, June 21, 1861, published June 26, 1861.

45. *Ibid.*

46. *Charleston Mercury*, June 25, 1861, published June 29, 1861.

47. *Charleston Mercury*, June 24, 1861.

48. *Ibid.*

49. *Ibid.*

50. *Ibid.*

51. *Charleston Mercury*, June 26, 1861.

52. *Ibid.*

53. *Charleston Mercury*, July 6, 1861.

54. *Charleston Mercury*, July 9, 1861.

55. *Ibid.*

56. In other accounts, the Federals were credited with having 12,000 men while the Confederates were believed to have 4,000. E.B. Long with Barbara Long, *The Civil War Day by Day* (Garden City: N.Y.: DeCapo, 1971), 93.

57. *Charleston Mercury*, July 19, 1861, published July 24, 1861.

58. *Ibid.*

59. *Ibid.*

60. *Ibid.*

61. *Charleston Mercury*, July 18, 1861, published July 25, 1861.

62. *Richmond Daily Dispatch*, July 21, 1861.

63. *Charleston Mercury*, July 27, 1861.

64. *Ibid.*

65. Spratt apparently could not see all of the battle area because he said his first reports of the battle were not accurate. He thought the Federals had attacked near Mitchell Ford, but he corrected his report and described the rest of the battle in bulletins. *Charleston Mercury*, July 21, 1861, published July 25, 1861.

66. *Ibid.*

67. *Charleston Mercury*, July 27, 1861.

68. *Ibid.*

69. *Charleston Mercury*, July 23, 1861, published July 29, 1861.

70. The article that he wrote on July 20 was published in the *Charleston Mercury* on July 25, and the articles written on July 22 and July 24 were published on July 29.

71. Congressman John Spratt (D-S.C.). Telephone interview, June 30, 2008.

72. *Charleston Mercury*, dateline July 24, 1861, published July 25, 1861.

73. *Charleston Mercury*, dateline July 29, 1861, published August 3, 1861.

74. *Daily Dispatch*, September 12, 1861.

75. *Daily Dispatch*, September 23, 1861.

76. *Charleston Mercury*, September 30, 1861.

77. *Ibid.*

78. Compiled Service Records, Microcopy M267 of CW 0544, No. 642, 1st Mounted Militia, D.W., 1861–1865, F602736, South Carolina Department of Archives and History.

79. Compiled Service Records, Microcopy No. 642 of CW 0544, Op. cit.

80. *Charleston Mercury*, April 28, 1862, and *Daily Dispatch*, April 30, 1862.

81. *Daily Dispatch*, June 24, 1862.

82. Records of Confederate General and Staff Officers, CW 1161, Microcopy No. M 331, 1861–1865, South Carolina Department of Archives and History.

83. "Col. L. Spratt," *Confederate Veteran*, 11 (November 1903), 516.

84. Records of Confederate General and Staff Officers, CW 1161, Microcopy No. M 331, 1861–1865, South Carolina Department of Archives and History.

85. Congressman Spratt said that Zack Spratt wrote that his father came home after Appomattox to find his uncle Leonidas hiding at the Spratt homeplace, telephone interview, June 30, 2008.

86. The wording on the Fort Mill marker describes the William Elliott White house as the site of the last cabinet meeting. The marker was created by Elliot White Springs from correspondence with Nora Davis of the South Carolina Department of Archives and History, April 26, 1939, to March 18, 1940, 32. Subsequent meetings were held in Abbeville, S.C., and Washington County, Georgia, where the Confederate government disbanded. Louise Pettus, *The White Homestead: The Story of a House, the People who lived in it, and the Land around it,"* privately published, undated.

87. During the Great Fire of 1901, James Spratt moved the land records from his title company, the Florida Abstract and Title Company, to a sailboat and across the river. After the courthouse burned, these records became the only surviving records for the county and were later legislated to be the only credible evidence of county land transactions.

88. 1880 Florida Census, Soundex and Population Schedules, United States, Bureau of the Census, 10th Census, Spratt was listed as 59 years old, Mary was listed as 55 years old. They had two sons, James W., who was 12 and born in South Carolina, and Charles Brewster, who was 10 and born in South Carolina.

89. Johnson, 33. Also, Thomas Dryden Spratt, 46.

90. Spratt, *Man in Continuation at this Earth of a Nature of Reality Throughout the Universe by Tradition of that Reality from its Original Universe of Force* (Washington, D.C.: Gibson Brothers Printers, 1894).

91. Spratt, *Nature of an Universe of Life* (Jacksonville, Fla.: Vance Printing Co., 1896).

92. Spratt, *Man At This Earth to the Man Possible of an Essential Being of the Universe* (Jacksonville, Fla.: Press of H. & W.B. Drew Company, 1902).

93. May and Faunt, 213; also, "Col. L. Spratt," *Confederate Veteran*, 11 (1903), 516.

Chapter 8, Henry Timrod

1. Motoko Rich, "It ain't me, babe," *New York Times, The State*, Columbia, S.C., September 16, 2006, 1-D.

2. Henry T. Thompson, *Henry Timrod: Laureate of the Confederacy* (Columbia, S.C.: The State Company, 1928), 9.

3. Paul H. Hayne, *The Poems of Henry Timrod* (New York: Arno Press, 1972), 9.

4. Edd Winfield Parks, *Henry Timrod* (New York: Twayne Publishers, Inc., 1964), 19.

5. A.H.Leopoldt, "A Memorial for Henry Timrod," *The Literary News*, (February 1899), 48, said Timrod's father died in 1835. Paul H. Hayne, *The Poems of Henry Timrod*, 16, said Timrod's father died in about 1837.

6. Timrod Papers, Emily Timrod Goodwin, South Caroliniana Library, University of South Carolina, Columbia, December 2, 1867.

7. *Ibid.*

8. Guy A.Cardwell, Jr., *The Uncollected Poems of Henry Timrod*, edited with an introduction by Guy A. Cardwell, Jr. (Athens, Ga.: University of Georgia Press, 1942), 23.

9. Thompson, 15.

10. Cardwell, 34.

11. *Ibid.*, 92, 95.

12. Hayne, 20.

13. Thompson, 24; also, Hayne, 22–23.

14. Hayne, 20.

15. Thompson, 20.

16. *Ibid.*, 22.

17. J.P. Kennedy Bryan, "Introduction" to the "Memorial Edition" of Timrod's Poems, 1899, 9; also Thompson, 30.

18. Sculley Bradley, Richmond Croom Beatty, and E. Hudson Long, *The American Tradition in Literature,* vol. 1, (New York: W.W. Norton & Co., 1956), 1287.

19. Thompson, 31, 32.

20. Letter to Emily, February 21, 1862, Timrod papers.

21. Letter to Emily, Charleston, February 25, 1862, Timrod papers.

22. Walter Brian Cisco, *Henry Timrod: A Biography* (Cranbury, N.J.: Fairleigh Dickinson University Press, Associated University Press, 2004), 78.

23. De Fontaine and Peter W. Alexander, the correspondent for the *Savannah Republican*, were the two leading reporters in the South.

24. Letter from Timrod to Emily written from Charleston, April 15, 1862, Timrod papers.

25. *Ibid.*

26. *Ibid.*

27. *Charleston Mercury*, May 7, 1862.

28. James M. McPherson, *The Atlas of the Civil War* (Philadelphia: Courage Books, Colin Gower Enterprises, Running Press Book Publishers, 2005), 413.

29. *Ibid,* 416.

30. *Ibid.*

31. *Charleston Mercury*, May 7, 1862.

32. *Charleston Daily Courier*, May 29, 1862.

33. McPherson, 56.

34. *Charleston Mercury*, dateline April 30, 1862.

35. *Ibid.*

36. *Ibid.*

37. *Charleston Mercury*, May 10, 1862.

38. *Ibid.*

39. *Ibid.*

40. *Charleston Mercury*, May 13, 1862.

41. *Ibid.*

42. *Ibid.*

43. *Ibid.*

44. *Ibid.*

45. *Charleston Mercury*, May 14, 1864.

46. *Ibid.*

47. *Charleston Mercury*, May 16, 1864.

48. *Charleston Mercury,* May 20, 1862.

49. *Ibid.*

50. *Charleston Mercury,* dateline May 9, 1862.

51. *Ibid.*

52. *Charleston Mercury,* May 20, 1862.

53. *Charleston Mercury,* May 20, 1862.

54. *Charleston Daily News,* May 20, 1862.

55. *Charleston Mercury,* May 31, 1862.

56. *Ibid.*

57. McPherson, 417.

58. Cisco, 81.

59. Parks, 39; also Cisco, 81.

60. *Ibid.*

61. Hayne, 42.

62. *Ibid.*

63. Parks, 39.

64. *Ibid.*

65. Cisco, 83.

66. Hayne, 134; also Bradley, Beatty, Long, 1296.

67. Parks, 103.

68. *Ibid.,* 104.

69. Robert A. Rosen, *Confederate Charleston* (Columbia: University of South Carolina Press, 1994), 151.

70. Thompson, 36.

71. Parks, 41.

72. Jay B. Hubbell, *The Last Years of Henry Timrod, 1864–1867* (Durham, N.C.: Duke University Press, 1941), 12, 16, 17; also Mary C. Simms Oliphant, Alfred Taylor Odell, and T.C. Duncan Eaves, *Letters of William Gilmore Simms* (Columbia: University of South Carolina Press, 1952–1982), 451.

73. Parks, 127.

74. *Ibid.,* 41, 42.

75. *Ibid.,* 89.

76. Hayne, 47–51.

77. Timrod papers, Letter to his sister Edith, Charleston, April 29, 1864.

78. Parks, 40; Rosen, 151.

79. James Morris Morgan, *Recollections of a Rebel Reefer* (New York: Houghton Mifflin, 1917), 244.

80. Hayne, July 20, 1864; Hubbell, 36–37.

81. Parks, 104.

82. Parks, 42, 43; Letter from Hayne to Clara Dargan, April 23, 1870, quoted in Hubbell, 17, 30–33, and 36–39; the second letter to Clara Dargan, August 20, 1864, also in Hubbell, 40–41.

83. Parks, 42; also Oliphant, 450–451.

84. William A. Courtenay, *Timrod Souvenir* (Aiken, S.C.: W.L. Washburn, publisher, 1901), South Caroliniana Library, University of South Carolina, Columbia.

85. Julian A. Selby, *Memorabilia and Anecdotal Reminiscences of Columbia, South Carolina* (Columbia, S.C.: R.L. Bryan Co., 1905), 121–124.

86. Thompson, 22.

87. Parks, 43, 44; Hayne, 45.

88. John Hammond Moore, *South Carolina Newspapers* (Columbia: University of South Carolina Press, 1988), 202.

89. *Daily South Carolinian*, April 19, 1865.

90. Rosen, 153.

91. Parks, 46.

92. *Ibid.*, 44.

93. *Ibid.*, 44, 45.

94. *Ibid.*, 45.

95. Cisco, 108.

96. Parks, 50, 51.

97. *Ibid.*, 45.

98. Mary C. Oliphant, *Letters of William Gilmore Simms* (Columbia: University of South Carolina Press, 1952); Letter to William Hawkins Ferry from Charleston, March 24, 1866, 547, 548.

99. Parks, 45.

100. *Ibid.*, 45, 46; also Letter to Hayne, March 30, 1866, quoted in Hubbell, 59–63.

101. Oliphant, Letter to William Hawkins Ferris from Charleston, April 13, 1866, 552.

102. *Charleston Courier*, June 18, 1866.

103. Douglas A. Robillard, Henry Timrod, John R. Thompson, and the "Ladies of Richmond," *South Carolina Historical Magazine*, vol. 62 (Charleston: South Carolina Historical Society, 1961), 129.

104. Emily Timrod Goodwin, November 19, 1866, letter to Hayne, Timrod papers, 51, 52. Also, Douglas J. Robillard, "Henry Timrod, John R. Thompson and the Ladies of Richmond," *S.C. Historical Magazine*, vol. 62, p. 129,130, 1961.

105. Timrod letter to Edith from Columbia, April 16, 1867, Timrod papers.

106. *Ibid;*, Letter to Edith, Columbia, April 16, 1867.

107. Parks, 50.

108. Hayne, 59.

109. Letter to Hayne from Columbia, September 20, 1867, Timrod papers.

110. Letter from Emily to Hayne, October 22, 1867, Timrod papers.

111. *The Columbia Record*, April 1, 1948.

112. Letter to Henry Timrod Goodwin from William A. Courtenay, Innisfallen, Newry, S.C., November 21, 1898, Timrod papers.

113. Timrod papers, unidentified and undated newspaper article.

114. Timrod papers, unidentified newspaper article, May 24, 1905.

Chapter 9, L.H. Mathews

1. Mark E. Neely Jr., *Southern Rights: Political Prisoners and the Myth of Confederate Constitutionalism* (Charlottesville: University Press of Virginia, 1999), 1. (While Mark Neely cites Mathews as the first civilian prisoner held by the Confederate military, *New*

York Times correspondent George Salter, writing under the pseudonym "Jasper," was detained by a group of men in Charleston, S.C., on April 12, 1861, the day Fort Sumter was fired on to begin the Civil War. Taken to the city jail, Salter was later released and hurriedly departed Charleston. (Louis M. Starr, *Bohemian Brigade, Civil War Newsmen in Action*, 28; J. Cutler Andrews, *The North Reports the Civil War*, 18.)

2. Robin Sterling, from a series of books including *L.H. Mathews, Editor of the Blount County News-Dispatch*, covering the history of Blount County, Alabama. http://home.hiwaay.net/~bobwonda/books/mathews.html (accessed February 13, 2009).

3. *Memphis Appeal*, May 31, 1861 (The correspondent "Nagle," who interviewed Nemo, is known only as "Dr. Nagle.").

4. George F. Pearce, *Pensacola During the Civil War* (Gainesville: University Press of Florida, 2000), 8–13.

5. Paul Taylor, *Discovering the Civil War in Florida* (Sarasota, Fla.: Pineapple Press, 2001), 27–29.

6. Pearce, 34.

7. Pearce, 56.

8. *New Orleans Daily Delta*, April 2, 1861. The article that Mathews wrote on March 28 was not published in the *Daily Delta* until April 2.

9. *Daily Delta*, April 2, 1861.

10. *Daily Delta*, April 4, 1861.

11. *Philadelphia Inquirer*, April 15, 1861.

12. *Daily Delta*, April 17, 1861. (Mathews wrote on April 13 that Fort Pickens had been reinforced, but the *Delta* did not publish his story until April 17. By that time, Mathews had been released from custody in Montgomery.).

13. *Ibid.*

14. *Daily Delta*, April 17, 1861.

15. Albert D. Richardson, *The Secret Service, the Field, the Dungeon and the Escape* (Hartford, Conn.: American Publishing Company, 1865), 106.

16. *Charleston Mercury*, April 20, 1861.

17. *Charleston Mercury*, April 18, 1861.

18. Lawrence H. Mathews' letter from the Exchange Hotel in Montgomery, Alabama, April 19, 1861, to Confederate Secretary of War Leroy Pope Walker; Record Division, Rebel Archives, Letters to the War Department.

19. *Ibid.*

20. *Ibid.*

21. Richardson, 95.

22. *Ibid.*, 96–104.

23. Richardson, 105.

24. Richardson, 109.

25. *Charleston Mercury*, April 18, 1861.

26. *Montgomery Advertiser*, April 17, 1861.

27. Neely, 1, 2.

28. *Ibid.*

29. *Memphis Appeal*, May 31, 1861. (Mathews was a follower of John Mitchel, who advocated race war between Ireland and England. He was a convert to Fenianism, which

represented the journalist sons of the Irish farming classes. Mitchel's *Jail Journal* and other writings constructed a tale of 800 years of national struggle against "sadistic" oppressors. British authorities sentenced him to prison and his followers dispersed in 1848. See *Oxford Illustrated History of Ireland* (New York: Oxford University Press, 1991) 209, 210.

30. *Ibid.*

31. *Pensacola Observer,* June 9, 1861.

32. *Ibid.*

33. *Ibid.*

34. *Ibid.*

35. Pearce, 111.

36. Taylor, 29, 30.

37. Pearce, 135.

38. *Ibid.*, 142, 143.

39. *Ibid.*, 144.

40. Records Division, Rebel Archives, War Department.

41. Pearce, 146–157.

42. *Ibid.*, 160–168.

43. *History of Fort Pickens* (Pensacola, Fla.: Pensacola Historical Society, 1989), 10.

44. *Photographic History of the Civil War,* Vol. IV, by Deering J. Edwards, M.D., Surgeon, Confederate States Army.

45. The Hospital Steward's Tent, www.geocities.com/hospital_steward (accessed February 13, 2009).

46. Records Division, Rebel Archives, War Department.

47. Civil War Database, Alabama Department of Archives and History, Montgomery, Alabama.

48. George M. Cruikshank, *History of Birmingham and Its Environs* (Chicago and New York: Lewis Publishing Company, 1920), 100–103 (Digital Collection at the Birmingham Public Library).

49. *Blount County News-Dispatch*, December 8, 1892.

50. Cruikshank, 100–102.

51. Rhoda Coleman Ellison, *History and Bibliography of Alabama Newspapers in the Nineteenth Century* (Tuscaloosa: University of Alabama Press, 1954), 16–17.

52. *Gadsden Times*, May 28, 1875.

53. Sterling, "Mathews, Editor of the *Blount County News-Dispatch*."

54. *Guntersville Democrat*, February 1, 1883.

55. *Ibid.*

56. Sterling noted that Mathews used *News and Dispatch* and *News-Dispatch* interchangeably, but he tended to use the "and" while his newspaper competitors hyphenated.

57. Sterling, "Mathews, Editor of the *Blount County News-Dispatch*."

58. *News-Dispatch*, November 7, 1889.

59. *News-Dispatch*, October 22, 1885.

60. *Birmingham Age-Herald*, October 2, 1892.

61. *News-Dispatch*, December 19, 1895.

62. *Southern Democrat*, April 11, 1901.

63. *News-Dispatch*, December 18, 1896.

64. *News-Dispatch,* October 17, 1889.

Chapter 10, John Forsyth

1. Thomas Cooper DeLeon, *Centennial Remembrance Book of Col. John Forsyth* (Mobile, Alabama, 1912).

2. *Annals of Congress of the United States*, 1st Cong., 1st sess., 89; *Annals of Congress of the United States*, 3rd Cong., 1st sess., 78–79; Jennie Jeffries, *A History of the Forsyth Family* (Indianapolis: W.B. Burford, 1920); William H. Forsyth, *Two Thousand Years of Forsyth History* (Atlanta, 1973).

3. "John Forsyth," In Allen Johnson and Dumas Malone, eds., *Dictionary of American Biography*, vol. 3 (New York: Charles Scribner's Sons, 1959), 533–535; Alvin Laroy Duckett, *John Forsyth: Political Tactician* (Athens: University of Georgia Press, 1962); James F. Cook, *Governors of Georgia* (Huntsville, Ala.: Strode Publishing, 1979).

4. DeLeon, *Centennial Remembrance Book*.

5. U.S. Congress, *Senate Exec. Journal*, 24th Cong., 1st sess., 499, 504, 520; Andrew Jackson to John Forsyth, September 29, 1835, Appointment Papers of the Department of State: Applications and Recommendations for Public Office, 1829–1836, National Archives, Washington, D.C.

6. *Mobile Register*, September 8, 1837, December 16, 1837, December 23, 1837, January 18, 1838, February 2, 1838, July 1, 1838, July 28, 1838, November 10, 1840, November 16, 1840.

7. *Mobile Register*, December 1, 1841; *Savannah Georgian*, June 18 1849; U.S. Congress, *Senate Exec. Journal*, 29th Cong., 1st sess., 15–16, 35, 41; *Columbus Times*, August 27, 1845, June 24, 1846, weekly from late July to late November.

8. *Columbus Times*, July 11, 1848, November 14, 1848, November 28, 1848, December 5, 1848, February 12, 1850, February 19, 1850, April 9, 1850, June 8, 1850, August 10, 1850, September 10, 1850, September 28, 1850, October 22, 1850, April 1, 1851, July 16, 1851; *Mobile Register*, January 5, 1853, May 3, 1877.

9. Lonnie A. Burnett, *The Pen Makes A Good Sword: John Forsyth of the* Mobile Register (Tuscaloosa: University of Alabama Press, 2006), 57.

10. *Mobile Register*, October 9, 1855, November 6, 1855, December 11, 1855, December 15, 1855, February 14, 1856, February 16, 1856; *New York Herald*, reprinted in *Mobile Register*, May 5, 1877.

11. *Mobile Register*, January 1, 1856.

12. *Mobile Register*, April 19, 1856.

13. *Mobile Register*, June 13, 1856, June 29, 1856, July 1, 1856.

14. *Mobile Register*, July 11, 1856.

15. *Mobile Register*, May 3, 1877; Burnett, *The Pen Makes a Good Sword*, 75–96.

16. *Mobile Register*, December 19, 1859, January 27, 1860, February 4, 1860, February 8, 1860, February 10, 1860, February 12, 1860, February 24, 1860, February 25, 1860, May 15, 1860; *Montgomery Advertiser*, June 20, 1860.

17. Bailey Thomson, "Douglas awaited 1860 election results in Register office," *Mobile Press-Register,* August 30, 1992; *New York Times*, December 7, 1860; John Forsyth

to Stephen Douglas, December 28, 1860, Stephen A. Douglas Papers, Regenstein Library, University of Chicago, Illinois.

18. "Ordinances and Constitution of the State of Alabama, with the Constitution of the Provisional Government and of the Confederate States of America, 1861," Alabama Department of Archives and History, Montgomery; *Journal of the Congress of the Confederate States of America, 1861–1865*, vol. 1 (Washington, D.C.: Government Printing Office, 1904), 55, 85–86; various letters, *The War of the Rebellion: A Compilation of the Official Records of the Union and Confederate Armies* (Washington, D.C.: Government Printing Office, 1880–1901), ser. 1, vol. 1, and ser. 4, vol. 1; various letters, James D. Richardson, comp., *A Compilation of Messages and Papers of the Confederacy, including the Diplomatic Correspondence* (Nashville, Tenn.: United States Publishing Co., 1905); "War Inevitable: Opinion of the Southern Commissioners," *New York Evening Post*, April 10, 1861.

19. City of Mobile: Alderman's Minute Books, Book 4, 1857–61, 441, Mobile Municipal Archives, Alabama; Stewart Sifakis, *Compendium of the Confederate Armies: Alabama* (New York: Facts on File Books, 1992); Charles Forsyth, *History of the Third Alabama Regiment, C.S.A.* (Montgomery, Ala.: Confederate Publishing Co., 1866).

20. Lawrence H. Mathews to Leroy Pope Walker, April 19, 1861, in *Letters Received by the Confederate Secretary of War, 1861–1865*, National Archives microfilms, M437, no. 379-1861, reel 1; Memphis *Daily Appeal*, November 5, 1863; New York *Daily Tribune*, September 1, 1862; Samuel Chester Reid, Jr., Diary, quoted in Judith Lee Hallock, *Braxton Bragg and Confederate Defeat*, vol. II (Tuscaloosa: University of Alabama Press, 1991), 162; J. Cutler Andrews, *The South Reports the Civil War* (Princeton, N.J.: Princeton University Press, 1970), 62–64, 146–147.

21. "Letter from Gen. Bragg's Army," *Mobile Advertiser and Register*, October 14, 1862. A short item titled "Release of Col. Forsyth and Others" in the October 9, 1862, *Register* announced receipt of the September 27 letter and briefly relayed the group's abduction to Gen. Buell's camp in Cave City and release on parole.

22. *Mobile Advertiser and Register*, October 14. 1862.

23. *Ibid.*

24. *Ibid.* If Forsyth carried out his plan to publish "Bragg's Army Register," no record of it could be found.

25. *Mobile Advertiser and Register*, October 14, 1862.

26. *Ibid.*

27. *Ibid.*

28. *Mobile Advertiser and Register*, October 22, 1862.

29. "Two Victories in One Day," *Mobile Advertiser and Register*, October 18, 1862.

30. *Ibid.*

31. *Mobile Advertiser and Register*, October 24, 1862, October 26, 1862.

32. "Gen. Bragg's Kentucky Campaign," *Mobile Advertiser and Register*, November 9, 1862.

33. *Ibid.*

34. *Ibid.*

35. *Ibid.*

36. *Mobile Advertiser and Register*, November 16, 1862.

37. *Ibid.*

38. *Ibid.*

39. *Mobile Advertiser and Register*, December 5, 1862.

40. *Ibid.*; emphasis retained from original.

41. Burnett, *The Pen Makes a Good Sword*, 139–144; *Mobile Register*, December 31, 1865; Ralph Poore, "Alabama's Enterprising Newspaper: *The Mobile Register* and Its Forebears, 1813–1991," unpublished manuscript, Mobile Public Library, Alabama.

42. *Mobile Advertiser and Register*, July 21, 1865, July 28, 1865, May 9, 1866, September 27, 1867, October 8, 1867, October 25, 1867, February 1, 1868, February 4,1868, February 11, 1868, May 27, 1868, June 27, 1868, July 21, 1868, July 23, 1868, September 23, 1868, September 26, 1868, October 14, 1868, November 5, 1868.

43. *Mobile Advertiser and Register*, November 4, 1874, November 5, 1874, November 21, 1874, November 24, 1874, May 3, 1877, May 5,1877.

44. *Mobile Advertiser and Register*, August 1, 1865, reprinted in the *New York Times*, August 20, 1865.

45. *New York Times*, May 3, 1877; *New York Sun*, reprinted in *Mobile Register*, May 5, 1877.

Chapter 11, Henry Hotze

1. Terry L. Jones, *The A to Z of the Civil War*, Vol. 1, A–L (Lanham, Md.: The Scarecrow Press, 2006), 689.

2. Douglas Southall Freeman, *The South to Posterity* (New York: 1939) 24–25, cited in Charles L. DuFour, *Nine Men in Gray* (Garden City, N.Y.: Doubleday & Company, 1963), 268.

3. Jon L. Wakelyn, *Biographical Dictionary of the Confederacy* (Westport, Conn.: Greenwood Press, 1977), 239–240.

4. *Ibid.*; also *Mobile Daily Register*, May 11, 1887; D.P. Crook American National Biography, Vol. II, edited by John A. Garraty and Mark C. Carnes (New York: Oxford University Press, 1999), 245–247. (Some sources say he was naturalized in 1855, and some say 1856.)

5. DuFour, 269.

6. Henry Hotze, *Three Months in the Confederate Army* (printed in facsimile from *The* (London) *Index*, 1862, with an introduction by Richard Barksdale Harwell, University of Alabama Press, 1952), 3, 4.

7. DuFour, 269; *Mobile Daily Register*, May 2, 1858, May 11, 1887.

8. *Ibid.*, 269.

9. Dufour, 269.

10. Hotze, 14.

11. Hotze, 15.

12. Hotze, 14.

13. *Mobile Advertiser & Register*, July 2, 1861.

14. Hotze, 20.

15. Hotze, 30–31.

16. Muster Roll, Third Alabama Regiment, June 30, 1861, manuscript, National Archives, Washington; also Harwell, Introduction, Army, 4. (Hotze does not mention his change in duties in his journal.)

17. Hotze, 33.

18. Walker to Hotze, August 31, 1861, ORA, series IV, vol. 1, 596.

19. W.L. Yancey and P.A. Rost to Hunter, October 5, 1861, Official Records of the Union and Confederate Navies in the War of the Rebellion, II, Vol. 3 (Harrisburg, Pa.: National Historical Society, 1987), 280.

20. DuFour, 270.

21. W.L. Yancey and P.L. Rost to Hunter, October 5, 1861, ORN, series II, vol. 3, 280.

22. Hotze presented his plan orally to Hunter. Hotze to Hunter, no. 3, February 23, 1862, ORN, series II, vol. 3, 347.

23. ORN, series II, vol. 3, 347.

24. Hunter to Hotze, 293–294.

25. Hunter to Hotze, November 14, 1861, ORN, 293, 294; letter of appointment, 117.

26. Henry Hotze's Dispatch Book, Records of the Confederate States of America, 1854–1889 (bulk 1861–1865) ID no.: MSS16550 Library of Congress. Hereafter cited as Hotze, Dispatch Book.

27. *Ibid.*

28. Frank Lawrence Owsley, *King Cotton Diplomacy,* 2nd ed. (Chicago: University of Chicago Press, 1959), 156.

29. ORN, 293, 294.

30. *Ibid.,* 294.

31. *Ibid.*

32. Owsley, 156.

33. John S. Bowman, *The Civil War* (North Dighton, Mass.: World Publications Group, 2006), 51.

34. Hotze to Hunter, February 1, 1862, ORN, 325, 326.

35. *Ibid.*

36. *Ibid.*

37. *Ibid.*

38. Hotze, February 23, 1862, ORN, 346, 347.

39. *Ibid.*

40. Hotze, ORN, February 28, 1862, ORN, 353.

41. *Ibid.,* 352.

42. Hotze, ORN, March 11, 1862, ORN, 361, 362.

43. The term *public relations professional* will also be used even though the first historical use of this term was not until 1932.

44. ORN, 354.

45. Hotze, March 11, 1862, ORN, 361.

46. *Ibid.*

47. *Ibid.,* 360.

48. Hotze to Hunter, March 11, 1862, ORN, 360–362.

49. Hotze to Benjamin, March 24, 1862, ORN, 371.

50. *Ibid.*

51. Hotze to Hunter, April 25, 1862, ORN, 400, 401.

52. *Ibid.*

53. *The Index*, May 1, 1862.

54. Hotze to Benjamin, August 4, 1862, ORN, 506.

55. *Ibid.*

56. *Index*, August 14, 1862.

57. Hotze to Benjamin, September 26, 1862, ORN, 534, 537.

58. Edwin DeLeon to Hotze, October 1, 1862, Dispatch Book.

59. Crook, 247.

60. Hotze to Benjamin, September 26, 1862, ORN, 535, 537.

61. Hotze, November 7, 1862, ORN, 601, 602.

62. Hotze to Benjamin, December 20, 1862, ORN, 633.

63. Benjamin to Hotze, January 16, 1863, ORN, series 2, vol. III, 659–660.

64. Benjamin to Hotze, January 16, 1863, ORN, 660.

65. Hotze, January 17, 1863, ORN, 661.

66. *Index*, for dates cited.

67. Hotze to Benjamin, January 17, 1863, ORN, 661.

68. Hotze to Benjamin, May 14, 1863, ORN, 768.

69. Owsley, 248, 249.

70. Hotze to Benjamin, June 6, 1863, ORN, 783–785.

71. Crook, 246.

72. Hotze, ORN, August 27, 1863, 871.

73. *Ibid.*

74. Benjamin, September 19, 1863, ORN, 902, 903.

75. Hotze to Benjamin, February 13, 1864, ORN, 1025.

76. *Ibid.*

77. Paul Pecquet du Bellet, The Diplomacy of the Confederate Cabinet of Richmond and Its Agents Abroad; being memorandum notes taken in Paris during the Rebellion of the Southern States from 1861 to 1865. Edited with an introduction by William Stanley Hoole (Tuscaloosa, Ala.: Confederate Publishing Company, 1963), 27.

78. *Ibid.*

79. Bulloch to Hotze, April 25, 1865; Hotze, Dispatch Book.

80. Hotze, Dispatch Book, June 1, 1865.

81. *Index*, August 12, 1865.

82. Hotze Dispatch Book, August 27, 1863, ORN, 879.

83. Crook, 247.

84. Wakelyn, 239, 240.

Chapter 12, John H. Linebaugh

1. Obituary, the *Montgomery Daily Mail*, November 16, 1864, as reported in Barbara G. Ellis, *The Moving Appeal: Mr. McClanahan, Mrs. Dill, and the Civil War's Great Newspaper Run* (Macon, Ga.: Mercer University Press, 2003), Appendix E, 600.

2. *The Moving Appeal*, 331, 600.

3. Thomas H. Baker, "Refugee Newspaper: The *Memphis Daily Appeal*, 1862–1865," *Journal of Southern History*, 29:3 (August 1963), 329.

4. *The Moving Appeal*, 331, 600.

5. *Ibid.*, 6, 25.

6. *Ibid.*, 12–13.

7. *Ibid.*, 22.

8. Ellis, 598.

9. Annual Convention of the Protestant Episcopal Church in the Diocese of Alabama, May 1849, 44.

10. *Ibid.*, May 1850, 35.

11. Ellis, 599.

12. *Ibid.*, 598.

13. *Ibid.*, 599.

14. Obituary, *Montgomery Daily Mail*, November 16, 1864, as reported in Ellis, 600.

15. *Memphis Daily Appeal*, June 6, 1863.

16. Ellis, 243.

17. J. Cutler Andrews, *The South Reports the Civil War* (Princeton, N.J.: Princeton University Press, 1985), 346.

18. Ellis, 245.

19. Andrews, 543–544.

20. Ellis and Steven J. Dick, "Who Was 'Shadow'?" The Computer Knows: Using Grammar-Program Statistics in Content Analyses Finally May Solve This Civil War Riddle and Other Writing Mysteries. *Journalism & Mass Communication Quarterly*, 73/4 (Winter 1996), 947–962.

21. Obituary, *Montgomery Daily Mail*, November 16, 1864, as reported in Ellis, *The Moving Appeal*, Appendix E, 600.

22. Ellis and Dick, "Who Was 'Shadow'?" The Computer Knows," 947–962.

23. Ellis, 243.

24. *Ibid.*, 259.

25. Ellis and Dick, 947–962

26. Baker, "Refugee Newspaper," 335.

27. *Memphis Daily Appeal*, November 5, 1863.

28. *Ibid.*

29. Ellis, 248.

30. *Memphis Daily Appeal*, November 5, 1863.

31. *Memphis Daily Appeal*, November 7, 1863.

32. *Memphis Daily Appeal*, November 5, 1863.

33. Baker, "Refugee Newspaper," 335.

34. *Memphis Daily Appeal*, July 16, 1863.

35. George Sisler, "The Arrest of a Memphis Daily Appeal War Correspondent on Charges of Treason," XI (1957) *Western Tennessee Historical Society Papers*, 76.

36. Baker, 336.

37. *Ibid.*, 337.

38. *Memphis Daily Appeal*, November 5, 1863.

39. Ellis, 592.

40. *Ibid.*, 251; Andrews, *The South Reports the Civil War*, 349.

41. Baker, 337.

42. *Memphis Daily Appeal*, October 7, 1863.

43. Ellis, 593.

44. Baker, 337.

45. *Memphis Daily Appeal*, November 5, 1863.

46. *Ibid.*

47. *Ibid.*

48. *Huntsville Confederate*, October 27, 1863, as reported in Ellis, *The Moving Appeal*, 516, n.103.

49. Ellis, 252.

50. Baker, 335.

51. Richmond, Virginia, *Whig*, November 23, 1864.

Chapter 13, Samuel C. Reid, Jr.

1. *The Twentieth Century Biographical Dictionary of Notable Americans*, Rossiter Johnson, ed. (Boston: The Biographical Society, 1904), not paginated. The entry for Reid provides valuable biographical information on him. For more on Reid's life, J.G. Wilson & J. Fiske, eds., *Appleton's Encyclopedia of American Biography*. 6 vols. (New York: 1887–89). See also, J. Cutler Andrews, *The South Reports the Civil War* (Princeton, N.J.: Princeton University Press, 1970), 52–53.

2. *Ibid.*

3. *Ibid.*

4. *Ibid.*

5. *Ibid.*

6. Samuel C. Reid, Jr., *The Scouting Expeditions of McCulloch's Texas Rangers* (Philadelphia: G.B. Zieber and Co., 1848), 5.

7. *Ibid.*, 31.

8. *Ibid.*, 31.

9. *Ibid.*, 28.

10. Reid, *The Scouting Expeditions of McCulloch's Texas Rangers*, 13.

11. *Ibid.*

12. *Ibid*, preface.

13. Lisa M. Daigle, "Samuel Chester Reid, Jr.: Confederate Correspondent, 1861–1864," In *The Civil War and the Press*, David B. Sachsman, S. Kittrell Rushing, and Debra Reddin van Tuyll, eds. (New Brunswick, N.J.: Transaction Publishers, 2000).

14. Andrews, 47–48.

15. Virginia Pettigrew Claire, *Harp of the South* (Georgia: Oglethorpe University Press, 1936), 65.

16. Daigle, 375.

17. *Ibid.*

18. *New Orleans Picayune*, September 4, 1861.

19. *Mobile Advertiser and Register*, October 15, 1862.

20. *New Orleans Picayune*, September 4, 1861.

21. *New Orleans Picayune*, February 16, 1862.

22. Daigle, 381.

23. *New Orleans Picayune*, February 16, 1862.

24. *New Orleans Picayune*, April 10, 1862.

25. *New Orleans Picayune*, February 18, 1862.

26. *New Orleans Picayune*, March 30, 1862.

27. *Ibid.*

28. As harbor master of New York, Reid's father invented and erected the first marine telegraph between New Jersey and New York. In 1826, he invented a new system of land telegraphs to send a message from Washington to New Orleans in two hours. See Johnson.

29. *New Orleans Picayune*, March 30, 1862.

30. *Mobile Advertiser and Register*, April 14, 1862.

31. *Mobile Advertiser and Register*, August 15, 1862.

32. *New Orleans Picayune*, March 28, 1862.

33. *Ibid.*

34. *New Orleans Picayune*, March 30, 1862.

35. *New Orleans Picayune*, April 6, 1862.

36. *Ibid.*

37. *New Orleans Picayune*, April 10, 1862.

38. *Ibid.*

39. *Mobile Advertiser and Register*, April 19, 1862.

40. *Ibid.*

41. *Charleston Mercury*, September 26, 1862.

42. *Memphis Daily Appeal*, May 22, 1862.

43. *Ibid.*

44. *Ibid.*

45. *Charleston Daily Courier*, June 21, 1862.

46. *Memphis Daily Appeal*, September 18, 1863.

47. *New Orleans Picayune*, March 30, 1862.

48. *Ibid.*

49. *Charleston Mercury*, September 26, 1862.

50. Andrews, *The South Reports the Civil War*, 146–147. Taken from Bragg Papers, Western Reserve Historical Society.

51. "General Braxton Bragg," *Chattanooga Times*, August 22, 1862.

52. *Ibid.*

53. *Ibid.*

54. "From the Seat of War," *New Orleans Picayune*, March 30, 1862.

55. "Letter from Cumberland Gap," *Mobile Advertiser and Register*, October 15, 1862.

56. *Ibid.*

57. "From Tennessee: Entry of Yankee Army Into Knoxville," *Memphis Daily Appeal*, May 22, 1862.

58. *Mobile Advertiser and Register*, June 10, 1862.

59. "Shelling of Chattanooga," *Mobile Advertiser and Register*, June 11, 1862.

60. "Letter from Cumberland Gap," *Mobile Advertiser and Register*, October 1, 1862.

61. *Mobile Advertiser and Register*, October 15, 1862.

62. "Our Army Correspondence," *Mobile Advertiser and Register*, October 3, 1862.

63. "From the Seat of War," *New Orleans Picayune*, March 28, 1862.

64. "Special Correspondence of the Appeal," *Memphis Daily Appeal*, May 21, 1862.

65. Claire, 65; Diary of Samuel Chester Reid, Jr., Samuel Chester Reid Papers, Santa Cruz, California.

66. *Ibid.*

67. "Letters From the Seat of War," *New Orleans Picayune*, April 6, 1862.

68. M*obile Advertiser and Register*, June 11, 1862.

69. "Letter from Chattanooga," *Mobile Advertiser and Register*, June 10, 1862.

70. *Mobile Advertiser and Register*, January 4, 1863.

71. "Letter from the Seat of War," *New Orleans Picayune*, February 18, 1862.

72. "From Our Special Correspondent," *Mobile Advertiser and Register*, February 19, 1863.

73. "Letter From Charleston," *Mobile Advertiser and Register*, February 19, 1863.

74. *Ibid.*

75. "Tornado at Shelbyville, Tenn.," *Memphis Daily Appeal*, March 9, 1863.

76. "Letter From Tennessee," *Mobile Advertiser and Register*, April 12, 1863.

77. "Letter From Chattanooga," *Mobile Advertiser and Register*, April 12, 1863.

78. Rossiter Johnson.

79. *Ibid.*

80. *Ibid.*

Chapter 14, William W. Screws

1. J. Ford Risley, "William Wallace Screws," in John A. Garraty and Mark C. Carnes, ed., *American National Biography*, vol. 19 (New York: Oxford University Press, 1999), 521–522.

2. *Ibid.*

3. *Montgomery Daily Advertiser,* July 9, 1862.

4. *Ibid.*

5. *Ibid.*

6. J. Cutler Andrews, *The South Reports the Civil War* (Princeton, N.J.: Princeton University Press, 1970), 237.

7. *Daily Advertiser*, August 27, 1862.

8. Andrews, 237.

9. *Daily Advertiser*, August 27, 1862.

10. J. Cutler Andrews, "The Confederate Press and Public Morale," *The Journal of Southern History* 32:4 (November 1966), 445–465, 456.

11. *Ibid.*

12. J. Ford Risley, "William Wallace Screws," in John A. Garraty and Mark C. Carnes, ed., *American National Biography*, vol. 19 (New York: Oxford University Press, 1999).

13. Certificate of Disability for Leave of Absence, William W. Screws Confederate Service File; May 19, 1864. National Archives, Washington, D.C.

14. Civil War Service Database, Alabama Department of Archives and History. http://www.archives.state.al.us/civilwar/soldier.cfm?id=172032 (accessed January 10, 2009).

15. Historic Structure Report, The Confederate Monument at the Alabama State Capitol, July 1, 2002, 1–27, 15. www.monumentpreservation.com/history.pdf (accessed June 9, 2008).

16. *Daily Advertiser,* May 6, 1864.

17. *Daily Advertiser,* May 29, 1864.

18. *Daily Advertiser,* June 26, 1864.

19. Andrews, 548–551.

20. *Ibid.*

21. *Daily Advertiser,* May 29, 1864, and June 13, 1864.

22. *Daily Advertiser,* May 6, 1864.

23. *Daily Advertiser,* June 27, 1864.

24. *Daily Advertiser,* July 9, 1864.

25. *Historic Structure Report, The Confederate Monument at the Alabama State Capitol,* July 1, 2002, 1–27, 15. www.monument preservation.com/history.pdf.

26. *Daily Advertiser,* November 14, 1865.

27. William Wallace Screws, "Alabama Journalism," in *Memorial Record of Alabama: A Concise Account of the State's Political, Military, Professional and Industrial Progress, Together with the Personal Memoirs of Many of its People,* vol. 2, 158–235. (Spartanburg, S.C.: Reprint Company, 1976; original, Madison, Wis.: Brant & Fuller, 1893).

28. Thomas McAdory Owen, *History of Alabama and Dictionary of Alabama Biography,* vol. 4 (Chicago: The S. J. Clarke Publishing Company, 1921), 1516.

29. King E. Williams, Jr., *The Press of Alabama: A History of the Alabama Press Association* (Birmingham: Alabama Press Association, 1997).

30. Screws, "Alabama Journalism," 189.

31. "The Alabama Democrats; Phases of the Late Convention. Colored Delegates and Southern Manhood—Why Col. Langdon Was Rejected—the Significance of the Platform," *New York Times,* June 17, 1878.

32. *Northern Alabama Historical and Biographical Illustrated* (Spartanburg, S.C.: The Reprint Company, Publishers, 1976; original, Birmingham, Alabama: Smith & De-Land, 1888), 621.

33. "The Alliance in Alabama: Its Relation to the Democratic Party and its Prospects," *New York Times,* June 28, 1891, 13:7.

34. *New York Times,* June 28, 1891.

35. Risley, 521–523.

36. Samuel L. Webb, "A Jacksonian Democrat in Postbellum Alabama: The Ideology and Influence of Journalist Robert McKee, 1869–1896," *The Journal of Southern History* 62:2 (May 1996), 239–274, 255, 265.

37. Williams, Jr., 7.

38. *Ibid.*

39. Williams, Jr., 33.

40. W.W. Screws, *Report of W.W. Screws, historian to Alabama Press Association,* Meeting at Dothan, June 16 and 17, 1909.

41. Screws, "Alabama Journalism," 161.

42. *Northern Alabama Historical and Biographical Illustrated* (Spartanburg, S.C.: The Reprint Company, Publishers, 1976; original, Birmingham, Alabama: Smith & De-Land, 1888), 621.

43. Owen, 1516.

44. Andrews, 24.

45. Owen, 1516.

Chapter 15, William G. Shepardson

1. *Richmond Daily Dispatch*, February 3, 1862.

2. War Songs, 1862. The theme of "Waiting" is a widow's yearning for the return of her soldier husband, who she discovers was slain at Manassas, 136. "The Midnight Ride" is about scouting the countryside on a cold, dark night, 172. Special Collections, Library of Virginia, Richmond. Also see the *Daily Dispatch*, which republished Bohemian's translation on December 27, 1861. Some verses were camp songs and some originated with "more than one fair daughter of the South."

3. Despite the best efforts of the author and librarians, Shepardson's birthplace, his date of death, and burial site have never been located. They cannot be found in his military records.

4. *Daily Dispatch*, October 9, 1861.

5. *Daily Dispatch*, January 16, 1862.

6. *Ibid.*, October 18, 1861.

7. James M. Perry, *A Bohemian Brigade, the Civil War Correspondents, Mostly Rough, Sometimes Ready* (New York: John Wiley and Sons, Inc.), preface, xi. The author writes that objectivity was not expected. He adds, "They were rowdy and boisterous. They competed hard to be the first with the news, and got it wrong more often than they should have. They were frequently arrogant and pompous. They lied; they cheated; they spied on one another and on the generals they wrote about . . . They drank too much. But out of all this turmoil and chaos came distinguished reporting."

8. *New Orleans Daily True Delta*, July 31, 1861.

9. *Daily Dispatch*, September 6, 1861.

10. *Daily Dispatch*, October 9, 1861.

11. *Daily Dispatch*, September 23, 1861.

12. *Ibid.*

13. *Daily Dispatch*, September 30, 1861.

14. *Daily Dispatch*, October 4, 1861.

15. *Ibid.*

16. *Daily Dispatch*, October 7, 1861.

17. *Daily Dispatch*, October 14, 1861.

18. *Daily Dispatch*, October 15, 1861.

19. *Daily Dispatch*, October 21, 1861.

20. *Ibid.*

21. *Daily Dispatch*, October 26, 1861. See also E.B. Long with Barbara Long, *The Civil War Day by Day* (Garden City, New York: Doubleday, 1971), whose count was approximately 1,700 men on each side, 129.

22. *Ibid.*

23. *Ibid.*

24. In the reportage of the Civil War, the comma was often omitted after an introductory clause. Writers revealed a fondness for hyphens, as in "to-day." Frequently,

all parts of proper names were not capitalized, as in "Anna river," "Libby prison," and "Conscript act." In Shepardson's case, many spelling errors occurred, but they may have been the fault of compositors, who were not likely to have been college educated.

25. *Daily Dispatch*, October 29, 1861.

26. *Daily Dispatch*, October 25, 1861.

27. *Ibid*. See also Long and Long, *Civil War Day by Day*, 129. This source puts casualties at 36 killed and 117 wounded.

28. *Daily Dispatch*, October 29, 1861.

29. *Daily Dispatch*, October 26, 1861.

30. *Ibid*. See also *Civil War Day by Day*, 129, "The federals had 49 killed, 158 wounded, and 714 missing, many of whom drowned . . . It was a dramatic, terrible, costly Federal defeat and a well-fought Confederate victory. The repercussions 'would far outweigh its relatively secondary strategic value.'"

31. *Daily Dispatch*, October 31, 1861.

32. *Ibid*.

33. *Daily Dispatch*, October 25, 1861.

34. *Daily Dispatch*, November 29, 1861.

35. *Ibid*.

36. Johnston was the commanding officer of the Armies of the Shenandoah and of the Potomac. A sutler is "one who follows an army for the purpose of selling the troops provisions, liquor, etc.," *Webster's Dictionary*, 1839.

37. *Daily Dispatch*, December 21, 1861.

38. *Ibid*.; *Daily Dispatch*, November 26, 1861. On November 19, the correspondent wrote that candles were scarce and cost twenty cents each.

39. *Daily Dispatch*, December 30, 1861.

40. *Ibid*.

41. *The War of the Rebellion: A Compilation of the Official Records of the Union and Confederate Armies, Correspondence, Etc.—Confederate* (Washington: Government Printing Office, 1880–1901), series I, vol. 5, 1014 (Republication).

42. *The War of the Rebellion*, series I, vol. 5, 1021.

43. *Daily Dispatch*, December 17, 1861.

44. *Daily Dispatch*, January 6, 1862.

45. *Ibid*.

46. *Ibid*., January 3, 1862.

47. *Daily Dispatch*, March 14, 1862.

48. Randolph was secretary of war from April 15, 1862, to November 15, 1862.

49. *War of the Rebellion*, series I, vol. 5, part III, 636.

50. *War of the Rebellion*, series I, vol. 2, 459.

51. See General Orders, 1861–1863, No. 78, issued by the Adjutant and Inspector General's Office from Richmond, October 28, 1862, Special Collections, Library of Virginia, Richmond.

52. *Daily Dispatch*, January 22, 1862.

53. Unidentified correspondent, "From Norfolk, runaway negroes—'Bohemian' gone to North Carolina—the news, &c.," *Daily Dispatch*, February 5, 1862. In the same piece, this correspondent speculated that the "crippled fleet" of the enemy, "with all

its shivering Hessian troops, will accomplish but little more than the stealing of a few negroes, and the plundering at unprotected points of the barns, smoke-houses, and hen roosts of the thrifty farmers in the productive section of Carolina, which they are so anxiously hoping to possess."

54. *Daily Dispatch*, February 28, 1862.

55. *Ibid.*

56. *Daily Dispatch*, February 11, 1862.

57. *Daily Dispatch*, February 27, 1862.

58. An anodyne is a medicine that relieves pain, *Webster's Dictionary.*

59. *Daily Dispatch*, February 27, 1862.

60. *Daily Dispatch*, February 28, 1862. See also Long and Long, *Civil War Day by Day*, 168. "While a relatively small engagement from the standpoint of forces and casualties, Roanoke Island had considerable importance. Control of Pamlico Sound gave the Federals a first-rate base on the Atlantic coast for operations against North Carolina." See also James McPherson, *Battle Cry for Freedom* (Oxford: Oxford University Press, 1988), 372–373, in which the author describes the island as "the key to Richmond's back door."

61. *Daily Dispatch*, February 10, 1862.

62. *Daily Dispatch*, February 20, 1862.

63. *Daily Dispatch*, February 26, 1862. The Richmond paper often billed Shepardson as "Our own Correspondent."

64. *Ibid.*

65. Wise, son of General Henry A. Wise, "as brave and gallant a man as ever breathed, constantly exposed himself to protect his men, and finally fell mortally wounded," in *Daily Dispatch*, February 28, 1862.

66. *Daily Dispatch*, February 27, 1862. McPherson, in *Battle Cry*, points out that Henry A. Wise, commander of Confederate troops on the island, recognizing that his "mosquito-fleet" gunboats were substandard, his batteries "badly sited," and his troops poorly trained and outnumbered, "pleaded with Richmond for more men and more guns, but Richmond seemed strangely indifferent," 372.

67. *Daily Dispatch*, February 27, 1862.

68. *Daily Dispatch*, February 28, 1862.

69. *Daily Dispatch*, March 4, 1862. See also Mitchel P. Roth, *Historical Dictionary of War Journalism* (Westport, Conn.: Greenwood Press, 1997), 283. Roth believes Shepardson was "one of the most outstanding reporters for the Confederate press during the American Civil War."

70. *Daily Dispatch*, March 14, 1862.

71. *Ibid.*

72. "Register of the Commissioned and Warrant Officers of the Navy of the Confederate States to January 1, 1864," Surgeons (Richmond, Va.: MacFarlane & Fergusson, Printers, 1864), National Archives of the United States, Record Group 109, 11, 56, 60.

73. *Ibid.*

74. *Mobile Advertiser and Register*, March 17, 1863.

75. *Mobile Advertiser and Register*, June 7, 1863.

76. *Mobile Advertiser and Register*, July 12, 1863.

77. *Mobile Advertiser and Register*, June 14, 1863.

78. *Civil War Day by Day*, 351.

79. *Mobile Advertiser and Register*, June 14, 1863.

80. Vicksburg was surrendered to the Federals on July 4, 1863, and the Confederate unconditional surrender occurred at Port Hudson, Louisiana, on July 8, 1862, in Long and Long, *The Civil War Day by Day*, 1112 and 1053, respectively.

81. *Mobile Advertiser and Register*, July 22, 1863.

82. *Mobile Advertiser and Register*, July 23, 1863.

83. *Ibid.*

84. *Ibid.*

85. *Mobile Advertiser and Register*, July 26, 1863.

86. *Ibid.*

87. *Ibid.*

88. *Ibid.*

89. *Mobile Advertiser and Register*, July 22, 1863.

90. *Mobile Advertiser and Register*, July 28, 1863.

91. *Ibid.*

92. *Mobile Advertiser and Register*, August 5, 1863.

93. John Bell, *Confederate Seadog: John Taylor Wood in War and Exile* (Jefferson, N.C.; McFarland & Co., 2002) 28.

94. *Daily Dispatch*, September 2, 1864.

95. *Ibid.*

96. *Ibid.*

97. Probably the Painkatank River, *Seadog*, 28.

98. *Daily Dispatch*, September 2, 1863.

99. *Ibid.*

100. *Ibid.*

101. *Ibid.*

102. Bell, *Confederate Seadog*, 28. See also Shepardson, "The Capture of Gunboats on the Rappahannock," *Daily Dispatch*, September 2, 1863.

103. *Daily Dispatch*, September 2, 1863.

104. *Ibid.*

105. *Ibid.*

106. *Ibid.*

107. *Ibid.*

108. *Ibid.*

109. Bell, *Confederate Seadog*, 28.

110. *Daily Dispatch*, September 2, 1863.

111. *Ibid.*

112. *Ibid.*

113. *Ibid.*

114. *Ibid.*

115. *Ibid.*

116. *Daily Dispatch*, August 30, 1863.

117. *Ibid.*

118. Arthur Thurston, *Tallahassee Skipper* (Yarmouth, Nova Scotia: Lescarbot Press, 1981), 357–364, in *Confederate Seadog*, 29.

119. Today the city's name is spelled New Bern.

120. *Daily Dispatch*, February 10, 1864.

121. Bell, *Confederate Seadog*, 140.

122. *Ibid.*

123. *Daily Dispatch*, February 10, 1864.

124. *Ibid.*

125. *Ibid.*

126. *Daily Dispatch*, February 12, 1864.

127. Bell, *Confederate Seadog*, 141.

128. *Daily Dispatch*, February 10, 1864.

129. *Ibid.*

130. *Ibid.*

131. *Ibid.*

132. *Daily Dispatch*, February 12, 1864.

133. *Daily Dispatch*, February 10, 1864.

134. *Daily Dispatch*, September 7, 1864.

135. *Daily Dispatch*, September 19, 1864. See also *Confederate Veteran*, a source that published information about Shepardson's diary, Broadfoot's Bookmark reprint, September 1910, 446. The entry about Bohemian states: "Robert H. Cunningham, 1932 Franklin Street, Baltimore, Md., has in his possession a diary kept during the war by one William Shepardson, who was assistant surgeon in the 5th Virginia Cavalry, commanded by Colonel Rosser, and afterward transferred to the navy as assistant surgeon on the Confederate States Steamer *Tallahassee* . . . Thinking that some of his family might like to have this diary, Mr. Cunningham sends this notece [sic]." "The Cruise of the Tallahassee" apparently is a portion of the original.

136. Official Records of Union and Confederate Navies, Operations of the Cruisers, series I, vol. 3, 706. See also Shelby Foote, *The Civil War, A Narrative: Red River to Appomattox* (New York: Random House, 1974), 508.

137. Official Records of Union and Confederate Navies, series II, vol. 1, 268. The C.S.S. *Tallahassee* was purchased in Wilmington in 1864. It was described as a "two-screw steam sloop cruiser," 220 feet in length, with a beam of 22 feet and a speed of 17 knots. The *Tallahassee* was known earlier as the blockade runner *Atlanta*. Afterward, the name was changed to *Olustee* and then to *Chameleon*.

138. Official Records of Union and Confederate Navies, Operations of the Cruisers, series I, vol. 3, 703–704.

139. Foote, *The Civil War, a Narrative*, 509.

140. *Daily Dispatch*, September 23, 1864. J. Thomas Scharf, however, included a chart of 33 ships in his *History of the Confederate States Navy from Its Organization to the Surrender of Its Last Vessel* (New York: Rogers and Sherwood, 1887), vol. 2, 814–816.

141. Foote, *The Civil War, a Narrative*, vol. 3, 508.

142. *Daily Dispatch*, September 19, 1864.

143. Foote, *The Civil War, a Narrative*, 508–509.

144. *Daily Dispatch*, September 19, 1864.

145. *Ibid.*

146. *Ibid.*

147. *Ibid.*

148. *Daily Dispatch,* September 19, 1864.

149. *Ibid.*

150. *Daily Dispatch,* September 19, 1864. The list of captured vessels was not finished. Next was the schooner *Lemot Du Pont,* of Wilmington, *Delaware,* from Glace Bay, and *Cape Breton,* with a cargo of coal. The correspondent noted that by Saturday night, August 13, a week from the *Tallahassee's* departure from Wilmington, the crew had destroyed one ship, three barques, three brigs, and eight schooners. Approximately 200 prisoners had been taken, exclusive of the passengers aboard the *Adriatic.*

151. *Daily Dispatch,* September 19, 1864.

152. *Daily Dispatch,* September 19, 1864.

153. *Ibid.*

154. *Daily Dispatch,* September 19, 1864.

155. *Ibid.*

156. *Ibid.*

157. *Daily Dispatch,* September 19, 1864.

158. Official Records of Union and Confederate Navies, Operations of the Cruisers, series I, vol. 3, 702.

159. Official Records of Union and Confederate Navies, Operations of the Cruisers, series I, vol. 3, 705.

160. *Daily Dispatch,* September 19, 1864.

161. *Ibid.*

162. *Ibid.*

163. Official Records of Union and Confederate Navies, North Atlantic Blockading Squadron, series I, vol. 10, 603.

164. Shepardson, December 24, 1864, *Daily Dispatch,* December 30, 1864.

165. *Ibid.*

Chapter 16, Peter W. Alexander

1. *Savannah Republican,* September 10, 1862, 1. A version of this chapter appeared as Ford Risley, "Peter W. Alexander: Confederate Chronicler & Conscience," *American Journalism,* 15:1 (1998), 35–50.

2. Rabun Lee Brantley, *Georgia Journalism of the Civil War Period* (Nashville, Tenn.: George Peabody College, 1929), 100; Louis Turner Griffith and John Erwin Talmadge, *Georgia Journalism, 1763–1850* (Athens: University of Georgia Press, 1951), 43–65; Jon L. Wakelyn, *Biographical Dictionary of the Confederacy* (Westport, Conn.: Greenwood Press, 1977), 71; David E. Paterson, "Lawyer, Journalist, and War Correspondent," *Upson County Historical Society Newsletter,* August–September, 1998 (available from http://files.usgwarchives.net/ga/upson/bios/pwalexander.txt; accessed November 2, 2008); F.D. Lee, *Historical Record of the City of Savannah* (Savannah, Ga.: J.H. Estill, 1869), 191–192.

3. William B. Styple, *Writing and Fighting the Confederate War: The Letters of Peter Wellington Alexander Confederate War Correspondent* (Kearny, N.J.: Belle Grove Publishing Co., 2002); Lucian Lamar Knight, *Georgia's Landmarks, Memories, and Legends,* vol. 2 (Atlanta: Byrd Printing Co., 1914), 720; Peterson, "Lawyer, Journalist and War Correspondent."

4. *Atlanta Constitution*, September 24, 1886, 2; *Upson Pilot*, December 8, 1860, 2.

5. However, he did write a letter to Thomaston resident Loula Kendall, daughter of a local physician, in which he described the national flag design under consideration by delegates. The young woman made a flag according to the pattern Alexander described: a broad white bar between two equally broad bars, with a hoist of blue decorated with a circle of seven stars, one for each of the seceded states. According to Miss Kendall, this was the first Confederate flag manufactured in Georgia.

6. It was not unusual for full-time reporters to work for more than one paper during the war to supplement their incomes. Alexander also wrote at various times for the *Mobile Advertiser and Register* and the *Richmond Dispatch*. See J. Cutler Andrews, *The South Reports the Civil War* (Princeton, N.J.: Princeton University Press, 1970), 50–51; Paterson, "Lawyer, Journalist and War Correspondent."

7. According to Upson County tradition, Alexander was in Montgomery for the convention that organized the Confederate government and in Charleston for the bombardment of Fort Sumter. That tradition maintains that Alexander collected the first cannonball fired at Fort Sumter from mud near the fort and sent it home to the B.B. White family. Today, a cannonball is affixed to a marble pedestal in front of the Upson County Courthouse that purports to be that first ball. However, the claim must be considered with skepticism. Confederate guns flung more than 3,000 balls and shells at Fort Sumter during the 34-hour bombardment. While the Upson story maintains Alexander knew how to determine the first ball fired, such a claim requires considerable credulity. However, the story does possibly put him at the moment and place where the Civil War began.

8. Walter J. Fraser, *Savannah in the Old South* (Athens: University of Georgia Press, 2003), 333.

9. Letter dated June 11, 1861, cited in Styple, *Writing and Fighting,*10.

10. Letter dated June 25, 1861, cited in Styple, *Writing and Fighting*, 14.

11. *Ibid.*

12. Letter dated June 28, 1861, cited in Styple, *Writing and Fighting*, 15.

13. *Ibid.*

14. In several instances, the North and South gave different names to Civil War battles. In most cases, the Confederates named a battle after the town that served as their base, while the Federals chose the landmark nearest to the fighting, usually a river or stream. Because this study examines a Confederate correspondent, the Southern name is used when referring to a battle.

15. *Savannah Republican*, July 23, 1861.

16. *Savannah Republican*, August 19, 1861.

17. *Savannah Republican*, August 27, 1861.

18. Letter dated August 12, 1861, cited in Styple, *Writing and Fighting*, 30.

19. *Savannah Republican*, August 26, 1861.

20. *Savannah Republican*, August 16, 1861.

21. Letter dated November 18, 1861, cited in Styple, *Writing and Fighting*, 53.

22. E.B. Long with Barbara Long, *The Civil War Day by Day* (Garden City, N.J.: Doubleday, 1971), 151.

23. *Savannah Republican*, December 6, 1861.

24. *Ibid.*

25. *Savannah Republican*, December 20, 1861, 1. For more on problems with the Quartermaster Corps, see Richard D. Goff, *Confederate Supply* (Durham: University of North Carolina Press, 1969), 34–39. Shortages of drugs and medicines in the Confederacy are discussed in Mary Elizabeth Massey, *Ersatz in the Confederacy* (Columbia: University of South Carolina Press, 1952).

26. Letter dated December 15, 1861, cited in Styple, *Writing and Fighting*, 58.

27. *Ibid.*

28. *Ibid.*

29. In May 1862, Alexander was among a group of correspondents reporting from Corinth, Mississippi, who were ordered to leave the army after a reporter for the *Memphis Appeal* allegedly disobeyed an order. For Alexander's report on the incident, see *Savannah Republican*, June 6, 1862.

30. *Savannah Republican*, September 15, 1861.

31. *Savannah Republican*, September 14, 1864.

32. *Richmond Daily Dispatch*, May 18, 1864.

33. Letter dated February 18, 1862, cited in Styple, *Writing and Fighting*, 70.

34. *Savannah Republican*, January 26, 1862.

35. Letter dated January 25, 1862, cited in Styple, *Writing and Fighting*, 64.

36. *Ibid.*

37. *Ibid.*

38. *Ibid.*

39. *Savannah Republican*, February 26, 1862.

40. *Savannah Republican*, April 17, 1862.

41. *Savannah* Republican, April 14, 1862.

42. *Ibid.*

43. *Savannah Republican*, May 26, 1862.

44. Andrews, *The South Reports the Civil War*, 173, 192–193, 246; *Savannah Republican*, June 6, 1862.

45. *Savannah Republican*, June 2, 1862.

46. *Savannah Republican*, June 16, 1862.

47. Letter dated July 3, 1862, cited in Styple, *Writing and Fighting*, 88.

48. *Atlanta Southern Confederacy*, March 12, 1862.

49. *Savannah Republican*, September 10, 1862.

50. Mobile *Daily Advertiser and Register*, October 24, 1862. Although not identifying Alexander by name, quotes from the correspondent's reports are used in Horace Herndon Cunnigham, *Doctors in Gray: The Confederate Medical Service* (Baton Rouge: Louisiana State University Press, 1958), 259.

51. For background, see Russell B. Nye, "Freedom of the Press and the Antislavery Controversy," *Journalism Quarterly*, 22 (March 1945), 1–11.

52. *Savannah Republican*, September 24, 1862.

53. *Ibid.*

54. *Ibid.*

55. *Mobile Advertiser and Register*, September 25, 1862.

56. *Ibid.*

57. *Savannah Republican*, September 22, 1862.

58. *Savannah Republican*, October 1, 1862.

59. Letter dated September 18, 1862, cited in Styple, *Writing and Fighting*, 108.

60. *Ibid.*

61. *Savannah Republican*, October 1, 1862.

62. *Savannah Republican*, October 2, 1862.

63. *Savannah Republican*, November 23, 1862.

64. *Richmond Dispatch*, October 9, 1862; *Athens Southern Banner*, October 3, 1862; *Savannah Republican*, October 22, 1862.

65. *Mobile Advertiser and Register*, December 5, 1862.

66. Andrews, 225–226.

67. *Mobile Advertiser and Register*, December 25, 1862.

68. *Ibid.*

69. *Savannah Republican*, March 4, 1863.

70. *Savannah Republican*, March 10, 1863.

71. *Savannah Republican*, April 10, 1863.

72. *Savannah Republican*, April 13, 1863.

73. *Savannah Republican*, May 22, 1863.

74. *Savannah Republican*, July 19, 1863.

75. *Savannah Republican*, July 19, 1863.

76. *Ibid.* For one of the best military studies of Gettysburg, which raises some of the same questions as Alexander, see Edwin B. Coddington, *The Gettysburg Campaign: A Study in Command* (New York: Charles Scribner's, 1968).

77. *Mobile Advertiser and Register*, September 29, 1863.

78. Letter dated September 23, 1863, cited in Styple, *Writing and Fighting*, 191.

79. *Savannah Republican*, November 16, 1863; Andrews, *The South Reports the Civil War*, 369.

80. *Savannah Republican*, December 1, 1863. Historians generally agree that the conduct of Confederate troops at Missionary Ridge was poor, although they also cite poor planning by officers as a reason for the disaster. See, for example, James Lee McDonough, *Chattanooga: A Death Grip on the Confederacy* (Knoxville: University of Tennessee Press, 1984), 205.

81. Letter dated December 20, 1863, cited in Styple, *Writing and Fighting*, 206.

82. *Ibid.*

83. *Savannah Republican*, May 25, 1864.

84. *Richmond Dispatch*, May 19, 1864; Andrews, *The South Reports the Civil War*, 389.

85. Letter dated May 7, 1864, cited in Styple, *Writing and Fighting* 209.

86. *Richmond Dispatch*, May 30, 1864.

87. *Mobile Advertiser and Register*, June 16, 1864.

88. *Savannah Republican*, July 14, 1864.

89. Letter dated July 4, 1864, cited in Styple, *Writing and Fighting*, 230.

90. Letter dated August 24, 1864, cited in Styple, *Writing and Fighting*, 240.

91. John E. Talmadge, "Savannah's Yankee Newspapers," *Georgia Review* 7 (1958): 66.

92. *Mobile Advertiser and Register*, January 12, 1865.

93. Alexander apparently did not return to Savannah but instead traveled to Macon where he discussed continuing as a correspondent with the editor of the *Macon Telegraph and Confederate*. On April 3, the newspaper announced that Alexander had been employed as a correspondent and that he had left to cover the fighting in Virginia. However, no correspondence from Alexander ever appeared in the paper.

94. "A Bitter Political Fight," *New York Times*, December 30, 1883.

95. Lucien Lamar Knight, *Georgia's Landmarks, Memorials and Legends* (Atlanta: Byrd Printing Co., 1914), 720.

96. 1870 census for Columbus, Georgia.

97. Anne Kendrick Walker, *Older Shorter Houses and Gardens* (New York: Tobias A. Wright, 1911), 53, 55, 160.

98. *Ibid.*, 66; 1880 U.S. Census for Georgia.

99. 1870 U.S. Census for Georgia.

100. *Atlanta Constitution*, September 24, 1886; Wakelyn, *Biographical Dictionary*, 71.

Chapter 17, James R. Sneed

1. He was a widower who raised five of his children alone for 10 years. The Federal Census for 1860 lists the Sneed family as James R. aged 40, editor *Savannah Republican,* and five children age 10 to 16; "James Roddy Sneed," Broadsides Collection of Hargrett Library.

2. *Savannah Morning News,*March 13, 1862; *Memphis Daily Appeal,* June 17, 1862; *The Press Association of the Confederate States of America* (Griffin, Ga.: Hill and Swayze's Printing House, 1863), May 13, 1863, 26, 29, 54–56.

3. Louis Turner Griffith and John Win Talmadge, *Georgia Journalism 1763–1950* (Athens: The University of Georgia Press, 1951), 53; *Ibid.*, 55.

4. F.D. Lee, *Historical Record of the City of Savannah* (Savannah, Ga.: J.H. Estill, 1869), 192.

5. Martha Galludet Waring, "Reminiscences of Charles Seton Henry Hardee's Recollections of Old Savannah, Part I," *Georgia Historical Quarterly* 12:3 (September 1928), 16.

6. Frederick J. Walker, Willis Sneed Family Historical Notes, Granville County, North Carolina. http://files.usgwarchives.org/nc/granville/bios/sneed01.txt (accessed August 22, 2007).

7. *Savannah Republican*, April 15, 1861.

8. *Ibid.*

9. *Ibid.*

10. *Ibid.*

11. *Ibid.*

12. *Ibid.*

13. *Ibid.*

14. *Savannah Morning News*, March 13, 1862; *Memphis Daily Appeal*, June 17, 1862.

15. *Savannah Republican*, October 14, 1861.

16. *Savannah Republican*, June 24, 1861.

17. *Savannah Republican*, March 5, 1863.

18. *Charleston Mercury*, July 6, 1861.

19. *Savannah Republican*, January 16, 1862.

20. *Richmond Daily Dispatch*, December 30, 1861.

21. *The War of the Rebellion: A Compilation of the Official Records of the Union and Confederate Armies*, series I, vol. 5 (Washington, D.C.: Government Printing Office, 1881), 1014, 1015.

22. *The War of the Rebellion*, 1021.

23. *Savannah Republican*, January 16, 1862.

24. *Ibid.*

25. *Savannah Republican*, January 18, 1862.

26. *Ibid.*

27. *Savannah Republican*, February 1, 1862.

28. *Ibid.*

29. *Savannah Republican*, January 17, 1862.

30. *Richmond Daily Dispatch*, March 14, 1862; *Savannah Republican*, March 14, 1862.

31. *Ibid.*

32. E. Merton Coulter, *A History of the South, Volume VII, The Confederate States of America 1861–1865* (Baton Rouge: Louisiana State University Press, 1950), 503.

33. *Savannah Republican*, April 12, 1862.

34. Mark M. Boatner, III, *The Civil War Dictionary* (New York: Random House, 1991), 296.

35. *Savannah Republican*, May 22, 1862. Mrs. Sneed was listed as Nora C. in the 1880 U.S. Census.

36. The city directory of 1860 lists the Sneed family as residing on Tattnall Street between Liberty and Harris streets and his office at the newspaper was on Bay between Bull and Whitaker.

37. *Savannah Republican*, June 5, 1862.

38. *Ibid.*

39. *Savannah Republican*, June 10, 1862.

40. *Ibid.*

41. *Ibid.*

42. U.T., "Letter from the Thirteenth Georgia, Frederick's Hall, Central R. R. Va., June 22, 1862," *Savannah Republican*, July 2, 1862.

43. *The Press Association of the Confederate States of America*, May 13, 1863, 26, 29, 54–56.

44. *Savannah Republican*, February 18, 1863.

45. *Ibid.*

46. *Ibid*; *New York Times*, February 12, 1863.

47. E.B. Long with Barbara Long, *Day by Day, An Almanac 1861–1865*, (New York: Da Capo, 1975), 335, 336; Robert N. Rosen, *Confederate Charleston* (Columbia: University of South Carolina Press, 1994), 137.

48. *Savannah Republican*, July 15, 1863.

49. *Ibid.*

50. *Savannah Republican*, July 17, 1863.

51. *Ibid.*

52. *Ibid.*

53. *Ibid.*

54. *Savannah Republican*, August 26, 1863.

55. *Ibid.*

56. *Ibid.*

57. *Ibid*

58. *Ibid.*

59. *Ibid.*

60. *Day by Day*, 405

61. *Savannah Republican*, July 17, 1863.

62. *Savannah Republican*, August 28, 1862.

63. *Savannah Republican*, October 12, 1863.

64. Jefferson Davis Papers, Sneed to Jefferson Davis, November 17, 1864, Duke University.

65. *Ibid.*, George A. Trenholm to Sneed, November 27, 1864, Duke University.

66. *Savannah Republican* editorial, December 21, 1864.

67. *Day by Day, an Almanac 1861–1865*, 613, 614.

68. Griffith and Talmadge, 83.

69. Waring, 25–26.

70. Brantley, 74.

71. No author listed, "James Roddy Sneed," Broadsides Collection of Hargrett Library, University of Georgia, available from http://fax.libs.uga.edu/common/qfullhit.htw?Ci WebHitsFile=%2Fbro%2Fbro1869%2Fbro246a%2Edjvu&CiRestriction=sneed&CiHilite Color=0xff6600&CiBold=3&CiUserParam3=/common/query.asp&CiHilite Type=Full#CiTag0, (accessed December 16, 2008).

72. *Savannah Republican*, August 18, 1865.

73. Brantley, 77.

74. *Savannah Morning News*, October 7, 1868.

75. *Savannah Morning News*, February 27, 1869.

76. Martha Galludet Waring, "The Striving 'Seventies in Savannah," *Georgia Historical Quarterly* 20:2 (June 1936), 159.

77. "James Roddy Sneed," part of a collection of many separate loose pages, no date, no page number.

78. Courtesy of Cheryl Brundle, Sneed relative.

79. *Savannah Morning News*, March 21, 1891.

80. *Ibid.*

81. *Daily Inter Ocean, Chicago*, March 18, 1891.

Chapter 18, John S. Thrasher

1. James Grant Wilson and John Fiske, eds. "Thrasher, John S," Appleton's Cyclopedia of American Biography, 106; Rev. B.F. Tefft, Webster and His Masterpieces, 441;

Handbook of Texas on Line, available at http://www.tshaonline.org/handbook/onlin/
articles/GG/eegzb.html (accessed February 20, 2008); Tom Chaffin, Fatal Glory, 145;
Cubans in the Confederacy.

2. Ruby Florence Tucker, "The Press Association of the Confederate States of America in Georgia," (master's thesis, University of South Carolina, 1950), 27; Wilson, 106.

3. With the Federal District Court of Northern Georgia.

4. Wilson, 165.

5. *The Press Association of the Confederate States of America* (Griffin, Ga.: Hill and
Swayze's Printing House, 1863), 41.

6. "John Sydney Thrasher," *Directory of American Biography* (New York: Charles
Scribner's, 1936), 18: 509–510.

7. Wilson and Fiske, 106.

8. "Mr. Thrasher's Last Address to His Countrymen," *Bangor Daily Whig & Courier*
(Maine), Friday, December 12, 1851.

9. Barbara G. Ellis, *The Moving Appeal: Mr. McClanahan, Mrs. Dill and the Civil
War's Great Newspaper Run* (Macon, Ga.: Mercer University Press, 2003), 75.

10. "Washington. Presidential Levee," *New York Times*, December 12, 1851.

11. "In the U.S. House of Representatives," *Daily Morning News* (Savannah, Ga.), December 20, 1851; Henry Wheaton, *Elements of International Law* (Boston: Little, Brown,
and Co., 1855), 123–125; Tefft, 41; "The Case of Mr. Thrasher," *New York Times*, October
25, 1851; "Washington. Presidential Levee," *New York Times*, December 12, 1851.

12. Wilson, 106.

13. "The Works of Humboldt and J.S. Thrasher on Cuba," *New York Herald*, August
13, 1856, 8; J.S. Thrasher, "Cuba and the United States: How the Interests of Louisiana
Would Be Affected by Annexation," *De Bow's Review*, XVII (July 1854), 47.

14. J.S. Thrasher, ed., *The Island of Cuba* by Alexander Humboldt, Translated from
the Spanish (New York: Derby & Jackson, 1856), 55.

15. Texas Handbook; *The Scotch-Irish in America: Proceeding and Addresses of the
Second Congress* (Cincinnati: Robert Clark & Co., 1890), 167.

16. Press Association, 5–7.

17. *Augusta* (Georgia) *Chronicle and Sentinel*, January 21, 1862; *Columbus* (Geor-
gia) *Enquirer*, October 1, 1862; Minutes of the Board of Directors of the Press Asso-
ciation, Embracing the Quarterly Reports of the Superintendent, October and January
(Atlanta: Franklin Steam Publishing House, 1864); First Annual Meeting of the Press
Association (Montgomery: Appeal Job Printing Establishment, 1864); J. Ford Risley,
"Wartime News Over the Wires"; Quintus C. Wilson, "Confederate Press Association:
A Pioneer News Agency," *Journalism Quarterly* (June 27, 1949), 160; Tucker, 4.

18. *Columbus Enquirer*, October 1, 1862.

19. *Augusta Chronicle and Sentinel*, October 25, 1864.

20. *Augusta Chronicle and Sentinel*, January 21, 1862.

21. Press Association, 6–7; *Savannah Republican*, March 17, 1862; William Herbert
Wilken, "As the Telegraph Saw It: A Study of the Editorial Policy of the *Macon Telegraph* (And *Confederate*), 1860–1865," (Unpublished master's thesis, Emory University,
1964), 12–13; Quintus C. Wilson, "Confederate Press Association: A Pioneer News

Agency," *Journalism Quarterly* 26 (June 1949), 160; J. Cutler Andrews, *The South Reports the Civil War* (Pittsburgh: University of Pittsburgh Press, 1970) 55–56; Ruby Florence Tucker, "The Press Association of the Confederate States of America in Georgia," (unpublished master's thesis, University of Georgia, 1950), 2; J. Ford Risley, "Georgia's Civil War Newspapers: Partisan, Sanguine, Enterprising," (PhD dissertation, University of Florida, 1996) 114.

22. Press Association, 6–7.

23. *Ibid.*,11, 16.

24. J. Ford Risley, "The Confederate Press Association: Cooperative News Reporting of the War," *Civil War History* (September 2001): 222, 225.

25. Thrasher chose Atlanta because it "combines the advantages of a central geographical position, communication by telegraphy and rail with all parts of the country, lies on one of the branches of the telegraphy system, most liable to work ill to the disadvantage of a portion of our members." Press Association, 37.

26. Press Association, 1863, 37.

27. *Ibid.*, 19–20, 25.

28. *Ibid.*, 53.

29. *Ibid.*, 40.

30. *Ibid.*, 9.

31. *Ibid.*, 23.

32. *Ibid.*, 22.

33. Andrews, 339.

34. Press Association, 28.

35. *Ibid.*, 26.

36. *Ibid.*, 28.

37. *Ibid.*, 29, 54–56.

38. *Ibid.*, 29.

39. *Ibid.*, 30.

40. *Ibid.*, 29.

41. *Ibid.*, 47.

42. *Ibid.*, 47.

43. *Ibid.*, 47, 48.

44. Andrews, 274.

45. Press Association, 29, 30.

46. *Ibid.*, 36.

47. *Ibid.*, 30.

48. *Ibid.*, 49.

49. *Ibid.*, 50.

50. Risley, 224.

51. Risley, 238–239.

52. Press Association, 54, 55.

53. *Ibid.*, 29.

54. *Ibid.*, 21.

55. *Ibid.*, 25, 21.

56. *Ibid.*, 24, 25.

57. Risley, 232.

58. Press Association, 36.

59. *Ibid.*, 36.

60. *Ibid.*, 37

61. *Ibid.*, 36–37.

62. Wilson, 161.

63. Debra Reddin van Tuyll, "The Rebels Yell: Conscription and Freedom of Expression in the Civil War South," *American Journalism,* Spring 2000.

64. Press Association, 22.

65. Risley, 239; Andrews, 515–516.

66. Risley, 232.

67. Andrews, 464, 463.

68. Wilson and Fiske, 106.

69. W.T. Block, "Hamilton Stuart and Benjamin Chambers Stuart: A Century of Distinguished East Texas Journalism and History." Texas Gulf Historical and Biographical Record, November 1997, 33.

Chapter 19, Durant da Ponte

1. Elliott Ashkenazi, *The Civil War Diary of Clara Solomon* (Baton Rouge and London: Louisiana State University Press, 1995), 3.

2. Durant da Ponte and Clara and Rosa Solomon, as well as other members of the family in New Orleans, spelled the surname with a lower case "d" as in "da Ponte." However, Durant's grandfather and father spelled the name with a capital D. Most current descendants appear to spell the name with a capital D. The author is using the spelling of the name preferred by Durant da Ponte.

3. Shield Hodges, *Lorenzo Da Ponte: The Life and Times of Mozart's Librettist* (Madison: The University of Wisconsin Press, 2002), 4.

4. *Ibid.*, 15.

5. Lorenzo Da Ponte, translated by Elisabeth Abbott, *Memoirs* (New York: New York Review of Books, 1957), 5.

6. Abbott, 347.

7. Hodges, 198.

8. The Jewish Museum Vienna, brochure accompanying the exhibit "Lorenzo Da Ponte: Challenging the New World," March 21, 2006.

9. In 1889, Durant da Ponte swore under oath in a passport application that his birthday was February 16, 1832. This disagrees with the conclusions of earlier biographical sketches, but this writer is using the 1832 date because it corresponds to the ages he gave on both of his marriage records.

10. Adam Goodyear, "Don Giovanni: A Historical Intermessa," *Washington College Magazine*, Summer 2006.

11. John Howard Brown, ed., *Cyclopaedia of American Biography: Comprising the Men and Women of the United States Who Have Been Identified With the Growth of the Nation,* vol. 2 (Boston: James H. Lamb Company, 1890. Reprinted by Kessinger Publishing, 2006), 342.

12. *Ibid.*, 556.

13. Durant da Ponte, "Whitman's Young Fellow Named da Ponte," *Walt Whitman Review*, March 5, 1959, 16–17.

14. Lota M. Spell, "The Anglo Saxon Press in Mexico, 1846–1848," *The American Historical Review*, 36 (1), October 1932, 24. Note: Durant's widow received a pension for his Mexican War service from the U.S. government while she lived in New Orleans and California.

15. *New Orleans Daily Picayune*, January 9, 1850, 2.

16. J. Cutler Andrews, *The South Reports the Civil War* (Princeton, NJ: Princeton University Press, 1970), 35.

17. Andrews, 69.

18. Andrews, 68.

19. *New Orleans Daily Delta*, June 8, 1861, 1.

20. Solomon, 26.

21. *Ibid.*

22. *Daily Delta*, June 25, 1861, 1.

23. *Ibid.*

24. Solomon, 36.

25. The exact battle to which da Ponte was referring cannot be identified because most of that day's newspaper was smeared before microfilming.

26. *Daily Delta*, June 26, 1861, 2.

27. *Ibid.*

28. Solomon, 40.

29. *Daily Delta*, June 25, 1861, 1.

30. *Daily Delta*, June 27, 1861, 1.

31. *Daily Delta*, June 29, 1961, 1.

32. Solomon, 48.

33. *Ibid.*

34. *Ibid.*

35. *Ibid.*

36. *Daily Delta*, July 14, 1861.

37. Solomon, 74.

38. Solomon, 95.

39. Andrews, 94.

40. *Daily Delta*, September 4, 1861.

41. *Daily Delta*, September 28, 1861, 1.

42. *Daily Delta*, October 4, 1861, 1.

43. Solomon, 234.

44. *Daily Delta*, November 12, 1861, 1.

45. Solomon, 242.

46. *Daily Delta*, December 19, 1861, 1.

47. *Daily Delta*, January 30, 1862, 1.

48. *Daily Delta*, February 11, 1862.

49. *Ibid.*

50. *Ibid.*

51. *Ibid.*

52. *Ibid.*

53. *Ibid.*

54. Solomon, 286.

55. Solomon, 339–340.

56. Admiral David Farrabut, quoted in Charles Dufour, *The Night the War Was Lost* (Lincoln and London: The University of Nebraska Press, 1960), 300.

57. Dufour, 301.

58. Dufour, 306.

59. Monroe to Farragut, quoted in Dufour, 306.

60. Chester G. Hearn, *The Capture of New Orleans 1862* (Baton Rouge: Louisiana State University Press, 1995), 257.

61. Solomon, 344.

62. Solomon, 348.

63. Solomon, 349.

64. Solomon, 368.

65. *Daily Picayune*, August 8, 1894, 11.

66. The National Archives, Compiled Service Records of Confederate General and Staff Officers and Nonregimental Enlisted Men, file of Durant da Ponte, 1861–1862 and Confederate Papers Relating to Citizens or Business Firms, 1861–1865, file of Charles Helm.

67. John Howard Brown, ed., *Lamb's Biographical Dictionary of the United States*, vol. 7 (Publisher unknown, 1900–1903). The book has been digitalized and placed online by Google.com. The web site location is : http://www.archive.org/details/lambsbiodic01 browrich.

68. Ashkenazi, ed., 443.

69. *Daily Picayune*, August 8, 1894, 11.

Chapter 20, Henry H. Perry

1. See, for example, J. Cutler Andrews, *The South Reports the Civil War* (Princeton, N.J.: Princeton University Press, 1970).

2. See, for example, *New Orleans Daily Picayune,* May 12, 1861, and May 29, 1861.

3. *Ibid.*

4. *New Orleans Daily Picayune*, May 12, 1861.

5. *New Orleans Daily Picayune*, May 28, 1861.

6. William M. Owen, *In Camp and Battle with the Washington Artillery of New Orleans* (Gretna, La.: Pelican Publishing Company, 1964), 512.

7. *New Orleans Daily Picayune*, May 28, 1861.

8. See, for example, *New Orleans Daily Picayune*, June 18, 1861, July 13, 1861, August 1, 1861.

9. The Cabildo, "The Civil War" (available at lsm.crt.state.la.us/cabildo/cab10.htm; accessed November 21, 2007); Federal Records, "Report from the Confederate War Department, Dec. 1861," (available at http://www.archives.gov/research/guide-fed-records/groups/109.html; accessed November 21, 2007).

10. *New Orleans Daily Picayune,* May 28, 1861.

11. *New Orleans Daily Picayune,* June 20, 1861.

12. *New Orleans Daily Picayune,* May 29, 1861.

13. *New Orleans Daily Picayune,* June 1, 1861.

14. Owen, *In Camp and Battle with the Washington Artillery of New Orleans,* 11.

15. *New Orleans Daily Picayune,* August 1, 1861.

16. *New Orleans Daily Picayune,* July 30, 1861.

17. *Ibid.*

18. *New Orleans Daily Picayune,* August 1, 1861.

19. *New Orleans Daily Picayune,* June 19, 1861.

20. *New Orleans Daily Picayune,* June 19, 1861.

21. *New Orleans Daily Picayune,* June 19, 1861.

22. *Alexandria Gazette,* sec. D, January 1, 1929.

23. *New Orleans Daily Picayune,* October 23, 1861.

24. *New Orleans Daily Picayune,* February 2, 1862.

25. *Ibid.*

26. *New Orleans Daily Picayune,* February 6, 1862.

27. *New Orleans Daily Picayune,* February 14, 1862.

28. *New Orleans Daily Picayune,* March 21, 1862.

29. *New Orleans Daily Picayune,* April 11, 1862.

30. *Ibid.*

31. *New Orleans Daily Picayune,* April 13, 1862.

32. *Ibid.*

33. *Memphis Daily Appeal,* May 19, 1862.

34. *Memphis Daily Appeal,* June 6, 1862.

35. Owen, *In Camp and Battle with the Washington Artillery of New Orleans,* 512; Andrews, *The South Reports the Civil War,* 813.

36. *New Orleans Daily Picayune,* June 19, 1861.

37. *Ibid.*

38. *Ibid.*

39. *New Orleans Daily Picayune,* April 21, 1862.

40. *Ibid.,* 4.

41. *New Orleans Daily Picayune,* January 3, 1862.

42. *New Orleans Daily Picayune,* March 22, 1862.

43. *New Orleans Daily Picayune,* March 18, 1862.

44. National Park Service, "US Department of the Interior: American Battlefield Protection Program CWSAC 2006" (available at http://www.nps.gov/history/hps/abpp/; Internet; accessed December 10, 2007).

45. *New Orleans Daily Picayune,* September 18, 1861.

46. *New Orleans Daily Picayune,* January 3, 1862.

47. *Ibid.*

48. James M. McPherson, *Battle Cry of Freedom: The Civil War Era* (Oxford: Oxford University Press, 2003), 952.

49. *New Orleans Daily Picayune,* January 3, 1862.

50. *New Orleans Daily Picayune,* February 3, 1862.

51. *New Orleans Daily Picayune*, April 13, 1862.

52. *New Orleans Daily Picayune*, October 10, 1861.

53. *New Orleans Daily Picayune*, January 16, 1862.

54. *New Orleans Daily Picayune*, February 21, 1893.

55. T. Harry Williams, *P.G.T. Beauregard: Napoleon in Gray* (Baton Rouge: Louisiana State University Press, 1955), 346.

56. B.G. Ellis, *The Moving Appeal: Mr. McClanahan, Mrs. Dill, and the Civil War's Great Newspaper Run* (Macon, Ga.: Mercer University Press, 2003), 677.

Chapter 21, Charles DeMorse

1. *Clarksville Standard*, February 8, 1862. Note: In order to give an accurate sense of DeMorse's writing, his grammar, spelling, and punctuation has not been changed. The use of the word "sic" has been used sparingly, only when needed for clarity.

2. Many Texas newsmen and printers enlisted, including James P. Douglas of the *Tyler Reporter* who served as an artillery officer; both publishers of the *Dallas Herald*; George H. Sweet of the *San Antonio Herald* who served as a captain (and, later, as a colonel) in Company A of the 15th Texas Cavalry; Joseph Lancaster of the *Texas Ranger* who served as a captain; S.H.B. Cundiff of the *Nacogdoches Chronicle*, who also served as a captain and escaped capture at the Battle of Arkansas Post; and the editors of the *Henderson Times*, the *Sentinel*, and the *Kaufman Democrat*. The entire staff of the LaGrange-based *States Rights Democrat* put enlisted en masse. The Editor, J.G. Wheeler, told readers in September 1861 that the newspaper was suspending, stating, "All hands; editors and printers, have considered it their duty to go to war, and none of us are likely to return before our independence is acknowledged."Quote reprinted from the *LaGrange True Issue*, September 15, 1861. On common public rhetoric associated with Confederate Nationalism, especially the link between patriotism and religion, see Drew Gilpin Faust, *The Creation of Confederate Nationalism: Ideology and Identity in the Civil War South* (Baton Rouge: Louisiana State University Press, 1988), 22.

3. Debra Reddin van Tuyll, "The Rebels Yell: Conscription and Freedom of Expression in the Civil War South," *American Journalism* 17:2 (Spring 2000), 17; Ernest Wallace, *Charles DeMorse: Pioneer Editor and Statesman* (Lubbock: Texas Tech University Press, 1943), 23. DeMorse, encouraged and backed by a group of prominent citizens from Clarksville and the Red River counties, began publishing the *Northern Standard* on August 20, 1842. Texas newspaper historian Marilyn McAdams Sibley states that although DeMorse managed to keep the newspaper running his entire life, the lack of cash in frontier communities in North Texas meant the editor at times had to resort to accepting produce in lieu of cash, a frequent practice in small towns across Texas. See Marilyn McAdams Sibley, *Lone Stars and State Gazettes: Texas Newspapers before the Civil War* (College Station: Texas A & M Press, 1983), 11. Even as war drew near, DeMorse still made appeals to exchange subscriptions for fresh food. See, for example, "Food Wanted," *Clarksville Standard*, July 7, 1860.

4. Van Tuyll, 17–19.

5. John Osterhout did serve in the Texas State Militia, but his duty kept him within the confines of the state itself.

6. DeMorse to the *Clarksville Standard*, May 12, 1862. DeMorse's letter noted that approval had been granted by the secretary of war on March 8, 1862. DeMorse was allowed to enlist volunteers for either a three-year term or for the duration of the war. His cavalry regiment was not to exceed 10 companies with each comprising between 60 and 125 privates.

7. Mark K. Christ, "All Cut to Pieces and Gone to Hell," in *The Civil War, Race Relations, and the Battle of Poison Spring* (Little Rock: August House Publishers, 2003), 22, 84.

8. Gregory J. W. Irwin, "'We Cannot Treat Negroes . . . As Prisoners of War:' Racial Atrocities and Reprisals in Civil War Arkansas," in Gregory J.W. Irwin, ed., *Black Flag Over Dixie: Racial Atrocities and Reprisals in the Civil War* (Carbondale: Southern Illinois University, 2004), 132–152.

9. Wallace, 145.

10. David Paul Smith, *Frontier Defense in the Civil War* (College Station: Texas A & M University Press, 1994), 3–40. Forts were constructed throughout the frontier areas of Texas and completed in 1852 to protect settlers from raids by Native Americans and Mexicans.

11. Other Confederate reporters, including the noted Peter Alexander, used more than one byline. Most reporters who did this wrote for more than one publication, however. See Ford Risley, "Peter Alexander: Confederate Chronicler & Conscience," *American Journalism*, 15:1 (Winter 1998), 35. For more on pen names, see J. Cutler Andrews, *The South Reports the Civil War* (Pittsburgh: University of Pittsburgh Press, 1985), 49.

12. DeMorse's biographer, Ernest Wallace, notes the same thing in his chapter on DeMorse's Civil War activities. See Wallace, 143–153.

13. Wallace, 1–2.

14. *Clarksville Standard*, April 25, 1863. The original letter was dated March 30.

15. Although Wallace wrote that DeMorse belonged to no church, the editor considered himself to be nominally Christian and had a large library of religious works at his home. See Wallace, 2–7. In explaining the religious rhetoric so common to Civil War literature and nonfiction, historian Drew Gilpin Faust has stated that Christianity was "the most fundamental source of legitimation for the Confederacy." See Faust, 22.

16. *Clarksville Standard*, May 25, 1861.

17. *Clarksville Standard*, July 18, 1863, April 30, 1864.

18. Alice Fahs, *The Imagined Civil War: Popular Literature of the North & South, 1861–1865* (Chapel Hill: University of North Carolina Press, 2001), 25. Phillip Knightley, *The First Casualty: The War Correspondent as Hero and Myth-Maker from the Crimea to Kosovo* (Baltimore: Johns Hopkins University Press, 2000), 25–26.

19. "Telegraphic Despatches and War News," *Clarksville Standard*, May 12, 1862.

20. Omissions due to the Southern press' booster role were common throughout the Confederate states.

21. Wallace, 148.

22. DeMorse to *Clarksville Standard*, October 15, 1864. The original letter was dated September 29.

23. John C. Waugh, *Sam Bell Maxey and the Confederate Indians* (Abilene, Texas: McWhiney Foundation Press, 1998), 71.

24. James M. McPherson, *For Cause & Comrades: Why Men Fought in the Civil War* (New York: Oxford University Press, 1997), 11.

25. George Robinson of the *Huntsville Item* exemplified the typical prewar Texas newspaperman. He served as his journal's editor, the writer, business manager, printer, and pressman. " . . . this economy is absolutely necessary, or we should soon have to shut up shop," he noted in the late 1850s. Robinson also engaged in job printing, including handbills, pamphlets, occasional books, and public printing contracts. See Sibley, *Lone Stars and State Gazettes*, 10.

26. Knightley, 24.

27. James P. Douglas of the *Tyler Reporter* sent clippings from other newspapers along with reports for publication of the battles in which he fought. See Lucia Rutherford Douglas, ed., *Douglas's Texas Battery, CSA* (Tyler, Texas: Smith County Historical Society, 1966), 112.

28. Ford Risley, "'Dear Courier': The Civil War Correspondence of Editor Melvin Dwinell," *Journalism History*, vol. 31 (3) (Fall 2005), 163.

29. Wallace, 10–11.

30. Wallace, 16–17.

31. Wallace, 20–22. Wallace notes that although the newspaper was not named by DeMorse, it most likely was the *Daily Bulletin*, Austin's first daily newspaper that largely contained news of the proceedings of the House of Representatives along with a few news items and editorial matter.

32. Wallace, 22–23.

33. His editorials throughout the 1850s encouraged railroad development, road improvements, and navigational improvements throughout Texas as well as support and encouragement of slavery and cotton culture.

34. Immigrants to the Texas Republic established the institution of slavery there because they believed slavery was the best and quickest means of achieving economic development. See Billy D. Ledbetter, "White Over Black in Texas: Racial Attitudes in the Ante-Bellum Period," *Phylon* 34:4 (Winter 1973), 406; Randolph B. Campbell, *Gone to Texas: A History of the Lone Star State* (New York: Oxford University Press, 2003), 111.

35. For a full examination of all of the issues involved in the boundary dispute, see Mark J. Stegmaier, *Texas, New Mexico, and the Compromise of 1850: Boundary Dispute and Sectional Crisis* (Kent, Ohio: Kent State University Press, 1996). On DeMorse's views of slavery and the Texas Boundary dispute, see Wallace, 30–33, 110–111. Also, see Sibley, 274.

36. Wallace, 125.

37. Quoted in Wallace, 116.

38. "Fugitive Slave Law," *Clarksville Standard*, December 7, 1850.

39. "The Compromise," *Clarksville Standard*, June 29, 1850. An important section of this editorial explained DeMorse's beliefs about both the Union and slavery when he stated: "God knows we love this Union. We love her for the sake of her loveliness, for her undefiled purity, for her republican institutions and equal rights; but we cannot consent to the elevation of the negroes by placing them upon the same footing with ourselves. Neither are we willing that the happiness and safety of eighteen millions of free white people should be put in jeopardy in the vain hopes of liberating three

millions of negroes, one-half of whom would starve in less than one year after their liberation."

40. Quoted in Wallace, 115, 123.

41. *Clarksville Standard*, April 23, 1859.

42. Wallace, 130. See the November 26, 1859, and December 10, 1859, issues of the *Standard*. DeMorse reiterated his desire to see the Union remain intact in a February 1860 editorial, but recognized that secession may have been near: "It is quite possible that the South may have to draw a line and defend it . . . But we are opposed to taking trouble by anticipation. We are not yet oppressed—perhaps the point at which resistence would be proper may never arrive," he wrote. See *Clarksville Standard*, February 4, 1860.

43. Texas newspaper historian Marilyn McAdams Sibley has stated that DeMorse, like other moderates in Texas, faced a dilemma as war approached. He didn't unquestioningly follow the party line. He supported Breckinridge in 1860 and "deplored the stalemate of the Democrats at Charleston that led to the breakup of the party." See Sibley, *Lone Stars and State Gazettes*, 292.

44. Wallace, 134–135.

45. "The Crisis," *Clarksville Standard*, January 19, 1861.

46. "The Election," *Clarksville Standard*, February 23, 1861.

47. Sibley, *Lone Stars and State Gazettes*, 292.

48. Quoted in Sibley, *Lone Stars and State Gazettes*, 292.

49. Sibley, *Lone Stars and State Gazettes*, 293.

50. Wallace, 143.

51. "War," *Clarksville Standard*, April 27, 1861.

52. *Clarksville Standard*, May 25, 1861.

53. *Clarksville Standard*, February 15, 1862.

54. *Clarksville Standard*, March 1, 1862.

55. Military records show that two and one-half times as many Texans joined cavalry regiments than the infantry. In a state where no one walked if they possessed a horse, this is not surprising. See Statement of Organized Confederate Units, September 1861, Official Records, series IV, vol. 1, 628; McCulloch to Walker, July 18, 1861, series I, vol. III, 611–612.

56. *Clarksville Standard*, March 29, 1862.

57. The latter issue is ironic given that DeMorse referred to Union soldiers as mercenaries fighting for money, while Southerners, he claimed, fought for principle, home defense, and their way of life. For more on the relationship between manhood, duty, honor, and calls to war, see McPherson, *For Cause & Comrades*, 25–26.

58. *Clarksville Standard*, May 5, 1862.

59. *Ibid.*

60. *Ibid.*

61. John J. Hennessy, *Return to Bull Run: The Campaign and Battle of Second Manassas* (Norman: University of Oklahoma Press, 1999).

62. On DeMorse's early political career, see Wallace, 22. In 1842, DeMorse also served as the first mayor of Clarksville and was congressman-elect at the time of annexation.

63. *Clarksville Standard*, September 13, 1862.

64. On Alexander, see Ford Risley, "Peter Alexander: Confederate Chronicler & Conscience," *American Journalism,* 15, no. 1 (Winter 1998), 40.

65. *Clarksville Standard*, September 13, 1862.

66. Christopher Gustavus Memminger was born in Germany in 1803 and moved to Charleston, South Carolina, as a young child. He was appointed secretary of the Confederate Treasury on February 21, 1861. Scholars disagree as to the role that Memminger played in the Confederate government's flagging economic policies. See, for example, Douglas B. Ball, *Financial Failure and Confederate Defeat* (Urbana: University of Illinois Press, 1991); Larry Schweikart, *Banking in the American South from the Age of Jackson to Reconstruction* (Baton Rouge: Louisiana State University Press, 1987); Robert Cecil Todd, *Confederate Finance* (Athens: University of Georgia Press, 1954).

67. *Clarksville Standard*, September 13, 1862.

68. *Ibid.*

69. Faust, 42.

70. *Ibid.,* 43.

71. This letter also was published in the *Dallas Herald*, September 20, 1862.

72. *Clarksville Standard*, September 13, 1862.

73. Gary W. Gallagher, ed., *The Richmond Campaign of 1862: The Peninsula and the Seven Days* (Chapel Hill: University of North Carolina Press, 2000). Gallagher and other historians have noted that the Seven Days Battles and the Battle of Second Manassas were tremendous tactical and psychological victories for the Confederacy. Southerners believed that a slaveholding nation might become an actuality, while moderate voices in the North realized that harder tactics were needed if the Union was to be re-established and slavery ended.

74. *Clarksville Standard*, October 13, 1862.

75. *Clarksville Standard*, October 13, 1862. This letter was written from Cady's Hotel in Columbus, Mississippi, on September 14, 1862, as DeMorse was returning to Texas. Note the month's delay from the time the editor sent the letter to his newspaper and the time it was published.

76. Sibley, 9.

77. *Clarksville Standard*, October 13, 1862. John Marshall died after being struck in the neck by a bullet while lining his men up for their charge.

78. *Clarksville Standard*, October 18, 1862.

79. *Ibid.*

80. The Col. Cumby to which DeMorse refers is Robert H. Cumby who briefly commanded Greer's 3rd Texas Cavalry in 1862 when the regiment was reorganized after it departed Corinth, Mississippi, in late May 1862.

81. *Clarksville Standard*, October 18, 1862.

82. *Clarksville Standard*, October 13, 1862.

83. *Clarksville Standard*, February 28, 1863, July 23, 1863; Campbell, 266–267.

84. Wallace, 146.

85. Murray R. Wickett, *Contested Territory: Whites, Native Americans, and African Americans in Oklahoma, 1865–1907* (Shreveport: Louisiana State University Press, 2000), 4.

86. Alvin M. Josephy, Jr., *The Civil War in the American West* (New York: Alfred A. Knopf, 1992), 354; Laurence M. Hauptman, *Between Two Fires: American Indians in the Civil War* (New York: Free Press, 1995), 41–63.

87. The fort was completed in 1851.

88. *Clarksville Standard*, April 25, 1863.

89. John C. Waugh, *Sam Bell Maxey and the Confederate Indians* (Abilene, Texas: McWhiney Foundation Press, 1995), 47.

90. The Civil War created deep divisions within and between tribes in Indian Territory and led to intertribal warfare. The ensuing fighting forced many Indians allied with the Union cause to head for Kansas, often fleeing for their lives and pursued by Confederate-supporting Indians. The land became devastated by repeated attacks. Even many of the Confederate Indians stayed close to Southern camps and forts to receive aid and protection. For more, see Wickett, *Contested Territory*, 5–6; Hauptman, *Between Two Fires*, 41–63.

91. *Clarksville Standard*, April 25, 1863.

92. *Clarksville Standard*, May 2, 1863.

93. *Ibid.*

94. *Clarksville Standard*, May 30, 1863.

95. *Clarksville Standard*, June 16, 1863.

96. DeMorse admitted that in the confusion, a lieutenant colonel riding in the ambulance got away from the Confederate troops, leaving only his coat behind.

97. Historian James McPherson has noted that the "initial combat experience produced a winnowing effect in many regiments, with the chaff drifting to the rear or finding their ways into noncombatant duties. Among them were some who had expressed the greatest eagerness to fight." See McPherson, *For Cause & Comrades*, 35.

98. *Clarksville Standard*, June 16, 1863. Despite his detailed descriptions of days of skirmishes and maneuvers near the Arkansas River, DeMorse, true to his nature, included a detailed description of the plants, trees, and terrain where the troops fought.

99. *Clarksville Standard*, June 16, 1863.

100. *Ibid.* DeMorse was referring to Colonel Leonidas Martin, commander of the 5th Texas Partisan Rangers Cavalry Regiment.

101. *Clarksville Standard*, June 16, 1863.

102. Larry C. Rampp, "Negro Troop Activity in Indian Territory, 1863–1865," in Martin H. Greenberg and Charles G. Waugh, eds., *The Price of Freedom: Slavery and the Civil War*, vol. I (Nashville, Tenn.: Cumberland House Publishing, 2000), 183.

103. Frank Arey, "The First Kansas Colored at Honey Springs," in Mark Christ, ed., *All Cut to Pieces and Gone to Hell: The Civil War, Race Relations, and the Battle of Poison Spring* (Little Rock, Ark.: August House Publishers, 2003), 81.

104. *Ibid.*, 79–97; Wallace, 147; http://www.nps.gov/history/hps/abpp/battles/ar014.htm (accessed June 23, 2007).

105. "The Battle of Elk Creek," *Clarksville Standard*, September 12, 1863. In DeMorse's official report to Brigadier General Cooper, the editor detailed, as best he knew, the placement of the various Confederate regiments and how the Union supply train eluded them. "Had we known at the outset; the true position and strength of the enemy, we should easily have killed or captured their entire force, but being deceived as to their strength, and mistaken as to their position, and after its ascertainment and the falling

back on both sides, all my guides being cut off, and time lost before others came in, I missed a capture which I feel that my force would have commanded," DeMorse stated. See *Clarksville Standard*, July 18, 1863.

106. Wallace, 147–148.

107. "Deserters," *Clarksville Standard*, November 28, 1863, 1; "Deserters," *Clarksville Standard*, January 16, 1864.

108. General S.B. Maxey to Col. S.S. Anderson, February 7, 1864, reprinted in the Official Records, series I, vol. 53, 963–965.

109. *Clarksville Standard*, April 30, 1864. The original letter was written on April 21, 1864.

110. Mark K. Christ, "All Cut to Pieces and Gone to Hell," 22; Gary Dillard Joiner, *One Damn Blunder From Beginning To End: The Red River Campaign of 1864* (Wilmington, Del.: Scholarly Resources, 2003), 129.

111. *Clarksville Standard*, April 30, 1864.

112. For more on this, see Wallace, 149–150.

113. George S. Burkhardt, *Confederate Rage, Yankee Wrath: No Quarter in the Civil War* (Carbondale: Southern Illinois University Press, 2007), 126.

114. Marvin J. Hancock, "The Second Battle of Cabin Creek, 1864," *The Chronicles of Oklahoma*, 39:4 (1961), 415–416.

115. Hancock, 417–418.

116. *Clarksville Standard*, October 15, 1864. The letter was dated September 29.

117. *Clarksville Standard*, October 15, 1864.

118. Hancock, 419–420.

119. *Clarksville Standard*, October 15, 1864.

120. *Ibid.*

121. *Clarksville Standard*, June 10, 1865.

Chapter 22, William Doran

1. Most of Col. A.W. Spaight's 11th Texas Battalion also took part. Note: In order to provide readers with as accurate a picture of Doran's writing as possible, his grammar, spelling, and punctuation were not changed for this chapter.

2. The story of Doran's Paul Revere-like ride was compiled by Texas historian W.T. Block a: W.T. Block, "News of attack traveled a circuitous route," *Beaumont Enterprise*, February 5, 1984, 2CC.

3. For more on the retaking of Galveston, see Edward T. Cotham, Jr., *Battle on the Bay: The Civil War Struggle for Galveston* (Austin, Texas: University of Austin, 1998); Donald S. Frazier, *Cottonclads!: The Battle of Galveston and the Defense of the Texas Coast* (Abilene, Texas: McWhiney Foundation Press, 1998), 64–85.

4. Edward T. Cotham, Jr., *Sabine Pass* (Austin, Texas: University of Texas Press, 2004), 125–158; Block, "News of attack," 2CC.

5. A number of correspondents aided the military, although many worked as secretaries to earn additional money. See Phillip Knightley, *The First Casualty: The War Correspondent as Hero and Myth-Maker from the Crimea to Kosovo* (Baltimore: Johns Hopkins University Press, 2002), 24.

6. *Houston Tri-Weekly Telegraph*, February 10, 1865.

7. David P. Smith, "Conscription and Conflict on the Texas Frontier, 1863–1865," *Civil War History* 35 (Sept. 1990), 250–261; James M. McPherson, *For Cause & Comrades: Why Men Fought in the Civil War* (New York: Oxford University Press, 1997), 138.

8. *Houston Daily Telegraph*, August 8, 1864.

9. *Houston Tri-Weekly Telegraph*, May 30, 1862; *Tri-Weekly Telegraph*, June 20, 1862.

10. *Houston Tri-Weekly Telegraph*, May 15, 1863.

11. Three works that give examples of the best and worst of Civil War reporting are Knightley, *The First Casualty*, 19–42; J. Cutler Andrews, *The South Reports the Civil War* (Pittsburgh: University of Pittsburgh Press, 1985); and Brayton Harris, *Blue & Gray in Black & White* (Washington, D.C.: Batsford Brassey, 1999).

12. *Houston Tri-Weekly Telegraph*, April 4, 1862.

13. Knightley, *The First Casualty*, 26.

14. *Houston Tri-Weekly Telegraph*, November 13, 1861.

15. *Houston Tri-Weekly Telegraph*, April 16, 1862.

16. *Houston Tri-Weekly Telegraph*, May 15, 1863.

17. *Houston Tri-Weekly Telegraph*, May 30, 1862.

18. Randolph B. Campbell, *Gone to Texas: A History of the Lone Star State* (New York: Oxford University Press, 2003), 261.

19. *Houston Tri-Weekly Telegraph*, April 4, 1862.

20. *Houston Tri-Weekly Telegraph*, February 15, 1865.

21. *Ibid.*

22. Cotham, *Battle on the Bay*, 160, 176.

23. *Galveston Daily News*, November 26, 1901, 21.

24. *Ibid.*

25. Colonel Benjamin McCulloch, a veteran of the Texas Rangers and a hero during the fight for independence from Mexico, led 500 volunteers to San Antonio where they surrounded the regimental headquarters of Major General David E. Twiggs, the commander of all Union troops in Texas. Twiggs agreed to surrender all Union property and evacuate all Union troops (approximately 2,700 men). For more, see Alvin M. Josephy, Jr., *The Civil War in the American West* (New York: Alfred A. Knopf, 1992), 3–30.

26. *Houston Tri-Weekly Telegraph*, March 19, 1861; *Galveston Weekly News*, September 3, 1861; *Tri-Weekly Telegraph*, December 30, 1861, 2.

27. *Houston Tri-Weekly Telegraph*, March 19, 1861.

28. *Galveston Daily News*, February 22, 1896, 7.

29. *Houston Tri-Weekly Telegraph*, March 19, 1861.

30. *Galveston Weekly News*, October 15, 1862.

31. *Houston Tri-Weekly Telegraph*, March 19, 1861.

32. William W. Freehling, *The South vs. The South: How Anti-Confederate Southerners Shaped the Course of the Civil War* (New York: Oxford University Press, 2001), 40.

33. Walter L. Buenger, "Secession and the Texas German Community: Editor Lindheimer vs. Editor Flake," *Southwestern Historical Quarterly*, 82 (April 1979), 379–402; James Smallwood, "Disaffection in Confederate Texas: The Great Handing at Gainesville," *Civil War History*, 22 (December 1976), 349–360.

34. Claude Elliot, "Union Sentiment in Texas, 1861–1865," *Southwestern Historical Quarterly*, 50 (April 1947), online. http://www.tshaonline.org/publications/journals/shq/online/v050/n4/contrib_DIVL7560.html

35. *Sioux*, "From the Rio Grande," *Galveston Weekly News*, September 3, 1861.

36. *Houston Tri-Weekly Telegraph*, December 30, 1861. The first four lines of the poem were as follows: Up with the Lone Star banner!/Its hues are still as bright/As when its glories braved the breeze/At San Jacinto's Fight.

37. *Houston Tri-Weekly Telegraph*, January 13, 1862.

38. *Ibid.*

39. *Houston Tri-Weekly Telegraph*, April 16, 1862.

40. *Ibid.*

41. *Houston Tri-Weekly Telegraph*, April 4, 1862.

42. *Houston Tri-Weekly Telegraph*, April 4, 1862. Historian James M. McPherson has stated that many rebel soldiers understood "that the best way to defend their state was to win the war, even if that meant fighting on a front a thousand miles from home." See McPherson, *For Cause & Comrades*, 97.

43. William P. Doran, "A 35th Anniversary," *Galveston Daily News*, February 22, 1896, 7.

44. *Houston Tri-Weekly Telegraph*, May 9, 1862.

45. *Ibid.*

46. *Houston Tri-Weekly Telegraph*, May 30, 1862. Note the 24-day lag time between the writing of this letter and its publication.

47. *Houston Tri-Weekly Telegraph*, June 27, 1862.

48. Of his injury, Doran recounted years later: "When we were marching to aid in the capture of General Prentiss' division a bullet struck the side of my left heel, pitting the bone, about 1 p.m., and I thought my leg was gone. I rolled over and over, and seeing Colonel Moore and Captain Christian in a ravine I rolled in there. They both laughed heartily at my antics." See *Galveston Daily News*, February 22, 1896, 7.

49. *Houston Tri-Weekly Telegraph*, June 20, 1862.

50. Sioux, *Houston Tri-Weekly Telegraph*, June 20, 1862, 2.

51. *Ibid.*

52. *Ibid.*

53. *Galveston Daily News*, November 26, 1901, 21.

54. *Houston Tri-Weekly Telegraph*, January 14, 1863.

55. "A 35th Anniversary," 7.

56. Sioux, 21.

57. *Houston Tri-Weekly Telegraph*, October 22, 1863.

58. Theodore P. Savas, David A. Woodbury, and Gary D. Joiner, eds., *The Red River Campaign: Union and Confederate Leadership and the War in Louisiana* (Shreveport, La.: Parabellum Press, 2003).

59. "A 35th Anniversary," 7.

60. *Austin State Gazette*, June 29, 1864. Copies of the *Houston Tri-Weekly Telegraph* during the period of the Red River Campaign no longer exist. This article on prisoner exchanges from the *Austin State Gazette* is a reprint of one of Doran's *Telegraph* articles.

61. *Houston Tri-Weekly Telegraph*, November 14, 1864.

62. *Houston Tri-Weekly Telegraph*, November 25, 1864.

63. *Houston Tri-Weekly Telegraph*, December 19, 1864.

64. *Houston Tri-Weekly Telegraph*, November 25, 1864.

65. *Houston Tri-Weekly Telegraph*, November 21, 1864.

66. *Houston Daily Telegraph*, January 2, 1865.

67. *Houston Tri-Weekly Telegraph*, April 5, 1865.

68. *Houston Tri-Weekly Telegraph*, March 22, 1865.

69. *Galveston Weekly News*, March 29, 1865.

70. *Houston Daily Telegraph*, June 3, 1865. He did not appear to have covered the final battle of the Civil War at Palmetto Ranch the previous month.

71. Sioux, 21.

72. *Ibid.*

Chapter 23, James P. Douglas

1. J.P. Douglas, "Editorial Correspondence," *Tyler Reporter*, August 1, 1861.

2. David C. Humphrey, "A 'Very Muddy and Conflicting' View: The Civil War as Seen from Austin, Texas,") *Southwestern Historical Quarterly*, 94, no. 3 (1991, 369–375.

3. Humphrey, 368–414.

4. Phillip Knightley, *The First Casualty: The War Correspondent as Hero and Myth-Maker from the Crimea to Kosovo* (Baltimore: Johns Hopkins University Press, 2004), 21.

5. Lucia Rutherford Douglas, ed., *Douglas's Texas Battery, CSA* (Tyler, Texas: Smith County Historical Society, 1966), 103. Also see Douglas' letter to his fiancé on page 108. He states: "I suppose the quickest news you receive from here is from Yankee papers. These accounts are nearly always false. Even the accounts in our own papers won't do to rely on."

6. These Texas editor-correspondents may also have been given incorrect casualty figures by superiors. It is impossible to know for certain.

7. Douglas, viii.

8. *Ibid*, vii.

9. The best account of Douglas' political, social, and economic views is contained in his collected letters in a book his daughter issued. See Douglas, *Douglas's Texas Battery*.

10. James B. Lunsford, "Douglas' First Texas Battery," *Dallas Morning News*, August 4, 1907, 8.

11. Lunsford, 8

12. *Ibid.*

13. Debra Reddin van Tuyll, "The Rebels Yell: Conscription and Freedom of Expression in the Civil War South," *American Journalism*, 17 (2), (Spring 2000), 15.

14. *Bellville Countryman*, September 11, 1861.

15. *Texas Republican*, November 25, 1864, 2; *Dallas Herald*, February 19, 1862, 2; Larry Jay Gage, "The Texas Road to Secession and War: John Marshall and the Texas State Gazette, 1860–1861," *Southwestern Historical Quarterly*, 62 (October 1958), 191–226. Also see Sibley, *Lone Stars and State Gazettes*, 298.

16. *Dallas Herald*, June 26, 1861.

17. J.P. Douglas, "Editorial Correspondence," *Tyler Reporter*, August 1, 1861.

18. Lunsford, "Douglas' First Texas Battery," 8.

19. The leading scholarly works on the battle are by William Shea, Earl Hess, and Mark K. Christ. See William L. Shea and Earl J. Hess, *Pea Ridge: Civil War Campaign*

in the West (Chapel Hill: University of North Carolina Press, 1992) and Mark K. Christ, ed., *Rugged and Sublime: The Civil War in Arkansas* (Fayetteville: University of Arkansas Press, 1994).

20. William L. Shea, "1862: A Continual Thunder," in Christ, ed., *Rugged and Sublime*, 31–38.

21. *Ibid.*, 31.

22. *Houston Tri-Weekly Telegraph*, April 4, 1862.

23. Shea, "1862: A Continual Thunder," 32; Shea and Hess, *Pea Ridge*, 110.

24. Shea: "1862: A Continual Thunder," 33.

25. *Houston Tri-Weekly Telegraph*, April 4, 1862.

26. Shea: "1862: A Continual Thunder," 33; Shea and Hess, *Pea Ridge*, 144–145.

27. *Houston Tri-Weekly Telegraph*, April 4, 1862.

28. Shea, "1862: A Continual Thunder," 35.

29. *Houston Tri-Weekly Telegraph*, April 4, 1862.

30. Shea and Hess, *Pea Ridge*, 248–252.

31. *Houston Tri-Weekly Telegraph*, April 4, 1862.

32. *Ibid.*

33. Shea, "1862: A Continual Thunder," 37.

34. *Houston Tri-Weekly Telegraph*, April 4, 1862.

35. *Ibid.*

36. Douglas, *Douglas's Texas Battery*, 124.

37. Ibid., viii.

38. Ibid., ix, 157.

39. Ibid., viii.

40. Ibid., x.

Chapter 24, R.R. Gilbert

1. Gilbert's first name was spelled at least five different ways on documents. For example, the Tyler newspaper spelled his first name differently than it appeared on the pension application.

2. *Houston Tri-Weekly Telegraph*, December 8, 1863.

3. J. Cutler Andrews, *The South Reports the Civil War* (Pittsburgh: University of Pittsburgh Press, 1985), 24.

4. J. Ford Risley, "Peter W. Alexander: Confederate Chronicler & Conscience," *American Journalism*, 15, no. 1 (Winter 1998), 39. On the Confederacy and its southern press, see Phillip Knightley, *The First Casualty: The War Correspondent as Hero and Myth-Maker From the Crimea to Kosovo* (Baltimore: Johns Hopkins University Press, 2000), 24–25; Andrews, *The South Reports the Civil War*.

5. Risley, "Peter W. Alexander," 35. The original article was published in the *Savannah Republican*, May 26, 1862, 2. Among the best scholarly assessments of the strengths and weaknesses of Southern correspondents are Knightley, *The First Casualty*; Andrews, *The South Reports the Civil War*; and Brayton Harris, *Blue & Gray in Black & White* (Washington, D.C.: Batsford Brassey, 1999).

6. Knightley, 22.

7. Ralph A. Wooster and Robert Wooster, "'Rarin' for a Fight': Texans in the Confederate Army," in Ralph A. Wooster, ed., *Lone Star Blue and Gray: Essays on Texas in the Civil War* (Austin: Texas State Historical Association, 1995), 71. For biographical information on Gilbert and his military service, see R.R. Gilbert, *High Private's Second Edition of Confederate Letters Written for the Houston Telegraph During the Late War, with the Addition of the Secrets of Success or Business Advice to the Young Men of the South* (Austin, Texas: Eugene Von Boeckmann, 1894), 3–4.

8. Mark K. Christ, *Rugged and Sublime: The Civil War in Arkansas* (Fayetteville: University of Arkansas Press, 1994), 61–65. Editors were exempt from military service. See Debra Reddin van Tuyll, "The Rebels Yell: Conscription and Freedom of Expression in the Civil War South," *American Journalism*, 17, no. 2 (Spring 2000), 15.

9. Alice Fahs, *The Imagined Civil War: Popular Literature of the North & South 1861–1865* (Chapel Hill: University of North Carolina Press, 2001), 96.

10. Jim Turner, "Jim Turner," 152.

11. Gilbert, *High Private's Second Edition of Confederate Letters*, 6.

12. *Ibid.*, 4.

13. Fahs, *The Imagined Civil War*, 200–201.

14. Gilbert entered and left the Army as a private. Gilbert always used "R.R. Gilbert" as his name for census and city directory purposes. His first name was constantly spelled differently in various newspaper articles, city directories, etc. The spelling used in this article is taken from his widow's Confederate Pension Application, available at the Texas State Archives in Austin, Texas.

15. Gilbert's own obituary, for example, noted that he died at his daughter's house in Houston, that he was born in Vermont, and provided a list of pallbearers. Nothing was mentioned of his life prior to the Civil War, although the *Houston Post* noted that he worked for a number of the state's newspapers, including the *Post*, following the War. See "R.R. Gilbert (High Private)," *Houston Post*, October 7, 1899, 6.

16. R.R. Gilbert, *High Private's Confederate Letters*, written for the *Houston Telegraph*. During the War of 1861-2-3-4-5, With a Short Autobiographical Sketch of the Author (Austin: Eugene Von Boeckmann, 1890). 31.

17. *Houston Post*, October 7, 1899, 6; 1880 Census, Anderson County, Precinct 1 (Palestine), series: T9, roll: 1288, page 46D.

18. R.R. Gilbert, *High Private's Confederate Letters*, 15. His obituary in the *Houston Post* also notes that Gilbert arrived in Texas shortly before the war's outbreak. See "R.R. Gilbert," 6.

19. Reprinted in Gilbert, *High Private's Confederate Letters*, 13–14.

20. This information is mentioned in his widow's Confederate Pension application available at the Texas State Archives in Austin.

21. Gilbert noted in 1894 that the *Victoria Advocate* as well as *Telegraph* Editor Edward Cushing's residence burned a few years after the war. All of the letters used for this chapter come from the *Telegraph*.

22. Emory M. Thomas, "Rebel Nationalism: E.H. Cushing and the Confederate Experience," *Southwestern Historical Quarterly*, vol. 73, no. 3 (1970), 343–355; E.B. Cushing, "Edward Hopkins Cushing: An Appreciation by His Son," *Southwestern Historical Quarterly*, vol. 25 (April 1922), 261–273.

23. *Telegraph*, June 9, 1862. The editor of the "Item" noted in July 1862 that he was disappointed that High Private was out of town at the time as he was looking forward to making jokes with him.

24. R.R. Gilbert, *High Private's Second Edition of Confederate Letters*, 49.

25. The song is reprinted in Gilbert, *High Private's Second Edition of Confederate Letters*, 49.

26. For more of Gilbert's poetry that lampooned military and social conditions, see Gilbert, *High Private's Second Edition of Confederate Letters*, 8, 9, 10, 31. For more on poetry during the War, see Fahs, *The Imagined Civil War*.

27. *Telegraph*, January 3, 1865. For more on Abbott and the commercial value of war reporting, see Alice Fahs, "The Market Value of Memory: Popular War Histories and the Northern Literary Marketplace, 1861–1868," *Book History*, 1, no. 1 (1998), 107–139.

28. It's unclear whether Gilbert was injured or ill, but based on this comment, he was somehow medically unable to continue the service for which he volunteered. See Gilbert, *High Private's Confederate Letters*, 39–40, for his account of eight months of service with the "Bloody Sixth" at Camp Henry E. McCulloch. He noted: "For eight long months I 'fought, bled and died,' side by side, with the members of the 'Bloody Sixth;' fought fleas, bled the sutler and died (probably dyed) my memory with military recollections."

29. According to some of the articles' subheads, some material was sent by pony express. For more on his whereabouts during the war, see Gilbert, *High Private's Second Edition of Confederate Letters*, 3–4.

30. *Telegraph*, February 18, 1865.

31. *Telegraph*, January 7, 1864, 2. When Gilbert did get to Houston, it was announced in the newspaper. See, for example, *Houston Tri-Weekly Telegraph*, January 16, 1865.

32. *Telegraph*, May 4, 1864.

33. Gilbert's reports from Louisiana and Arkansas could add up to three columns. He composed throughout the day, updating as newspapers came in or as he obtained news himself.

34. *Telegraph*, August 11, 1863.

35. *Telegraph*, February 17, 1865.

36. Knightley, *The First Casualty*, 24–25.

37. Despite archival searches, identities of these other correspondents could not be discovered.

38. Gilbert, *High Private's Second Edition of Confederate Letters*, 4.

39. *Telegraph*, April 17, 1862, 2; *Telegraph*, July 18, 1862, 1. The *Telegraph* was cautious in reporting the capture of Union troops, questioning whether the rumors were true. At other times similar information was printed from other Southern newspapers, the *Telegraph* satisfied that if other newspapers published Union losses, they must be true.

40. *Telegraph*, October 27, 1863.

41. *Telegraph*, January 19, 1864.

42. The documents to which Gilbert referred were Confederate dispatches. The information was told to Gilbert by a man identified as Captain Hughes. See *Telegraph*, January 21, 1864.

43. "The Situation," *Texas Weekly Record*, April 21, 1865, 1. Although the date of the publication was almost two weeks after General Lee's surrender at Appomattox, Texas

still had not heard the news. Ironically, Gilbert also stated in this article that news of the evacuation of Petersburg and Richmond were nothing more than "Yankee Lies." He predicted that when Generals Lee and Johnston came together, "they will give the enemy battle."

44. *Weekly Record*, April 14, 1865. This was the salutary editorial of his postwar newspaper. Gilbert laid out his views on journalism and editing. He stated that "a high-toned, reliable journal is never out of place in any community and such we aim to make this sheet."

45. *Telegraph*, January 17, 1865.

46. Reprinted in the *Telegraph*, July 29, 1863. Gilbert had produced a number of humorous poems for the *Telegraph*, and the Huntsville editor was mimicking Gilbert's form.

47. *Texas Weekly Record*, April 21, 1865.

48. Knightley, 25–26.

49. *Telegraph*, October 27, 1863.

50. High Private, "High Private's Proclamation," reprinted in Gilbert, *High Private's Second Edition of Confederate Letters,* 17–18.

51. *Texas Weekly Record*, May 5, 1865.

52. Knightley, *The First Casualty*, 25.

53. For more on Confederate casualties during the Battle of Chickamauga, see Peter Cozzens, *This Terrible Sound* (Urbana: University of Illinois, 1996); James Arnold, *Chickamauga 1863: The River of Death* (Sterling Heights, Mich.: Osprey Publishing, 1992), 85; Grady McWhiney, *Confederate Crackers and Cavaliers* (Abilene, Texas: McWhiney Foundation Press, 2002), 130.

54. Reprinted in Gilbert, *High Private's Confederate Letters*, 9.

55. For more about Confederate writings about extortionist prices, which most Southerners considered one of the greatest failings of the Confederacy, see Drew Gilpin Faust, *The Creation of Confederate Nationalism: Ideology and Identity in the Civil War South* (Baton Rouge: Louisiana State University Press, 1988), 41–57.

56. Gilbert probably meant crippled.

57. *Telegraph*, May 30, 1862. Gilbert castigated the rich who made a profit from war and sent men to their deaths in an earlier dispatch from February 12, 1862. That letter contained a lengthy poem titled, "The Power of Gold." See *Telegraph*, February 12, 1862.

58. Reprinted in Gilbert, 46.

59. *Telegraph*, January 1, 1864.

60. *Telegraph*, January 11, 1864.

61. *Telegraph*, October 14, 1863.

62. *Telegraph*, February 22, 1865, 3.

63. This is another example of the different ways that Gilbert's first name was spelled at least five different ways on documents.

64. 1880 Census, Anderson County, Precinct 1 (Palestine), series: T9, roll: 1288, page 46D. For more on Gilbert's family, see 1900 Census, Travis County, Austin, series: t623, roll 1673, page 51; 1910 Census, Bexar County, San Antonio, series: T624, roll: 1532, page: 43; 1920 Census, Bexar County, Alamo Heights, series: T625, roll: 1777, page: 30; 1930 Census, Bexar County, Alamo Heights, series: T626, roll: 2298, page: 35.

65. Cemetery information provided by Ana Sanchez, a librarian at the Palestine Public Library.

66. *Texas Weekly Record*, April 21, 1865. Despite the date, Gilbert and other Texas editors had yet to hear of General Lee's surrender.

67. *Record*, May 5, 1865.

68. *Ibid.*

69. *Telegraph*, June 14, 1865.

70. Column reprinted in Gilbert, *High Private's Confederate Letters*, 70.

71. Column reprinted in Gilbert, *High Private's Confederate Letters*, 69–70.

72. Column reprinted in Gilbert, *High Private's Confederate Letters*, 62–63.

73. This newspaper was published for an unknown period. The Center for American History at the University of Texas at Austin is the only known holder of this newspaper: three copies, April 14 and 21, 1865, and May 5, 1865.

74. *Austin State Gazette*, April 12, 1865, 2. The story, called "Philanthropos," was serialized in the newspaper. Only three issues of this paper exist, all at the Center for American History at the University of Texas at Austin. These may have been the only three issues printed.

75. The prospectus ran in a number of newspapers. See, for example, the *Dallas Herald*, April 20, 1865, 2.

76. *Texas Weekly Record*, April 21, 1865, 1. He clearly was hoping for more advertising. His rate was listed as 10 cents per line.

77. A small editorial notice on page 2 of the January 20, 1866, issue of the *Dallas Herald* notes that "Dr. R.B. Gilbert, Esq., is the only authorized agent for the *Dallas Herald* in New Orleans." Tracking Gilbert's whereabouts has proven extremely difficult. What he did in New Orleans is uncertain.

78. *Dallas Herald*, November 20, 1869, 2; April 16, 1870, 2.

79. *Dallas Herald*, July 2, 1870, 2.

80. *Dallas Herald*, August 10, 1872, 2.

81. Copies of this newspaper do not appear to exist in any holdings in the country, so Gilbert's reconstruction views from editorials cannot be known.

82. See http://www.brazosgenealogy.org/data/esupporters.txt., accessed April 28, 2007. The original petition is found in Brazos County Commissioners Book A, 316–318.

83. The notice appeared in the March 25, 1881, edition of the *Galveston News*. This information was provided by Karla Lang of the Palestine Public Library.

84. High Private, "The Average Texas Hotel," *Texas Siftings*, June 4, 1881, n.p. Note: *Texas Siftings* exists in its entirety at the Center for American History at the University of Texas–Austin.

85. *Dallas Morning News*, October 31, 1885, 4. A search did not reveal any copies of this title. It's unclear from which town this publication was issued.

86. Austin city directories were used to obtain information on Gilbert's residences and jobs while in Austin.

87. R.R. Gilbert, *High Private's Confederate Letters*, written for the *HoustonTelegraph*. During the War of 1861-2-3-4-5, With a Short Autobiographical Sketch of the Author (Austin, Texas: Eugene Von Boeckmann, 1890).

88. The Austin city directories for the years 1887–1896 provided all of the information about Gilbert's jobs during his nine years in Austin. For unknown reasons, perhaps financial, the editor and his wife moved five times.

89. *Dallas News,* October 9, 1899, 7. Gilbert's wife remained in Austin after her husband moved to Houston in the mid-1880s to live with his daughter. Louella is buried in Austin at Oakwood Cemetery, but R.R. Gilbert's burial site has not been located despite extensive searching by the author and five archivists and scholars throughout Texas. On Louella Gilbert's death, see: *San Antonio Express,* September 18, 1932, 3.

90. *Dallas Morning News,* October 31, 1885, 4.

Chapter 25, George W. Bagby, Jr.

Abbreviations: VHS: George W. Bagby, Jr., Papers, Virginia Historical Society

1. That photograph was published in historian J. Cutler Andrews' *The South Reports the Civil War* (Princeton, N.J.: Princeton University Press, 1970), unnumbered page.

2. The early portrait can be viewed at the Virginia Historical Society, Richmond.

3. *Ibid.*; Andrews, unnumbered page.

4. William B. Matthews to Dr. George W. Bagby, Jr., March 14, 1862, VHS.

5. Joseph Leonard King, Jr., *Dr. George William Bagby: A Study of Virginia Literature, 1850–1880* (New York: Columbia University Press, 1927), 22.

6. Robert Barnwell Rhett, Jr., to George W. Bagby, Jr., April 9, 1862, VHS.

7. King, 22.

8. Edward S. Gregory, "George William Bagby," In *The Writings of Dr. Bagby, vol. 1, George W. Bagby* (Richmond, Va.: Whittet & Shepperson, Co., 1884), xvi; Steven H. Gale, ed., "George William Bagby," In *Encyclopedia of American Humorists* (New York: Garland Publishing, Inc., 1988), 18; King, 1–4; Ritchie Devon Watson, Jr., "George William Bagby," In *American National Biography,* vol. 1 (New York: Oxford University Press, 1999), 868.

9. King, 4–5.

10. King, 4.

11. George W. Bagby, Jr., "Good Eatings," *Southern Literary Messenger,* May 1863.

12. Gale, 18; King, 6–7.

13. King, 12–13; personal communication with Lisa Gensel, assistant archivist, University of Delaware, January 26, 2007; Watson, 868.

14. George W. Bagby, *Reminiscences: Recollections of Travel in the Old Days on the James River and Kanawha Canal* (Richmond, Va.: West, Johnston, and Co., 1879), 27; King, 12–13.

15. Gale, 19; King, 15, 18–19; Watson, 868.

16. Edward S. Gregory, "George William Bagby," In *George W. Bagby, Selections from the Miscellaneous Writings of Dr. George W. Bagby,* vol. 1 (Richmond: Whittet & Shepperson, 1884), xx.

17. 1850 U.S. Manuscript Census (available with subscription from http://www.ancestry.com, accessed February 7, 2007); King, 19–20, 24–25; Watson, 868.

18. George W. Bagby, Jr., *The Virginia Editor, Selections from the Miscellaneous Writings of Dr. George W. Bagby,* vol. 1 (Richmond, Va.: Whittet & Shepperson, 1884), 109–120.

19. *Ibid.*

20. Gregory, xxi; Gale, 19; King, 26–28.

21. King, 29.

22. Gale, 19; King, 30.

23. George William Bagby to Robert Ridgeway, March 31, 1858, Brock Collection, Huntington Library, Pasadena, Calif.

24. Bagby Diary, Bagby Family Papers, George William Bagby file, Virginia Historical Society, Richmond; George W. Bagby to Robert Ridgeway, March 31, 1858, Brock Collection, Huntington Library, Pasadena, Calif.; Andrews, 49; Robert Barnwell Rhett, Jr., to George W. Bagby, Jr., January 27, 1858, VHS.

25. King, 53.

26. Bagby to Ellen A. Turner, April 14, 1858, VHS; Bagby to Ellen A. Turner, May 24, 1858, VHS; King, 54.

27. King, 58.

28. King, 58–59; Watson, 868.

29. George W. Bagby, *Letter Wun, The New Mozis Addums Letters* (Richmond, Va.: McFarlane and Fergusson, 1860), under "Wright American Fiction 1851–1875" (available at http://www.letrs.indiana.edu/cgi/t/text/text-idx?c=wright2;idno=Wright2-0180, accessed November 14, 2007).

30. King, 58–59, 62; Bagby, Preface to Mozis Addums, Writings, vol. II, 40.

31. King, 68.

32. *New Orleans Crescent*, March 5, 1859.

33. King, 69.

34. N.F. Cabell to George W. Bagby, Jr., A.L.S. July 30, 1860. BR Box 48, Brock Collection, Huntington Library, Pasadena, Calif.; King, 71.

35. King, 73.

36. Bagby, "The Ups and Downs of a Southern Lecturer," unpublished; King, 73.

37. Bagby Diary, May 28, 1860, and June 3, 1860, VHS.

38. Bagby Diary, May 2, 1860, VHS; S. Morgan Friedman, creator, The Inflation Calculator [web site] available from http://www.westegg.com/inflation/, accessed January 30, 2009 (2008 figure was not yet available).

39. Bagby Diary, May 30, 1860, VHS.

40. Bagby Diary, May 31, 1860, VHS.

41. Bagby Diary, June 6, 1860, VHS.

42. Cecil D. Eby, Jr, "Dr. George William Bagby: Professional Virginia," *Iron Worker*, Autumn 1960, I.

43. *Boston Daily Advertiser*, November 7, 1865.

44. Joseph Leonard King, Jr., *Dr. George William Bagby: A Study of Virginia Literature, 1850–1880* (New York: Columbia University Press, 1927), vii.

45. King, viii.

46. King, 58.

47. Robert B. Rhett, Jr., to George W. Bagby, Jr., January 11, 1861, VHS.

48. 1860 U.S.Manuscript Census for South Carolina.

49. Robert B. Rhett, Jr., to George W. Bagby, Jr., January 18, 1861, VHS.

50. Robert B. Rhett, Jr., to George W. Bagby, Jr., January 31, 1861, VHS.

51. *Ibid.*

52. *Ibid.*

53. Robert Barnwell Rhett, Jr., to George W. Bagby, Jr., January 31, 1861, VHS.

54. King, 92–93.

55. King, 93.

56. Robert Barnwell Rhett to George William Bagby, Jr., undated telegraph, VHS.

57. Robert Barnwell Rhett to George William Bagby, Jr., April 21 (year not given, but most likely 1861), VHS.

58. Robert Barnwell Rhett, Jr., to George William Bagby, Jr., May 29, 1861, VHS.

59. King, 93.

60. Eby, "Dr. George William Bagby: Professional Virginia," 1–7; King, 94.

61. King, 94.

62. King, 95.

63. "An Unrenowned Warrior: The Record of a Man Who Shivered Through the Manassas Campaign," *Selections from the Miscellaneous Writings of Dr. George W. Bagby,* 2 vols. (Richmond, Va.: Whittet and Shepperson, 1884–85), cited in King, 95.

64. Richard E. Beringer, Herman Hattaway, Archer Jones, and William N. Still, Jr., *Why the South Lost the Civil War* (Athens: University of Georgia Press, 1986).

65. Bartholemew Riordan to George William Bagby, Jr., September 20 (no year, but must be 1861) VHS; Eby, "Dr. George William Bagby: Professional Virginia"; Bartholemew Riordan to George William Bagby, September 29, 1861; Bagby Diary, November 6, 9, 1861, VHS.

66. Bartholemew Riordan to George William Bagby, Jr., March 27 (no year given), VHS.

67. Bartholemew Riordan to George William Bagby, Jr., February 3 (no year given), VHS.

68. *Charleston Mercury,* October 18, 1861.

69. *Charleston Mercury,* November 28, 1862.

70. Robert Barnwell Rhett, Jr., to George W. Bagby, Jr., April 21 (no year given), VHS.

71. Bartholemew Riordan to George William Bagby, Jr., April 3 (no year, but probably 1862), VHS.

72. *Charleston Mercury,* October 5, 8–12, 14–19, 21–23, 25, 26, 28–30; November 1, 2, 4, 5, 1861.

73. *Charleston Mercury,* October 8, 1861; February 3, 1862; October 30, 1862; March 7, 1863; October 5, 1863. These are only a sampling of stories that illustrate Bagby's correspondence on the question of recognition.

74. *Charleston Mercury,* April 11, 1862.

75. *Charleston Mercury,* October 14, 1861.

76. *Ibid.*

77. *Charleston Mercury,* February 2, 1863.

78. *Charleston Mercury,* November 4, 1862.

79. *Charleston Mercury,* November 12, 1862.

80. *Charleston Mercury,* April 17, 1862.

81. *Charleston Mercury,* October 14, 1861.

82. For an example, see *Charleston Mercury,* September 8, 1862.

83. For an example, see *Charleston Mercury*, November 14, 1861.

84. For a full discussion of the effect of libertarians on the Confederacy, see Paul D. Escott, *After Secession: Jefferson Davis and the Failure of Confederate Nationalism* (Baton Rouge: Louisiana State University, 1978).

85. *Charleston Mercury*, October 22, 1861.

86. *Charleston Mercury*, October 30, 1861.

87. *Charleston Mercury*, October 3, 5, 8, 30, 1861; February 15, 20, 24, 27, 1862; April 5, 1862; July 26, 28, 1862; October 3, 6, 7, 17, 1862; April 10, 8, 1863.

88. *Charleston Mercury*, July 28, 1863.

89. Horace W. Raper and William W. Holden, *North Carolina's Political Enigma, James Spunt Studies in History and Political Science*, vol. 59 (Chapel Hill: University of North Carolina Press, 1985); Horace W. Raper, "William W. Holden and the Peace Movement in North Carolina," *North Carolina Historical Review*, 31 (1954): 493–516; Richard Reid, "William W. Holden and 'Disloyalty' in the Civil War," *Canadian Journal of History/Annales Canadiennes d'Histoire*, 20 (April 1985), 23–44; *Raleigh State Journal*, January 11, 1862.

90. *Charleston Mercury*, October 10, 1861.

91. *Charleston Mercury*, October 7, 1861.

92. For Davis' message to Congress on this veto, see Lynda Lasswell Crist and Mary Seaton Dix, *Papers of Jefferson Davis*, vol. 7 (Baton Rouge: Louisiana State University, 1992), 301.

93. *Charleston Mercury*, October 9, 1861.

94. *Charleston Mercury*, November 5, 1861.

95. *Charleston Mercury*, October 10, 1861.

96. Bartholomew Riordan to George W. Bagby, Jr., November 2 (no year given, but probably 1862), VHS.

97. The sample included the first month of Bagby's correspondence, October 1861 and each October of the war thereafter, as well as each February, April, and July. Those months were chosen because they were key times in the Confederate experience when Bagby might be writing evaluative stories. In October, the summer campaigning was winding down and armies were moving toward winter quarters or at least (usually) were not as actively engaged in battle. In February, Congress was generally convened in Richmond, so political issues were under way that might trigger commentary. In April, armies were gearing up for summer campaigning and, in July, summer campaigns were fully under way.

98. Andrews, *The South Reports the Civil War*, 36; W.L. King, *The Newspaper Press of Charleston, S.C.* (Charleston, 1872), 155.

99. The *Charleston Southern Standard* was owned by Spratt and E.H. Britton from 1853 to 1858. John Hammond Moore, *South Carolina Newspapers* (Columbia: University of South Carolina Press, 1988), 39.

100. William C. Davis, *Rhett: The Turbulent Life and Times of a Fire-Eater* (Columbia: University of South Carolina Press, 2001), 364, 365.

101. Spratt was listed as the editor of the *Charleston Mercury* on February 13, 1861, in "The Philosophy of Secession: A Southern View, Presented in a Letter addressed to the Hon. Mr. Perkins of Louisiana, in criticism on the Provisional Constitution adopted

by the Southern Congress at Montgomery, Alabama," February 13, 1861, documenting the American South (Chapel Hill: University of North Carolina at Chapel Hill, 2001), (available at http://docsouth.unc.edu/imls/secession/secession.html, accessed December 2, 2007).

102. *Charleston Mercury*, August 15, 1862.

103. *Charleston Mercury*, October, 2, 4, 7, 10, 11, 15, 29, 1861.

104. Robert Barnwell Rhett, Jr., to George William Bagby, Jr., November 25, 1861, VHS.

105. Robert Barnwell Rhett, Jr., to George William Bagby, April 9, 1862, VHS.

106. Gale, 19.

107. Bagby, "Editor's Table," *Southern Literary Messenger*, June 1860, 466.

108. King, 89; *Southern Literary Messenger*, December 1860, 468–474.

109. Bagby, "Editor's Table," *Southern Literary Messenger*, January 1861, 71.

110. *Charleston Mercury*, November 29, 1862.

111. *Charleston Mercury*, October 25, 1861; October 4, 1862; October 27, 1863.

112. *Charleston Mercury*, October, 7, 25, 30, 1862.

113. *Southern Literary Messenger*, January 1863, 57.

114. *Ibid.*

115. *Ibid.*

116. Story reprinted in the *Richmond Sentinel*, January 11, 1864.

117. Statement from William C. Wickham and P.W. Alexander, May 2, 1864, VHS.

118. *Ibid.*

119. *Ibid.*

120. Captain Carey to John Forsyth, undated but included with W.G. Clarke to George William Bagby, Jr., February 15, 1864, VHS.

121. *Ibid.*

122. Joseph S. Wickham, "Williams Carter Wickham (1820–1888)" [web site]; available from http://www.geocities.com/joewickham/williams.htm?200719, accessed February 19, 2007.

123. King, 102, 107–108; Gregory, xxvii.

124. Virginia (an unpublished biographical sketch of his daughter), reprinted in King, 118–119.

125. Durante DaPonte to George W. Bagby, Jr., August 19, 1865; A.F. Crutchfield to George W. Bagby, Jr., May 20, 1865; Charles Dimity to George W. Bagby, Jr., December 27, 1866; Robert Barnwell Rhett, Jr., to George W. Bagby, Jr., November 16, 1866, all from the Bagby Collection, VHS; Bagby to unknown recipient, November 6, 1866, Brock Collection, Huntington Library, Pasadena, Calif.; George W. Bagby, Jr., to "Dear George (probably George C. Wedderburn, April 5, 1866, Brock Collection, Huntington Library, Pasadena, Calif.

126. Felix G. de Fontaine to George W. Bagby, Jr., September 4, 1866, VHS; Gale 19–20; Watson, 868–69; Gregory, xxx.

127. Felix G. de Fontaine to George W. Bagby, Jr., September 4, 1866, VHS.

128. Watson, 868–69; King, 184–86.

129. King, 182.

Chapter 26, James B. Sener

1. "Bloodiest landscape in North America" is the headline used on the National Parks Service website devoted to the Fredericksburg and Spotsylvania County Battlefield Memorial (http://www.nps.gov/frsp/ (accessed May 6, 2008).

2. "The Battles of the Rappahannock," *Richmond Enquirer,* May 14, 1863; "From Gen. Lee's Army," *Richmond Enquirer,* August 12, 1863.

3. "Affairs at Fredericksburg," *Richmond Dispatch,* November 25, 1862.

4. "From Fredericksburg," *Richmond Enquirer,* December 15, 1862.

5. 1860 Manuscript Census listing for Joseph W. Sener in the White Schedule and listing for Waite and Sener in the Manufacturing Schedule, White Schedule available from www.ancestry.com (accessed May 18, 2008) and Manufacturing Schedule available from http://www.historypoint.org/1885_business_directory.asp (accessed May 17, 2008); Fredericksburg City Directory for 1885, available from http://www.historypoint .org/1885_business_directory.asp (accessed May 17, 2008).

6. Sylvanius Jackson Quinn, *The History of the City of Fredericksburg, Virginia* (Richmond, Va.: The Hermitage Press, 1908), 227; History of Fredericksburg Masonic Cemetery, available from http://ftp.rootsweb.ancestry.com/pub/usgenweb/va/fredericksburg/ cemeteries/masonic.txt (accessed May 17, 2008).

7. University of Virginia Matriculation Book, 1855–1856, 1856–1857, Special Collections, University of Virginia Library, Charlottesville.

8. "Judge Brockenborough Visits Gen. Lee About That College Business," *New York Times,* September 3, 1865; James Grant Wilson and John Fiske, eds., "James B. Sener," In *Appleton's Cyclopaedia of American Biography,* vol. 5 (New York: D. Appleton and Co., 1900), 461; "James B. Sener," Biographical Directory of the United States Congress, available from http://bioguide.congress.gov/scripts/biodisplay.pl?index= S000240 (accessed May 16, 2008); Lawrence M. Woods, *Wyoming Biographies* (Worland, Wyo.: High Plains Press, 1991), 168–169; *Atlanta Constitution,* December 16, 1879.

9. "Correspondence of the Richmond Dispatch. Match Race," *Richmond Dispatch,* February 4, 1861; "Hanover," *Richmond Dispatch,* April 25, 1861; "The Federal forces— returning fugitive slaves—the steam gun–examining baggage—insults to ladies, &c," *Richmond Dispatch,* May 31, 1861.

10. "Affairs at Fredericksburg," *Richmond Dispatch,* November 24, 1862.

11. "From Fredericksburg" (letter of December 13, 1862), *Richmond Enquirer,* December 13, 1862.

12. "From Fredericksburg," *Richmond Enquirer,* December 15, 1862.

13. *Ibid.*

14. *Ibid.*

15. *Ibid.*

16. *Ibid.*

17. *Ibid.*

18. *Ibid.*

19. *Ibid.*

20. "From Fredericksburg" (letter of December 14, 1862), *Richmond Enquirer*, December 15, 1863.

21. "From Fredericksburg" (letter of December 16, 1863), *Richmond Enquirer*, December 18, 1862.

22. "From Fredericksburg" (letter of December 16, 1863), *Richmond Enquirer*, December 17, 1862; "From Fredericksburg" (letter of December 16, 1863), *Richmond Enquirer*, December 18, 1862.

23. "From Fredericksburg" (letter of December 17, 1862), *Richmond Enquirer*, December 18, 1862.

24. *Richmond Enquirer*, January 2, 1863.

25. *Richmond Enquirer*, February 6, 1863.

26. *Ibid.*

27. *Richmond Enquirer*, February 28, 1863.

28. *Richmond Enquirer*, February 6, 1863.

29. *Ibid.*

30. "From Fredericksburg," *Richmond Enquirer*, April 7, 1863.

31. "From the Rappahannock," *Richmond Enquirer*, May 2, 1863.

32. "The Battles of Chancellorsville and Fredericksburg," *Richmond Enquirer*, May 8, 1863.

33. "From Fredericksburg," *Richmond Enquirer*, May 9, 1863.

34. "The Battles of the Rappahannock," *Richmond Enquirer*, May 14, 1863.

35. *Ibid.*

36. *Ibid.*

37. *Ibid.*

38. J. Cutler Andrews, *The South Reports the Civil War* (Princeton, N.J.: Princeton University Press, 1970), 298–299).

39. *Richmond Enquirer*, June 13, 15, 17, 1863.

40. "Our Correspondent with the Army of Northern Virginia," *Richmond Enquirer*, July 7, 1863.

41. "Interesting Details of the Battles Near Gettysburg," *Richmond Enquirer*, July 13, 1863.

42. *Ibid.*

43. *Ibid.*

44. *Ibid.*

45. *Richmond Enquirer*, July 17, 1863.

46. *Richmond Enquirer*, July 21, 1863.

47. *Ibid.*

48. *Richmond Enquirer*, July 22, 1863.

49. *Richmond Enquirer*, August 7, 10, 15, 1863.

50. *Richmond Enquirer*, August 10, 1863.

51. Andrews, 330, 331.

52. *Richmond Enquirer*, September 2, 1863.

53. *Richmond Enquirer*, September 12, 1863.

54. *Ibid.*

55. *Richmond Dispatch*, November 26, 27, 1863.

56. *Richmond Dispatch*, November 26, 1863.

57. *Richmond Dispatch*, December 29, 1863.

58. *Ibid.*

59. *Richmond Dispatch*, November 26, 1863.

60. *Richmond Dispatch*, November 27, 1863.

61. *Richmond Dispatch*, November 30, 1863.

62. *Richmond Dispatch*, December 11, 1863.

63. *Richmond Dispatch*, December 8, 1863.

64. *Ibid.*

65. *Richmond Dispatch*, December 19, 1863.

66. *Richmond Dispatch*, December 11, 1863.

67. *Richmond Dispatch*, December 23, 25, 1863.

68. *Richmond Dispatch*, December 23, 1863.

69. *Richmond Dispatch*, December 29, 1863.

70. *Richmond Dispatch,* January 7, 1864; "Review of the Pennsylvania Campaign," *Richmond Dispatch*, March 9, 1864; "Pennsylvania campaign–second day at Gettysburg," *Richmond Dispatch*, March 19, 1864; "Pennsylvania campaign–third day at Gettysburg," *Richmond Dispatch*, April 15, 1864.

71. *Richmond Dispatch*, February 5, 1864.

72. *Richmond Dispatch*, March 4, 1864.

73. *Richmond Dispatch,* March 9, 1864.

74. *Richmond Dispatch,* May 6, 1864.

75. *Ibid.*

76. *Richmond Dispatch*, May 10, 1864.

77. *Ibid.*

78. *Ibid.*

79. *Richmond Dispatch,* May 16, 1864.

80. *Richmond Dispatch*, May 18, 1864.

81. *Richmond Dispatch*, May 23, 27, 1864; "From General Lee's Army," *Richmond Dispatch*, May 24, 1864.

82. *Richmond Dispatch*, June 8, 1864.

83. *Richmond Dispatch*, June 3, 1864.

84. *Richmond Dispatch*, June 4, 1864.

85. *Richmond Dispatch*, June 8, 1864.

86. *Richmond Dispatch*, June15, 1864.

87. *Richmond Dispatch*, June 22, 1864.

88. *Ibid.*

89. *Richmond Dispatch*, June 25, 1864.

90. *Richmond Dispatch*, July 1, 1864.

91. *Richmond Dispatch*, July 7, 1864.

92. *Ibid.*

93. *Ibid.*

94. *Ibid.*

95. *Richmond Dispatch*, July 23, 1864.

96. *Richmond Dispatch*, August 1, 1864.

97. *Richmond Dispatch*, August 3, 1864.

98. *Ibid.*

99. *Richmond Dispatch,* August 23, 1864.

100. *Ibid.*

101. *Richmond Dispatch*, September 5, 1864.

102. *Richmond Dispatch*, September 8, 1864.

103. *Ibid.*

104. *Richmond Dispatch*, September 12, 1864.

105. *Ibid.*

106. *Richmond Dispatch*, November 8, 1864.

107. Andrews, 52.

108. *Richmond Enquirer,* August 25, 1863.

109. Fredericksburg Research Records, available from http://departments.umw.edu/hipr/www/fredburg.htm, accessed May 28, 2008.

110. "James Beverley Sener," James Grant Wilson, John Fiske, and Stanley L Klos, eds., *Appleton's Cyclopedia of American Biography* (New York: D. Appleton and Company, 1887–1889), available from http://famousamericans.net/jamesbeverlysener, accessed May 28, 2008; Richard H. Abbott, *For Free Press and Equal Rights: Republican Newspapers in the Reconstruction South* (Athens: University of Georgia Press, 2004), 134; "In General," *Atlanta Constitution*, December 16, 1879.

111. "James Beverley Sener," Biographical Directory of the United States Congress, available from http://bioguide.congress.gov/scripts/biodisplay.pl?index=S000240, accessed May 28, 2007; Sylvanius Jackson Quinn, *The History of the City of Fredericksburg, Virginia* (Richmond, Va.: Hermitage Press, 1908), 157; "Virginia Politics," *New York Times*, November 11, 1874; Lawrence M. Woods, *Wyoming Biographies* (Worland, Wyo.: High Plains Press, 1991), 168–169.

112. *Decatur Daily Republican*, December 12, 1879.

113. *New York Times,* December 19, 1879.

114. *New York Times*, March 19, 1884.

115. *New York Times*, March 11, 1884.

Chapter 27, John R. Thompson

1. "A Poem for the Times," *Daily Register* (Raleigh, N.C.), May 18, 1861.

2. John S. Patton, *Poems of John R. Thompson Edited with a Biographical Introduction* (New York: Charles Scribner's Sons, 1920), xxxiii.

3. Patton, lvii–lviii; Jay B. Hubbell, *The South in American Literature, 1607–1900* (Durham, NC: Duke University Press, 1954), 522; Allan Nevins, *The Evening Post: A Century of Journalism* (New York: Boni and Liveright, 1922), 409.

4. Nevins, 409.

5. Patton, xi.

6. Gerald M. Garmon, *John Reuben Thompso,* (Boston: Twayne Publishers, 1979).

7. Jay B. Hubbell, *The South in American Literature, 1607–1900* (Durham: Duke University Press, 1954).

8. Samuel A. Link, *Pioneers of Southern Literature* (Nashville, Tenn.: Publishing House of M.E. Church, South, 1899).

9. Louise Manly, *Southern Literature, from 1579–1895* (Richmond, Va.: B.F. Johnson Company, 1900).

10. Joseph M. Flora and Amber Vogel, eds., *Southern Writers: A New Bibliographical Dictionary* (Baton Rouge: Louisiana State University Press, 2006).

11. J. Cutler Andrews, *The South Reports the Civil War* (Princeton, N.J.: Princeton University Press, 1970).

12. Nevins.

13. Barbara G. Ellis, *The Moving Appeal: Mr. McClanahan, Mrs. Dill, and the Civil War's Great Newspaper Run* (Macon, Ga.:Mercer University Press, 2003).

14. Flora and Vogel, 400.

15. Patton, 112.

16. Patton, xx.

17. Hubbell, 526.

18. Hubbell, 522.

19. Hubbell, 392–393.

20. Patton, xxvii.

21. Hubbell, 523.

22. Patton, xxviii.

23. Patton, xxx.

24. Andrews, 175–176.

25. Andrews, 49.

26. Ellis, 119.

27. "The *Commercial Appeal:* A History," *Memphis Commercial Appeal,* http://www.commercialappeal.com/news/2003/Oct/17/the-commercial-appeal-a-history/ (accessed February 12, 2009).

28. *Memphis Daily Appeal,* June 6, 1863.

29. Ellis, 168.

30. *Ibid.,* 467, n. 34.

31. Letters from "Virginius" appeared from June 11 to July 25, 1861. "Dixie" debuted July 31, 1861.

32. Ellis, 288.

33. *Ibid.,* 520, n. 43.

34. *Ibid.,* 186.

35. *Memphis Daily Appeal,* February 2, 1862.

36. *Memphis Daily Appeal,* October 16, 1861.

37. *Memphis Daily Appeal,* August 9, 1861.

38. *Memphis Daily Appeal,* September 10, 1861.

39. *Memphis Daily Appeal,* July 31, 1861.

40. *Ibid.*

41. *Memphis Daily Appeal,* August 9, 1861.

42. Patton, 2.

43. *Memphis Daily Appeal*, August 6, 1861.

44. *Memphis Daily Appeal*, June 15, 1863.

45. *Memphis Daily Appeal*, October 3, 1863.

46. Andrews, 287; Patton, 10.

47. Garmon, 115.

48. *Memphis Daily Appeal*, November 1, 1863.

49. *Memphis Daily Appeal*, August 6, 1861.

50. *Ibid.*

51. *Memphis Daily Appeal*, September 7, 1861.

52. *Memphis Daily Appeal*, September 22, 1861.

53. *Memphis Daily Appeal*, August 9, 1861.

54. *Memphis Daily Appeal*, June 21, 1862.

55. *Memphis Daily Appeal*, May 22, 1862.

56. *Memphis Daily Appeal*, October 29, 1862.

57. *Memphis Daily Appeal*, March 12, 1862, and April 11, 1863; Andrews, 386.

58. *Memphis Daily Appeal*, May 3, 1864.

59. *Memphis Daily Appeal*, October 29, 1862

60. *Memphis Daily Appeal*, January 5, 1862.

61. *Memphis Daily Appeal*, January 10, 1862.

62. *Memphis Daily Appeal*, June 27, 1862.

63. *Memphis Daily Appeal*, June 30, 1862.

64. *Memphis Daily Appeal*, November 8, 1862.

65. *Ibid.*

66. *Memphis Daily Appeal*, August 24, 1861.

67. Ellis, 171.

68. *Memphis Daily Appeal*, September 3, 1861.

69. *Memphis Daily Appeal*, November 25, 1862.

70. Andrews, *The South Reports the Civil War*, 401 n 49.

71. Hubbell, 524.

72. Patton, xlviii.

73. Patton, xIvii.

74. Hubbell, 524.

75. Nevins, 408–409.

76. *Daily Arkansan*, October 15, 1866.

77. Patton, lii–liv.

78. Patton, lv–lvii.

79. Patton, lvii; Hubbell, 522.

Chapter 28, Virginia

1. *Mobile Advertiser and Register,* August 17, 1861.

2. *Ibid.*

3. *Ibid.*

4. *Ibid.*

5. William S. Hoole and Shirley Addie, eds., *Confederate Norfolk: The Letters of a Virginia Lady To the Mobile Press Register, 1861–1862* (University, Ala.: Confederate Publishing Co., 1984), 5.

6. *Mobile Advertiser and Register,* August 17, 1861.

7. *Ibid.*

8. *Ibid.*

9. Cullen A. Battle and Brandon H. Beech, *Third Alabama! The Civil War Memoirs of Brig. Gen. Cullen Andrews Battle, CSA* (Tuscaloosa: University of Alabama Press, 1999), 2, 9.

10. *Ibid.*

11. Stephanie McCurry, *Masters of Small Worlds: Yeoman Households, Gender Relations, and the Political Culture of the Antebellum South Carolina Low Country* (New York: Oxford University Press, 1995).

12. *Mobile Advertiser and Register,* August 18, 1861.

13. J. Cutler Andrews, *The South Reports the Civil War* (Princeton, N.J.: Princeton University Press, 1985), 95; Hoole and Addie, eds.

14. Hoole, 7.

15. Cullen and Beck, 10; letter from Grandson to Grand Pa, published in the August 31, 1861, *Mobile Advertiser and Register,* August 31, 1861.

16. The edition of the *Charleston Courier* in which Joan's letter was published has not been preserved. However, it was reprinted in the *Richmond Enquirer,* July 19, 1861.

17. *Mobile Advertiser and Register,* August 24, 1861.

18. *Ibid.*

19. *Ibid.*

20. *Ibid.*

21. *Ibid.*

22. *Mobile Advertiser and Register,* August 31, 1861.

23. *Mobile Advertiser and Register,* September 7, 1861.

24. *Mobile Advertiser and Register,* August 28, 1861.

25. *Mobile Advertiser and Register,* September 7, 1861.

26. *Mobile Advertiser and Register,* August 24, 1861, and August 28, 1861.

27. *Mobile Advertiser and Register,* August 18, 1861.

28. *Mobile Advertiser and Register,* September 15, 1861.

29. *Mobile Advertiser and Register,* September 7, 1861.

30. *Mobile Advertiser and Register,* September 15, 1861.

31. *Ibid.*

32. The Civil War Soldiers and Sailors website operated by the U.S. National Parks Department identified two soldiers with the last name Cleveland who served in the 3rd Alabama, but neither of them was in the company nicknamed the Mobile Rifles.

33. *Mobile Advertiser and Register,* September 7, 1861.

34. *Mobile Advertiser and Register,* August 31, 1861.

35. *Mobile Advertiser and Register,* September 15, 1861.

36. *Ibid.*

37. *Mobile Advertiser and Register,* August 28, 1861.

38. *Mobile Advertiser and Register,* September 7, 1861.

39. *Mobile Advertiser and Register,* September 22, 1861.

40. Cullen, 5.

41. *Mobile Advertiser and Register,* October 29, 1861.

Chapter 29, Henry Watterson

1. Henry Watterson, *Marse Henry,* vol. I (New York: Beekman Publishers, 1974), 33.

2. *Ibid.,*36–37, 76–77.

3. Young E. Allison, "Likens Watterson to the Militant Roosevelt of America and Fox of England," *Register of Kentucky State Historical Society,* vol. 22, no. 59 (May 1922), 115, 116.

4. Joseph Frazier Wall, *Henry Watterson, Reconstructed Rebel* (New York: Oxford University Press, 1956), 35.

5. *Ibid,* 9; Watterson, *Marse Henry,* vol. II (New York: Beekman Publishers, 1974), 298.

6. Wall, 35.

7. *Ibid.*

8. Barbara G. Ellis and Steven J. Dick, "A unique accession number assigned to each record in the database; also referred to as ERIC Document Number (ED Number) and ERIC Journal Number (EJ Number).Who Was 'Shadow'?" The Computer Knows: Applying Grammar-Program Statistics in Content Analyses to Solve Mysteries about Authorship," EJ542518, *The name assigned to the document by the author. This field may also contain sub-titles, series names, and report numbers.The entity from which ERIC acquires the content, including journal, organization, and conference names, or by means of online submission from the author. Journalism and Mass Communication Quarterly,* vol. 73, no. 4, (1996), 947–962. J. Cutler Andrews made a significant case supporting Watterson as Shadow in *The South Reports the Civil War* (Princeton, N.J.: Princeton University Press, 1970), 543–547.

9. Shadow's byline appeared between June 1863 and July 1863 and May 1864 through September 1864 in the *Memphis Daily Appeal.* An indication of whether the document came from a peer-reviewed journal or U.S. Department of Education publication. Note: Used from 2005 on war the date the document or article was published.

10. Wall, 36, 44, 47, 48.

11. Marse is a regional variation of "Master."

12. One example is in the *Washington Post,* January 5, 1907. A political cartoon titled, "Col. Watterson's Secret of Perpetual Youth" shows Watterson smoking and playing cards in front of large piles of poker chips.

13. Daniel S. Margolies, *Henry Watterson and the New South, The Politics of Empire, Free Trade, and Globalization* (Lexington, Ky., University Press of Kentucky, 1969), 6.

14. Margolies, 54, 55.

15. *Ibid.,* 8.

16. *New York Times,* April 5, 1922.

17. Watterson, *Marse Henry,* vol. I, 24, 25.

18. Watterson, *Marse Henry,* vol. I, 25, 26.

19. Perry J. Ashley, *Dictionary of Literary Biography: American Newspaper Journalists, 1901–1925,* vol. 25 (Detroit, Mich.: Gale Research Company, 1984), 321.

20. Watterson, *Marse Henry*, vol. 1, 27.

21. Ashley, 322.

22. *Ibid.*

23. Watterson, *Marse Henry*, vol. 1, 17, 18.

24. *Ibid.*, 54–55.

25. Cameron would become Abraham Lincoln's first secretary of war.

26. Watterson loved to quote essayist and historian Carlisle. Writing as Shadow, Watterson also quoted Carlisle in an article under his Shadow byline in the *Mobile Advertiser and Register* on June 22, 1864.

27. *Ibid.*, 17.

28. Ashley, 322.

29. Watterson, *Marse Henry*, vol. 1, 17, 18.

30. *Ibid.*, 81.

31. Jeb Stuart was promoted to major general in 1862.

32. Wall, 27.

33. Watterson, *Marse Henry*, vol. I, 149.

34. *Ibid.*, 149.

35. *Ibid.*, 76, 77.

36. *Ibid.*, 77, 78.

37. *Ibid.*, 78.

38. *Ibid.*, 83, 84.

39. *Ibid*, 81, 82.

40. *Ibid.*, 82.

41. *Ibid.*, 84.

42. Watterson, *Marse* Henry, vol. I, 82.

43. Watterson, *Marse Henry*, vol. II, 127.

44. Watterson, *Marse Henry*, vol. I, 82.

45. *Ibid.*, 79.

46. *Ibid.*, 84, 85.

47. Forrest did not become a general until July 1862.

48. *Ibid.*, 85.

49. Wall, 37.

50. Watterson, *Marse Henry*, vol. I, 85.

51. *Ibid.*, 92.

52. *Ibid.*, 93.

53. *Ibid.*, 93, 94.

54. *Ibid.*, 94, 95.

55. *Ibid.*

56. *Ibid.*, 93–95.

57. Wall, 36–37.

58. Wall, 39.

59. Watterson and his chief biographer, Wall, said Watterson named the *Rebel*; however, several historians, including Steven Cox, head of Special Collections & University Archives at the University of Tennessee at Chattanooga, claim that the *Rebel* began publishing in August 1862 and that Watterson did not join the staff until later.

60. Watterson, *Marse Henry*, vol. I, 85. Louis M. Parham, the printer who may have stayed with Watterson and Roberts during the siege of Chattanooga, wrote a history around 1889 in the *Atlanta Constitution* that was reprinted in the *Chattanooga Times* on January 9, 1949. Parham said the first issue of the *Daily Rebel* appeared in Chattanooga about August 1, 1862, with Frank (sic) M. Paul of Nashville as publisher. "It was a four-column folio, printed mostly in minion and nonpareil types," he wrote. "Shortly after the publication began, Henry Watterson and Albert Roberts (John Happy) became the editors."

61. Zella Armstrong, *The Daily Rebel*, undated newspaper article, Historical Collection, Chattanooga Public Library. Of the 800 or more editions of the *Rebel* published between August 1, 1862, and 1865, only about 200 copies survive. Several issues that survive today were copies that were reprinted as souvenirs during military gatherings in Chattanooga.

62. Long, 380.

63. *The Chattanooga Daily Rebel*, February 12, 1863.

64. *Ibid.*

65. *Ibid.*

66. Wall, 40.

67. Roy Morris, "The Chattanooga Rebel: That Improbably, Praiseworthy Paper," *Civil War Times*, vol. 32, No. 7 (1984), 21, from the *Rebel*, February 14, 1863 (I have been unable to find a copy of the February 14, 1863, *Rebel.*).

68. *Chattanooga Daily Rebel*, February 17, 1863.

69. *Ibid.*, August 6, 1863.

70. *Ibid.*

71. *Ibid.*

72. Colonel Bennett H. Young, *Kentucky Eloquence* (Louisville, Ky.: Ben La Bree Jr., 1907), 379–391; Editorials of Henry Watterson, compiled with an introduction and notes by Arthur Krock (New York: George H. Doran Company, 1923), 187–208.

73. *Daily Rebel*, August 6, 1863.

74. *Ibid.*

75. *Ibid.*

76. *Ibid.*

77. *Ibid.*

78. *Ibid.*

79. *Ibid.*

80. *Ibid.*

81. E.B. Long with Barbara Long, *The Civil War Day by Day, an Almanac 1861–1865* (Garden City, N.Y.: Da Capa, 1971), 399.

82. *Daily Rebel*, August 25, 1863.

83. Watterson, *Marse Henry*, vol. II, 308, 309.

84. *Ibid.*

85. *Daily Rebel*, August 25, 1863.

86. *Daily Rebel*, August 30, 1863; *Chattanooga News*, July 2, 1890.

87. *Chattanooga Times*, January 9, 1949; Wall, 23.

88. *Daily Rebel*, August 30, 1863.

89. *Ibid.*

90. Long, 403.

91. *Daily Rebel,* August 30, 1863.

92. *Ibid.*

93. *Ibid.*

94. Looking Backward, *Chattanooga Times,* January 9, 1949, Historical Collection, Chattanooga Public Library. The article was originally published in the *Atlanta Constitution* and reprinted in Chattanooga in 1890. Louis L. Parham said he was a compositor, "having been with the paper continuously since its inception till it reached Griffin," where he left the newspaper a short time before it left for Selma.

95. *Ibid.*

96. Long, 407.

97. Long, 427.

98. Wall, 43, 44.

99. *Chattanooga News,* July 2, 1890; Wall, 43. The last edition of the *Rebel* was published on April 27, 1865.

100. *Chattanooga Daily Rebel* marker, 523 Market Street, Chattanooga, Tennessee.

101. Wall, 44.

102. Long, 437–439.

103. Long, 440–441; Wall, 44.

104. Wall, 44; Watterson, *Marse Henry,* vol. I, 85.

105. The *Daily Constitutionalist* published a note on May 12, 1864, announcing the appointments and locations but not the real names of their new correspondents. Watterson was one of the correspondents who was in Dalton, Georgia, at the time. "Our Correspondents.—Having secured the services of several competent writers to act as regular correspondents of the Constitutionalist, we flatter ourselves that in this respect as well as in every other, our paper will compare favorably with the leading journals of the country. The letters now being published are written with ability and cannot fail to be interesting to our readers. This is especially true of letters written from Richmond over the signature of 'Tyrone Powers' and 'Sigma.' In a few days we will have letters from a special correspondent with the Army of Northern Virginia, narrating the events of the present campaign. At Dalton and other points of interest we have also correspondents, so that we have now a regular organized corps of army correspondents." *Daily Constitutionalist,* May 12, 1864.

106. Wall, 46.

107. *Mobile Advertiser and Register,* dateline May 24, 1864, published May 28, 1864.

108. *Ibid.*

109. *Mobile Advertiser and Register,* dateline May 26, 1864, published June 4, 1864.

110. *Ibid.*

111. After the war, the Federals offered a $100,000 reward for the capture of Governor Isham Harris, who fled in May to Cordova, Mexico, to live in exile. The emperor of Mexico issued a decree on September 5, 1865, opening Mexico to immigration and colonization. Others living in exile included "General Magruder, Gov. Allen and Judge Perkins of Louisiana, Gov. Reynolds of Missouri and Gov. Murrah and General Clarke of Texas and many other and lesser Confederate lights." Robert Adamson, *Atlanta*

Constitution, August 1, 1897, excerpted as "Gov. Harris at the Close of the War," *Confederate Veteran*, vol. 5, no. 8, (Nashville, Tenn., August, 1897), 402–405.

112. Watterson, *Marse Henry*, vol. 1, 80, 81.

113. Watterson, *Marse Henry*, vol. 1, 81. Watterson told this same story as Shadow in an article datelined June 30, 1862, from Marietta in the *Mobile Register and Advertiser*.

114. *Daily Constitutionalist* (Augusta, Ga.), May 29, 1864,

115. *Ibid.*

116. Long, 519.

117. *Daily Constitutionalist* (Augusta, Ga.), June 9, 1864. Although Watterson was no longer associated with the *Rebel*, the *Constitutionalist* reported that the Chattanooga newspaper had moved to Griffin by June 9, where Paul continued as the publisher with Leon Trousdale as editor. Louis L. Parham, who was the printer for the *Rebel*, said that Charlie Faxon, who was later on the *Courier-Journal*, was the temporary editor. Faxon may have been replaced by Trousdale by the time the *Rebel* reached Griffin.

118. Long, 521, 522.

119. *Mobile Daily Advertiser and Register*, June 15, 21, 1864; Wall, 46.

120. *Ibid.*, July 17, 1864.

121. Long, 529.

122. *Daily Constitutionalist* (Augusta, Ga.), July 1, 1864.

123. *Ibid.*, July 5, 1864.

124. *Mobile Advertiser and Register*, dateline Atlanta July 12, 1864, published July 17, 1864.

125. Long, 540.

126. Wall, 46, 47.

127. *Daily Constitutionalist* (Augusta, Ga.), July 22, 1864.

128. *Ibid.*

129. *Ibid.*

130. Long, 542.

131. *Daily Constitutionalist* (Augusta, Ga.), July 29, 1864.

132. *Ibid.*

133. *Ibid.*, August 10, 1864.

134. *Ibid.*

135. *Ibid.*

136. *Ibid.*

137. Writing for the *Daily Constitutionalist* (Augusta, Ga.), August 28, 1864, Lavengro described the decimated corps of journalists on August 28: "John E. Hatcher, a bright humorist, a tender poet and genial gentleman and editor of the "Register" had gone to … North Mississippi. Dumble, with the courage of a hero, who withstands the shells as resolutely as the ravages of ill-health, is still here, and runs the 'Appeal Extra.' John Happy, Waterson (sic) and Baker, a trio of inseparables are also to be seen with wizzard [sic] tread accurately determining the range of the shells as they peregniate [sic] the haunts of old associations, and sigh for the pretty faces of Marietta and Peachtree, and the excellent vintage of Signor Cora. Genial, big hearted John H. Stute is in Macon. He and Dr. Nagle are engineering the "Intelligence' there. Mr. Watson, of the 'Confederacy,' a man of very decided genius, whose poetical merit is just beginning to

be appreciated in the South, is busily engaged at the some [sic] point over news columns and political leaders. The 'Register' corps excepting Mr. Hatcher, has gone to Augusta."

138. Lavengro, *Daily Constitutionalist* (Augusta, Ga.), August 28, 1864.

139. *Daily Constitutionalist,* August 28, 1864.

140. *Ibid.*

141. *Ibid.*

142. Long, 563, 564.

143. Watterson, *Marse Henry,* vol. I , 85, 86.

144. *Ibid.,* 97.

145. *Ibid.*

146. *Ibid.*

147. *Ibid.*

148. Adamson, *Confederate Veteran,* 402–405.

149. Long, 565.

150. Watterson, *Marse Henry,* vol. 1, 85, 86.

151. *Ibid.,* 161.

152. *Ibid.*

153. *Ibid.,* 165.

154. *Ibid.,* 166.

155. *Ibid.,* 166, 167.

156. *Ibid.,* 169.

157. *Ibid.,* 170.

158. *Ibid,* 171.

159. *Ibid.,* 172.

160. *Ibid.,* 67.

161. Vice President Alben W. Barkley, Wall, xiii.

162. Wall, 327–329.

163. *New York Times,* April 5, 1922.

164. Wall, xiii.

Epilogue

1. Gary W. Gallagher, *Causes Won, Lost, and Forgotten: How Hollywood and Popular Art Shape What We Know about the Civil War* (Chapel Hill: University of North Carolina Press, 2008), 25–29.

2. Frederic Hudson, *Journalism in the United States, from 1690 to 1872* (New York: Harper and Row Publishers, 1969), 283.

Index

Many newspapers have undergone frequent changes in owners and names, particularly during the Civil War, and some were published as multiple editions under similar names. For example, the *Charleston Courier* became the *Charleston Daily Courier* and was subsequently published as the *News and Courier* before becoming the *News and Courier and Evening Post* and finally publishing as the *Post and Courier*. For the sake of clarity, such newspapers cited in the index are cross-referenced.

In addition, page numbers set in italics indicate photographs or illustrations.

1st Indian Brigade, 432
1st Kansas Colored, 410, 428, 429, 431, 432, 433
1st Texas Battery (Douglas Battery), 455, 456
2nd Texas Brigade, 430
3rd Alabama Regiment, 564–65, 567
3rd Alabama volunteers, Company A, 219
6th Texas Infantry, 466, 467, 469
8th Texas Cavalry, 469
11th Louisiana, 254
14th Tennessee, 553
15th Virginia Cavalry letter, 532
29th Texas Cavalry, 409–10, 429, 430
31st North Carolina, 290
33rd Texas Cavalry, 438
47th Massachusetts Regiment, 436
54th Massachusetts Colored Infantry, 83, 355

Abbott, John S. C., 469–70
Adair, Colonel George W., 593
Adams, General D. W., 212
Address to Christians Throughout the World (convention of ministers, Richmond, VA, 1863), 234
Adriatic, a British ship, 304, 305
Advertiser and Mail, 272–73
Alabama, *201*, 208
"Alabama" (Timrod), 173
Alabama Press Association, 274
Albertson, Jonathan, 603 *table*
Albertson, J. W., 528
Albion, 554

Alexander, Peter W.
    on abuses of civilians by quartermaster corps, 320–21
    acerbic political rhetoric of, 317
    on acquiring a passport, 316
    on the Army of Northern Virginia, 313
    on the Army's welcome to Maryland, 329
    on Bagby's false report on Major Alfred M. Barbour, 509
    balanced criticism of Confederate government and military, 321–22
    on Battle at Fredericksburg, 332–33
    on Battle at Shiloh, 324–25
    on Battle at the Wilderness, 337–38
    battlefield illness of, 318–19
    on Battle of Chickamauga, 336
    on Battle of Fort Donelson, 322
    on Battle of Gettysburg, 334–36
    on the Battle of Sharpsburg, 329–30
    on Battle of Spotsylvania Court House, 337
    on bombardment of Fort Fisher, 339
    on the buildup for war, 316
    censorship and, 325
    children of, 339–40
    on Cold Harbor assault, 338
    concern for Confederate troops, 313, 320, 327, 330–31, 336
    condemnation of the Confederate government, 313–14
    controversy over correspondent "A" and, 528
    criticism of Confederate Medical Department, 320

Alexander, Peter W. (*continued*)
  criticism of the conduct of Southern
    troops, 336–37
  criticism of war correspondents, 325
  date and place of birth, 315
  death of, 340
  defense of freedom of the press, 322–23
  on a dying Union soldier, 319
  education of, 4, 315
  on First Manassas, 317–18
  on General Order No. 98, 322–23
  on General Robert E. Lee, 332, 338
  on General Stonewall Jackson, 328–29, 334
  on General Ulysses S. Grant, 338
  on inauguration of Jefferson Davis, 323–24
  intention of his criticism of war effort, 321,
    327
  James Roddy Sneed and, 18, 315, 332,
    345–46
  J. Cutler Andrews on, 316, 493
  legal practice of, 339, 346
  marriage to Maria Teresa Shorter, 339
  methods of working, 12
  Mobile Advertiser and Register and, 339, 528
  on naval battle at Charleston, 333–34
  "An Old Soldier" letter to, 332
  parents of, 315
  political activities of, 315
  political controversy and, 339
  portrait of, *314*
  on press restrictions, 13–14
  private note to James Roddy Sneed, 332
  pseudonym of, 312
  purple prose of, 322
  quality of his correspondence, 18–19, 318,
    322, 325–26
  reputation of, 325
  Savannah Republican and, 311, 316, 326,
    337, 493
  secession and, 311, 315, 653 *note* 7
  on siege of Petersburg, Virginia, 338–39
  on soldiers carrying side arms and knives,
    319
  Southern Confederacy and, 316
  on the Trent Affair, 319–20
Allen, Laura S. (de Fontaine), 46
Almon, W. J., 308
amateur Confederate war correspondents, 7–9

See also citizen journalism; soldier correspondents
American Magazine, 573
American Pioneer, 382
The American Union (Spence), 226, 234
Anderson (South Carolina) *Intelligencer*, 8
Anderson, Benedict on importance of newspapers, 23
Anderson, Major Robert, 342, 343, 344
Andrews, J. Cutler
  on Confederate press and public morale,
    267
  on correspondent "A," 528
  on George William Bagby, Jr., 493
  on Peter W. Alexander, 316
  and pseudonyms of Civil War correspon-
    dents, 269
  on quality of Southern journalism, 17–18
  on "Virginia," 560
Antietam Creek, 77
army hospital near Richmond, *106*
Army Letters of Personne, magazine, 19, 91,
  92, 93
Arthur, Mayor E. J., 97–98
Arthur, President Chester A., 542
"Ashby" (Thompson), 555
Associated Press, 574
Association of the Richmond Press, 365
Athens (Georgia) Southern Banner, 332
Athens Southern Watchman, 23
Atlanta, Georgia
  the burning of, *311, 374*
  destruction of its railroad tracks, *18*
  evacuation of, *589*
  prior to Sherman's capture of, *367*
  Sherman's headquarters in, *375*
  surrender of, 374
Atlanta Constitution, 573
Atlanta Daily Intelligencer, 261
Atlanta Southern Confederacy, 348, 541, 572,
  583, 585, 586, 593, 594
  See also *Southern* (Atlanta) *Confederacy*
Atlantic, a ship, 303, *305*
Atlantic Monthly, 252, 487
Augusta (Georgia) Daily Constitutionalist, 572
Augusta Chronicle and Sentinel, 16, 503
Augusta Constitutionalist, 365
Augusta Daily Chronicle and Sentinel, 365

Austin City Gazette, 415
Austin State Gazette, 408, 456, 478
Austin Statesman, 480

Bagby, George W., Jr.
   "An Apology for Fools" lecture, 492
   Bartholomew Rochefort Riordan and, 132,
      497, 498
   Boston Daily Advertiser on, 493
   characterizing the typical Virginia news-
      paper editor, 488–89
   Charleston Mercury and, 20, 484, 490,
      494–95, 497, 505
   color stories and, 501
   common themes in his writing, 499
   his concern for Confederate soldiers,
      500–1
   on corruption and the Confederacy, 502–3
   criticism of General Robert E. Lee, 483,
      501–2, 507–8
   criticism of Jefferson Davis, 20, 483, 503,
      504, 506
   criticism of the Confederacy and its citi-
      zens, 500–1, 502–3, 504–5
   date and place of birth, 486
   death and burial place of, 512
   deceptive portraits of, 483–84
   demographic data on, 602 *table*
   on desertions, 503
   dichotomy of, 484–86
   duel of, 489–90
   dyspepsia and, 487, 512
   education of, 4, 487
   on Elizabeth Hobson, 486–87
   ending his career in journalism, 510
   enlistment in Lynchburg Rifle Grays, 495
   establishing the *Native Virginian*, 511
   eulogy of, 512
   on European recognition of Confederacy,
      498–99
   The Express and, 487–88
   his false report on Major Alfred M.
      Barbour, 509–10
   on General Ambrose Burnside, 508
   on General Braxton Bragg, 508
   Harper's and, 487, 490
   J. Cutler Andrews on, 493–94
   lecturing career of, 492, 511, 512

   letter from William B. Matthews, 484–85
   libertarian perspective of, 502
   Memphis Daily Appeal and, 554
   on military politics/gossip, 507–9
   on his military service, 496
   Mobile Advertiser and Register and, 497, 509
   his Mozis Addums stories, 491–92
   Nashville Union and American and, 497
   New Orleans Crescent and, 490
   peace movement and, 504
   political reporting and, 502
   portrait of, *484*
   postwar careers of, 511–12
   prolificacy of, 498
   pseudonym of, 20, 155, 483, 508
   publications using his work, 487–88
   his rationale for publishing bad news, 505
   readers' opinion of, 482
   Richmond Examiner and, 510
   on Richmond of 1862, 497–98
   Richmond Whig and, 487, 490, 510
   Robert Barnwell Rhett, Jr. and, 20, 494–96,
      505
   salary of as a war correspondent, 10–11
   sources for his war reporting, 502
   Southern Illustrated News and, 510
   Southern Literary Messenger and, 487, 490,
      491, 492–93, 498, 506–7, 508, 509
   states rights and, 502
   on Virginia secession, 507
   Washington experience of, 492
   as Washington political correspondent,
      490–91
   weather reports of, 499–500
Baltimore American, 546
Banks, General Nathaniel P., 436, 449
Barbour, Major Alfred M., 509–10
Barker, Captain E. A., 432
Barkley, Vice President Alben W., 596
Barksdale, General William, 520
Barr, William D., 604 *table*
Barton, Clara, 134
Bass, J. N., 603 *table*
Battery Wagner on Morris Island, Federal
   bombardment of, 83, 132, 135, 352–55
*The Battle of Chickamauga, A Concise His-
   tory of Events from the Evacuation of
   Chattanooga* (Reid), 263

Baylor University, 450

Bayly, Thomas Henry, 364

Beacon of Cuba, 364

Beal, General George, 253–54

Beauregard, General Pierre G. T.
censorship and, 13, 15
on Corinth, 164, 170
Edward Hopkins Cushing on, 447
evacuation of Savannah and Charleston, 351, 355
Felix Gregory de Fontaine and, 46
Henry Timrod on, 163, 169
James Roddy Sneed on, 354
popularity of, 343
portrait of, *48*
Press Association of the Confederate States of America and, 371
replaced by General Braxton Bragg, 170
retreat from Corinth, 403
Samuel Chester Reid, Jr. and, 256–57

Bee, General Bernard, 26, *141*, 155–56

Bellville Countryman, 409

Benjamin, Judah P. (Secretary of War), 61, 221, 284–85, 346

Bennett, James Gordon, 47, 49–50

Bethel Church, 52

Billow, a ship, 305

Birds of a Feather Flock Together: Or Talks with Sothern (de Fontaine), 91

Birmingham Age-Herald, 198, 199

Birmingham Independent, 195

Birmingham State Herald, 198

Birmingham Sun, 195

Black, Tabitha (Watterson), 573

Black Republicans, 206

black soldiers, use of, 533, 537–38

black troops, massacres of, 410, 428, 429, 431

"Bloody 11th Louisiana," 254

Blount County News, 196

Blount County News and Dispatch, 196–97, 198, 636 *note* 56

Blount Springs Advance, 196

Blount Springs News, 196

Blunt, General James G., 428

Boston Daily Advertiser, 493

Boston Herald, 46

Bothwich, A., 224

Bowen, Josephine (Reid), 264

Bragg, General Braxton
arrest of Lawrence H. Mathews, 180, 186–88, 208–9
arrest of William W. Screws, 202, 209, 265–67
assault on Santa Rosa Island, 193
censorship and, 12, 15, 287, 372
correcting abuse by officers, 336
excluding the *Chattanooga Rebel* from his army, 584–85
Fort Pickens and, 180, 182–83, 191
George W. Bagby, Jr. on, 508
Henry Watterson and, 570, 584
Huntsville Confederate and, 245–46
John Forsyth and, 208–10, 212–14
John Linebaugh and, 202, 209, 243
John S. Thrasher and, 371
Memphis Daily Appeal and, 243–45
ordered to the defense of the Tennessee line, 193–94
portrait of, *182*
relationship with the press, 208, 267
relieving Lawrence H. Mathews of duty, 195
replacing General Beauregard, 170
resignation from the army, 585
Samuel Chester Reid, Jr. and, 257–59

Brazos Eagle, 479

Breckenridge, John, 416

Brewer, H. O., 228

Bright, William, 226

Briton, E. H., demographic data on, 604 *table*

Brockenbrough, John, 515

Brooke, Sophia (da Ponte), 382, 385, 392

Brown, John, 574

Bruns, John Dickson, 171, 602 *table*

Bryant, William Cullen, 554

Buchanan, President James, 143, 207

Buell, General Don Carlos, 64, 166, 211

Bulloch, James D., 235

Bull Run, Battle of, *37*, 75, 152–55

Bunting, Robert Franklin, 604 *table*

Burdell, John, 98

Burnside, General Ambrose
at Battle of Chattanooga, 86
defeats at Fredericksburg, 508
at Knoxville, Tennessee, 583
at Rappahannock, 516

replaced as commander of Union Army, 520
at Roanoke Island, 400, 469– 70
at the siege of Petersburg, 537–38
Butler, General Benjamin
    insulting order to Confederate women of
        New Orleans, 65
    at New Orleans, 390–91

Cabin Creek, Battle of, 410, 431–32
The Cabinet of the Confederate States, *218*
Caldwell, Colonel A. W., 244
Calhoun, Mayor James, 593
Campbell, Lord, 226, 227
Carey, James W., his description of
    journalism, 5
"Carolina" (Timrod), 178
Carolina Planter, 97
Carrie Estelle, a ship, 303
Carroll, a ship, 303
Carter, Hodding II, 17
Carter, Theodoric, 2, 604 *table*
*The Case of the Private-Armed Brig-of-War
    General Armstrong* (Reid), 249
censorship
    Felix Gregory de Fontaine and, 55–56, 59,
        61, 62
    General Order No. 98 and, 285, 322
    General Orders No. 158 and, 287
    James Roddy Sneed and, 312, 345, 346–48
    Joan and, 123–24
    John S. Thrasher and, 15–16, 81–82, 372–73
    Peter W. Alexander and, 325
    R. R. Gilbert on, 473
    Samuel Chester Reid, Jr. and, 254–55,
        258–59, 261
    self-censorship, 16
    See also press restrictions in the
        Confederacy
Central Journal, 479
    See also *Crockett Journal*
Centreville, retreat from, 399–400
Chancellorsville, Battle of, 521–23, *522, 525*
"Charleston" (Timrod), 172
Charleston, siege of, 352–54
Charleston, South Carolina, *242*
Charleston Courier
    Felix Gregory de Fontaine and, 25, 494
    Joan and, 25, 105, 106–7, 110

Samuel Chester Reid, Jr. and, 256–57
    See also *Post and Courier*
Charleston Daily Courier, 69
Charleston Mercury
    announcement of secession, *30*
    on arrest of Lawrence H. Mathews, 186, 189
    Bartholomew Riordan and, 127
    Bartholomew Rochefort Riordan and, 128,
        135
    educational level of staff, 4
    George W. Bagby, Jr. and, 20, 484, 490, 505
    Henry Timrod and, 163
    and the importance of newspapers, 23
    influence and circulation of, 505
    Leonidas William Spratt and, 26, 143, 147,
        505
    on Peter W. Alexander, 18
    on protecting military secrets, 16–17
    Robert Barnwell Rhett, Jr. and, 505
    Robert Barnwell Rhett, Sr. and, 143
    secession and, 50
    on secret Congressional sessions, 505–6
Charleston News, 27–28, 135–36, 137, *138*
Charleston Southern Standard, 141, 505
Charleston Sunday News, 177
Chattanooga Advertiser, 578
Chattanooga Advocate, 578
Chattanooga Daily Rebel, 261
Chattanooga Gazette, 578
Chattanooga Rebel
    design of, 578
    destruction of its printing equipment, 570
    excluded from General Bragg's Army,
        584–85
    final destruction of, 585
    Francis M. Paul and, 578, 585
    Henry Watterson and, 570, 572, 578, 583,
        584
    nomadic travels of, 583, 585
    popularity of, 578
    wartime difficulties of, 569–70
Chickahominy, Battle of, *68*
Chickamauga, Battle of, 83, 244, 263, 336
Chickasaw Indians, 456
Choctaw Indians, 429, 456
citizen journalism, 105
    See also amateur Confederate war corre-
        spondents; soldier correspondents

Civil War correspondents' memorial arch, *21, 22*

Clarke, W. G., 509

Clarksville Standard
    Charles DeMorse and, 408, 411, 414, 428, 429, 433, 456
    demise of, 435
    "Democracy and Disunion"editorial, 416
    desertions and, 413, 429
    encouraging enlistment, 418
    establishment of, 415
    nameplate and motto of, 417
    on the Union capture of New Orleans, 418

Clay, Clement C., 235

Clisby, Joseph, 366

Cohen, Leonora (Sneed), 349, 361

Colcock, Colonel Charles J., 40

Cold Harbor, Battle of, 338, 534–35

Collier's Weekly, 572

Columbia, South Carolina, destruction of, *102, 103*

Columbia Banner, 97

Columbia Daily South Carolinian, 512

Columbus (Georgia) *Times*, 202

Columbus Times, 205

Commercial Appeal. See *Memphis Daily Appeal*

Company A., 3rd Alabama volunteers, 219

Compromise of 1850, 205

The Compromises of Life (Watterson), 595

Confederate camp at Warrington, Florida, *189*

Confederate Conscription Act of 1862, 409, 456

Confederate Custom House, Richmond, Virginia, 1865, *510*

Confederate entrenchments outside of Petersburg, Virginia, *270*

Confederate forces recaptured the city of Galveston, New Year's Day, 1863, *448*

Confederate fort near Atlanta, *463*

Confederate law and Native Americans, 424

Confederate lines outside of Petersburg, Virginia, *268*

Confederate press and modern journalism, 6, 598–99

Confederate prisoners at the Chattanooga railroad depot, *585*

Confederate Ram at Wilmington, North Carolina, *303*

Confederates evacuating Brownsville, Texas, *443*

Confederate spies Williams and Peters, *253*

Confederate troops at White Springs, Virginia, *53*

Confederate troops ford the Potomac as they enter Maryland, *328*

conscription of journalists, 86, 373

Cooke, John Esten, 493, 512, 604 *table*

copyright of news stories, 7, 95, 100–101, 312, 363

Coquette, a Philadelphia anchor-sweeper, 297

Corinth, Battle of, 446–47

Corinth, First Battle of, 403

Corinth, Mississippi, 1862, *164, 165, 171*

Cosmopolitan, 573

"The Cotton Boll" (Timrod), 162

Courtenay, William Ashmead
    advertisement for his book shop, *29*
    Captain G. B. Cuthbert and, 37
    Captain W. E. Earle and, 38
    Charleston News and Courier on, 27–28
    children of, 42
    on Civil War camp life, 32–36
    controversial postscript of, 31, 36
    criticism of the direction of the war, 30–33, 38
    date and place of birth, 28
    death and burial place of, 44
    defending his honor (duels), 27, 37, *37*, 38–40, 41–42
    demographic data on, 602 *table*
    education of, 28
    in Hardeeville, South Carolina, 38–41
    on Henry Timrod, 177, 178
    Henry Timrod and, 26, 27, 32, 43–44, 174
    honors awarded to, 42–43, 44
    investigation into mistreatment of army horses, 38–40
    marriage to Julia Anna Francis, 42
    as mayor of Charleston, 42
    military career of, 28, 33, 38, 613 *note* 33
    Peabody Educational Trust board member, 42
    portrait of, *28*
    postwar career of, 42–44
    preserving South Carolina's history, 44
    pseudonym of, 26, 30

South Carolina Palmetto Guard and, 27, 33, 36, 37
  W. L. DePass and, 38–40, 41–42
Crawford, Martin, 208
Creek Indians, 426–27, 428
Crockett Journal, 479
  See also *Central Journal*
CSS *Tallahassee*, 202, 301–8, *302*, *305*
Cumberland Gap, Tennessee, *251*, 258–59
Curtis, General Samuel R., 460
Cushing, Edward Hopkins
  Confederate Conscription Act and, 409
  on General Beauregard, 447
  R. R. Gilbert and, 408, 466, 467, 469, 470
  William P. Doran and, 408, 444
Cuthbert, Captain G. B., 37

Daily Appeal (Memphis), 66
  See also *Memphis Daily Appeal*
Daily Constitutionalist, 586
Daily Dispatch, 276, 288, 301
Daily Inter Ocean, 361
Daily Morning News, 358, 359
Daily South Carolinian, 89, 172, 174, 175, 177
  See also *South Carolinian*
Daily States, 574
Dallas Herald, 456, 479
Dana, General N. B., 594
da Ponte, Durant
  American Pioneer and, 382
  Battle of New Orleans and, 390–91
  on capture of Commodore Lynch's fleet, 389
  children of, 393
  Clara Solomon and, 378, 380, 382–83, 385–386
  Confederate approval of his writing, 387
  on Confederate defeat at Fishing Greek, Kentucky, 388
  a Confederate military policy, 386–87
  date and place of birth, 381, 661 *note* 9
  death and burial place of, 393
  demographic data on, 603 *table*, 604 *table*
  dismissing Northern victories, 384
  on enthusiasm for the Confederacy, 382
  on Fortress Monroe, 384–85, *385*
  General Ulysses S. Grant and, 392
  importance of his writing, 394
  injury of, 392
  on intentions of Union army, 389
  marriage to Rosa Solomon, 392
  marriage to Sophia Brooke, 382
  on mood in Richmond, 387, 388
  on mortally wounded Captain O. Jennings Wise, 388
  New Orleans Crescent and, 381
  New Orleans Daily Delta and, 381, 382, 387
  on the *New York Herald* reporting, 384
  portrait of, *380*, 393
  pseudonym of, 378
  his report on the kindness of a Virginia family, 384
  his title as "Captain," 387
  volunteering for the Confederate army, 392
Da Ponte, Lorenzo, 381
Da Ponte, Lorenzo Luigi, 381
The Daring Raid of General John H. Morgan, in Ohio, His Capture and Wonderful Escape with Captain T. Henry Hines (Reid), 263
Davis, Jefferson
  on cost of attacking Fort Pickens, 192
  on destroying Charleston, South Carolina, 135
  at Fort Mill, 158–59
  on freedom of the press, 12–13
  George W. Bagby, Jr. on, 503, 504
  Joan on, 111–12
  John R. Thompson on, 550–51
  Leonidas William Spatt on, 154–55
  at Manassas, 154–55
  Peter W. Alexander on, 323–24
  replacing General Joseph E. Johnston, 590
  William G. Shepardson on, 279
Davis, Richard T., 603 *table*
Davis, Varina Howell, 192
Dawson, Francis Warrington, 135, 136, 628 *note* 45
De Bow's Review, 105, 142, 364
Decatur (Illinois) *Daily Republican*, 541
defense of freedom of the press, 95, 97–99
de Fontaine, Chevalier Louis Antoine, 46
de Fontaine, Edith, 91
de Fontaine, Felix Gregory
  Army Letters from Personne (magazine), 19, 91, *92*, *93*
  on Atlanta, Georgia, July, 1864, 86–87
  on Ball's Bluff battle scene, 58–59

de Fontaine, Felix Gregory (*continued*)
  battles and skirmishes covered by, 51
  on bombardment of Battery Wagner on
    Morris Island, 83
  books and major magazine articles of, 91,
    621 *note* 196
  Boston Herald and, 46–47
  on Bull Run battle, 52–54
  on camp deaths, 60
  censorship and, 55–56, 59, 61, 62
  on Charles Mason execution, 73
  Charleston Courier and, 25, 494
  on Christmas of 1861, 60–61
  Columbia Daily South Carolinian and, 512
  on conditions at Corinth, Mississippi,
    April, 1862, 63–65, 169–70
  on Confederate defeat in Tennessee, 62
  date and place of birth, 46, 622 *note* 198
  death and burial place of, 92–94
  defending General Nathan "Shanks"
    Evans, 59
  demographic data on, 602 *table*
  descriptive writing of, 55–57
  on desertion, 88
  on diet and health care of the army, 67–68
  on difficulties of writing on the move,
    73–74
  education of, 4
  on ending of one-year enlistments, 60
  escape from Memphis, 67
  establishing *Die Charlestoner Zeitung*, 91
  establishing the War Record Publishing
    Company, 91
  evacuating Columbia, 89, 174
  family portrait of, *90*
  on Fort Sumter, 45–46, 50
  on Fredericksburg battle, 80
  on General Butler's insulting order about
    Confederate women, 66
  General Pierre G. T. Beauregard and, 46
  George W. Bagby, Jr. and, 511–12
  on Glendale battle, 69–70
  on Henry Timrod, 172–73, 177–78
  injury of, 17
  James Gordon Bennett and, 47, 49–50
  on James River skirmishes, 51–52
  James Roddy Sneed and, 346
  on Kinston, North Carolina, 79

  on Lookout Mountain and Missionary
    Ridge, 83–86
  loyalty to the South, 50
  marriage to Georgia Vigneron Moore, 83
  on Memphis naval battle, 66
  newspapers using his work, 51
  New York Evening Telegram and, 91
  New York Herald and, 25, 47–48, 177
  New York Times on, 19, 51, 90
  parents of, 46
  portrait of, *46*
  Progress editor on, 79–80
  pseudonyms of, 51, 163
  reissued writings of, 91
  on repulse of Federals at Bethel Church, 52
  rescue of abandoned Confederate
    papers, 89
  on Richmond, January 23, 1863, 80
  on rumor, 55
  salary of during the Civil War, 50–51
  on scavenging for food, 74–75
  on Second Battle of Manassas, 75–76
  on Seven Days Campaign, 70–71
  on Seven Pines battle, 69
  on Sharpsburg battle, 77–79
  on shelling of Fort McAllister, 82
  on Shepherdstown, Virginia, 79
  on Shiloh Church battle, 62–63
  on South Carolina's secession, 50
  South Carolinian and, 86, 90, 172, 174, 175,
    177
  on South Mountain battle, 76–77
  on strengthening of Confederate money, 88
  on the war and religion, 72
  William Gilmore Simms on, 46
  writing style of, 12, 19–20, 51, 74
de Fontaine, Georgia (Schuyler), 94
de Fontaine, Wade Hampton, 90
de Gournay, Francis F., 603 *table*
Delaware College, 487
DeLeon, Edwin, 230
D. Ellis, a schooner, 306
DeMorse, Charles
  on Abraham Lincoln, 416
  accuracy of his reports, 413, 414, 454
  on accuracy of Telegraphic Dispatches, 413
  at Battle at Elk Creek, 428–29, 670 *note* 105
  on Battle of Cabin Creek, 431–34

on Battle of Gaines Mill, 422

birthplace of, 414

on Choctaw Indians, 429

civil career after the war, 434–35

Clarksville Standard and, 408, 409, 411, 415

on Confederate self-sufficiency, 422–23

criticism of the Confederacy, 419–21

death of, 435

"Democracy and Disunion"editorial, 416

demographic data on, 604 *table*

desertion and, 430

disagreement with General Samuel Bell
 Maxey, 424

early careers of, 414–15

education of, 4, 414

enlistment drive of, 417–18, 668 *note* 57

establishing the 29th Texas Cavalry,
 409–10, 419–23

feud with General Richard Gano, 414

on Fort Arbuckle, 423–24, 426

on Fort Arbuckle region, 412–13

on the Fugitive Slave Law, 416

on Indian allies of the Confederacy,
 424–26, 427–28, 429

on Indian allies of the Union, 426–27

on John Breckenridge for president, 416

on just and moral cause for the war, 417

marriage to Lodiska Wooldridge, 415

on the Missouri Compromise, 416

on the need for Texas wool, 423

original reporting and, 408

patriotic declaration of, 409

on the Peninsula Campaign, 421–22

Perryville retreat and, 429

personality and personal interests of, 412

portrait of, *410*

position on secession, 415, 416–17, 667 *note*
 39, 668 *note* 42

profession of, 4

pseudonyms of, 411–12

on regiment moved to Camp Butler, 426

on skirmishes around Fort Gibson, 426–28

on the slaughter of the 1st Kansas Colored,
 433

on slavery, 415

supporting the Pearce Compromise Bill,
 415

as typical frontier editor, 414

on Union capture of New Orleans, 418–19

on victory at Poison Spring, Arkansas,
 430–31

wounding of, 429

writing style of, 412, 413

DePass, W. L., 38–40, 41–42

desertion

 Charles DeMorse and, 413, 430

 Felix Gregory de Fontaine on, 88

 George William Bagby, Jr. on, 503

 Henry H. Perry on, 403

 Henry Timrod on, 170

 James Beverley Sener on execution of
  deserters, 528–29

 William P. Doran on, 438–39, 440

Diadem, a schooner, 306

Die Charlestoner Zeitung, 91

Dill, America, 546

Dill, Benjamin F., 238, 244, 246, 546

Doran, William P.

 accuracy of his writing, 439, 454

 accused of being an abolitionist, 441–42

 on Battle of Corinth, 446–47

 on Battle of Shiloh, 445–46

 children of, 452

 on conditions in Texas in 1864, 449–52

 criticism of the Confederacy, 440–41

 demographic data on, 604 *table*

 on desertion, 438–39, 440

 enlistment in Co. A of Capt. Christian, 445

 enlistment in the Galveston Rifles
  Company, 442

 establishing *The Freeman's Champion*, 452

 Galveston News and, 436, 438, 442

 on health and well-being of Confederate
  troops, 440, 441–42, 445, 446, 447, 451

 heroism and devotion to the Confederate
  cause, 438

 Houston Tri-Weekly Telegraph and, 436,
  438

 ideology and sympathies of, 441

 invasion of Texas at the Sabine Pass, *407*,
  414, 436–38

 letter from Galveston, January 10, 1862, 444

 marriage to Sallie M. Linsicum, 452

 name-dropping and, 443

 on operation to regain Galveston, 448–49,
  452

Doran, William P. (*continued*)
  original reporting and, 408
  patriotic rhetoric of, 439–40, 441, 444, 445
  portrait of, *437*
  on pro-Union sentiments in Texas, 443
  pseudonym of, 438
  purple prose and, 439
  quality and importance of his reporting,
    452
  recruiting calls of, 444, 445
  Red River campaign and, 449, *450*
  on retreat from Corinth, 447
  as roving state news reporter, 449–52
  Union capture of, 436
  on Union prisoners, 449
  on Union troops, 446
  Willard Richardson on, 452
  wounding of, 447, 673 *note* 48
  writing style of, 438, 439–40
Douglas, James P.
  1st Texas Battery (Douglas Battery) and,
    455–57, 461–62
  accuracy of his reports, 454
  on accuracy of news accounts, 454
  on the Battle of Elkhorn Tavern, 457–61
  business career of, 463
  on Choctaw and Chickasaw Indians, 456
  Dallas Herald on, 456
  date and birthplace of, 455
  death and burial place of, 464
  on the death of General Benjamin
    McCulloch, 458–59
  on the death of General Macintosh, 458, 459
  demographic data on, 604 *table*
  education of, 455
  on General Earl Van Dorn, 459
  loss of his correspondence, 455
  marriage to Alice Earle Smith, 464
  marriage to Sallie Susan White, 463
  as member of the 12th Senate of Texas, 462
  military ranks of, 455
  original reporting and, 408
  portrait of, *454, 464*
  purple prose of, 460
  on retreat from Elkhorn Tavern, 460–61
  romanticizing battle, 461
  Rutherford Douglas on, 462, 463
  Tyler Reporter and, 408, 414, 453, 455
  Union spy story of, 453

Douglas, Rutherford, 462, 463
Douglas, Stephen A., 206, 207
Douglas Battery. *See* 1st Texas Battery
  (Douglas Battery)
Drewry's Bluff, 269, 292–93
Duggan, Ivy W., 17
Durant, Cornelia (Da Ponte), 381
Duryea Zouaves, 75
Dwinell, Melvin, 8
Dylan, Bob, 26, 160, 178

Earle, Captain W. E., 38
Elk Creek, Battle of, 410, *411*, 428–29, 670
  note 105
Elkhorn Tavern, Battle of, 457–61
Elliott, Captain George P., 40
"E.L. McE.": a Southern woman
  correspondent, 7–8
Emory, General William H., 436
Encyclopedia of Military History, 114
Enquirer (Columbus, Georgia), 52, 365
Etta Caroline, a fishing schooner, 306
Eubank, Captain John L., 531
European recognition of the Confederacy,
  216, 221, 232, 233, 404–5, 498–99
Ewell, General Richard S., 533
Ewin, Rebecca (Watterson), 582
Express, 487

Fahs, Alice, 467–68
"Farewell to Savannah" (Sneed), 361
Farmington, Battle of, 166–70
Faro Industrial, 363
Farragut, Admiral David, 390
Faust, Drew Gilpin on prosperity of the
  American nation, 421
Federal and Confederate pickets exchange
  newspapers in the Rappahannock, *81*
*The Fireside Dickens: A Cyclopaedia of the
  Best Thoughts of Charles Dickens* (de
  Fontaine), 91
Flag of Truce, a steamer, 405
Flash, Henry Lynden, 493
Florida
  as breadbasket for the Confederacy, 180
  secession of, 143, 179–80
  See also Fort Pickens, Florida; Pensacola,
    Florida
Flournoy, J. G., 604 *table*

Floyd, General John, 62

The Foreign Slave Trade: the Source of Political Power and of Material Social Integrity, and Social Emancipation to the South (Spratt), 142

Forrest, General Nathan, 62

Forsyth, Charles, 208

Forsyth, John
  appointed local postmaster, 205
  on battles at Harrodsburg, 211–12
  on Black Republicans, 206–7
  on "Bragg's Army Register," 210
  calling for secession, 208
  children of, 204
  Columbus (Georgia) *Times* and, 202
  date and place of birth, 203
  death of, 215
  on the "Democratic faith," 206
  demographic data on, 602 *table*
  describing Confederate troop positions in Kentucky, 210
  education of, 204
  elected state legislator, 215
  Federal capture of, 210
  General Braxton Bragg and, 208–10, 212–14
  Henry Hotze and, 218
  influence of, 203
  on Kentuckians, 211, 213
  legal career of, 204–5
  loyalty to the Democratic Party, 206, 215
  marriage to Margaret Hull, 204
  as mayor of Mobile, 208
  as minister to Mexico, 207
  Mobile Commercial Register and Patriot and, 205, 206, 214
  portrait of, *204*
  praise for, 215
  purchase of the *Columbus Times*, 205
  rebuking Kentucky Provisional Governor Richard Hawes, 214
  Samuel Chester Reid, Jr. and, 259
  sectional diatribes of, 207
  his stance on Reconstruction, 215
  support for Stephen A. Douglas, 206, 207, 208
  support of slavery, 207, 208
  as an Ultraist in the Southern Rights Party, 205

"Virginia" and, 560
  as a war correspondent, 208–13

Forsyth, John III, 208

Forsyth, John (Senior), 203

Forsyth, Robert, 203

Fort Arbuckle, Texas, 412–13, *412*, 423–24

Fort Barrancas, Florida, 181, 182, *183*

Fort Donelson, Battle of, 62, 77, 167, 322

Fort Fisher, bombardment of, 339

Fort McAllister, shelling of, 82

Fort McRee, Florida, 182

Fort Pickens, Florida, *179, 183, 184, 185, 187, 396*
  Albert Richardson on, 186
  General Braxton Bragg and, 180, 183
  importance of, 181–82
  Jefferson Davis on attack of, 192
  Lawrence H. Mathews and, 180
  as a prison, 194

Fort Pickens truce, 180, 182

Fort Powhatan capture, 292

Fort Pulaski, Savannah, Georgia, 125, 348–49, *348*

Fortress Monroe, 384–85, *385*

Fort Sumter, South Carolina, *25, 47, 84, 133, 136*
  Bartholomew Riordan on, 132–33
  Felix Gregory de Fontaine on, 45–46
  James Roddy Sneed on, 342–44, 354
  William Seward and, 208

Fourteen Months in American Bastilles (Howard), 234

Fourth South Carolina regiment working in the trenches at night, *54*

Fowle, Lieutenant Colonel Daniel G., 290

Fox-Genovese, Elizabeth on female authorship, 104

Francis, Julie Anna (Courtenay), 42

Frank Leslie's Illustrated Newspaper, 81, 95, 99, 375

Fredericksburg, Battle of, 80, 332–33, 516–20, *519, 540*

Fredericksburg, Virginia, 513, *515*

Fredericksburg Ledger, 541

Fredericksburg Democratic Recorder, 514

freedom of the press defense, 95, 97–99

The Freeman's Champion, 452

Free Soil Know-Nothings, 206

Fugitive Slave Law, 416

Gadsden Times, 195

Gaines Mill, Battle of, 422

Galbreath, W. B., 604 *table*

Gallagher, Gary, 598

Galveston News, 408, 436, 438, 442, 480

Galveston Weekly News, 478, 479

Gano, General Richard, 414, 424, 432

Garland, Colonel Robert R., 467

Garland, Hudson, 487

Garmon, Gerald, 544

Garner, Geo. G., 287

Garnett, General Robert S., 151

General Order No. 98, 285

General Orders No. 158, 287

Georgia, secession of, 311

   See also Atlanta, Georgia

Gettysburg, Battle of, 334–36, *334, 335*

Gibbes, Elizabeth Guignard, 101

Gibbes, Mary Phillip Wilson, 97

Gibbes, Robert W., Jr.

   copyright of news stories, 100–101

   death and burial place of, 103

   death of his wife, Carolina Elizabeth

     Guignard Gibbes, 101

   defense of freedom of the press, 95, 97–99

   demographic data on, 603 *table*

   destruction of Columbia, South Carolina

     and, 101–3

   education of, 97

   Frank Leslie's Illustrated Newspaper on,

     95, 99

   letter to Congress on power of the press, 86

   ownership of newspapers, 97, 101

   Palmetto-State Banner and, 97

   portrait of, *96*

   Press Association of the Confederate States

     of America and, 26, 81, 86, 95, 100

   scientific writings of, 97

   South Carolina Press Association and,

     95, 97

   South Carolinian and, 97, 101

   as student at South Carolina College, 97

   as surgeon general of South Carolina, 86

   William Gilmore Simms on, 97

Gibbes, William Hasell, 97

Gilbert, R. R.

   accuracy of his reporting, 471–73, 474

   acknowledging Southern losses and

     retreats, 473

   on Alexandria prison exchange, 475

   Austin Statesman and, 480

   biographical information on, 86, 468–69

   children of, 476

   collected humor of, 480

   on Colonel Robert R. Garland, 467

   his concern for maimed Confederate

     soldiers, 476

   on men shirking enlistment, 473

   on consequences of the fall of Vicksburg,

     471

   contents of his reports, 471, 479

   criticism of Confederate soldiers, 473

   date and place of birth, 468

   death and burial place of, 480, 676 *note* 15

   demographic data on, 604 *table*

   Edward Hopkins Cushing and, 408, 466,

     467, 469, 470

   enlistment in Company B, 6th Texas

     Infantry, 469, 677 *note* 28

   establishing the *Brazos Eagle*, 479

   establishing the *Central Journal*, 479

   establishing the *Crockett Journal*, 479

   establishing the *New South*, 480

   establishing the *Palestine News*, 479

   establishing the *Texas Tidings*, 480

   establishing the *Texas Weekly Record*, 478

   on the failures of the Confederacy, 476–77

   full name of, 465, 676 *note* 14

   Galveston Weekly News on, 478

   Houston Tri-Weekly Telegraph and, 465,

     466, 476, 478–79

   on John S. C. Abbott, 469–70

   lampooning gubernatorial candidates,

     474–75

   lampooning Southern society, 474

   lampooning the Union Army, 474

   letter to his Northern relatives, 468

   marriage to Louella Lyon, 475–76

   on mistreatment of Confederate soldiers,

     465

   on the "negro question," 477

   original reporting and, 408

   as a physician, 468, 473

   popularity of, 469, 470

   portrait of, *466*

   on postwar uncertainties, 477

   postwar years of, 478–80

   on press censorship, 473

prolificacy of, 470
pseudonym of, 408, 467, 468
on rumor as news, 472
on Texas hotels, 479
Tyler Journal on, 475–76
his use of humor, 467–68, 469, 474–75
West Texas Star and, 479
his "The Yankee President" song, 469
Gleaner, an English schooner, 437
Glenavron, a ship, 305
Glendale, battle of, 69–70
Glory, a movie, 355
Golden Rod, a Baltimore schooner, 297, 298
Goodwin, Katie (Timrod), 162, 173
Gorman, A. M., 104
Gracie, General Archibald, 269
Grady, Henry, 573
Graeme, John, 350
Grant, General Ulysses S.
    Battle of Spotsylvania, 533–34
    Battle of the Wilderness, 533
    Durant da Ponte and, 392
    James Beverley Sener on, 536–37
    Petersburg battles, 535–40
    William Wallace Screws on, 271
Greeley, Horace, 142, 375
Greenhow, Rose, 13
Greer, Colonel Elkanah, 455
Greg, Percy, 230
Gregg, General Maxcy, 158
Grey, Jane Swisshelm, 104
Guignard, Carolina Elizabeth (Gibbes), 101
Guntersville Democrat, 196

H. A. correspondent, 408
Hagood, General Johnson, 269
Halleck, General Henry Wager, 170, 255, 403
Halpine, Charles Graham, 3
Hamilton, Hanse Van, 455
Hanson, Major H. T., 339
Hardee, Charles Seton, 361
Hardee, General William J., 325, 337, 358, 585
Hardeeville, South Carolina, 39, 40–41
Harper's, 81, 487, 490, 545
Harper's Monthly, 572
Harris, Isham, 588, 695 *note* 111
Harris, Jacob, 206
Hatcher, John E., 603 *table*
Hathaway, John R., 562

Hawes, Richard, 214
Hay, Anna Maria (Sneed), 342
Hayes, John E., 359–60
Hayne, Paul H., 161, 162, 171, 174–75, 176, 493, 545
Heckman, General Charles, 269
Henderson Times, 456
Henley, Robert H., 195
"Heroic Deeds of Heroic Men" (Abbott), 469
Heron, Ann, 564
Hill, Adams Sherman, 3
Hill, Benjamin H., 11, 315
A History of the Florentine Republic and of the Age of Rule of the Medici (Da Ponte), 381
History of the Spanish-American War (Watterson), 595
Hobson, Elizabeth, 486
Hoke, General Robert Frederick, 269
Holden, William W., 270, 503–4, 532
Holt, Emily Frances (Screws), 272
Honey Springs, Battle of. *See* Elk Creek, Battle of
Hood, General John Bell, 75, 590, 593
Hooker, General Joseph, 2, 70, 520–21, 522, 523, 533
Hopkins, Major Henry, 433
Hotze, Henry
    on army life, 220
    as Confederate propaganda agent in London, 221–27
    his contribution to the Confederacy, 202
    criticism of, 235
    date and place of birth, 217
    death and burial place of, 237
    demographic data on, 602 *table*
    education of, 217
    on English sentiment toward the Confederacy, 224
    on European recognition of Confederacy, 216, 221
    immigration and naturalization of, 217
    on importance of the border states, 226
    The Index and, 216–17, 227–37
    on James Spence, 226
    John Forsyth and, 218
    journal entries aboard the *St. Nicholas*, 219
    Judah P. Benjamin and, 221, 228, 229, 231, 233, 234, 235
    Leroy Pope Walker and, 218, 220

Hotze, Henry (*continued*)
  in London, October, 1861, 220
  on Lord Campbell, 226
  military career of, 219–21
  Mobile Advertiser and Register and, 218, 219
  Mobile Cadets and, 219
  pamphleteering of, 234–35
  plan to seize the transport ship *Illinois*, 218
  portrait of, *217*
  propaganda plan of, 220–21
  pseudonym of, 219
  reputation of, 216
  R. M. T. Hunter and, 221–22, 227
  as secretary of the U.S. Legation at Brussels, 217–18
  as secretary to the Mobile Board of Harbor Commissioners, 218
  on the Southern press, 227
  on Thurlow Weed, 224
  travel observations of, 220
  his use of symbols, 233-234
Hotze, Rudolph, 217
Houghton Mifflin, 178
Houston, Sam, 365
Houston Daily Telegraph, 451
Houston Telegraph, 408, 452, 456, 480
Houston Tri-Weekly Telegraph
  Edward Hopkins Cushing and, 409
  R. R. Gilbert and, 465, 466
  William F. Doran and, 436, 438
Howard, a schooner, 306
Howell, A. D., 196
Hull, Margaret (Forsyth), 204
Humboldt, Alexander, 364
Humphreys, W. W., 8
Hunter, R. M. T., 221–22, 227
Huntsville (Texas) *Item*, 472
Huntsville Confederate, 245–46

Independence, a schooner, 414
Independent, 195
The Index, a newspaper
  appearance and contents of, 229, 233
  blockade statistics and, 233
  circulation figures for, 231
  as Confederacy's main propaganda tool abroad, 235
  cost to produce, 231

  criticism of, 230, 235
  date of first issue, 228
  Edwin DeLeon on, 230, 231
  on European recognition of Confederacy, 232, 233
  final edition of, 235
  funding of, 216, 228, 230
  John R. Thompson and, 554
  praise for, 216
  price of, 228
  purpose of, 227–28
  significance of name of, 228
  stable writers for, 230–31
  subtitle of, 228
  support for, 234, 235
  value of, 231
  See also Hotze, Henry
the Indian Territory region, 423, 670 *note* 90

Jackson, Andrew, 205, 551
Jackson, General Thomas "Stonewall"
  in camp, *156*
  death of, 292, 334, 521, 523–24, 533
  legend of, 155–56
  Leonidas William Spratt and, 26
  portrait of, *142*
James L. Littlefield, a schooner, 305
Jenkins, Donelson Caffrey, 603 *table*
Joan
  on Abraham Lincoln, 124
  on accommodation of soldiers in Richmond, 119
  advocating for hospital reform, 118–19
  on Alexander Stephens, 111
  attitude toward the war, 112–13
  in camp with her son, 117–18
  on casualty numbers, 114
  censorship and, 123–24
  Charleston Courier and, 25, 105, 106–7, 110, 561
  clues to her place of residence, 107–8
  color stories of, 115–17
  compared to "Virginia," 558, 561, 567
  on Confederate leaders, 111
  demographic data on, 602 *table*
  diatribes of, 561
  on fall of Fort Pulaski, 125
  on First Manassas, 114–15
  hatred of the Yankees, 113, 116–17

importance of her work, 7, 106, 110–11, 125–26

on Jefferson Davis, 111–12

Mason plantation story, 118

military skirmishes and, 114

motive for writing, 107

news stories of, 120–21

nickname of, 112

her "an old negro" story, 115

on Northern journalism, 125

personal opinion and, 115

on the power of the newspaper press, 23, 125

rigid social standards of, 109–10

on sobriety of Confederate troops, 109

Southern yeomen and, 5, 108

topics of, 120, 123

trip to Fairfax from Richmond, 116–18

uniqueness of, 104, 105–6

on women, 121–23

Johnston, General Albert Sidney, 62, 63, 415, 445

Johnston, General Joseph E.

  banning reporters from his army, 15, 285, 346, 348, 552

  death of, 62, 361

  his General Orders No. 98, 285, 286, 322

  James Roddy Sneed and, 346–48

  John S. Thrasher and, 371

  portrait of, *283*

  relieved of his command, 590

  retreat to Centreville, 399–400

  on sutlers, 282

  William G. Shepardson and, 61, 202, 276, 284–85

Johnston, Thomas, 273

Jones, Doctor C. A., 520

Jones, Thomas, 274–75

Jones, William S., 22

Jones Valley Times, 195

Jordan, Thomas, 496

Josiah Achom, a schooner, 306

journalism and women, 104–5

Judah, a ship, 192

Kansas-Nebraska Act of 1854, 206

"Katie" (Timrod), 178

Kaufman Democrat, 408, 456

Kearny, General Philip, 70

Ketchum, John H., 196

Kibby, Epapheas, 205

Kirk, Charles D., 604 *table*

Knickerbocker, 545

Knightley, Phillip, 17

"knights of the quill," use of term, 4 -5

LaGrange (Georgia) *Reporter*, 312

Lancaster, John, 408

"L": a Southern war correspondent, 17

Latham, G. Woodville, 487

Lee, General Robert E.

  Battle of Cold Harbor, 534–35

  Battle of Spotsylvania, 533–34

  censorship and, 15

  on death of General "Stonewall" Jackson, 524

  Fort Pulaski and, 348–49

  George W. Bagby, Jr. on, 483, 501–2, 507–8

  James Beverley Sener on, 530

  John R. Thompson on, 549– 50

  Petersburg battles, 535–40

  Peter W. Alexander on, 332

  surrender of, 235

  war strategy of, 327–28

  William G. Shepardson on, 291–92

Leesburg, Battle of, 280–82

"Lee to the Rear" (Thompson), 549

Leopard, a schooner, 306

LePrince, Sergeant Julius page, 40–41

The Life and Times of Aaron Burr, a Vindication (Reid), 249

Lincoln, Abraham

  Charles DeMorse on, 416

  Henry Watterson on, 574–75, 579–80

  Joan on, 124

Linebaugh, John

  arrest of, 202, 209, 243–45

  his concern for Charleston, South Carolina, 242–43, *242*

  criticism of, 241, 246

  death of, 238, 246

  deficiencies in reporting, 240, 241, 246

  demographic data on, 604 *table*

  as an Episcopal priest, 239–40

  General Braxton Bragg and, 202, 209, 243, 244

  journalistic inexperience of, 238–39

  Memphis Daily Appeal and, 238–39, 240, 243–45, 246

Linebaugh, John (*continued*)
  obituary of, 246
  professions of, 4, 239
  pseudonym of, 202, 240–41
  writing style of, 241, 246
Linsicum, Sallie M. (Doran), 452
Lloyd, Catherine, 178
Locke, David Ross, 469
London Times, 227, 526–27
Long Bridge, Alexandria, Virginia, *130*
Longfellow, Henry W. on Henry Timrod, 178
Longstreet, General James, 76, *159*, 533
Lookout Mountain, Battle of, 83–86, *569*, *581*,
  584, 585
Loughery, Robert, 409
Louisiana
  date of secession, 377
  effect of the Civil War on, 377–78
  fall of New Orleans, 378
  number of Louisiana troops in
    Confederacy, 397
  soldier resting in a Louisiana swamp, *377*
Louisville Courier-Journal, 572, 594, 595
Loyal Georgian, 359
Luce, Colonel W. A., 520
Lynchburg Daily Virginian, 487
Lyon, Louella (Gilbert), 475–76

MacDonnell, Richard Graves, 307
Macintosh, General James M., 458, 459
Macon Daily Telegraph, 360
Macon Telegraph, 9, 366
Macon Telegraph and Confederate, 493
Macon Telegraph and Messenger, 339, 340
Magnolia, a schooner, 306
Magruder, General John B., 392, 436, 437, 469
Mahone, General William, 530
Mallory, Lee, 292
Manassas, First Battle of, *153*
  casualty figures for, 404
  effect of, 319
  Henry H. Perry on, 398–99, 403
  Joan on, 114–15
  Peter W. Alexander on, 317–18
  William G. Shepardson and, 277
Manassas, Second Battle of
  dates of, 419
  effect of, 327
  Felix Gregory de Fontaine on,

General Robert E. Lee and. 332, 419
  Peter W. Alexander on, 313
Mann, A. Dudley, 220
*Marginalia, or Gleanings from an Army Note-
  book* (de Fontaine), 19, 49, 86, 88, 91
Marietta, Battle of, 588–89
Marks, Colonel Sam, 254
'Marse Henry': An Autobiography,
  (Watterson), 595
Marshall, John, 422
Mary A. Howes, a schooner, 306
Mason, Charles, 73
Mason, James M., 60, 222, 223, 231, *232*, 319
  See also Trent Affair
Mathews, Lawrence H.
  Albert Richardson on arrest of, 186, 188
  arrest and acquittal of, 180, 186–90,
    208–9
  criticism of, 195, 196, 198
  date and place of birth, 181
  death of, 198
  on demise of *Mineral Age*, 197
  demographic data on, 602 *table*
  establishing the *Blount County News and
    Dispatch*, 196–97, 198, 636 *note* 56
  establishing the *Blount Springs News*, 196
  on Fort Pickens, 180, 184–86
  Gunterville Democrat on, 196
  interview with the *Memphis Appeal*,
    190–91
  on his Irish heritage, 199
  John Mitchel and, 191, 635 *note* 128
  letter to Confederate Secretary of War
    Leroy Pope Walker, 186–88
  Mark E. Neely, Jr. on, 190
  military service of, 194–95
  on the Pensacola Guards, 192
  praise for, 197, 198
  pseudonym of, 186
  purchase of the *Birmingham Sun*, 195
  Southern Aegis on, 197
  on victory at Fairfax Courthouse, 192
Matthews, William B., 484–85
Maxey, General Samuel Bell, 424, 431
McClanahan, John Reid, 238, 246, 546
McClellan, General George B., 76, 319, 537
McCord, Louisa S., 104–5
 ⋯lloch, General Benjamin, 458–59, 672
             ⋯5

McDowell, General Irvin, 319

McJunkin, C. M., 8

McKeen, Captain A. C., 442

McKinstry, Colonel Alexander, 246

McLaughlin, Thomas A., 195

McLaws, General Lafayette, 78, 335

McPherson, James, 414

Meade, General George G., 293, 530

Meigs, Clara (Forsyth), 203

Memminger, Christopher G., 88, *218*, 420, 669 *note* 66

Memphis, Tennessee, March 1862, *401*

Memphis Appeal
  Battle of Shiloh report, 8–9
  Henry H. Perry and, 406
  Henry Watterson and, 570
  interview with Lawrence H. Mathews, 190–91
  on a newspaper's rights and responsibilities, 6
  wartime difficulties of, 569

Memphis Daily Appeal
  George W. Bagby, Jr. and, 554
  Henry H. Perry and, 378, 395, 396, 406
  John H. Linebaugh and, 202, 238, 243–45, 246
  John R. Thompson and, 482, 543, 545, 546, 547, 548, 549–50, 553, 554
  persistence of, 547
  present day name of, 546
  quality and design of, 547
  on release of John S. Thrasher, 378
  Samuel Chester Reid, Jr. and, 261

Memphis Eagle and Enquirer, 490

Menard, Menard Doswell, 365

Menard, Michel B., 364

Menard, Rebecca Mary Bass (Thrasher), 364–65

Merrimac, destruction of, 65

"The Midnight Ride" (Shepardson), 277

Mills House Hotel in 1865, *137*

Milton, John, 179

Mineral Age, 197

Missionary Ridge, Battle of, 83–85, 336–37, 461, *462*, 584, 585

Mississippians practice with the Bowie knife, *56*

Mitchell, General John G., 259–60

Mitchel, John, 191, 635 *note* 128

Mobile (Alabama) Daily Advertiser and Register, 572

Mobile Advertiser and Chronicle, 205

Mobile Advertiser and Register
  George W. Bagby, Jr. and, 497, 508–9
  Henry Hotze and, 218, 219
  Henry Watterson and, 240
  John Forsyth and, 202, 203, 259
  Peter W. Alexander and, 339, 528
  Samuel Chester Reid, Jr. and, 256, 258, 259
  "Virginia" and, 556, 565
  William G. Shepardson and, 276

Mobile Cadets, 219

Mobile Commercial Register and Patriot, 205, 206

Mobile Daily Advertiser and Register, 261

Mobile Daily News, 215

Mobile Daily Tribune, 259

Modern Times (Dylan), 26, 160, 178

Monroe, John T., 390

Montgomery Advertiser, 189, 208, 265, 268, 271–72, 277, 583

Montgomery Journal, 198

Montgomery Mail, 572, 593

Moore, Clement, 381

Moore, Georgia Vigneron (de Fontaine), 83, 94

Moore, John V., 83

Morehouse, Major Edwin, 414

Morning Herald, 227

Morning Post, 224, 227

Morse, Nathan S., 16, 503, 504

"A Mother's Wail" (Timrod), 175, 178

Moving Appeal. See *Memphis Appeal*

Munson's Hill, October 5, 1861, *31*

Mutual Benefit Association, 365

Nacogdoches Chronicle, 456

"Names of the Months Phonetically Expressive" (Timrod), 173

Nashville (Tennessee) *Union and American*, 11

Nashville, Tennessee, 62, *576*

Nashville American, 574

Nashville Banner, 572

Nashville Union, 573

Nashville Union and American, 497

Native Americans and Confederate law, 424

Native Virginian, 511

Neely, Mark E., Jr., 190

Neva, a brig, 307

Nevins, Allan, 554
Newbern, North Carolina, 299
"Newbern expedition," 299–301
New Era, 574
New Orleans, Battle of, 390–91, *390*, *391*
New Orleans Crescent, 378, 381, 490
New Orleans Daily Delta
    Bartholomew Riordan and, 128
    Durant da Ponte and, 378, 379, 381, 382, 387
    on Fort Pickens, 184–86
    L. H. Mathews and, 184–86
    shutdown of, 392
New Orleans Daily Picayune, 378, 396, 401, 403
New Orleans Picayune
    Bartholomew Riordan and, 128
    Henry H. Perry and, 395
    lost records of, 396
    Samuel Chester Reid, Jr. and, 202, 249, 260
New Orleans Sunday Delta, 487
News and Courier, 127, 136, 137
New South, 480
newspapers, importance of, 22–23
New York Associated Press, 81
New York Evening Telegram, 91
New York Herald, 50, 115, 206, 285, 304, 364, 384, 527, 599
New York Post, 544, 554
New York Times, 19, 51, 273, 361, 364, 499, 542, 573, 574
New York Tribune, 186, 188
Norfork, Virginia, 556–57, *557*, *558*, *567*
Norfork Day Book, 562
Norfork Naval Hospital, 564
North Carolina peace movement, 504, 532
Noticioso de Nuevo York, 364

"Ode" (Timrod), 175–76
The Old Men's Regiment, 353
"The Old Virginia Gentleman" (Bagby), 511
Osterhout, John, 409
"Our Willie" (Timrod), 175, 178
Overall, Edwin E., 479
Owsley, Frank L., 222

Palestine News, 479
Palmer, James W., 195
Palmetto-State Banner, 97
Palmetto State Song, 146, *146*

Parham, Louis L., 583, 584, 694 *note* 60, 695 *note* 94
Patterson, General Robert, 151
Patton, John S., 544
Paul, Francis M., 578, 585
pay and benefits of war correspondents, 10–11
P. C. Alexander, a schooner, 306
Peabody Educational Trust, 42
Pearce, George on Jefferson Davis, 192
Pearce Compromise Bill, 415
Pearl, a schooner, 306
Pemberton, General John C., 371, 508
Peninsula Campaign, 421–22
Pensacola, Florida
    attack on Confederate navy dry dock, 192, *193*
    Confederate troop pullout, 193–94
    Federal occupation of, 194
    importance of, 180–82
Pensacola Guards, 192
Pensacola Observer, 180, 181, 191
Perkins, John R., 196
Perry, Henry H.
    accuracy of his reports, 397–98
    on Battle of Roanoke Island, 400–401
    on Battle of Shiloh, 402
    demographic data on, 603 *table*
    description of Louisiana troops, 397
    on desertion, 403
    effect of his writing, 406
    elusiveness of, 395–96
    on European recognition of Confederacy, 401–2, 404–5
    on First Battle of Manassas, 398–99
    on Louisiana troop movements, 395, 396
    Memphis Appeal and, 66, 406
    Memphis Daily Appeal and, 395, 396, 406
    multiple topic dispatches, 405
    New Orleans Daily Picayune and, 66, 378, 395, 396
    on picket fighting, 404
    pseudonym of, 378, 395
    quantity and quality of his writing, 405–6
    on retreat from Centreville, 400
    on Union soldiers and generals, 399, 403–4
    on the Washington Artillery, 398
    writing style of, 378, 397, 398
Perryville, Battle of, *209*

Petersburg (Virginia), siege of, 338–39
Petersburg, siege of, 535–40
Pickens, Governor Francis W., 143, 495
picket fighting, 404
Pickett, General George, 299–300, 335
Pierce, Franklin, 207
Pillow, General Gideon Johnson, 62
Pinkney, John Bell, 604 *table*
Pleasants, John Hampden, 487
Poe, Edgar Allan, 545, 562
Poets and Poetry of the South (Thompson), 555
Poison Spring, Battle of, 410, 430–31
political reporting in the South, 502
Polk, General James H., 205, 586, *587*, 588–89
Pope, General John, 169
Port, General David, 390
Post and Courier, 127
    See also *Charleston Courier*
Powell, James R., 195
Press Association of the Confederate States of America
    Article No. 8 of its constitution, 367
    Bartholomew Riordan and, 26, 132
    Benjamin and America Dill and, 546
    censorship and, 372–73
    "code of the instructions" of, 367
    conscription of journalists and, 86
    copyright of news stories, 312
    creation of, 6–7, 351, 365–66, 546
    General Braxton Bragg and, 267
    general rules for telegraphic press reports of, 368–71
    headquarters of, 366, 660 *note* 25
    John Reid McClanahan and, 546
    John S. Thrasher and, 81–82, 312, 351, 366–73
    Joseph Clisby and, 366
    membership in, 366
    professional standards of, 368
    Robert W. Gibbes and, 26, 81, 86, 95, 100
    sale of its news dispatches, 373–74
    staffing of, 366, 368
press culture in the antebellum and Civil War South, 5–6
press restrictions in the Confederacy, 12–17
    Charleston Mercury and, 16–17
    civilian tolerance for dissent and, 13
    of General Braxton Bragg, 15, 372

of General Earl Van Dorn, 15
of General Joseph E. Johnston, 15, 61, 62
of General Pierre G. T. Beauregard, 325
General Robert E. Lee on, 15
Jefferson Davis on, 12–13, 15
John S. Thrasher on, 12, 15–16
military secrets and, 13–14
rules of military conduct and, 15
Secretary of War Leroy Walker on, 14
telegraphic restrictions of news, 12, 59
    See also censorship
Price, General Sterling, 211, 446
Price, W. P., 8
Prince, Thyrza E. (Timrod), 160
Printers Union, 360–61
Pritchard, William H., Jr., 349–50
Pritchard, William, Sr., 365
Progress, 79
propaganda and Confederate correspondents, 5, 598
Pryor, General Roger A., 75, 217
Purvis, George E., 594, 603 *table*

Quitman, General John A., 247, 249

Raleigh (North Carolina) Daily Register, 543
Raleigh (North Carolina) *Standard*, 13
Raleigh Standard, 503
Randall, James Ryder on Henry Timrod, 170
Randolph, George W. (Confederate Secretary of War), 15, 332, 409
Raymond, Henry J., 3
Reagan, Postmaster General John, 506
Reid, Samuel Chester, Jr.
    accuracy of his reporting, 249–50, 251–52, 255, 263
    age of at the time of enlistment, 202
    Atlantic Monthly and, 252
    authorship of, 248–49
    battles witnessed by, 250
    careers of, 247
    censorship and, 254–55, 258–59, 261
    criticism of, 253–54, 259
    date and place of birth, 247
    death of, 264
    demographic data on, 602 *table*
    entrepreneurial skills of, 261–62
    on Federal advance near Corinth, Mississippi, 1862, 260–61

Reid, Samuel Chester, Jr. (*continued*)
General Braxton Bragg and, 257–59
on General George Beal, 253–54
on General John G. Mitchell's attack on
Chattanooga, 259–60
General Pierre G. T. Beauregard and,
256–57, 325
legal studies of, 247
marriage to Josephine Bowen, 264
New Orleans Picayune and, 249, 261
newspapers he worked for, 249, 261
on number of enemy forces in the South,
256
optimism of, 254
portrait of, *248*
postwar career of, 264
pseudonyms of, 249
report from Cumberland Gap, 258–59
on spies, 252, *253*, 262
as a Texas Ranger, 247–49, 254
his use of humor, 250
writing style of, 255, 260–63
Reid, Samuel G., 265, 266–67, 271–72
Reilly, J. B., 408
Republican Banner, 594
Restless, a fishing schooner, 306
"The Restoration of Southern Trade and
Commerce" (Reid), 264
Rhett, Albert, 14
Rhett, Robert Barnwell, Jr.
Charleston Mercury and, 505
duels of, 37
education of, 4, 505
on fees for Washington correspondence,
490, 494
George W. Bagby, Jr. and, 20, 494–96, 505,
506
Governor Francis W. Pickens and, 495
William Ashmead Courtenay and, 31, 36
Rhett, Robert Barnwell, Sr.
Charleston Mercury and, 143
Charleston Southern Standard and, 505
as a strident secessionist, 36
Richardson, Albert, 186, 188
Richardson, Willard, 408, 444, 452
Richmond, Virginia, *383*
Richmond Daily Dispatch, 15
Richmond Dispatch, 157, 331, 339, 514, 529

Richmond Enquirer, 214, 514, 516, 520, 523,
524
Richmond Examiner, 13, 135, 510
Richmond Mutual Press Association, 238
Richmond Press Association, 516
Richmond Record, 546
Richmond Sentinel, 299
Richmond Whig, 246, 487, 490
Riordan, Bartholomew Rochefort
on Alexandria, Virginia, 129–31
Charleston Mercury and, 128–29, 132, 135
Charleston News and, 135–36, 137, *138*
contribution to American journalism, 127
date and place of birth, 127
date and place of death, 139
education of, 127
on Fort Sumter bombardment, 132, 134
founding of Riordan & Co., Cotton Commission Merchants, 139
Francis Warrington Dawson and, 135, 136
George W. Bagby, Jr. and, 132, 497, 498
Mason Cotton Gin Cylinder Company and,
139
as moody and melancholy, 138–39
News and Courier and, 136, 137
on paper shortage, 498
portrait of, *128*
possible stroke of, 137–38
Press Association of the Confederate States
and, 132
pseudonym of, 26, 129
Richmond Examiner and, 135
on siege of Charleston, 132, *133*, *134*
on South Carolina volunteers at Richmond,
129–30
on Washington, DC, 131–32
Roan, a ship, 308
Roanoke Island, Battle of, 287–89, 400–401
Roberts, Albert ("John Happy"), 583, 593, 594,
604 *table*
Roberts, Hiram, 360
Robinson, George, 472
Roddy, Abigail Latham, 342
Roebuck, J. A., 234
Roman, Alfred, 208
Rosser, Colonel T. L., 295
Rost, Pierre A., 220
"Rover": a Southern war correspondent, 17

Rowe, George Henry Clay, 604 *table*
Ruffin, Edmund, 153, 217
Runnels, Hal G., 442
Russell, Earl, 226, 227, 229
Russell, William Howard, 1, 526
Russell's Magazine, 162

Sabine Pass and the invasion of Texas, *407*,
  436–38
Sales, Colonel John, 449
San Antonio Herald, 456
Sanford, Thaddeus, 205
Sarah A. Boyce, a schooner, 302–3
Sarah B. Harris, a schooner, 306
Sarah Louise, a schooner, 306
Saturday Evening Post, 572
Saturday Review, 230, 231
Savannah (Georgia) *Republican*
  Charles Seton Hardee and, 361
  on Florida's corn crop, 180
  General Sherman's takeover of, 339,
    359–60, *359*
  Hiram Roberts and, 360
  James Roddy Sneed and, 312, 339, 341, 343,
    345, 360–61
  John E. Hayes and, 359–60
  letter of warning to, 350
  Peter W. Alexander and, 311, 313, 315, 316,
    325, 328, 331, 333, 337
  suspension of publication, 356
Savannah, Georgia
  chart of approaches to, *352*
  evacuation of, 355, 357–58, *358*
  surrender of, 357–58
Savannah Daily Morning News, 342
Savannah Republican, 311, 315–16, 326, 337,
  493
Sayler's Creek, Battle of, 392
Scott, John, 194
*The Scouting Expeditions of McCulloch's
  Texas Rangers* (Reid), 248
Screws, William Wallace
  Advertiser and Mail and, 272–73
  Alabama Press Association and, 274
  arrest of, 202, 265
  battlefield experience of, 267
  criticism of other newspapers, 273
  date and place of birth, 272

death of, 274
demographic data on, 603 *table*
on events on the battle field at Drewry's
  Bluff, 269
on the Farmer's Alliance of 1891, 273
General Braxton Bragg and, 202, 265–67
legal career of, 272
his letters from Gracie's Brigade, 268–69
marriage to Emily Frances Holt, 272
Montgomery Advertiser and, 272
mystery of what he wrote, 268–71
New Orleans Picayune and, 265
New York Times on, 273
opposing secession, 265
on Petersburg, Virginia, June, 1864, 271
political career of, 273
portrait of, *266*, *275*
probable pseudonym of, 268–70
report on the history of Alabama
  newspapers, 274
reputation of, 274–75
taken prisoner, 267
his title of "Major," 272
on Ulysses S. Grant, 271
war wound of, 267
writing style of, 271
Sea Flower, a schooner, 306
"The Secrets of Success: Or Business Advice to the Young Men of the South"
  (Gilbert), 480
Seddon, Confederate Secretary of War James
  A., 533
Sedgwick, General John, 522
Selby, Julian A., 88–89, 172, 174
Semmes, T. J., 15
Senac, Ruby (Hotze), 237
Sener, James Beverley
  access to military correspondence, 513–14,
    516
  accuracy of his reporting, 521, 522, 523,
    524, 535
  advocating for citizens of Fredericksburg,
    520
  assessment of his reporting on the Battle of
    Chancellorsville, 524
  on an attack on Fredericksburg, 514
  on Battle for Fredericksburg, 516–20
  on Battle of Chancellorsville, 521–23

Sener, James Beverley (*continued*)
  on Battle of Cold Harbor, 534–35
  on Battle of Spotsylvania, 533–34
  on Battle of the Wilderness, 533
  on black soldiers, 533
  on camp life, winter 1863–1864, 531–32
  as chief justice, Wyoming territorial
    Supreme Court, 541–42
  his concern about Maryland, 526
  his concern for Confederate troops, 530
  on Confederate brigades contributing to
    the citizens of Fredericksburg, 520
  on the Confederate cavalry, 536
  on controversy over correspondent "A,"
    527–28
  correspondent X stories, 515–16
  date and place of birth, 514
  death and burial place of, 542
  on the death of General "Stonewall"
    Jackson, 523–24
  demographic data on, 604 *table*
  on desertion, 529, 532
  education of, 4, 515
  on execution of deserters, 528–29
  Fredericksburg, Virginia and, 513
  Fredericksburg Ledger and, 541
  on General Grant's opening gambit,
    532–33
  on General Joseph Hooker, 520–21
  historical assessment of his war
    correspondence, 541
  on Lee's retreat from Gettysburg, 525
  legal studies of, 515
  letter from the 15th Virginia Cavalry, 532
  on Martinsburg, Virginia, 526
  on the *New York Herald's* story concerning
    Lee's force, 527
  parents of, 514
  on Petersburg siege, 535–40
  portrait of, *514*
  postwar career of, 541–42
  profession of, 4
  on the renewal of fighting of April, 1863,
    521
  Richmond Dispatch and, 514
  Richmond Enquirer and, 514, 516, 524, 529
  Richmond Press Association and, 516
  on state of affairs in Virginia, 1863, 530–31
  on state of religious feeling throughout the
    army, 531
  on treatment of *London Times*
    correspondents, 526–27
  on Ulysses S. Grant, 536–37
  on Union General George Meade, 530
  on the value of war correspondents, 541
  weather reports of, 515
  on Winchester, Virginia, 525, 526
Seven Pines, battle of, 69
Seward, William, 208
Sharpsburg, Battle of, 77–79, *77, 78,* 329–30,
  329, 331
Shaw, Colonel H. M., 400
Shepardson, William G.
  on Army of the Potomac's winter quarters,
    284, 286
  arrest of, 202, 276
  on Battle of Leesburg (*Ball's Bluff*),
    October 21, 1861, 280–82
  on Battle of Roanoke Island, 287–90
  battles reported on, 277
  breaching Confederate security, 61
  on captured Yankees, 306–7
  capture of, 288–89
  on the capture of the fishing schooner *Etta
    Caroline,* 306
  controversy concerning the 31st North
    Carolina, 290
  criticism of Confederate generals, 308–9
  on CSS *Tallahassee,* 301–8
  Daily Dispatch and, 61, 276
  date and place of birth, 277
  demographic data on, 602 *table*
  on the destruction of the British ship
    Adriatic, 304–5
  on the destruction of the *William Bell,* 304
  on Drewry's Bluff, 292–93
  enraging General Joseph E. Johnston, 61
  European travels of, 277
  on Fort Powhatan, 292
  on gathering news, 278–79
  on General George G. Meade, 293
  on General George Pickett, 299–300
  General Joseph E. Johnston and, 202, 276,
    284–85
  on General Robert E. Lee, 291–92
  on General Stonewall Jackson, 292

humor of, 278
on importance of newspapers, 279, 282
on Jefferson Davis, 279
Mobile Advertiser and Register and, 276
on "Newbern expedition," 299–301
on *New York Herald's* article detailing the
  Confederate Army, 285–86
on non-reenlistment of officers, 293
on problems of civilians during war, 290–91
pseudonyms of, 277
raid on Federal ships in Chesapeake Bay,
  294–99, *296*
reporting bizarre occurrences, 279–80
serving aboard the cruiser *Tallahassee*, 276
on Southerners abandoning Fairfax, 280
on spoils of war, 282
on substitute soldiers, 293–94
as a surgeon, 276, 278, 288, 290, 294, 297,
  298, 308
on sutlers, 282–83
transfer to the Confederate Navy, 290
writing style of, 277, 278–79
Sheridan, Union General Phil, 534
Sherman, General William T.
  march on Atlanta, 40, 87, 590–93
  march on Columbia, South Carolina, 89
  capture of Savannah, 41, 135, 339
  destroying railroad tracks in Atlanta, *18*
  destruction of Columbia, *102, 103*
  Savannah headquarters of, *357*
  surrender of Savannah, 357–58
  takeover of the *Savannah* (Georgia) *Repub-
    lican*, 339, 359–60, *359*
Shiloh, Battle of
  Felix Gregory de Fontaine on, 62–63
  Henry Perry on, 402
  Henry Timrod on, 164–66, 168–70
  Peter W. Alexander on, 324–25
  William P. Doran on, 445–46
Shirley Plantation, 292–93
shortages
  of basic goods, 120
  and Confederate bureaucracy, 419
  and desertions, 413, 439
  of horses, 336
  of housing and basic necessities, 551
  of printing supplies, 86, 312, 345, 356, 498
Shorter, Marie Teresa (Alexander), 339

Sibley, Marilyn McAdams on Charles
  DeMorse, 417
Siegel, General Franz, 457
Siege of Corinth. *See* Corinth, First Battle of
Simms, William Gilmore, 97, 162, 173, 175
Sims, F. W., 350
Slaughter, Montgomery, 513, 516
Sledge, James B., 603 *table*
Slemmer, Lieutenant Adam, 181, 186
Slidell, John, 60, *223*, 230, 319
  See also Trent Affair
Sloan, Joe Mather, 261
Smith, Alice Earle (Douglas), 464
Smith, James M., 339
Smith, J. Henly, 11, 62, 348
Sneed, Archibald Henderson, 342
Sneed, James Roddy
  on the 54th Massachusetts Colored
    Infantry, 355
  on Battery Wagner on Morris Island,
    352–55
  on bombardment of Fort Sumter, 342–44,
    354
  capture of Savannah and, 339
  censorship and, 312, 345, 346–48
  children of, 342, 349
  criticism of Confederate Navy, 355
  criticism of General Beauregard, 354
  criticism of General Joseph E. Johnston, 62
  his curse on nonpaying readers, 345
  dealing with shortages of ink and paper,
    312, 345, 356
  date and place of birth, 342
  death and burial place of, 361
  demographic data on, 603 *table*
  disunion and, 341
  editorial guidelines of, 351
  on evacuation of Savannah and Charleston,
    352
  Felix Gregory de Fontaine and, 346
  on General Johnston's expulsion of news-
    paper correspondents, 346–48
  John E. Hayes on, 360
  letter from General W. H. T. Walker, 347
  Macon Daily Telegraph and, 360
  marriage to Anna Maria Hay, 342
  marriage to Leonora Cohen, 349
  on The Old Men's Regiment, 353

Sneed, James Roddy (*continued*)
  parents of, 342
  his perspective on the practice of news-
     papering, 346
  Peter W. Alexander and, 18, 315, 332,
     345–46
  as a poet, 361
  Press Association of the Confederate States
     of America and, 312
  on the Printers Union, 360–61
  pseudonym of, 341
  Savannah (Georgia) *Republican* and, 312,
     341, 342, 345, 360–61
  on the Southern Associated Press, 349–51
  spelling of his name, 342
  on the surrender of Savannah, 357–58
  on suspension of publication of the *Savan-
     nah* (Georgia) *Republican*, 356
  wartime appointment as collector of the
     port of Savannah, 341
  William H. Pritchard, Jr. and, 350
Sneed, William A. H., 361
soldier correspondents
  Battle of Shiloh report and, 8–9
  private letters from soldiers, 9–10
  quality of writing of, 10
Solomon, Clara, 378, 379–80, 382–83,
     385–86, 388, 389–92, 394
Solomon, Rosa (da Ponte), 392, 393
Sophy, a schooner, 306
Soule, Captain C. C., 41
South Carolina
  city of Charleston, 1862, *485*
  destruction of Columbia, *102, 103*
  influential newspapers of, 25
  newspaper correspondents of, 25–26
  Ordinance of Secession, *144, 145*
  Palmetto Guard of, 27, 33, 36, 37
  secession of, 145
South Carolina Audubon Society, 44
South Carolina College (University of South
     Carolina), 97, 140
South Carolina Palmetto Guard, 27, 33, 36, 37
South Carolina Press Association, 95–96
South Carolinian, 86, 97, 101, 174
  See also *Daily South Carolinian*
Southern (Atlanta) *Confederacy*, 316
  See also *Atlanta Southern Confederacy*
Southern Aegis, 197

Southern Associated Press, 11, 54, 349–51, 365
Southern Confederacy, 593
Southern Democrat, 198
Southern Field and Fireside, 492, 545, 546
Southern Illustrated News, 172, 510, 546
Southern Know-Nothings, 206
Southern Literary Messenger
  Edgar Allan Poe and, 506, 545
  George W. Bagby, Jr. and, 488, 490, 491,
     498, 506–7, 508, 509
  Henry Timrod and, 162
  John R. Thompson and, 492, 506, 545, 546
  Thomas W. White and, 545
  "Virginia"on, 563
Southern Quarterly Review, 105
Southern Republic, 506
South Mountain, battle of, 76–77
Southwestern Telegraph Company, 100
A Souvenir of Zurich (Thompson), 545
Spence, James, 226, 230
Spencer, Cornelia Phillips, 23
Spotsylvania, Battle of, 533–34
Spotsylvania Court House, Battle of, 337
Spratt, John, 4, 155, 628 *note* 4, 631 *note* 85
Spratt, Leonidas William
  accused of spying, 140, 157–58
  army career of, 158
  on attack at Blackburn's Ford, 151–52
  on availability of firearms, 150
  on Bull Run, 152–53
  his campaign to reopen the slave trade,
     141–42, 143–47
  the *Charleston Mercury* and, 26, 143, 147,
     505, 629 *note* 16
  the *Charleston Southern Standard* and,
     141, 505
  on Charlottesville, Virginia of 1861, 147
  children of, 159
  creating a Civil War legend, 26, 140,
     155–56
  criticism of Confederate Congress, 143–45
  date and place of birth, 140
  death and burial place of, 159
  on defeat at Loral Hill of General Robert S.
     Garnett, 151
  defending the crew of the brig *Echo*, 143
  demographic data on, 602 *table*
  on difficulties of creating an army of the
     new republic, 147–48

editorializing of, 150

education of, 4, 140

on Federal advance toward Fairfax, 149–50

on formation of a Slave Republic, 144, 147

F. W. Pickens on, 143

on General Bernard Bee, 155–56

on Harpers Ferry, May 14, 1861, 147

Horace Greeley on, 142

on Jefferson Davis, 154

on Manassas Junction, June 26, 1861, 150

marriage to Mary A. Wadsworth, 158

on measles in Camp Davis, 148

physical description of, 140

practice of law, 140–41

pseudonym of, 26

quality of his war correspondence, 20

quitting as a war correspondent, 156–57

South Carolina Ordinance of Secession and, 143, *144*, *145*

on South Carolina's secession, 145–46

on Southern women, 150–51

speech before the secession convention, 143

on wagon transportation, 150

on the Washington Artillery, 152

"Spring's Lessons" (Timrod), 173

Standard, 227

Stark, Madison, 179

States Rights Democrat, 456

Stephens, Alexander H., 111, 323–24, 504

Stoddard, Richard Henry, 174

Stuart, J. E. B., 76, 284, 528, 550, 555, 574

Suliote, a ship, 305

Sumner, General E. V., 513, 516

Swett Battery, 167

Tallahassee, a cruiser, 276

Taylor, General Dick, 449

Taylor, Zachary, 205, 247

telegraphic press reports, 368–71

Tennessee

    Memphis, Tennessee, March 1862, *401*

    problems of newspapers in, 569–70, 583–84

    secession of, 481, 569

Texas

    difficulties of newspapers operating in, 407–8

    effect of Civil War on, 449–50

    Galveston, Texas, 448, *448*, 469

    the Indian Territory region, 423, 670 *note* 90

    invasion of at the Sabine Pass, *407*

    number of Texas men fighting in the Civil War, 407, 453

    percentage of Texans supporting secession, 443

    soldier-editors of Texas, 454, 665 *note* 2

Texas Ranger, 408, 456

Texas Siftings, 479

Texas State Gazette, 422

Texas Tidings, 480

Texas Weekly Record, 478

Thompson, John R.

    accounts of Richmond life, 551–52

    Albion and, 554

    "Ashby" poem, 555

    on the battlefield after the Battle of Fair Oaks, 552

    on casualties from the 14th Tennessee, 553

    on Centreville, Virginia, 552–53

    his concerns for Confederate soldiers, 553–54

    on confusion over flags, 553

    date and place of birth, 543

    death and burial place of, 555

    demographic data on, 604 *table*

    on demoralizing effect of gambling, 548

    description of, 543

    descriptive language of, 547–48

    on General Robert E. Lee, 549

    Harper's and, 545

    Henry Timrod and, 545

    The Index and, 554

    J. E. B. Stuart and, 550

    on Jefferson Davis, 550–51

    on John Wilkes Booth, 554

    Knickerbocker and, 545

    Memphis Daily Appeal and, 482, 543, 545, 546

    New York Post and, 554

    Paul Hamilton Hayne and, 545

    poetry of, 543, 544, 545

    portrait of, *544*

    pseudonyms of, 482, 547

    publishing setbacks of, 554–55

    Richmond, Virginia and, 543–44

    Richmond Record and, 546

    on rumors, 548–49

    on the Seven Day Campaign, 553

Thompson, John R. (*continued*)
  sources covering his life, 544–45
  Southern Field and Fireside and, 492, 545, 546
  Southern Illustrated News and, 546
  Southern Literary Messenger and, 491, 545
  tuberculosis and, 544
  on *Uncle Tom's Cabin* (Stowe), 545
  his use of imagery, 548
  William Cullen Bryant and, 554
Thompson, John Y., 205–6
Thompson, William Tappan, 11–12, 342
Thrasher, John S.
  arrest of, 363–64
  Beacon of Cuba and, 364
  biographical data on, 603 *table*
  concern for Cuba, 362, 364
  conscription of journalists and, 373
  copyright of news stories, 7, 95, 101, 312, 363
  Daniel Webster on, 362, 364
  date and place of birth, 363
  death and burial place of, 375
  Faro Industrial and, 363
  Frank Leslie's Illustrated Newspaper and, 375
  marriage to Rebecca Mary Bass Menard, 364–65
  meeting with Confederate generals, 371–72
  on military censorship, 12, 15–16, 81–82, 372–73
  Noticioso de Nuevo York and, 364
  notoriety of, 362
  Press Association of the Confederate States of America and, 81–82, 312, 351, 366–73, 660 *note* 25
  reforming Southern journalistic practices, 6, 363, 368, 371
  regaining access to military camps, 348
  as a revolutionary journalist, 362, 363
  Sam Houston on, 365
  telegraphic press reports, 368–71
Timrod, Adeline Rebecca, 160
Timrod, Edyth, 161
Timrod, Emily, 160, 176–77
Timrod, Henry
  army enlistment of, 163
  on battle at Farmington, 166–70
  at Corinth, Mississippi, 64, 65, 163–64, *164, 165*

"The Cotton Boll" (a poem), 162
  date and place of birth, 160
  death and burial place of, 91, 160, 177
  on desertion of Confederate troops, 170
  education of, 4, 161, 162
  evacuating Columbia, 174
  Felix Gregory de Fontaine on, 173, 177–78
  Henry W. Longfellow on, 178
  illness of, 68
  James Ryder Randall on, 170
  J. Dickson Bruns on, 171
  John R. Thompson and, 545
  letter to Paul H. Hayne, 174–75, 176
  letter to Richard Henry Stoddard, 174
  marriage to Katie Goodwin, 162, 172–73
  memorials to, 178
  on "needless loss" of battle at Shiloh, 164–66, 168–70
  nickname of, 160
  nom de plume of, 162
  on ominous warnings from a book titled *Armageddon*, 166
  Paul H. Hayne on, 171
  poetry of, 26, 160, 161, 162–63, 172, 177–78
  portrait of, *161*
  pseudonym of, 26, 65
  publishing "thumb sheets," 89
  salary of as war correspondent, 10, 163
  siblings of, 160–61
  his son, Willie, 173, 175
  and the *South Carolinian*, 86, 172, 173, 174, 175, 176
  Southern Literary Messenger and, 162
  on Theodore Wagner, 172, 173
  tuberculosis and, 170–71, 176–77
  William Ashmead Courtenay and, 26, 27, 32, 43–44, 174, 178
  William Gilmore Simms and, 162, 173, 175
Timrod, William Henry, 160
Timrod, Willie, 173, 175
Timrod Memorial Association, 178
Tonkaway Indian tribe, 424, 426
Toombs, Robert, *218*, 501
Trenholm, George A., 88, 172
Trent, a British mail packet, 319
Trent Affair, 60, 121, 223, 224, 319–20, 405
Tubman, Harriet, 134
Tulane University and Hurricane Katrina, 396

Turner, Jim on Colonel Robert R. Garland, 467

Two Brothers, a Philadelphia anchor-sweeper, 297

Tyler Journal, 475– 76

Tyler Reporter
  issues destroyed by fire, 455
  James P. Douglas and, 408, 414, 453

Uncle Tom's Cabin (Stowe), 545

Union flotilla during the Red River expedition, *450*

Union troops attacking Confederate prisoners in the streets of Washington, D.C., *131*

Union troops burning the bridge over the Tennessee
  River at Decatur, 201

University of Virginia, 544

"The Unknown Dead" (Timrod), 172

U.S. Act of 1820, 143

The U.S. Bankruptcy Law of 1841, With a Synopsis and Notes (Reid), 248

USS *Reliance*, 295, *296*, 297

USS *San Jacinto*, 121, 319

USS *Satellite*, 295, 296, 297, 298

USS *Underwriter*, 299

Van Dorn, General Earl, 15, 16, 244, 387, 446, 447, 457, 459

Varner, Herbert, 9–10

Victoria Advocate, 466

Virginia
  Capitol Square, Richmond, Virginia, *481*
  city of Richmond, *485*
  secession of, 481
  war correspondents of, 482
  Washington Monument at, *489*

"Virginia"
  on the 3rd Alabama Regiment, 564–65, 567
  compared to Joan, 558, 561, 567
  on the death of Private John O'Connor, 565
  demographic data on, 602 *table*
  her concern for Confederate troops, 564, 565
  her devotion to the South, 562–63
  her humor, 563–64
  J. Cutler Andrews on, 560
  keys to her identity, 562

  and the letter defending Norfork, Virginia, 556–60
  Mobile Advertiser and Register and, 556, 565
  on Norfolk Naval Hospital, 564
  praise of John R. Hathaway, 562
  religion and, 562
  reporting of rumors, 565–66
  sentiments of, 561–62
  on the *Southern Literary Messenger*, 563
  value of her work, 482, 561, 566–68
  writing style of, 566

Wadsworth, Mary A. (Spratt), 158

Wagner, A. J., 368–71

Wagner, General Henry, 40

Wagner, Theodore, 172, 173

"Waiting" (Shepardson), 277

Walker, General W. H. T., 347

Walker, Leroy Pope (Confederate Secretary of War), 14, 186, 192, 218, 220

Waller, John R., 442, 443

war correspondence, quality of
  Felix Gregory de Fontaine, 19–20
  Hodding Carter, II on, 17
  impediments to, 20–21
  and the importance of newspapers, 22–23
  J. Cutler Andrews on, 17, 18
  Leonidas William Spratt, 20
  overview of, 21–23
  Peter W. Alexander, 18–19
  Phillip Knightley on, 17

war correspondents, differences between Northern and Southern, 5, 598

war correspondents defined, 1–3

War Record Publishing Company, 177

War Songs of the South (Shepardson), 277, 647 *note* 2

Washington and Lee University, 515

Washington Artillery, 152, 395–98, 520

Washington Union, 127, 573, 574

Waters, A. P., 228

Watie, Indian General Stand, 428, 432

Watterson, Harvey Magee, 573

Watterson, Henry
  on Abraham Lincoln, 574–75, 579–80
  Atlanta Constitution and, 573
  Atlanta Southern Confederacy and, 585, 586

Watterson, Henry (*continued*)
on attack at Chattanooga, 240
on Battle of Marietta, 588–89
books by, 595
capture of by Federal Colonel Shook,
577–78
capture of by General N. B. Dana, 593–94
Chattanooga Rebel and, 570, 572, 578, 583,
584, 693 *note* 59, 694 *note* 60
as chief of scouts for General Johnson, 586
on conduct of Confederate soldiers in
Middle Tennessee, 579
Daily Constitutionalist and, 586, 695 *note*
94
Daily States and, 574
date and place of birth, 573
death and burial place of, 595–96
demographic data on, 604 *table*
education of, 573–74
enlistment in the Confederate Army, 576
on evacuation of Chattanooga, 582–84
General Braxton Bragg and, 570
General James H. Polk and, 586, 588–89
on General John Bell Hood, 593
on General Nathan Forrest, 576, 577
on Governor Isham Harris, 588, 695 *note*
111
on importance of defending the mountains
of East Tennessee, 581–82
on indiscretions of the press, 580
interview with John Brown, 574
Louisville Courier- Journal and, 572, 594,
595
his meeting with General Bragg, 584
Memphis Appeal and, 570, 586
military career of, 571, 585
Montgomery Mail and, 572, 593
Nashville Banner and, 576
national magazines published in, 572–73
New Era and, 574
on newspapers leaving Atlanta, 590
newspapers worked for, 572
parents of, 573
Philadelphia Press and, 574
physical description of, 571

poetry of, 592
portrait of, *572, 595*
postwar career of, 594–95
pseudonyms of, 570, 572, 586
Pulitzer Prize, 595
Rebecca Ewing and, 582
Republican Banner and, 594
reputation of, 3, 570, 572–73
on Sherman's taking of Atlanta, 590–93
on Southern refugees, 586–88
on secession, 575–76
on his tour of the army, 588
writing style of, 570
Webster, Daniel, 362
Weed, Thurlow, 121, 224, *225*
Welch, O. G., 429
West Texas Star, 479
White, Sallie Susan (Douglas), 463–64
White, Thomas W., 545
Whitman, Walt, 381
Whitten, J. L., 198
Wigfall, Louis, 11
Wilderness, Battle of the, 337–38, 533, *549*
Wilkes, Captain Charles, 319
William Bell, a ship, 303–4
William Elliott White house, 158, 631 *note* 86
Williams, Talcott on importance of
newspapers, 23
Willington, A. S., *49*
Wilmot Proviso, 205
Wilson, Hugh, 8
Wilson, Samuel F., 205
Wise, O. Jennings, 388
Withers, Jones M., 219
Wood, Benjamin, 135, 136
Wood, Captain John Taylor, 294–99, 301,
306, 307, 308
Woodson, Will O., 372
Wooldridge, Colonel Thomas, 415
Wooldridge, Lodiska (DeMorse), 415
Woolridge, John, 411

Yancey, William Lowndes, 207, 217, 220
Yates, W. J., 22
Yeadon, Richard, 349

About the Authors

Patricia Gantt McNeely is the Eleanor M. and R. Frank Mundy Distinguished Professor Emerita at the University of South Carolina (USC) where she taught writing and reporting for 34 years. She was chair of the Print Sequence in the journalism school for 25 years and associate dean for four years. Before joining the USC faculty, she was a reporter and editor for the *Greenville News*, the *Columbia Record*, and *The State*. She is the author of *Fighting Words: A Media History of South Carolina*. She and her husband, Al, have two children, Allison and Alan, daughter-in-law Gretchen, and two grandchildren, Jordan and Julia McNeely.

Debra Reddin van Tuyll is a professor of communications at Augusta State University (Georgia). Prior to entering academia, she worked in both public relations and journalism. She was co-editor of *WINDOWS* magazine at the Texas Engineering Experiment Station, assistant editor of the *Journal of the Islamic Medical Association of North America*, a reporter at the *Decatur* (Alabama) *Daily*, and a reporter and editor at the *Robertsdale* (Alabama) *Independent*. She is author of the *Southern Press in the Civil War* and co-editor of *The Civil War and the Press*.

Henry H. Schulte is retired from Ohio State University, where he was Kiplinger Professor of Public Affairs Reporting. He was also the Frank Gannett professor of public affairs reporting at Marshall University and an associate professor at the University of South Carolina. Earlier, he was a reporter and editor for 25 years with the *St. Petersburg Times*, the *Nashville Tennessean*, the *Louisville Times*, the *Savannah Morning News*, and the *Chicago Daily News*. He is the author of two reporting textbooks, *Reporting Public Affairs* and *Getting the Story, An Advanced Reporting Guide to Beats, Records and Sources*, both published by Macmillan Company.

Contributors to *Knights of the Quill*

Matthew J. Bosisio is an associate professor of journalism at Augusta State University (Georgia), where he also advises the award-winning campus newspaper, the *Bell Ringer*. Prior to teaching, he worked in newsrooms across the country, including the *Roswell Daily Record*, the *Richmond Daily News*, and the *Portland Chronicle*.

Mary M. Cronin teaches in the Department of Journalism and Mass Communications at New Mexico State University in Las Cruces. A former newspaper reporter and editor, Cronin's research interests focus on the 19th century press, specifically press coverage of the U.S. Civil War and publications produced by women and minorities.

Jinx Coleman Broussard teaches in the Manship School of Mass Communication at Louisiana State University where she is the William Dickinson Distinguished Professor. Broussard conducts research on public relations and on the black press. She is the author of *Voice to the Voiceless: Four Pioneering Black Women Journalists*.

Skye Chance Cooley is a doctoral student in Communications and Information Sciences at the University of Alabama. He earned his master's degree in mass communication at Louisiana State University. His research interests include international communications, online social networking, theoretical development, and historical research studies. During football season, he is still torn between supporting the Tigers and the Tide.

Mark K. Dolan earned his Ph.D. in journalism and mass communications from the University of South Carolina in 2003. His research areas include journalism as literature and history of the black press. He has reported for the *Savannah Morning News*, the *Naples Daily News*, and *The State* in Columbia.

Nancy McKenzie Dupont, Ph.D., is an associate professor in the School of Journalism at the University of Mississippi. Her teaching follows a 17-year career in television news. She concentrates her research interests on journalism history, particularly the Southern secession newspapers. She is author of seven book chapters.

Bradley J. Hamm is dean of the School of Journalism at Indiana University. His Ph.D. is in mass communication research at the University of North Carolina, following a master's degree in journalism from the University of South Carolina and an undergraduate degree from Catawba College in North Carolina.

Bruce Mallard, a native of Tennessee, holds the Ph.D. in political science from the University of Tennessee. At the time his chapter was researched and written, Mallard was living in Savannah, Georgia, where he was dean of academic affairs at South University.

Erika Pribanic-Smith teaches media history and journalism courses at the University of Alabama's College of Communication and Information Sciences. Armed with experience at daily and suburban weekly newspapers, national magazines, and public relations firms, Pribanic-Smith focuses on media history and journalism skills courses. Her research focus is on antebellum era and Southern newspapers during the Civil War.

Amy Ransford Purvis is a doctoral student at the Indiana University School of Journalism. She received her master's degree in journalism from Indiana University and her undergraduate degree from Hanover College in Indiana.

Ford Risley is head of the department of Journalism at Penn State University. He is the author of *Abolition and the Press: The Moral Struggle Against Slavery* (Northwestern University Press, 2008) and *The Civil War: Primary Document From 1860 to 1865* (Greenwood, 2004). He has also published articles in *American Journalism, Civil War History, Georgia Historical Quarterly,* and *Journalism History.*

Joseph V. Trahan, III, is president and chief executive officer of Trahan & Associates. He earned his Ph.D. in mass communication from the University of Southern Mississippi and a master's degree in public relations from Ball State University. His undergraduate degree is in American military history from Tulane University. Trahan has more than 25 years experience in public affairs training programs.

Carol Wilcox, Ph.D., teaches journalism at Virginia State University in Petersburg. She and her late husband, Gary Stiff, founded the *Clear Creek Courant* in Colorado in 1973. Wilcox has worked at newspapers in Mexico, France, and Canada. In 1993, she was a National Press Foundation fellow in Mexico and, in 1995, she was a North American Journalist Exchange fellow in Mexico City and Montreal.

Janice Ruth Wood is an assistant professor in the Department of Communication and Dramatic Arts at Auburn University in Montgomery, Alabama. She holds the Ph.D. from Southern Illinois University in Carbondale. A former journalist, Wood is the author of *The Struggle for Free Speech in the United States, 1872-1915: Edward Bliss Foote, Edward Bond Foote, and Anti-Comstock Operations* (Routledge, 2008).